media,
minorities,
and meaning

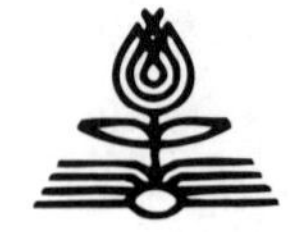

PETER LANG
New York • Washington, D.C./Baltimore • Bern
Frankfurt • Berlin • Brussels • Vienna • Oxford

Debra L. Merskin

media, minorities, and meaning

a critical introduction

PETER LANG
New York • Washington, D.C./Baltimore • Bern
Frankfurt • Berlin • Brussels • Vienna • Oxford

Library of Congress Cataloging-in-Publication Data

Merskin, Debra L.
Media, minorities, and meaning: a critical introduction / Debra L. Merskin.
p. cm.
Includes bibliographical references and index.
1. Minorities in mass media. 2. Stereotypes (Social psychology) in mass media.
3. Racism in mass media. 4. Difference (Psychology) in mass media.
5. Other (Philosophy) in mass media.
6. Mass media and ethnic relations—United States.
7. Difference (Psychology)—Social aspects—United States.
8. Multiculturalism—United States. I. Title.
P94.5.M552U655   305.5'6—dc22   2010035258
ISBN 978-1-4331-1141-9 (hardcover)
ISBN 978-1-4331-1140-2 (paperback)

Bibliographic information published by **Die Deutsche Nationalbibliothek**.
Die Deutsche Nationalbibliothek lists this publication in the "Deutsche
Nationalbibliografie"; detailed bibliographic data is available
on the Internet at http://dnb.d-nb.de/.

The paper in this book meets the guidelines for permanence and durability
of the Committee on Production Guidelines for Book Longevity
of the Council of Library Resources.

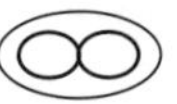

We don't see things as they are,
we see things as we are.

Anaïs Nin

To Myszka, Nib, Wicker, Luna, Sweet Pea, and Douglas.
Above all to Don and Virgie, who did the best they could with what they had.
I love you all.

Table of Contents

Section One: Foundations

Section Two: The Articulation of Difference

❈ Illustrations

❈ **Preface**

> *What are stories if not the container of culture, the body, and its inner worlds? Myth encompasses many elements; the human and divine, the history of a people, their thought, their way of being, the terrain in which they live.*
>
> Linda Hogan

Twelfth-century Sufi mystic poet Rumi (1207–1273) tells the story of an elephant that invites us to explore how human beings come to perceive, conceptualize, and define "reality." Roughly translated the story goes something like this:

> Some Hindus were exhibiting an elephant in a dark room, and many people collected to see it. But as the place was too dark to permit them to see the elephant, they all felt it with their hands, to gain an idea of what it was like. One felt its trunk, and declared that the beast resembled a water pipe; another felt its ear, and said it must be a large fan; another its leg, and thought it must be a pillar; another felt its back, and declared the beast must be like a great throne. According to the part which each felt, he gave a different description of the animal. (1993, p. 208)

In the United States, the proverbial elephant is in the living room. Everyone knows it is there, but few are willing to acknowledge it in its full scope—the racism, sexism, ageism, and other "isms" that continue to permeate our culture, society, and psyches. Many of us feel those parts that most resonate with our own experiences. Others have had the experience of being defined only by one aspect of themselves—appearance, voice, mannerisms, origin, or perhaps by skin color. Rumi's tale is a reminder of the importance of asking questions and examining our preconceptions. It invites exploration of unfamiliar terrain and encourages us to be open to different experiences. In a similar fashion, this book proceeds in a grass-roots manner: from the bottom up, rather than the top down. Problems associated with racism, sexism, ageism, and other "isms" clearly exist, are persistent, consistent, and corroborated in many forms of mass media and popular culture. Each deserves examination, but first we need to understand the historical, psychological, cultural, sociological, economic, and political circumstances that contribute to the maintenance of the status quo in mainstream society—the core of the elephant.

In this book, I examine historical and cultural narratives underlying mass media and advertising sustained stereotypes and/or mis-representations of women, people of color, and other minorities.[1]

For more than a century, the mass media have been America's primary tellers of tales. Along with education, government, religion, and the family, the mass media comprise a major social institution and locus of learning. The messages the media deliver to us are at least, if not more, influential than other sources of institutionalized learning. Books, newspapers, and magazines, and electronic sources such as television, radio, music, and the Internet, provide the news, information, and entertainment that contribute to our understanding of the world around us.

As early as 1922, journalist Walter Lippmann pointed out how the media are skilled in constructing pictures in our heads, which support the status quo as opposed to an external, experiential reality. Today, individuals form impressions of themselves and of others, particularly those whom they have not met in person, largely based on what "the box," the "silver screen," and other mass media show, making the media some of the most powerful arbiters of racial, ethnic, and gender identity and inequity. Rather than drawing on first-hand personal experience for shared cultural definitions of who is one of "Us" and who becomes one of "Them," Americans are largely dependent on the kind of second-hand knowledge the media deliver. For example, stereotypical portrayals of Native Americans as savage sports mascots largely go unquestioned. If someone raises ethical questions he or she is often dismissed as being "too P.C." (politically correct).

In order to understand how many of these representations and media-defined relationships have come to seem normal, natural, and unremarkable to many of us, I begin by looking below the surface of media content and explore the psychological, social, and economic underpinnings of our system of beliefs (ideology). In America, the ideology of an elite is one that not only permits the continued existence of dehumanizing portrayals but also participates in their construction and maintenance. Similarly, the *lack* of representations (symbolic annihilation) of particular groups of people speaks as loudly as images and words.

Why, as a society, are we inclined to accept media messages as truth? In the United States, which is the focus of this book's examples, the mass media reflect stereotypical beliefs about people, places, and things that have their foundation in the pre-mass-mediated past. From pictograms on cave walls to pixels on computer screens, human communication efforts display a "truth," a "reality," and a "world view" which become the voice and vision of a society reflected in its recorded words and images. In Western society, the beneficiaries of the power and resources, those who author and/or legitimize these expressions, have been and continue to be White, male, heterosexual, and middle class. One only has to look at the captains of media industry to see the faces of patriarchal power: Michael Eisner (Disney, until 2005; replaced by Robert Iger), Sumner Redstone (Viacom), Jean-Bernard Lévy (Vivendi Universal), Jeffrey R. Immelt (GE/owns NBC), and Rupert Murdoch (News Corp.)

This book begins with an exploration of cognitive and analytic psychological explanations for questions such as: Why do we stereotype? What functions do stereotypes serve? What harm is there in stereotyping? These views provide tools for exploring questions of why human beings categorize and stereotype and what purpose this kind of thinking serves. Understanding the function of stereotypes comes by way of the ideas of Carl Jung, Joseph Campbell, Emile Durkheim, Erving Goffman and others, along with several media effects theories such as cultivation, media dependency, social learning, and accumulation theory. Other than the obvious impact on self-esteem, belonging, and community, stereotypes de-legitimize groups of people in the minds and eyes of those who hold power and access to resources. Perceptions of difference thought of in this way impact public policy decisions, economic outcomes, and access to medical care, education, employment, and legal representation. Through examples, my goal is to work toward undoing some of the basic psychological programming that continues to fuel the fires of discrimination in American society and to encourage readers to become activists in making changes to the ways people are presented in advertising, television programs, magazines, and other media.

Once upon a time, children learned morals, rules, attitudes, and behaviors from their parents and elders. Lessons about morality, religious, and social beliefs, and other protocols for coexistence were largely taught through stories, which were and are effective means of communicating important information to children. If, for example, the behavioral lesson for children is not to go into the world alone (where danger lurks) without a parent's permission, the story inevitably includes brushes with death and frightening creatures, stories about what happens when little boys and girls disobey their parents (think about the silenced Ariel in Disney's *Little Mermaid*). Similarly, morality tales stress conformity to a culture's beliefs about sex, love, romance, and appropriate partners. These tales hold as much truth and cultural weight as do Native American tales of Trickster Coyote's adventures, ghost stories told over a campfire, or film portrayals.

Memorabilia, sheet music, movie posters, brand images, jokes, television, film, news, radio, and the Internet create a seemingly seamless flow of ideas about people, places, and things that take on an aura of truth, of naturalness. Stereotypically loaded information remains current in ways that, drawing upon Goffman (1979), should prompt us to ask, "Why don't these words and images seem strange to us?"

While perceptions and beliefs shift and change over time, old views never completely disappear. These "master narratives" are simply transformed into culturally relevant tales that have the weight of policy behind them (Lyotard, 1984, p. xii). For example, while the Latino Frito Bandito stereotype is no longer visibly with us, he continues to live in the collective unconscious. Modern representations have transformed him into the inner city gang member or renegade border crosser, as shown in films, in books, in the news, and on television. According to the stereotype, he is as violent as ever, still of low social class, lazy, and less intelligent than the majority non-Hispanic White audience. These mutually reinforcing stereotypes have deep and ancient roots that remain fertile should the right circumstances arise to reenlist their service. Before the tragedy of September 11, 2001, for example, an evil Arab stereotype was already in place, based on decades of action adventure movie Arab bad guys, constructed and available to those in power. For more than 50 years, movies, cartoons, and news stories told of the monolithic Arab terrorist (see Chapter 6 for more on this topic). Therefore, when the enemy was defined as "those of Arab descent," it seemed a natural and normal conceptualization.

How can we interrupt the flow of (dis)information and (mis)representation? What can you and I do to change the enduring, dehumanizing stereotypes in the media and replace them with rich, diverse, and complex representations? How can we, as Stuart Hall advocates, contest and interrogate stereotypes in order to make them uninhabitable? This book is a step in that direction. It joins the voices of other books that appeal to all of us, some as students, media professionals, educators, legislators, and all of us always as consumers of media products, that change is needed in attitudes that underlie the perpetuation of beliefs and hence representations that present non-majority individuals as "lesser than." Why? Simply because it is the right, the honorable, the ethical thing to do. Awareness of the constitutive nature of stereotypes, of their psychological, cultural, historical, and economic origins, creates the condition in which their meaning need not be fixed.

Books such as this one and courses about the (mis)representation of women, people of color, and other marginalized people, will pave the way for change and be the impetus for activism. The next generation, our students, are where the fire of hope burns. A lofty goal? Yes. But one by one, student by student, *you*, can make a difference in the way media messages are created and consumed.

The first four chapters of this book establish the foundation for thinking about why and how stereotyping seems to be a natural and nearly seamless process in human consciousness. In Chapter 1, I present a model for understanding the power media have in maintaining and perpetuating stereotypes, one that begins with storytelling and myth. This chapter calls for a renewal of the definition of myth, not as lies but as culturally specific truths about concepts greater than ourselves. In this chapter we consider the place of myth in traditional and modern life, see how storytelling is a central part of human consciousness and creative thought, and look at how people come to "know" something is "true" (epistemology). Chapter 2 is a psychological exploration of questions of meaning—and how difference is constructed based on racial, ethnic, sexual, and other differences (isms). This chapter connects meaning with the human psychological tendency to categorize and provides fundamental definitions for terms that appear throughout the book. The goal is to deconstruct the impulse to "Other" so we can learn to interrupt and thereby stop repeating past responses which have led to harm throughout millennia.

Once we understand the psychological processes behind categorizing others it becomes easier to understand and interpret problematic media representations and suggest ways of improving them. Chapter 3 examines the major articulations of "Otherness" in the mass media, the role of stereotypical representations in perpetuating and maintaining differences between a social and psychological construction of who is one of "Us" and who is one of "Them," and theories of media effects. Chapter 4 describes how differences are articulated in American society. It includes a discussion of the major divisions according to class, race, ethnicity, sex, gender, and sexual orientation.

Illustrative case studies of media representations of particular groups of people based on constructed differences (race, ethnicity, gender, ableness, and combinations of these qualities and characteristics) comprise Chapters 4 through 13. These chapters apply theory to practice. Finally, the book offers resources (Internet sites, films and documentaries, and readings) as part of a vision of what you and I can do, as educators, students, citizens, consumers, and human beings, to interrupt the flow of limiting words and images to create a better world. Key terms, which are listed at the end of each chapter, are highlighted in bold.

Endnote

1   The term "minorities" is used as a way of describing individuals who hold the minority of power in a society. This is not a numerical designation. Also used in this book is the expression "people of color." Given that every individual has a preferred way of being referred to, for example, African American and Black or Native American and Indian, these designations will be used interchangeably as a way of respecting preferences.

Images referred to in Chapter 9 are available online at http://mediaminorities andmeaning.wordpress.com

❁ Acknowledgments

I would like to thank several people who provided support and guidance throughout this process. First, my family and friends who continued to hear about "the book" but stayed around anyway. My thanks as well for time and support to the School of Journalism & Communication, the Center for the Study of Women and Society, and the Center on Diversity and Community at the University of Oregon.

Thank you as well to Mary Savigar at Peter Lang for believing in this project. This book represents more than the years it took writing it and even the years spent teaching about these issues. It represents the sorting out and questioning that began within me as a child who wondered why certain people were treated differently than others, why it seemed ok for one group to denigrate another in images and in words, and knowing what it feels like to be an outsider. Although I didn't know her long, I'd like to acknowledge the influence of my mother, a woman who felt the constraints of many wires of the metaphorical birdcage in terms of her ability to fully comprehend, have access to, and be a part of the world. She was an uneducated, Southern, Native American, whose beauty, wisdom, and sophistication propelled me into questioning what labels mean. Grateful acknowledgement is hereby made to copyright holders for permission to use copyrighted materials: University of Georgia, Department of Entomology, Library and Archives Canada, photographer Donald Schneider, The John Hay Library, Brown University, Library of Congress Prints and Photographs Division, Washington, DC, the National Park Service, Statue of Liberty-Ellis Island Foundation, Office of the Clerk, U.S. House of Representatives, and Festival Internacional de Cine en Guadalajara.

Not every certainty is worth preserving.
David Berreby

Foundations

 Introduction

We are like sculptors, constantly carving out of others the image we long for, need, love or desire, often against reality, against their benefit, and always, in the end, a disappointment, because it does not fit them.

Anaïs Nin

Seeing comes before words. The child looks and recognizes before it can speak.

John Berger

There are many truths. If you happen upon one, it may be comforting. But don't dwell too long there, or you will miss the next truth, which will be equally important.

Thomas Moore

All the world's a stage and all the men and women merely players; they have their exits and entrances; and one man in his time plays many parts.

William Shakespeare

The purpose of this book is to analyze how American mass media, including advertising, presents Otherness (anyone or anything constructed as different from an established norm) in terms of gender, race, sex, disabilities, and other markers of difference. I have two primary goals for this book: (1) to offer it as a consciousness-raising tool by revealing the foundations of historically based inequities in the American social, cultural, and economic milieu that are maintained, at least in part, by mass media, popular culture and advertising representations of Otherness, and (2) to increase awareness of stereotyping in the media by, as expressed by John Berger (1977), learning ways of seeing how people are constructed as Others and how their marginalization becomes normalized in our media environment. The underlying premise is that the mass media are powerful sources of learning that have assumed the position of a dominant social institution in American society (joining education, religion, family, and government). These communication outlets are effective means of creating, sustaining, and perpetuating limited and limiting representations of people, places, and things through the retelling of **myths**, defined as the stories we tell ourselves about ourselves.

A **cultural studies** approach guides readers toward an understanding of the roots of stereotype formation and the role mass media play in constructing, reinforcing, perpetuating, and maintaining stereotypes. This is accomplished by describing the context (psychological, historical, economic) within which limited and limiting thinking about others arises. A cognitive developmental foundation is constructed upon those fundamental issues of human understandings of identity, power, and the symbolic mechanisms through which learning and meaning making take place. This book positions the mass media as modern storytellers that serve as conduits to the human psyche, or in the words of psychologist Carl Jung (1974, p. 122), the "**collective unconscious**." The collective unconscious contains "the entire psychic heritage" of human beings, and its existence is most visible in our dreams, in the symbols we use to express meaning, and universally in timeless stories and fairy tales (Stevens, 1994, p. 23). This perspective is important as what we regard as **stereotypes** (overgeneralizations that treat all members of a group as the same) and stereotypical portrayals in fact, developed from fundamental psychological constructs, germinated in myths. These narratives are peopled by recognizable **archetypes** (multi-dimensional timeless figures) that become concretized in stereotypes (one-dimensional limited representations), limiting their meaning and interpretation. Continually recycled, stereotypes generate ideological rewards that are financially reaped by the owners of mass media corporations in a system, such as that in the United States, of concentrated ownership.

This chapter introduces basic ideas about the historically grounded symbolic power of mass media, the media's relationship with society, and individual processing of media information about self and others. To begin, I'll tell a story once told to me.

The World Outside versus the Pictures in Our Heads

In October 1914, on an island somewhere in the Pacific Ocean lived a few English, French, and German people. Back then, no telegraph or telephone lines reached the island and television did not exist. Newspapers and mail arrived only every two to three months. So, in October, the islanders greatly anticipated and excitedly awaited the September delivery, as it would bring word of the verdict in a very exciting trial. It seems in March 1914, on the eve of World War I, Madame Caillaux, wife of a powerful French cabinet minister, had murdered her husband's enemy, *Le Figaro* editor Gaston Calmette. The outcome of her trial would be revealed by this delivery.

When the ship arrived, the people not only learned the verdict of the trial, but also that, during the six-week interim between updates, thousands of miles away in Europe, those who were French and those who were English had been fighting for the sanctity of treaties against those who were German. All this time the islanders had been friends. When word arrived from a world apart from the island, they found out they were now enemies. During the six-week window, the people on the island had conducted their business as usual, it "was a time for each man who [had] adjusted to an environment that no longer existed" (Lippmann, 1922, p. 4). In Europe, as late as July 25, 1914, "men were making goods that they would not be able to ship, buying goods they would not be able to import" (p. 4). Everything had changed, but for a period, the people on this island did not know it. "They trusted the pictures in their heads," not the world outside (p. 4).

Journalist Walter Lippmann wrote this story in 1922, but the lesson is well worth considering today. How do you and I know about events happening and people living in other parts of the world? Mostly by the stories the media tell us. When we hear or read about an event, our mind's eye goes to work drawing a picture based on information we have received in the past, either through others or through our own direct or indirect experiences that may or may not be accurate but become a kind of "truth." Yet, somehow, these pictures in our heads seem as real and informed as if we'd experienced the situation first-hand. Lippmann (1922, p. 29) asked, "Who actually saw, heard, felt, counted, named the thing, about which you have an opinion? Was it the man who told you, or the man who told him, or someone still further removed?" Today, more than ever before, our **knowl-edge** of people, places, and things comes by way of the mass media, "the world that we have to deal with politically is out of reach, out of sight, and out of mind. It has to be explored, reported, and imagined" (p. 7).

> Those features of the world outside which have to do with the behavior of other human beings, in so far as that behavior crosses ours, is dependent upon us, or is interesting to us, we call roughly public affairs. The pictures inside the heads of these human beings, the pictures of themselves, of others, of their needs, purposes, and relationship, are their public opinions. (Lippmann, 1922, p. 18)

Why are the pictures inside our heads so often distorted? Because of six factors that limit people's access to facts: artificial censorships, limitations of social contact, limited time, distortions, limited vocabulary, and fear.

1. *Artificial censorships.* This is the selective presentation of facts (verbal or visual) on the part of politicians and the mass media. According to Lippmann (1922, p. 7), "[Man]…has invented ways of seeing what no naked eye could see, of hearing what no ear could hear.…He is learning to see with his mind vast portions of the world that he could never see, touch, smell, hear, or remember. Gradually he makes for himself a trustworthy picture inside his head of the world beyond his reach."

2. *Limitations of social contact.* People tend to socialize with others who are, in some way, like them. Sometimes it is economically based, but often it is ideological—Democrats spend time with Democrats, conservatives know other conservatives, Catholics mingle with other Catholics—not exclusively, but certainly regularly. Typically this behavior results in within-group reinforcement of values, attitudes, and ideals, yielding group solidarity.

3. *Limited time available.* Today we seem always in a hurry—running errands, trying to make it to class or to jobs on time. There is little *time* available to contemplate assumptions or presumptions about those who are somehow different from us.

4. *Distortions.* The bulk of what we know about the world outside comes to us through words and images produced by the media. At every level of telling the information goes through the individual reporter's internal censors. This is natural, we are subjective beings. What makes sense to one person may or may not to another. What gets reported on and into the media is the result of decisions made by **gatekeepers** (editors, producers) who decide for us what is important. This is called the **agenda-setting function** of the media, telling us what to think about and sometimes what to think about the information we are given.

5. *Limited vocabulary.* A word choice that might be innocuous to one individual might offend another. Journalists and advertisers have tremendous power to fuel perceptions or misperceptions of the world outside. For example, what

comes to mind when you hear the word "immigrant?" As is discussed in Chapter 14, the meaning of the word changed remarkably in 2006 on the National Day of the Immigrant, for example, when thousands of legal and illegal workers demonstrated solidarity. The meaning of the word "terrorist" also shifted after the September 11 disaster, as discussed in Chapter 6. What does the word "freedom" mean to you? Does it mean the same thing to your friends? Family? We have many more ideas than we do words to express them. "Words, like currency, are turned over and over again, to evoke one set of images today, another tomorrow" (Lippmann, 1922, p. 42).

6. *Fear.* Finally, and perhaps most potent and compelling, is the power of fear to motivate and dictate what we hear, see, feel, and do. Allowing new information in, information that might be contradictory to long-held ideas, is risky, it upsets our psychic balance. It takes courage to suspend one's disbelief, prejudices, or reframe the pictures in our heads in order to consider the views of other people. Fear of the unknown, fear of loss of resources, fear of change are all powerful, if not the most powerful, motivations for the maintenance and perpetuation of limited views of others.

Now the question is, how "this trickle of messages from the outside is affected by the stored up images…preconceptions and prejudices which interpret, fill them out, and in their turn powerfully directly" influence the way we look at and think about others and ourselves?" (Lippmann, 1922, p. 18). The first step toward answering this question is to look to the past and to the process of narratively relaying information as one of the powers of myth, using signs, gestures, and stories.

Understanding Myth

One of the great intellectuals who thought about how people live in the world, the meanings they make, and the stories they tell was Joseph Campbell (1904–1987). Campbell stood on the shoulders of giants such as philosopher Arthur Schopenhauer, analytical psychologist Carl Jung, historian of religion Mircea Eliade, as well perspectives of Native Americans, and the philosophies behind Buddhism, Christianity, and Judaism.

Campbell influenced contemporary thinking about how people's relationships to one another are reflected in a shared and enduring mythological past. He was convinced that human **cultures** share Big Themes about life, love, death, and origins. The stories differ in culturally specific ways, but all societies have them. In 1985, Campbell was awarded the National Arts Club Gold Medal of Honor in Literature. At the ceremony, psychologist James Hillman (1985) stated, "No one in our century—not Freud, not Thomas Mann, not Lévi-Strauss—has so brought the mythical sense of the world and its **eternal figures** back into our everyday consciousness."

What is a "mythical sense of the world" and who are "its eternal figures"? Campbell posited what we know, the meaning we give to people, places, and things come from the stories we tell each other and that these stories are continually retold in ways that are relevant to a particular time and place. Paraphrasing the work of Schopenhauer, Campbell notes

> The experiences and illuminations of childhood and early youth become in later life the types, standards and patterns of all subsequent knowledge and experience, or as it were, the categories according to which all later things are classified—not always consciously, however. And so it is that in our childhood years the foundation is laid of our later view of the world, and with that, our perception of its superficiality or depth: it will be in later years unfolded and fulfilled, not essentially changed. (as quoted in Walter, n.d.)

Campbell (1988, p. 38) recognized early on the power myths have for structuring reality. He said they perform four crucial functions:

1. *Metaphysical.* A sense of the transcendent, of someone or something greater than the self "out there."
2. *Cosmological.* An idea of connectedness to a mysterious external reality and that we play an important role in the order of things, real and imagined.
3. *Sociological.* Passing down of the "correct" order of things, the **codes** and rules people need to follow that present a coordinated social order that affirms dominant social structure (see Ideology, p. 13).
4. *Pedagogical.* Myths also teach us about how to be in the world, in relation to individual development and ourselves as well as how to interact with others.

This perspective explains in part modern-day constructions of, for example, masculinity, spawned from fundamental psychological constructs germinated in myths about heroism, courage, strength, and order that are perpetuated in popular culture. Today these might take the form of Bruce Willis action adventure films and might even explain the popularity of the television phenomenon World Wide Wrestling.

Campbell also noted, albeit indirectly, how the social and pedagogical functions of myths not only energize a culture but also how they can be used oppressively and repressively in terms of limiting views of gender, race, class, sexuality, and religion, by turning archetypes (multi-dimensional, fluid symbols of personality) into stereotypes (one-dimensional, concretized signs of Otherness) in ways that made "stereotypes seem archetypal by way of the power and beauty of mythic narrative and image" (Miller, 1995, p. 171). He knew that "mythicizing the archetype has given the status quo metaphysical sanction and has supported political atrocity" (as he wrote, for example, about the Chinese view of Tibet) (p. 171). For this reason Campbell (1959, p. 12) cautioned us to use myths carefully and wisely:

> Clearly mythology is no toy for children, nor is it a matter of archaic, merely scholarly concern, of no moment to…action…. The world is now far too small, and [the]…stake in sanity too great, for any more of those old games of Chosen Folk…by which tribesmen were sustained against their enemies in the days when the serpent still could talk.

What Is Myth?

> The big stories that shape our lives…are very often those that came to us in our childhood. (McElroy, 2004, p. 12)

A myth, which has been defined in many ways, is a "true" story (Eliade, 1962/1998, p. 1) "woven into a culture which dictates belief, defines ritual, and acts as a chart of the social order" (Malinowski, 1962, p. 249). One of the powers of myth is that people believe in the story (s) they see and hear while growing up, whether or not they are factually provable. Unfortunately, and incorrectly, myth in common parlance has come to mean something untrue, false, fake, or distorted. Instead, the real meaning of myths is they are "not just delightful stories but also…revelations about human nature and human values with human impact" (Galician, 2004, p. 35). French semiologist Roland Barthes (1972) regarded myths not only as classical fables about gods and heroes, but more. Similar to Campbell's pedagogical functions, myths to Barthes reflect the dominant ideologies of our times and take on the appearance of naturalness, of truth, he notes "the very principle of myth: [is] it transforms history into nature…" (p. 129). "Myth does not deny aspects of [life], on the contrary, its function is to talk about them; simply, it purifies them. Simply put, it makes them innocent, it gives them a natural and eternal justification, it gives them a clarity which is not that of an explanation but that of a statement of fact" (p. 143).

To any given situation, we each bring our own set of cultural understandings, experiences, and opinions. In this respect the modern Western worldview is every bit as mythological as was the medieval one. A way of thinking about myths is to regard them as ideologies expressed in stories, for example, myth = ideology + narrative. The everydayness of myths can be thought of metaphorically as "the lenses of a pair of glasses in the sense that they are not the things people see when they look at the world, they are the things they see with. Myths are the truths about society that are taken for granted" (Bennett, 1980, p. 167).

Myths are extended metaphors that help us comprehend our experiences in our own culture and apprehend the world around us. They stand in for something or someone else and work as meaning-making tools that help naturalize culture and function as "instruments by which we continually struggle to make our experiences intelligible to ourselves" (Shorer, 1946, p. 355). **Metaphors**, which can be visual or verbal, stand in for something else from which meaning is made, whereas myths are the entire constructed story. Thus, **metaphorical discourse** is the constructed narrative that accompanies the tale which itself might be allusion. Myths are lived extensions of speech from which we make laws, rules, regulations, social relationships, beliefs, and values seem natural and normal, and simply how things are and forever have been. This is accomplished through language, narrative structures, images, and sounds. Words such as "good" and "evil," emotions such as "hatred" and "vengeance," and many of our highest ideals for the civilized world are, in part, products of our culture: myths, heroes, legends, and rituals" (Zehnder & Calvert, 2004, p. 123). William Doty (2000, p. 331) observes, "It is striking how many myths reflect societal polarities: rich: poor, servant: king, hero: monster, chaos: order, male: female, older: younger, light: darkness, destructive: constructive, socially approved: socially disapproved, gods: humans."

In a society with ancient and deep roots into what Jung (1974, p. 221) calls the "collective unconscious," myths fill the empty containers of authority with information that appears to be natural, normal, and commonsensical. The collective unconscious, while part of the **psyche** (unconscious), "does not…owe its existence to personal experience" (Jung, 1976, p. 59), rather it is a collection of cognitive (thinking), affective (feeling), and behavioral (doing) characteristics passed down to all members of society generation to generation. This kind of unconscious group-thinking is composed of archetypes, or forms that are "present always and everywhere" (Jung, 1936/1976, p. 60). Archetypes are generalized and often idealized versions of human behavior patterns, sometimes positive and sometimes not. While they take many forms, Jung identified four **primary archetypes** (eternal figures) in the human psyche: Self (individual identity), Shadow (usually darker side of personality), Anima (female nature in men), and Animus (male nature in women). These are eternal, archetypal figures found in dreams and stories (myth). They encompass practically all of the characters we find in modern films, television programs, advertising, books, and other media re-presentations. As will become clear in later chapters in this book, the concretization of archetypes forms the foundation for racial and sexual stereotypes which are found consistently in the media and popular culture. Plato called these invisible energies the Eternal "Ideas" (or Forms). The only way we are able to "see" this invisible pattern of the psyche is by way of an intermediary word or image. So-called "larger-than-life" figures such as heroes and monsters, real or imagined, play important roles. Jung called them "hooks" in story telling. Characters that typically take the form of archetypal figures in art, media, and popular culture include the hero, king/father, great mother, *puer* (eternal boy), child, trickster, and the shadow. An archetypal view assumes that people are influenced by universal instincts that manifest themselves in ways of thinking. Examples of this include the ubiquity of ideas about the creation of human beings, importance of the mother and father in development, and self in relation to society. When re-presented in story form this narrative construction can become naturalized as *the* one and only way to think about someone or something. Archetypes thereby help us make sense out of the world, find answers to questions associated with everyday living, and serve as guides through the complex web of information we are flooded with on a daily basis. There are seven primary archetypes, each fulfilling a specific function in narrative (Voytilla, 1999, p. 13). When you read the descriptions, think about what characters might play these roles in books or news stories you have read or in movies you have seen:

1. Hero—"to serve and sacrifice"
2. Mentor—"to guide"
3. Threshold Guardian—"to test"
4. Herald—"to warn and challenge"
5. Shape shifter—"to question and deceive"
6. Shadow—"to destroy"
7. Trickster—"to disrupt"

For a myth to remain relevant, credible, and viable, people need to believe it accurately reflects present day and, importantly, *their* realities. Today we live in a complicated, interconnected, fast-paced world from which we are always trying to extract meaning, to uncover answers to who we are and where we are going. It is a search for soulfulness, for an understanding of our and others' cultures and values. While the underpinnings of a myth remain true through time, religious and popular culture portrayals help define, refine, reproduce, and distribute it. Social changes such as women's movements, civil rights movements as well as technological advancements in media affect a culture's telling, remembering, and retelling of its stories. Thus, "ancient myths inform (though in disguised form) our arts, our media, and our everyday lives" (Berger, 2004, p. 136). Examples include the ubiquitous romantic belief that there is only one perfect person who will make all our dreams come true. This concretized view of a partner perpetuates not only a search for "the one" but also leads to dissatisfaction in otherwise positive relationships. The myth of "the one" in our everyday lives, the search for the soul mate, is the subject of countless movies, such as the classic *Casablanca* or contemporary hits such as *Sleepless in Seattle*. While the ancient epic of Gilgamesh was relevant in Sumerian times, it doesn't seem as applicable today in its original form. However, Neo, hero of *The Matrix*, similarly goes out into the world, faces a series of three challenges, and returns somehow changed and the better for it. Other popular examples of the hero motif include Luke Skywalker in *Star Wars* and Robin Hood. It is not that the film directors consciously draw on these myths (although they might have), rather the idea of the hero is such a deeply rooted story in the collective unconscious it is continually re-circulated because it makes immediate sense to an audience. These narratives are the familiar structures behind often-repeated versions of a story.

One way of apprehending how this complex process works is to think about an experiment you probably did in your pre-college education. It required three things: a magnet, a piece of cardboard, and some metal shavings. The three-step process goes something like this: (1) put the magnet on a table and place the cardboard on top of it, (2) sprinkle the metal shavings onto the cardboard, and (3) gently blow. What happens? The shavings organize themselves into a series of patterns around the magnet's invisible energy field. Archetypes work this way (although they aren't visible like shavings). Rather, archetypes (inherent predispositions) are unseen psychic, unconscious energy that become visible through images. A constellation of characteristics form a type, with ancient origins that make it familiar and comfortable. Archetypes can manifest themselves in ordinary beliefs, behaviors, and representations of everyday life as expressions of our cultural unconscious. Some characteristics are brought together and re-presented in mediated representations of our lives. If we use film as an example, Tollefson (1998, p. 108) refers to them as **"cinemyths,"** where familiar constructions are revealed through film. Tollefson (1998) identifies three mythological systems operating in new garb in media, all based on the idea of a "Return to the Garden of Eden":

1. *Biblical version*. This pattern has two patterns—dominant and subversive. This is a "lover's triangle" tale. *Fatal Attraction* is an example of the dominant version in which Glenn Close plays "the other woman" to Michael Douglas as the husband. Close's character Alex is of the type who "lures men away from their wives or steady girlfriends into an intoxicating vortex of sex, secrecy, and violence" (p. 109). This representation of the temptress who controls and sometimes destroys men and their families has ancient origins that can be traced, in Judeo-Christian traditions, to the ancient tale of Adam, Lilith, and Eve. Eve is the good wife who kills the wild demonic interloper. Other film tellings that use this pattern include *Presumed Innocent* and *Dick Tracy*. In the subversion version, "Adam prefers Lilith," to Eve and is evident in films such as the Sharon Stone and Michael Douglas hit *Basic Instinct*.

2. *Greek version.* This is the fantasy that a woman can be remade or retooled to meet the higher male standard. A classic example is *My Fair Lady* in which Henry Higgins asks, "Why can't a woman be more like a man?" Other examples include *Children of a Lesser God* and *Educating Rita.*

3. *Garden of Eden with a twist.* This version focuses on the relationship between the women, between Lilith and Eve. In this telling, the Adam figure (whether lawyer, husband, sheriff, or father) is left to work out his issues. The women are intent on healing and growth. Examples of this cinemyth include *The Color Purple, Fried Green Tomatoes,* and *Thelma and Louise.* These gender outlaws often buck the system and travel together (literally or metaphorically) and are liberated through love and respect for each other.

How do we learn these stories?

Important to studying the presence of myth in media content is the idea that myths are "used to transmit a culture's basic belief system to a younger generation and to explain natural and supernatural phenomena" (Berger, 2004, p. 181). "Understanding the difference between what is real and what is represented," says Trbic (2007, p. 87), "is vital to our understanding of any medium." Myths therefore inform a culture's ideology through their ability to teach young people the rules and norms of the culture they will participate in. Linguistic and visual markers of myth are found in the codes a dominant social group uses to construct meaning from art, books, and mediated culture. These narratives strike a chord that is consistent with the point of view of dominant society.

Ideology is defined as a belief system that, "in order to be effective, must be perceived as the truth, rather than seen as one of many possible belief systems" (Gaffney, 2008, p. 136). Importantly, the truths are established and the meanings are made in ways that appear to be common sense. A more detailed definition says, ideology

> is about the "ideas" held in common by social groups in their everyday lives. It also suggests that these ideas are organized in certain ways. An ideology is a "logic of ideas" indicating that the groups who hold various ideologies perceive and understand the world in a certain consistent way. (Thwaites, Davis, & Mules, 2002, p. 158)

This logic of ideas is formed on the individual level and even more so, on the public level. A way of thinking about how ideology works is to think of looking at the world through a pair of special glasses. You might not be aware you are wearing these glasses, but they are constructed in a way so that what you see is framed according to a particular worldview. What you see appears to be the normal and natural way of looking at the world. People often do not recognize they are acceding to beliefs and values of the dominant system because of the process Stuart Hall (1986, p. 53) calls "articulation." **Articulation Theory** makes sense out of otherwise, and previously, unrelated concepts. This view conceptualizes the mental moment when people "knit together disparate and apparently contradictory practices, beliefs, and discourses in order to give their world some semblance of meaning and coherence" (Trimbur, 1993). **Hegemony,** defined as ruling of society through the power of ideas versus physical force and where the governed consent to their sublimation, relies on the power of myth. Myths are the frames within which the lenses (ideologies) are contained. These concepts work closely together as psychological (rather than physical) forms of social control.

In French Marxist theorist Ferdinand Althusser's (1971) view, this is accomplished through **Ideological State Apparatus** (ISA), instruments of power that operate as a force "in ways that are subtle, disguised, and accepted as everyday social practice" (Allison, 1991, p. 195). Althusser (1971) identified two sources of power: Repressive State Apparatus and Ideological State Apparatus. Whereas the first uses physical coercion and/or laws to force compliance with dominant system of beliefs, the second uses ways of thinking, usually through ideas, laws, mores, and rules taught by social institutions such as schools, education, and mass media through an ideological "interpellation" (Althusser, 2001).

The mass media are particularly powerful as they contain a wide variety of symbolic vehicles such as television, film, news, books, magazines, that carry messages consistent with views of the role of women, people of color, and children in society. Essentially, these tools (lenses) reproduce the ideas, values, and beliefs **dominant culture** wants to appear as agreed-upon. A television program (the apparatus) such as *Friends*, for example, presents middle class values, definitions of femininity and masculinity, and, by virtue of the absence of people of color, racial hierarchy.

How we form associations and make meaning is the foundation of mythic thinking. Diarist Anaïs Nin points out at the beginning of this chapter how and what we see, the meanings we ascribe to people, places, and things, depend largely on who we are and how we are raised, that is, our subjective natures: "We don't see things as they are, we see things as we are." Individual ways of apprehending images, words, and events based upon differences such as nationality, individual experiences, age, race, ethnicity, and sex are components of **subjectivity**, which is

> an abstract or general principle that defies our separation into distinct selves and that encourages us to imagine that, or simply helps us to understand why, our interior lives inevitably seem to involve other people either as objects of need, desire, and interest or as necessary sharers of common experience. (Mansfield, 2000, p. 3)

The development of individual identity involves learning the "general truths and shared principles" at the intersection of common experience and self, where self is recognized not as a separate and independent entity rather as a part of it, as "one is always subject *to* or *of* something" (italics orig.) (Mansfield, 1994, p. 3). Thus we subjectively encounter the world. Repeated exposure to myths, the tenets of ideologies, or mythic motifs instead of intentional conscious learning and actual experience is responsible for embedding these mythic stories into the structure of our consciousnesses. These deep structures influence how we engage with the world around us. They manifest in the modern world not so much as fully formed mythical narratives but rather as "fragmentary references, indirect allusions, watchwords, slogans, visual symbols, echoes in literature, film, songs, public ceremonies, and other forms of everyday situations, often highly condensed and emotionally charged" (Flood, 1996, p. 84).

How Do We Study Myths?

There are two compatible, interrelated ways to "read" myths as **text**: semiotics and mythological analysis.

Semiotics

Semiotics, based on the Greek word *semeîon*, is a useful way of deciphering the coding of cultural myths. This interdisciplinary method draws on fields as diverse as philosophy, anthropology, sociology, literary studies, psychology, and education. A semiotic analysis explores signs and symbols used to articulate myths. Essentially, semiotics is about the meaning people make from the words and images they see. Semiotics helps us **denaturalize** words, symbols, and signs in order to peel off the layer of applied (preferred) meaning that, for example, suggests portraying women as sex objects, African Americans as lazy, or Native Americans as drunkards is a natural and normal reflection of reality.

The theory of semiotics was originally articulated by two primary individuals: Swiss linguist Ferdinand de Saussure (1857–1913) and American philosopher C. S. Peirce (1839–1914). Saussure's (1916) *sémiologie* originated in the book *A Course on General Linguistics*. He sought to explain "the role of signs in social life" (1983, p. 15). Saussure made an important distinction between ***langue*** (language) and ***parole*** (speech). *Langue* is the system or rules around language use such as syntax. *Parole* is use of language. For example, a film uses language as dialogue, but film genres such as mysteries, science fiction, or horror adhere to specific stylistic *conventions* (see Chapter 13 for more on this topic). **Conventions** include a particular way of shooting a scene, use of lighting, shadows, or music. The viewer can anticipate these being included as a specific form of syntax in the film. In Saussure's view, language is comprised of signs that are made up of two components, signifiers (sounds or images) and the signifieds (concepts or ideas). The relationship between signifier, signified, and sign is illustrated in mathematical form:

$$\text{Signifier} + \text{Signified} = \text{Sign}$$

The **sign** is an empty container that is filled by meaning, meaning made by a particular culture. The **signified** is the mental concept, the idea of someone or something that exists between "a mental image, a concept, and a psychological reality" (Eco, 1976, pp. 14–15). The **signifier** is the material object, the tangible person or thing that can be seen, touched, tasted, or otherwise experienced. The sign is therefore the result of the interaction of these two components through the process of *signification.*

Whereas Saussure saw a science of signs, C.S. Peirce's (pronounced "purse") conception of signs was philosophical. He called the field "semeiotic" or "semiotic." Peirce created a taxonomy of signs, comprised of three types: (1) icons are signs that take meaning because they *resemble* someone or something, such as a photograph of Marilyn Monroe. It is a realistic *image* of someone or something but not the real thing, (2) **indexes** illustrate a cause and effect relationship, for example, an image of smoke coming out of a house indicates fire, and (3) **symbols** are signs that, through convention, take on a particular meaning, such as a flag, Star of David, or a swastika. Peirce created a triadic model comprised of three elements:

1. The ***representamen*** is the form the sign takes (not necessarily material, though usually interpreted as such), called by some the "sign vehicle."
2. An **interpretant** is the *sense* made of the sign, not an interpretation per se.
3. An **object** which exists beyond the sign, but to which it refers (***referent***)

Of this model Peirce (1931/1958, 2.228) said

> a sign…is something which stands to somebody for something in some respect or capacity. It addresses somebody, that is, creates in the mind of that person an equivalent sign, or perhaps a more developed sign. That sign which creates I call the *interpretant* of the first sign. The sign stands for something, its *object*. It stands for that object, not in all respects, but in reference to a sort of idea, which I have sometimes called the *ground* of the representamen.

Therefore, the sign is made up of the meaning constructed for it is the product of a dynamic relationship between the ways sounds, words, and images are combined that produces meaning. These texts, whether visual, verbal, or written, are constructed according to a kind of cultural semiotic logic that makes them make sense to us. According to Fredric Jameson (1972, p. 32–33)

> It is not so much the individual word or sentence that "stands for" or "reflects" the individual object or event in the real world, but rather that the entire system of signs, the entire field of the *langue*, lies parallel to reality itself; that it is the totality of systematic language, in other words, which is analogous to whatever organized structures exist in the world of reality, and that our understanding proceeds from one whole or Gestalt to the other, rather than on a one-to-one basis.

How does this system operate in media? In advertising, for example, literal signs that advertise an establishment such as restaurant, bar, or grocery store stand in for a place or a thing and convey something about the essence of it. Logos operate in a similar way, conveying corporate identity along with an intangible something about the product or service through the use of particular colors and shapes. Thus, by looking at a particular text, for example an ad, it is possible to read it, that is, ascertain the message communicated. This meaning operates at two levels: connotative and denotative. The connotative meaning (from the Latin *connotare*) is filled with a specific culture content; it is the deeper level meaning, below the surface. The denotative meaning (from the Latin *denotare*) is the surface, literal meaning.

Semiotician Roland Barthes drew on his own (French) culture to explore objects such as the Citroen automobile, wrestling, and steak and *frites*. Connotative (deeper level) meanings are inferred and they take us into the realm of myth. A sign's denotative meaning is on the surface, it is what we first take away, the explicit versus implicit meaning. Meaning is coded into a text by its creator based on his or her understanding of the culture and the goals of the form of communication. Codes are defined as "complex patterns of associations that all members of a given society and culture learn" (Berger, 2005, p. 30). The codes are learned structures that influence how we interpret what we hear and see. They produce a "symbolic convergence with a text" and the reader (Alfino, Caputo, & Wynyard, 1998, p. 43).

A Barbie doll is an example of a text that can be decoded. The denotative meaning of Barbie is a female doll which has specific anatomical measurements. However, the connotative meaning of Barbie is complex—she is the only *adult* doll, and her proportions *mean something* in an image-obsessed, consumer-driven culture, such as America's. Hence, the entire package of and about Barbie, including her friends and possessions teach developing girls (the pedagogical role of myth) about what it means to be a woman in American culture. Understanding and using semiotics as method and perspective are important if, for no other reason, than to be literate in the underlying meaning structures of the information that circulates so widely around us. A study of signs "can assist us to become more aware of the mediating role" they play in our lives and the roles played by others in response to them (Chandler, 2007, p. 10). Learning to decipher the codes that construct a text empowers informed choices. Not only is it important to be aware of the polysemy (multiple meanings) a sign might have, but also how, as Saussure warned us, a sign can be used as a devious agent for the propagation of an ideology. All signs exist in relation to the society within which they are created and "reveal whose realities are privileged and those who are suppressed" (Chandler, 2007, p. 11). Meaning can thereby be constructed in ways that conceal or reveal its intent.

> Everything we do sends messages about us in a variety of codes, semiologists contend. We are also on the receiving end of innumerable messages encoded in music, gestures, foods, rituals, books, movies, or advertisements. Yet we seldom realize that we have received such messages, and would have trouble explaining the rules under which we operate. (Pines, 1982, n. p.)

In the essay "Myth Today," Barthes (1972, p. 142) notes, "Semiology has taught us that myth has the task of giving an historical intention a natural justification, making contingency appear eternal. Now this process is exactly that of bourgeois ideology." What signs share is an overarching context of vast human experience. These Big Stories are myths and appear in a variety of story telling modes, including the mass media. The style in which we wear our hair, whether a woman wears makeup or not (see Chapter 10 for more on this), our body language, and tone of voice say something about us to other people. In some cases, these artifacts suggest participation in a specific religion, political party, or value system and meaning is not arbitrary. Just as myths do, what something stands for naturally changes over time, evolving to remain relevant, based on conventions, and learned patterns. Moreover, these meanings are reinforced over our life, sometimes as the correct, natural, and right thing to do, wear, suggest, or carry. Thus, to interpret them, we must recognize the shared codes and conventions of language and symbols (and language as symbol) that govern a culture. An example that illustrates this point comes from politics.

On May 1, 2003, President George W. Bush arrived via jetfighter and boarded an aircraft carrier. He had declared the U.S. attack on Iraq a success under the banner "Mission Accomplished." The event, arranged to stabilize the president's image as protector of the country, heroic leader, and powerful president. Press photos and coverage sought to ground the president in this story of stability by providing what Barthes (1977, p. 40) termed **anchorage**, which is amplification of the meaning of a text and fixing it at a moment in time to mean something specific. This anchorage was, however, undone, by the reality of the situation there and thereafter when it became clear that the United States had no way out of the situation in Iraq, there were no "weapons of mass destruction" hidden there, and overall uncertainty as to why the military was in Iraq in the first place given the attacks on the Pentagon and World Trade Center in 2001 came from forces in Afghanistan. However, how or if the story of presidential power and progress was de-stabilized depended also on the point of view of the reader of the text (age, race, political perspective, education). The psychological location therefore relies on whether or not a person possesses a guiding mythology and/or participates in the mythology of his or her culture.

A mythological model of the media

Mircea Eliade (1967, p. 28) pointed out, "Certain mythical themes still survive in modern societies, but are not readily recognizable since they have undergone a long process of laicization." An "**onion of culture**" metaphor described what Eliade meant (Asa Berger, 2003). This metaphor suggests it takes peeling away each layer to find more at the core that's central to the tale. Each stage (layer) brings us deeper and further back in time to what seems to be the origins of the story. For example, in the modern-day film genre the Western can be traced to the original Adam and Eve story. *Star Wars* is an example that clearly draws both on the modern Western formulas as well as mythological origins of the hero's journey. A basic mythic mode for analyzing media images and stories was creatively constructed by Asa Berger (2005, p. 71). It recognizes "many of our activities are desacralized manifestations of ancient myths" and provides a framework with which we can **deconstruct** (take apart) a media text according to the following elements (see Table 1.1):

1. A myth (a sacred/ancient story)
2. A historical event related to the myth
3. The text or work from elite culture based on the myth
4. The text or work for popular culture based on the myth
5. Some aspects of everyday life based on the myth

An example of the application of this model is to deconstruct the main title sequence for the ABC television program *Desperate Housewives*. Every Sunday evening the program begins with a scene from the previous episode, pauses after a dramatic, introductory moment, and flips to the complex main title sequence of the Garden of Eden in a style reminiscent of German Renaissance painter Lucas Cranach's oil *Adam and Eve* (1526).

The viewer is transported from the sacred story/myth through high and popular culture portrayals of the interactions between men and women, to the everyday world of Anystreet, United States, where suburban life carries the promise of freedom from the temptations of city life but lived reality is something quite different, particularly on Wisteria Lane. This flow makes sense immediately to

Table 1.1: Asa Berger's Mythic Model of Media

Myth/Sacred Story	Adam in the Garden of Eden. Theme of natural innocence	Oedipus Myth. Theme of son unknowingly killing father and marrying mother.
Historical experience	Puritans come to United States to escape corrupt European civilization	Revolutions
Elite culture	American Adam figure in American novels. Henry James' *The American*	Sophocles, *Oedipus Rex* Shakespeare, *Hamlet*
Popular culture	Westerns…restore natural innocence to Virgin Land. *Shane.*	Jack the Giant Killer
Everyday life	Escape from city and move to suburbs so kids can play on grass (and with grass).	Oedipus period in little children

Source Asa Berger, A. (2005, p. 71). *Shop 'til You Drop: Consumer Behavior and American Culture.* Lanham, MD: Rowman & Littlefield.

American viewers. Although we do not consciously process it, we are able to understand it in a mere twelve seconds because it is mythic, because it resonates with deeply held, puritanical visions of earthly paradise. In this animatronics version, Adam and Eve come alive in pop-up paper doll fashion. The apple falls, Eve (subtitle for actor Terri Hatcher enters) catches it under a tree in the Garden of Eden, hair tendrils wafting behind, and, according to creators yU+co., "in a Monty Python-esque moment, Eve lowers the boom on her disagreeable hubby with an apple the size of a Volkswagen" (Title sequence, n.d.). Next, an Egyptian woman, with four highly stylized Egyptian children slide in. The mother is subsumed by the little ones and then disappears amongst them (subtitles enter for actors Felicity Huffman and Marcia Cross).

This three-second moment is pushed aside by the famous van Eyck oil painting *The Arnolfini Portrait (The Marriage of Giovanni Arnolfini and Giovanna Cenami)* (1434) (Figure 1.1). In the *Desperate Housewives* version, however, the man is animated, eats a banana (actor Eva Longoria Parker's name enters), tosses the peel over his shoulder (actor Nicolette Sheridan's name replaces Parker's) and his wife sweeps it away.

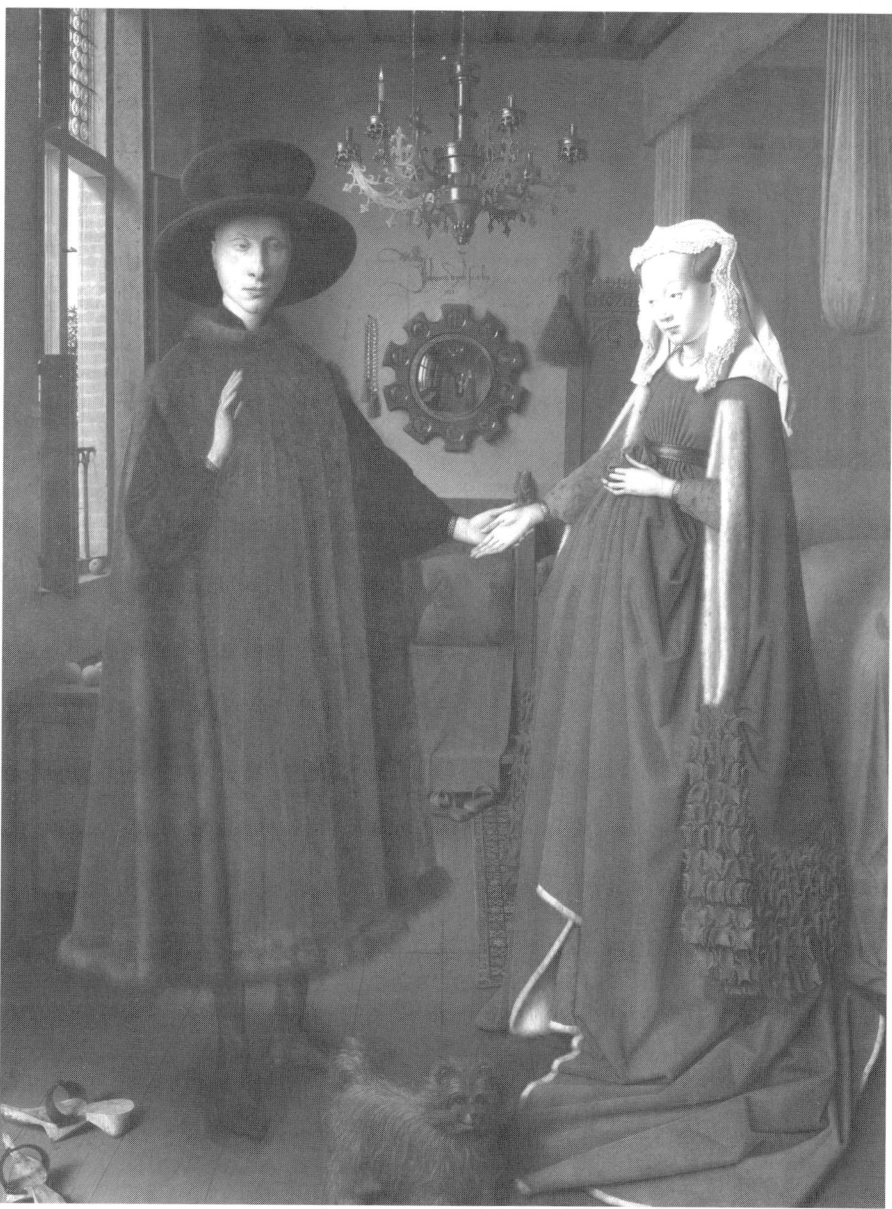

Figure 1.1: Jan van Eyck. The Arnolfini portrait (the marriage of Giovanni Arnolfini and Giovanna Cenami) (1434).

Source: *National Gallery*, London / Art Resource, NY.

Next, the iconic Grant Wood painting *American Gothic* (1930) pushes out the Van Eyck.

In the *Desperate Housewives* version, however, the farmer has a wandering eye and smiles as he is tickled under the chin by World War II pin-up girl. His dismayed wife melds into the cover of a sardine can, supplanted by what appears to be homage to Andy Warhol's Campbell's Soup can, ending in Lichtenstein-like cartoon character couple of Robert Dale's *Couple Arguing* and *Romantic Couple*. The tearful woman punches the man, and the subtitle of omniscient (dead) narrator Mary Alice enters. The final image is of the glamorous foursome (main characters Susan, Bree, Gabrielle, and Lynette), as bright red apples land in each well-manicured hand and the serpent dangles from a branch behind. Male actor names float in and out. Image producer Lane Jensen adds, "Each [image] calls to mind one of the gripes women have faced over the years from infidelity to a husband who can't pick up after himself." The core message: According to one of the sequence creators, Garson Yu, the creators used "iconic imagery to convey the anguish of the feminine mind." The sequence shows allegedly untrustworthy and wily women throughout time who, as do the women of Wisteria Lane, come out on top.

Psychologist James Hillman (1975, p. 3) states, "by telling mythical stories about our lives we can direct fantasy into organized, deeply life-giving psychological patterns." The media tell stories composed of various signs and symbols that reflect agreed-upon, common understandings, that is, patterns. How these representations are communicated in society and reified through rituals, images, symbols, and language, is central to understanding the media as mechanisms through which meaning is made. Meaning making practices are central to any culture, serving as social glue that binds people together over what are thought to be shared beliefs. Although the term "myth" is often used to indicate something that is not true, this is misuse of the word. Myths make stories seem "natural and eternal" and

> in passing from history to nature, myth acts economically: it abolishes the complexity of human acts, it gives them the simplicity of essences, it does away with all dialectics, with any going back beyond what is immediately visible, it organizes a world which is without contradictions, because it is without depth, a world wide open and wallowing in the evident, it establishes a blissful clarity: things appear to mean something by themselves. (Barthes, 1957/1973, p. 143)

Popular culture narratives function in this way. In movies, television programs, and advertisements a world is created that denies "the human complexity of acts" and the realities of human history. A simple, clear, peaceful world is presented devoid of the complexity of real human interactions. Thus, as metaphors, myths are "comparisons by which we hope to gain some useful insight into our condition and our place in the cosmos" (Voytilla, 1999, p. 9).

Myth in the Modern World

> Media stories provide the symbols, myths, and resources through which we constitute a common culture and through which we insert ourselves into this culture. (Kellner, 1995, p. 5)

Myth analysis has been used in media studies primarily to examine films and news. In news, this approach has been applied to study differences between events and the symbols used to construct stories about them (Coman & Rothenbuhler, 2005; Marvin & Ingle, 1999; Campbell, 1995; Bird & Dardenne, 1988; Graham & Dean, 1982). For example, we see how the news media present the American flag (Marvin & Ingle, 1999), how the events of 9/11 were contextualized (Rothenbuhler, 2005), and how news operates as cultural narrative in the construction of history (Liebes & Blondheim, 2005). In an analysis of drama-as-myth and the Peking Opera in the People's Republic of China, Denton (1987) describes how myth can be used to sustain a point of view but at the same time disguises political intentions of its creator, when in what otherwise might be seen as a simple play or story "myth becomes a devious agent for the propagation of an ideology" (p. 120). Furthermore,

> an ideology requires myth to promote and sustain itself; it needs myth to transform 'history into nature.' If the supremacy of Mao Zedong's Thought is simply stated or explained in dry theoretical treatises or newspaper articles it does not appear as a natural image of reality: it is cold and unappealing. In myth, the meaningful sign on the first level of signification lends a naturalness and ineluctability to its emptied form on the mythic level. (p. 133)

Researchers argue that news follows a mythological narrative pattern that is communal, orienting, and ritualistic. Myth helps explain the inexplicable, organizes the disorganized. News helps us with that as well as "news is a particular kind of mythological narrative with its own symbolic codes that are recognized by its audience" (Bird & Dardenne, 1988, p. 71). Journalists, who are raised in the same culture as their readers, operate by the same narrative codes and draw upon this knowledge when writing stories. Thus, by reading newspaper stories we can learn the mythic codes, value, and symbols of a culture.

It is probably easier to see how mythic narratives are used in film because so much of film is obviously story telling and fantasy, whereas in news the hero archetype might be less obvious when articulated as a politician, sports figure, or celebrity who faces challenges and transcends limitations. Voytilla's (1999) seven archetypes described earlier present a model for thinking about how myth operates in movies. Film analyses using a mythic approach include studies of *An Inconvenient Truth* (Rosteck & Frentz, 2007); *2001: A Space Odyssey* (Kuberski, 2008); *The*

Matrix (Cook, 2007); a mythic analysis of the western films of director John Ford (Bohnke, 2001); and an analysis of the films of director David Cronenberg (Lasiera, 2008).

With news, our expectations of truth are of a certain kind, and we look to experts to help us fill in the blanks for what we don't understand. Film varies more widely depending on whether it is a documentary, presented as history, or presented as fantasy. Yet, even fantasy carries a kind of universal truth. But how do we know what is true? Are there different truths? Whose reality is presented as the right, correct, and true one? Whose myth are we living today? We can approach answering these questions by examining the study of knowledge (**epistemology**) and consider how we learn about how something influences what we believe we know to be "the truth."

Epistemology

> You're going to find that many of the truths we cling to depend
> greatly on our point of view. (Obi-Wan Kenobi)

What do we believe about what we see in life and what we see presented in the mass media? How do we *know* something is real or false, a truth or a lie? Our access to a sense of certainty about "truth" or "reality" traditionally comes from central social institutions such as the church (or other religious group), the government, the family, and education. It is from these sources and the individuals in charge of them that a child learns what is right or wrong, what qualities make for a good boy or a good girl, a real man or a real woman. The philosophy of ways of knowing, the study of knowledge, is epistemology and has been explored by countless philosophers, linguists, and sociologists (Kerlinger, 1973; Kuhn, 1962). There are many ways of "knowing" and evaluating a truth and/or a fiction. They include:

1. *Scientific knowledge.* Looking to science is one of the most common ways people feeling they can know something to be true. This method "attempts to define a process for defining truth that produces results verifiable by others and is self-correcting" (Huitt, 1998, n.p.) using categorizations and taxonomic models.

2. *Faith based knowledge.* Here "truth is established through a trusted source such as God, tradition, or public sanction" (Huitt, 1998, n.p.) or in holy writings such as the Talmud, Bible, and Koran.

3. *Intuition or personal knowledge/experience.* Also known as the method of tenacity advocated by Peirce (Kerlinger, 1973). In this case, "truth is what is

known to the individual or group. It simply is true by the individual or group's method of assessment" (Huitt, 1998, n.p.) always and forever.

4. *Folk knowledge.* This is everyday knowledge and theories of everyday people. Someone might say, "I have a theory about that...." It doesn't mean she or he has scientifically tested an idea according to some set of criteria but rather, based on experience, stories, or second-hand knowledge, put together a sense of what is true.

5. *Expert knowledge.* Also known as an authority, a social authority such as a teacher, judge, police officer, or other public figure.

6. *Media-generated knowledge draws on the previous five sources.* Today, given the centrality of media in many people's lives and the ubiquity of advertising and public relations, the mass media function with other major social institutions as sources of knowledge of "truth." Although the reliability of journalism has come under intense scrutiny in the last few years, many people still use print and electronic media to find out what is going on in the world. Television news in particular is the primary source of most people's information, and within that, particularly during emergencies, the cable network CNN and FOX are the choice of millions.

Once we have identified something as being true, whether it is a statement, an image, or an idea we then have "knowledge," which can be classified into six categories (Huitt, Hummel, & Kaeck, 2001):

1. *Facts.* An idea or action that can be verified. Examples include names and dates of important activities or the population of the United States according to the latest census.

2. *Concepts.* Rules that allow for categorization of events, places, and/or people and ideas. For example a desk is a piece of furniture (also a concept) designed with a flat top for writing; a chair is a piece of furniture designed for sitting; a chair with a flat surface attached to it that is designed for writing is also called a desk.

3. *Principles.* Relationship(s) between/among facts and/or concepts. For example, the number of children in the family is not related to the average scores on nationally standardized achievement tests for those children.

4. *Hypotheses.* Educated guess about relationships (principles). For example, for lower-division, undergraduate students study habits are a better predictor of success in a college course than is a measure of intelligence or reading comprehension.

5. *Theories.* Set of facts, concepts, and principles that allow description and explanation. Examples include Piaget's (1969) theory of cognitive development that identified four stages of child development (each with cognitive

opportunities and limitations), Erikson's (1950) theory of socio-emotional development, and Skinner's (1953) theory of operant conditioning.

6. *Laws.* Firmly established, thoroughly tested, principle or theory. For example, a fixed interval schedule for delivering reinforcement produces a specific effect on behavior.

Collectively we have ways of seeking out, verifying, and understanding something we come to believe as true. This does not necessarily mean everyone believes the same thing or sees a situation through the same eyes. What constitutes beauty, for example, varies by culture, particularly ideal female beauty and is an example of **cultural relativity**. Having the "correct" religion, believing in the same basic values, and regarding one another as equal (or not) varies not only by nation, but also by culture and by individual. In the same way views of beauty, status, or differences across cultures are the meanings words hold in different languages. If you have ever seen a foreign language film, for example, and know the language, the translations might not seem to capture the essence of the meaning of the words of the original film. Linguists Sapir and Whorf developed a theory of **linguistic relativity** to account for differences in meanings or sheer numbers of words used in a particular language based on the importance of the person, place, or thing to that culture. For example, a place that receives a great deal of rain or snow might have many more words for this precipitation than would a desert community simply because it is more relevant. Individual or societal definitions of truth can be liberating or constraining:

> The idea of truth is a fence that keeps out others who have a different truth. It is the grandest illusion, in which we believe and to which we attach our hopes. It is generally opaque, while the illusions that lead to understanding and justice are transparent. They allow life to pass through them, whereas truth is a sentry keeping life out. (Moore, 2003, p. 9)

If myths are the stories we tell ourselves about ourselves, and if myths transcend time and space while being constantly reconstituted to fit current ideas and goals, how are they communicated to present day, technologically sophisticated people? What importance does the retelling serve?

Myth Making and Media

The mass media warn us of danger, inform us of the goings on of government, employ us, and keep us in touch with different parts of society, such as individuals we might not otherwise meet in person. The stories are told in the form of films, television programs, news, magazine articles, books, and in the embedded advertising and public relations. What kinds of stories do they tell? Boy meets girl, the hero's journey, lovers' triangle, and tragic resolution are common themes. They are all based on stories that have circulated through hundreds of years of history and are universal, with in some cases, variations on places, names, and details that reflect local culture.

Myths in modern times also arrive by way of advertising. Advertisements for shampoos that bring intense sexual pleasure, young men who attract supermodels by drinking lots of beer, and perfumes that operate as love potions present a world with no relationship to reality. Nearly as direct as injection, advertising gives us "immediate access to the world of desire, eroticism, and even love" (Jhally, 1997). Media critic Sut Jhally (1997) posits "if an anthropologist from Mars analyzed these ads they might conclude that our culture is dominated by a belief in magic," as the "magic system" presented in ads suggests these products have tremendous powers. For example, by the use of a particular brand of lotion, women turn from alligators into supermodels, and the correct choice of breakfast cereals is a substitute for steroid injections. What these advertisements rely upon is the transformative quality products are shown to possess and that these qualities can be yours through purchase.

While the mythological basis for shared understandings helps to explain the basis for the **social construction** of particular types of individuals and story lines, there are other approaches for understanding how archetypes (symbols) become concretized into stereotypes (signs). The underlying construct is, of course, the process of creating and maintaining difference, the subject of the next chapter (Chapter 2).

Questions for Discussion

1. What is an example of a myth that is common to action adventure films?
2. Why does this remain a popular theme?
3. Was there a time when you were told a story and it had an impact on you?
4. How do you know an actor is playing a doctor in a film? Is this person a man or woman?
5. Is story telling an important part of the way media communicate information?

Key Words

Agenda-setting function	Anchorage
Archetype	Articulation Theory
Cinemyths	Code

Collective unconscious
Convention
Cultural relativity
Cultural studies
Culture
Deconstruct
Denaturalize
Dominant culture
Epistemology
Eternal figures
Gatekeeper
Hegemony
Ideology
Ideological State Apparatus (ISA)
Index
Interpretant
Knowledge
Langue
Linguistic relativity
Metaphor
Metaphorical discourse
Myth
Object
Onion of culture
Parole
Primary archetypes
Psyche
Referent
Representamen
Semiotics
Sign
Signified
Signifier
Social construction
Stereotype
Subjectivity
Symbol
Text

CHAPTER TWO

Constructing Categories of Difference

As a demeaned outsider, the Other can become an easy target, blamed
for the problems that society cannot or will not solve.

Belenky, Field, Bond, & Weinstock

We see what we believe, and not just the contrary;
and to change what we see,
it is sometimes necessary to change what we believe.

Narby

All good people agree,
And all good people say,
All nice people, like Us, are We
And everyone else is They.

Rudyard Kipling

What does it mean to be an American in the 21st century? Is there a typical American? At different times in the nation's history, who may become an American has changed and what it means to be American shifts. The focus of this book is on American stereotypical constructs, but this limit in scope does not suggest the same thought process and actions don't exist in other parts of the world, they do. Otherwise, how would one account for the horrors of Nazi Germany, the genocides of Armenia, Rwanda, Darfur, the former Yugoslavia, and others? In the post-9/11 world, and the resultant era of American global conflict, who is an American and what it means to be an American are subjects of debate. Immigration, citizenship, and patriotism are all topics that are under microscopic examination at the national, regional, local, and personal level. While the founders of the United States may have had a vision of homogenization, of oneness among different peoples, the reality of lived experience has indeed proven quite different. In one sense, this is positive. The antiquated melting-pot idea of stirring together racial, ethnic, cultural **differences** into one thick soup leaves no room for individuality, no flavor of different cultures, religions, or ideas. This metaphor for **assimilation** of immigrants into a common American culture originated in a 1908 play by writer **Israel Zangwill**, who, in the late 1800s, escaped persecution and certain death in Russia. In the play *The Melting Pot,* Zangwill told a Romeo and Juliet tale that featured star-crossed lovers: one a Russian Jew and the other with a Russian Cossack heritage. At the dénouement of the play the hero declares: "Understanding that America is God's crucible, the great **melting pot** where all races of Europe are melting and reforming! A fig for your feuds and vendettas! Germans and Frenchmen, Irishmen and Englishmen, Jews and Russians— into the Crucible with you all! God is making the American." The story was retold in the 1917 Charlie Chaplin film *The Immigrant.*

A metaphor closer to the reality of lived experience in the United States is the **salad bowl**. Early in the colonization of the United States, most of the people moving in were White Europeans. Although ethnically different, there were many shared characteristics. However, by the mid-19th century, with forced enslavement of Native Americans, African Americans, and others, the population of Others grew. A melting pot suggests the longer all the vegetables (human beings) simmer together, the more alike they will become. That, however, has not been the case. A problem with homogenization is the erasure of differences. However, awareness of diversity can also be used to discriminate. Fertile ground for conflict between groups of people is separating human beings to create in-groups (the Us) and out-groups (the Them). Should we stress our similarities and build upon shared beliefs? Or celebrate differences? America is a nation of both immigrants and indigenous peoples. From the beginning, there was land that one group wanted to acquire and another group wanted to retain. The drive for acquisition of resources and **power** has shaped who Americans are. The arrival of every subsequent group of immigrants raised questions and concerns among those who were already ashore. Rumors spread often before the newcomers arrived about who they were, what they believed in, whether they were honorable or dishonorable. Every group who considers the United States to be their home country has its own history, one made up of experiences and viewpoints rich in tales of both economic and cultural riches and poverty. The United States has remained one of the most diverse countries in the world. A person can travel from one state to the next, one city to the next, and in some cases, one street to the next and find completely different food, clothing, complexions, and perspectives from his or her own. So instead of melting pot, the tossed salad metaphor is often used to describe the heterogenic cultural, racial, ethnic and other variations in society.

Individual and national identities, constructs of sex, gender, race, ethnicity, and other categories of difference (dissimilarity) change over time. For example, after the tragedy of September 11, 2001, the definition of who is an American underwent serious scrutiny as those who had once been neighbors and friends, if of "Arab descent," were made to feel like outsiders. The same thing happened during World War II to Japanese citizens who were made to live in internment camps. Author Toni Morrison (1992, p. 47) says, "Race has functioned as a metaphor necessary to the construction of American-ness."

In this chapter we explore how and why identity categories are constructed, what they mean in terms of quality of life for those who vary from the socially constructed norm, and the economic, cultural, political, health, and media consequences of these divisions for a democratic society. In the following sections, key concepts are defined and contexts provided that are used in the chapters that follow. Understanding the process of categorization and defining difference is foundational and critical to understanding Othering and identity. For purposes of this chapter, **Othering** is defined as identification of another person on the basis of some real or imagined, visible or invisible, difference that is used to sustain and maintain inequities in power. In other words, it is the "process which serves to mark and name those thought to be different from oneself" (Weis, 1995, p. 18). Othering creates a web of contingencies that informs the construction, perpetuation, and persistence of historically grounded limiting beliefs about people, places, and things. This includes theories that explain and predict the way human beings make meaning from and construct difference among Others. The arbitrary nature of marking someone as Other was exemplified on the popular television series *Lost*, which ran on ABC from 2004 to 2010. In this series, different groups of people are called Others, but there is always such a group "albeit an amorphous, ill-defined group" (Gaffney, 2008, p. 140) (see Chapter 11 for more on *Lost*). The slippery nature of their identity makes explicit the way Otherness is constructed— that it "creates fear and is created by fear, how it serves as a divide-and-conquer strategy, how it creates an "us" versus "them," and importantly, "how those who are associated with otherness are linked to savagery and to a lack of civilization" (p. 140).

Defining Difference

Difference

> Noun. 1. a. The condition, quality, or fact of being different, or not the same in quality or in essence; dissimilarity, distinction, diversity; the relation of non-agreement or non-identity between two or more things, disagreement. (OED)

In an individualistic society such as the United States, strong emphasis is placed on the value of individual achievement, decision-making, and well-being as opposed to what is best for the group. This ideology comes into conflict when the nation as a whole needs citizens to come together in support for or to rally against some important issue or group.

In the following sections, several approaches are described that attempt to explain why human beings so often narrowly define other human beings as Other. Is it biologically hardwired into us to do this or are we taught? The identification of difference and the mechanisms that underlie its construction is at the core of the onion for understanding the how and why human beings categorize and label each other.

Making meaning/constructing categories

The first time in human history one individual saw another who differed in some way, for example, not being from his or her tribe or possessed something another wanted, difference was established. From then onwards, humans thought in terms of an "I" and a "you" or, collectively, an "Us" and a "Them." This response was and is not only fundamental to both individual and group survival but also continues to be a part of modern psychology. Many behaviorists argue that the need to define someone as "Other" is part of a basic cognitive structure that needs to categorize as part of one's mental **schema**. Schemata are defined as "knowledge structures based on experiences that organize people's perceptions of the world" (Samsup, 2003, p. 406). **Schema theory** suggests, "the absorption and processing of information depends on learned, relatively stable cognitive structures of knowl-edge," called schemata or visualizations (p. 406). A way of thinking about schema is as a blueprint that maps out our mental world, that organizes and makes sense of our relationship to other people, places, and things, and what we have in com-mon and what we do not. This cognitive tool is based on the assumption that people are "cognitive misers," who have well defined limits on what they perceive and what they are willing to understand (p. 406).

The process of categorizing has long been used to create divisions amongst human beings for a variety of reasons. A result of marking distinctions between the constructed "Us" and the similarly created comparative group of "Them" is **discrimination**, treating someone or some group unfairly on the basis of some shared difference. An early example of the difference between what people think (**prejudice**) and what they do (**discriminate**) is illustrated by the experience of a Chinese couple. In the 1930s, sociologist Robert La Piere escorted a Chinese husband and wife on a trip around the United States. During this period, all Asian peoples, Chinese included, were victims of extreme and widespread discrimination and exclusion. Surprisingly, while traveling La Piere and the couple experienced discrimination only once. They stayed at hotels and ate in restaurants all without incident. However, six months after the trip, La Piere found something different when he contacted each place they visited and inquired about making reservations. In his letters, he told the establishments that some in his group were Chinese and asked if that would be a problem. Half of the businesses replied and 92% said they would not be able to accommodate the group. What happened between the in-person visits and the later inquiry? It seems that anti-Asian prejudice was in place when the trio arrived in person, but to avoid a scene and because a non-Asian accompanied the couple, the proprietors did not express their feelings. However, in a more distant and impersonal interaction of letters, the restaurant and hotel employees openly expressed their prejudice. Was the group simply victims of circumstances of the past? Unfortunately not. While individuals discriminate, so do institutions. **Institutionalized discrimination** operates at the ideological level and includes patterns, policies, and procedures that work to overlook, overpower, or otherwise maintain control of individuals who do not belong to the dominant group. In the early 1990s, the restaurant chain Denny's was sued for denying or providing unsatisfactory service to minority customers, primarily African Americans. Some were made to pay for meals in advance; others were not seated or were made to wait inordinately long periods of time for seats or meals. The 1994 class action lawsuit settlement of $54.4 million was the largest and broadest under Federal laws having to do with restaurants and public spaces ("In a surprising act," 1999). In 2000, Coca-Cola agreed to pay $192 million as settlement in which four current and former African American employees (on behalf of 2,200 others) claimed racial discrimination in pay, promotions, and performance evaluations. While the company denied the allegations, major changes were made in the company's personnel policies ("Case profile," n.d.). In 2010, two American International Group (AIG) subsidiaries agreed to pay more than $6 million in the first cases in which banks were charged with discriminating against racial minorities in terms of lending and terms of loans (Brown, 2010).

Power is both cultural and ideological. Unlike individual prejudice "ideological racism is part of the cultural heritage and exists apart from the people who inhabit a society at a specific time" (O'Sullivan & Wilson, 1988, p. 227). These obstacles stand in the way of getting onto the path of opportunity as the American playing field is far from level. Oppression is "the systematic, institutionalized mistreatment of one group of people by another for whatever reason" (Yamato, 1995, p. 66). An example is slavery in the American South. Supporting this systematic oppression was an elaborate system designed to justify slavery and its economies and ameliorate slaveholders' feelings of guilt. This included thinking of slaves as childlike, thereby unable to take care of themselves on their own and "explaining" the oppression on the basis of innate racial/biological differences.

Chapter 12 describes how American films, such as *Birth of a Nation,* were replete with examples of the self-less Mammy or the carefree and mindless Sambo. Unfortunately, the end of slavery did not end these beliefs. It may be possible to legislate behavior but attitudes endure, living on as each new generation is socialized into a system that supports their maintenance.

The other side of this macro level practice is the micro level experience of what happens to individuals who are affected by acts of oppression. **Internalized oppression** occurs when members of the oppressed group are "emotionally, physically, and spiritually battered to the point that they begin to actually believe that their oppression is deserved, is their lot in life, is natural and right" (Yamato, 2001, p. 20). Yamato (2001) uses the metaphor of a virus to explain how racism, or any other **ism**, exists. She says, "it's hard to beat racism, because by the time you come up with a cure it's mutated to a 'new cure-resistant' form" (p. 20).

What motivates prejudice, discrimination, and oppression? Fear. While groups of people might be defined by what they look like, how they talk, the shape of their lips, or the color of their hair, what drives the continued insistence on the part of White, middle-upper **class**, heteronormative patriarchal society is fear, fear of losing the position of majority member, fear of the real abilities of people who are different, and fear of paying the price for the centuries of suffering endured by anyone regarded and coded as "Other."

A contemporary example to this process comes from Indiana University's Professor Dennis Rome (2004) who researched how the image and idea of a criminal are formed in people's minds. Rome found the mass media, particularly in gangsta rap and reality police shows, connect the stereotypical image of the criminal to African American men using a three-step process that results in "conceptual entrapment by imagery" (p. 8):

1. The media report on crimes, showing images that viewers then associate with crime.
2. The media report on crimes without showing images. Viewers have in mind the images shown previously, part of their schema.
3. When viewers later think about crimes, they look for indications that support their conception of crime, which was formed by what they saw in the media reports.

Rome's goal is for "people to understand the conceptualization, the entrapment by second-hand knowledge. If we understand how we conceptualize these media images, we can begin to change our behavior" (p. 8). Understanding this process comes closer to helping us answer questions about why and how we categorize in the first place, the subject of the following sections.

Creating Categories

Category

a. Certain general classes of terms, things, or notions; b. A class, or division, in any general scheme of classification (*OED*)

Human beings categorize in ways that make thinking about and getting on with the business of life more efficient. As non-neutral neural beings we categorize in response to and in anticipation of positive and negative experiences. **Categorization** is the process of grouping things (or people) together based on what they have in common from which an ideal type emerges. It is a method of organizing through our thoughts, perceptions, actions, and speech on the basis of differences. "Most categorization is automatic and unconscious" (Lakoff, 1987, p. 6), and most categories are not of things, rather "they are categories of abstract entities…essentially a matter of both human experience and imagination" (p. 8). Because we cannot experience everyone and everything in the world, we rely on what others have seen and heard and then file this information in our mental data bank. Over time this second-hand information can become its own form of truth, used as a substitute for first-hand experiences. In Chapter 1 this process was described as articulation.

Sometimes categories are used to express a preference or hierarchical arrangement of most to least favored, such as foods, restaurants, or colors. Other times we use categorical thinking to determine who or what represents a perceived threat, challenge, or competition for resources. The division of educational disciplines is another example. In colleges of arts and sciences, for example, there are chemistry, sociology, physics, and English departments. Another way of dividing groups and/

or ideas is class standing. There are freshmen (first-year students), sophomores, juniors, and seniors. Implicit in these divisions is the assumption of hierarchy. The higher up one goes in class standing, for example, the greater the privileges (such as registering first for classes). There is nothing written or universally true that says the world should be arranged in this way. Rather, it is through social agreement, through the social construction of reality that this occurs.

In the following sections, two approaches to unpacking the phenomena of categorization and marking difference are explored through two perspectives: the first philosophical and the second psychological. A brief discussion of each helps explain how and why we operate in the ways that we do and contributes to the argument of this book that the way we think about and respond to individuals and groups perceived as somehow different from ourselves (and thus Other) is a product of both nature (biological processes) and nurture (cultural conditioning).

What does philosophy say?

In the Western way of thinking, the world is typically divided into either/or, Black/White, good/bad, dichotomous thinking that often functions to polarize our beliefs and our behaviors. It is the nature of dualistic thought that encourages construction of binary categories as natural, a priori conceptions that are mutually exclusive. Thus, over time, with enough use and repetition, the divisions begin to seem normal and natural, hence remain largely unquestioned and meanings appear to be fixed. Categories have long served the practical purpose of placing people, animals, plants, and objects into defined groups that are labeled for a particular set of reasons.

Western consciousness is built around ancient essentialist ideas of perfection, prototype, and dualisms traceable to philosophers such as Plato and Aristotle. Plato devoted considerable time to the speculative idea of perfection. He believed that ideas are held first as non-material, unachievable concepts that are approximated in the real world. Thus, through effort, perfection and idealized types are thought to be at least theoretically possible. A perfect circle is an example.

Whereas Plato thought in terms of the ideal, Aristotle thought in terms of essences. The **Essences** are ideas that metaphorically connect mind and world. His goal was to create an inventory of everything—a catalog of sorts. Essences are not real per se, rather our *ideas* of them are. Essences ignore the conditions under which they emerge. In his famous *Statesman* dialogue, Plato introduced the idea of shared properties as the basis for grouping of objects and categorization which

Aristotle explored further in *Categories*. It is through essences that categories emerge.

Aristotle argued that an achievable ideal/perfect anything is a generalization and that abstract notions include what elements someone or something has in common, but can never be fully realized in reality. Whereas phenomena (via the senses) come and go, ideals are eternal. In *Categories,* Aristotle worked from the general to the specific, asking questions that increasingly narrowed the fields of discrimination between objects creating definitions. Definitions are essential for they give "us real causal knowledge of why things behave as they do" (Lakoff & Johnson, 1999, p. 379). There are three forms or theories of categorization: (1) classical, (2) conceptual, and (3) prototypical.

1. **Classical categorization** was developed from Plato's concept of the ideal. This philosophical position posits that categories can be determined by objectively established understandings of characteristics common to all. Both objects and people, he argued, share properties that are common to the category, and all categories share properties common to the objects, which are mutually exclusive and exhaustive. The **Category-as-Container** concept is a central element of classical theory of categorization. For hundreds of years in the West, the idea of common shared properties dominated thought about differences and was considered to be the only way to categorize and create order. A consequence is the example of courage and cowardice. At opposite ends of the spectrum, courage is an ideal state of being, and therefore good, a goal to hold. Cowardice, however, is not an ideal state, but instead the other end of the spectrum that says, "lack of a courageous state" is a deficit (p. 369), therefore undesirable and inappropriate to human beings. This metaphor thereby links essences with morality. For Plato, "the pious person… is the virtuous person who performs actions that are good," thereby "realizing an ideal of what a human being can be" (p. 369). Thus the coward lacks the essence (the virtue) that makes us human. By this point it should be frighteningly clear how the concept of an ideal type could and has become perverted when used to construct human beings considered less than fully human by virtue of constructed categories of lack.

2. **Conceptual categories** are developed based on qualitative, conceptual qualities, not strict descriptions. An example is *fair judges* or *honest lawyers*. This cognitive concept of conceptual clustering is further explored in later sections of this chapter, but it accepts the idea of shared or inherent characteristics that might exist across as well as within categories. Linguist George Lakoff's (1987) example of "mother" as a **cluster category** includes subcategories such as *foster* mother or *surrogate* mother. The women are still mothers, but the

biological status of "mother" is qualified by status. Mother is also a **radial concept**, around which stereotypical ideas of "motherness" are organized. What comes to mind when you hear related concepts of "working mother," "single mother," and others that are in relation to the normalized description of stereotypical definition of who and what a mother is? In this case, the ideal (prototypical) mother in American society is one who isn't in the workplace. In this way, there is the concept of "mother" and the qualifier, a mother who works, which distinguishes her from mothers who do not. The same is not true for fathers, wherein "working father" sounds odd because it is the presumed role for men.

Idealized Cognitive Models (ICM) are mapping tools used to study how one group of people, based on some visible or invisible shared characteristic, (dis)regards another group of people (Lakoff, 1987, p. 126). ICMs, "provide a conventionalized way of comprehending experience in an oversimplified manner." An ICM of Seeing, for example, has the following aspects:

1. You see things as they are.
2. You are aware of what you see.
3. You see what is in front of your eyes. (p. 128)

Of course we do not all categorize in the same way, given our individual experiences and traits, yet we all use a variation of this. ICMs are important in establishing a theory of meaning for two reasons: (1) the cognitive status of ICMs permits us to make sense of what presuppositions (background assumptions) are and, (2) they allow us to understand the problem with the notion of analytic truth (defined as a sentence that is true "solely by virtue of the meaning of its words") (Lakoff, 1987, p. 128). The mental processing behind what we see forms the context from which we formulate views of ourselves and of others.

3. **Prototype theory** posits that a category can be constructed on the basis of the best examples of that category. Members of a group are related on some level by the principles of "best qualities." This is similar to the notion of an *ideal*. Aristotle generated the concept of **taxonomy**, the practice of classification, which comes from the Greek word *taxis*, or order. In Western thought, taxonomies are hierarchically constructed as subsets. This began with the concept of classifying organisms, but today it applies to anything organized in this manner—people, places, and things—and can be purely mental construct or function in an applied manner.

What does psychology say?

The second approach for unpacking the phenomenon of categorization is based in the sciences. Many theologians, biologists, and behaviorists look to what is thought of as our instinctual animal nature in order to understand motivations for articulating differences between Others and ourselves. Biologists and neurologists argue that the impulse to categorize is instinctual reaction found in the parts, development, and chemical responses in the brain. According to this view, the human (triune) brain consists of three parts that developed in the following order: the **reptilian** (primitive) brain, the **mammalian** (limbic) brain, and the **neocortex**. The **reptilian brain** (R-complex), the oldest part, is responsible for swallowing, breathing, and heartbeat. Its needs are basic and immediate, tied to the physical survival of the organism. Automatic responses such as flight or fight originate here. Many scholars suggest the reptilian part of our brains contains the survivalist mechanism that, unlike more modern brain development, responds primarily to what Freud called our basic (instinctual) drives: sex and aggression, which does not include the contemplative notion of "to be or not to be," rather it is "to eat, or to be eaten" (Campbell, 1988). This is where what we sometimes call "gut instincts" originate. Fundamentally, this part of the brain activates basic needs and desires such as those associated with procreation and survival. While we never, or at least rarely, need this sense in the same ways or for the same reasons as we did in the past, this instinct fuels new functions such as competition for jobs or for romantic partners.

The second part of the brain to develop, the **limbic system**, carries out the primary responses initiated by the reptilian brain and mediates our emotions. Not only does this level of brain activity detect danger (or opportunity), it also figures out the quickest escape route. This is the quick response part of the brain that works in terms of generalizations rather than specifics. As such the limbic system has "difficulty conceptualizing uniqueness" (Dozier, 2003, p. 17). This "**primitive neural system**" sizes up others in terms of perceived threat or opportunity.

The relationship between these parts of the brain gets at what we have in common with other animals, what makes us *human* animals, and importantly, what aspects of ourselves we have control over and which we do not. The limbic system is present in all mammals, is located in the brain stem, and is a learning area comprised of the **amygdala, hypothalamus**, and several other nuclei. Drives and impulses are located in this part of the brain including visceral responses (circulatory, respiratory, and digestive activities), thermoregulation (shivering and sweating), and cause-and-effect thinking. The hypothalamus modulates hunger, fighting, fleeing, sex, and thirst. While drives from the reptilian brain are constant, they shift among themselves and when satisfied, this area stimulates feelings of pleasure. When feelings such as outrage, fear, aggression, anger, pity, and predation are stimulated the amygdala is called into service to help mediate the situation. Thus, the limbic system is the site of our emotions, behaviors, and attachments, and often plays traffic cop to the desires and drives of the reptilian brain. Whereas a reptile might eat its young, the limbic system steps in and constrains this impulse in most mammals and operates below our level of (conscious) awareness.

The neocortex, which is the "**advanced neural system**," makes up 80% of the brain and is the most recent part to develop. It houses functions such as reasoning, language, writing, and abstract thought. The **prefrontal cortex** is the site of morality and conscience. When this portion of the brain is injured, individuals lose their sense of responsibility. Substances such as alcohol impede the functioning of this part of the brain, resulting in a less predictable and often irrational individual.

These are, of course, biological findings (nature) and have been challenged by sociological theories (nurture) that suggest human beings are taught in particular ways based on sex and inculcated into particular gender roles. A combination of the two might bring us closer to the truth. As such, if science tells us males are physically constructed (based on thousands of years of evolution) in ways that have resulted in larger brain sizes for these responses (with larger pre-optic areas and amygdala), cultures with narrowly defined gender roles tend to build on what is already there. Rather than teaching an old dog new tricks, the system simply facilitates the development of preexisting tendencies and dispositions. Research shows significant correlation between levels of testosterone, sexual activity, and crime, for example. Young men and adults incarcerated for violent crimes have, on average, twice the testosterone levels of the non-aggressive male population (Rubin, Reinisch, & Haskett, 1981, pp. 1318–1324). Male criminals also tend to be taller, have more acne, and are equally intelligent as other males. On a much more basic level, these differences might help explain why men are more likely to participate in aggressive, competitive sports (and enjoy watching them), thrive in competitive environments, hunt, build a stronger body, and amass particular kinds of cultural objects (such as cars, guns).

Epistemology, as described in Chapter 1, is the study of different ways of knowing. Intuitively, it seems, women exhibit signs of being more emotional, thoughtful, patient, cooperative, compassionate, and empathetic than men are. Personal experience has also shown this to be true. Some of this behavior has been shown at the beginning of life (Blum, 2002). Other studies have found day-old infant girls' emotional responses to the sound of another baby's cries (i.e., too young for socialization) were more empathetic than those of boy infants. Blum's (2002, pp. 460–463) research shows that women are more aware of nonverbal behavior (such as micro emotional response), have access to better language about emotions, stronger emotional support systems, and are able to recover more quickly from the loss of a parent or spouse. Further evidence suggests "women may be programmed by evolution to deal with stress by 'tending and befriending,' that is, turning to each other for moral support" (Foreman, 2002, n.p.). A coarser description is that "it appears that testosterone has two, and only two drives: fuck it or kill it. Males are saddled with this biological nightmare almost from day one" (Wilber, 2000, p. 4). Female aggression is found intensely and fiercely around childcare, particularly when faced with danger to offspring, and is associated with the hormone prolactin present in milk production (Moyer, 1976). Whereas responses to a baby's cries result in a strong, biological, protective reaction in mothers, fathers must learn this behavior.

Thinking of people as categories is not only a matter of cultural perceptions and beliefs—there is some nature in with the nurture. By this, I mean a physiological process of responding to and thinking about those different from ourselves. Activities of the limbic system are reflexive. Responses are so quick, such as jerking back your hand from something hot, that we do not process them on a conscious level. Jumping back or being startled from a sudden noise, such as a car backfiring, is another example of the speed at which our mind/body connection operates. A small gland in the "new brain" (neocortex) part of brain is responsible for this instant reaction (the amygdala). Our conscious mind becomes involved afterward, sorting out exactly what happened. This primitive "flight-or-fight" response can be a lifesaver, as it especially was when humans were hunting and gathering in the natural world. Today, however, these kinds of threats are less frequent, and many times we are rather embarrassed by our strong reactions—our primitive (reptilian) brains were trained to over-respond as the consequences were potentially life threatening. Under these circumstances and conditions, we tend to think in stereotypes, in generalizations, because when we are frightened or startled, we cannot take the time to make fine distinctions. A delay of seconds might cost us our lives.

While the limbic system is present in all mammals, it seems humans are the only ones to keep theirs on autopilot. A rabbit fears the coyote, but not constantly. When it is necessary to respond, the fear is there, but otherwise the creature goes on about his or her business attending to other details of life (such as having or raising young, finding food, grooming) as a more efficient use of energy. Human beings, however, seem unable to let go of their ever-present vigilance, fear-based beliefs, and this is where hate grows—in the space between the conscious and unconscious mind, the space that ordinarily calms the primitive brain down and returns to a state that places threat more efficiently aside for when it is most useful.

The most recent, and perhaps powerful, example of this is the ability of so-called "suicide-bombers" to maintain this constant state in order to carry out their deeds.

> Islamic terrorists of the kind we witnessed on September 11, 2001, have an elaborately rationalized fanatical meaning system—based on a misguided religious interpretation—which holds that committing a suicidal attack as an act of holy war, or 'jihad,' will ensure the survival of their souls at the top of the hierarchy in an eternal paradise. Thus, the objectively irrational becomes perfectly rational in the mind of the terrorist, at both the conscious and primitive levels. To this person's limbic system, suicide is ensuring the individual's eternal survival—even reproduction (some interpretations of paradise include sexual activity). In fact, within this frame of reference the act of dying is not even defined as suicide but rather as martyrdom for a higher cause. The brain's capacity for mixing the rational and the irrational makes the conquest of hate urgently important but exceptionally challenging. (Dozier, 2003, p. 12)

Because human beings remember with neurons, "we are disposed to see more of what we have already seen, hear anew what we have heard most often, think just what we have always thought" (Lewis, Amini, & Lannon, 2000, p. 141). Since these "**limbic lessons**" occur below the level of consciousness, sometimes called preconscious, and take place during formative years, they become set in a way that makes them difficult to deconstruct and become the core of our beliefs about ourselves and others and color the way we see the world around us. Unfortunately, many of the emotions are negative, and responses "can manifest in humans as… greed, lust, arrogance, brutality, and impulsiveness…tribalism, cults, prejudices, stereotypes, superstition, rationalization, 'us against them' thinking, and group thinking" (Whitesell, 2002, p. 1). The extreme of this is the psychopath who lacks empathy for others.

Research using functional magnetic resonance imaging (fMRI) reveals that amygdala responses to face stimuli (subjects who identified themselves as Black or White viewed photographs of White and Black faces) were affected by perceived **race** of the stimulus face (Hart et al., 2000). Thus, the brain categorizes based on racial stimuli as a part of identifying in-group versus out-group members. Some of this response is based on the unfamiliarity of the faces, but is as likely to be a result of learned stereotypes or contribute to the development and maintenance of them.

In Malcolm Gladwell's (2005) bestseller *Blink: The Power of Thinking without Thinking*, he describes the part of our brain that leaps to conclusions as our "internal computer" (p. 11). This adaptive unconscious instantly processes data we need to function in the world. The response to perceived threat is ancient, having helped humans survive for thousands of years when making a quick decision meant the difference between life and death. The first time we meet someone we make decisions about him or her—does he seem safe to talk to? Does a potential employer come across as honest? We use a different part of our brain and a different aspect of our personality when making quick decisions. They are sometimes called snap decisions, gut instincts, or intuition. While we might be suspicious of the outcome, nevertheless we do this all the time. Gladwell (2005, p. 23) calls these responses "**thin slicing**," it is "the ability of our unconscious to find patterns in situations and behavior based on very narrow slices of experience." In sports, for example, basketball players who survey the scene are said to have "court sense" (p. 44) and Hollywood directors often say they know someone is right for a part the moment he or she auditions. The question is "How do we know these things?"

How do we categorize?

Thin slices originate at a level below consciousness and happen so quickly it is difficult to say exactly what informs them. In psychology, a technique used to elicit responses buried in memory is called **priming**. Particular words, images, or sounds (semantics) can stimulate and enhance responses. Hansen and Hansen's (1988) activation recency approach posits that subjects primed with media content are more likely to use that content in other situations. In particular they note, "the distorted appraisal of a subsequent stimulus induced by activation is unlikely to be consciously corrected" (p. 290). In other words, if we watch a reductive representation in the media we are less likely to consciously correct what we see, particularly if this portrayal is consistent with other forms of information about a group. For example, as discussed in Chapter 4, African American women are stereotypically presented in ways that activate both female and Black schema as "nurturing-asexual mammies, domineering matriarchs, sexually aggressive jezebels, and lazy welfare mothers," information, if not contradicted in other areas of life, that has significant impact on whether or not Black women receive equitable treatment and regard in social life, medical and legal care (Monahan, Brown Givens, & Shtrulis, 2003). Furthermore, this view, if heard often enough, tends to be internalized, affecting a minority person's self-esteem, identity, and hence ability to function in situations where race might be used evaluatively. **Stereotype threat**, defined as fear of being viewed through the lens of a negative stereotype, or the fear of doing something that would inadvertently confirm the stereotype (Steele, 2006, p. 253) is evident in educational settings.

For example, Steele and colleagues (2006) asked a group of twenty African American students twenty questions taken from the Graduate Record Exam (GRE). On a pre-test questionnaire, when respondents were asked to identify their race, their performance on the test was half (50%) of what it was when they were not asked about their race, even though Black and White students were matched in terms of ability. Given stereotypes surrounding race and intelligence, reminding someone of his or her race served as a reminder of static images of identity. While no overt references are made, we pick up clues in our environment, visual and verbal, from which these deeply embedded ideas activate internalized limitations. Words are powerful associative mechanisms. For example, "old," "shuffleboard," and "wrinkles" when followed by the word "Florida," can prime people to affect a particular attitude or exhibit opinions based on stereotypical information about the Sunshine State. Colors, pictures, sounds, and scents can also trigger associations that result in thin slicing. Prejudicial thoughts, statements, and acts are some of the darker effects of rapid cognition/thin slicing. Gladwell (2005, p. 73) terms this the "**Warren Harding Error**," referring to this former U.S. president's propensity to stimulate admiration and confidence in his political skills based on his attractive physical appearance. He proved to be one of the worst presidents in U.S. history—he had the look, but not the talent.

The Implicit Association Test (IAT) is an experimental tool used to measure the strength of associations and pairings of categories of differences and for ascertaining outcomes when two words or images with deep associations within us are presented along with unfamiliar ideas. While any one of us might proclaim to be liberal, non-biased, or egalitarian, and consciously committed to change, we often hold elements of deeply embedded "residue," retrievable by asking the right kinds or series of questions. You can participate in the test yourself by going to the Harvard University-based Web site at https://implicit.harvard.edu/implicit/ and select among options such as religion, weapons, disability, skin-tone, or race. The most widely cited test is associated with race, "this IAT requires the ability to distinguish faces of European and African origin. It indicates that most Americans have an automatic preference for White over Black," but there are also implicit association tests for sexuality, age, skin-tone, and even more specific investigations of Arab-Muslim names.

Selective perception theory essentially says that we see what we want to see, filtering out conflicting information. This psychological theory demonstrates how **cognitive biases** (a situation-specific deviation in judgment) affect our perceptions. For example, in a famous study of sports fans, Princeton and Dartmouth football fans watched a film of an especially violent game between the two teams. Princeton viewers reported seeing nearly twice as many rule infractions by the Dartmouth team than did Dartmouth viewers and vice versa (Hastorf & Cantril, 1954). Other examples include group behavior, mob madness and manias, framing, and status quo bias.

Optical illusions are a common and accessible tool to explore the concept that each of us can see something or someone different in an identical image.

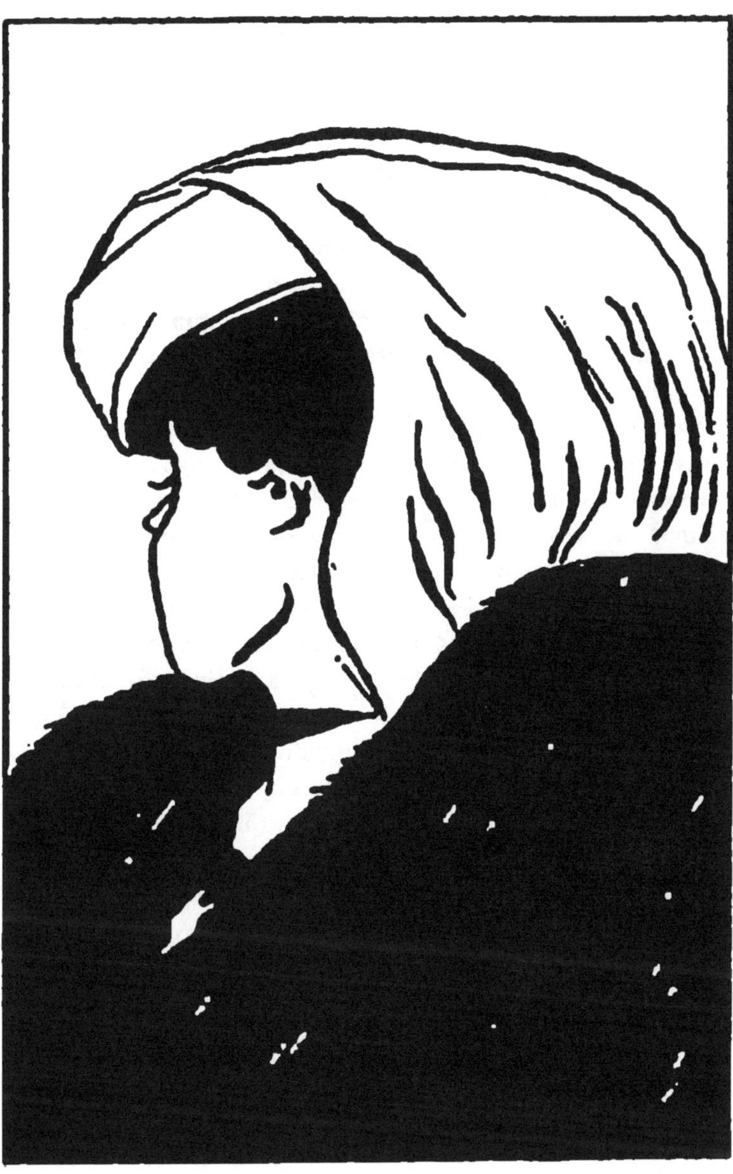

Figure 2.1: My wife and my mother-in-law, by the cartoonist W. E. Hill, 1915 (adapted from a picture going back to a 1888 German postcard). *Puck Magazine, 6,* Nov. 1915.

Pre-conceived ideas influence what we (think we) see has to do with perception. For example, in the figure (Figure 2.1), what do you first see? An old woman or a young girl?

Figure 2.1 originally came from an 1888 German postcard, but is often used to illustrate **perceptions** (ways of seeing). What you see is a **visual paradox** or optical illusion. These are tricks, creatively drawn or with pieces arranged, that fool the eye into seeing something that is or isn't there. In some cases, the clever design causes an **afterimage** because of confusion between what the eye sees and how the brain tries to organize that information, resulting in a physiological imbalance. Our brains try to grab onto what seems familiar and connect it with patternings. These ways of seeing are influenced by individual socialization as well as social constructions of reality. Researchers who explore this phenomenon might say that if you first saw a young woman, you might prefer youthful looks. If it was the older woman who first appeared this might indicate your thoughts about aging or your grandmother. Nevertheless, these selective ways of responding are very much like the IAT—our first responses are always the truest to what we have been taught but might not recognize that we believe or express.

What benefit is there to an individual or group of constructing categories of difference? What purpose, if any, does this process serve? Some theorists argue that the expression of this self serves as a way of venting frustrations associated with repressing forbidden desires or animosities or that carving out territory is an instinctive behavior designed for group and individual survival. It is also efficient to make distinctions between people or make quick judgments in order to compartmentalize thinking in order to get on with the business of living. Equally possible is that envisioning oneself and/or one's group as superior makes dealing with those who are different easier, such as in times of war, making unequal or even inhumane treatment seem justified. Generalizations "are appealing in part because they satisfy the desire to perceive existing forms of social and economic arrangements as fair, legitimate, and justified" (Jost & Kay, 2003, p. 835).

Making distinctions between people who are perceived as "good" and "one of Us" and those who are "bad" and "not one of Us," are useful mechanisms for maintaining social order. Societies that are disorganized quickly fail. Those in positions of power maintain their situations by identifying others who represent a threat to that stability. If divisions are drawn between groups, this also prevents marginalized people from forming alliances against the dominant system. Stanford professor John Jost and graduate student Aaron Kay (2003) explored the implications of spontaneous decisions in terms of stifling social change and maintaining the status quo. Some, on the surface seem benevolent. For example "women who accept the [frame] that they are nurturing and kind (whereas men are powerful and agentic) are also more likely to justify **gender inequality,** often at an unconscious level." Jost and Banaji's (1994) **system justification theory** explains why people hold strongly to as well as rationalize and justify their views that maintain the status quo. SJT is the process "by which existing social arrangements are legitimized, even at the expense of personal and group interest" (p. 2). Thus, inequities become self-perpetuating and reinforcing, even if seemingly positive because they come to seem natural, as "just the way things are." "Us and Them" distinctions operate at two levels (1) the *individual level* beginning with formation of individual identity and the self, and (2) the *generalizable, social level* where groupthink and the collective unconscious reside and intermingle with individual level constructions. What is important to recognize is that while we all learn and sometimes retain attitudes and beliefs based in hidden biases, we can learn how to inform our decisions and control our responses.

What are the categories of difference?

The very qualities that make individuals special and cultures distinctive are some of the very ones that can lead to discrimination. Groups whose members have significantly less control and/or less autonomy over the quality of their own lives and access to material resources than do members of a dominant group belong to a **minority group**. Minority status is not a numerical distinction about the number of individuals, belonging to a particular group, rather, assignation is based on lack of resources and narrowing of opportunities (success, education, wealth, access to quality health care) that are disproportionately few compared to the number of individuals in society. For example, in the United States, women constitute nearly 52% of the population and yet are regarded as a minority group because of social, cultural, and economic inequities. Similarly, Blacks in South Africa during apartheid suffered under the power of numerically fewer Whites. Four common themes, none of which are mutually exclusive, are typically used to define (and defend) a minority group: (1) inequality, (2) visibility, (3) self-consciousness as a political, economic, cultural social unit, and (4) ascribed status.

1. *Inequality* is a pattern of disadvantage or disability typically falling somewhere along a continuum. At the most extreme end is torture, slavery, and genocide. At the other end we find circumstances such as lack of access to left-handed desks. In either sense, this pattern of disadvantage is the most defining characteristic of a minority group. Because members of the majority/dominant group are valued more than the minority group, accommodations for differences are lacking all the way to outward patterns of aggression. This includes

a narrowing or even elimination of opportunities such as access to quality health care, education, wealth, and political representation.

2. *Visibility.* Psychosocial and physical characteristics by which members of a group are identified are singled out. In many cases, the defining characteristic of someone belonging to a minority group is physical. Color of complexion, anatomical build, shape of nose or mouth are examples of physical differences and are the basis of racial minority status. Religion, dress, food, or speech patterns are cultural examples that articulate cultural difference and are considered aspects of ethnic minority groups. Someone's faith might not identify his or her visibility, or it might, as in the case of Hasidic Jews. Latinos, Italians, and Greek people are part of this category whereas Native Americans, African Americans, and Arab Americans signify racial groups. Of course many of these characteristics overlap.

3. *Self-conscious social units* are another way of describing how people who belong to a particular group are aware of distinctions made by the majority group. Collectively and individually, awareness of being different from what is regarded as "the norm" (in the case of the United States, White) can be the foundation for group cohesion.

4. *Ascribed status.* This fourth characteristic used to define a member of a minority group is typically assigned at birth and cannot be easily changed. For example, being born into a Jewish family or raised in a Latino family. This status is involuntary and lasts a person's lifetime. Feelings of lack of self-determination are a key psychological restraint for members of minority groups.

At one time, an additional characteristic of minority groups was a tendency to marry within one's group, but this is increasingly not the case. While in-group marriages are changing in America, many traditional families still expect or hope their son or daughter will marry someone from the same group. Legal sanctions against interracial marriage have existed since the mid-1800s. Some laws banned interracial marriages (**miscegenation**) between other-than-white racial groups as well, such as between Asian and Native Americans. Laws akin to the U.S. law have been enforced in other places during other times. For example, between 1935 and 1945 in Nazi Germany, and from 1949 to 1985 in South Africa during apartheid.

Not long ago many states forbid miscegenation. While the U.S. Supreme Court declared this unconstitutional in the late 1960s, many states were slow in officially removing the laws from their books. The court case of *Loving versus Virginia* (U.S.) is an example of an interracial couple's fight to win the right to marry. In 1958, Richard and Mildred Loving were married in Washington, D.C., because their home state of Virginia still upheld the anti-miscegenation law. They married and lived together in Caroline County, Virginia. However, in 1959, they were prosecuted and convicted of violating the state's anti-miscegenation law. Each was sentenced to a one-year term in jail but was told the sentences would be suspended if they left the state for 25 years. Forced to move, they returned to Washington, D.C., where, in 1963, they initiated a suit challenging the constitutionality of the anti-miscegenation law. In March 1966, the Virginia Supreme Court of Appeals upheld the law, but in June 1967, the U.S. Supreme Court unanimously ruled the law unconstitutional. Thus, in 1967, 16 states that still had anti-miscegenation laws on their books were forced to remove them (see Table 2.1 for view of all states with anti-miscegenation laws). While such laws were clearly intended to prevent intermarriage of so-called "traditional" groups, such as African Americans and Whites, they can also be applied to same sex marriages. While behavior can be legislated, attitudes cannot, as evidenced by the 2009 refusal of a Louisiana justice of the peace to issue a marriage license to a White woman and a Black man. Judge Keith Bardwell said, in defense of his decision, that he was, "concerned for the children who might be born of the relationship and that, in his experience, most interracial marriages don't last" (Deslatte, 2009, n.p.).

Whether differences are based on racial, ethnic, sexual, gender, or age differences, the bottom line is they are used to establish borders and boundaries with which the majority culture can quickly identify minority cultures. In some ways, these markers are similar to signs to mark group membership (in group and out group, depending on one's perspective). In this way, by establishing vast, monolithic generalities about a group of people, patterns of oppression, and racism become institutionalized and incorporated into the structure of business, political, educational, and cultural practices. Without these markers it would be difficult, if not impossible, for the dominant group to determine who belonged to another group and thereby required engagement with people on the individual level. What are the major categories of difference in the United States? On what basis were they created? These questions are addressed in the following section and detailed in Chapter 4.

On the basis of race, the collective "We" in the United States (+ 300 million people) is characterized according to categories and percentages shown in Table 2.2. In 2009, the estimated U.S. population was 307,006,550 people (census.gov). About 20% of the U.S. population is under age 14, 67% between 15–64 years, and approximately 13% are over age 65. Women, although a minority in terms of power and access to resources, are slightly in the majority when it comes to population—roughly 52% of the nation's population is female.

Demography is the statistical study of populations on the basis of size, patterns of birth and death, geographic mobility and other patterns or changes.

Table 2.1: Anti-miscegenation Laws Enacted in the Thirteen Colonies and the United States

Anti-Miscegenation Laws Repealed by 1887

State	First Passed	Law Repealed	"Races" Banned from Marrying Whites	Other Information
Illinois	1829	1874	Black	
Iowa	1839	1851	Black	
Kansas	1855	1859	Black	Law repealed prior to statehood
New Mexico	1857	1866	Black	Law repealed prior to statehood
Maine	1821	1883	Black, Native American	
Massachusetts	1705	1845	Black, Native American	1913 law prevented out-of-state couples from going around their home state anti-miscegenation laws
Michigan	1838	1883	Black	
Ohio	1861	1887	Black	Last state to repeal before California did in 1948
Pennsylvania	1725	1780	Black	
Washington	1855	1868	Black, Native American	Law repealed prior to statehood

Anti-Miscegenation Laws Repealed 1948–1967

State	First Law Passed	Law Repealed	"Races" Banned from Marrying Whites	Other Information
Arizona	1865	1962	Black, Asian, Filipino, Native Americans, Malay, and Indians (Hindus added 1931)	

(Table continued on next page)

California	1850	1948	Black, Asian, Filipino	Supreme Court overturned the law in *Perez v. Sharp*
Colorado	1864	1957	Black	
Idaho	1864	1959	Black, Native American, Asian	
Indiana	1818	1965	Black	
Maryland	1692	1967	Black, Filipino	Law repealed as result *Loving v. Virginia*
Montana	1909	1953	Black, Asian	
Nebraska	1855	1963	Black, Asian	
Nevada	1861	1959	Black, Native American, Asian, Filipino	
North Dakota	1909	1955	Black	
Oregon	1862	1951	Black, Asian, Native American, Native Hawaiian	
South Dakota	1909	1957	Black, Asian, Filipino	
Utah	1852	1963	Black, Asian, Filipino	
Wyoming	1913	1965	Black, Asian, Filipino	

Demographics refer to specific statistically measurable characteristics of groups of people such as age, education, income, race, gender, and employment. In the United States, the census is taken every ten years. A census is an attempt to capture information about an entire population, rather than **sampling** from a subset and generalizing to the whole. A questionnaire is used to obtain this information. Once obtained, the statistical information is organized into categories defined by the United States Census and the Federal Office of Management and Budget. These figures on race, age, occupation, language, employment, family size, and other characteristics are used to apportion federal funds and political representation to populations. The Census is controversial in many ways. Those most relevant to this book have to do with three areas: (1) the limited number of self-identification categories among which individuals must choose, (2) challenges as to the accuracy of this form of information retrieval due to variations in understandings of terms and willingness to participate, and (3) lack of category flexibility for self-identification (Siegel, Swanson, & Shyrock, 2004, p. 176). The difficulty in defining who belongs to which group and why has plagued census makers and takers since its inception in 1790.

In early forms of the census (1850) choices were limited to White, Black, and Mulatto (Farley & Haaga, 2005, p. 333). In 1880, the list was expanded to White, Black, Mulatto, Chinese, and Indian reflecting specific political issues of the time. In 1978, there were still only four racial categories (White, Black, Indian/Alaskan Native, Asia/Pacific Islander) and ethnicities. In a 1997 directive, five categories were created for racial self-identification: American Indian/Alaskan Native, Asian, Black or African American, Native Hawaiian or other Pacific Islander, and White (census.gov). By 2000, respondents were given more choices when defining race than before. A person could select from 126 categories. The malleability of these categories is evident in Cape Verdeans being added as a 127th choice. According to Kirsanow (2006, n.p.), two thirds of states have populations of fewer than 100, and Cape Verdeans themselves are multi-racial (78% are Creole, 21% are African,

Table 2.2: Population by Race and Hispanic Origin for the United States: 2000

Race	Number	Percent of Total Population
RACE		
Total population	**281,421,906**	**100.0**
One race	274,595,678	97.6
White	211,460,626	75.1
Black or African American	34,658,190	12.3
American Indian and Alaska Native	2,475,956	0.9
Asian	10,242,996	3.6
Native Hawaiian and Other Pacific Islander	398,835	0.1
Some other race	15,359,073	5.5
Two or more races	6,826,228	2.4
Hispanic or Latino	35,305,818	12.5
Not Hispanic or Latino	246,116,088	87.5

Source: U.S. Census Bureau, *Census 2000 Brief.*

and 1% are of European origins). Yet, the propensity is to lump all members of the group into the category "Black."

The most significant change was the option of selecting more than one race. Nearly seven million individuals chose this designation. While Table 2.2 describes the general categories of race and ethnicity as defined by the U.S. Census, the following sections and tables provide more detailed descriptions of the many groupings under which people are classified. The order of description is on the basis of percentage of the population. According to census text, racial categories are defined as follows:

- *White*. A person having origins in any of the original peoples of Europe, the Middle East, or North Africa. It includes people who indicate their race as "White" or report entries such as Irish, German, Italian, Near Eastern, Arab, or Polish.
- *Black or African American*. A person having origins in any of the Black racial groups of Africa. It includes people who indicate their race as "Black, African Am., or Negro," or provide written entries such as African American, Afro-American, Kenyan, Nigerian, or Haitian.
- *Asian*. A person having origins in any of the original peoples of the Far East, Southeast Asia, or the Indian subcontinent including, for example, Cambodia, China, India, Japan, Korea, Malaysia, Pakistan, the Philippine Islands, Thailand, and Vietnam. It includes "Asian Indian," "Chinese," "Filipino," "Korean," "Japanese," "Vietnamese," and "Other Asian."
- Similar to the American Indian and Alaskan Native designation, the Asian group is comprised of dozens of language, cultural, and other differences. Among Asians, some groups trace their U.S. history back more than a century while others, such as Vietnamese, Laotians, Hmong, and Cambodians immigrated relatively recently. The U.S. Census identifies 11 groups that comprise at least 1% of the total Asian population.
- *Native Hawaiian and Other Pacific Islander*. A person having origins in any of the original peoples of Hawaii, Guam, Samoa, or other Pacific Islands. This includes people who indicate their race as "Native Hawaiian," "Guamanian or Chamorro," "Samoan," and "Other Pacific Islander."
- *Native American/American Indian/Alaska Native*. Although census data has been collected since 1790, Native Americans weren't identified as a group until the 1860 census. Individual Indians weren't counted until the 1890 census, 100 years after the first census was taken. Alaskan Natives were first identified as a separate group from other indigenous Americans in 1970. The Census describes people in this group as follows: "'American Indian' and 'Alaska Native.' A person having origins in any of the original

peoples of North and South America (including Central America) and who maintains tribal affiliation or community attachment."

- *Some other race.* This category includes all other responses not included in the "White," "Black or African American," "American Indian and Alaska Native," "Asian" and "Native Hawaiian and Other Pacific Islander" race categories described above. Respondents providing write-in entries such as multiracial, mixed, interracial, or a Hispanic/Latino group (for example, Mexican, Puerto Rican, or Cuban) in the "Some other race" category are included here.

- *Two or more races.* People may have chosen to provide two or more races either by checking two or more race response check boxes, by providing multiple write-in responses, or by some combination of check boxes and write-in responses.

After reading these divisions it quickly becomes clear how, for purposes of efficiency, many different groups of people are lumped together under a limited number of categories that lose all distinctiveness. In addition to race, individuals are asked to classify themselves according to one of two ethnic identities: Hispanic or Latino origin or Not Hispanic or Latino.

People who are Hispanic are, according to the U.S. Census, not members of a racial group but rather are defined by ethnicity, or being a person of Latin American descent. The Census definition of Hispanic or Latino is "a person of Cuban, Mexican, Puerto Rican, South or Central American or other Spanish culture or origin regardless of race." Therefore, someone from Spain, for example, is not considered Hispanic or Latino, but instead is European. Thus, the population breakout with this factor included shows Hispanic/Latinos comprising approximately 15% of the U.S. population.

In the 2000 census, race and Hispanic origin were noted as two separate concepts. Hispanic is the term the U.S. government uses when defining a person of "Mexican, Puerto Rican, Cuban, South or Central American, or other Spanish culture or origin regardless of race." Thus, Hispanics may identify among any racial group. People who considered themselves Hispanic could choose among four categories: Mexican, Puerto Rican, Cuban, or other Spanish/Hispanic/Latino. For the latter option, individuals could write in a group, such as Spaniard or Dominican. Many individuals living in the United States identify themselves first with country of origin, such as Mexico, followed, by American. Others use labels such as Latina or Latino, Chicano or Chicana, while others have adopted the general category of Hispanic for self-identification.

The decade 1990–2000 was the greatest growth period for foreign-born Mexicans and South Americans coming to the United States. Nearly 50% arrived during this time. This was the smallest immigration period for foreign-born Cubans, however, only 26% entered during this time, most having arrived before 1970. Over 75% speak a language other than English at home.

The findings of the 2010 census are likely to reveal even more about the many differences and similarities among American citizens.

Summary

So far in this chapter we have examined the philosophical, psychological, and sociological process of defining difference through the construction of categories. The purpose of doing so varies widely from making an intellectual argument as to the necessity of labeling in order to organize thought (philosophy), the primal urge to defend what one believes to be his or her own from someone else (psychology), and practical reasons for dividing society into measurable and locatable groups for purposes of the allocation (or not) of economic resources. But, as was set out in Chapter 1, the purpose of this book is to go deeper. The goal of this chapter is interpreting how "reality" is created, the mechanisms through which we, as societies and as individuals, construct "reality," which includes who is defined as one of Us and who is defined as one of Them and why, and to demystify the process. This includes identifying who is included and who excluded from policy-making decisions, has access to material resources, and how and what we believe about others and ourselves including our motivations and treatment of others.

This process is important, not only to understand the basic arguments for human processing of information that results in the construction of categories of difference but also for knowing how this is passed on in the stories we tell ourselves about others and ourselves in myths.

Who has the power to decide about the welfare and well-being of others in American society? How is that decided? Who is one of us and who is one of them and why? What is at stake in definitions of self and Other? These questions are addressed in Chapter 3 when we examine the nature of power and power relations that are at the core of categories of difference that are more complex than simple numerical tabulations and strike at the core of racial, ethnic, sexual, cultural, and economic Othering. In the next chapter, the study of difference is not regarded as an objective, neutral intellectual inquiry. Rather, motivated by a commitment to social justice, the underpinnings of limited thinking, its origins, foundations, and the extent to which mass media and popular culture contribute to and perpetuate this way of thinking are considered. While it is important to know that people are categorized, how and why this is done, and how this process is manifested in formalized, institutionalized ways, what also matters are the very real consequences of this activity in terms of physical and mental health.

Questions for Discussion

1. Can you think of a film or television program that fits Asa Berger's Myth Model?
2. Do the mass media rely on mythic tales to relay news stories? Why?
3. In what form of media is the super-muscular hero typically found?
4. In what form of media is the super-thin female beauty typically found?
5. What purpose does dividing human beings into groups serve in society?

Key Words

Advanced neural system	Afterimage
Amygdala	Articulation
Assimilation	Category-as-container
Categorization	Class
Classical category	Cluster category
Cognitive biases	Conceptual Category
Demographics	Demography
Difference	Discriminate
Discrimination	Essences
Gender inequality	Hypothalamus
Idealized cognitive model (ICM)	Inequality
Institutionalized discrimination	Internalized oppression
Isms	Limbic system
Limbic lessons	Mammalian brain
Melting pot	Minority group
Miscegenation	Neocortex
Oppression	Optical illusion(s)
Othering	Patriarchy
Perceptions	Power
Prefrontal cortex	Prejudice

Priming	Primitive neural system
Prototype theory	Race
Radial Concept	Reptilian
Reptilian brain	Salad bowl
Sampling	Schema
Schema Theory	Stereotype threat
System justification theory	Taxonomy
Thin slicing	Visual paradox
Warren Harding Error	Israel Zangwill

CHAPTER THREE

Minorities, Meaning, and Mass Media

If I differ from you, far from wronging you, I enhance you.
Antoine de Saint-Exupèry

If you differ from me, far from wronging me, you enhance me.
Leyens, Yzerbyt, & Schadron

It is the white man who creates the Negro.

Frantz Fanon

Are people with blue eyes smarter than people with brown eyes? Do people with brown eyes deserve better treatment than people with blue eyes? These were questions a third-grade teacher posited to her class in April 1968. In a now-famous study of the arbitrary nature of defining difference and how it feels to be marked as Other, educator Jane Elliott created a powerful classroom learning experience. Elliott had been talking with her Riceville, Iowa, students (who were White and Christian) about racism. Dr. Martin Luther King was their hero of the month. When the news media announced Dr. King had been assassinated the students came to class confused—if Dr. King was a hero, why would someone kill him?

Elliott saw the tragedy as an opportunity to try an unusual experiment—for her students to experience first hand what it feels like to be discriminated against.

Riceville, Iowa is a small farming community and most of the children had never met a Black person. Describing racism was one thing, but what might it feel like to be discriminated against on the basis of some shared characteristic you had nothing to do with acquiring? To explore this, Elliott divided the students into two groups: blue-eyed and brown-eyed and told them that those with blue eyes were superior to those with brown eyes. On the first day, the brown-eyed children had to wear special collars, were not allowed seconds at lunch, because they would take more than their share, she said. Blue-eyed children would get five extra minutes of recess while the brown-eyed students waited in the classroom. Brown-eyed children would not be allowed to use the water fountain—they had to drink out of paper cups. The brown-eyed children had to wear special collars so they could be quickly identified as belonging to that group. The next day she reversed the roles. This experience proved to be profound for the children, to experience first-hand what it felt like to be discriminated against on the basis of some arbitrary physical trait.

> What happened over the course of the unique two-day exercise astonished both students and teacher. On both days, children who were designated as inferior took on the look and behavior of genuinely inferior students, performing poorly on tests and other work. In contrast, the 'superior' students—students who had been sweet and tolerant before the exercise—became mean-spirited and seemed to like discriminating against the 'inferior group' (*A Class Divided*, 1985).

Some cried, some were angry, but all felt the terrible sense of frustration, loneliness, and misunderstanding that accompanies being singled out as lesser-than on the basis of some assigned characteristic. Elliott said, "I watched what had been marvelous, cooperative, wonderful, thoughtful children turn into nasty, vicious, discriminating little third-graders in a space of fifteen minutes." Elliott realized then that she had "created a microcosm of society in a third-grade classroom" (*A Class Divided*, 1985).

In a powerful documentary filmed sixteen years later (*A Class Divided*, 1985), the eleven students in this first group reported the experience had changed their lives forever. In the interviews a young woman said, "Nobody likes to be looked down upon. Nobody likes to be hated, teased, or discriminated against." Another student, Sandra, said,

> You hear these people talking about different people and how they'd like to have them out of the country. And sometimes I just wish I had that collar in my pocket. I could whip it out and put it on and say 'Wear this, and put yourself in their place.' I wish they would go through what I went through, you know.

The psychosocial process of drawing distinctions is articulated in many ways, as was discussed in Chapter 2. The focus of this chapter is on how difference and otherness is constructed and ultimately turned into forms of (mis)representation in various forms of mass communication and popular culture. In addition, some of the consequences for lived experience of those who are discriminated against are explored. First, we examine in greater detail divisions created in American society on the basis of race, gender, **ethnicity**, and other distinctions. This is followed by a discussion of the ways markers of difference are constructed through the process of **stigmatization** (marking as different), which is then articulated in the form of stereotypes.

How Are Others Constructed?

We live in a land where the past is always erased and America is the innocent future in which immigrants can come and start over, where the slate is clean. The past is absent, or it's romanticized. This culture doesn't encourage dwelling on the past, let alone coming to terms with, the truth about the past.

Toni Morrison (as cited in Gilroy, 1995, p. 180)

As is discussed in Chapters 1 and 2, the process of categorization takes a socially agreed upon, often arbitrary visible or invisible characteristic or trait of a person and uses it to define him or her as Other. Dominant (also known as elite) cultures are replete with limiting discourse, reflected in law, religion, mass media, politics, and education, that make the minority designation, differential treatment, and exclusion seem like common sense, as if they were naturally occurring divisions. Several historical experiences contribute to the construction of subordinate groups. Three primary phenomena are migration, annexation, and colonialization.

Migration

When individuals or a population leave an area or a country and move to another they **emigrate** (to leave one's home country) and **immigrate** (enter and settle in another). This migratory transfer of a population may be voluntary (such as Japanese and other Asians who came to the United States as workers around the turn of the 20th century) or involuntary (such as Africans who were brought as slaves). Immigrations can occur within a country as well such as the movement of newly freed slaves from the South to the North after the abolition of slavery.

The relocation of indigenous North American peoples to reservations by White Europeans is an example of **forced migration**. In 1824, by directive of President Andrew Jackson, the government established the Indian Bureau in the War Department. Thousands of Native people were slaughtered, maimed, raped, starved, and those who survived were relocated to reservations. These acts included murdering mothers and babies, forced sterilization, and kidnapping Indian children, taking them to boarding schools to be "re-educated" as part of federal assimilation policies. These extermination efforts were deemed the final solution to the "Indian problem" as result of "the refusal or inability of Native people to assimilate into American society" (Stremlau, 2005, p. 265). In 1889, in his annual report to the Secretary of the Interior, Thomas Jefferson Morgan wrote, "the Indian must conform 'to the White man's ways,' peaceably if they will, forcibly if they must" (Reyhner, 2006, n.p.).

A term related to forced migration is the experience of diaspora. The term comes from the Greek verb *speiro*, "to sow," and the preposition *dia*, means "over" (Cohen, 1997, p. ix). Originally, used to describe Jewish, Greek, and Armenian people who also experienced genocide, this word is generally taken to mean an interconnected community whose ties are sustained through communication, contacts, trade, kinship, shared culture, language, rituals, and media (Peters, 1999) and who share a "history of displacement, suffering, adaptation, and resistance" (Agnew, 2005, p. 4). The diaspora connects multiple groups who are moved and systematically dispersed across borders, among which are forms of shared identification, memory, and longings, as well as collective memory. In a seminal article, Clifford (1994, p. 305) defines diaspora by the following characteristics: "A history of dispersal, myths/memories of the homeland, and alienation in the host (bad host?) country, desire for eventual return, ongoing support of the homeland, and a collective identity importantly defined by this relationship."

Diasporic individuals may live separately in the world but identify with one another, their country of origin, and with their current location. When diaspora is defined as a type of consciousness, individuals may be geographically dispersed, but "emphasize their sense of belonging or exclusion, their states of mind, and their sense of identity" (Agnew, 2005, p. 5). Memory and longing are key aspects of this experience. Can one speak of a diaspora if forced removal/relocation occurs within the same nation? Yes, says Hua (Agnew, 2005, p. 4), who argues the term diaspora refers to, "the dispersion of a group of people from a centre to two or more peripheral places, as well as to the collective memory and trauma involved in such a dispersion," traditionally so by "slavery, pogroms, genocide, coercion and expulsion, war in conflict zones, indentured labor, economic migration, political exile, or refugee exodus" (Hua, 2005, p. 193).

A diaspora is also a mode of cultural production concerned with the reproduction of cultural phenomena through the processes of creolization and/or hybridization. For example, individuals who are displaced might adopt some of the qualities and characteristics of the culture within which they live and combine them with those they brought with them. In some cases, an entirely new, composite identity is constructed. As a result, regardless of the conformation, individuals living within and without the dominant culture are thereby forced to assume multi-level consciousness. Adding to W. E. B. Du Bois' notion of **double consciousness** (living in two worlds simultaneously), Native Americans, for example, must maintain a quadruple consciousness as American, as Native American, as a tribal member, and as a man or a woman. Thus, to be active in dominant culture is to be aware and continuously reminded of these distinctions.

Annexation

The incorporation or attachment of contiguous land is called **annexation**. It can result from war (such as Mexican Americans in Treaty of Guadalupe Hidalgo) or by purchase (such as Native Americans and Inuit in Alaska). This external re-designation of land has been pivotal in determining who qualifies as a citizen of a country. With annexation, the dominant group typically works to suppress the language and culture of minority groups. For example, Native American boarding schools were set up to reconstruct Native American children into what was regarded as "proper" Americans in terms of dress or by banning original language. African American slaves were prevented from becoming literate. The human history of Hawaii is filled with stories of invasion and annexation. The overthrow of the Hawaiian kingdom is an example of American **imperialism**, defined as "the creation and maintenance of an unequal economic, cultural and territorial relationship, usually between states and often in the form of an empire, based on domination and subordination" (Johnston, 2000, p. 375).

In 1845, the state now called Texas was annexed to the United States from Mexico, for example. This government-imposed geographical distinction rarely occurs with the involvement of those whose homes and land are divided, taken, and re-allocated. Sometimes across-the-road neighbors find themselves citizens of different countries virtually overnight. Native American lands were annexed by treaties in order to acquire additional lands for political and economic gains of primarily White Europeans seeking to expand scope of control, gain mineral rights, and secure borders.

In 1898, by a joint resolution of Congress, the United States annexed the Hawaiian Islands. Hawaii was one among many new U.S. "possessions" that the government conquered and occupied during this time, but "the only one to be formally annexed to the United States" (Basson, 2005, p. 580). In the 19th century, Christian missionaries arrived on the islands with the intent of converting the indigenous population. Later, land speculators and those with business interests followed. The interest was primarily in sugar plantations upon which Asian contract laborers worked. Over time, Hawaiian residents wanted to maintain political and economic powers and certain guarantees for sugar prices and other concessions were promised. In 1887, radical White groups forced the abdication of the Hawaiian king, and the **Bayonet Constitution** was instituted, which reduced his control in government. Queen Liliukalani tried to replace this group after the king died, to no avail. The Chinese Exclusion Act (discussed in Chapter 11) and **denial** of U.S. citizenship to Hawaiian citizens took place at the same time as it did on the mainland. On February 22, 1900, under U.S. President William McKinley, the **Newlands Resolution** officially made Hawaii a territory. Discomfort with extending citizenship to indigenous Hawaiians crossed Democratic and Republican party lines. Statehood was not granted to Hawaii until 1959.

In 1993, the U.S. Congress officially apologized to the people of Hawaii for overthrowing the monarchy under Law 103-150, otherwise known as **The Apology Bill** (Kinzer, 2006).

Colonization

The sustained political, social, economic, and cultural domination over people by a foreign power is one definition of **colonization**. It is the process by which "European powers," for example, "reached positions of economic, military, political, and cultural hegemony in much of Asia, Africa, and the Americas" (Shohat & Stam, 1994, p. 2). Colonialism is based on two kinds of power: the power of the "individual to appropriate the resources, labor, and territory of another group or individual, creating hierarchy and inequality," and "the capacity to deny responsibility for having done so to silence resistance and opposition, and to normalize the outcome" (Lorenz & Watkins, 2000, p. 1). To normalize means "the resultant inequities and suffering are made to appear as if they are completely natural through mythologies of **scientific racism**, gender role, ethnic identity, national destiny, and social Darwinism" (p. 4). Thus, mainstream culture takes its position of power as one of natural superiority and the result of fate, whereas other groups' supposed inferiority is presumed to be the result of biology, that is, fact.

Colonization can be both external (ruling from afar) and internal (ruling from within). The internal experience is what Taylor and Stern (1997) calls "**percepticide**"—a form of renunciation that "turns the violence on oneself" it "blinds, maims, kills through the senses" (p. 124). A split within oneself internalizes violence resulting in a state of sustained dissociation or internalized oppression and continues to be the case for many Native Americans in the United States, Native Hawaiians, Puerto Ricans, and Filipino/as.

Eurocentrism is the engine that drives colonialism. It is the belief in the natural supremacy of Europe/Europeans and, by extension, America/Americans, over other countries and peoples. Harmand (quoted in Shohat & Stam, 1994, p. 18) states, the "basic legitimation of conquest over native peoples is the conviction of our superiority, not merely our mechanical, economic, and military superiority, but our moral superiority." Thus, Eurocentrism includes feelings of moral supremacy, ontological superiority, and intellectual ascendancy. Although Eurocentrism is not necessarily racist (or sexist, or ageist), it is a way of seeing the world through a specific cultural lens. However, "what is racist is the stigmatizing of difference in order to justify unfair advantage or the abuse of power, whether that advantage be economic, political, cultural, or psychological" (Shohat & Stam, 1994, p. 22).

The writer, revolutionary, and psychoanalyst Frantz Fanon, a Black man from Martinique, wrote about the psychopathologizing of **colonization** (domination and control by outsiders) and the emphasis on difference. His first experience with **Whiteness** came in the 1940s with Vichy French occupation of the island. Fanon (1952/1965) identified early on how colonization is not only a process of physical oppression, torture, and suffering but also a mental one (hegemony), attainable through the use of language. In the following quote, Fanon addresses the experience of not knowing one is "raced" until placed in a situation of comparison and judgment by the colonizer. The quote is long, but is worth reading in its entirety as Fanon's actions and words had tremendous influence on other writers and revolutionaries such as Malcolm X in the United States and Ernesto "Che" Guevara de la Serna in Cuba.

> As long as the black man is among his own, he will have no occasion, except in minor internal conflicts, to experience his being through others. There is of course the moment of 'being for others,' of which Hegel speaks, but every ontology is made unattainable in a colonized and civilized society [. . . .] In the Weltanschauung of a colonized people there is an impurity, a flaw that outlaws any ontological explanation. Someone may object that this is the case with every individual, but such an objection merely conceals a basic problem. Ontology—once it is finally admitted as leaving existence by the wayside—does not permit us to understand the being of the black man. For not only must the black man be black; he must be black in relation to the white man [. . . .] His metaphysics, or, less pretentiously, his customs and the sources on which they were based, were wiped out because they were in conflict with a civilization that he did not know and that imposed itself on him. The real world challenged my claims. In the white world the man of color encounters difficulties in the development of his bodily schema. Consciousness of the body is solely a negating activity [. . . .]

Just as Jane Elliott's students felt what it is like to become Other for reasons that defy logic or soul, Fanon described his in-betweeness in country, category, and consciousness. What they all experienced is prejudice (belief), and prejudice leads to discrimination (behavior), both of which are discussed in the next section.

Prejudice

> Preconceived opinion not based on reason or actual experience; bias, partiality; (now) spec. unreasoned dislike, hostility, or antagonism towards, or discrimination against, a race, sex, or other class of people. (*OED*)

Derived from the Latin words *prae* "before" and *judicum* "a judgment," the word "prejudice" refers to the concept of making a judgment before knowing the facts, *praejudicium*, meaning "an opinion or judgment formed…without due examination." Prejudice refers to "a set of rigidly held negative attitudes, beliefs, and feelings toward members of another group" (Yetman, 2004, p. 8). In 1954, Harvard psychologist Gordon Allport defined prejudice as "an antipathy based on faulty and inflexible **generalization**. It may be felt or expressed. It may be directed toward a group or an individual of that group" (p. 8). In other words, prejudice is "an aversive or hostile attitude toward a person who belongs to a group, simply because he [or she] belongs to that group, and is therefore presumed to have the objectionable qualities ascribed to the group" (p. 8). It is any belief that serves to discriminate against another human being that has its foundation somewhere in the past.

As described in Chapter 6, long before September 11, 2001, prejudice was in place that constructed an evil Arab stereotype. Long before the first Africans were enslaved in the United States, attitudes and beliefs sprung from a set of particular cultural, economic, and political conditions that made doing so seem natural and normal. Sometimes prejudicial beliefs are used to survive, particularly in ancient times, when humans were always on the lookout for other humans who wanted their food, shelter, or other resources. Healy points out a common factor in the origins of prejudice: "competition between groups: some episode in which one group successfully dominates, takes resources from, or eliminates a threat from some other group" (2007, p. 16). Thus the group that is successful, that wins the battle or the prize, becomes dominant. But prejudice is usually the result of a competitive situation and not the cause. In order to "win," the other must become the enemy, more a thing than a person. Typically prejudice is regarded as hostile or negative attitudes toward another individual and/or social group. George Mason University economics professor Walter E. Williams (2006, n.p.) describes the attitude this way:

> In a world of costly information, people seek to economize on information costs. Imagine heading off to work, you open your front door, only to be greeted by a full-grown tiger. The uninteresting prediction is the average person would slam the door or otherwise seek safety. Why they do so is more interesting. It's unlikely that person's decision is based on any detailed information held about that particular tiger. More likely his decision is based on tiger folklore or how he's seen other tigers behave. He prejudges, or stereotypes, that tiger.

Therefore, if an individual didn't prejudge, he or she would seek additional information before coming to this conclusion. However, given the circumstances and the immediacy of the many situations that might not be the route taken. In a mediated world filled with rapid transference of symbolic information, people often don't have or don't take the time to stop the process of belief formation from moving into the action of discrimination.

Discrimination

The behavior that usually results from prejudice is discrimination. Whereas prejudice is the thought pattern, an intellectualized point of view, discrimination is the behavior that results. Being prejudiced is holding the view that unfavorable or discriminatory treatment of individuals because they belong to a particular group is appropriate. Discrimination involves the unfair treatment of an individual or a group on the basis of some stigmatized characteristic such as race, class, gender, age, ethnicity, religion, national origin, **sexual orientation**, political views, disability, and other characteristics.

The system of discrimination can be formal or informal. Formally (lists, laws) or informally (casual observation, attitudes) classifying people into different groups accords members of each group distinct, and typically unequal, treatments, rights, and obligations. The criteria delineating the groups, such as gender, race, or class, determine the form of discrimination. Examples of the many ways discrimination is demonstrated include "simple" forms such as racial slurs and jokes, intimidation, to unequal job treatment (such as refusing to hire or promote someone), and, its most extreme expression, the "systematic oppression" (slavery) and "outright violence" (vandalism, arson, terrorism, lynching, pogroms, massacres) (Yetman, 2007, p. 9).

As early as 1949, sociologist Robert Merton (1948) identified four types of people in whom prejudice, attitude, and discrimination work together as a spectrum of types:

1.   The unprejudiced non-discriminator—*the all-weather liberal*
2.   The unprejudiced discriminator—*the fair-weather liberal*
3.   The prejudiced nondiscriminator—*the fair-weather bigot*

4. The prejudiced discriminator—*the all-weather bigot*

In the class of the first type (all-weather liberal), the individual believes strongly in the American creed of equality in belief and in practice. The view is fixed and stable. The second type of person, the unprejudiced discriminator (fair-weather liberal), might state belief in the American creed but cave in to pressures from a larger group and discriminate. The prejudiced nondiscriminatory individual (fair-weather bigot) goes along with societal pressures *not* to discriminate, all the while harboring deep-seated hatreds and aggressions toward racial and ethnic minorities. Finally, the prejudiced discriminator (full-blown bigot) is upfront, open about his or her feelings, and consistent in beliefs that discrimination is the correct thing to do. In many ways, what is important about Merton's array is the social context within which discrimination occurs. It is not enough to know that discrimination exists, but one must understand that prejudice "is a product of situations, historical situations, economic situations, political situations; it is not a little demon that emerges in people because they are depraved" (Schermerhorn, 1970, p. 6).

As with prejudice, discrimination is not usually based on actual experience with someone different from us; rather it is based on information passed down or on to others from another person or the media. Typically, conceptions of oppressed people are that they are somehow genetically inferior, less intelligent, less able to adapt to majority society, and more likely to harm majority members. Very often discriminatory attitudes and beliefs about others are institutionalized. In other words, governments, schools, churches, and other institutions enact discrimination through formal mechanisms. The effects of discrimination extend from the seemingly mild cases of covert acts such as unhelpful or slow service, to more overt acts such as ethnic, racial or sexual slurs, the denial of jobs or housing, to life-threatening hate crimes. Some examples are unequal welfare payments to unemployed citizens and non-citizens, inequitable availability of health care to Native Americans and poor citizens, and unfair arrest of both citizens and non-citizens through the dictates of the Bush administration's Homeland Security measures.

Governments have routinely and formally supported discrimination—apartheid in South Africa, the U.S. institutionalizing slavery before and during the Civil War, the so-called "Indian problem" in the United States, and the so-called "Jewish problem" in Nazi Germany. The 1960s U.S. Civil Rights Movement is an example of the government working to lessen discrimination through polices of affirmative action. In 2001–2009, despite declared policies designed to protect human rights, the American government's actions in Guantanamo Bay, Cuba, were found to include torture, "bizarre, even sadistic treatment of detainees in the American prison camp" (Leung, 2005, n.p.).

How does prejudice live longer than the original situation that created it? How and why do prejudices persist through time and place? In the mid-1940s, Swedish economist Gunnar Myrdal suggested prejudice is perpetuated as part of a vicious cycle. First, the dominant group has a goal in mind and uses its power to force the minority group into an inferior position. In order to justify this stratification and to create a construct that supports its perpetuation, the wider social group must adopt the prejudicial beliefs. Over time, these beliefs become so widespread and common that they come to seem normal, that the inferior status of the oppressed group appears to be the natural order of things. For example, White slaveholders oppressed Blacks by confining them to plantations and treating them like children and justified these actions by saying Blacks were lazy, performed poorly, and were unable to assimilate. These simplified, inaccurate, constructed traits were used as rationalization for the oppression.

As discussed earlier, beliefs, including prejudices, are learned. Identifying a group of people as different, and thereby lesser-than, for example, as an animal or childlike is one way prejudicial beliefs are instilled as part of generational passing-on of values, attitudes, and beliefs. The long and deep roots that lead to the source of prejudice are persistent and are difficult to destroy. How does someone become a member of a group of "Others"? One route is by being stigmatized.

Stigma

Race/**ethnicity** is perhaps the most clearly visible distinction by which people have been separated from dominant culture and is used as a primary example in this chapter. Other categories (referred to as "isms") such as sex, sexuality, gender, religion, health status, (dis)ability, and class-based discrimination follow similar patterns. Conceptualizing race (or another marker of difference) as a **stigma,** defined as visible and invisible markings of difference, highlights the way race-as-stigma operates to produce and maintain inequities as a form of meaning making and social reproduction. Howarth (2006) identifies at least four ways (embodied, practiced, constituted, and imposed) race-as-stigma is imposed:

1. *Embodied.* Whether it is the color of skin, size of eyes or nose, or other bodily inscriptions, stigma marks a person or group of people as somehow different from those with the majority of power. Inherent in this is also the idea of the stigmatized person as somehow sullied or impure, thus needing to be policed and controlled least they "infect" the pure quality and nature of the oppressor (Foucault, 1973, 1977; Douglas, 2002). Furthermore, "a blemished person, ritually polluted, is to be avoided, especially in public places" (Goffman, 1968, p. 11). Embodied stigma is viewed as psychological marking that

impacts an individual's sense of self, value, ambition, expectations, and fears and becomes internalized.

2. *Practiced.* For the dominating social system to remain in control, it is important that the person is identifiable and observable in all aspects of life. Goffman (1968, p. 3) noted that stigma reduces a person "from a whole and usual person to a tainted, discounted one." Thus, this "**spoiled identity**" positions the stigmatized person as Other, less than, non-normative. Foucault (1980) identified how a social system informed by stigmatic demarcation uses surveillance, or the panoptic gaze to fulfill its hegemonic potential. This theory built upon Jeremy Bentham's (1785/1995) design of the panopticon-type of prison in which the inmate is always observable, even if he or she can't see who is watching. Bentham described this structure (also used in mental hospitals) as "a new mode of obtaining power of mind over mind, in a quantity hitherto without example." Stigmatization is also a disciplinary practice. It requires one group be easily identifiable and those with interests in maintaining the system able to observe. Those who are observed thereby structure their behavior, attitudes, and beliefs in ways that are consistent with that system. This requires

   > asn inspecting gaze which each individual under its weight will end by interiorizing to the point that he is his own overseer, each individual thus exercising this surveillance over, and against, himself. A superb formula: power exercised continuously and for what turns out to be minimal cost. (Foucault, 1980, p. 155)

3. *Constituted.* Inequities in societies make their appearance in terms of unequal distribution of resources and access to power. Histories of domination, migration, annexation, colonization, globalization, representation, and resource allocation reveal the stigmatized category as constituted through prejudice and anchored in experiences of exclusion, poverty, and psychological oppression. These systems of enacted regulations are in many ways invisible or at least not as overt today as they were in the past. Foucault refers to these as "bio-politics" as they take place both inside and outside social, economic, and cultural institutions. In this way, stigma is enacted as ordered text written "on" bodies as forms of, in some cases literal, but many times metaphorical social control. Anorexia, for example, is an act of inscribing on the (primarily) female body the ideology of ideal female beauty that constrains both thought and act. Tatooing is another example of inscribing culture onto physical form.

4. *Imposed.* Race is "stigma in the eye of the beholder" (Howarth, 2006, p. 443). Race or other such identity is variable, socially constructed, and then marked *on* someone by another. The imposed stigmatized category usually clashes

with one's claimed identity, depresses self-esteem, and operates at its hegemonic fullest when the stigmatized cooperate in their own oppression, that is, begins to think of him or herself in the same terms as the oppressor does. For example, the systematic observation of bodies through medical care (or lack thereof) is an example wherein race-as-stigma becomes associated with treatment. Furthermore, certain categories of being that are thereby marked as somehow lesser-than, impure, or dangerous are used as justification for exclusion from care or **attribution** of socially constructed categories of illness even though many times particular illnesses result from the stress of being stigmatized.

Embodied socially constructed, practiced, constituted, and imposed, identities are identifiable not only by what is present, but also by what is absent. A "Black person" is never just that but is also young or old, male or female, a professor or a lab technician, well or poorly dressed, tall or short, friendly or hostile, from the South or the North, and above all not White. Therefore, the first question involving perception of an individual must be: Which category is used and when?

As discussed in Chapter 2, identity is created, constructed, and operates categorically at both the individual (**shadow**) level and the collective (archetypal) level in the form of projection. **Projection**, defined as the "unperceived and unintentional transfer of subjective psychic elements onto an outer object" (von Franz, 1995, p. 3), is the psychological process of taking unconscious thoughts, ideas, and constructs and applying them to someone or something outside of ourselves as if they were a part of Them when in fact they are a part of Us. In other words, "what is projected is not only a memory-image, as one might at first conclude, but rather a sum of characteristic qualities that constitutes a part of the person observed" (von Franz, 1995, p. 2). Thus, projection is not about the person upon which these ideas about impurity, danger, authority, and threat are placed but rather about the insecurities, fears, and undealt-with past experiences of the one doing the projecting. The outcome of projections of this inner authority appear on the collective level in ways that appear to be normal and natural distinctions but are born out of fear of psychological disequilibrium and physical threat. We use ego defense mechanisms to support long held points of view that even if uncomfortable, feel familiar.

Three **anxiety and ego-defense mechanisms** are used to maintain a sense of balance and peace of mind: **repression**, denial, and projection. While our first response might be to try to determine whatever person, place, or thing is causing this rupture in our psychological well-being, repression (also called defensiveness) is a powerful way of fending off ideas which conflict with those long held. This is not usually done consciously. By repressing, we can deny our thoughts or reactions to others are who are "bad" and rather project that they *are* "bad" and what we are feeling is "good" and right (see Chapter 6 for more on this topic). Denial is another tool for fending off the anxiety produced by uncertainty. By pretending the situation or persons do not exist, psychological equilibrium is restored. **Scapegoating** is an example of the projection process, wherein a person or group is identified as problematic. The shadow, or the darker part of our personalities, underlies prejudice and discrimination and is used to justify oppression, persecution, and stereotyping. Prejudice and discrimination are outcomes.

The cultural studies approach of this book, described in Chapter 1, posits that in order to understand social relationships and media (re)presentation, it is critical to understand the nature of power and how it is articulated in social institutions and practices. Power is the overarching framework within which attitudes, beliefs, and behaviors associated with categorization, prejudice, and discrimination operate. As Jordan and Weedon (1994, p. 11) emphasize, "*everything* in social and cultural life is fundamentally to do with power. Power is at the centre of cultural politics. It is integral to culture. *All signifying practices, that is, all practices that have meaning—involve relations of power.*" [ital. orig]. Thus, the primary determinant of difference is power. In the following sections, power, and its articulation in differences, stereotypes, and privilege are discussed in detail.

Power

> \Pow"er\, n. [OE. pouer, poer, OF. poeir, pooir, F. pouvoir, n. &
> v., fr. LL. potere, for L. posse, potesse, to be able, to have power.
> Control or authority over others; dominion, rule; government,
> command, sway. Capacity to direct or influence the behaviour
> of others; personal or social influence. (*OED*)

One of the most insidious, and yet less obvious, ways of establishing difference is by withholding power—the power to act, to govern, and to achieve equity. Power is control over the distribution of resources (capital), which can be tangible or intangible. Often differences in expectations, perceived ability (or lack thereof), and intelligence are established and reinforced in ways that, to those with power, justify paying lower wages, limiting access to health care, legal representation, and education, higher incarceration rates, and general lack of access to the means to improve one's life.

The unequal distribution of goods and services is a trait of most societies, creating haves and have-nots. In the United States, men have more power than women; White men and women have more power than do people of color; wealthy more than poor; heterosexual over homosexual; young over old, and owners of corporations over workers. Power comes not from individual men, who certainly vary in their participation in a system of patriarchy, but as a group of (typically) White men enjoy privileges not afforded to or at a higher level than women (White and women of color) and men of color. As John Stuart Mill (1864, p. 151) noted, "human affairs are not entirely governed by mechanical laws, nor men's characters wholly and irrevocably formed by their situation in life; ideas are not always mere signs and effects of social circumstances, they are themselves a power in history." In the United States and other Western societies, social class is a primary source and marker of difference that extends to all areas of life. The many ways difference is articulated that reflect ideological interests are referred to as "isms," which structure social attitudes. Those discussed in this book fall within a group related to race, gender, ethnicity, sexuality, and belong to a particular family of marked identity.

Meet the "ism" family

Individuals who do not fit the definition of "normal" experience a set of challenges for each characteristic that differs from it. Isms are defined as institutionally based disadvantages usually based on physically, socially, culturally, and economically stigmatized characteristics that are identifiable by systems of advantage and disadvantage that construct and maintain inequities. They are examples of oppression, which is the combination of the desire to maintain or achieve power and prejudice. Both factors historically and contemporarily create systems of advantage (privilege) that benefit some and disadvantage others based on some socially constructed, shared characteristic used to define everyone belonging to that group. The oppression individuals and groups experience can be thought of metaphorically as wires on a birdcage (Frye, 1983). They work like this: If you look closely at a single wire on the cage, it is easy to miss the others, and wonder why the bird doesn't simply fly away. However, by stepping back, by examining the elements that comprise each wire, it becomes clear how and why freedom and equity (spaces outside of the cage) are difficult if not impossible goals to reach. Each bar is identifiable as an "ism" (categories of difference: racism, sexism, heterosexism, ageism, classism, and ableism). The **"bird cage metaphor"** suggests that the so-called "playing field" is far from level, available with few hindrances unless the individual is White, male, middle class, educated, and heterosexual. A 54-year-old working class lesbian Latina, for example, will find it much more difficult to get the same wages or the same consideration as a White male or a White woman of the same age. If age, sexuality, ethnicity, or mobility are considered alone, each might appear to offer little hindrance in reaching the playing field. The more wires added, the more the challenges. Frye (1983, pp. 4–5) writes, "One can study the elements of an oppressive structure with great care and some good will without seeing or being able to understand that one is looking at a cage and that there are people there who are caged, whose motion and mobility are restricted, whose lives are shaped and reduced." The isms (wires) are characterized by several key mechanisms:

1. *The positing of lack.* Seeing others (non-European Whites) as deficient in areas such as intelligence, materiality, civilization, discourse, and modesty.
2. *The mania for hierarchy.* Not only are people ranked (European Whites at the top) but so are cultural practices and beliefs.
3. *Blaming the victim.* Viewing a person as responsible for his or her oppression, thus deserving of the consequences no matter how harsh.
4. *The refusal of empathy.* This mechanism is closely connected with blaming the victim as it is demonstrated by lack of feelings of care or compassion for those who have been victimized by the social structure.

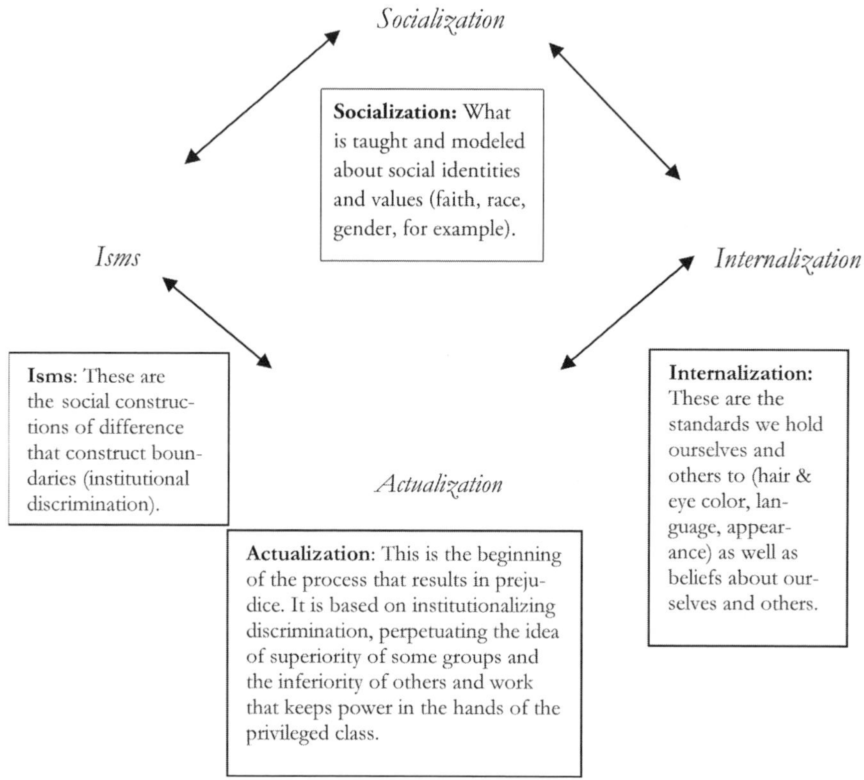

Figure 3.1: Web of oppression.

Source: The Inclusion Center for Community and Justice.

5. *The systematic devalorization of life.* Lives of racially White people have long been held up (by racially White people) as more important and valuable than those of people of color. Inequitable treatment of groups on the basis of race following Hurricane Katrina is an example. Thus, racial/ethnic others are regarded as expendable, in the most extreme circumstances.

Another way of thinking about the interconnectedness of the isms is the **Web of Oppression** (Figure 3.1). This model demonstrates the process by which we learn what our society and culture value and believe in, and how those beliefs then become a barometer of truth and reality (**internalization**).

These beliefs are enacted/actualized through levels of discrimination, which are: (1) socialization, (2) internationalization (standards, inner conflict, beliefs), (3) actualization, and (4) institutional groups (that perpetuate and maintain). The process begins during childhood and is repeated throughout our lifetime by exposure to ideas and images that typically affirm, confirm, and concretize ways of meaning-making consistent with the goals of dominant society. As you will read in the case studies in Chapters 5 to 14, laws, cultural values, policies, and various social systems such as education and occupation construct and fix isms in ways that they appear to be naturally created eternally recurring phenomena. As a result, symbolic representation based on categorization and construction of Otherness in media, for example, is practically seamless to the uncritical eye. Institutionalized practices advantage some groups (privilege) and disadvantage others (discrimination). These are discussed in the next section.

Privilege

The persistence of hierarchies in the United States contributes to the maintenance of the system of power. Differences are explained and rationalized based on physiognomic (judging someone by their facial features) and cultural (transmitted patterns, beliefs, attitudes) characteristics. This system gives unearned power and resources to one group, thereby making them unavailable to others as a way of retaining and maintaining positions of authority. The result is that people who are unmarked enjoy the privilege.

Privilege keeps restrictive, institutionalized structures in place in part because it is largely invisible to those who enjoy the majority of freedoms. Privilege speaks to the many unearned advantages in day-to-day life that those who happen to be born into the normative group enjoy. There are many things someone who is privileged simply does not have to think about, such as whether a job will be suddenly filled when the employer sees him or her, an apartment will suddenly become unavailable, or that he or she will be followed around a department store or arrested on the basis of race. Thus, privilege is a kind of social blindness available to those in power who are the builders and keepers of culture and consciousness.

Gloria Yamato's (1998) foundational work, *Something About the Subject Makes It Hard to Name,*" describes how unarticulated privilege makes access to life's political, social, and cultural playing field more difficult. These unmarked (and, to members of the group to whom they apply, invisible) aspects of privilege construct the boundaries between who does and who does not have access to America's playing field of social, cultural, and economic life:

> Privilege generally allows people to assume a certain level of acceptance, inclusion, and respect in the world; to operate within a relatively wide comfort zone....It allows people to define reality and to have prevailing definitions of reality fit their experience. Privilege means being able to decide who gets taken seriously, who receives attention, who is accountable to whom and for what. (Johnson, 2001, p. 33)

Jones (n.d.) uses the example of right-handed and left-handed people to illustrate this tender topic as an example that is not as loaded with as much "historical baggage" as is race or gender, or other culturally inscribed differences. "Do we live in a right-handed or left-handed world?" he asks. Americans shake hands, pledge allegiance, salute, take legal and governmental oaths with our right hand.

> My answer is that we live in a right-handed world. Look at the systems that have been created to support the successful functioning of the group called the right-handed people. School desks are set up for right-handed people; most baseball mitts are designed for right-handed people...I recently went into a store called the Left-handed Store in San Diego, CA. When was the last time you walked into your local Wal-Mart, Target, or department store and thought about the fact that you were in a right-handed store?

In "Unpacking the Invisible Backpack," McIntosh (1989) lists 42 ways in which privilege is institutionalized (built into a social system) and constructed that both grants and denies opportunities on the basis of group membership or the basis of race and gender. Rather than thinking, as she had been trained to do, about the disadvantage racism causes others, McIntosh challenges Whites to think about how the present system advantages them. Examples include:

- I can arrange to be in the company of people of my own race most of the time.
- If I should need to move, I can be pretty sure of renting or purchasing housing in an area which I can afford and in which I want to live.
- I can turn on the television or open to the front page of the paper and see people of my race widely represented.
- I can do well in a challenging situation without being called a credit to my race.

- I can choose blemish cover or bandages in flesh color and have them more or less match my skin.

What informs the isms and supports privilege? Generalizations made from categories. As described in Chapters 1 and 2, all statements of fact or truth require generalization. A generalization is a statement based on a finite set of observations and experiences which claims to hold true for the larger set, even for those cases that have not been seen or experienced. All generalizations, then, can be said to be theoretical. They offer a theory about how things are in general and are predictive. Thus the statement "All trees have leaves" is a useful generalization. Although the observation is made on the basis of only a few trees, it isn't necessary to see every tree on the planet to come to this conclusion. However, while most trees have some leaves at different times of the year, it is not true that all trees have leaves—pine and fir trees have needles. Generalization comes from our mind's efforts to organize knowledge, not necessarily with the intent to oversimplify or oppress but to categorize. As such, in the tree example, the intention is to form a general sense of trees and their needs, not to harm them. The goal might be to manipulate trees-as-nature in order to benefit human beings' needs. Thus, "the effect of the generalization is to increase people's ability to manipulate nature to human ends, and so like all acts of knowledge this one affects the power balance between knower and thing known" (Jay, 2007, n.p.). Similar to the function of categories discussed in Chapter 2, generalizations produce a form of knowledge that organizes thoughts. Not all generalizations, however, are neutral or positive, for example, the stereotype.

What are stereotypes?

It would be nearly impossible to function in the world without simplifying visual and verbal information to manageable units. As available methods for organizing the "great blooming, buzzing confusion of the outer world" (Lippmann, 1922, p. 81), **stereotypes** "…get hold of the few simple, vivid, memorable, easily grasped, and widely recognized characteristics about a person, reduce everything about the person to those traits, exaggerate and simplify them, and fix them without change or development to eternity" (Hall, 1997, p. 258).

As discussed in Chapter 2, the process of categorizing, or organizing meaning in and about the world has been discussed for thousands of years. The word stereotype comes from the Greek words *stereos* (rigid) and *túpos* (trace). It was coined in 1798 to describe a unit of type cast from a mould. These individual units together were used to create text to uniformly create a document. Each letter had to be the same as the others in terms of height and shape. A similar term was used by early psychiatrists—stereotypy or stereotypie—to describe repetitive gestures, postures, or speech patterns.

In the context of this book, stereotyping is a signifying mental practice. It provides convenient shorthand in the identification of a particular group of people. In 1922, journalist and political pundit Walter Lippmann brought the term stereotype into the domain of social science. Lippmann's story of islanders in Chapter 1 is an example of how "the world outside" (reality) does not necessarily correspond to the "pictures in our heads" (stereotypes). In his view, people do not respond directly to reality but rather to representations of "reality" that may be entirely constructed in their minds. Thus, defining "reality" is a profoundly personal and political act.

Stereotype formation begins during early childhood. "It seems likely that stereotypes become part of our understanding of our surroundings from the first moments of our efforts to make sense of the world around us" (Gandy, 1998, p. 83). Stereotypes are tools that provide justification, reinforcement, and maintenance of the status quo. They are the foundations of social tradition and maintain the social and symbolic order by binding people together as an Us and sending those who are not Us into "symbolic exile" as Them (Hall, 1997, p. 258). Stereotypes have the following characteristics (Jay, 2007):

1. Originate within a group or individual and are caused by a history of sociopolitical struggle between unequal groups within a region, nation, or society
2. Present generalizations which function to create or sustain inequalities of value, power, and/or wealth among socially constructed groups (by race, age, sex, class, religion)
3. Are intended to harm or have a negative effect as regards the object of the stereotype or can reasonably be predicted to do so
4. Circulate repeatedly and systematically in a culture so that many people in the culture, even those who are the object of the stereotype come to accept them as "common sense" truths
5. Disguise or distort the truth through caricature and misrepresentation based on only partial aspects of a person or situation
6. Appeal to the prejudices of the audience, exploiting these by attaching them to emotions of pleasure or hatred that are reinforced often by casting stereotypes within frameworks of entertainment

According to Tajfel (1981), stereotypes perform three social functions: (1) causal explanation, (2) justification, and (3) differentiation. A **social causal explanation** looks outward to explain something that happened that appears to be beyond the control of a group, for example, blaming immigrants for low-paying jobs or economic recession. The **social justification function** occurs when a stereotype is created in order to justify action against a particular group. An example discussed earlier is how colonial slaveholders created the stereotype of the unredeemable, happy-go-lucky childlike slave who was incapable of acculturating in order to justify keeping other human beings enslaved by saying it was for their "own good." The Uncle Tom and Zeb Coon characters of American cinema and popular culture are illustrations of this portrayal and are discussed in Chapter 12.

The **social differentiation function** establishes specific differences between one group and another in order to create a dominant in-group and subordinate out-group. Pinning yellow stars on Jews by German Nazis during World War II is an example of externalized social differentiation used to stand in for or mark, a stigmatized group.

Summary

This chapter has explored the theoretical and psychological mechanisms behind divisions created by the thought process that categorizes, generalizes, and thus stigmatizes individuals who belong to particular groups; the primary reason being to support a system of power that seeks to keep order and control in the hands of the privileged. The next step is to articulate the primary divisions between groups in American society. What are the major divisions and how are they then articulated in mass media? These questions are explored in the next chapter (Chapter 4).

Questions for Discussion

1. Have you ever felt the effects of prejudice or discrimination? What was the situation and how did you resolve it

2. What purpose does stereotyping serve?

3. How might stereotypes of masculinity or femininity affect social interactions?

4. Who are your five favorite Latina/o actors? Native American? What does this tell you about visibility of people of color in the media?

5. What roles do social institutions other than the mass media play in the formation of stereotypes?

Key Words

Annexation	Anxiety and ego-defense mechanisms
Apology Bill	Attribution
Bird cage metaphor	Bayonet Constitution
Colonization	Denial
Double consciousness	Emigrate
Ethnicity	Eurocentism
Forced migration	Generalization
Imperialism	Immigrate
Internalization	Newlands Resolution
Percepticide	Projection
Repression	Scapegoating
Scientific racism	Sexual orientation
Shadow	Social causal explanation
Social differentiation function	Social justification
Spoiled identity	Stereotype
Stigma	Stigmatization
Web of Oppression	Whiteness

 The Articulation of Difference

Collective fear stimulates herd instinct, and tends to produce ferocity toward those who are not regarded as members of the herd.

Bertrand Russell

This is no simple reform. It really is a revolution. Sex and race because they are easy and visible differences have been the primary ways of organizing human beings into superior and inferior groups and into the cheap labour on which this system still depends. We are talking about a society in which there will be no roles other than those chosen or those earned. We are really talking about humanism.

Gloria Steinem

I, with a deeper instinct, choose a man who compels my strength, who makes enormous demands on me, who does not doubt my courage or my toughness, who does not believe me naïve or innocent, who has the courage to treat me like a woman.

Anaïs Nin

A cultural studies approach to studying popular representations in media "unmasks the deeply embedded power structures that attempt to sustain dominant ideologies" (Bell-Jordan, 2008, p. 353). These ideologies are political, economic, social, and legal and reflect historical constructions of identity. One of the most powerful ways that Otherness is constructed is through articulations of difference. As Fiske (1986) notes, "the structure of meanings in a text is a miniaturization of the structure...of society—both exist in a network of power relations, and the textual struggle for meaning is the precise equivalent of the social struggle for power" (p. 392). Thus, whether seen on television, in films, in ads, or heard in music or radio programs, the way dominant society wants the world to be seen is typically reflected in the products mainstream culture produces. While there is room for resistance and redefinition, what the majority of people see, hear, and read is filtered through the lens of the majority power holders.

While Chapter 3 focused on the historical, cultural, and economic underpinnings for how difference and Otherness are constructed, the resulting beliefs (prejudices) are then enacted overtly in behaviors such as discrimination and covertly in the form of stereotypes. This chapter examines the major divisions in American society in terms of class, race, gender, sexuality, and other differences. The resulting isms are then interrogated as they apply to major categories or racial and ethnic differences, which appear in the mass media and popular culture in the form of reoccurring stereotypes. These stereotypes are examined further in the case study chapters that follow.

What Are the Major Divisions?

Class

> \Class\ (kl[.a]s), n. [F. classe, fr. L. classis class, collection, fleet; akin to Gr. klh^sis a calling, kalei^n to call, E. claim, haul.] A division or order of society according to status; a rank or grade of society. (*OED*)

In American society, class is the overarching expression of power/powerlessness, along with race, gender, and sexuality. Intimately connected to power is social class, a central component of social structures. Social class is considered the "**master identity**," the "category through which all other social identities are to be mediated" (du Gay, Evans, & Redman, 2000, p. 1). The American class structure exists despite the persistence of belief that America is a "classless society" (Coleman & Rainwater, 1978).

Despite lived realities, there has been a general cultural denial or "disinclination to accord differences (educational or otherwise) on the basis of class" (North, Snyder, & Bulfin, 2008, p. 895). Polarities inherent in Western dualistic thinking about class, such as high and low class, function as hierarchically "at one end as a value sought. The other represents its opposite, a negative to be avoided" (Belenky, Bond, & Weinstock, 1999, p. 20). While social class is discussed extensively in Chapter 5, it is important to briefly describe the nature of social-class-as-power in order to understand how differences are constructed to keep resources and power away from some while remaining with others. French theorist Pierre Bourdieu (as cited in Swartz, 1998, p. 92) described social class as a structured space of symbolic capital. Whereas capital is typically thought of as money and resources, according to this view, individuals also create **symbolic capital,** defined as the aspects of goods that say something about the owner, out of three other forms of capital: economic (financial), social (networks of relationships with people), and cultural (values, tastes, knowledge, customs, skills). Briefly, capital becomes part of social relationships as "it relates goods, material and symbolic, without distinction, that present themselves as rare and worthy of being sought after in a particular social formation" (as cited in Harker, Mahar, & Wilkes, 1990, p. 13). Cultural capital acts as a social relation within a system of exchange that includes the accumulated cultural knowledge that confers power and status.

Classism

In his classic work *Distinction*, Bourdieu further describes the inscription of social class by upper classes who move away, or distance themselves from other groups, via shared and agreed-upon recognition and valuation of life's material resources. Gated communities are an example. Thus, *distinction* operates as a privileging of the abstract and idealized over the real and the material. An example is the concept of *nouveau cuisine* in which tiny portions of food are served and high prices charged. Classical music or minimalist decorating thus becomes valued over country music and early American decor. Yet, as economist Thorstein Veblen (1912/1994, p. 49) identified at the turn of the 20th century, it is considered in poor taste to overdo emblems of "conspicuous consumption." Similarly, "privilege publicly worn is an affront to democracy, and the American elite discovered that inverse snobbery is more effective in masking social class difference and weeding out patricians from *parvenus* than flagrant snobbery and public displays of financial superiority" (Cookson & Persell, 1985, p. 29).

There is a relatively recent trend, however, amongst upper classes to return to the more "authentic" or "real" in life—highly textured fabrics, folk art, and indigenous food and music become highly valued commodities. These "Bohemian bourgeois" (Bobos) are "educated trekkers" who "are not looking for fun," rather they "want to spend their precious weeks torturing themselves in ways that will be intellectually and spiritually enhancing" (Brooks, 2001, p. 208). Ecotourism, baking artisan breads, or back-to-the-land living are examples, all done with limited amounts of roughness and a great deal of comfort.

But social class is about more than money or things. The reality is that less than one-half of one percent of the total American population comprises the American upper class. In terms of both economic and cultural dominance, the elite are numerically smaller but wield the bulk of the power. Therefore, "class is defined not on the terrain of the economic but on each of the levels of economic, political, and ideological structure. Class is the complex effect of these three structural levels, which are the loci at once of determination and of struggle" (Frow, 1995, p. 103).

As mentioned in the Preface, owners of media corporations and other CEOs tend to be upper class, White, and male. These representatives of American patriarchal power and privilege exert and reinforce classism, a system of oppression that operates on multiple levels in both institutional and individual terms. The roots of classism in American capitalistic economic structures are found most clearly in acts of classist discrimination. As discussed in greater detail in Chapter 5, the interrelationships between social class, race, and gender, and the articulation of discrimination and prejudice occur in the categorical construction of difference. Attitudes of middle-class Americans, for example, about those poor in material

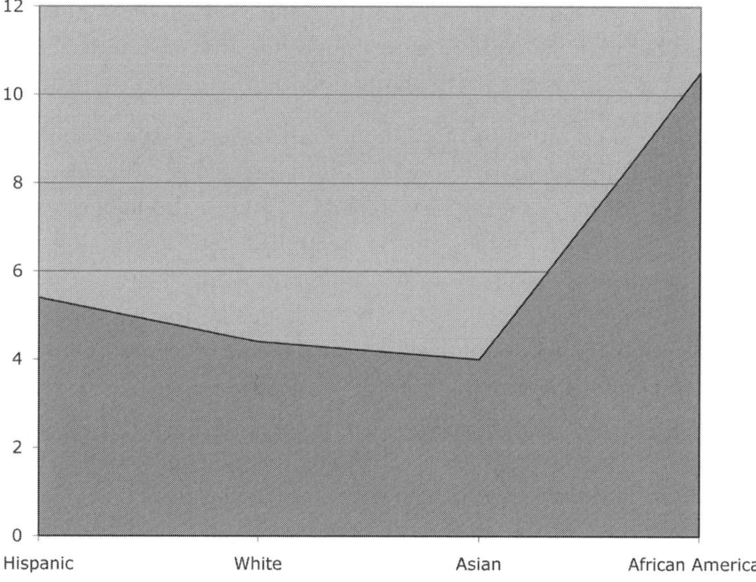

Figure 4.1: Unemployment by race

Source: Bureau of Labor Statistics, 2005.

goods constellate around raced constructs of welfare recipients as "typically characterized as dishonest, dependent, lazy, uninterested in education, and promiscuous" (Bullock, 1995, p.125). Figure 4.1 shows, based on census data, the percentage of Americans who are unemployed, by race.

Langston (1992, p. 112) offers, "when we experience classism, it will be because of our lack of money (i.e., choices and power in this society) and because of the way we talk, think, act, move—because of our culture." These visible and invisible markers of difference thereby result in "oppression of the poor through a network of everyday practices, attitudes, assumptions, behaviors, and institutional rules" (Bullock, 1995, p. 119). Differences and prejudices intersect around race, class, and gender; studies show, for example, young Black men have higher incarceration rates. Bullock (1995) studied over 3,500 Texas State Prison inmates and found African American men's sentences were longer when their victims were White than those of Whites whose victims were Black. Bullock's study has yet to be disproved.

Race

> \Race\, n. [F. race; cf. Pr. & Sp. raza, It. razza]. A group of persons, animals, or plants, connected by common descent or origin. In the widest sense the term includes all descendants from the original stock, but may also be limited to a single line of descent or to the group, as it exists at a particular period. (*OED*)

There is less—and more—to race than meets the eye. Race does not exist as a biological fact. Scientists have known this for years and yet, despite more than half a century of writings by geneticists, biologists, and anthropologists, the belief persists among the general public that there are substantial genetic differences between human beings classified as White, Black, Asian, Native American, or other groups. Race persists as a concept but cuts deeply and widely as a tool to mark differences for purposes of exclusion and is one of the more obvious and persistent markers of difference in American society. The continual belief in racial difference was used as justification for enslavement of millions of Black Africans, for example, by White European colonizers throughout the Americas, the Caribbean, Africa, and Asia. The persistent belief in the existence of human races, "constitutes one of man's most damnable masses of misinformation, and…has led to wars, strife, murder and waste of natural resources" (Calloway & Harris, 1977).

While "the human genetic code (genome) is 99.9% identical throughout the world" (Shreve, 2001, p. 15), the belief in human biological variation, hence differences, remains intact. Because of this, and the way the American economic and political system is organized, were this fact to be widely endorsed, groups that have suffered inequities due to race and ethnicity would no longer receive the modicum of assistance given today. If we were to consider other species of animals, of which humans are one, we'd say all domesticated cats, for example, belong to the genus *felis*. While there might be some differences in physical appearance between, say, a Persian and a Tabby or a Devon Rex, as a group they are all cats. For some reason, however, among our own genus *homos*, human beings are narrowly defined on the basis of perceived physical, phenotypical, or belief differences and we call them biological. Therefore, race is "an arbitrary classification system of populations conceived in Europe, using actual or assumed genetic traits to classify populations of the world into a hierarchical order, with Europeans [listed as] superior to all others" (Christensen, 1989, p. 275). Race as a "self-evident 'fact' requiring no protracted thought" (Hannaford, 1996, p. 3), consistently masks ideologies, making difference appear to be natural, normal, and eternal. Biological distinctions have been and are used as the basis for prejudice and discrimination in the darkest chapters in human history.

Racism

If race is based on socially constructed differences based on physical appearance, what is racism? Racism is "the systematic, institutionalized mistreatment of one group of people, based on race, by another for whatever reason" (Frye, 1983, p. 81). The term was first used in the 1930s by **Magnus Hirschfeld** (in German) to describe anti-Semitism directed at Jews—he intended the word to denote a *system* of racialized oppression in order to inspire thinking about the social circumstances of oppression that generated specific negative attitudes, beliefs, and behaviors. Racism can be enacted by political, educational, religious, or governmental institutions (Hirshfeld, 1938). As such, racism is defined as a concept, as the psychological practice of dividing human beings into groups and labeling them as biologically distinct categories. **Racism** is the practice that results from holding and enacting the following beliefs:

1. Human beings can be divided into races.
2. Some races are morally or intellectually inferior (or conversely superior) to others.
3. It is morally permissible for the "superior" races to treat the supposedly inferior races as less than full moral persons.

There is an important distinction between *individual* racism (discriminatory actions of one racist/bigoted individual, such as suddenly filling a job opening) and *institutional* racism (institutional practices that result in oppression of large numbers of people of a named group—such as Black children suffering from malnutrition).

In the next section Whiteness is interrogated as the norm by which other groups are compared and as the primary (along with sex) identifiable visual characteristic that the majority society uses to oppress and discriminate. Only in the last few years has Whiteness-as-race been a topic of classroom discussions. Whether White people see themselves as raced and the role Whiteness-as-the-norm plays in reifying privilege and racial inequality are also addressed. As Hacker (2003, p. 4) notes

> America is inherently a 'white' country: in character, in structure, in culture. Needless to say, black Americans create lives of their own. Yet as a people, they face boundaries and constrictions set by the white majority. America's version of apartheid, while lacking overt legal sanction, comes closest to the system even now…reformed in the land of its invention.

One of the most effective ways to discuss difference, be it racial, ethnic, or sexual, is to talk about what many Americans fail to notice: Whiteness. For roughly 75% of the American public, issues of job preferences, discrimination, inequitable medical and child care, legal services, and educational quality are not something to be evaluated in terms of whether or not their race had anything to do with decisions that were made. Height? Perhaps. Weight? Probably. Most inequities based on physical appearance do not get onto the radar of White Americans. If the boss says "you're fired" to a White person, he or she can be pretty certain skin color didn't have anything to do with the decision. What is Whiteness? What does it mean to be White in American society?

Deconstructing Whiteness

White

> Applied to those of ethnic types (chiefly European or of European extraction) characterized by light complexion, as distinguished from black, red, yellow, etc.

If you are White, you probably don't describe yourself in terms of your race. Why not? Because you don't have to. It is not unusual for Whites to feel everyone else belongs to a race. Whether aware of it or not, if you are a White person you experience the privilege of *not* having to think about whether you got the job (or didn't) because of your race, religion, ethnicity or if you'll be followed in department stores. In American society, White (along with middle-to-upper-middle class, educated, and male) is the default category, the norm against which members of other groups are measured. For example, in news stories it is not unusual to see a person identified by race, but it would look strange to see something like the following: "Jim Jenkins, white, a candidate for office in the next local election." Why does this look strange to us? Plug in another racial group and what happens? What "pictures in your head" does this information trigger? White studies is a growing area of research that examines the social construction of race by first exploring what being White is about, what the economic, social, cultural advantages have been and are for what is regarded as master status, as a way of unpacking White (and concurrently male) privilege. As long as Whiteness isn't regarded as race, "as long as White people are not racially seen/named, they/we function as a human norm. Other people are raced, we are just people" (Dyer, 1997, p. 1).

Critical consideration of White as a race can be traced to the late 1880s (Dyer, 1997), when "White" became a social designator and the defining criterion for who could vote, who could be enslaved, who could be a citizen, who could attend which schools, who could marry whom, and who could drink from which water fountain. Laws and social interactions were built upon the false idea that Whites are a naturally superior race that automatically deserves special privileges and protections, "Many, perhaps most, of our white students in the U.S. think that racism doesn't affect them because they are not people of color; they do not see 'whiteness' as a racial identity" (McIntosh, 1988, p. 9).

Ethnicity

Ethnic character or peculiarity. *(OED)*

In the United States, groups who are differentiated based on culture such as language, food, music, religion, or other practices are considered ethnic minorities. **Ethnicity** refers "to broad groupings of Americans on the basis of both race and culture of origin" (Phinney, 1996, p. 919). While racial minority groups also have distinctive cultural traditions, members of ethnic minority groups such as Hispanics or Latinos, include Mexican Americans, Chicanos, Puerto Ricans, and Cubans. People of the Jewish faith are also considered cultural minorities. It is important to note that ethnic minority members can be Black, White, Asian American, or Native American. For example, a person can be both Black and Hispanic. Religious minorities are those people who have a religion other than the dominant faith, which in the case of the United States is Christianity. U.S. religious minorities include Jews, Muslims, Amish, Mormons, Quakers, and Wiccans. Table 4.1 shows America's major religious groups (self-identified).

Three psychological dimensions to ethnicity are key to making this designation: (1) cultural norms and values' strength, salience, and meaning of ethnic

Table 4.1: Top 20 Religions in the United States (2001)

Religion	1990 Est. Adult Pop.	2001 Est. Adult Pop.	2004 Est. Total Pop.	% of U.S. Pop., 2000	% Change 1990—2000
Christianity	151,225,000	159,030,000	224,437,959	76.5%	+5%
Nonreligious/ Secular	13,116,000	27,539,000	38,865,604	13.2%	+110%
Judaism	3,137,000	2,831,000	3,995,371	1.3%	-10%
Islam	527,000	1,104,000	1,558,068	0.5%	+109%
Buddhism	401,000	1,082,000	1,527,019	0.5%	+170%
Agnostic	1,186,000	991,000	1,398,592	0.5%	-16%
Atheism		902,000	1,272,986	0.4%	
Hinduism	227,000	766,000	1,081,051	0.4%	+237%
Unitarian Universalism	502,000	629,000	887,703	0.3%	+25%
Wiccan/ Pagan/Druid		307,000	433,267	0.1%	
Spiritualism		116,000	163,710	0.05%	
Native American Religion	47,000	103,000	145,363	0.05%	+119%
Baha'i	28,000	84,000	118,549	0.04%	+200%
New Age	20,000	68,000	95,968	0.03%	+240%
Sikhism	13,000	57,000	80,444	0.03%	+338%
Scientology	45,000	55,000	77,621	0.02%	+22%
Humanism	29,000	49,000	69,153	0.02%	+69%
Deism (Deist)	6,000	49,000	69,153	0.02%	+717%
Taoism	23,000	40,000	56,452	0.02%	+74%
Eckankar	18,000	26,000	36,694	0.01%	+44%

Source: Religioustolerance.org

identity, and experiences and attitudes associated with minority status, (2) a subjective sense of ethnic group membership (i.e., ethnic identity) that is held by group members, and (3) shared experiences associated with minority status, including powerlessness, discrimination, and prejudice (Phinney, 1996, p. 919).

Political, economic, and historical factors are also relevant and overlap with ethnicity. Sociologically, there is a problem with ethnic categories in terms of what being labeled means psychologically because there are "social constructions rather than natural entities that are simply 'out there' in the world" (Waters & Eschbach, 1995, p. 421). The U.S. census, as described in Chapter 2, for example, has only recently changed its basic four-category array to five to include Hispanic and non-Hispanic White as ethnicity options. Many people believe this non-racial designation minimizes the importance of the discrimination Latino/as face. What is also problematic about ethnicity as a category, like race, is the tremendous variation among groups, for example, education, geographical region, social class, family structure, and size of ethnic community. Increasing numbers of individuals' self-identify as mixed ethnicity and race and use a wide variety of self-labels: Black, African American; Mexican, Latino, Hispanic, Chicano, Mexican American; and Native American, Indian—all of which have different psychological correlates. The same label can have different individual meanings as well. Thereby, "self-categories do not represent fixed, absolute properties…but relative, varying, context-dependent properties" (Turner, Oakes, Haslam, & McGarty, 1994, p. 456). Self-labels can change depending on the situation as political choice. Chicano/a is as much or more a label of political activism as it is a group. Usage is also impacted by the way an individual is perceived by others. Thus, "race [and] ethnicity . . . are dimensions, not categories, of human experience" (Goodchilds, 1991, p. 1).

Sex

> \Sex\, n. [L. sexus: cf. F. sexe.] Either of the two divisions of organic beings distinguished as male and female respectively; the males or the females (of a species, etc., esp. of the human race) viewed collectively. *(OED)*

There is little doubt that physical attributes largely determine how an individual is or is not regarded within a society, the effect of which includes presence or absence of fair and equitable consideration by others, access to quality health care, legal rights, job opportunities, and many other so-called privileges which, by most accounts, are basic human rights. **Sex**, as used here, denotes the biological binary applied to physiological differences between males and females. The presence or absence of specific genitalia, just as the presence or absence of certain levels of melatonin in the skin, is both a precursor and predictor of treatment of an individual in a society.

When we speak of sexuality, extended from the purely biological to the qualities associated with being one sex or another, we enter into the common mindset of binaries (consisting of two parts) and dualities (twofold classification system). The presumption exists that a person is born either wholly male or wholly female. That is not necessarily the case. On the basis of this distinction, social roles of **masculinity** and **femininity** are socially constructed and constitute gender (discussed in the next section).

Gender

> A euphemism for the sex of a human being, often intended to emphasize the social and cultural, as opposed to the biological, distinctions between the sexes. (*OED*)

Gender has been part of language since at least the 14th century. If you have ever studied a Romance language such as French, Spanish, or Italian, the words are gendered. For example, in Spanish, words that end in –o- are masculine and those that end in –a- are feminine. Used in this way, gendered language communicates perceived value and status in a culture. Whereas sex, except under conditions of surgical alternation, does not change, gender can and does. As described in the previous section, sex is a set of biologically inscribed characteristics (male or female), whereas gender characteristics are socially and culturally inscribed (femininity or masculinity). In American culture, there is a performative aspect to gender, constructed through the clothing we wear, the ways we walk, and the ways we talk (Butler, 1990). An example of gender, or more specifically gender roles, is the social definition of masculinity and femininity. Neither individual men nor women define what is feminine or masculine. Rather, these concepts, built on thousands of years socially constructed behaviors and expectations, make non-compliance non-normative. For example, for many years, women wearing pants was considered a violation of gender norms and today, wearing of skirts by men still is. Some people use affective characteristics such as caring, feeling, compassion or the opposite to describe femaleness or maleness. Sugar and spice and everything nice? Girls. Snips and snails, and puppy dog tails? Boys. These ideas are culturally relative and are part of individual identity construction as well as hegemonic gender constructions. As discussed earlier in this chapter, individual identity (supported and informed by social identity) is constructed from the meaning ascribed to people and places and intergenerationally transferred through the stories we tell each other.

What are the stories (myths) American culture tells us about what it means to be a man (masculine) and what it means to be a woman (feminine)? The following section describes each of these constructions in greater detail. Some of the socially constructed characteristics used to define "normal" gender roles include the stereotypical "real" woman as passive, whereas men are active. Women work in teams; "real" men work alone. Women are small and fair, while men are large and dark. Women are emotional, while "real" men are rational.

Femininity

> Feminine quality; the characteristic quality or assemblage of qualities pertaining to the female sex, womanliness; in early use also, female nature. (*OED*)

One is not born a woman, said French feminist Simone de Beauvoir, rather she is made. This social constructionist view appeared in de Beauvoir's 1949 tome *The Second Sex*. What she so clearly identified is while sex distinguishes individuals on the basis of body parts; the mental construct of gender roles is psychological and must be systematically applied. Both boys and girls experience puberty (the biological process/sex distinctions) and adolescence (the physical and emotional process/gender formation), but each faces a unique set of challenges. Whereas boys' moods and self-image improve during adolescence, particularly with weight gains, physical development for girls often triggers the opposite reaction (Offer, Schonert-Reichl, & Boxer, 1996). Widening hips, developing breasts, and emerging curves are inconsistent with media-generated and sustained images of ideal female beauty, often resulting in unrealistic expectations and lowered self-esteem. The media play an important role in cultivating and perpetuating the thin body, flawless skin, perfect-haired image that only a tiny percent of girls naturally come by. Stereotypical representations of femininity emphasize:

- Beauty (within narrow conventions)
- Size/physique (again, within narrow conventions)
- Sexuality (as expressed by the above)
- Emotional (as opposed to intellectual) dealings
- Relationships (as opposed to independence/freedom)

Chapter 9 examines these ideas in relationship to how women are presented in fashion advertising and Chapter 10 explores the performance of femininity by exploring the role cosmetics play in that construction.

Masculinity

> The state or fact of being masculine; the assemblage of qualities
> regarded as characteristic of men; maleness, manliness. (*OED*)

As a learned behavior, masculinity and femininity are assigned particular characteristics and social expectations, "masculinity is what a culture expects of its men" (Craig, 1992, p. 3). For example, traits of masculinity include the following:

- Strength (physical and intellectual)
- Power
- Sexual attractiveness (which may be based on the above)
- Physique
- Independence (of thought, action)

In American society in general, masculine traits have been "fluid, evolving, and dialectically progressive" (Stern, 2003, p. 216). Social science research shows that mediated violence can "increase aggressive behavior in children" and "teaches that violence is acceptable, and that mediated violence increases viewers' local perceptions of violent crime" (Bates & Garner, 2001, p. 141). Violent representations are particularly powerful if the violence goes unpunished or is rewarded. Equating masculinity to violence as a normal expression of manliness supports a social system built upon acceptance of violence as a "natural" male trait.

Sexual Orientation

Sexual orientation refers to an individual's behavioral and/or erotic proclivities or focus of desires. **Heterosexuality** is sexual orientation/attraction to the opposite sex (male and female). This arrangement is privileged in American society (see Chapter 13 for more on this topic). Laws, rights, and regulations are structured to support this orientation in terms of who can marry, right of survivorship, and economic benefits. **Homosexuality** is attraction to or being in a relationship with someone of the same sex. The term used to describe homosexual men is gay and homosexual women is lesbian. These relationships are stigmatized as are bisexual relationships (attraction both to the same and opposite sex). At times, non-heterosexual relationships have been regarded as mental health problems, the result of physical health problems, or the result of trauma. People ask if being homosexual or bisexual is a choice? Is it genetic? Regardless of origin, the impact of social labeling has had tremendous negative effects, resulting in the need to hide one's orientation. Increasingly, the term sexual identity is used instead of orientation because it refers to the individual as entire person, rather than only to his or her sexual preferences. It also moves away from the scientific stigmatization of sexuality. **Queer theory** emerged out of gay and lesbian studies and is a growing area of theory and research that challenges binary thinking (good/bad; right/wrong; straight/gay). Identities are not fixed in this view but rather are fluid, able to be defined and redefined. However, given the nature of the social construction of gender categories, this theory addresses sexual identity issues of anyone regarded as non-normative (heterosexual).

This leads us to how to identify the major stereotypes assigned to the groups so far identified. Unlike representations of Euro-Americans that are many and varied, popular culture and media representations of people of color tend to be polarized at the extremes of sexuality and physicality. Representation refers both to product and process "to the construction of…aspects of 'reality' such as people, places, objects, events, cultural identities and other abstract concepts" (Chandler, n.d.). These "realities," are therefore constructed not only in content (encoded) but also processed in the minds of recipients (decoded). Thus, systems of symbolic representation, which are supported for and by ideologies, come to seem unremarkable and common. If these portrayals, concretized in stereotypes, persist over time and space, and are reinforced in mass media and advertising, the effects can be even more complex and complete. **Social identity theory** says that stereotypes inform individuals about their "proper" place in society (Taijfel & Turner, 1986), and "once stereotypes become embedded in the social consciousness," they affect not only how individuals and groups are perceived but also how they perceive themselves (Nieman, 2001, p. 59).

Group belonging and referential information include uniform attitudes, beliefs, and behaviors that make a clear distinction between an "us" (good) and a "them" (not good). Hence, in-group people perceive themselves as belonging to and possessing all of the same positive qualities and characteristics of other members of their group and those who do not are constructed as possessing the opposite/bad qualities.

What role do the mass media play in the reproduction and maintenance of this system of one-dimensional, limiting portrayals? That is the subject of the next section of the chapter and Section II of this book.

What Are the Major Stereotypes?

Mammy and Uncle Tom salt and pepper shakers. Hattie McDaniel in *Gone with the Wind* (Fleming, 1939). J. J. Walker on the 1980s sitcom *Good Times*. Actor Diane Amos as the Pinesol Lady in the late 1990s. The Indian princess on boxes of Land O'Lakes butter. Anna May Wong as the Dragon Lady in von Sternberg's *Shanghai Express* (von Sternberg, 1932). Lucy Liu as sharp-tongued Ling Woo on *Ally McBeal* (1998–2002) and as underworld queen O-Ren Ishii in Quentin Tarentino's *Kill Bill I* (2003) (see Chapter 11). These are just a few examples of the persistent, consistent, and corroborated visual representations of race, ethnicity, and gender in American mass media and advertising. What do these portrayals have in common? The answer is the subject of this section in which the **Matrix of Mass Media Stereotypes** is introduced to examine the limiting representations that consistently appear across groups, time, and media.

> The real environment is altogether too big, too complex, and too fleeting for direct acquaintance. We are not equipped to deal with so much subtlety, so much variety, so many permutations and combinations. And although we have to act in that environment, we have to reconstruct it on a simpler model before we can manage with it. To traverse the world men must have maps of the world. (Lippmann, 1922, p. 8)

Stereotyping, as a media effect, gains power and credibility the longer and more regularly the same information is presented, in the same way, to the same audiences. The longer these (re)presentations remain unchallenged, mediated constructions of race, ethnicity, sexuality, and gender become normalized as a "regime of truth" (Coombes, 1998, p. 190) in the American popular imagination. This discourse thereby "fixes otherness in an ideological discourse" by requiring "that which is already known to be continuously presented, represented, and repeated" (p. 191).

Thus images in our heads and these maps of the world outside "clarify people's itinerary in the windings of social reality." Lippmann (1922, p. 60) warned us, however, "they will prove erroneous if used wrongly or with gullibility." In the absence of direct personal experience, stereotypes serve as a way of filling in the blanks in terms of expectations (or lack thereof) of those different from the individual imagining them.

By using specific signs and symbols, articulated in particular images, racial/ethnic and sexual stereotypes draw strength from a shared cultural reservoir of thought-to-be-truths about particular groups of people. Based on a history of cultural, social, and psychological infusions of one-dimensional and distorted presentations of qualities (or lack thereof), these "truths" serve the interests of those in power who aim to retain their status and resources. This system of representation has thereby become a "stable cultural convention…taught and learned by members of…society" (Kates & Shaw-Garlock, 1999, p. 34) as a mythological narrative of a romanticized past. As Alvarado, Gutch, and Wollen (1987, p. 177) point out, "the media, along with other socializing agencies, are constantly constructing that apparently natural 'reality.'"

Academic research about stereotypes reveals a consistent pattern of stereotypes identifiable by sexuality and gender in films, on television programs, in magazine advertising, and in branding. These patterns indicate the characteristics that are emphasized, to the exclusion of others, ultimately constructing one-dimensional, pan-racial/ethnic dichotomized narratives that result in limited ideas of people who appear to be different from oneself. This information is internalized, resulting in oppression of members of the represented group. Hence, the stories the media told through stereotypes are based on deeply entrenched cultural beliefs and values that cultivate and build support for a system of symbolic representation that benefits the financial, cultural, economic, and social interests of the ruling elite through the reinforcement of racialized heteronormative beliefs and values. Bobo (1995, p. 36) points out, speaking of Black women but certainly this applies to all women of color, "fictionalized creations of Black women," for example, "are not innocent; they do not lack the effect of ideological force in the lives of those presented in that Black women are rendered as objects and useful commodities in a very serious power struggle."

People bring a shared set of beliefs to every film, television program, magazine advertisement, or newspaper story they see or hear that serves as a frame of reference for understanding the world around them. Beyond their obvious informational or selling roles, the media are relational, they are about making meaning. Advertising, for example, must "take into account not only the inherent qualities and attributes of the products they are trying to sell, but also the way in which they can make those properties mean something to us" (Williamson, 1978, p. 12). When we see people of color represented in the media, when we see them at all, the re-presentations follow a predictable pattern based on race/ethnicity and gender. As described in Chapter 2, the many differences contained within U.S. government established categories for race (White, Black, Asian/Pacific Islander and Native American/Alaskan Native) and ethnicity (Hispanic) are lost when lumped together. In "*La vida es loca*," Valdivia (1999, p. 484) points out how the social construction of race and these categories is "a narrative that structures our symbolic and material order." The patterns of portrayals become obvious when representative studies are looked at collectively.

African American stereotypes in media

In 1898, a children's book was published that gave tremendous visibility to a Black stereotype—*Lil Black Sambo*. In the story, even though Sambo outwitted the tigers, he still became a visual type. Throughout the 19th and early 20th centuries, sheet music covers presented two primary forms of Black masculinity: Uncle Tom and the Coon (see Chapter 12 for more on this topic).

Goings' (1994) study of African American stereotypes and Black collectibles and memorabilia from the 1880s to the 1950s is a useful example for understanding the trail of racist constructions in popular culture. So-called "collectible" items such as salt and pepper shakers, trading cards, and sheet music with images of happy Sambos, plump mammies, and wide-eyed pickaninnies served as non-verbal articulations of racism made manifest in everyday goods. By exaggerating the physical features of African American men and women and making them comical and powerless, seemingly banal household objects reinforced beliefs about the place of Blacks in American society. Aunt Jemima, the roly-poly mammy of syrup bottles, and Uncle Rastus, the happy chef slave on the Cream of Wheat box, remain with us today. Both were and are used to help make Whites feel more comfortable with, and less guilty about, maintenance of distinctions based on race well after Reconstruction (Manring, 1998). These items were meant for daily use, hence constantly circulated, subtly reinforcing stereotypical beliefs, later articulated in mass-produced goods. Leonard (2005, p. 14) notes, "From pancakes and breakfast cereal to alcoholic beverages and sports apparel, businesses have historically used a palpable blackness defined by either clownish qualities or physical control to draw in White consumers." Goings (1994, p. xix) adds, "It is important to note Black memorabilia are figures from White American history. White Americans developed the stereotypes; White Americans produced the collectibles; and White American manufacturers and advertisers disseminated both the images and the objects to a White audience."

Studies of African Americans on branded products on shelves to the present day have found although Aunt Jemima, Rastus, and Mrs. Butterworth are with us still, the majority of overtly racist representations are gone. What appears instead, in advertising, in print, and in broadcast media is much more subtle, or what Jhally and Lewis (1992, p. 94) refer to as "**enlightened racism.**" *The Cosby Show* illustrates enlightened racism, which the authors suggest is a "new, more insidious, and apparently enlightened" form. As such racism, which is unfortunately alive and well and lives in all forms of media, masquerades as liberalism by those who watched the Huxtables each week. They note, "Beneath this progressive attitude, however, lies an implicit and unstated rejection of the majority of Black people, who are not like the Huxtables and, by implication, not 'one of us'" (p. 97). Thus television and other mass media present a different, but nonetheless consistent, view of Blackness.

Similarly, Hall (1997) argues that a central component of British imperial representations of Black people is the theme of non-Christian savages who require civilizing by British missionaries and adventurers. These images were subsequently transformed into what he calls "commodity racism," whereby "images of colonial conquest were stamped on soap boxes…biscuit tins, whisky bottles, tea tins and chocolate bars" (p. 240). At the height of colonization, physical annihilation and oppression gradually attached "imperial conquest to advertised images of domestic products," placing scientific racism alongside the rise in consumerism (Roediger, 2002, p. 52). This "marriage of commerce, racism," and in the case of Aunt Jemima, "sexism," along with the corresponding "historical baggage," makes race-based images effective tools for the maintenance and perpetuation of racism (Manring, 1998, pp. 182–183).

News presentations also consistently show the Black criminal in stereotypical ways: guilty-until-proven innocent mode, with arms behind (usually) his back, and women disproportionately over-represented as "welfare moms." Film portrayals consistently present the dichotomized male and female roles of Uncle Tom/ Black buck and Mammy/Jezebel. Studies of Black representations on television tell us that when African Americans appear on television at all, it is usually in a comedy setting and typically, whether in advertising or on programs, skin color is consistently light. Fuller's (2001) study of the Black woman character in a Pine-Sol commercial and Aunt Jemima found that, "the mammy and the Aunt Jemima images are creeping back into our television commercials." Why? Edwards (1993) suggests it is a cultural love for the large-figured mammy, and further attributes Oprah Winfrey's success to this love "for the big, warm-hearted Black woman" (as quoted in Fuller, p. 13). As a further example, in the television hit *Touched by an Angel*, Della Reese's role, as the large lady caring and watching out for the other angels is consistent with this argument. An important question is how this portrayal might influence Black women's images of themselves. Popular beliefs about African Americans that contribute to and support stereotypes in the mass media include:

1. Athletic
2. Lazy/Slovenly
3. Rhythmic
4. Unintelligent/Stupid
5. Ignorant
6. Poor
7. Musical
8. Loud
9. Ostentatious
10. Criminal
11. Very Religious
12. Hostile

13. Dirty (physically)
14. Naive
15. Unreliable

Primary media stereotypes of African Americans:

- Men—Uncle Tom/Black Buck
- Women—Mammy/Jezebel

Native American stereotypes in media

Native Americans are conceivably the most invisible minority group in mass media. However, when seen, the portrayals are almost always in the past. Overgeneralizations about Native Americans can be traced to the arrival of Europeans in North America. Natives were considered "biologically and morally 'inferior' to the more 'civilized' newcomers who were only doing God's will in conquering the natives and taking their land (Hess, Markson, & Stein, 1995). Stereotypes were established at this time, many of which remain with us today: the noble savage and Indian Princess, for example (see Chapter 8 for more on this topic).

Stereotypical images of Native Americans were constructed in children's games, toys, tales, art, sculpture, the covers of sheet music, and in theater of the 1800s. The cigar store Indian, for example, presents the stoic, static noble savage, with a hand extended and offering, simultaneously "guarding" the entrance and exit to the store and complying with White rules. Similarly, the Indian "princess" conveys natural, wholesome virginity, and freshness. These representations, including the male versions of stoic chief and savage warrior, found their way into books, newspapers, and magazines and later on in film, on television and in the advertising that supported these outlets.

Rarely is an American Indian seen in movies as a complex, multi-dimensional human being. The television program *Northern Exposure* attempted to do this but is an aberration in television programming. In the case of Native American portrayals, a wide array of individual qualities, experiences, histories, and characteristics is truncated by stereotyping into a single Pan-Indian identity based on a unilateral conception of "Indianness." Consistently repeated representations have power as "these are the ideas we have been hearing for a long time and that we've ended up believing out of truth, custom, or repetition" (Dávila, 2001, p. 56). Regarded as a "dying race," Native Americans have been romanticized into idealized remainders of America's past. Research about Native American portrayals focuses primarily on film, advertised products and brand images, and television programs. Increasingly scholars are examining tribal casinos and Web sites.

Common misbeliefs about Native Americans that support and inform stereotypes in the mass media include the ideas that they:

1. Are all alike
2. Exist only in the past
3. Were "conquered" because they are naturally inferior
4. Had no civilization until Europeans brought it
5. Are warlike and treacherous
6. Are children of nature
7. Had no religion until Europeans brought it
8. Are confined to reservations
9. Live in tipis
10. Wear braids
11. Ride horses
12. Stoic, with no sense of humor
13. Naturally tend toward alcoholism
14. Naturally tend toward violence
15. Naturally over sexed
16. And that all Indians know all histories of all tribes

Primary mediated stereotypes of Native Americans:

- Men—Chief/Savage
- Women—Squaw/Princess

Latino/a stereotypes in mass media

"Finally, a Cold Latina," was the headline on a billboard advertising Tecate beer. The uproar was so loud and sustained that California congresswoman Lucille Roybal-Allard demanded the outdoor board come down. She said it made light of "one of many negative and misguided stereotypes about Latinas, such as that Latinas are to be viewed as sex objects" (Martinez, 2007, n.p.). Although some people in the advertising industry, including the campaign's Chicago-based ad agency *L piz*, didn't see the problem, many others did. Similarly, the Taco Bell campaign, featuring tiny Chihuahua Gidget, was similarly indicted for being an insult to the Latino community for making fun of language, accent, and connecting the culture with fast food. The hot "Cantina Girl" and the lazy Mexican stereotypes are pervasive in American mass media and advertising. Ramírez Berg (2002) identified three types of representations of Latinas that have been historically and contemporarily consistent in cinema: the Cantina Girl, the Vamp, and the Suffering Senorita. These are discussed in greater detail in Chapter 7. This taxonomy is consistently found in magazines, news, and prime time television programs such as *Desperate Housewives* and *Cane*, films such as *Maid in Manhattan*, and popular culture. Below are common beliefs about Latino/as that contribute to and support mass media stereotypes:

1. Drug Dealers
2. Gang members
3. Hypersexual
4. Poor
5. Drunks
6. Boxers
7. Overweight
8. Overbearing
9. Mysterious
10. Hostile
11. Passionate
12. Musical
13. Lazy
14. All are immigrants

Primary media stereotypes of Latino/as

- Men—bandito/gang member/Old Man
- Women—Cantina Girl/Vamp

Asian American stereotypes in mass media

"Wok-n-Bowl—Let the Good Times Roll—Chinese Food & Bowling," and "Wong Brothers Laundry Service—Two Wongs Can Make It White" were Abercrombie & Fitch t-shirts that, in 2002, created such a controversy that the shirts were pulled from store racks. Emblazoned on the front were two buck-toothed smiling men in conical hats, images harkening back to the days of stereotypical anti-Asian propaganda. Twenty-three-year-old Austin Chung, who manages an Asian-targeted magazine *Monolid*, said

> Abercrombie & Fitch is producing popular culture, and they cater to the views of the majority. You have to ask yourself, who benefits, who gets empowerment, from these kinds of images? It denigrates Asian men. (Strasburg, 2002, n.p.).

Recent fashion faux pas such as this are, unfortunately, still a part of modern popular culture. Although most of the time offensive stereotypes operate below the radar of national consciousness, occasionally an incident such as A & F's comes through, reminding us of the persistence of these limited and hurtful views. Pan-Asian stereotypes have filled popular culture and mass media portrayals for as long as Asians have immigrated to the United States. The group targeted has varied considerably. During World War II, for example, Japanese Americans were interred in camps, families broken apart, forced to abandon homes and property in the interest of "national security" and were collectively constructed as the "**Yellow Peril.**" Yet, these were individuals who were U.S. citizens, born and raised, in some cases multi-generationally in the United States, and yet they became suspect. The same requirements and discrimination were not imposed on German or Italian citizens at the time. Why the difference? Scholars such as Edward Said (1978) would attribute this Othering to the concept of **Orientalism**. It is not appropriate to refer to Asians as Orientals, rather the term applies to the European invention of the concept of Other that poured all members of other groups into the category of Other. Exoticism, novelty, danger, and cruelty were all characteristics applied to people from Middle East and Asian countries, including India.

A powerful, positive-seeming stereotype applied to Asians is the **model minority**. This defines Asians, all Asians, as scholarly, good at math and science, productive, complacent, passive, and hardworking. While some of these qualities apply to some of the people some of the time, they certainly cannot be attributed to everyone. An important aspect is to consider how it might feel to be an Asian and not be good at math? A seemingly positive trait can be internalized as individual failure, a sense of never living up to society's expectations.

As in all the major stereotypes, there are four primary classifications—the good, the bad, the pure, and the defiled. In the case of Asian stereotypes, dominant images of men are either Evil Fu Manchu (later transmogrified into Gang Member), or passive, techno-nerd effeminate male. For women, the virgin/whore dichotomy prevails with Dragon Lady on one end (think of the character Ling in *Ally McBeal* or *Kill Bill 2*, for example) or China Doll/Geisha Girl, the pure, innocent, subservient girl (see Chapter 11 for more on this topic).

Beliefs about Asian Americans that contribute to and support stereotypes in the mass media include:

1. Rude
2. Selfish
3. Aggressive
4. Nerd
5. Good at math
6. Hypersexual beings
7. Submissive

8. Sneaky
9. Naïve

Primary media stereotypes of Asians

- Men—Fu Manchu/Nerd
- Women—Dragon Lady/China Doll (Geisha Girl)

Summary

By now you would have probably noticed a pattern in representations on the basis of race/ethnicity and gender. Women and people of color are not (re)presented in a range of roles, instead whether in films, on television programs, in books, magazines, or newspapers, they are dichotomized: old/young; sexual/asexual; threat/non-threat. This patterning, which will be even clearer after you read the case study chapters (5–14), fits into the **Matrix of Mass Mediated Stereotypes**, shown in Table 4.2.

If there were varied representations of minorities along a continuum these might be less problematic, but there are not. What this analysis reveals is a pattern of polarization on the basis of sexuality (or lack thereof) and physical appearance that impacts development of individual and social identity. According to Westerman (1989, p. 28), when minority groups speak, businesses are beginning to listen: "That's why 'Lil Black Sambo' and the Frito Bandito are dead. They were killed by the very ethnic groups they portrayed."

Not only does stereotyping communicate inaccurate beliefs about, for example, Natives to Whites, but also to Indians. Children are perhaps the most important recipients of this information. If, during the transition of adolescence, Native children internalize these representations that suggest Indians are lazy, obligated to "willingly" provide their native/natural bounty to Whites, alcoholic by nature, and violent, this misinformation can have a lifelong impact on perceptions of self and others. As Lippmann (1922, p. 89) wrote, "The subtlest and most pervasive of all influences are those which create and maintain the repertory of stereotypes. We are told about the world before we see it. We imagine most things before we experience them." By playing a game of substitution, by inserting other ethnic groups or races into the same advertisement, the problem is clear. Stereotypical images do not reside only in the past, because the social control mechanisms that helped to create them remain with us today. Instead, they have gone mainstream, working smoothly through media and popular culture representations, relying on connotative understandings deeply rooted in the collective unconscious. Manring (1998, p. 181), drawing on the remarks of Eldridge Cleaver, refers to this phenom-

Table 4.2: Matrix of Mass Mediated Stereotypes

Group	Man	Woman	Man	Woman
Arab American	Sheik	Burka-clad slave	Terrorist	Belly dancer
African American	Sambo	Mammy	Buck	Jezebel
Asian American	Tech geek	China doll/ Geisha Girl	Fu Manchu	Dragon Lady
Latino/Latina	Bandito/ Gang Member	Suffering Senorita	Latin lover	Cantina girl
Native American	Noble savage	Squaw	Ruthless savage	Indian princess
Gay/lesbian	Sissy	Lipstick	Predator	Dike

enon as "the secret of Aunt Jemima's bandana." Just as the bandana-clad mammy situated White male desires for the proper place of Blacks and White women, in the case of Native Americans, race and gender are tools through which advertisers reify stereotypical images of savages and princesses, and ensconce them safely in the past to fulfill their proper roles as historical relics. Howard Adams (quoted in Yellow Bird, 2004, p. 1) points out the consequences of this discourse:

> The colonizer's falsified stories have become universal truths to mainstream society, and have reduced Aboriginal culture to a caricature. This destroyed reality is one of the most powerful shackles subjugating Aboriginal people. It distorts all Indigenous experiences, past and present, and blocks the road to self-determination.

This matrix offers the opportunity to go beyond what separate groups of researchers already know about representation among members of a single group and bring together similar studies of other marginalized groups to demonstrate the universality of stereotypes. Below is a list of suggested questions to ask of media representations in order to be an informed viewer, listener, and reader:

1. What or who is being represented?
2. How is it (are they) represented?
3. Is the representation made to seem "true," "commonsense," or "natural"?
4. Who created the representation? Whose interests does it reflect? How do you know?
5. At whom is this representation targeted? How do you know?
6. What does the representation mean to you?
7. What does the representation mean to others?

8. How do people make sense of it?
9. What alternative representations are possible?

This chapter has been an excursion through the many ways difference is defined and how it is articulated. As you can tell by now, the distinctions, while few within groups, are precise as projections from dominant society. Ultimately, for every major minority group, as defined by the U.S. Census, there is a pan-ethnic/racial identity that lumps everyone who is a member of these very diverse groups together, as if everyone shared all of the stereotypical characteristics all of the time. In terms of social construction of stereotypes, a pattern emerges that is clearly visible in mass media and popular culture. Hence, the Matrix of Mass Mediated Stereotypes becomes a useful road map for tracing the articulation of these projections in popular culture forms. Now that the foundation is in place for deconstructing these types, and we have explored the underpinnings of stereotyping (prejudice, discrimination, isms) along with brief introductions to their expression in mass media and the potential real-life consequences, we now turn to specific examples in specific media. In the following chapters specific stereotypical portrayals are described in detail. In Chapters 5 through 14 you will find examples of specific stereotypes communicated in mass media. Chapter 5 examines the social class stereotype of the redneck in Gretchen Wilson's hit country single "Redneck Woman." The pan-Arab enemy image is illustrated in the post-9/11 rhetoric of presidential speeches in Chapter 6. In Chapter 7, the Suffering Senorita/Vamp Latina stereotype is explored in the television program *Desperate Housewives*. The appropriation of images and words of Native Americans to sell products is explored in Chapter 8. In Chapter 9, fashion advertising in mainstream fashion magazines is examined according to the argument that pornography finds its way into everyday media. Chapter 10 also takes up the topic of gender by examining the naming of lipsticks and the connection to women's construction of self and representation to others. Chapter 11 explores gender and race by interrogating the character of Sun on the ABC hit television series *Lost*. Chapter 12 is an historical journey into stereotypes of Black men in media, particularly on the covers of sheet music, while reminding us how contemporary images reflect the past. Chapter 13 describes the history of representations of homosexuals in film, focusing on the construction of lesbians as vampires in the horror film genre. Chapter 14 brings race, gender, ethnicity, and gender together by examining U.S. immigration and specifically television news coverage of the 2006 "Day without an Immigrant."

You will find many of the guiding concepts of this book repeated in these chapters. This is intentional so that they may be used as stand-alone topics. This is also to emphasize how prevalent the patterns are, how consistently they have remained with us, and that they are corroborated in multiple forms of public expression.

Questions for Discussion

1. If race is not a biological reality, why does it persist as a defining category of Otherness?
2. Why is social class a hidden, yet powerful distinction in American society?
3. What are some examples in film of stereotypes discussed in the Matrix of Mass Mediated Stereotypes?
4. Have you ever seen a representation that you felt was inaccurate in media of a group that you identify with?
5. Is it possible for creators of media content to change the pattern of presentations and stereotypes viewers are accustomed to seeing?

Key Words

Enlightened racism	Femininity
Heterosexuality	Magnus Hirschfeld
Homosexuality	Masculinity
Master identity	Matrix of Mass Mediated Stereotypes
Model minority	Orientalism
Queer theory	Racism
Sex	Social identity theory
Symbolic capital	Yellow peril

SECTION II:
Articulations

 Country Music and "Redneck Woman"

[It is]…a contingent consciousness, burdened with matter which here makes its appearance in the form of agitated layers of air, sounds, in short, of language. Language is as old as consciousness, language is practical consciousness that exists also for other men, and for that reason alone it really exists for me personally as well; language like consciousness, only arises from the need, the necessity of intercourse with other men.…Consciousness is, therefore, from the very beginning a social product, and remains so as long as men exist at all.

Karl Marx

A generation ago, when you sent your kids to private school, it was because you didn't like black people. And now when you send your kids to private school, it's 'cause you don't like poor people. It's all about class, it's all about, 'I want my kid to go to school with the right kinds of people so that he can get into Harvard'…it's all about class.

Joe Queenan

Tammy Wynette worked as a beautician before moving to Nashville in 1966, and she kept her license current just in case her records stopped selling.

Country Music Hall of Fame

The word 'class' is fraught with unpleasant associations, so that to linger upon it is apt to be interpreted as the symptom of a perverted mind and a jaundiced spirit.

R. H. Tawney

When you hear the expression "the poor," who or what first comes to mind? A man or woman? Is this person Black, White, Asian, Native American, or Mexican? Do television shows, for example, present positive or negative portrayals of people with few material resources? How about music? The Karl Marx quote at the beginning of this chapter describes how language is voice for those with and for those without social power and social/symbolic capital. Music, as a form of voice, has been used throughout human history to express life's frustrations, joys, and challenges as well as serving as a medium for the distribution of news and gossip. In the book *Real Country: Music and Language in Working Class Culture*, Fox (2004, p. 20) notes, "voice is a privileged medium for the construction of meaning and identity, and thus for the production of a distinctive 'class culture.'" In his study of working-class Texans, Fox identified the importance of songs and music as forms of critical and playful talk and narrative as well as expressions of technical skill. Furthermore, through country music, working-class people "construct and preserve a self-consciously rustic, '**redneck**,' ordinary, and country ethos in their everyday life" (p. 20).

The importance of the everyday and its expression in story and in song are central arguments behind this chapter. This **phenomenological** approach to cultural exploration points to the importance of experience, memory, and local expression (the everyday) in affirming the bonds and boundaries of the collective unconscious. As Malone (2002, p. 13) points out, "country music is America's truest music. It does not address every issue and problem in our lives" but it "lays bare the uncertainties that lie at the heart of American life."

This chapter focuses on media representations of social class and gender in order to understand the complexity of the interrelationship between socially defined categories of gender, race, ethnicity, education, and assets. A brief discussion of social class and American discomfort with the topic is followed by a case study that focuses on a specific music entertainer and the song she made popular involving women, country music, and class: **Gretchen Wilson**'s "Redneck Woman." The lyrics to Gretchen Wilson's 2004 hit, "Redneck Woman" are analyzed using Barthes' (1988) procedure for **textual analysis**, by asking the following research question: Do the song's lyrics rally against or reinforce a poor Southern woman stereotype? Four themes are revealed in the lyrics: defiance/ pride, physical appearance, consumption, and legitimacy. In the first section, I briefly describe the American reticence toward speaking about social class. This is followed by a discussion of the ideology of social inequality, social class and stigma, and concludes with a discussion of country music and the song "Redneck Woman."

A Touchy Subject

Social class

A division or order of society according to status; a rank or grade of society. (*OED*)

One of the most understudied areas in mass media is the portrayal and issue of social class. Sociologist Paul Blumberg (1980) calls social class "America's forbidden thought." Society columnist R. Couri Hay ("People Like Us") says, "It's basically against the American principle to belong to a class. So naturally, Americans have a really hard time talking about the class system, because they really don't want to admit that the class system exists." Many people are embarrassed by their economic status, are suspicious of others asking about it, and generally feel income is a private matter. It is interesting how money, income, and class (and concerns about keeping and getting them) underlie most, if not all, of the isms. What is social class and why is it a neglected area of study?

While most people have a sense of which social class they belong to, among scholars there is little agreement on definitions. Some view it as power, income, prestige, and others as the amount of income and property someone has, and others look at shared social networks. For purposes of this chapter **social class** is defined as hierarchical distinctions between individuals and groups in society based on differences in access to material resources, power, authority, living conditions, health, work, and education with significant psychological impact. Social class is the economic "pecking order" of a particular society. **Social stratification** is the study of unequal distribution of resources. For example, in industrialized countries, 1 in 10 children live in poverty. Although we have the first African American president of the United States, in 2008 40% of Black children under age five lived in poverty (Ayers, 2009, p. 13). Whereas the proverbial elephant of Othering was presented in Chapter 1, the 800-pound grizzly in America's living room is the taboo topic of social class. Economist Paul Fussell (1992, p. 1) says, "You can outrage people today simply by mentioning social class." Why? one way of finding out about someone's social class is by how outraged they get when asked about it. For example, high-income people tend to be the most reactive; they generally base values, style, ideas, and disposable income as the markers of class. Those nearer the bottom—that is, of a lower social class—consider education on equal footing with the amount of money someone has. Historian Studs Terkel (1967/1997), in *Division Street: America*, interviewed a woman who revealed her class not only by how quickly she reacted to being asked about it but also how quickly she stated occupation as the critical criterion: "We have right on this street almost every class," she said. "But I shouldn't say class," she went on, "because we don't live in a nation of classes." Then, the occupational criterion came forth: "But we have janitors living on the street, we have doctors, we have businessmen, CPAs."

The construction of social class

Social class is commonly determined by several components: personal performance (occupation, education, income, achievement), wealth (the amount and the source of it), and social orientation (class consciousness, interactions, and value orientation) (Coleman, 1965). In some cases, markers of class are visible. Others, such as accents and traditions are less so. The reality is that income, education, appearance, attitudes, and family background are all social class markers—some verbal, some nonverbal, some intentional, and some unavoidable. Some we are born into, others we arrive at. Marilyn Frye's bird cage metaphor discussed in Chapter 3 describes how each of these characteristics is one more bar on the cage (an ism) limiting access to the playing field of equality. **Intersectionality** is a term that describes how individuals live at the intersections of multiple identities such as race, gender, age, class, and physical abilities that are shaped by self and by others. The "interlocking matrix of relationships" (Collins, 1990, p. 20) that constructs and comprises identity is important to remember as to isolate one characteristic overlooks important dimensions of difference and power. Kitch (1994, p. 88) notes, "All identities, even those conforming to mainstream or dominant norms are…fabricated by political structures and operations that conceal the mechanisms through which they function." Gaining, let alone accessing, a *level* playing field, is a near impossibility for many people as social institutions shape and constrain opportunity.

A Fable of Equality

'Underclass' describes a state of mind and a way of life. (Goldberg, 1993, p. 43)

When English novelist Frances Trollope toured America in 1832, she noted how reticent the government was in acknowledging the reality of class. After all, the nation billed itself as the land of opportunity and freedom, while simultaneously "enslaving Africans and killing its native people" (as quoted in Buis, 2007, n.p.). Much to the embarrassment of government officials and citizens, Trollope pointed out the hypocrisy:

They inveigh against the governments of Europe, because, as they say, they favour the powerful and oppress the weak. You may hear this declaimed upon in Congress, roared out in taverns, discussed in every drawing-room, satirized upon the stage, nay, even anathematized from the pulpit: listen to it, and then look at them at home; you will see them with one hand hoisting the cap of liberty, and with the other flogging their slaves. You will see them one hour lecturing their mob on the indefeasible rights of man, and the next driving from their homes the children of the soil, whom they have bound themselves to protect by the most solemn treaties.

Perhaps more than any country in the world, the United States defines itself by several beliefs about itself in what is called the "**American model**." This model presents capitalism as the culmination of the American Dream—economic mobility and economic opportunity for all. What is the American Dream? Hochschild (1995, p. 18) articulates four beliefs that constitute the "ideology of the American Dream": (1) everyone can participate equally and can always start over, (2) it is reasonable to anticipate success, (3) success is a result of individual characteristics and actions are under one's control, and (4) success is associated with virtue and merit. This concept of equality suggests everyone's economic situation is improving, that there are support services for the very poor, and finally that *everyone* regardless of religion, race, ethnicity, sexual orientation, age, or gender has the same opportunity to climb the economic ladder. According to *The Economist* (2006, n.p.), eight out of ten Americans believe that, even though a person may start out poor, with enough hard work, drive, and desire "you can make pots of money." The contradiction is sustained by what is called the **bootstrap philosophy** that says all that is required for success is individual effort and desire. As author James Joyce (1922/2002, p. 601) says in *Ulysses*, "There were others who had forced their way to the top from the lowest rung by the aid of their bootstraps." The **Horatio Alger** stories, a genre of 19th-century popular American fiction, are tales of a poor boy's escape from his conditions and achievement of riches and power through moral determination and effort.

This fable of equal access to occupations, education, and social justice is deeply embedded in the American collective unconscious as it is predicated on the values of individualism and independence in achieving one's goals and realizing the American Dream. This rags-to-riches fiction promised unlimited success to those who have the will power, desire, and drive to accomplish whatever tasks are put before him or her. The lacunae are the interrelated complexities of gender, age, physical ability, and sexuality that influence one's ability to access resources such as the education needed to obtain a good paying job, for example. It is not true that "*all* the people...can lift themselves up by their bootstraps, get educated, spend thriftily, save, invest, and get out of poverty—that is, to get decent housing in a safe neighborhood, adequate food, health care and education for their children"

(Lakoff, 2002, p. 420). In fact, as we will see, it is not in the interest of capitalist economy that any significant number of people are able to do this. What matters is that they believe they can.

While these stories contain a grain of collective truth, or perhaps aspiration to them, the lived reality is something quite different. The potency of these tales has, however, attracted more immigrants to the United States than to any other country. In fact the American Dream thrives most among the nation's poorest people. It is motivating and encouraging—even if lived reality is quite different. For example, corporate bosses often earn 300 times more than a worker. In 2003, more than 12 million (1 in 6) American children lived in poverty (U.S. Census, 2003). While corporate profits over the last decade have soared, individual income, particularly among the lower percentiles, has dropped precipitously. These realities, discussed briefly below, frame discussions of economy and social class.

The reality of inequality

> If you're upper middle class you really are grasping opportunities…rising through the world. And if you're part of the working class, you may stay at the same factory for thirty years or for your whole life or even for three generations. And that is a totally different mentality. (David Brooks, magazine editor)

The gap between rich and poor is wider in the United States than in any other developed nation. When adjusted for inflation, between 2000 and 2005, workers' wages, at the exact middle of income distribution, rose less than 1%. United States statistics on income, education, wealth, crime, and race reveal that the median U.S. household income was $40,816. In 2007, the figure was $61,355. This puts "middle class" quite clearly at that mark, as the definition of "middle class" income is $32,653 to $48,979. Today, more Americans live in single adult households than ever before. When adjusted for the times (including employer paid benefits) the median income of middle class has risen 33% since 1979 (Rose, 2007). Many people consider themselves "middle class" and yet, when actual figures are applied, something quite different appears.

According to an analyst at the Brookings Institution, "about 50% of Americans consider themselves middle class, but politicians define it quite differently, depending on what they are promoting." For example, during President Barack Obama's campaign for office he promised a tax cut for the middle class—this meant families earning up to $200,000 per year. Harvard College defines middle class as families earning between $60,000 and $180,000 per year whereas most U.S. citizens define it in the range of $45,000 to $200,000 per year. According to a 2008 Pew Research Center study 4 in 10 Americans with incomes below $20,000 consider themselves middle class as do one-third with incomes over $150,000. Race is relevant too: about 50% of Hispanics, Blacks, and Whites consider themselves middle class even though racial minority group members have significantly lower income overall than do Whites. When asked whether wealth comes primarily from hard work (ambition, education) or good connections (being born into money, knowing the right people), overall, 42% of people believe it is hard work, but this varies by class. More than half of upper-class individuals (56%) believe wealth comes primarily from hard work, whereas only 42% of lower-class people do (53% of lower-class persons believe knowing the right people or being born to wealth is the primary route).

> Even if *all* the present lower-tier workers moved into the upper tier, the country would still need a quarter of the population, working at low wages, to take care of the children, clean the house, work in fast-food places, pick the lettuce, weed the lawns, wait on tables, wash the cars and so on. This economy absolutely relies on hard-working people whose pay does not reflect their contribution to the economy. (Lakoff, 2002, p. 421)

Social class is sometimes called the master identity of a society. It is the pivot point, the "category through which all other social identities are to be mediated" (du Gay, Evans, & Redman, 2004, p. 1) and a hierarchical method of organizing groups and individuals into collections of upper and lower class based on income, education, and other characteristics. Because prejudice and discrimination are about power and resources, those who have them (dominant or elite society), do everything they can to keep them. Distinctions are not only numerical but rather, vary according to race. Whiteness is a resource that affords access to and control over power and resources that might be available to others.

Two scholars are most associated with historical writings about social class: Karl Marx and Max Weber. Marx (1818–1883) stated there are three relational classes: those who own the means of production (**capitalists**), those who do the work, and the petty bourgeois (those who owned small business, the self-employed professionals). All that the workers owned, said Marx, is their ability to work (**labor power**). Because the owners of production determine what workers are paid for their labor, they have power over them. Marx felt that the capitalists exploited the workers by convincing them the amount paid was appropriate for the work done, thereby resulting in worker's participation in their own oppression, what he called **false consciousness**. Thus, Marx was most interested in the social relations of production and saw conflict as the trajectory for change.

Max Weber (1864–1920) regarded class as stratified economic interests and that economic positions are those that share a set of common lifestyle values and sense of status and prestige that was part of one's market situation. Weber (quoted in Swedberg, 1998) identified three variables of economic strength:

1. *Power.* The extent to which people control other people
2. *Wealth.* The objects or signs/symbols of wealth and status people own and the value ascribed to them
3. *Prestige.* The amount of regard, importance, and/or respect, favorably given to an individual by society.

Weber said there are three kinds of power: Class power (class), social power (status), and political power (party). In the first case, lack of power, or "unequal access to material resources," was the true definition of class. Weber was interested in how power, wealth, and prestige affected human consciousness through the **stratification of social classes**. Weber believed that social class position has economic implications. Status and power, including political power, are important determinants of where an individual is located. Weber saw class designations as hierarchical and the relationships dependent on domination and suppression of so-called "lower" classes by "upper" privileged classes who have more material resources. These resources include land, social respect, physical strength, and intellectual ability, resulting in measurable assets (capital) or symbolic or sensed. As an example, if one has something the other person wants or needs (food, a good grade in class, protection) the person with the resources holds a kind of power. Social power/status involves respect of one by another as a resource (what one has and the other does not). Both status and interest groups that advance the interests of particular social sectors or groups who are in decision-making roles evidence political/party power. Thus, power comes from a variety of tangible and intangible resources, later referred to as **capital** by French theorist **Pierre Bourdieu.**

Whereas Marx saw capitalism as exploitative and that a compromise was necessary in the interests of both parties, Weber saw it as the natural development of a system, as highly rational and ultimately the best arrangement for both interests. Instead of conflict as the avenue to change, Weber saw opportunities or chances as the route to improved quality of life through education and income. Writing later than Marx, and further into social conditions of industrialization, modernization, and urbanization, Weber witnessed a growing complexity in the market system. Thus, it is not only occupation that leads to an individual or group's class but also shared lifestyles and norms that influence social class. As is seen in other chapters, characteristics such as race and gender are highly influential in status and social class availability. Inclusion or exclusion in particular organizations, for example, perceived appropriateness for certain occupations on the basis of race or gender all influence whether or not someone is admitted to a status circle. Thus non-class forms of inequality, as described in Chapter 4, pivot on differences such as gender and race, and thus pose significant challenges to economic success.

Bourdieu (1993) drew from Weber the importance of domination and symbol systems for the maintenance of social orders. He saw society as groups of **fields** in which particular professions such as law, medicine, and education, are sites of struggle over the appropriation of kinds of capital. That capital being whatever is important within that group such as knowledge, times of practice, or control over teaching schedules. Whereas the field is an objective concept, **habitus** is the subjective set of feelings, habits, or experiences of those associated with a particular field. As a form of symbolic capital, knowledge, to Bourdieu, is one of the most important ways power is articulated and perceived through socially constructed and inculcated classificatory systems (see Chapter 3 for more on this). In Chapter 2, we examined the function of classification in the human mind as method of creating and maintaining order. In the process of constructing the in-group (Us) and, as a result, an out-group (Them), the stigmatized out-group may be met with stares, negative non-verbal responses, or otherwise discriminatory actions called **symbolic violence**. While feelings of discrimination and oppression might be purely emotional, this way of establishing superiority over another person is an act of power and an act of psychological abuse. If the persons receiving the looks or disparaging words begin to believe what they hear, they are then participating in their own oppression, thereby satisfying a goal of a hegemonic system. Many individuals physically and psychologically distance themselves from those deemed "poor" (Lott & Saxon, 2002; Chafel, 1997; Leahy, 1983). Thus symbolic capital, in the form of the imposition of thought categories, is a very powerful way of enacting forms of prejudice and discrimination that may not be physically violent but can impart significant psychological pain. Conversely, bestowing praise and positive reinforcement with a thumbs up or smile can elicit the opposite feeling. The latter being sought after and enjoyed as evidence of doing the "right thing" or being the "right type." Bourdieu (1993) saw the patriarchal system of Western societies as an example of symbolic violence, as "paradoxical submission," or what he called **doxa**, the "sum of social beliefs or practices which are seen as normative, as going unsaid, as being outside the framework of challenge and criticism":

> Throughout my life I have been amazed at what one might call the paradox of the doxa: the fact that the order of the world as we know it, with its one-way streets and its no entry signs (both literally and figuratively), its obligations and its penalties, is generally speaking respected.

Cultural capital (skills, qualifications) is evident in the role education plays in determining income and social success. For example, those who are wealthy in experience and "street smarts" will not be afforded the same kinds of jobs or opportunities given to those with formal education. Determining what a particular set of qualifications consists of or how an individual goes about attaining them is a social construction designed to feed the dominant system more of what it needs to self-perpetuate. Language, according to Bourdieu and other theorists, is a form of cultural knowledge and power. Not simply a method of communication, the words one uses provide a powerful method of framing thought. For example, the idea of "working" mother, described in Chapter 2 functions in what seems to be a normal fashion, whereas "working father," seems unnecessary and redundant. Furthermore, as novelist Virginia Woolf (1998) noted, power through structures such as language, lifestyle, or beliefs seems invisible because they are normalized in everyday practice; she called this "the hypnotic power of domination":

> Inevitably, we look upon societies as conspiracies that sink the private brother, whom many of us have reason to respect, and inflate in his stead a monstrous male, loud of voice, hard of fist, childishly intent upon scoring the floor of the earth with chalk marks, within whose mystic boundaries human beings are penned rigidly, separately, artificially; where, daubed red and gold, decorated like a savage with feathers he goes through mystic rites and enjoys his dubious pleasures of power and dominion while we, 'his' women, are locked in the private house without share in the many societies of which his society is composed.

Social Class Stereotypes

Income isn't always the determining characteristic of social class status because people engaged in different kinds of occupations might in fact make similar amounts of money but are regarded quite differently. Hence the expressions **blue-collar** (labor), pink-collar (women), and white-collar (executive/managerial) workers linguistically privilege color and gender. One's class and subsequent prestige (or lack thereof) are often visible in the kinds of clothing worn, manners (or lack thereof), as well as cultural refinement, reputation, title, and use of language. Categories such as race, gender, and age are fluid and can influence or are influenced by social standing. Ethnicity and race are probably the most consistent indicators of class distinctions in some societies (such as apartheid), and standing as religious group, such as in the Indian caste system, can also be such an indicator.

Are people aware of the class to which they belong? Class-consciousness, says Mclaurin (n.d.), is "recognition by a particular group that they occupy a common, usually inferior, position within a society, and a commitment to changing that position through some type of political activity." This Marxist approach to class recognizes the oppositional relationship that results from awareness of one's "place" in the social, economic, and cultural hierarchy. Historian E. P. Thompson (1963) says class-consciousness

> … happens when some men, as a result of common experiences (inherited or shared) feel and articulate the identity of their interests as between themselves, and as against other men whose interests are different from (and usually opposed to) theirs. The productive relations into which men are born or enter voluntarily, largely determine the class experience.

Studies have examined beliefs about the poor, poverty, and stereotypes (humble, hardworking, lazy, uneducated) from the perspective of the impact on social mobility. There is evidence that awareness of one's social class plays a role in underperformance in school. Similar to racial stereotype threat discussed in Chapter 2, scholars have identified the impact awareness of low socioeconomic background has on academic achievement. In a study of students from poor families, the authors found that those who feared confirming negative stereotypes (such as the poor are lazy, dishonest, uninterested, and disinterested) did less well in intellectual performance whereas scores of those to whom a test was not presented as a measure of intellectual ability did not suffer (Croizet & Claire, 1998). Another study (Woods, Kurtz-Costes, & Rowley, 2005) of Black and White 4th, 6th, and 8th graders found that children in both groups regarded the rich as "more competent in academics than the poor," but that Black youth particularly carried this belief. Older White and more affluent children felt the poor were better at sports. African American youth are at a "double-risk," according to this study, because they must not only overcome social class stereotypes but also racial stereotypes, both of which influence academic success if internalized during development.

The internalization of stereotypical information by poor students certainly affects self and others' perception as well as social policy decisions and beliefs by those in institutions who are in positions to make decisions that impact the quality of life for those who are stereotyped. While upper and middle class individuals stereotype "lower or *underclass* individuals as inherently violent, dirty, and incapable of improving themselves," middle, working, and upper-class individuals are generalized as "snooty, aloof, condescending and phony." Furthermore, "Some stereotypes held about middle-class people (by both the upper class and the working class) are that they are overly ambitious, striving and obsessed with 'keeping up with the Joneses'" (Andersen & Taylor, 2005, p. 276). These findings point to the importance of information that influences early beliefs and identity development, such as mass media portrayals of social class.

Social Class and Media

How many forms of media can you think of where the primary characters struggle to make ends meet? Work more than one job to pay the bills? There aren't many—a few films such as *Coal Miner's Daughter* (1980), *Flashdance* (1983), *Norma Rae* (1979), *Boyz 'n the Hood* (1991), *Frankie & Johnnie* (1991), and *Cadillac Man* (1990) and some television programs.

Television, one of the more democratized forms of mass media, is one of the few that include working-class people, and yet even there, they are not a popular group. Not many television programs take place among individuals or families who are not members of middle-or upper-class status. Most television programs, particularly dramas, have middle-and upper-class characters. Comedy is the genre of choice for telling stories about those with fewer material goods. One of the earliest was the popular situation comedy *The Honeymooners* (1955–1956) starring Jackie Gleason as New York City bus driver Ralph Cramdon. His next-door neighbor and best friend Ed Norton (Art Carney) worked in the city sewer system. Most of the show's action took place in Ralph and his wife Alice's (Audrey Meadows) kitchen. Ralph and Ed were working men, trying to earn a living for their families. The frustrations of blue-collar work, however, followed each of them home long after the day was done. Though only airing (live) for one year, the program remains in syndication today. In retrospect, Ralph's incessant yelling at and threatening of Alice verged on domestic violence. One of the more famous, and often repeated, of his sayings was: "One of these days, Alice, bang, zoom, straight to the moon!"

Archie Bunker (Mr. Bigot in the original British version) was the bigoted father/husband in the White working-class television show *All in the Family*. Using irony and humor, Archie was presented as a dumb stereotypical working-class man. *The Jeffersons*, which spun off *All in the Family*, was a rags-to-riches tale of a Black Harlem family who owned a dry-cleaning business. One study examined two television programs by director Garry Marshall—*Happy Days* and *Laverne and Shirley*—and found these comedies gave more dignity to working-class characters such as the Fonz (Henry Winkler). Winkler's character, however, was presented as a hypersexual womanizer. A study of seven television comedies found that working-class families were sentimentalized but provided strong pro-consumption messages (Lipsitz, 1986). Studies of social-class representations from the 1950s to 1980s found under-representation of blue-collar workers and over-representation of white-collar workers. In most cases, when present at all, working-class individuals were peripheral to the story. In other studies of working-class families from 1946 to 1990, Butsch (1992, 1995, 2000), and Butsch and Glennon (1983) found consistent representations in **situation comedies**. The findings include:

- Working-class families were disproportionately under-represented compared to their proportion of the U.S. population.
- For more than 20 years, there was only one working-class based program on the air.

- From 1955 to 1971 there was not a single working-class domestic situation comedy.
- In most family situations, fathers were in professional/managerial roles.
- More specifically, Butsch found the following consistent patterns of representation:

  - Working-class men were portrayed as incompetent and ineffectual buffoons who were in some way flawed. Examples include Ralph Cramden, Fred Flintstone, Archie Bunker, and Homer Simpson.
  - Despite being well intended and loveable, the men are failures in their roles as fathers and husbands, therefore are not respected.
  - Working-class women, in order to compensate for the failings of the men, are shown as more intelligent and sensible than their husbands and generally run the family.

By depicting working-class men as de-masculinized, they are treated more like children than as husbands or fathers and the wives act more like mothers. Thus, working-class representations are also coded in terms of gender. The 1980s sitcom *Roseanne*, however, worked to overturn these gendered stereotypes. Roseanne (Roseanne Barr) was strong and opinionated. Dan (John Goodman) was a sensitive man who took responsibility. Humor and sarcasm were used to represent the Connors' working-class family life.

In her study of social class, media use, and temporal orientation (time), Jordan (1992) worked with 21 White families (5 working class, 9 middle class, and 7 upper middle class) in order to gain an understanding of their use of media and other ways of living. Rather than considering media use in terms of amount, Jordan looked at how often media are used and how they are used in relationship to concepts of time. She found that higher social class families saw time as something to be organized and managed. Therefore, these families were more likely to substitute media use "at the exclusion of other activities" (p. 386). This group tended to be concerned with the amount of time their children spent with television. Lower socioeconomic (SES) groups were more likely to consume media in combination with other activities and were more concerned with the content of programs. Upper SES families were more likely to encourage their children to limit time with and concentrate attention on the single activity of television viewing. Therefore, television "may be cultivating children's beliefs about the worthiness of the medium in overall time allocation" (p. 386). Working-class parents, however, seemed more concerned about the effects of television on their children.

Not all White working-class people are regarded the same in society or in the media. Hicks, hayseeds, hillbillies, crackers, trailer trash, White trash, and rednecks are related stereotypes. As discussed in Chapters 2 and 3, a stereotype is used to refer to overgeneralized attitudes, beliefs, and behaviors about and toward someone based on his/her group membership. **White trash** is a specific kind of marked stereotyped Whiteness that suggests a symbolic border between working-class status and a form of "failed" Whiteness. Wray (2006, p. 23) refers to this as a **stigmatype**, a "stigmatizing boundary term that simultaneously denote[s] and enact[s] cultural and cognitive divides between in-groups and out-groups, between acceptable and unacceptable identities, between proper and improper behaviors." Berube (1997, p. 18) describes the trailer park trash designation in *White Trash*. He describes the precariousness of this form of Whiteness: "If we failed and fell to the bottom, we were in danger of also losing, in the eyes of other White people, our own claims to the racial privileges that came with being accepted as White Americans."

During the Civil Rights Movement of the 1960s, many poor White Southerners felt left out as dominant, middle-class White culture stereotyped them as "red necked, bigoted, conformist, and stupid" (Bufwack & Oermann, 2003, p. 270). The expression *White trash* is itself a stereotype, one that has become nearly synonymous with racist labeling of someone who is essentially worthless. The identity however includes a variety of class-based characteristics and attitudes including "parochialism, nationalism, patriarchy, inscrutability, a penchant for violence, and an ingrained racism" (Fox, 2004, p. 25). White trash, cracker, and redneck are stereotypes of a White person typically originating in rural regions such as the Appalachians and Ozark Mountains, Texas, Alabama, and Tennessee. "Cracker" is used as part of branding for Georgia peaches on this sign (Figure 5.1)

The term "White trash" was used in the 1991 film *The Silence of the Lambs* in which killer cannibal Hannibal Lecter (Anthony Hopkins) tried to intimidate FBI agent Clarice Starling (Jodi Foster) by calling her "White trash" because of her West Virginia accent: "Good nutrition has given you some length of bone, but

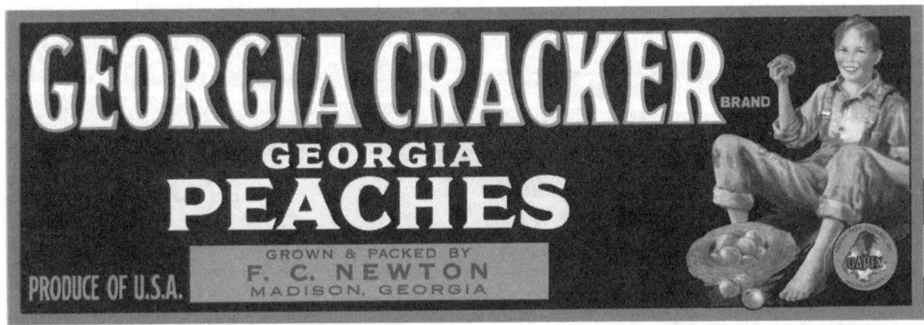

Figure 5.1: Georgia Cracker Georgia Peaches

Source: Courtesy of University of Georgia, Department of Entomology.

you're not more than one generation from poor White trash, are you, Agent Starling?"

Redneck, a related stereotype, is, "canonically bound up with a defensive articulation of Whiteness—a particular class-positioned way of being 'White'" (p. 25).

The Redneck Stereotype

> I am a redneck myself, born and bred on a submarginal farm in Appalachia, descended from an endless line of dark-complected, lug-eared, beetle-browed, insolent barbarian peasants, a line reaching back to the dark forests of central Europe and the alpine caves of my Neanderthal primogenitors. (Edward Abbey, 1979, p. 162)

The term redneck can be used as a derogatory term, or, when spoken by someone within the group who claims the identity, it can also function as a measure of pride (Fox, 2004). In *The Redneck Manifesto*, Goad (1998) images the stereotype, based on mass media representations:

> Gradually we come to believe that working-class whites are two-dimensional cartoons— rifle totin,' booger-eatin,' beer-bellied swine flesh. Skeeter-bitten, ball-tuggin,' homohatin,' pig fuckin,' daughter-gropin,'' slugs…. Unwashed, uncomprehending kids with cavity-peppered teeth. The stereotypes aren't new, just more persistently cruel of late.

In 1998, Goad searched Internet newspaper archives of the *Detroit Free Press* and *San Francisco Chronicle* to see how the mainstream press handled the term. He found several categories, including obese, curler-wearing women standing unashamed in orange bikinis, their sloping boobs slung over caesarean scars: Contemptible clowns (which included psychotic, in-breeding, incestuous, alcoholics), foreigners (terms such as "far-flung redneck burgs" and "redneck territory), and ethnic identity ("redneck Klansman," "bigoted redneck"). Using Lexis/Nexis database, in January 2008, I searched the *New York Times* for use of the term. Other than one story describing the behavior of a particular bird, the 109 stories in the last two years included self-labeling, when a group of White teenage boys accused of yelling racial slurs at a young Black girl referred to themselves as rednecks. In horse breeding country, Ocala, Florida was described as still looking "more like the blue grass state than the Redneck Riviera." An environmentally focused story said, "Paul Bunyan is now seen by enlightened urbanites as a redneck vandal." Finally, in a movie review, a group of problematic White men were called "redneck buddies." It seems, under many guises, the use of the word redneck is alive and well in America.

Conventional understanding of the term "redneck" is that it comes from a designation of working people, particularly those who worked on farms, in fields, and other outdoor jobs, who often were sunburned across the back of their necks. A red neck functioned as an indicator of working-class status, most particularly the marker of a poor White, farmer who worked in poor soil and lived a poor existence. To those outside the group, redneck is often used as a stereotypical insult. To insiders, however, while the term recognizes the working-class nature of origins, it is also a mark of pride.

In the 1970s, popular culture television shows such as *Hee Haw* and the *Dukes of Hazard* took advantage of the term to create stock, Southern characters. In recent years, the word has shown up in comedy routines of people such as Jeff Foxworthy, Ron White, Bill Engvall, Larry the Cable Guy, and Lee Roy Mercer who have become popular with their *Blue Collar Comedy Tour*. The Fox animated television show *King of the Hill* portrays a suburban family in Arlen, Texas, who are sometimes disparagingly called Rednecks and Hillbillies (a related term). A 2008 Country Music Television program hosted by Tom Arnold, *My Big Redneck Wedding*, features a "different redneck wedding" each week, "each with its own rustic eccentricities, whether it is a four-legged best man, a romantic beer can canopy, a celebratory shotgun salute or a reception filled with mattress surfing and mud wrestling" (CMT).

Thus "redneck," as the term has evolved, is also an ambivalent and fluid concept that floats between urban and rural, White and non-White. "'Redneck' is emblematic of a much less clear contemporary historical moment too, in which American blue-collar workers and small town communities feel a profound sense of political disempowerment and economic and cultural insecurity" (Fox, 2004, p. 25). In particular, as a form of identity politics and as a performative act, self-labeling as redneck, White working-class Southerners "found self-esteem and a defensive voice in country music" (Bufwack & Oermann, 2003, p. 270).

Class-consciousness and Country Music

Country….Now *that's* American. (WQYK radio, 2008)

Country music, a widely popular genre, has long borne the image of working class, poor, Southern identity. Most country music performers are Southern, often born into laboring, rural class families; their songs articulated the struggles, challenges, and occasionally joys of shared community. In *Don't Get Above Your Raisin'*, Bill Malone (2002, p. 15) says, "The bulk of the major performers still come, overwhelmingly, from the South, and they exhibit their Southernness through their dialects, speech patterns, and lifestyles and through the values and themes of the music that they perform." Symbolically and iconically located in the American South, country music espouses values that are quite similar to those of dominant society: patriotism, freedom, individualism, self-sufficiency, and self-government. Country music addresses these beliefs indirectly and differently than other genres. McLaurin (n.d.) notes

> The music portrays a keen awareness of the plight of the worker, of the necessity for daily toil, of the long odds against achieving wealth or position. It is also evident that the music offers mechanisms of rationalization, acceptance, hope and revenge.

The first country music record was recorded in 1923 in Atlanta, Georgia (Peterson, 1997, p. 5). Although the New York music executive involved with the project described the music as "awful," a local record distributor got hold of the record and got 500 copies made, which sold out, quickly. The music of Fiddlin' John Carson, and country music generally, had a more difficult time receiving airplay and becoming institutionalized than other forms of music for several reasons. Prejudice was one explanation. Country music was seen as the antithesis to other forms of music, placing it low on the totem pole of culture. Regarded as rural (when the focus was on urban), poor (when the focus was on social class), and traditional (in a time of modernism and change), the makers of the music were poor relatives come to call who lacked the sophistication of the urban set.

Earlier in this chapter, the discussion of class-consciousness pointed to research that says people in lower social classes are less aware of their position. Country music lyrics suggest the opposite is true—that every day in every way those in lower social classes are reminded of who they are not and what they do not have in terms of material goods. Van Sickel (2005) studied the lyrics of all of **Billboard magazine**'s number one country songs (1,217) for the period from 1960 to 2000. His work revealed that very few songs referred to politics or ideology. Every song that reached the Number 1 position during this time, dealt primarily with "interpersonal issues, romantic love, marital relationships" (p. 329). When the world outside was mentioned, it was often in a nostalgic way, a longed-for return to familiar roots. Politics was not dealt with and economic issues were few.

A study of a Western Texas blue-collar community found country music to be "an essential resource for the preservation of community and the expression of White (but not only White …) working-class identity" (Andsager & Roe, 1999, p. 21). Country music is also the constellation of stars and recordings that form and reify it as a form of communication. McLaurin (n.d.) identified the singer Jimmie Rodgers as among the first to reach a national audience and noted that his songs epitomized the working-man's life. His narrator was often the stylized rambling man down on his luck, to be pitied for his lack of material wealth and envied for his freedom. Yet, during the Great Depression, when many of Rodgers' songs were recorded, drifters were very much a reality. In such songs as "Brakeman's Blues," "Waiting for a Train," or "Hobo's Meditation," Rodgers voiced the all too real condition of millions of American workers. Alfred Reed's "How can a man stand such things and live?" connects feelings of despair, resignation, and debilitating feelings of impoverishment.

Other singers, such as Merle Travis, gave voice to coal miners. Tennessee Ernie Ford epitomized this spirit in his 1955 hit "Sixteen Tons" as did the Jimmy Dean hit "Big Bad John." Truckers replaced trainmen in the 1960s, as in Dave Dudley's album *Truck Drivin' Son-of-a-Gun*. The lives of factory laborers, loggers, cotton-mill workers, and farmers all reached the charts throughout the 1970s. During the late 1960s and 1970s, many of the songs carried political content, referencing restlessness, individualism, and nostalgia ("Hungry Eyes," "Sing Me Back Home," "Folsom Prison Blues"), a working-class pride ("Workin' Man Blues"), and a dislike and distrust for the then visible counterculture in the song "Okie from Muskogee." "There's too much month at the end of the money," sings Billy Hill (Sherrill, Dipiero, & Robbins, 1989), who articulated the common theme in country music of being *broke*.

Women in Country Music

As in other musical genres, working women were few and far between in country music. Loretta Lynn sang of her origins in "Coal Miner's Daughter" as did Dolly Parton in her song of hardship "Coat of Many Colors." in 1968, Norma Jean presented the waitress point of view in "Heaven Help the Working Girl." Professional women remained invisible in country music until Dolly Parton's crossover hit "9 to 5." Yet, what these songs don't do is compare the working-class life with that of higher social classes. Singers talk about the difficulties of life but not in comparison to those of higher classes. This suggests lack of class-consciousness as defined by McLaurin and no particular vision to changing things. Typically, however, these songs have four mechanisms for coping with the hardships: rationalization, acceptance, hope, and revenge. The most common type is "I'm poor but I'm happy," which identifies the rich but states they are unhappy. In other songs, the singer has achieved the fame, wealth, and glamour he or she dreamed of but yearns for the simpler life he or she knew before. Loretta Lynn's song "One's on the Way," illustrates the second theme—acceptance. In this tune the narrator imagines the life of the rich and famous but without protest says that children need to be fed, the house needs cleaning. Change is presented but in a dreamy way in the form of hope—hope that one day things will be easier, different, more comfortable. According to McLaurin, the most basic and common revenge theme is sexual. This might be striking back at a cheating spouse, boyfriend, or girlfriend or attaining the rich man or woman. The common message is that only poor folk can know true love. In a study of 1,400 hit country songs, nearly three-fourths had the trials and tribulations of love as a central theme (Stack & Gundlach, 1992).

Women's voices came through loud and clear from the 1960s to the 1980s. Feminism's second wave brought ashore opportunities for women to sing about issues in their lives: sexual harassment, loneliness, trouble with men, divorce, lack of equity, and lack of respect. "Harper Valley, PTA," by Jeannie C. Riley and Tom T. Hall (1968), challenged the idea of conservative small town sexual and alcohol hypocrisy. This song resulted in a made for TV movie and television show starring Barbara Eden as Stella Johnson, a widowed single mom whose tight jeans and makeup raise the ire of the community and the school board. But mom and the kids got even. One of most famous of these songs is Tammy Wynette's "Stand by Your Man" (1968), which infuriated people working for women's equity because it talks about overlooking a man's faults if a woman really loves him. Wynette later said it meant standing next to him as an equal. Although she later apologized, Hillary Clinton raised a row when, in a CBS *Sixty Minutes* interview describing her relationship with husband Bill, she said, "You know, I'm not sitting here like some little woman standing by my man like Tammy Wynette" (Cockburn & St. Clair, 2007, n.p.). Also in 1968, Wynette created a stir with her hit "D.I.V.O.R.C.E" that soared to the top of the charts. The song told the story of a mother spelling out the word *divorce* so that her young children wouldn't understand what she was talking about. Wynette had warned us, however, in her 1967 song "Your Good Girl's Gonna Go Bad." In many ways, Wynette brought a strong woman's voice to the sound of country music. "(W)hen the end of the road was reached, she also spoke plainly of the hard issues facing modern day couples" (Wolff, 2000, p. 335).

In 1980, Dolly Parton starred (with Jane Fonda and Lily Tomlin) in the movie (and later television series) *9 to 5*. The film and song are about three working woman who fantasize about getting even with their "sexist, egotistical, lying, hypocritical bigot" boss (Dabney Coleman). Parton won an Academy Award for best original song in a motion picture (which she wrote and performed), two Grammy awards, and it reached the #1 position in *Billboard*'s Hot 100 list.

Throughout the 1990s, women appeared on the music scene in more roles than ever before. In the country music genre, female stars such as Mary Chapin Carpenter and Wynonna Judd, led the call for women's success resulting in sold-out concert tours and platinum albums. Shania Twain's 1996 album, *The Woman in Me*, catapulted her to the all-time top-selling female country album (CMA Marketing, 1998). LeAnn Rimes followed closely with her hit single *Blue*. Women's success, changing sound of the music and lyrics, and cross over to pop popularity prompted critics to question their validity as "real" country singers. As Steve Jones (2002) points out, the entire, synergistic country music industry, comprised of theme parks, radio, records, tours, and fan groups, depends on the distinction between country and other musical genres. The industry asked, "Can good country music be commercially successful, and creative or original, but also untraditional, at least in part, at least when done by women?" (p. 191)

Picturing Country Women

If women were performing in concerts and creating financially successful hit songs, how were they appearing in music videos? Just as MTV and VH1 market performers and their music in videos, so too do Country Music Television and The Nashville network. Powerful marketing tools, music videos are also, "powerful, if playful, postmodern art. Their raw materials are aspects of commercial popular culture, their structures those of dreams, their premise the constant permutation of identity in a world without social relationships" (Aufderheide, 1986, p. 77). Motivated by the entertainment industry's declaration that 1997 was the "year of the woman," Andsager and Roe (1999, p. 71), asked: "Do country music videos symbolically annihilate women?" Furthermore, "How are female and male artists portrayed in country music video in terms of their roles and appearance?" and "How are female characters portrayed in this genre? Whose vision is represented?" In an analysis of 285 Country Music Television videos, they found that females' videos portrayed women more progressively than men's videos did that included women (the ratio of male to female artists was 4:1). This is similar to other genres in terms of the numbers of women and men represented in which the ratio of male artists to female artists is 3:1. Therefore, both in terms of the number of women performers and the ratio of male to female performers in videos, women were not on the same playing field as male performers, hence not achieving the same status as men. Men's videos were also played three times more often than were women's. In addition, when female artists were represented, they were of two types: early 30s "equal" women, who were direct, assertive who, while heartbroken perhaps, also spoke of emancipation or the scantily clad, sexually hungry, lamenting-objectified woman. Mary Chapin Carpenter's "Tender When I Want to Be" is an example of the first kind. In the opposite portrayal, the women were missing their men even though they were sometimes mistreated. Faith Hill's "It Matters to Me," is an example of this representation. When women appeared in men's videos, they were often in very traditional roles and completely dedicated to the man—often as brides and pregnant wives.

Sut Jhally's (1991, 1995, 2007) powerful visual exploration of the power of music videos to construct and reinforce stereotypical feminine and masculine roles shows just how narrow representations of women are—and in fact how ubiquitous women are in these videos that we rarely notice them anymore. He notes that, because 90% or more of the directors of these videos are men and most of the videos are by men, the volume of material that presents women primarily as sexual objects or predators is dangerous. These dangerous and dehumanizing portrayals thereby contribute to a climate of female objectification and violence easily internalized by girls. Very often, visuals in videos are only tangentially related to the lyrics, forming "thin narrative threads" from song lyric to video image (Aufderheid, 1986, p. 77). In country music, female performers have less airtime on radio and television than male stars do, are often scantily clad, referred to as girls, treated as insignificant, and most often portrayed as sex objects in music videos (Andsager & Roe, 1999, p. 71).

How have country women fared since then? At the end of the 20th century, a new movement emerged among the women of country music. While loud and angry artists such as Fiona Apple, Alanis Morissette, and PJ Harvey voiced their opinions of female body image, men, and female sexuality, country music was having its own revolution. According to Keel (2004, p. 155), "although largely ignored by the mainstream music press, this movement has revolutionized the way women are portrayed in popular music's most conservative genre."

While the storm may have quieted, female country music singers have had to navigate an industry in which sexism and double standards are as strong as ever (Chandler & Chalfant, 1985). Traditionally, country fans are similarly conservative. Shania Twain was one of the first women to really rock roles the country music industry proscribed. Twain, "frustrated by the fact that she faced constraints in the country genre," told the *Hartford Courant*, "I don't listen to the industry at all. I'm much more interested in what the fans think" (Herzig, 2003, p. 249). The fans loved her. Mercury Nashville Records President Luke Lewis said

> I think it's a Southern tendency as well as a tendency in country music very slowly to change. I don't think she and [husband/producer] Mutt [Lange] meant to come in and kick the doors down, but in a lot of ways that's what happened. She was ahead of a lot of us in this town in that she recognized that the audience had become far more sophisticated than we seemed to recognize. People in rural communities have satellite dishes now. I credit her with figuring out before us that you can push the envelope in terms of style and music and clothing. She was much more in tune to the audience than most of us in Nashville were. (Quoted in Keel, 2004, p. 172)

Thus, the women had to ease feminist messages into songs in a slower and more tempered way sister singers did in other genres. It worked, says Keel (2004, p. 156), "today virtually every top female artist's songs reflect a feminist stance, and if record sales are any indication, this new way of thinking has been received warmly by country record buyers." In fact, more women have dominated the Top 10 charts than have men in the last few years. Shania Twain, Faith Hill, Martina McBride, Trisha Yearwood, Wyonna Judd, the Dixie Chicks, and Gretchen Wilson worked their way to the top of *Billboard's* charts.

While songs of heartache remained, feminist political themes emerged. Although Tammy Wynette selflessly stood by her man, today's country women haven't abandoned him. Shania Twain said, when asked if she was a feminist, "I guess you could say that I am, but I'm not an *angry* [ital. orig.] feminist, you know? I'm a very old fashioned person, so I enjoy it when a man opens the door for me— I'm not offended by those things. I still believe in the theory of standing by your man, as long as the man is willing to stand by his woman!" The doormat days are gone. Not only have women country music performers crossed boundaries between genres, but are reaping immense financial rewards, and are making their marks as performers, producers, and writers.[1]

Redneck Woman

> She's has seen too much brutality to retain any vestigial wisps of daintiness. But what she's lost in frilly femininity, she's gained in scrappy, cynical spirit that comes from having survived. Hard knocks make for hard women… They're better hard-line feminists than many of the sheltered gals who so loudly espouse vagino-supremacy. (Goad, 1998, p. 143)

In 2004, Gretchen Wilson boldly stepped forward and announced to the world that she's a redneck woman on a multi-platinum hit album, "Here for the Party." In a popular press story, she is described as a "proud beer-drinking, tobacco-chewing, jeans-wearing tomboy" who "had a painful upbringing, including a life of poverty, her ogre of a stepfather, and dropping out of school after the eighth grade" (Mumbi Moody, 2007, n.p.).

Wilson's (2006) autobiography *Redneck Woman: Stories from My Life* describes Pocahontas, Illinois, the one stop-light town she grew up in, "no one comes to Pocahontas that doesn't already live there" (p. 2). The town's credentials include "country music, stock car racing, pickup trucks, and Jack Daniel's whiskey" (p. 3). Although located in Illinois, Wilson defends Pocahontas as Southern by describing how close the community is to Kentucky and Tennessee (even though Illinois fought for the North during the Civil War). The fact that this history is mentioned in her book attests to the importance of being Southern to be legitimate in country music. In body, geography, and attitude, Gretchen Wilson wants everyone to know she is a *Southern* country girl; and, even more importantly, a *redneck* country girl. This analysis draws on **feminist theory**, an interdisciplinary, philosophical, and theoretical extension of feminism that examines inequities in power relations, and differential treatment on the basis of differences such as sexuality, aesthetics, media representations, and contemporary art. Barthes' (1988) four procedures for conducting a textual analysis is the analytical approach used (Barthes does not use the term *method*), to study meanings within and behind the lyrics of "Redneck Woman." **Textual analysis** is a method for not only examining specific words in a **media text** but more so the meanings hidden with them, "the finest possible sieves, thanks to which we shall 'cream off' meanings, connotations" (1994, p. 7). According to Barthes (1994, p. 273), textual analysis

> Does not try to describe the structure of a work; it is not a matter of recording a structure, but rather of producing a mobile structuration of the text…of staying in the signifying volume of the work, in its 'significance.' Our aim is not to find the meaning, nor even a meaning of the text [...] Our aim is to manage to conceive, to imagine, to live the plurality of text, the opening of its 'significance.' [...Textual analysis] touches on a theory, a practice, a choice, which are caught up in the struggle of [men] and signs.

Given earlier definitions of redneck, the research question driving this case study asks: "Is 'Redneck Woman' an example of class-based internalized oppression or liberation?" As defined in Chapter 2, internalized oppression is the acceptance and internalization of tools of oppression such as dehumanization through denigration based on stereotypes.

Method and analysis

A Barthesian textual analysis has four steps (procedures):
1. Cut up the text into segments ("lexia"), which are arbitrary observations.
2. Observe meanings of the lexia, the connotations, associations, and relations (linking).
3. Use a slow, progressive, step-by-step approach to reading the lexia, what Stuart Hall calls "a deep soak" of the material.
4. Look for the plurality of the text, "departures of meaning, not arrivals." (Barthes, 1988)

Barthes recognizes it is impossible to catch every meaning, particularly given the **intertextuality** (multiple interrelationships) of media as "symbolically dense" texts. Four themes, or lexia, revealed themselves during analysis of "Redneck Woman" as text: Defiance/ pride, physical appearance, consumption, and legitimacy.

Defiance/pride

A redneck, according to Wilson (2006, p. 121), "is a lifestyle, an attitude toward the world. It's about people who work hard, often in blue-collar jobs, and play hard. And they don't take no crap from anyone about who they are and where they come from." In the song, the only ones looking down on Wilson are the people in the posters on her wall. She is not about to be defined by or judged by the ubiquitous "they" or "them" "out there." Her defiance is clear when she says, "I don't give a rip," although she does, otherwise why write the song? The lyrics further embrace the pregnant and barefoot stereotype as Wilson is proudly "standing [barefoot] in [her] own front yard" with a baby on her hip.

Physical appearance

The genesis of "Redneck Woman" is telling. According to her book, the idea came when she and fellow band members wanted to write a new song. For inspiration, Wilson watched three videos, one each by Shania Twain, Faith Hill, and Martina McBride, while herself wearing a wife-beater tank top, a pair of sweatpants, and flip flops. She says, "I had no makeup on and I had a cigarette in one hand and a bottle of beer in another" (Wilson, 2007, p. 120). She says she felt discouraged and in no way thought she could be or do what she saw on the screen. "That's just not what I am," she said, "I guess I'm just a redneck woman!" Rich replied, "You are not the Barbie Doll type" (p. 121).

Consumption

Not only does Wilson tout the literal consumption of beer over champagne on tailgates and in honky tonks, but also by naming Barbie Doll, Victoria's Secret, and Wal-Mart. It isn't the money Wilson lusts for, but to be sexy to her man, thereby reinforcing the heteronormative subscript in the song. She is a discriminating shopper, not about to be taken in by flash and glamour of Victoria's Secret.

Legitimacy

The chorus reinforces what Wilson is as much as what she is not by choice of house decoration, knowing the "right" performers (Charlie Daniels, Lynard Skynard, Tanya Tucker, Hank Williams) so well that she knows the lyrics to all their songs that make her Southern, and her connection to a working-class community. She demonstrates this through swearing and yelling. She asks other country women to join her in preserving this attitude and music by "keeping it country."

The second stanza of the song defines "What is sexy?" about Victoria's Secret and "models on TV." Is this reminiscence perhaps of sexy videos of other country women that motivated the song in the first place? Wilson demonstrates her ability to work with a low-income group by showing how she can be just as sexy by shopping at Wal-Mart—and that she *is* sexy but not impure. Being strong, self-assured, drinkin' and swearin' with the best of them doesn't make a woman sexually indiscriminate, she is a new woman of country music, and fits in to her community.

Finally, Wilson adjusts the final chorus to pay homage to Hank Williams, Jr., affirming her membership in the country club by demonstrating women can be rednecks too.

Summary

This chapter focuses on the construction of social class and, as a case study, how "Redneck Woman" creates meaning about being Southern, being a woman, being a Southern woman, and the connection of that identity with consumption practices and brand choices. In "Redneck Woman" do the lyrics rally against or reinforce the poor Southern woman stereotype? Is it an example of internalized working-class oppression or is it liberation? Through re-appropriation of the term *redneck* and her rally for women's inclusion in the term, is Wilson affirming her right and role in the club? In her autobiography she claims the song is anti-stereotypical, that "it has nothing to do with the racist, stupid, hateful, backward 'redneck' stereotype that will hopefully…disappear from the language" (Wilson, 2007, p. 121). This analysis is a first step in an examination of whether or not adoption of a hateful word, used as a slur by outsiders, can ever really be re-appropriated by the target group. Even if it does become positive within a group, does its circulation in popular culture further reify its negative associations among the out-group?

Country music is by no means the only form of music that represents and reflects the intersectional complexities of gender, race, sexuality, and class. Hip-hop has been called "the new Black minstrelsy" and *Birth of a Nation* with a black beat" by cultural critic Stanley Crouch (as quoted in Boyton, 1995, n.p.), as "affirmation of collective self in the face of a society that despised the black and the brown poor" by Patricia Rose (as quoted in Kennedy, 2005, n.p.), as the "advanced sound track of the storm" preceding Hurricane Katrina, and as "protest poetry and danceable entertainment version of African American take on life" (Lydon, 2008). For more than 25 years, angry, clever with beat and bite it can be homophobic and misogynistic but also a unifying voice for injustices replete with anger and passion. Language is a form of power that circulates in the social field and can attach to strategies of domination as well as those of resistance (Diamond &

Quinby, 1988, p. 185). If language is, as Samuel Johnson (1888, p. 279) said, "the dress of thought," is the emperor not wearing clothes?

Drawing on Goodwin's (1992) analysis of rock music videos, it is important to highlight the importance of *context* within which songs and videos are seen and heard. Audiences for music and television "[inhabit] a culture that has in common various discourses, attitudes and structures of feeling"; people are consuming the product in particular times and places (p. xix). Adorno wrote that music serves a variety of functions, including its use amongst social movements. Music is universal, spanning time, people and place in its ability to connect people to shared values and ideals, to bring comfort, entertainment, humor and catharsis. Music can function as a kind of social glue for affirming shared social ideologies (Eyerman & Jamison, 1998). Similar to other forms of media, which are the loci of meaning making, lyrics can affirm group membership, emphasize sameness and difference, and provide information about characteristics of a person belonging to a particular group. The intertexuality among words and song and, today, performance in a video creates a discursive field ripe with meaning.

Bakhtin's (1981, p. 281) term, "dialogic" describes how a word, as in a lyric, in its symbolic form, exists within a network of meaning. Thus "redneck" operates from an "apperceptive background of understanding" in which the audience of the song experiences the music and lyrics with a primed openness to certain perspectives and within a particular social and cultural milieu, which Bahktin calls "background" (p. 281). It is within this background that audience members secure a specific understanding of the meaning of the word(s). In this view, it is impossible to dislodge a culturally specific word, such as redneck, from its context. The mega hit "Redneck Woman" used the term "redneck" as a bridge to a more contemporary encounter, and perhaps, re-appropriation.

"Redneck Woman" was an anomaly in country music and is a worthwhile text in its own right, worthy of analysis for what it says about the performative nature not only of gender but also class. In 2007, Wilson said of the song, "I think the girls, the blue-collar women in America, had just been waiting for ["Redneck Woman"] so long. It was just perfect timing" ("Blue Collar," 2007, p. 20). Described as "anthemic," the song and video reclaim an otherwise derogatory word and reframe it to connect country to the modern and the feminist, thus demonstrating the mutability of language and meaning. The stereotypical characterizations of women, poor women, poor country women, and redneck women are thus confronted and reclaimed in "Redneck Woman."

Questions for Discussion

1. Do you agree or disagree with Hochschild's (1995) beliefs and the American Dream? Why or why not?
2. The Declaration of Independence states, "all men are created equal." Has that ideal ever been realized in the United States? In the introduction to *Democracy in America*, Alexis de Tocqueville (1831) states: "Among the novel objects that attracted my attention during my stay in the United States, nothing struck me more forcibly than the general equality of condition among the people." Was de Tocqueville accurate in his observation?
3. What do the television characters Al Bundy, Archie Bunker, and Homer Simpson have in common? What kind of relationship do they have with their wives and families? Are they respected?
4. It has been said that history is told from the perspective of the victors. Today it can be said the tales are told in the mass media. What is the tale of social class told in mass media? Does this shape our worldview?
5. Similar to the argument in hip hop culture around use of the term "bitch," does in-group use of redneck diminish the stinging power and damage of this label?

Key Words

American model	*Billboard* magazine
Blue collar	Bootstrap philosophy
Capital	Capitalists
Cultural capital	Doxa
False consciousness	Feminist theory
Fields	Gretchen Wilson
Habitus	Horatio Alger
Intersectionality	Intertextuality
Labor power	Max Weber
Media text	Phenomenological
Pierre Bourdieu	Redneck
Situation comedies	Social class
Social stratification	Stigmatype

Stratification of social classes	Symbolic violence
Textual analysis	White trash

Endnote

1. Over the history of country music, duos, particularly opposite sex duos have persisted. While a very important part of the story, it is beyond the scope of this chapter.

CHAPTER SIX

The Construction of Arabs as Enemies

Make no mistake, we will find the enemy and we will kill the enemy.
The Siege (1998)

Make no mistake, the United States government will hunt down and punish those responsible for these cowardly acts.
George W. Bush (2001)

Let me tell you about Ahab the Arab the sheik of the burning sand
Ray Stevens, "Ahab the Arab" (1962)

The 21st century dawned with alarming clarity and frightening images as the towers of New York's World Trade Center toppled. Shortly thereafter, groups of people (immigrants and American born) were rounded up, detained, interrogated, and even tortured at the direction of a controversial American president and his cabinet. Citizens spoke out about the loss of individual rights, privacy, due process, and intellectual freedom. W.E. B. Du Bois stated that the problem of the 20th century was the **color line,** and, unfortunately, the 20th century did not end concepts of "color," as a method of marking difference for purposes of oppression.

In fact, in the newness of the 21st century, we are also facing problems of the "difference line." Guerrero (1993) points out

> Certainly, many of these *differences* have always been with us in one brutal form or another as dark historical nightmares, genocides, socially structured oppressions, clashing religions, class struggles, homophobic persecutions and so on. The list is necessarily long. But what has changed, especially here in the United States as we rush into this new century/millennium, is that the 'problem' once defined and brutally contained under the binary model of color (with 'black' versus 'white' being the absolute poles of disenfranchisement and privilege) has shifted toward a more complex 'multicultural' model.

This chapter explores the responses, evidenced in political **rhetoric**, following the September 11 tragedy and the process of constructing those "of Arab descent" as enemy Others. The following sections introduce the ideas of **propaganda**, stereotyping, and the construction of enemy images that serve as the platform from which limiting, dehumanizing portrayals grow.

Just as the media have anthropomorphized courage and bravery in the post-September 11 world, a face has also been put on terror and it is Arab. The political rhetoric of George W. Bush following the September 11, 2001, attacks on the World Trade Center and Pentagon employed words and expressions—"us," "them," "they," "evil," "those people," "demons," "wanted: dead or alive"—to characterize people of Arab/Middle Eastern descent. While these descriptions have largely been applied to non-U.S. citizens, they cannot help but include the approximately three million Arab individuals living in the United States, many of whom were born in the States as well as others who have adopted America as home—Iraqis, Iranians, Palestinians, Egyptians, Arabs, Yemenis, and others. Table 6.1 shows the variety of groups of Americans with Arab ancestry based on 2003 Census estimates."

Popular culture and mass media in the United States have generated and sustained stereotypes of a monolithic evil Arab; these stereotypes constructed all Muslims as Arabs and all Arabs as terrorists. Using representations and language in news, movies, cartoons, and magazine stories, the media and popular culture have participated in the construction of an evil **Arab stereotype** that encompasses a wide variety of people, ideas, beliefs, religions, and assumptions. For example, movies such as those listed above and several news magazines presented dark images of Middle Eastern men, or what Shaheen (1995, p. 191) calls "America's bogeyman." In recent films, "barbarism and cruelty are the most common traits associated with Arabs" (Jackson, 1996, p. 65). These stereotypes, "which tend to lump Arabs, Muslim, Middle East into one highly negative image of violence and danger," are composed largely from collective memory, rather than from actual experience (Jackson, 1996, p. 65).

Historically, a combination of (mis)information has worked to construct an enemy image in the popular imagination that has an important function in the

Table 6.1: Population with Arab Ancestry by Detailed Group: 2000

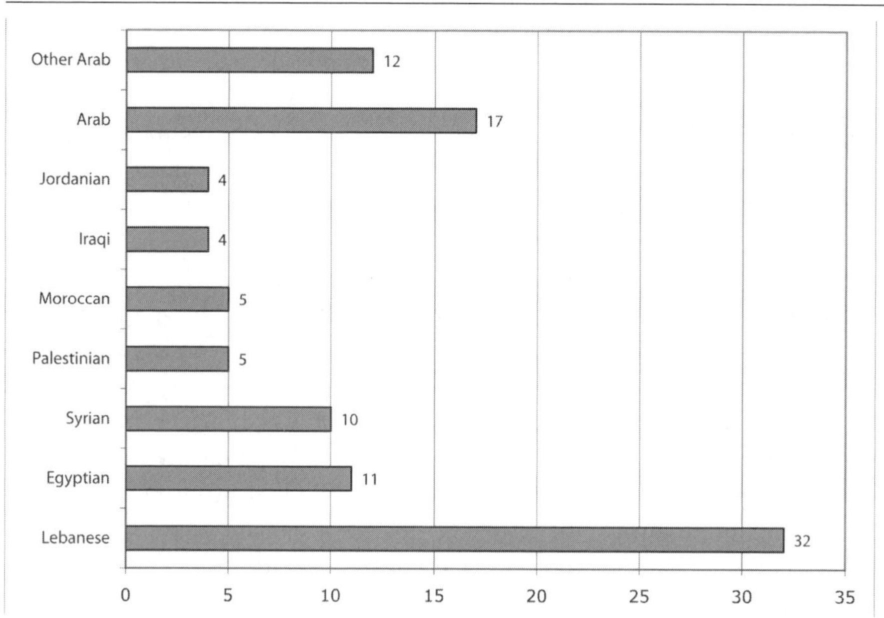

1　Includes people who report Arab ancestry only, regardless of whether they reported one or two Arab ancestors.

2　Includes 68,614 people who reported one Arab ancestor not listed above and 13,140 people who reported two Arab ancestors, whether listed above or not.

Source: U.S. Census Bureau, Census 2000.

maintenance of political power, or hegemony, through ideology. Consequently, the "Face of Terror" is not only that of Osama bin Laden and Saddam Hussein but also all persons of Arab descent, evoking the simulacrum of all Middle Eastern-looking males as the face of terror/ism (Ghareeb, 1983; Hamada, 2001; Suleiman, 1999).

This essay links stereotypes of Arabs, enemy image construction, and ideology to the rhetoric of President George W. Bush as delivered during five speeches and a memorial service subsequent to the September 11, 2001, attacks.[1] Spillmann and Spillmann's (1997, pp. 50–51) **model of enemy image construction** is used as a framework for an interpretive textual analysis (Chandler, 2002; Hall, 1975) that chronologically traces the development of the Arab enemy image in this rhetoric. This model posits that feelings and reactions to enmity can be described as a syndrome, one that draws on a historically constructed foundation from which stereotypes are built and enemy images emerge. The resultant extraction of an enemy image reinforces ancient ideological dichotomies of good versus evil and us versus them, rigidifying an agreed-upon stereotype with referential function. Over time, an **enemy image**, defined as a "culturally influenced, very negative, and stereotyped evaluation of the 'other'" (Fiebig-von Hase, 1997, p. 2), is reinforced and reinvigorated via the words of political opinion leaders and mass media representations. The present study reveals that the accumulation of historically, politically, and culturally cultivated negative images of Arabs resembles the word choices and allusions used in the carefully constructed, post-September 11 speeches of President George W. Bush. A necessary part of this analysis is to "bracket the historical question of guilt and innocence, and focus on the recurring images that have been used…to characterize the enemy" (Keen, 1986, p. 13). The analysis demonstrates how presidential verbal rhetoric built upon and was informed by cultural artifacts (movies, television, newspaper stories, and comics) and is consistent with Spillmann and Spillmann's (1997) model of enemy image construction. There is a standard repertoire of propagandistic words and images that serves to dehumanize the "other" as part of the construction of an enemy image in the popular imagination and thus makes a retaliatory backlash against human beings seem logical and natural. The results of this study are important for scholars, governmental decision-makers, media creators, and citizens. They add to the limited literature on the construction of enemy images and Arab stereotyping in the media and extend and exemplify the Spillman and Spillman (1997) model. As evidenced by policies such as those enacted by the newly created Department of Homeland Security, the **Patriot Act**, and detainment of suspects without due process of the law, these findings have human rights as well as foreign and domestic policy implications (Feehan, 2003; Valbrun, 2003).

Making Enemies

Nations "need" enemies. Governments use the idea of a common enemy as a method of social control, of reinforcing values of the dominant system, and of garnering participation in the maintenance of those beliefs (Keen, 1986; Spillmann & Spillmann, 1997). As a hegemonic device, a common enemy can serve to distract attention and divert aggression and energy toward a common threat. In addition, a common enemy is important in organizing evolutionary-based survival strategies that rely on perceptual and behavioral patterns that are a fundamental part of human nature.

Differences in age, race, religion, culture, age, or appearance can be the characteristics that stimulate resentment toward other groups. The unfamiliar and strange evoke strong emotions and reactions such as aggression, fear, hate, aversion, and expulsion. Xenophobic and racist reactions create "an artificial binary opposition that is resolved through the physical annihilation of one side by the other" (Kibbey, 2003, p. 2). The resultant "we–they" dichotomy produces a kind of "group think" that supports separation of particular racial, religious, ethnic, or cultural groups, positioning them as hostile and alien. As Said (1997) points out, "Sensationalism, crude xenophobia, and insensitive belligerence are the order of the day, with results on both sides of the imaginary line between "us" and "them" that are extremely unedifying"(p. xlviii).

Cultural factors also play an important role in forming and regulating human behavior as part of the "phenomenology of the **hostile imagination**" (Keen, 1986, p. 13). Despite changing times and circumstances, the "hostile imagination has a certain standard repertoire of images it uses to dehumanize the enemy" (Keen, 1986, p. 13). This process includes what Jung refers to as the shadow archetype, which, in this case, becomes the **archetype of the enemy** (Hyde & McGuinness, 1994, p. 86). In the collective sense, according to this theory, shadowy qualities and unsavory characteristics are often projected onto other people resulting in "paranoia, suspiciousness, and lack of intimacy, all of which afflict individuals, groups, and even entire nations" (Hopcke, 1989, p. 82). Spillmann and Spillmann (1997) explain the development of the collective unconscious that comes to support viewing others as enemies. They describe enemy image construction as a syndrome of deeply rooted perceptual evaluations that take on the following characteristics:

1. ***Negative anticipation.*** All acts of the enemy, in the past, present, and future become attributed to destructive intentions toward one's own group. Whatever the enemy undertakes is meant to harm us.

2. *Putting blame on the enemy.* The enemy is thought to be the source of any stress on a group. They are guilty of causing the existing strain and current negative conditions.

3. *Identification with evil.* The values of the enemy represent the negation of one's own value system and the enemy is intent on destroying the dominant value system as well. The enemy embodies the opposite of that which we are and strive for; the enemy wishes to destroy our highest values and must therefore be destroyed.

4. *Zero-sum thinking.* What is good for the enemy is bad for us and vice versa.

5. *Stereotyping and de-individualization.* Anyone who belongs to the enemy group is ipso facto our enemy.

6. *Refusal to show empathy.* Consideration for anyone in the enemy group is repressed due to perceived threat and feelings of opposition. There is nothing in common and no way to alter that perception. (pp. 50–51)

Stereotypes and Propaganda

First the image, then the enemy (Keen, 1986, p. 10)

Thought of as over-generalized, reductionist beliefs, stereotypes are collections of traits or characteristics that present members of a group as being all the same. This signifying mental practice provides convenient shorthand in the identification of a particular group of people. As available methods for organizing the "great blooming, buzzing confusion of the outer world" (Lippmann, 1922, p. 81), stereotypes "...get hold of the few simple, vivid, memorable, easily grasped, and widely recognized characteristics about a person, *reduce* everything about the person to those traits, *exaggerate* and *simplify* them, and *fix* them without change or development to eternity" (Hall, 1997, p. 258).

Certainly, it would be impossible to function in the world without simplifying visual and verbal information to manageable units. As Gandy (1998) suggests, "It seems likely that stereotypes become part of our understanding of our surroundings from the first moments of our efforts to make sense of the world around us" (p. 83). Stereotypes serve as building blocks of the "fortress" of social tradition (Lippmann, 1922, p. 96). They are part of the "maintenance of social and symbolic order" that facilitates the binding of people together as an us and sends those who are not *us* into "symbolic exile" as *them* (Hall, 1997, p. 258). Once an individual is constructed as an outsider, this person is no longer thought of as having humanity. The intimidating outsider is "surely an animal in human form" (Green, 1993, p. 327). In the absence of direct personal experience, stereotypes serve as a way of filling in the blanks in terms of expectations (or lack thereof) of those different from the individual imagining them. Construction of an enemy image becomes the "mental background for aggression, distrust, guilt, projection, identification with all evil, and stereotyping" (Fiebieg-von Hase, 1997, p. 2).

The people and government of the United States, for example, have a long history of selectively demonizing and dehumanizing others, including their own citizenry, in the interest of acquisition and preservation of resources and power (Said, 1997; Takaki, 1993; Zinn, 1995). Worth (2002) points out that

> America's discovery of an enemy who is not merely an enemy, but an 'evil,' has impeccable historical credentials. In a long history of responding to real and perceived threats, it seems clear that this large, heterogeneous country defines itself in part through its nemeses. Such bellicosity can serve as a convenient tool for unification where differences among 'us' can be minimized, erased, or overlooked with a powerful 'them' or 'other.' (p. 1)

Further, a joining of politics and religion is useful in propagating hegemonic beliefs. To accomplish this, both theologians and political rhetoricians frequently invoke images of Satan (Pagels, 1996). This practice can be traced at least as far back as Luther, when rebelling peasants were declared to be "agents of the devil" (Keen, 1986, p. 27). For purposes of this essay, however, there are ample examples in the recent past that can best be explained under the rubric of two structural factors tied to enmity: (1) "some concrete facts that permit the enemy image to appear as plausible and real" and (2) "the political system itself" (Fiebig-von Hase, 1997, p. 24). Attitudes among European Americans that would permit attempts to exterminate indigenous Americans, enslavement of Africans, and Japanese internment are a few examples of the extremes to which enemy construction has reached. These beliefs are not simply erased over the passage of time. Rather, through the messages of dominant social and cultural institutions, such as the government and the media, selective versions of "reality" are presented in a way that provides justification for past, present, and future action and reaction to constructed enemies.

The political system is the second structural source of social conflict and enmity (Fiebig-von Hase, 1997). In American bureaucracy, tension often arises between an individual's beliefs and expectations of government and political control. In the guise of political rhetoric, **propaganda,** defined in its broadest sense as "the technique of influencing human action by the manipulation of representations," is often used to ameliorate psychological dissonance (Lasswell, 1934/1995, p. 13). Propaganda can be found in "spoken, written, pictorial, or musical" forms and has been used as a way of mobilizing sentiment around an idea, image, or product. Moreover, it attains "eminence as the one means of mass mobilization that is cheaper than violence, bribery, or other possible control techniques" (Lasswell, 1934/1995, p. 17).

Embedded in official doctrine, hate propaganda draws strength and longevity from well-established underlying attitudes and beliefs: "For mobilization of national hatred the enemy must be represented as a menacing, murderous aggressor, a satanic violator of the moral and conventional standards, an obstacle to the cherished aims, and ideals of the nation as a whole and of each constituent part. Through the elaboration of war aims, the obstructive role of the enemy becomes particularly evident" (Lasswell, 1934/1995, pp. 18–19). In the 1980s, for example, when Ronald Reagan identified the Soviet Union as "the focus of evil in the modern world," he asked Americans "to pray for the salvation of all those who live in totalitarian darkness" and to "pray they will discover the joys of knowing God" (Keen, 1986, p. 31). In 1982, as a result of Reagan's Speech to the House of Commons, the expression "evil empire" came to embody the Soviet Union in the Western world, and "fears of terrorism" took "root in the national psyche" (Kakutani, 2001). The official website of the White House adopts Reagan's rhetoric in its historical description of his tenure in the White House: the White House stood "witness as the great moral crusader Ronald Reagan would crush the evil Soviet Empire from the Oval Office, and re-invent what it means to portray an honest, faith-loving American" (White House History, 2004). During the Persian Gulf War, the September 1990 *Atlantic Monthly* cover titled "The Roots of Muslim Rage," featured the image of a large, turbaned, slanty-eyed man whose angry eyes had irises in the shape of the American flag. There is nothing to suggest that the man has any humanity; rather, what is important is that he is "unlike us. We need have no sympathy, no guilt, when we destroy him" (Keen, 1986, p. 16).

Through the use of symbols or symbolic words that are not only popular but also resonate with preexisting points of view, propagandist representations must spontaneously induce acceptance and elicit necessary changes in order to bring about permanent adaptation. Stereotypes, "especially negative ones of Arabs, have been used as a weapon that has proved to be as effective as some of the military, economic, or political weapons" (Suleiman, 1988, p. 9).

The Arab Stereotype in American Popular Culture

Al tikrar biallem il hmar. By repetition, even the donkey learns.
(Arab proverb)

All the information a child or a young adult learns becomes assimilated into a particular worldview and is compressed into categories of understanding (stereotypes) that are consistent with widespread social norms (Gandy, 1998; Hall, 1997; Merskin, 2001; Spyrou, 2002). From early childhood onwards, media and popular culture teach both Arabs and non-Arabs about "Arab-ness" by bombarding them "with rigid, repetitive, and repulsive depictions that demonize and delegitimize the Arab" (Shaheen, 1990, p. 7) and appear to represent consensus. These distorted representations can be found in music (remember "Ahab the Arab"?), cartoons, advertisements, comic strips, editorials, political rhetoric, and even children's textbooks (Ghareeb, 1983; Hamada, 2001; Shaheen, 1988, 2001; Terry, 1985). The movie quotation at the beginning of this chapter suggests Hollywood has been a particularly powerful and consistent outlet for vilification of others. According to Basinger (Lyman, 2001, E1) "we've had the IRA as villains, we've had international drug dealers, we've had Arabs, we've had vague Asians who weren't quite sure what country they were from." In other words, "the media are not simply institutions that reflect consensus but also institutions that produce consensus and 'manufacture consent'" (Hall, 2002, p. 428). The system of representation thereby "becomes a stable cultural convention that is taught and learned by members of a society" (Kates & Shaw-Garlock, 1999, p. 34). Markers of the nation state, these signifiers serve as key components of ideology in a hegemonic system that requires a great number of people to "buy in" to the dominant belief system, the one held to be "right." Stories and beliefs about what is "true" thereby become fertile fodder for the construction and maintenance of Arab stereotypes.

In an exhaustive study of more than 900 films over the last 20 years that portray Arab men, women, and children, Shaheen (2001) found that, in all but a few, Arabs were presented as "Public Enemy#1—brutal, heartless, uncivilized religious fanatics, and money-mad cultural 'others' bent on terrorizing civilized Westerners, especially Christians and Jews." Other examples include stereotypical representations such as "brute murderers, sleazy rapists, religious fanatics, oil-rich dimwits, and abusers of women" (Shaheen, 2001, pp. 1–2), as well as "A-rabs, camel jockeys, towel-heads, sand-niggers, genie, sheik, greasy merchant, ruthless, violent, treacherous, barbaric, all Arabs as Muslims—all Muslims as Arabs" (http://www.adc.org, 2002).

Since the dismemberment of the Soviet Union and the end of the Cold War, America needed a new enemy, a global bad guy, "a new foreign devil" (Said, 1997, p. xxviii). Cultural, political, educational, and media environments were well in place to make the threat Arab. The 1991 Gulf War provoked "an ugly wave of anti-Arab racism in the United States with Arab Americans insulted or beaten or threatened with death. Bumper stickers said, "I don't brake for Iraqis" (Zinn, 1995, p. 587). By then, the construction of an enemy "of Middle Eastern descent" was well established, as evidenced by the rush to judgment when an Arab American man (Abraham Ahmad) was arrested only a few hours after the April 19, 1995, Oklahoma City bombing. Ahmad said that he was singled out, "because of his Middle Eastern appearance and name and because he was flying to Jordan" ("Suspect Sues," 1995, 3A).

A lack of representation (symbolic annihilation) can also reinforce stereotypes. In an extensive three-year study (1993–1996) of TV content on ABC, CNN, PBS, and NPR, Lind and Danowski (1998) found very little coverage of Arabs and less of Arab culture. This reinforcement of dominant stereotypes through an overwhelming association with war, violence, and threats resulted in the representation of Arabs who "were identified most strongly in terms of their relations with Israel" (p. 165).

According to a study of Arabs in the news, Nacos and Torres-Reyna (2003) found that news before September 11, 2001, emphasized Muslim and Arab Americans and their participation in the political process during elections and those who sympathized or supported Middle East terrorists. They argue the point is not whether or not the press should have covered these topics, but other aspects of Arab American life were ignored. There was more use of Muslim and Arab

American sources prior to 9/11. After September 11, the predominant themes, in addition to terrorism and status of civil liberties, focused primarily on domestic issues such as concern with Arabs being singled out. This study found that, while there was a more favorable view after 9/11, fewer people had heard of Muslim Americans, and there was evidence of increasing doubts as to their ability to be loyal to the United States.

In a 1996 article in the *Journal of Media Psychology,* Narmeen El-Farra pointed out that news media routinely use particular words to describe Arabs, such as terrorists, extremists, and fanatics. According to Shaheen (1984), "The present day Arab stereotype parallels the image of Jews in pre-Nazi Germany, where Jews were painted as dark, shifty-eyed, venal and threateningly different people." These distortions of the Arab people have created a general mistrust and dislike for Arabs among Americans, even Arab Americans.

Thus, to identify Arabs with terrorism is to classify them as enemies. In research conducted by Martin (1985), results showed that the word "terrorism" was used by the press in describing events and individuals they disapproved of. Yet, when describing these same acts by individuals who are not Arabs, the media were careful to appear neutral and unbiased. Shaheen (1981, p. 89) reminds us that, "The racism that led to the internment of Japanese Americans during World War II was created partly by the motion picture industry, which for years typecast Orientals as villains, and partly by the press, especially the newspapers of William Randolph Hearst....The 'yellow peril' hysteria and the stereotyping which helped produce that myth have retreated into history. The Arab has now become the latest victim of media stereotyping."

With regard to the conflict with Osama bin Laden, Pilon quoted Attorney General John Ashcroft at a National Press Club luncheon as saying that Americans had "seen the face of evil" (Pilon, 2001), that they were dealing with "irrational madmen," and that they were "at war against international terrorism" (Fish, 2001, A19). The "axis of evil" became the presidential mantra of the moment. Fish (2001, A19) points out, "We have not seen the face of evil; we have seen the face of an enemy who comes at us with a full roster of grievances, goals, and strategies. If we reduce the enemy to 'evil,' we conjure up a shape-shifting demon, a wild-card moral anarchist beyond our comprehension." In a *New York Times* article following George W. Bush's September 15, 2001, speech, D. T. Max (2001) wrote:

> He called the terrorists 'folks' and referred to the coming battle as a 'crusade.' He called for 'revenge,' called Osama bin Laden the 'prime suspect,' and asked for him 'dead or alive.' He said 'make no mistake' at least eight times in public remarks. It was beginning to look like 'bring me the head of Osama bin Laden.' (p. 1)

Presidential Speeches

An interpretive textual analysis was used to examine six speeches, remarks, and a memorial address given by President George W. Bush shortly after September 11, 2001; specifically, the September 11 presidential address to the nation; remarks in a photo opportunity with the National Security Team on the 12th; a September 14 prayer service at Washington National Cathedral for the September 11 victims; remarks Bush made upon arrival at the White House from the South Lawn on September 16; a speech before a joint meeting of Congress on September 20; and the State of the Union address on January 29, 2002. These speeches were selected because the discourse provides insight into the enemy-building process that Spillmann and Spillmann (1997) describe.

The first step of the analysis involved "a long preliminary soak" (Hall, 1975, p. 15) in the text by studying complete speeches. This was followed by a "close reading" to identify the rhetorical characteristics of enemy image construction and an interpretation of the findings within the Spillmann and Spillmann (1997) model (Feldstein & Acosta-Alzuru, 2003, p. 159). Representative quotes of each characteristic (negative anticipation, putting blame on the enemy, identification with evil, zero-sum thinking, stereotyping and de-individualization, and refusal to show empathy) are presented in this analysis. Transcripts were collected from http://www.whitehouse.gov. Since the Spillmann and Spillmann (1997) categories are not mutually exclusive, the results are presented and discussed chronologically.

September 11, 2001: Statement by the president in his address to the nation

In this brief (593-word) address to the nation, President Bush laid the foundation upon which his future rhetoric would build, solidifying the evil enemy image. The term "evil" was mentioned four times in this first address, God once, and Psalm 23, "Even though I walk through the valley of the shadow of death, I fear no evil, for You are with me" was recited. The Spillmann and Spillmann (1997) characteristics of enemy construction, negative anticipation, blaming the enemy, identification with evil, stereotyping and de-individualization, are pulled together in this rhetoric. For example, in the first few sentences, Bush invoked the concepts of good versus evil and us versus them when he provided an initial reason for the attack: "Our very freedom came under attack….America was targeted for attack because we're the brightest beacon for freedom and opportunity in the world… thousands of lives were suddenly ended by evil, despicable acts of terror." This is the first of many uses of the word *evil* that transmogrified into "evil folks" and "evil-doers" in later addresses. He noted that "[t]oday, our nation saw evil" and that "the search is underway for those who are behind these evil acts." Zero-sum thinking, stereotyping, and de-individualization are evident in the statement "we will make no distinction between the terrorists who committed these acts and those who harbor them."

September 12, 2001: Remarks by the president in photo opportunity with the National Security Team

Animalistic stereotypical Jungian shadow imagery was evoked in these remarks by Bush in references to an enemy who "hides in the shadows and has no regard for human life" and is different from those of previous conflicts because "this is an enemy who preys on innocent and unsuspecting people, then runs for cover. This is an enemy who tries to hide."

Bush reminded Americans that "Freedom and democracy are under attack" not only in America but also among "all freedom-loving people everywhere in the world." He said that U.S. retaliation "will be a monumental struggle of good versus evil…but good will prevail." Drawing from the movie *Siege* (1998), in which the villains were Islamic terrorists, he declared, "Make no mistake about it: we will win." This expression was repeated in the State of the Union Address on January 29, 2002.

September 14, 2001: Washington prayer service

On September 14, Bush delivered a prayer service, which on its face is not unusual. However, such an intensely religious, Christian event suggests an administration more zealous than that of Carter. Critics have called the Bush presidency the "most resolutely 'faith based' in modern times"(Fineman, 2003, p. 22) and noted President George W. Bush's high level of public, Evangelical Christian religiosity (Balmer, 2003; Carver, 2003; Fineman, 2003; McNamara & George, 2001). While Carter is also an Evangelical Christian, "Bush's God is the 'eye for an eye' God, the God of vengeance and retribution" (Balmer, 2003, p. 7). During the December 13, 2000, Republican debate, for example, Bush was asked who his favorite philosopher was, to which he replied "Jesus" (Balmer, 2003, p. 7). Although on at least two occasions Bush "made a point of praising Islam as 'a religion of peace'" (Fineman, 2003, p. 22), this effort was adumbrated by persistent mentions of evil, God's power, and fire and brimstone imagery: "we have seen the images of fire and ashes and bent steel."

In this address, Bush referred to God or the Lord no less than seven times and made references to evil as well. Bush reassured the nation that "God's signs are not always the ones we look for. We learn in tragedy that his purposes are not always our own. The world he created is of moral design. And the Lord of life holds all who die and all who mourn." The power of prayer was declared when Bush proselytized, "Yet the prayers and private suffering…are prayers that help us last through the day or endure the night. There are prayers of friends and strangers.…There are prayers that yield our will to a will greater than our own." He concluded this speech with the words, "Neither death nor life, nor angels, nor principalities, nor powers, nor things to come, nor height, nor depth, can separate us from God's love. May He bless the souls of the departed, may he comfort our own." According to Balmer (2003, p. 7), rather than drawing upon "twentieth century liberal nostrums about human goodness," Bush applied Protestant theologian Reinhold Niebuhr's "theology of crisis" which demands "that people of faith abandon their quaint naïveté about human progress and unite to resist evil—by force if necessary."

Shadow imagery and the word *evil* have historically and contemporarily been used to summon the image of a dark, ominous, stereotypical threat—and they were used, too, in Bush's rhetoric. By referring to the enemy as a dark, faceless, soul-less source of evil, and referencing the forthcoming war as a "crusade," Bush positioned the retaliation as a battle between the forces of good and evil. While this kind of discourse is thought to bring a nation (tribe) closer together, it instead tends to have a polarizing effect. For example, Bush pointed out that the "civilized world" (which implies that "we" are civilized and the monolithic "they" are not) "was rallying to America's side." Spillman and Spillman's (1997) negative anticipation and stereotyping are evident in Bush's rallying cry to Americans that it is the United States' responsibility to "rid the world of evil" as "war has been waged against us by stealth and deceit and murder." Bush positioned America as the world's leader of obvious virtues when he declared, "we are freedom's defender" and "whether we bring our enemies to justice or bring justice to our enemies, justice will be done."

September 16, 2001: Remarks by the president upon arrival at the White House

George W. Bush's remarks to the nation from the South Lawn of the White House offered less scripted, more spontaneous rhetoric. At this point, terms such as "evil-doers," "evil folks," and "barbarism" had entered the vernacular. Arab enemy image construction is evident in the President's persistent references to evil in his speeches and the accompanying pervasive images of Arab suspects in the news media. In his remarks from the South Lawn, Bush said, "… we're a nation that can't be cowed by evil-doers....We will rid the world of evil-doers....There are evil people in this world....Evil folks still lurk out there, never did anybody's thought process *[sic]* about how to protect America did we think that the evil-doers would fly not one, but four commercial aircraft into precious U.S. targets. That's why I say to the American people we've never seen this kind of evil before. But the evil-doers have never seen the American people in action, before, either—and they're about to find out."

The idea of evil in Bush's remarks was accompanied by the idea of goodness, frequently expressed in Christian terms and expressions. In this speech, the word "faith" was used six times, either in references to Sunday, September 16, being "the Lord's day," "this day of faith," or of the American people, having "great faith." Bush said he had "faith in our military," and "faith in America," and "great faith in the resiliency of the economy."

The animalistic nature of stereotyping and de-individualization are evident as well in his assurance that "my administration is determined to find, to get 'em running, and to haunt *[sic]* 'em down, those who did this to America."

September 20, 2001: President Bush's address before a joint meeting of Congress

In this speech, Bush identified four questions he felt Americans were asking: (1) Who attacked our country? (2) Why do they hate us? (3) How will we fight this war? (4) What is expected of us? In response to the first question, Bush engaged negative anticipation by pointing out previous attacks and bombings by Arabic affiliated groups. At this time, he not only used terms such as "evil-doers" but also began referring to a more precise group identified as the Taliban. Bush described how the Taliban would pay a price for not meeting his demands. He drew upon the stereotypical, de-individualized characteristics of enemy image construction when he described the people as animalistic and brutal in act and ideology: "The terrorists may burrow deeper into caves and other entrenched hiding places. Our military action is also designed to clear the way for…relentless operations to drive them out and bring them to justice" since "they hide in your land." The statement to the Taliban that they must act immediately and "hand over the terrorists or they will share in their fate" illustrates zero sum thinking.

In commenting that the Muslim faith is respected and freely practiced by individuals in America and around the world, Bush's ecumenical effort to be inclusive was subsumed by the statement that followed, one that was loaded with the return to identification with evil: "Those who commit evil in the name of Allah blaspheme the name of Allah." Many Americans are not well schooled in the details of Islamic faith and thus cannot make the fine distinctions necessary to understand the significance of this statement. According to Hathout (1999, p. 1), "Islam is probably the most misunderstood American reality" and "studies have shown that Americans' knowledge of the Islamic faith is 'tragically laughable.'" As a result, "Most of the time we're mentioned, it's sensationalized, ugly or weird. And when a group is generalized, it becomes an object of fear" (Hathout, 1999, p. 1).

"Why do they hate us?" was the second question Bush posed. His response: they hate us because "Americans show a deep commitment to one another and an abiding love for country." The implication was that "they" do not share a similar sense of national pride. Bush compared an unknown image to a known stereotype by stating, "Al Qaeda is to terror what the Mafia is to crime." The act of blaming the enemy—and the representation of the enemy as greedy, insatiable, and possessing no limits or boundaries—provides justification for doing whatever is necessary to preserve the American way of life. In this speech, Bush used the abstract concept of freedom as being under attack, not individuals. For example, he said, "[e]nemies of freedom committed an act of war against our country." He pointed out that the "terrorists' directive commands them to kill Christians and Jews." Negative anticipation is illustrated in this speech when Bush stated that America and Americans are hated because of "what they [the terrorists] see right here in this chamber, a democratically elected government. Their leaders are self-appointed. They hate our freedoms, our freedom of religion, our freedom of speech, our freedom to vote and assemble and disagree with each other."

A clear example of zero sum thinking is found in Bush's ultimatum, "Every nation in every region now has a decision to make. Either you are with us or you are with the terrorists. From this day forward, any nation that continues to harbor or support terrorism will be regarded by the United States as a hostile regime." Refusal to show empathy is illustrated when Bush made this declaration about sympathizing nations: "they will hand over the terrorists or they will share in their fate." The American military would either "bring our enemies to justice or bring justice to our enemies." It was alongside this statement that Bush announced the creation of a cabinet level position that would report directly to him—the Office of Homeland Security.

In this speech, Bush extended the evil paradigm when he drew parallels with Nazism: "We have seen their kind before. They are the heirs of all the murderous ideologies of the 20th century. By sacrificing human life to serve their radical visions, by abandoning every value except the will to power, they follow the path of fascism, Nazism and totalitarianism."

When he presented the third question, "How will we fight this war?" Bush's response returned to the characterization of the enemy as evil, barbaric, and animalistic when he said the U.S. military would "starve terrorists of funding, turn them one against another, drive them from place to place until there is no refuge or no rest."

Finally, negative anticipation, identification with evil, blaming the enemy for domestic tensions, zero-sum thinking, and stereotyping came together in Bush's response to the fourth question, "What is expected of us?" In describing the meaning of patriotism, Bush assimilated the U.S. economy into the symbolic meaning of the World Trade Center: "terrorists attacked a symbol of American prosperity." Religiosity also came into play when Bush implored Americans "to continue to pray," as "prayer has comforted us in sorrow and will help strengthen the journey ahead." Dark and light imagery again were used as points of opposition when Bush stated, "Our nation, this generation, will lift the dark threat of violence from our people and our future." He concluded with his own request: "God grant us wisdom and may he watch over the United States of America."

January 29, 2002: State of the Union Address

By the time of this important address, the enemy was fully constructed, infused by more than 20 years of media and popular culture images equating Muslim/ Arab as terrorists. The United States was firmly positioned, at least in the minds of the Bush administration, as global caretaker supported by faith in God. The enemy was a dirty, dehumanized animal that scurried to "caves" and dark places. Anyone or any country that empathized or harbored the enemy became the enemy. "They" clearly were no longer individuals but rather demonized as evildoers "who send other people's children on missions of suicide and murder. They embrace tyranny and death as a cause and a creed," and it is "equaled by the madness of the destruction they design."

In this speech, Spillmann and Spillmann's (1997) identification with evil was evident when Bush identified the nations of North Korea, Iran, and Iraq as the "axis of evil," a collection of countries that were "arming to threaten the peace of the world" with their "weapons of mass destruction." While going into detail about what these countries have done to their own and other countries' people, he pointed out, "This is a regime that has something to hide from the civilized world. States like these, and their terrorist allies, constitute an axis of evil, arming to threaten the peace of the world." Movie-speak entered presidential discourse as Bush again declared "Make no mistake about it: If they do not act [governments "timid in the face of terror"] America will."

Economy as sign/symbol and power was apparent with his pronouncement of the new budget, one that nearly doubled "funding for a sustained strategy of homeland security," designed to protect the "economic security for the American people." War, the goals of an impending war, and economics were conflated when Bush stated, "we will prevail in this war, and we will defeat this recession." He assured the nation that "we can overcome evil with greater good," that "evil is real, and it must be opposed," and that "God is near." "[O]ur enemies believed America was weak and materialistic, that we would splinter in fear and selfishness. They are as wrong, "Bush said, "as they are evil." By this point in time, America's enemy was fully constructed and retaliation fully justified.

Summary

The purpose of this study was to examine post-September 11, 2001 presidential **rhetoric** to see if the use of particular words, phrases, and allusions fits Spillmann and Spillmann's (1997, pp. 50–51) enemy image construction model. In this case, while some of the characteristics played a stronger role than others did (stereotyping and de-individualization, identification with evil, and zero-sum thinking), it is clear that the carefully chosen, mostly scripted words in President Bush's speech were grounded in powerful connections to universal notions of enmity. In particular, historical as well as current popular culture portrayals of people of Arab/Middle Eastern descent were coupled with a rhetoric that was able to draw upon collective consciousness in order to revivify, reinforce, and ratify the Arab as terrorist stereotype.

Preexisting stereotypical media portrayals and presidential verbiage consistent with dominant ideology about Arabs provided the context for rigidifying the constructed Arab terrorist stereotype in a way that made such associations seem normal and logical. Combined with verbal and visual portrayals that consistently construct Arabs as terrorists, the tragic events of September 11 showed a real face and, for many Americans, a real reason to retaliate. Presidential propaganda thereby became a powerful hegemonic tool in the organization of public support and energy in the "Hunt for bin Laden" and investment in homeland security.

The construction of all Arabs as terrorists and all Muslims as Arab terrorists—through political rhetoric reducing vast populations into a single dark image—has significant consequences not only for the civil rights of individuals living in the United States but also for many other citizens of the world. Ultimately, such patterns have not only consequences for organizing citizen support for government operations but also a serious impact on the quality of life for Arab Americans. Families have suffered violence, and there have been numerous hate crimes, illegal detentions, and even murders (May & Modood, 2001). Children have experienced humiliation and fear among their schoolmates, and the climate of prejudice and hate only deepens the wound of discrimination. The constitutionality of the Patriot Act, in conjunction with concerns over the legality of actions by the Department of Homeland Security, will also be topics of conversation, scholarship, debate, and media attention for years to come.

Are we likely to see an end to the construction of enemy images? Probably not. Television programming largely omits Arabs from stories, and movies continue to rely upon a monolithic Arab stereotype "complete with glinty eyes and a passionate desire to kill Americans" (Said, 1997, p. 27). In the absence of a continuum of roles, characters, and occupations, there are very few alternative media sources for non-Arabs to draw upon in their understanding of Arab cultures. Considering how all but European Americans are identified by some level of hyphenation, differences serve as constant reminders of "otherness" to some imaginary *real* American. If the United States truly is a democratic nation and Arabs and Muslims are truly "our friends," then it is important to reflect this not only in media content but also in the hiring of writers and producers who can work in cooperation with television, news, and movie executives. Delivery of a more balanced, informed, and fairer image of Arabs (and all other minorities for that matter) to viewers is a pedagogically crucial, long overdue move toward professional respect and responsibility to all persons in the United States and elsewhere in the world. Perhaps then, in an odd twist of fate, the experiences of Arab Americans after September 11 will ironically serve as a crucible of our times.

Questions for Discussion

1. Can you think of any examples in film in which the "bad guys" were Arab?
2. In the Disney film *Aladdin*, is the young prince stereotypical?
3. Do you think language that describes people in written text impacts lived experiences?
4. What is your first memory of a media portrayal of someone who appears Arab?
5. Did you know more about Arabic peoples after September 11? Was the information accurate?

Key Words

Arab stereotype	Archetype of the enemy
Color line	Enemy image
Hostile imagination	Model of enemy image construction

Negative anticipation	Patriot Act
Propaganda	Rhetoric

Endnotes

1. Rhetoric, as used in this essay, is defined as "discourse calculated to influence an audience toward some end" (Gill & Whedbee, 1997, p. 157).

CHAPTER SEVEN

Perpetuation of the Hot Latina Stereotype in *Desperate Housewives*

I've played every stereotype except the pregnant teenager.

Tony Plana

Pretty dresses aren't just for skinny girls.

Estela in *Real Women Have Curves*

The Latino image with a Latino perspective is rarely seen. Instead, what you see are non-Latinos' ideas of what a Latino is.

Bel Hernandez

One of most popular network television programs to come along in years, ***Desperate Housewives*** (*DH)*, enjoys a viewership of more than 21 million women and men (Arthur, 2006, E5). In its 9:00 P.M. Sunday night time slot, *DH* presents the intimate lives of five attractive women living in a middle-to-upper-middle class neighborhood somewhere in America. One of these women, **Gabrielle Solis** (played by **Eva Longoria Parker**) is **Latina** (Figure 7.1). At first blush, hers appears to be a breakthrough role in terms of media representations of Latinas. Visibility as a lead character in a highly successful television program is a rarity for Latino women and for men. While the television series *Ugly Betty* has America Ferrera in the title role, critics suggest the show is stereotypical, that Betty is "the faithful Latina/o with a heart of gold" and that the show itself is filled with "a revolving bar of stereotypes":

> Betty's father is an unemployed, illegal Mexican immigrant trying to obtain free medical coverage. Her sister, an unwed mother, "works" by selling an herbal health scam. The father of her son is a gangster thug who walked out on his family. Betty herself is, well, ugly. ("An Ugly Turn," 2007, n. p.)

Similarly, in the *DH* representation, a critical reading of the program shows that the opportunity to advance the image of Latinas is lost as dialogue, the presentation of Gabrielle, and the off-screen life of Longoria Parker, fulfill Keller's (1994) **tripartite typology of Latina stereotypes (Cantina Girl, Suffering Senorita**, and **Vamp). Accumulation Theory** (DeFleur & Dennis, 1998) suggests the media are likely to have powerful effects if the information is presented persistently, consistently, and corroborated among forms. As a media effect, stereotypes rely on repetition to perpetuate and sustain them. The **hot Latina stereotype** is one with great longevity.

In a "cultural climate where Latinas are hot and hot Latinas are on fire," *DH*'s Eva Longoria Parker sizzles (Papps, 2005, p. 21). As Wisteria Lane's hoop-earringed hottie Gabrielle Solis, Longoria Parker's role as well as her public persona consistently presents the entire spectrum of the hot Latina stereotype.[1] Longoria Parker's prime time pinup status and promotional positioning in magazines reinforce the already prominent, oversexed, under-dressed decisive and divisive character she embodies on *DH*. In an interview promoting her photo shoot for *Unleashed* magazine, readers are told, "When she's not seducing the gardener on *Desperate Housewives,* fiery Eva Longoria Parker is seducing newsstand readers!" and "Instead of being tempted to try new projects because she is often pigeonholed as the sexy Latina, Eva plays up the stereotype" (Askmen.com, 2005). The steamy similarity in character and promotion of Longoria Parker/Solis is seamless.

In this chapter, I examine the articulation of the "hot Latina" stereotype of the character Gabrielle Solis and the conflation of that character with actor Eva Longoria Parker. Media-sustained stereotypes of Latinas served as a guide for interpretation (Valdivia, 1998, 2000) of the twenty-three episodes that constituted Season 1 (2004–2005). These episodes were decoded to examine the presentation of the Latina body and behavior of both the character Gabrielle Solis and news media coverage of the actor Eva Longoria Parker. This study draws upon and extends Guzmán and Valdivia's (2004) analysis of media presentation and press coverage of three Latina icons (Selma Hayek, Frida Kahlo, Jennifer Lopez). My intent is to add to this perspective in two ways: (1) to examine the Gabrielle Solis character as a representation of dominant stereotypes of Latinas, and (2) to consider whether Longoria Parker's off-screen, print, and commercial personae reinforce those stereotypes. The following research questions led this study: (1) Does the Gabrielle Solis character fulfill Keller's (1994) definitions of dominant stereotypes of Latinas? and (2) Do actor Eva Longoria Parker's off-screen and in-print personae reinforce that stereotype?

Representational Politics

As sources of learning, the mass media in general, and television in particular, are powerful sites of cultural (re)production where dominant (Anglo, male) beliefs about race, ethnicity, sex, and gender (among other "isms") are reinforced and recirculated. An ideology of White/Anglo racial superiority is maintained in part using stereotypes designed to construct an "Other" which is regarded as lesser than the declared and constructed ideal. Stereotypes, as hegemonic tools, reduce individuals to a single, monolithic, one-dimensional type that appears and is presented as natural and normal (read true and accurate) as they fit into ideological patterns of representations that serve, among other functions, to establish "in-group categorizations of out-groups" (Ramíerez-Berg, 1990, p. 294). Stereotyping "puts people in boxes and creates images that result in false presumptions accepted as inconvertible truths" (Oboler, 1998, p. 27). Stereotypes persist because "they fulfill important identity needs for the dominant culture" thereby maintaining the status quo and preserving hegemony (Mastro & Behm-Morawitz, 2005, p. 112). Images of Latino/as "… exist not in a vacuum but as part of a larger discourse on Otherness in the United States …. Beyond their existence as mental constructs or film images, stereotypes are part of a social conversation that reveals the mainstream's attitudes about others" (Ramírez-Berg, 2002, p. 4). Rather than using physical force, this social control strategy (hegemony) is psychological, requiring the consent of those ruled. Consent is evident in the normalization of stereotypical, one-dimensional representations that under other circumstances would seem, at the least, inappropriate if not all together harmful and misleading. Thus, as Dyer notes, stereotyping works "to fashion the whole of society according to their own world view, value-system, sensibility and ideology" (quoted in Ramírez-Berg, 2002, p. 22).

The consistency of stereotypical portrayals is also key to their longevity as presentation of the same or similar stereotypes is likely to add credibility to the (re)presentations as they take on an aura of naturalness and truth. Hence this naturalization, or as Hall (1996) refers to it, articulation, is reified through the lack of contradictory images and information and is apparent in the story-telling/myth-building capabilities of the mass media. The stories the media tell are based on deeply entrenched cultural beliefs and values that cultivate and build support for a system of symbolic representation that benefits the financial, cultural, economic, and social interests of the ruling elite through the reinforcement of racialized heteronormative beliefs and values. Through the use of specific signs and symbols, articulated in particular words and images, racial/ethnic and sexual stereotypes draw strength from a shared cultural reservoir of thought-to-be-truths about particular groups of people based on a history of cultural, social, and psychological infusion of one-dimensional and distorted presentations of qualities (or lack thereof) which serve the interests of those in power who wish to retain their status and resources.

A related concept and partial explanation for the effectiveness of a hegemonic system of social control is Accumulation Theory (DeFleur & Dennis, 1998). This theory predicts, if the mass media, including advertising, present information in ways that are consistent, persistent, and corroborated, this instruction is likely to have long-term, powerful effects. Stereotyping, as a media effect, gains power and credibility the longer and more regularly the same information is presented, in the same way, to the same audiences. These (re)presentations remain largely unchallenged so that carefully cultivated cultural constructions of race, ethnicity, sexuality, and gender become normalized in the American popular imagination.

In the case of Latino/as portrayals, the wide variety of individual qualities, experiences, histories, and characteristics are truncated by stereotyping into a single Pan-Latina/o identity based on a unilateral conception of "Hispanic-ness" (Dávila, 2001, p. 56). Consistently repeated representations have power as "these are the ideas we have been hearing for a long time and that we've ended up believing out of truth, custom, or repetition" (p. 56). Markers of sex and sexuality in Latinas posit them as "exotic, sexual, and available, and as more in touch with their bodies and motivated by physical and sexual pleasure than white women" (Beltrán, 2002, p. 82). While curviness and a prominent derriere might be acceptable in the construction of Jennifer Lopez-as-Latina celebrity, this is not an attribute of mainstream (Anglo) ideal female beauty in American media. However, because an ample derriere is coded as an eroticized aspect of Latina-ness, she can be curvy and be considered attractive. This construction thereby complies with mainstream expectations of Latina beauty.

Latina Stereotypes in U.S. Popular Culture

I love you, that's why I make you miserable. (Carmen in *Real Women Have Curves,* 2002)

During the 1920s–1940s, Latina stars such as **Carmen Miranda** broke through racial/ethnic barriers to celebrity and success in U.S. popular entertainment. Yet, the physical and performative requirements for success simultaneously established not only the Latina "look" in film, but also the look as a symbol of lower social class. Carmen Miranda ("the lady in the tutti-frutti hat"), Dolores del Rio, and Lupe Velez (the "Mexican Spitfire") projected not only exotic, inviting, and flamboyant sexuality but also a particular social class look derived from a perceived ethnicity. In 1945, Carmen Miranda, for example, was America's highest paid woman (O'Neil, 2005). Her fame, however, carried a high price as fruit-filled hats, an accent thick as picante, and ever-zanier roles undermined whatever strides she had taken for Latinas in Hollywood (O'Neil, 2005).

The **dramaturgical display** (**Erving Goffman**, 1956) of each of these actors affected their celebrity, image, and subsequent success and illustrated the hierarchical nature and ambiguity of roles for Latinas in American popular entertainment (Cortés, 1997; López, 1991; Noriega, 1992; Ramírez-Berg, 1990; Rios-Bustamante, 1992; Rodriquez-Erastrada, 1992).

Stereotypical behavioral characteristics assigned to Latinas include "addictively romantic, sensual, sexual, and even exotically dangerous" (Mastro & Behm-Morawitz, 2005, p. 125), self-sacrificing, dependent, powerless, sexually naïve, childlike, pampered, and irresponsible (Arredondo, 1991; Gil, 1996; King, 1974; Lott & Saxon, 2002). Others include "they all make good domestics," mispronounce words, speak Spanish, are all Catholic, impulsive dancers, and are known for "cooking up a spicy storm" (Cofer, 2005, p. 247)—not only in a culinary sense. Comprised of "bright colors, rhythmic music, and olive or brown skin," Latina tropicalism erases differences between specific Latino groups and conflates characteristics of people from African, Caribbean, and Latin American cultures into a single, pan-Latino/a identity (Guzmán & Valdivia, 2004, p. 211). When stereotypical physical characteristics (red lips, big bottoms, large hips, voluptuous bosoms, and small waists), fashion extremes (high heels, huge hoop earrings, seductive clothing), sexual predation, and promiscuity (hot, exotic, experienced) are combined with behavioral generalities, the Latina is constructed as "mixed signifiers of sexual desire and fertility as well as bodily waste and racial contamination" (Guzmán & Valdivia, 2004, p. 212). Keller (1994, p. 40) organizes these stereotypes under three categories which "epitomize the range of representations of women in Hispanic" and Anglo television and film.

1. *Cantina Girl.* "Great sexual allure," teasing, dancing, and "behaving in an alluring fashion" are hallmark characteristics of this stereotype. She is most often represented as a sexual object, a "naughty lady of easy virtue" (p. 40).

2. *Faithful, self-sacrificing senorita.* This woman usually starts out good but goes bad by the middle of the film or television program. This character realizes she has gone wrong and is willing to protect her Anglo love interest by placing her body between the bullet/sword/posse/violence intended for him.

3. *Vamp.* While Cantina Girl is most often presented physically as an available sexual object, the Vamp uses her intellectual and devious sexual wiles to get what she wants. She often brings men to violence and enjoys doing so. She is a psychological menace to males who are ill equipped to handle her.

Keller (1994) notes that the three major stereotypes function mainly in relationship to an Anglo love interest. Sex, passion, manipulation, and physical beauty are common to each of the characters who are coded with particular types of clothing, postures, motivations, speech, and behavior. This portrait epitomizes stock Latina attributes that set the stage for the character of Gabrielle to appear (to Anglo audiences) as natural. While all of the women on *DH* are, in some way, sexual, Gabrielle's libido is on fast-forward in a way different from the highly sexual Edie, for example. Susan (Teri Hatcher) is meek, Lynette (Felicity Huffman), mother of five, avoids sex so as not to get pregnant again, Bree (Marcia Cross), described as "Martha Stewart on steroids," is repressed. Edie (Nicollette Sheridan) is single and uses sex to get what she wants in somewhat mindless and obvious manner, whereas Gabrielle is tactical, risky, and sensual (shown in her bra and panties or tiny teddies), and iconicized in the larger-than-life portrait that hangs above the Solis' fireplace.

The character Gabrielle and the actor Eva Longoria Parker present a mediated, pan-ethnic identity in the process of **tropicalization** (Aparicio & Chávez-Silverman, 1997). Both the role and the public appearance are consistent with one another. Through these representations both as character and celebrity, Gabrielle/Eva becomes a key tropicalizer embodying pan-ethnic traits of **Latinidad** that draw from and affirm dominant stereotypes of Latina-ness.

Analyzing *Desperate Housewives*

Textual analysis is a useful methodology for getting at race/ethnicity-based ideological assumptions expressed through the framing power of language and images (McKee, 2003; Kraidy & Goeddertz, 2003; Lester, 1994; Lule, 1993, 1995). A **critical/resistant reading** of visual and verbal rhetoric reveals much about the political and cultural climate within which media content appears. **Keller's** (1994) **typology** provides clear categories for examining the presence or absence of reductive qualities when informed by other studies of Latina stereotypes (Cortés, 1997;

López, 1991; Guzmán & Valdivia, 2004; Noriega, 1992; Ramírez-Berg, 1991; Rios-Bustamante 1992; Rodriquez-Erastrada, 1992; Valdivia, 1998, 2000).

Therefore, a close reading was conducted on the first season (2004–2005) of *DH*, consisting of twenty-three episodes. Transcripts were obtained from the website http://desperatehousewives.ahaava.com/episodes.htm. The coder confirmed accuracy by comparing them to viewing videotaped episodes of the show. Keller's stereotypes (Cantina Girl, Suffering Senorita, and Vamp) are not mutually exclusive. Thus, in the following section, illustrative episodes and relevant dialogues are presented thematically in order to demonstrate how these characterizations conflate into a unified stereotypical Latina portrayal in the character Gabrielle and reinforced in "real life" media exposure of actor Eva Longoria Parker (Figure 7.1).

Spicy paella

Most of the characters on *DH* enter *tabula rasa*. In nearly every episode, drop by delicious drop, the characters' personalities blossom, their pasts slowly revealed, and, however tarnished, their true natures shine through. In the show's pilot (Cherry & McDougall, 2004) episode, Whiteness is established as the central signifier of culture on Wisteria Lane. In this episode the viewer first meets Gabrielle Solis as the camera pans to her from a handsome Hispanic man we later come to know as her husband Carlos. In a skin-tight, slinky black dress, stunning jewelry, and spiky high-heeled shoes Gabrielle carefully navigates the front steps, all while carrying a steaming dish. Gabrielle and Carlos are on their way to a wake for a friend (Mary Alice) who committed suicide and becomes the disembodied, omniscient narrator/voiceover for the show. The omniscient narrator (Mary Alice) introduces Gabrielle to the audience: "Gabrielle Solis, who lives down the block, brought a spicy paella."

In this introductory scene, we learn a lot about Gabrielle. She is immediately constructed as Latina in her dress, mannerisms, and by the food she contributes to the wake. We learn she married Carlos not out of deep love but for economic reasons. That fact is no secret to Carlos who is well aware of, and takes seriously, this arrangement and his power to control it. Mary Alice tells the viewer, "Since her modeling days in New York, Gabrielle had developed a taste for rich food and rich men." We quickly learn that Gabrielle quit her high fashion modeling career (a form of bodily selling) with the understanding that Carlos would keep her bejeweled, pampered, and wanting for nothing. In return, she sleeps with him, makes herself available, and, because of her good looks, is an asset in his business dealings in the (implied) Anglo world. The audience is told, "Gabrielle liked her paella piping hot. However, her relationship with her husband was considerably cooler."

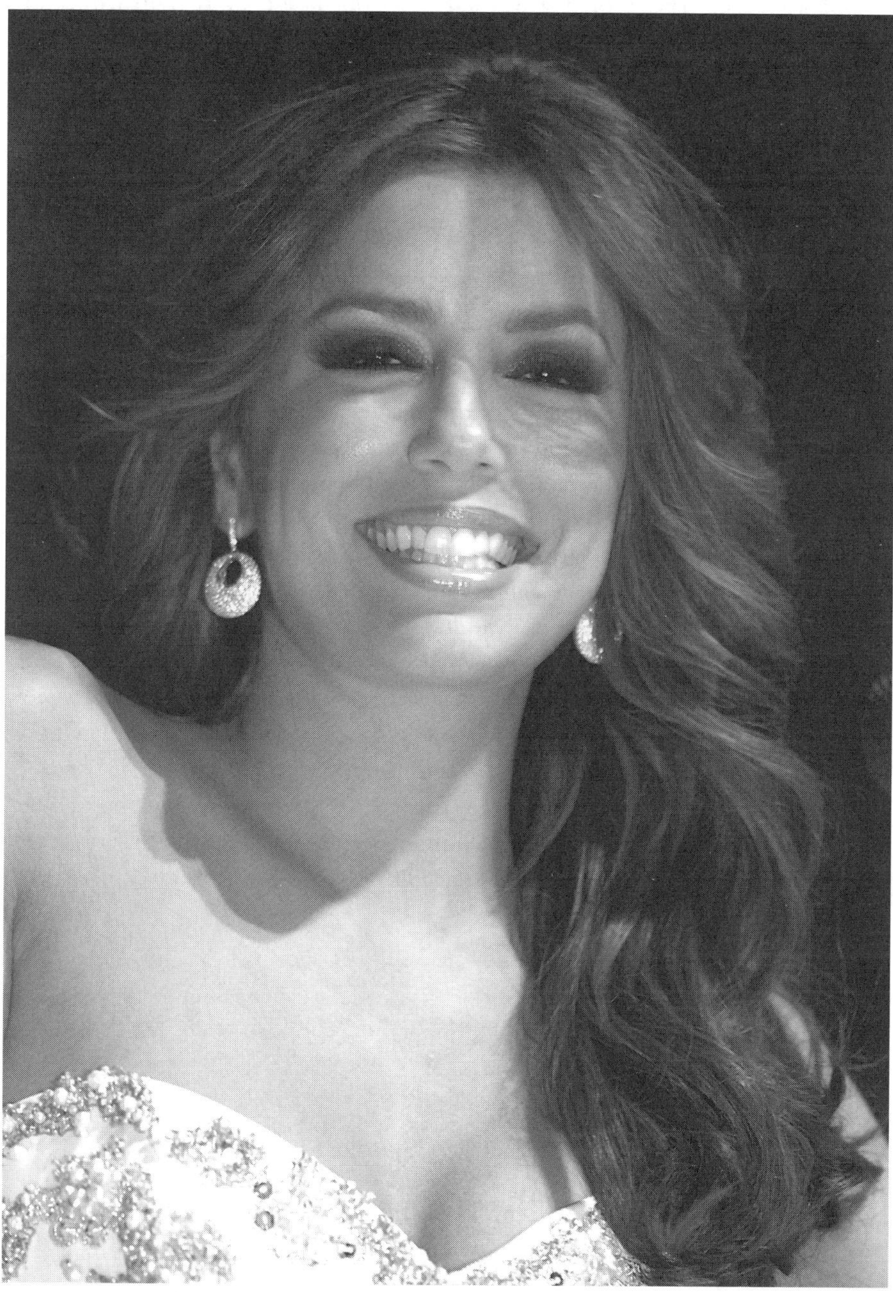

Figure 7.1: Eva Longoria Parker.

Source: Festival Internacional de Cine en Guadalajara.

Gabrielle is Carlos' property. More than a trophy wife, more than arm candy, Gabrielle makes herself available for his use (at least initially). This arrangement is evidenced by his willingness to "pimp" her for his own gain and her willingness to go along with it. As a Cantina Girl, she knows what she's got and as a Vamp, she works it to her advantage. For example, before a party with one of his important clients, Gabrielle shouts that Carlos cannot order her around or force her to go:

CARLOS: It's business. Tanaka expects everyone to bring their wives.

GABRIELLE: Every time I'm around that man, he tries to grab my ass.

CARLOS: I made over $200,000 with him last week. If he wants to grab your ass, you let him.

Gabrielle has mixed feelings about their agreement and how things are turning out in her life. Later in the same episode, Gabrielle tells Carlos she hates the way he talks to her, to which he replies, "and I really hate that I spent $50,000 on a diamond necklace that you couldn't live without. But I've learned to deal with it." When Carlos apologetically gives Gabrielle a convertible with a big red ribbon on it, she says, "Carlos, what have you done?" He replies, "I saw it when I drove by the dealership. I thought Gabrielle would look so beautiful in this." "Carlos!" she exclaims, playfully shoving him. Mary Alice's narration tells us "Gabrielle could see what this gesture had cost Carlos so *she responded the only way she knew how*" [italics added]. The scene ends with Gabrielle, in Cantina fashion, kissing Carlos, jumping up, and wrapping her legs around him.

In the second episode (Cherry & Shaw, 2004), anger quickly abates when Gabrielle-as-prize-and-property is plied into complacency. No matter how angry she gets, her fiery temper is quickly assuaged by bling, and the more expensive the bling the better.

GABRIELLE: Nope. No, no, no, no. You're not gonna buy your way out of this one.

CARLOS: It's a good gift.

GABRIELLE: Is that white gold?

CARLOS: Yeah. Put it on. And then make love to me.

GABRIELLE: I'm not in the mood. But, we could stay up and talk.

CARLOS: When a man buys a woman expensive jewelry, there are many things he may want in return. For future reference, conversation ain't one of them.

"To-be-looked-at-ness" is an important aspect of the construction of Gabrielle (Mulvey, 2001, p. 397). Her body is a central marker of Latinidad conflated with sexuality, therefore, her clothing is always bright and tight fitting, for example, to show off her toned and lithe body in a way that has "strong visual and erotic impact" and connotes availability and exudes willingness (p. 397). In Episode 17 ("Children Will Listen"), Gabrielle's priorities are reasserted: "There were many things Gabrielle Solis knew for certain. She knew red was her color. She knew diamonds went with everything and she knew men were all the same."

The Cantina Girl in Gabrielle thrives on and feels validated by attention to her appearance. In nearly every episode she is shown working out or on her way to or back from doing so. While Gabrielle wants her affair with John to be a secret, she does not mind attention and admiration from others. For example, in Episode 4, she asks John, her seventeen-year-old "gardening toy boy lover," (Papps, 2005, p. 21), "Why are your friends staring at me? Did you tell them about us?" John exclaims, "No! They're staring because they think you're hot." Gabrielle replies, smiling, "Oh! Okay!" (Cherry, Spezialy, & Melman, 2004). In Episode 5 (Cunningham, 2004), Gabrielle's vanity is apparent when she assures her friend Susan that she knows when people aren't looking at her: "Honey, trust me. When they're not staring at me, I notice."

While the Solises may be the wealthiest couple on Wisteria Lane, they often do not seem equal to their money. Gabrielle spends with abandon until she realizes there is none left. Carlos' sole focus is business and money and how to get more of each, even to the point of crime. The tension between Carlos and Gabrielle around power and autonomy are exaggerated examples of Macho/Machismo-Macha/Marianisma, or what Del Castillo (1998, p. 499) calls "Mexican gender ideology" in which "the family is hierarchical in structure…men have authority over women and the husband has authority over his wife" (p. 499). Gabrielle struggles to be a modern Latina, whereas Carlos holds a more traditional view about female/male power relationships. Carlos not only believes he "purchased" Gabrielle as a business arrangement, but also that he is entitled to renegotiate their arrangement after the fact. How much of herself did Gabrielle "sell" to Carlos? In Episode 8 (Murphy & Shaw, 2004), that subject comes up in front of dinner guests:

CARLOS: Can our lives have any meaning if all we ever do is buy stuff?

GABRIELLE: That depends on what we buy.

CARLOS: I want a child.

GABRIELLE: In case you've forgotten, before we got married, we made a deal. No kids!

CARLOS: Yeah, well, deals were meant to be renegotiated.

GABRIELLE: Well, we're not negotiating my uterus.

Gabrielle surprises Carlos with her demonstration of independence and clarity. She has the last word, which does not go over well in the possessive/submissive dance of their relationship. At the same time, this challenge sparks sexual energy between the two of them, a method of manipulation both Cantina Girl and the Vamp are well schooled in using.

Passion and promiscuity

Bodily ownership and sex conflate in a conversation between Carlos and Gabrielle in the first episode (Cherry & McDougall, 2004). Gabrielle has been instructed that if she talks to a particular person at Mary Alice's wake, she's to casually mention how much he paid for her necklace. Gabrielle retorts, "Why don't I just pin the receipt to my chest?" Undaunted, Carlos tells her to work it in, and she tells him it's not the kind of thing that can be "worked in" to a conversation. His comeback?

CARLOS: Why not? At the Donahue party, everyone was talking mutual funds and you found a way to mention you slept with half of the Yankee outfielders.

GABRIELLE: I'm telling you, it came up in the context of the conversation.

Promiscuity, passion, sex, and risk taking are characteristics of Gabrielle as her psychic (Vamp) personality emerges (Keller, 1994). For example, Gabrielle finds her encounters with John exciting, not only for the sex, but also because she is fooling Carlos and is stimulated by fear of his wrath. She spites Carlos and his money when she lures John into the kitchen (while Carlos is outside examining the lawn) (Papps, 2005, p. 21). John watches Gabrielle take off her blouse and lean back seductively on the kitchen table. She tells him the table is hand carved, imported from Italy, and cost Carlos $23,000. John laughs and asks her, "So you wanna do it on the table this time?" Gabrielle replies, "Absolutely."

In order to keep her affair with John going, yet secret, Gabrielle vacillates as she sacrifices for Anglo love interest John (as Carlos suspects it is not the garden John is tending). In the middle of the Tanaka party, for example, Gabrielle-the-Vamp makes sure her husband is well supplied with alcohol, and rushes home to mow the lawn. Wearing an elegant evening gown and spiky high heels, the Suffering Senorita pulls the lawn mower out of the garage and, under cover of darkness, frantically mows, rushes back to the party, no worse for wear (except for the telltale leaf she removes from her hair moments before returning, flirtatiously, to her husband's side).

Sexual passion conflates with violence in exchanges between Gabrielle and Carlos in later episodes. Between growing jealousy, anxiety about going to prison, and the death of his mother, Carlos becomes increasingly agitated and physically aggressive toward Gabrielle. In Episode 12 (Black & Grossman, 2004), Carlos returns from his first prison stint. Gabrielle is informed that, because of his electronic monitoring device, Carlos cannot work and their accounts are frozen. *She* will have to bring in the money. This is *not* what Gabrielle signed on for. Embarrassed and frustrated, she tells him, "Carlos, this is not like New York where I made thousands of dollars a day modeling haute couture. I'm doing boat shows. I spend eight hours a day doing this!" The saucy, spoiled Cantina Girl throws a fit and then assumes her Vampish, vengeful, manipulative nature when Carlos tells her "Things change!"

> GABRIELLE: Yeah, I know. The Feds towed away my Maserati. My husband is a felon, and I spend my days getting groped by fat tractor salesmen at trade shows. I am well aware things change!… I like my lifestyle, and I don't want you to kill it.

> CARLOS: Well, look around, Gabrielle, it's already dead. And there's nothing you can control.

> GABRIELLE: Maybe. But having a baby, that, I can control. You, I can control.

> CARLOS: Hey, you can't talk to me like that. [She goes outside] I'm still the man of this house.

> GABRIELLE: Oh, really?

With that said, Carlos starts to step off the front porch toward her and his ankle bracelet begins flashing and beeping. From her safe distance Gabrielle sarcastically shouts, "You're the man of the house? You can't even leave it!" Taunting him, she holds up a piece of meat, dangles it over her open mouth, and drops it slowly into her mouth. Her Vampish, predatory rebellion conflicts with Carlos' already threatened Machismo.

Carlos is convinced Gabrielle will leave him when he returns to prison. She promises she will not (although the look in her eye tells the viewer she has other ideas). At this point, Carlos begins tampering with Gabrielle's birth control pills, convinced a child will keep them together. He has badgered her about this, egged on by his mother, Juanita, who he calls *Mamá* and occasionally speaks Spanish with, much to Gabrielle's irritation. The tension between *Mamá* Solis and Gabrielle is consistent throughout the season. The matriarch feels dethroned by her son's gorgeous wife. Juanita, who now lives with the Solis', drives Gabrielle crazy, watching her every move and "watching her Mexican soap opera[s]," reminding viewers this is a Latino family after all. In a scene from Episode 5 ("Come in, Stranger"), we have this exchange:

GABRIELLE: You know, Juanita, this is so like you. I invite you on a nice shopping trip, and you find ways to upset me.

MAMA SOLIS: Oh, you didn't invite me. I invited myself. You keep looking at your watch. Is there someplace you have to be?

GABRIELLE: No! You know, and for the record, I am not one of those women who has a hole in her heart that can only be filled by a baby. I like my life a lot. It's very fulfilling.

MAMA SOLIS (TO A FELLOW CUSTOMER): Excuse my daughter-in-law. She's very fulfilled.

In no time at all (in fact, in the next episode) the fertile Gabrielle is pregnant, ordinarily a manipulative ploy of the Vamp. She blames the now-deceased Juanita for messing with her birth control pills. But, more importantly, who is the father? John? Carlos? A definitive behavior of the promiscuous Cantina and Vamp stereotypes. In Episode 13 (Etten & Sanford, 2004), John finds out the baby might be his and proposes to Gabrielle. She declines, leaving him, in true Vamp fashion.

GABRIELLE: I don't know. You know, every once in a while, even I want to do the right thing.

JOHN: Mrs. Solis, I love you so much! Doesn't that mean anything to you?

GABRIELLE: Honestly, no. John, you're a toy. A sweet, dumb toy, so you might as well go to college, because you and me, no future!

In Episode 18 (Murphy & Shaw, 2004), the tables are turned as Gabrielle's manipulation of Carlos backfires. He does not trust her and she does not trust him. Carlos insists she sign a postnuptial agreement stating that, should she divorce him while he is in prison, she will get nothing. She however, tells him she knows about his secret bank account in the Cayman Islands and taunts him with "so if I were you, Carlos, I wouldn't mention the words divorce, trust, post-nup ever again. You don't want to piss me off." As she walks away, Carlos grabs a vase and throws it against the wall, shattering it. Her response? "I know, baby. It hurts to lose."

The tit-for-tat exchange of threats continue as Carlos again tries to get Gabrielle to sign the post-nup, this time through threat of physical violence. She realizes he has moved the funds out of the Cayman Islands account but still refuses to sign the document. He gets angrier, she turns to run, Carlos chases her, grabs Gabrielle, picks her up, slams her down in a chair at the table, forcibly grabs her hand, puts the pen in it (again controlling her body) and makes her sign. No longer does Gabrielle's mental manipulation of Carlos work—he is on to her. This Suffering Senorita's promise or use of sex to manipulate no longer works.

GABRIELLE: Let me go. Ah! Stop! You're hurting me. Carlos!

CARLOS: Sign it. SIGN IT!

Gabrielle cries as she signs the paper. Carlos says, "I know baby. It hurts to lose." Later that night, in bed, they exchange other threats:

GABRIELLE: If you ever hurt me again, I will kill you.

CARLOS: If you ever leave me for another man, I'll kill you.

GABRIELLE: Boy, with all this passion, isn't it a shame that we're not having sex?

During the first season of *DH*, the Gabrielle Solis character transmogrifies from Cantina Girl to Suffering Senorita to Vamp. In the process, she does not lose any of the characteristics of the individual types; rather, as her character develops, the trio comes together as she becomes a fully realized hot Latina stereotype. In her public life, the actor Eva Longoria Parker picks up where Gabrielle leaves off. In her off-screen appearances, Longoria Parker, the "Latina temptress" (Papps, 2005, p. 21), does little to dispel a view of her behaviors, attitudes, and beliefs as identical to Gabrielle's. For example, in a magazine interview (in which she was later proclaimed number one out of 100 sexiest women), Longoria Parker said, "There's something very sexy about being submissive. Because your guard is down, you have to totally surrender to something like that" (Maximonline.com, 2003, p. 3). She plays the fantasy card when she admits she dresses a lot like her on-screen role: "I wear G-strings every day, all the time. I actually don't even own a full-bottom pair of underwear. I also love lingerie, and I love high heels, but I prefer total nakedness overall. That, to me, is so much sexier" (Maximonline.com, 2003, p. 3).

Because I'm worth it

In the late 1990s publicity, celebrity A-lister Jennifer Lopez stated she is an "actress who is Latin—not a Latin actress as in one who just does Latina roles" (Beltrán, 2002, p. 77). While this might have been part of a public relations strategy to position Lopez as an actor, moving away from previous publicity about her buttocks,[2] Longoria Parker presents a public and media persona consistent with her hot Latina *DH* role. In an interview, Longoria Parker responded to the question "What's the best thing about being a woman?" in a way consistent with Keller's (1994) stereotypical "triplets" in her *DH* role:

> Everything, everything. The sexiness that we get to exude. The femininity of having soft skin. The desire of always wanting to be pretty and put on make-up and wear heels. I love being a woman. I love shopping. I love wearing dresses and heels and jewelry. I love being sexy and feeling sexy. But the best thing about being a woman is the power we have over men. (oyemag.com, 2005)

In a *Rolling Stone* interview, Longoria Parker was described as "the hottest, juiciest of the Wisteria Lane housewives" who, "when she isn't shopping or mowing the front lawn in a pink party gown, she's doing the nasty with her seventeen-year-old hunk of a gardener." In response to the question, "What was the best sex you had all year?" in Gabrielle-esque Vamp form she replies

> Probably with my vibrator. I own two. I have the rabbit one, and I give that as a gift all the time to other girls for a birthday or the like. It's the best gift to give: an orgasm. And if I can't do it for ya, I'll give you the tools to succeed! I have one rabbit and a Pocket Rocket. (Hedeggard, 2005)

Longoria Parker's sexy girl-ness transcends her role in *DH* in the advertising arena. Wearing a black skin-tight, criss-cross backed evening gown she longingly and liquidly lounges on a white bedspread, slithering forward and rolling from stomach to back extolling the virtues of L'Oreal's VIVE shampoo. This commercial is the first among many she will do as the first and only Latina spokesmodel for the world's largest cosmetic company (Foster, 2005, p. 30) as she lends her name and body to the beauty product monolith's array of goods (L'Oreal, 2005). Longoria Parker went with the company because, "L'Oreal is one of the few companies that really reflect my values. Their company philosophy and their legendary phrase 'Because I'm Worth It' go hand-in-hand with who I am as a person. This is it, the best, the culmination of an amazing year" (Femalefirst.com, 2005).

Thirty-year-old Longoria Parker, "joins a bevy of beauties" who have contracted with L'Oreal including Andie MacDowell, Beyoncé Knowles, and Jennifer Aniston (Fashionspot.com, 2005). While Longoria Parker may have followed Aniston's footsteps to the door of the house of L'Oreal, it was to Aniston's former bedroom she volunteered her services. Intended as humor in light of publicity surrounding the Jennifer Aniston/Brad Pitt split (allegedly over Aniston's unwillingness and Pitt's desire to have children) Longoria Parker joined other American women in donning a pink "I'll have Brad's babies" t-shirt. Friends and fans were shocked by Longoria Parker's lapse in judgment. She later apologized for the display of poor taste and insult to Aniston. What is interesting, however, is Longoria Parker was keeping in character by playing the happy-when-pregnant hot Latina Cantina Girl stereotype.

Longoria Parker's public appearances do much to bolster her on-screen role. Voted by *Variety* as one of the "Ten New Faces of Fall" (quoted in torontofashion. com, 2004), she extends her seductive reach to daytime and evening (mostly female) viewing audiences with an appeal (and giggle) that will inevitably include men. Good marketing? Sure. However, as predicted by Accumulation Theory (DeFleur & Dennis, 1998), the combination of on-screen, off-screen, and in-print activities work to reinforce the hot Latina stereotype. In an interview, in defense of her role, and as a response to criticism of perpetuating Latina stereotypes, Longoria Parker stated:

> I don't think they're detrimental. It's great to be represented in any way. Ricardo Montalban said something about that in the documentary *The Brown Screen*. He said, "What's wrong with being a Latin Lover? Why is that a bad stereotype? I consider that a compliment." Same thing with Latinas always being cast as the sexy girl. It's a good thing! (oyemag.com/eva.html, 2005)

Summary

Gabrielle is characterized as a strong and willful Cantina Girl/Senorita/Vamp who knows what she wants and goes for it. However, the heroic and role model potential of this character are quickly undermined by this stereotypical presentation imbued with many of the qualities that have, for decades, perpetuated dehumanizing and limiting beliefs about Latinas' morality and potentiality. In Eva Longoria Parker's portrayal of Gabrielle Solis, the Latina stereotype genderizes and racializes physical appearance as well as character development. She is sexy, sultry, promiscuous, sexually experienced (to keep her lover John from seeing another girl, Gabrielle tells him "I can do things to you that she can't even pronounce"), quick tempered, materialistic, devious, desiring, not inclined to work, has an Anglo love interest for whom she will risk almost anything to keep, becomes pregnant quickly, uses her wiles to manipulate men, wears flashy, bright-colored and tight-fitting clothing she hopes people will notice, because "she's worth it." Harris (2005, p. D3) describes Longoria Parker in a way that demonstrates the synthesization of Keller's (1994) Cantina Girl, Suffering Senorita, and Vamp in Gabrielle.

> On the surface, it seems ideal to pair one of Hollywood's most narcissistic actresses with L'Oreal, a company whose slogan is "Because I'm worth it." But, as Longoria's diva reputation worsens—she recently complained that photographers don't fuss over her because she looks good in any light—hawking a product that underscores her vanity is hardly a savvy move. That said, Longoria's $2-million spokes model gig proves that beauty isn't the only thing that defines her life. Having a copious amount of money is meaningful to her, too. (Harris, 2005, p. D3)

Based on this analysis, the role of Gabrielle Solis contributes to and perpetuates long-standing stereotypes of Latinas in American movies and television programs as identified by Keller (1994). Longoria Parker's off-screen activities and antics further reinforce and conflate the character with the person. It is often difficult to determine whether the media are referring to Longoria Parker's character or to her as celebrity when they describe her as a "firecracker" (Fernandez, 2004, p 32), a "hot tempered siren" (Wittstock, 2005, p. 12), and one of the "titular horny homemakers" (FHM.com, 2004, p 1). Referring to Longoria Parker's "coverage" in its October 2004 issue, FHM magazine states, "Given the theme of Eva's new show, it seemed only appropriate that the 29-year-old's FHM photo shoot involved doing domestic work in her delicates. "It wasn't a new experience—that's standard operating procedure in my household," she says. "Who doesn't do housework in their underwear?" (FHM.com, 2004) Referring to her then-upcoming film role opposite Michael Douglas, she said, "I'm excited to not have to wear (just) bras and panties" (Keck, 2005, p. 8). Pre-premier publicity for Longoria Parker's *Sentinel* role tells audiences, "Longoria Parker looks forward to wearing clothes onscreen," and "she's thrilled she won't have to be flashing her flesh as she constantly does in hit TV show *Desperate Housewives*" (p. 8). Flesh flashing is a key component of Longoria Parker's on-screen and press promotion This study of the character Gabrielle Solis in *Desperate Housewives* and self-presentation and media constructions of actor Eva Longoria Parker demonstrate that not only does Gabrielle represent Kellner's typology, but also that Longoria Parker speaks and behaves in ways consistent with that role. Gabrielle is the Cantina Girl—she teases, flirts, is available as a sexual object, wears very high heels, short skirts, large earrings, and red lips. She is the Senorita—she is married, starts out the "good wife," and yet goes bad when she takes on an Anglo love interest who sparks physical violence between Carlos and John. And she is the Vamp. Gabrielle uses her body, her sexuality, and her intelligence in ways that manipulate men to her advantage. She might slip up a few times, but she largely succeeds in getting what she wants whatever the price.

The **representational politics** of Gabrielle/Eva positions the Latina character in a way that functions to provide justification for a narrow perception resulting in a continuation of the hot Latina stereotype. This "mainstreaming" of stereotypical images exists in a climate that supports hegemonic ideals of Anglo (White) heterosexual, male privilege (Gerbner, Gross, Morgan, & Signorielli, 1994). As it largely remains unchallenged by alternative portrayals, the Hot Latina stereotype takes on the appearance of naturalness. Accumulation Theory posits that if the same or similar image or information is presented consistently, persistently, and is corroborated in different media forms, it is likely to have long-term, powerful effects. Stereotyping is one of these effects. The character Gabrielle Solis and the actor Eva Longoria Parker conflate in the public eye, as both on-screen and off-screen women are consistent with one another. If Anglos, by way of media-supplied information, come not to expect much of Latinas and, because of the function of internalized oppression, Latinas do not expect much for themselves, the cycle of oppression continues uninterrupted.

The consequences of perpetuating stereotypes go beyond obvious manifestations such as name-calling or facile characterizations, rather they drive Latina educational challenges and disparities (Hughes, 2004) and contribute to disparate levels of domestic violence (Hyde, 2005; King, 1974), depression, internalized oppression (Román, 2000; Valdivia, 1998, 2000), as well as "distressing legal and societal treatment" (Bender, 2003, p. I). Hence, understanding media-engendered stereotypical images are, at least in part, responsible for the denial of opportunity for Latinas in their struggle for identity.

Questions for Discussion

1. Who are your top five Latina actors?
2. Can you think of other television actors whose on- and off-screen identities seem the same?
3. What roles have you seen Latinas play in movies? On television?
4. Is Carlos' role stereotypical of Latinos?
5. Do the other *Desperate Housewives* characters play stereotypical roles? Are they different than Longoria Parker's in terms of race/gender?

Key Words

Accumulation Theory	Cantina Girl
Carmen Miranda	Critical/resistant reading
Desperate Housewives	Dramaturgical display
Erving Goffman	Eva Longoria Parker
Gabrielle Solis	Hot Latina stereotype
Keller's typology	Latina
Latinidad	Representational politics
Roland Barthes	Suffering Senorita
Tripartite typology of Latina stereotypes	Tropicalization
Vamp	

Endnotes

1. In this chapter the terms "Hispanic," "Latino," "Latina," are used interchangeably as is consistent with marketing, media, and government terminology (Dávila, 2002).
2. Note: She made this announcement before *Maid in Manhattan* (2002) was released.

CHAPTER EIGHT

Commodified Racism: Brand Images of Native Americans

It is the repetitive regularity of the image in movies that refines and reinforces the societal stereotypes. Hollywood provides an endless parade in which we have "good Indians and bad Indians." Almost five hundred tribes, bands, and villages are thus reduced to the homogenized film Indian stereotypes.

Rennard Strickland

While Little Black Sambo and the Frito Bandito have gone the way of minstrel shows, Indians are still battling a red-faced, big-nosed Chief Wahoo and other stereotypes. No wonder people are confused about who Indians really are. When we're not hawking sticks of butter, or beer or chewing tobacco, we're scalping settlers. When we're not passed out drunk, we're living large off casinos. When we're not gyrating in Pocahoochie outfits at the Grammy Awards, we're leaping through the air at football games, represented by a white man in red face. One era's minstrel show is another's halftime entertainment.

Rita Pyrillis

If you are among the 99% non-Indian population and the only source of information you have about American Indians comes from product packages, advertising, and mass media portrayals, what would you conclude about the physical, emotional, and intellectual characteristics of indigenous North Americans? Bloodthirsty savages? Children of nature? Indian princesses? Defilers of White virgins? These are a few of the persistent stereotypes used in the media, particularly in advertising and product **branding** that feature images and attributes of Native Americans. Sue Bee Honey, Land O'Lakes dairy products, and Jeep Cherokee are contemporary examples of the commodification of racist representations. As Rosemary Coombe (1998, p. 186) points out

> From Red Man® chewing tobacco, Indian Spirit® air freshener, Indian-style™ popcorn, teams of Braves®, Red Indian® jeans, Warrior boxes, and Indian heads on everything from baking soda tins and neon beer signs to children's campgrounds, the corporeality of the 'Indian' continues to mark the privileges of the incorporated in commerce.

How and why pictorial metaphors of North American Indians on commercially produced product labels and promotions create and perpetuate commodified stereotypes is the focus of this chapter. In particular, I view these representations in and on consumer goods as a lens through which we can see how race is commodified and how stereotypes are reified. **Grant McCracken's** (1993) **Meaning Transfer Model** and Roland Barthes' (1972) semiotic analysis serve as the framework and method of analysis for four illustrative national **brands**. I expand on McCracken's (1993) framework by acknowledging the role of the viewer in the the process and add a reinforcement loop from the consumer back to the culture in which these stereotypes are constructed, experienced, and recirculated through the American (and global) system of goods and services. Because they are so common and everyday, these products become carriers of stereotypical, racist information that appears so normal and natural in American culture it largely goes unquestioned, thereby serving as a mechanism of **commodified racism**. I argue branding imbues certain products with racialized signifiers. Furthermore, such portrayals support a **White racist ideology** that benefits from the construction and maintenance of "Other" by incorporating racist tropes into commodities.

In the following sections, I briefly present the human developmental process and representational politics that underlie stereotyping in general and the mass media in particular. This is followed by a discussion of the development of stereotypes of Native Americans, leading to an analysis of four national brands that illustrate how the commodification of race works hand in hand with branding to support a system of physical and ideological dominance.

Childhood Development

During early childhood, Indians and non-Indians learn a definition of "Indianness" (Merskin, 2001, p. 159). Around 18 months of age, human beings begin to recognize themselves as distinct and separate beings from their mothers and others (Lacan, 1977). By age six, most attributes of personality formation are already established (Biber, 1984). The content of the information that consciously and unconsciously reaches children is critical for the formation of a healthy, grounded sense of self and respect for others. Today, in the absence of personal interaction with an indigenous person, for example, non-Indian perceptions inevitably come from other sources. These mental images, the "pictures in our heads" as Walter Lippmann (1922/1961, p. 33) calls them, come from parents, teachers, textbooks, movies, television programs, cartoons, songs, commercials, art, and product logos. American Indian images, music, and names have, since the beginning of the 20th century, been incorporated into many American advertising campaigns and marketing efforts, demarcating and consuming Indian as exotic "Other" in the popular imagination (Merskin, 2001). Whereas a century ago sheet music covers and patent medicine bottles featured the "coppery, feather-topped visage of the Indian" (Larson, 1937, p. 338), today's Land O' Lake's butter boxes display a doe-eyed, buckskin clad Indian "princess."

The fact that there never were Indian "princesses" (a European concept), and most Indians do not have the kind of European features and social "availability" that trade characters do, goes largely unquestioned. These stereotypes are pervasive, but not necessarily consistent, varying over time and place from the "artificially idealistic" (noble savage) to images of "mystical environmentalists or uneducated, alcoholic bingo-players confined to reservations" (Mihesuah, 1996, p. 9). Today, a trip down the grocery store aisle still reveals ice cream bars, beef jerky, corn meal, baking powder, malt liquor, butter, honey, sugar, sour cream, chewing tobacco packages, and a plethora of other products emblazoned with images of American Indians. To discern how labels on products and brand names reinforce long-held stereotypical beliefs, we must consider embedded ideological beliefs that perpetuate and reinforce this process.

Representational Politics

As sources of learning, the mass media in general, and advertising in particular, are powerful sites of cultural (re)production where dominant (White male) beliefs about race, ethnicity, sex, and gender (among other "isms") are reinforced and re-circulated. An ideology of White/Anglo racial superiority is maintained in part using stereotypes designed to construct an "Other" who is regarded as lesser-than the declared and constructed ideal. Stereotypes, as hegemonic tools, reduce individuals to a single, monolithic, one-dimensional type that appears, and is presented as, natural and normal as it fits into ideological patterns of representations that serve, among other functions, to establish "in-group categorizations of out-groups" (Ramierez-Berg, 1990, p. 294). Hegemonic beliefs and values are articulated through the construction, maintenance, and perpetuation of stereotypes that

> … get hold of the few simple, vivid, memorable, easily grasped, and widely recognized characteristics about a person, reduce everything about the person to those traits, exaggerate and simplify them, and fix them without change or development to eternity. (Hall, 1997, p. 258)

Oboler (1998, p. 27) writes stereotyping "puts people in boxes and creates images that result in false presumptions accepted as inconvertible truths." Furthermore, stereotypes persist because "they fulfill important identity needs for the dominant culture," thereby maintaining the status quo and preserving hegemony (Mastro & Behm-Morawitz, 2005, p. 112). Rather than using physical force as a social control strategy, hegemony employs psychological strategies that require the consent of those governed. This participation is evident when stereotypical, one-dimensional representations that under other circumstances would seem, at the least, inappropriate and misleading if not all together dangerous and dehumanizing, are normalized.

This naturalization, or as Hall (1997) refers to it, "articulation," is reified through the lack of contradictory images in media representations. The stories the media tell are based on deeply entrenched cultural beliefs and values that cultivate and build support for a system of symbolic representation that benefits the financial, cultural, economic, and social interests of the ruling elite through the reinforcement of racialized heteronormative beliefs and values. DeFleur and Dennis (1998) describe a related concept that offers a partial explanation for the effectiveness of a mediated hegemonic system of social control—Accumulation Theory. This theory predicts, if the mass media, including advertising, present information in ways that are consistent, persistent, and corroborated, it will have long term, powerful effects. Stereotyping, as a media effect, gains power and credibility the longer and more regularly the same information is presented, in the same way, to the same audiences. These (re)presentations remain largely unchallenged, so that carefully cultivated cultural constructions of race, ethnicity, sexuality, and gender become normalized as a "regime of truth" (Coombes, 1998, p. 190) in the American popular imagination. This colonial discourse thereby "fixes otherness in an ideological discourse" by requiring "that which is already known" to be continuously presented, represented, and repeated (p. 191).

Through the use of specific signs and symbols, articulated in particular words and images, racial/ethnic and sexual stereotypes draw strength from a shared cultural reservoir of thought-to-be-truths about particular groups of people. Based on a history of cultural, social, and psychological infusion of one-dimensional and distorted presentations of qualities (or lack thereof) these "truths" serve the interests of those in power who aim to retain their status and resources.

The maintenance of stereotypical beliefs also satisfies the human need for psychological equilibrium and order, finding support and reinforcement in ideology that distinguishes an "us" from a symbolic "them." Defined as "typical properties of the 'social mind' of a group" (van Dijk, 1996, p. 56), ideologies provide a frame of reference for understanding the world. *Racist* ideology functions psychologically, socially, and politically to reproduce racism by legitimating social inequalities, thereby justifying racially or ethnically constructed differences. **Racist ideology** serves three primary purposes, according to van Dijk: (1) it organizes specific social attitudes into an evaluative framework for perceiving otherness, (2) it provides the basis for "coordinated action and solidarity among Whites," and (3) it defines racial and ethnic identity of the dominant group (1996, p. 257). These beliefs and practices are thereby articulated in the production and distribution of racist discourse, the result of which, in this study, "is the creation of distance between the 'real' Indian and a manufactured replica of an Indian stereotype" (Staurowsky, 1998, p. 304).

One-dimensional racial and ethnic images became deeply entrenched in American popular culture and thought and have not disappeared. Instead, they have become naturalized into our visual environment. This system of representation has thereby become a "stable cultural convention...taught and learned by members of...society" (Kates & Shaw-Garlock, 1999, p. 34) as a mythological narrative of a romanticized past.

Goings' (1994) study of African American stereotypes and Black **collectibles** and **memorabilia** from the 1880s to the 1950s is a useful analogy for understanding the construction of Native American stereotypes in popular culture. So-called "collectible" items such as salt and pepper shakers, trade cards, and sheet music with images of happy Sambos, plump mammies, and wide-eyed pickaninnies served as nonverbal articulations of racism made manifest in everyday goods. By exaggerating the physical features of African American men and women and making them comical and powerless, seemingly banal household objects reinforced beliefs about the place of Blacks in American society. Aunt Jemima, the roly-poly mammy, and Uncle Rastus, the happy chef slave on the Cream of Wheat box, ironically remain with us today. Both were and are used to help make Whites feel more comfortable with, and less guilty about, maintenance of distinctions based on race well after reconstruction (Manring, 1998). These items were meant for daily use, hence constantly circulated, subtly reinforcing stereotypical beliefs, later articulated in mass-produced goods. Leonard (2005, p. 14) notes, "From pancakes and breakfast cereal to alcoholic beverages and sports apparel, businesses have historically used a palpable blackness defined by either clownish qualities or physical control to draw in White consumers." Goings (1994, p. xix) adds

> [that it] is important to note Black memorabilia are figures from white American history. White Americans developed the stereotypes; white Americans produced the collectibles; and white American manufacturers and advertisers disseminated both the images and the objects to a white audience.

Defining Indian-ness

Whereas "Little Black Sambo" tales reinforced the construction of racist beliefs about Blacks, songs such as "Ten Little Indians" or "Cowboy and Indian" games similarly framed Indian otherness in the White mind. Moreover, "the essence of the white image of the Indian has been the definition of American Indians in fact and in fancy as a separate and single other. Whether evaluated as noble or ignoble, whether seen as exotic or downgraded, the Indian as image was always alien to white" (Berkhofer, 1979, p. xv). Context is key. Anti-Indian sentiments did not begin with the subjugation and dislocation efforts of the 1800s. Rather, three major economic, social, and political movements or "fateful encounters" (Goings, 1994, p. 332) mark points in time when the "West encountered" Indian people, "giving rise to an avalanche of popular representations based on the marking of racial difference." First, 15th-century contact between European traders and explorers and the contamination and conquest of indigenous peoples on the North American continent. Second, European colonization of the Americas and the scramble for control of territories, markets, and raw materials, and third, pre- and post-Civil War migrations from the eastern United States to the west.

This cumulative evolution leads to the present with entrenched stereotypical alterity resulting in legal, medical, economic, and educational disparities. White images of Native Americans were similarly constructed through children's games, toys, tales, art, sculpture, and theater of the 1800s. The cigar store Indian, for example, presents the stoic, static noble savage, with a hand extended and offering, simultaneously "guarding" the entrance and exit to the store and complying with White rules. Similarly, the Indian "princess" conveys natural, wholesome, virginity, and freshness.

Thus, in the case of Native American portrayals, the wide array of individual qualities, experiences, histories, and characteristics are truncated by stereotyping into a single Pan-Indian identity based on a unilateral conception of "Indian-ness" (Merskin, 2001, p. 159). Consistently repeated representations have power as "these are the ideas we have been hearing for a long time and that we've ended up believing out of truth, custom, or repetition" (Dávila, 2001, p. 56).

In the 19th and 20th centuries, American Southwest and Niagara Falls tourism, as two examples, cashed in on the commodification of indigenous cultures as both spectacle and souvenir (Dubinsky, 1999). The Native community near Niagara Falls, for example, made available the spectacle of race because their lived experience often disappointed tourists in whose minds "Indians" "were supposed to be anachronistically suspended. The simultaneous sales of fake "Indian" artifacts and contempt for Indians-as-Other—culminated in romanticization of, enchantment with, and appropriation of the cultural trappings of the other or, as Rosaldo (1989, p. 109) calls it, "**imperialist nostalgia**." This so-called kitsch

> … reinscribed the power relations between triumphing tourist and subordinate Other. The reading of a sexually alluring Native woman into the Falls was a version of the eroticization of the unfamiliar, the feminization of Nature, common among European explorers and adventurers. (Dubinsky, 1999, p. 14)

While not in possession of this male gaze, female tourists, according to Dubinsky (1999, p. 14), "were no different from male tourists in their disdain for the racialized and economically marginalized others whose subservient labor made the very experience of tourism possible." As this example shows, these portrayals are consistent and persistent across media. Taken together, these studies suggest historically constructed images of and beliefs about American Indians are the core of stereotypical thinking and have been smoothly and easily translated into product images in a way that appears normal and natural and is at the root of commodified racism.

Advertising, Branding, and Commodity Racism

> No one knows the land like a Navajo. (Advertisement for 1991 Mazda Navajo truck)

Advertising

To every advertisement they see or hear, people bring a shared set of beliefs that serve as frames of reference for understanding the world around them. Beyond the obvious selling function, advertising images are about making meaning. Ads must "take into account not only the inherent qualities and attributes of the products they are trying to sell, but also the way in which they can make those properties mean something to us" (Williamson, 1978, p. 12). Barthes (1972) describes these articulations as myth, as "a type of speech" or mode of signification conveyed by discourse consisting of many possible modes of representation including, but not limited to, writing, photography, publicity, and advertising. Myth described by the process of semiology, "postulates a relation between two terms, a signifier and a signified" (p. 112). The correlation of the terms signifier, signified, and sign describes how associative meaning is made. What is experienced in an advertisement or product label are basic elements composed of linguistic signs (words) and iconic signs (visuals). Barthes uses a rose, for example, as a symbol of passion. Roses are not passion per se, but rather the roses (signifier) plus the concept of passion (signified) result in roses (sign). He states "the signifier is empty, the sign is full, it is a meaning" (1972, p. 113).

An example using race is the "savage" stereotype as mascot for the Florida State Seminoles football team or the University of Illinois Fighting Illini. The representation of an evil, angry generic Indian drawn from literary and photographic sources of earlier times suggests the savage (signified) has an immediate, obvious connection to the product—football and sports (King, 1998, 2001). However, savage-as-signifier of death, vengeance, evil, and rage, when placed on a t-shirt (sign), transfers meaning to the otherwise ambiguous product. The sign is formed at the intersection between the image, brand name, and meaning system articulated in a particular product. Quite simply, a sign, whether "object, word, or picture," has a "particular meaning to a person or group of people. It is neither the thing nor the meaning alone, but the two together" (Williamson, 1978, p. 17). So, to White consumers, the primary target audience, the product and image make sense, based on a collective history of defining Indian people in a one-dimensional way. When these views are not contradicted by other information, or alternative views are not provided, the stereotypes persist, full of hegemonic potential.

Branding

McCracken (1993, p. 125) defines a brand as a "bundle or container of meaning." He expanded on the Barthesian analysis and developed a framework for understanding the cultural relationship brands have within society. For example, a brand can have gendered meaning (maleness/femaleness), social standing (status), nationality (country meaning), and ethnicity/race (multicultural meaning). A brand can also stand for notions of tradition, trustworthiness, purity, family, nature, and so on. McCracken (1993) uses the Marlboro man as an example of these components with which a simple red and white box came to signify freedom, satisfaction, competence, maleness, and a quintessentially American, Western character. The product becomes part of the constellation of meanings that surround it and thereby "soaks up" meanings. When the rugged Marlboro man is situated on his horse, on the open plain, almost always alone, the meaning constellation becomes clear: he is freedom, love of the outdoors, release from the confines of industrialized society, he is a "real man," self-sufficient and individualistic. The meanings become part of a theme comprised of prototypical content while simultaneously being "idealizations and not reality itself" (Schmitt & Simonson, 1997, p. 124). McCracken's (1993) Meaning Transfer Model shows how brands assume meaning through advertising (Figure 8.1). Advertisements as vehicles of branding are used to boost the commodity value of product names by connecting them to images that resonate with the social and cultural values of a society. These images are loaded with established ideological assumptions that, when attached to a brand, create the commodity sign. Tools of branding are thereby used to draw upon and create a particular image in the mind of the consumer.

Advertising and branding are mechanisms through which visual and verbal discourse is distributed and "all successful brands have an underlying cognitive value...a cluster of attributes and associations that consumers connect to the brand name" (Ellwood, 2002, p. 71). Consistently, the American advertising industry has successfully employed racist "constructs and deploy[ed] racialized tropes and images in its efforts to sell a vision" (Leonard, 2005, p. 15). According to van Dijk (1996, p. 267), this pattern often serves to present an "us" versus "them" dichotomy, with "us" being White, "positive, tolerant, and modern," and "them" being minorities who are "problematic, deviant, and threatening." Hence, attitudes, beliefs, and behavior that are racist serve to support a dominant ideology that focuses on difference and separatism.

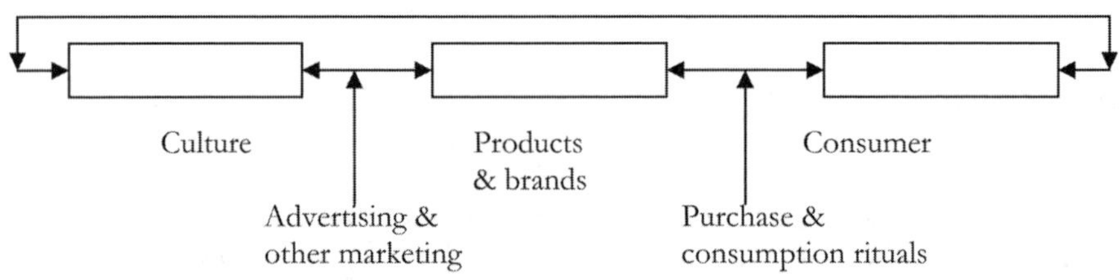

Fig. 8.1: Meaning Transfer Model

Source: G. McCracken, 1993

Commodity racism

An explanation for the persistent use of these images is found in the power and persuasiveness of popular culture representations. Simply put, they work. At the end of the 19th century, scientific racism transmogrified into commodity racism. Whereas scientific racism is "embodied in anthropological, scientific, and medical journals, travel writing and ethnographies," commodity racism, while also reflecting the narrative of White racial superiority, is translated into "mass produced consumer spectacles" (McClintock, 1995, p. 33). This was initially accomplished through photography. Raced bodies in 19th century ads, just like idealized White female bodies, were presented as decoration and illustration and "figured not as historic agents but as frames for the community, valued for *exhibition* alone" (p. 223).

Just as pseudo-scientific information provides support and rationale for male "superiority," so too photography in advertising provides "evidence" of Native "inferiority" without the requirement of literacy. Regarded as a "dying race," Native Americans were romanticized reminders of America's past (Domash, 2004, p. 7). Products such as Ivory Snow advertised using stereotypical dark caricatures designed to demonstrate how effective the soap was in washing away "ignorance and war," thereby fixing categories of difference between White and other cultures (p. 8). By fetishizing the product, in this case soap, the advertising promised "spiritual salvation and regeneration through commodity consumption" (McClintock, 1995, p. 211) and accomplished this by employing "racialized notions of empire" with images of removing, washing away darkness, blackness, and "color" (Mansvelt, 2005, p. 39). The Pears soap campaign of the time became famous for images of the blackness of little Black boys washing away by using the soap, "as if magically erasing the racial degeneration of Blackness" (Darian-Smith, 2002, p. 186).

Two "dialectally related forms of consciousness—scientific and commodity racism"—are tied to the transference of oppressive energy. The first is closely related to Said's (1978) concept of **Orientalism** and **Michel Foucault's** (1977) colonial **"power-knowledge" paradigm** wherein intellectual colonization is also tool of oppression, one that presupposes the role of "fiduciary of all knowledge" (Doxater, 2004, p. 618). The second occurred "in the specific forms of advertising and photography, the imperial Exhibitions, and the museum movement" (McClintock, 1995, p. 33). This form of racial narrative demonstrated the transition of "the narrative of imperial Progress into mass-produced spectacle" because "advertising translated *things* into a fantasy visual display consisting of signs and symbols" (p. 33). This process moved imperialist discourse from the arena of scientific publications and clubs to that of the commercial and domestic spheres.

McClintock (1995, p. 220) shows how commodity racism "was not just reflective of how the larger society's racism showed up in ads but also deeply constitutive of the very ways in which Whites connected race, pleasure, and service." A commodity occurs "on the threshold between culture and commerce, confusing the supposedly sacrosanct boundaries between aesthetics and economy, money and art" (p. 212). The resultant images and text draw upon the "collective unconscious" residing in a symbolic reservoir that revitalizes the latent racist point of view that exists just below the surface of conscious memory (Jung in Shamdasani, 2003, p. 340). At the same time, the advertising industry discovered that by manipulating "the semiotic space" around a commodity it simultaneously manipulated the "unconscious as a public space" (McClintock, 1995, p. 213).

In this way, the Native American portrayals served as a frame valued for its ability to do the associative work between signifier and signified. Semiotics provides the method with which we can explore the signs and symbols used to tease out the process of signification by doing a close reading of them as cultural text. Thus, four currently available national products (Land O'Lakes dairy products, Sue Bee Honey, Big Chief [Michigan] Sugar, and Crazy Horse Malt Liquor) are used to illustrate the racial commodification process, two featuring men, and two featuring women.

The Land O'Lakes maiden

Although not the first national manufacturer to draw on the mystique of Indian-ness (that honor goes to Redman Tobacco in 1904), Land O'Lakes continues to be perhaps the most prominent. In 1921, the Minnesota Cooperative Creameries Association opened for business in Arden Hills, Minnesota. This company served as the central shipping agent for a small group of small, farmer-owned dairy cooperatives (Morgan, 1986, p. 63). In 1924, the group wanted a different name and solicited ideas from farmers. Two came up with the winning name Land O'Lakes, "a tribute to Minnesota's thousands of sparkling lakes."

Until recently, the corporate Web site (www.landolakes.com) opened with a photograph of a quiet lake amid pine trees and blue sky (Merskin, 2001, p. 164). The copy under the image read

> Welcome to Land O'Lakes. A land unlike anywhere else on earth. A special place filled
> with clear, spring-fed lakes. Rivers and streams that dance to their own rhythms through
> rich, fertile fields. It's the land we call home. And from it has flowed the bounty and
> goodness we bring to you, our neighbors and friends.

In addition, the text tells us, "The now famous Indian maiden was also created during the search for a brand name and trademark. Because the regions of Minnesota and Wisconsin were the legendary lands of Hiawatha and Minnehaha, the idea of an Indian maiden took form" (Land O'Lakes). A painting was sent to the company of an Indian maiden facing the viewer, holding a butter carton with a background filled with lakes, pines, flowers, and grazing cows.

Today, the home page opens with recipe information, monthly updates, and the headline image of the classic butter-box maiden and the text "Where simple goodness begins."

At the Land O'Lakes corporate link, the director of communications includes a statement about the maiden image, where he agrees the logo, the "Indian Maiden," has powerful connotations (Land O'Lakes). Hardly changed since its introduction in the 1920s, he says Land O'Lakes has built on the "symbolism of the purity of the products" (Burnham, 1992, p. E1). The company "thought the Indian maiden would be a good image. She represents Hiawatha and the Land of Gitchygoomee and the names of Midwest towns and streets have their roots in the American Indian population" (p. E1).

The signifier is thereby the product, be it butter, sour cream, or other Land O'Lakes products, and the motto "… simple goodness." The Indian woman on the package is associated with youth, innocence, nature, and purity. The result is the generic "Indian maiden." Subsequently, the qualities stereotypically associated with this beaded, buckskinned, doe-eyed young woman are transferred to the company's products. Green's (1993) "noble savage" image is extended to include the female stereotype.

Sue Bee honey

The Sioux Honey Association, based in Sioux City, Iowa, is a cooperative of honey producers, yielding 40 million pounds of honey annually (Sioux Honey). Corporate communications describe a change of the product name in 1964 from Sioux Bee to Sue Bee, "to reflect the correct pronunciation of the name" (Sioux Honey). The brand name and image are reinforced on trucks (both real and toy), on the bottles and jars in which the honey is sold, and through collectibles such as coffee mugs and recipe books.

Sue Bee Honey also draws upon the child-of-nature imagery in an attempt to imbue qualities of purity into their products. If we were to view Sue Bee in her full form (as she is shown on many specialty items such as mugs, glasses, and jars) we would see that she is an Indian maiden on top, with braided hair and headband, and a bee below the waist. Changing the spelling of her name from "Sioux Bee" to "Sue Bee" could be interpreted in a variety of ways, possibly, as a matter of pronunciation as the company asserts or as an effort to draw attention away from the savage imagery stereotypically attributed to members of this tribe and toward the little-girlishness of the image. In this case, the product is honey, a paradisiacal product, traditionally associated with trees and forests and natural places. The homepage for Sue Bee Honey opens with the image of "Sue" and the words "Pure Delight. Mornings are sweeter with natural, pure Sue Bee Honey. The one more Americans pick" (Sioux Honey). The association of purity, virginity, availability, and naturalness works seamlessly with the girl child Indian stereotype. By placing the girl-bee on the package of honey, consumers can associate the innocence, purity, and naturalness attributed to stereotypical Native American females with the quality of the product.

In the tradition of Pocahontas and Sacajawea, both the Land O'Lakes and the Sue Bee maidens symbolize innocence, purity, and virginity of children of nature. The maiden image signifies a female "Indianness" (Merskin, 2001, p. 159). She is childlike, as she happily offers up perhaps honey or butter (or herself) that "is as pure and healthy as she is" (Dotz & Morton, 1996, p. 11). The maiden's image is used to represent attempts to embody nature, and association can accomplish this through the healthy, wholesome products of Land O'Lakes. Both images are encoded with socially constructed meanings about female Indian sexuality, purity, and nature, reinforcing the "proper place" of the subservient Native Woman: on her knees, legless, offering a pelvic honey pot or stick of butter for the taking.

Chief Sugar

Founded in 1901, the Michigan Sugar Company (michigansugar.com) processes approximately 4% of U.S. beet production into sugar (granulated, powdered, brown, and icing). For 60 years, the company has been producing sugar from beets, relying on a profile image of an American Indian in full-feathered headdress to sell the sugar goods. The products are available on grocery store shelves and in bulk for institutions, delivered by trucks with the Big Chief logo emblazoned on the sides. So, who does this Chief represent? Is he a legitimate tribal leader or a composite Indian designed to communicate naturalistic characteristics associated with Indians with the sugar? He shares the richness and abundance of the soil, and his presence implies and assures a natural "purity" and authority to the product. Green's (1993) savage typology suggests this individual is a combination of the noble savage (natural) and the bloodthirsty savage (ferocious). He is proud, noble, and natural, yet he is wearing a ceremonial headdress that communicates strength, stoicism, and authority.

Crazy Horse Malt liquor

A 40-ounce beverage that is sold in approximately 40 states (Metz & Thee, 1994), Crazy Horse Malt Liquor is brewed by the Heilman Brewing Company of

Brooklyn, New York. The company employs the image of Tasunke Witko (Crazy Horse) on the label The Malt Liquor. On the front of the bottle is the image of an American Indian man wearing a headdress that appears to be an eagle feather bonnet, and there is a symbol representing a medicine wheel of both sacred images in Lakota and other Native cultures. Image analysis shows the sign is that of an actual Indian chief and is therefore an icon. Signified, however, are beliefs about Indians as warriors, westward expansion, how mighty the consumer might be by drinking this brand, and wildness of the American Western frontier.

This brand, perhaps more than any other, has come under public scrutiny because it is the image of a particular person. A revered ancestor of the Oglala Sioux tribe of South Dakota, Crazy Horse died in 1877 (Blalock, 1992). The labels feature the prominent image of Chief Crazy Horse, who has long been the subject of stories, literature, and movies. Larger than life, he has played a role in American mythology.

Signifying Green's (1993) bloodthirsty savage image, Crazy Horse Malt Liquor makes use of American myths through image and association. Ironically, Crazy Horse objected to alcohol and warned his nation about the destructive effects of liquor (Specktor, 1995). As a sign, Crazy Horse represents a real person and symbol of early American life and westward expansionism. He was, according to the vice president of the Oglala Sioux Tribe, a "warrior, a spiritual leader, a traditional leader, a hero who has always been and is still revered by our people" (Hill, 1992; Metz & Thee, 1994, p. 50). This particular image brings together concise aspects of branding. Not only are the noble and bloodthirsty savage stereotypes brought together in a proud, but also ultimately defeated, Indian chief, but also this is an image of a real human being. The association of alcohol with that image, as well as targeting the Indian population, draws on assumptions of alcohol abuse.

Summary

Although there are dozens of Native images on product labels, ranging from cigarette packages to sports utility vehicles, the examples discussed above illustrate the principles behind semiotics. The four presented here are significant examples of national brands employing stereotypical representations. When people become aware of these products, they realize how these images consistently employ Indian stereotypes either in product names or in their logos. Many of these signs and symbols have been with us so long we no longer question them. Product images on packages, in advertisements, on television, in films, and sports mascots are usually the only images of Native Americans seen by non-Indians. We accept the covers of romance novels routinely featuring Indian men sweeping beautiful non-Indian women off their feet as their bodices tear away. These stereotypical representations of Natives deny humanity and present them as existing only in the past as single, monolithic Indians (Merskin, 1998).

American Indians are certainly not the only racial or ethnic group to be discriminated against, overtly or covertly. Aunt Jemima and Rastus certainly have their origins in dehumanizing, one-dimensional images based on a tragic past. Yet, like Betty Crocker, these images have been updated. Aunt Jemima has lost weight and the bandana, and the Frito Bandito has disappeared (Burnham, 1992). Nevertheless, the Indian image persists in corporate marketing and product labeling. An Absolut Vodka ad shows an Eskimo pulling a sled of vodka and a Grey Owl Wild Rice package features an Indian with braids, wearing a single feather, surrounded by a circle that represents (according to Grey Owl's distribution manager) the "oneness of nature" (Burnham, 1992, p. E1). A partial list of others includes Apache helicopter, Jeep Cherokee, Apache rib doormats, Red Man Tobacco, Kleek-O the Eskimo (Cliquot Club ginger ale), Dodge Dakota, Pontiac, the Cleveland Indians, Mutual of Omaha, Calumet Baking Powder, Mohawk Carpet Mills, American Spirit cigarettes, Eskimo pies, Tomahawk mulcher, Winnebago Motor Homes, Indian Motorcycles, Tomahawk missiles, many high school sports teams, and the music behind the Hamm's beer commercials that begins "From the land of sky blue waters."

Change is coming, albeit slowly. In 2000, British Petroleum Company changed the name of the largest-ever oil and gas find in the Gulf of Mexico from Crazy Horse to Thunder Horse after Tasunke Witko's (Crazy Horse) family approached the company. The name seemed harmless to the public, but "it proved offensive to the descendants of the Sioux war hero, who prohibit use of the name except during prayer or during meetings of the inner circle of Crazy Horse's family" (Crazy Horse).

In 2001, Stroh Brewing Company (who purchased bankrupt Heilman Breweries) settled with the Rosebud Reservation and Witko's descendents (Coombes, 1998). Company President John Stroh III journeyed to the reservation, offered a formal apology to the Nation, and gifted the estate with

> 32 Pendleton blankets, 32 braids of sweet grass, and 32 twists of tobacco (one for each of the 32 states in which the malt liquor is distributed). Stroh's also presented the Estate and the Rosebud Sioux Tribe with seven thoroughbred race horses (one for each of the seven bottling facilities). (Crazy Horse)

Still, despite requests from Crazy Horse's descendents (Walker, 2004), a Paris nude bar continues to be named Crazy Horse (Walker, 2004), as does a Liz Claiborne clothing line sold at J.C. Penney (Rave, 2003). Tootsie Rolls still carry the image of the Savage Chief (Smith, 2002, p. 27) on their wrappers and plastic cowboy and Indian figures, "this nation's most passionate, embedded form of hate talk," are still available for children's play (Yellow Bird, 2004, p. 42). One reason change is so difficult is that American Indians are not a significant target audience to advertisers. Representing less than 1% of the population, and the most economically destitute of all ethnic minority populations, American Indians are not particularly useful to marketers. Nearly 30% live below the official poverty line, in contrast with 13% of the general U.S. population (Cortese, 1999, p. 117). Without the population numbers or legal resources, it is nearly impossible for the voices of Natives to be heard, unlike other groups who have made some representational inroads. According to Westerman (1989, p. 28), when minority groups speak, businesses are beginning to listen: "That's why 'Lil Black Sambo' and the Frito Bandito are dead. They were killed by the very ethnic groups they portrayed."

Not only does stereotyping communicate inaccurate beliefs about Natives to Whites, but also to Indians. Children, Native American included, are perhaps the most important recipients of this information. If, during the transition of adolescence, Native children internalize these representations that suggest Indians are lazy, obligated to "willingly" provide their native/natural bounty to Whites, are alcoholic by nature, and violent, this misinformation can have a lifelong impact on perceptions of self and others. As Lippmann (1922/1961, p. 89) wrote, "The subtlest and most pervasive of all influences are those which create and maintain the repertory of stereotypes. We are told about the world before we see it. We imagine most things before we experience them." By playing a game of substitution, by inserting other ethnic groups or races into the same advertisement, the problem is clear. Stereotypical images do not reside only in the past, because the social control mechanisms that helped to create them remain with us today. Instead, they have gone mainstream, working smoothly through media and popular culture representations, relying on connotative understandings deeply rooted in the collective unconscious. Manring (1998, p. 181), drawing on the remarks of Eldridge Cleaver, refers to this phenomenon as "the secret of Aunt Jemima's bandana." Just as the bandana-clad mammy situated White male desires for the proper place of Black and White women, in the case of Native Americans, race and gender are similarly used tools through which advertisers reify stereotypical images of savages and princesses and ensconce them safely in the past to fulfill their proper roles as historical relics. Howard Adams (2004, quoted in Yellow Bird, p. 1) points out the consequences of this discourse

> The colonizer's falsified stories have become universal truths to mainstream society, and have reduced Aboriginal culture to a caricature. This destroyed reality is one of the most

powerful shackles subjugating Aboriginal people. It distorts all Indigenous experiences, past and present, and blocks the road to self-determination.

Commodified racism, as articulated in stereotypical representations in advertising and branding, works to maintain the values, ideals, and controls of mainstream White society. By pulling back the curtain, the camouflage, surrounding the everydayness of these portrayals, they become visible and can be changed.

Questions for Discussion

1. What is your first memory of seeing an American Indian in a film? In news?
2. Name your top five favorite Native American actors.
3. Can you think of another way Land O'Lakes might label their products that would still convey pure and natural but not use the image of a Native American?
4. What are some other images of human beings on products in the grocery store? Do these differ in any way from those of American Indians in numbers or styles?
5. Is the history of a people relevant to whether or not representations are problematic?

Key Words

Brand	Branding
Collectibles	Commodified Racism
Imperialist nostalgia	McCracken, Grant
Meaning Transfer Model	Memorabilia
Michel Foucault	Power-knowledge paradigm
Racist ideology	White racist ideology

 # The Pornographic Gaze in Mainstream American Magazine and Fashion Advertising

Being aroused to go out and purchase a lipstick or a car is definitely more acceptable than being sexually aroused. Seems you can't use sex to sell sex, but you can quite happily use sex to sell stuff.

Squires

We don't mind nudity if there is a very good reason for it, such as sex, bathing, or autopsy. The problem is, advertising seldom presents a very good reason for it.

Bob Garfield

The basic Female Body comes with the following accessories: garter belt, panti girdle, crinoline, bustle, brassiere, stomacher, chemise, virgin zone, spike heels, nose ring, veil, kid gloves, fish-net stockings, fichu, bandeau, Merry Widow, weepers, chokers, barrettes, bangles, beads, lorgnette, feather boa, basic black, compact Lycra stretch one-piece with modesty panel, designer peignoir, flannel nighties, lace teddy, bed head.

Margaret Atwood

She looks at you straight in the eye…defiantly, suggestively. Her thin arms hang loosely by her sides. She stands with legs apart, light shinning through her golden gauze-like gown…her wet hair drips down her shoulders and between her breasts. She knows you are looking at her…watching her perform for you. Just for you. Sounds like a scene straight out of **pornography** doesn't it? The truth is, this image is from a recent advertisement for clothing that ran in a *New York Times Magazine* fashion spread.

While Freud declared anatomy to be destiny, attraction is more complicated than repressed urges and drives. In fact, every society's vision of destiny (articulated through its mythology, social attitudes, cultural traditions) forms the basis for its understanding of the body and, by extension, sexuality. Whether in fashion, art, or advertising photography, representations of nude or semi-nude women are common and powerful cultural icons in the expression of sexual expectations, roles, and relations. Using female sexuality to sell clothing conflates capitalism and consumption and expresses it using popular mythology. The sexual sell of women's bodies in advertising is adjunct to the discussion of the social "control of women's bodies by men under a system of patriarchy" (Turner, 1984, p. 3). This includes framing and control of female sexuality.

As Berger (2000) points out "sexuality, sexual desire, sexual lust, and even intimations of sexual intercourse are fairly ubiquitous in contemporary advertising." **Advertising** depends heavily on the use of symbols, colors, and allusion to create parallels with the (implied male) spectator's world, presenting it in ways that seem natural and normal, hence plausible. "One of the most deeply seated traits of man, it is felt, is gender; femininity and masculinity are in a sense the prototypes of essential expression—something that strikes at the most basic characteristics of the individual" (Goffman, 1979, p. 7). By constructing what is "**feminine**," as discussed in Chapter 4, the media contribute to cultural discourse that defines gender differences in ways that support the dominant ideology of male dominance (patriarchy). Advertising is obsessed with gender and sexuality because "gender is one of our deepest and most important traits as human beings," and it "can be communicated at a glance (almost instantly)" because of our understanding of how advertising presents a view of the world (Jhally, 1990, p. 135). The world presented in fashion advertising is one of power, sexuality, and the sell. Foucault (1980) says, "the body is given meaning and wholly constituted by discourse. The body vanishes as a biological entity and becomes instead a socially constituted product which is infinitely malleable and highly unstable."

Under the guise of fashion (and the presence or absence of clothing), the fashioned body in advertising thus is marked with and inscribed by the culture and power relations within which it is presented. Fashion, and associated advertising, is thereby the material embodiment of ethnic, racial, and gender identities, as well as a staged performance of beauty, of health, and furthermore, it is a process, and "a way of knowing and marking the world, as well as a way of knowing and marking a 'self'" (Balsamo, 1995, p. 5).

A **feminist approach** is one that recognizes the situatedness of gender as a political construct. This perspective, which is both theoretical and methodological, "grounds women's sexuality in purely relational terrain, anchoring women's power and accounting for women's discontent in the same world they stand against" (McKinnon, 1991, p. 119) and is used in this chapter in which select, illustrative fashion advertisements from ordinary fashion magazines (such as *W, Elle,* and *Vogue*) are examined through the lens of Kuhn's (1985) Conventions of Photographic Pornography. The results show how particular production elements, such as the direct gaze, use of **objectification**, positional **hierarchy** of models, and violence present women in fashion ads in ways very much like they do in what is traditionally regarded as pornographic.

It is the goal of this chapter, through the use of examples, to show how pornographication of fashion advertising constructs a **pornographic stereotype.** It is stereotypical in that women are treated as the same, are one dimensional and valued only for their appearance. The pornographic aspect transcends pure image to include sexualized dehumanization, referencing race, ethnicity, and consumption. This stereotype is part of ongoing representations of sex role stereotypes, such as occupation and unrealistic standards of beauty, with over-generalized representations of female sexual availability that construct women as one-dimensional objects of male power.

The first section of this chapter briefly explores fashion advertising photography, followed by a discussion of definitions of pornography and definitions of advertising. The concluding section is an analysis and description of illustrative fashion advertisements that convey the pornographic stereotype.

The findings of this study reveal the assumptions within the anonymity and mystery that surround advertising and assist with "demystifying the images that parade before our lives" (Jhally, 1995, p. 86). From a feminist perspective, describing the persistent and pervasive stereotypes in fashion advertising images helps preserve women's hard-earned freedoms. These images in advertising are loaded with hegemonic potential. By not seeming unusual to us, the proliferation of these images gains acceptance by appearing to be normal reflections of heterosexuality.

Fashioning Advertising

Fashion is "a catalyst of popular culture and the reflection of the tenor of a period, the fashion photograph influences and is influenced by not only dress but also music, film, video, street culture, and art" (Wilkes, 1991, p. 1). Photography, as the current medium of expression of fashion advertising, lends a quality of **visual truth** to what we see (Newton, 2001). According to Kuhn (1985), "photography draws on an ideology of the visible as evidence. Whereas the eye of the camera is neutral, it sees the world as it is: we look at a photograph and see a slice of the world." Thus, seeing becomes a circuit of visibility and truth—someone is looking and someone is being looked at and that the exchange feels natural because it appears in everyday media.

Fashion photography and, by extension, fashion advertising have historically transgressed moral boundaries of what is commonly regarded as "appropriate." What passes for fashion advertising today would have been considered inappropriate for a general audience a few years ago. Why? According to *Advertising Age* editor Scott Danton, "it's not about advertising. It's about being noticed" (Ingrassia, 2000). "Sexuality provides a resource that can be used to get attention and communicate instantly" (Jhally, 1990, p. 5) and enables advertisers to rise above the clutter. Sex is an attention-getter and in "a particularly competitive and expansive era for American marketing, advertisers like to be on a sure thing—nothing cuts through the clutter like sex" (Solomon, 1990, p. 69). Very often sex, particularly female sex, is used to sell, whether or not the product is related to the body, "women…are used to sell everything from automobiles to toothpaste" (Asa Berger, 2000, p. 57). Sometimes it is difficult in fact to find the product in the ads, "sublimating product illustration to the creation of an independently arresting image" (Harrison, 1991, p. 248).

Fashion advertising presents a good opportunity to explore the relationship between portrayals of women's bodies since clothing has a natural relationship to bodies. Clothing, by virtue of its presence or absence, is a form of social communication that not only reflects culture but also marks "meaningful differences between categories" (Sahlins, 1976, p. 185). "Sex sells," says fashion historian Valerie Steele (1991, p. 81), and "sex ought to be even more effective at selling fashion, which is about bodies as much as it is about clothes." However, in recent years, many readers are asking of ads, "where are the clothes?" to (Brown, 2001, p. 162).

Selling it

After the economic and social liberation of the 1960s, advertisers were hot to move the line a bit further, waiting in the wings for permission to go ahead. In the 1970s, advertising agencies "commanded budgets large enough to hire flawlessly beautiful models, photographers had the technical finesse to place them in flattering light, and magazines finally possessed the requisite how-to to lend them a high gloss color" (Köhler, 1995, p. 129). The only hesitation was how far they could take **sex appeal** before "consumer stimulation gave way to aversion" since "the sex appeal of naked skin is one of the most irresistible stimuli to buying" (Köhler, 1995, p. 129).

While fashion photography has always dallied on the line between erotica and soft porn, fashion advertising tends to travel a slightly more restrained path. That is, until the 1970s when widely available birth control pills and a reinvigorated women's rights movement resulted in more openness toward female sexuality while simultaneously threatening patriarchal society. By relegating women to pejorative presentations that rely on nudity and semi-nudity, fashion advertising draws upon a long tradition in art and photography that reinforces societal beliefs about male superiority.

Representing a powerful element in the reinforcement of social mores, the media in general and advertising in particular construct gender difference in a way that appears to be a reflection of reality. Essentially, these messages are about power—reinforcing the existing power structure that relegates women and children to the position of other. No longer simply about presenting the body "in its most desirable and healthy form in order to sell a product, fashion photography is now an essential artistic medium which is highly semiotically charged and is increasingly self-reflexive and shocking" (Power, 2001). Fashion photographer Vince Alleti (1999, n.p.) points out how fashion advertising is, today, at a critical point, "this is truly a fashion moment. Perhaps because it has little to do with traditional ideas of beauty and even less to do with documenting a garment, fashion photography has never looked as smart, eccentric, inventive or as perverse."

While "the worlds of fashion and photography have been heavy petting for decades," the recent full-blown "explosion of pornography into the realm of mainstream fashion has given way to a new, transgressive glamour" (Browne, 2001, p. 162). The fashion industry is replete with information about how we, in particular, women, should look, should interact with others, and what we should buy to accomplish these goals. "Fashion magazines such as *Vogue* present images of women's bodies which tell us, as Goffman phrases it, "what our nature ought to be and how and when this nature ought to be exhibited" (Goffman, 1979, p. 225). Examples include the photographic work of Irving Penn, Helmut Newton, and Guy Bourdin. When speaking about Newton's photographs, *New York Times* writer Hilton Kramer wrote, "the interest in fashion is indistinguishable from an interest in murder, pornography, and terror" (Kramer, 1975, p. 28).

More than dirty pictures

To begin, we need a working definition of pornography. With due respect to **Chief Justice Potter**, it is not enough to know something is pornographic when we see it. While granting the importance of subjectivity, it is important to be clear about our terms and not rely on individual notions of what constitutes "dirty pictures." It is impossible to list the many definitions of pornography. For decades, scholars and the public have wrestled with this very question. There are dictionary definitions, personal definitions, and feminist definitions. The term *pornography* originates in the Greek words *graphein* and *pornographo*, which translates to writing about prostitutes. The *Oxford English Dictionary* defines pornography as "the explicit description or exhibition of sexual subjects or activity in literature, painting, films, etc., in a manner intended to stimulate erotic rather than aesthetic feelings; printed or visual material containing this."

Often, pornography is defined by efforts to regulate it. Since this chapter discusses mass-market heterosexual pornography, we can look at the widely understood definition in American culture as "the material sold in pornography shops for mostly male consumers" (Dines, Jensen, & Russo, 1998, p. 65). Critical feminist analyses define pornography as "a specific kind of sexual material that reflects and helps maintain the sexual subordination of women" (p. 65). McElroy (1995, p. 51) defines pornography as the "depiction of women and men as sexual beings." I suggest using a combination of these ideas. I contend that materials intended to arouse are not limited only to pornography shops or behind-the-counter materials and that present day mainstream fashion advertising meets the definitions of what constitutes soft-core pornography and occasionally crosses over to include elements that are used to define **hard-core pornography**. Thereby, for purposes of this chapter, pornography is defined as: material that depicts men and women as sexual beings with the purpose of sexually arousing mostly male desire in a way that reflects and helps to maintain the subordination of women.

It is important to further distinguish and describe the differences between soft-core and hard-core pornography. What is often used to distinguish these genres is the nature of power relationships. Pornographic representations run the gamut from mild versions of erotica on one end to the portrayal of actual deaths of women in snuff porn. In erotica, power relationships between individuals are equal and there is little exposure of bodies. Soft-core pornography typically presents women on their own with genitals covered. The lighting is soft and natural and attractive young women are romantically posed (Steele, 1991, p. 92). Sometimes grown women are made to appear like little girls.

In hard-core pornography, however, women are not alone and are often accompanied by one or several men, and possibly other women. The images are deliberately *strange*. "Hard core girls look like prostitutes or lesbians; they may even be dressed as boys" (Steele, 1991, p. 92). The lighting is often hard flash that draws attention to the fact that there is a photographer present. Since much of pornography is about control and power, the harder the porn, the clearer the disempowerment of the woman or women. With these definitions in mind it must be noted that not all images of women, clothed or not, are pornographic. There are pornographic fashion advertisements with women who are completely clothed and others with nude or semi-nude women that can be quite elegant. That's part of the challenge of figuring out what exactly is pornographic and where repetition fosters the pornographic stereotype.

The words sex, sexual, sexuality, and gender are used loosely in popular parlance and yet have very specific meanings. As described in Chapter 3, and for purposes of this chapter, *sex* (noun) means the biological differences/divisions between men and women; sexual (adjective) and sexuality are defined as:

> *Sex.* n. Either of the two divisions of organic beings distinguished as male and female respectively; the males or the females (of a species, etc., esp. of the human race) viewed collectively. (*Oxford English Dictionary*)

And gender means:

> *Gender.* n. In mod. (esp. feminist) use, a euphemism for the sex of a human being, often intended to emphasize the social and cultural, as opposed to the biological, distinctions between the sexes. (*Oxford English Dictionary*)

Or, drawing on Goffman (1979, p. 1), gender is the social construction of what is considered to be masculine and feminine differences. It is at the point of "what is considered to be," where this study inquires. Visual forms dominate pornography, drawing upon many conventions of visual representation. Kuhn (1995, p. 272) points out that while women may be the subject matter of photography, "it also constructs 'woman' as a set of meanings." This brings up important questions about how we think about the body, how we observe it socially, technologically, and libidinally. Pornography relies upon certain codes and conventions to communicate with the viewer. Broadly speaking, these **"gender displays"** (ritualistic, conventionalized portrayals) (Goffman, 1979, p. 3–4) fall within four categories or the four-part Conventions of Photographic Pornography (Dworkin, 1988) (hierarchy, objectification, **submission**, and violence):

1. *Hierarchy.* It is a question of power displayed when a man or men are presented on top or above a woman or group of women. Goffman (1979) refers to this positioning in advertisements as "rituals of subordination," "relative size," and "licensed withdrawal." These images include the use that looks like a parent-child relationship or treatment of a woman as child-like. Sometimes the woman is partially concealed by turning away from the camera

or psychologically disengaged from the situation. Sometimes she is shy, fearful, or laughing.

2. *Objectification.* When a "human being, through social means, is made less human, turned into a thing or commodity, bought, and sold …." And a "person is depersonalised, so that no individuality or integrity is available socially or in what is an extremely circumscribed privacy" (Dworkin, 2000, pp. 30–31). In Goffman's (1979, p. 29) work, objectification is realized through "feminine touch," which is when women use their fingers and hands to touch themselves, their lips, or to trace an outline or caress an object.

3. *Submission.* Acts of oppressed groups learn to anticipate the orders and desires of those who have power over them, and their compliance is then used by the dominant group to justify its dominance. This, according to Goffman (1979, p. 40) is a "classic stereotype of deference" of "lowering oneself physically." Beds and floors provide such places. Particular kinds of smiles engender subservience and submission as do "body clowning," "puckish styles," or "childlike guises" (Goffman, 1979, pp. 50–51).

4. *Violence:* "Subordination," according to Dworkin (2000, p. 31), "is *violence*" (italics orig.). When hierarchy, objectification, and submission are combined it makes violence seem like a normal and natural outcome. When it becomes systematic, endemic enough to be unremarkable and normative, this gender display is "usually taken as an implicit right of the one committing the violence" (p. 31). Thus, the presence of the first three conditions makes violence possible.

Construction of particular scenes or events in ads, in particular those containing the forementioned characteristics, trigger particular memories of sexual experiences (real or imagined) and nudity invites one to look—and be rewarded with pleasure for doing so. This pleasure of looking is called **scopophilia** of which voyeurism is a part.

Looking

Voyeurism is typically manifested in the "come on." The key tool for communicating this is facial expression (Kuhn, 1995, p. 276). While the woman in the advertisement might appear to be doing something sexually interesting, to the viewer it appears that the photograph was taken at the exact moment the model realized she was being looked at—and she likes it. Her head is tilted back or to the side so that her glance is at an angle. This look can appear to be a "come hither" or as a tease. Her lips are usually parted and the rest of her body can be read as an **invitation** to touch and possess her. This is a key moment in the construction of the subject-object relationship in photography.

This moment fuels desire on the part of the viewer who runs no risk of rejection or disappointment because the woman is not real. However, there is the coexistent appeal of being unable to possess her with the concurrent disappointment of that as well. The model acknowledges and welcomes the spectatorship. Her body is an object to be looked upon. What the viewer does with that information varies—he or she might simply flip the page or might find the image a useful fantasy and/or masturbation tool. The viewer is both Peeping Tom and subject of the look.

Pornography in Advertising

Defined as communication that is "paid for, delivered to an audience via mass media, and attempts to persuade" advertising is one of the most powerful relaters of cultural values that we have in modern world (O'Guinn, Allen, & Semenik, 2000, p. 9). O'Guinn et al. (2000, pp. 331–350) list several objectives for advertising that include promoting brand recall, scaring the consumer into action, defining the brand image, and instilling brand preference. While it is possible to use combinations of these objectives and related methods, it is under the category of Instill Brand Preference that we most commonly see sex appeal used as a tool to realize this objective. According to O'Guinn et al. (2000) sexual appeals are "attention getting and occasionally arousing, which may affect how consumers feel about a product" (2000, p. 337). "Calvin Klein and many other advertisers," such as Guess, "use sexual imagery in this way to successfully mold brand image"(O'Guinn et al., 2000, p. 337).

Advertising provides revealing insights into the culture in which it resides, serving as a "transparent cultural artifact" and taking the "stuff of everyday life and transforming it"(Jhally, 1990, p. 31). Where once advertising informed consumers, modern advertising is an "active strategy of selling and marketing" (Falk, 1997). Rather than simply telling consumers about the *use-value* of a product, the emphasis today, though branding, is on the product's *exchange value*. Advertising today is less concerned with communicating essential information and more concerned with recreating the social world. It makes assumptions about what it means to be a woman and presents ways of striving to reach that ideal. Goldman (1992, p. 19) points out that, "modern advertising thus teaches us to consume, not the product, but its sign. What the product stands for is more important that what it is. It is the voice that is added to the product." Related to this process is the concept of fetishism, meaning to invest something "with powers it does not have in itself" and "seeing the meaning…as an inherent part of their physical existence when in fact that meaning is created by their integration into a *system of meaning*"

(Jhally, 1990, p. 29). Humans produce this value that is added to an essentially empty container that is the product. "There is the very American, very modern faith in the possibility of continuous self-transformation. A life, after all, is commonly referred to as a *lifestyle*. Styles change" (Leibowitz & Sontag, 1999, p. 36).

What is it about sex and sexuality that seems to work in advertising? Since the turn of the century, advertising has been about cultivating a sense of lack and offering a (albeit temporary) solution. Advertising refers to the possibility of completion through possession of the product. A naked body works in this context to stimulate desire and the need for satisfaction. Advertising refers to eroticism by presenting a consumer good and the "projection of abstracted lack" (da Silva Martins, 1995, p. 54). In Lacan's view, lack for women is articulated in needs to make us more beautiful, more attractive, and more desirable because we lack "the lean and boyish, or in some cases, anorexic bodies that so many models" have (Asa Berger, 2000, p. 58). Cultural ideology tells women "that they will not be desirable to, or loved by, men unless they are physically perfect" (Cortese, 1999). For men, the formation affects male expectations of the female body, "who see these women and become dissatisfied with their sexual partners" (Asa Berger, 2000, p. 58).

Beyond its basic selling function, advertising has always been about creating desire. That desire might be as basic as satiating hunger with a hamburger or elevating low esteem with makeup. In advertising, the nude woman becomes an iconic device for perfume, jewelry, clothing, and hosiery. Sexuality thereby "became a catalyst for collapsing the distinction between high art and popular culture," (McDonald, 2001, p. 81). We commonly see these images in posters, pinups, and **"cheesecake" photographs** wherein the woman in the picture, and by extension all women, are interesting because of their body parts. Berger (1972) points out that **soft-core porn** draws on and transforms conventions through which the nude female body is represented in art, thus placing it in a mass-market context. These conventions include angling the woman's body toward the camera to offer the maximum display offering a view of her body and the part that is emphasized and accentuated breasts through particular placement of arms, elbows, and hands. The photograph says, "look at this, this body is there for you to look at, and you will enjoy looking at it. The formal arrangement of the body…solicits the spectator's gaze." (Kuhn, 1995, p. 275). Thereby, "voyeurism and exhibitionism are as intrinsic to fashion photography as they are to fashion itself" (Steele, 1991, p. 81).

In terms of constructing images of femininity, advertising establishes definitions and rules through the use of particular codes that help viewers understand what being a woman means and does so in such a way that it makes complete sense. The ubiquity of these images in the media suggests that these portrayals come to feel natural. Hall (1977) refers to this process as articulation. Articulation is part of the process of making meaning out of the images we see. Advertising takes meaning from a historical context (Budgeon, 1994, p. 62) and then uses them "to create new meanings" or **re-presentations** (Saco, 1992, p. 25; Williamson, 1978, p. 177). The appropriation of and reformulation of cultural values "take into account not only the inherent qualities and attributes of the product they are trying to sell, but also the way in which they can make those properties mean something to us" (Williamson, 1978, p. 12).

Advertising has to take advantage of this process because of time and space limitations. Certain objects and materials from our lives are reconstituted in such a way that advertisers are "selling us ourselves" (Williamson, 1978, p. 13). In doing so, what we see in an advertisement seems to be constructed from direct knowledge. A print ad, for example, has to make an immediate connection with the viewer, thereby employing signs and symbols that have been commonplace communicators in American society. Beliefs about what being a woman is about remain unchallenged within this environment because they appear to reflect reality and follow a kind of logic that makes whatever is going on in the ad seem natural and normal and that we are seeing women as they really are (Saco, 1992, p. 25).

Advertising works to create meanings based on an ideology, which is defined as "the discourses and narratives that circulate in a culture and determine, to a large extent, what can and can't be thought, what can and can't be done" (Schiarato & Yell, 2000, p. 73). According to Budgeon (1994, p. 60), and Hall (1977), advertising functions ideologically in three ways:

1. Advertising provides and selectively constructs social knowledge and social imagery through which we come to understand and interpret our social world and experiences. This is accomplished by making connections between products and images organized into **frames** (Goldman, 1992).
2. Advertising classifies and orders different types of "social knowledge" according to preferred meanings and **interpretations** that require the participation of the viewer by isolating "meaningful moments" (Budgeon, 1994, p. 60).
3. Advertising works to "organize, orchestrate, and bring together that which it has selectively represented and selectively classified," so that a particular meaning is presented.

To succeed, dominant ideology must "continually make and remake itself so as to contain meanings and values that lie outside of the dominant version," thereby reinforcing cultural hegemony (Budgeon, 1994, p. 65). According to Burgin (1982, p. 47):

> The total ideology of a society is imprinted in its production and consumption of material objects…all that constitutes reality for us is, then, impregnated with meanings. These meanings are the contingent products of history and, in sum, reflect our ideology….

> Objects present to the camera are already in use in the production of meanings, and photography has no choice but to operate upon such meanings.

So-called feminine qualities, such as softness, beauty, perfection, health, and sexiness, are thereby tied to consumption of products designed to achieve these ends. Advertising draws upon a rather limited definition of femininity through display, or, as Goffman (1979) showed, ads are not about the way men and women actually behave, rather they are about the ways we think men and women behave. These images strike at the core of individual identity and are key to "our understanding of ourselves as either male or female (socially defined within this society at this time)" and are central to "our understanding of who we are" (Jhally, 1990). Or, as Tickner (1989, p. 249) states: "art does not just make ideology explicit, but can be used, at a particular historical juncture, to rework it." Problems of vision have been and are "questions about the body and the operation of social power" (Crary, 1990, p. 3). Representation of the body is "central to society's construction not only of norms of sexual behavior, but of power relationships in general (Pultz, 1995, p. 7).

Female identity in advertising is almost exclusively defined in terms of female sexuality. In the case of women, this largely becomes a question about the *lack* of social power. The nude body of a woman in advertising is ubiquitous as it reflects "cultural norms about appearance, control, and attractiveness" (Bordo, 1993). As Schroeder and Borgerson (1998, p. 168) point out, "women are objectified in many ways, each suggesting and reinforcing the perspective that women are objects to be viewed voyeuristically, fantasized about, and possessed. Ambiguity arises when we think about these as images created of women for other women by "transmuting the 'male gaze' into a 'mirrored gaze' in which female readers become simultaneously the spectator and owner of the desired appearance" (Goldman, 1992, p. 11). While the eye "is an erogenous zone for both sexes," "men look, and women watch themselves being looked at."

Women also look, of course, and that is why fashion photography, and by extension fashion advertising works so well, as "photography is uniquely well suited to expressing the instinct for pleasure inherent in the libido for looking" (Steele, 1991, p. 96). "The allure that fashion photography creates and revels in is frequently that of ambiguity" (Ritchin, 1991, p. 121). Yet, the photographs use male-oriented conventions and, as women we see these women as if we were a man looking at her. The ambiguous zone of pornography is one, "that threatens and undermines society at the same time that it is the fullest expression of society's unspoken desires" (Turner, 1984, p. 83).

Image Analysis

Social science research methods for investigating portrayals of girls and women in the media have taught us a great deal. Experiments and content analyses have been particularly useful methodologies. Highly intellectualized feminist analyses have revealed a great deal about the existence of and problems with stereotypical portrayals of women. But, according to Jhally (1990), what often is missing is recognition of very real, very deep-seated, attraction. People are attracted to the images in these magazines and don't like being told that they shouldn't be. It is important to recognize that these attractions exist. Only then can we take the next step in revealing these desires as they are then articulated in the advertising images we see.

In this case, by combining nonverbal, symbolic, and sociological levels of analysis we can learn how techniques such as posture, touch, gesture, and gaze, communicate about power and authority. As Borgerson and Schroeder (2005, p. 174) point out, research in this area can move forward by "adopting alternative methods from the humanities and interpretive social sciences that emphasize the context in which advertising images are produced and consumed."

Most critics agree that the starting point of a visual analysis is **description**. In the case of this study, the medium is photography in the form of advertisements. In the tradition of Goffman (1979) I have assembled a selection of common advertisements from the contemporary fashion magazines *Vogue, W,* and *Elle* that illustrate how pornographic imagery has become commonplace in advertising. This method is supported by work in semiotics (Barthes, 1983; Williamson, 1978) and art history and criticism (Stokstad, 1995; Schroeder & Borgerson, 1998). The focus of these images is **interpretation** part of visual analysis. By combining Dines and Jensen's (1998) content model and Dworkin's (1998) four-part Conventions of Photographic Pornography (1985) (hierarchy, objectification, submission, and violence) with Kuhn's feminist framework for identifying **gendered codes** in mass marketed pornography (invitation, bits and pieces, and **caught unawares**), we can see how mainstream fashion advertisements contribute to the construction and perpetuation of the pornographic stereotype.

The **Conventions of Pornographic Photography and Gendered Codes** are (Kuhn, 1985):

1. Hierarchy

Invitation. In this imagery, the woman invites the viewer to look. She's aware of being looked at. Her head is tilted and angular; she's teasing, with a sort of come-on look. Her lips are slightly parted.

In a two-page spread for Marc Jacobs shoes, a woman is on her back (we learn from the small print that she is Victoria Beckham). All we can see of her, since she appears to be lying down in a large Marc Jacobs shopping bag are Beckham's bent legs. She appears only to be wearing patent leather pink and black shoes. Her legs are the only part of the body we see, hence the only part that matters. The surrounding space is entirely white and empty. Once again, the ad is for the shoes.

2. Objectification

Bits and pieces. Representing women only as parts has been a mainstay of fashion advertising for some time. In recent ads we can see a woman wrapped in two leather belts (not holding anything up because she is naked). She is looking forward, lips parted and wet, with her breast and nipple revealed in the crux of her elbow (Kieselstein-Cord). This type of image presents women as fragments, emphasizing particular body parts for the viewer's gaze. Often her head is missing and her body is angled toward the camera offering maximum display. Body parts are fetishized, such as breasts, buttocks, and lips.

3. Submission

Caught unawares. Here we see a woman enjoying her own body, often pleasuring herself, unaware that she is being watched, transported by her pleasure. Her eyes are often closed, she faces away from the camera, her body is open, her genitals concealed, yet vulnerable.

Christian Dior's Opium perfume, released in 1976 and described as an "addictive perfume" in its publicity slogan, "incarnates the fantasies and desires of the new bourgeoisie while suggesting the transgression of taboos, escape, and ecstasy. Because of its mysterious, magical, and sacred dimension, this perfume provides access to a superior spiritual existence, and the quest for the absolute" (International Perfume Council, 2001).

Banned in Great Britain and France because it was considered degrading to women, the Christian Dior Opium ad just took things too far, said the public. ("French Women," 2001). The ad displays a voluptuous red-haired woman viewed from the side, wearing only a necklace and a pair of high-heeled strap sandals reclining on her back. She is fondling a breast and appears to be enthralled in sexual rapture. Her lips are parted. This advertisement is clearly an example of a *caught unawares*—she is enjoying her own body and is transported by her pleasure ("Two Staples of Soft-core Porn," Kuhn, 1985). Her body is available for looking at, she faces away from the viewer whom she seems to be unaware of as she's so caught up in her own passions (or addictions?). This is an example of what Kuhn (1985, p. 30) refers to as "lawless seeing." The hierarchy of male (viewer subject) power over female (object) power is evident by her vulnerability and the appeal to scopophilia.

Other examples include a recent Yves Saint Laurent Paris perfume ad, in which the viewer sees a woman, dressed only in a man's unbuttoned black shirt, with her arms above her head gazing into the mirror (one way mirror?). Her back is arched revealing most of her breasts, all of her belly, and her bikini underwear. In the image she is accompanied by a shirtless young man/boy. The sleeve of a grown man appears in the corner. The viewer is invited to watch the goings on—a *menage a trois*? An incestuous encounter? A prostitute? The story telling is up to the viewer, but clearly something sexual is or could be going on.

4. Violence

Hard-core crossovers. This category presents violence in ways that combine many of the elements in the other categories in order to present situations where the woman is clearly not the one in control, or if she is, she is aggressively dominating the viewer or other people in the advertisement. Advertisements from a number of fashion houses featured women together (Lanvin, Gucci), a woman surrounded by three men (Gaultier), a woman with a whip (Dolce & Gabbana) (to my knowledge whips are not yet a fashion accessory), a woman in a leather jacket, tight, high black underwear standing in a bathroom, leaning against the sink, looking away with her purse and a naked man available (Bottega Veneta), a woman being overpowered by a man against a tree (Guess), and a female vampire with blood running out of her mouth while her red Francesco Biasia handbag (with cloves of garlic tied to the handles) stood safely nearby.

A particularly clear example is a series of Versace advertisements that appeared in many mainstream fashion magazines that feature what appears to be a scene from a pornographic movie. In the advertisements, which appeared individually or as a foldout, in a serial format, three women are shown in various states of dress and undress across beds adorned in bright aqua high-heeled shoes. The viewer only sees the faces of two of the models, while the third model is only viewed from behind, with the focus on her exposed buttocks, which are emphasized, by her black thong lace panties, garters, and hose. She is draped across a pillow, available for more pleasure. Her rumpled demeanor clearly indicates she has been active. The other women in the room are also on the bed or sitting in chairs available for the viewer and willing to be involved with one another. The ads present a scenario that combines hierarchy, objectification, and submission.

While the presumed gaze for these ads is male and heterosexual, it is also white, as the primary target for the magazine is white, evidenced by both content

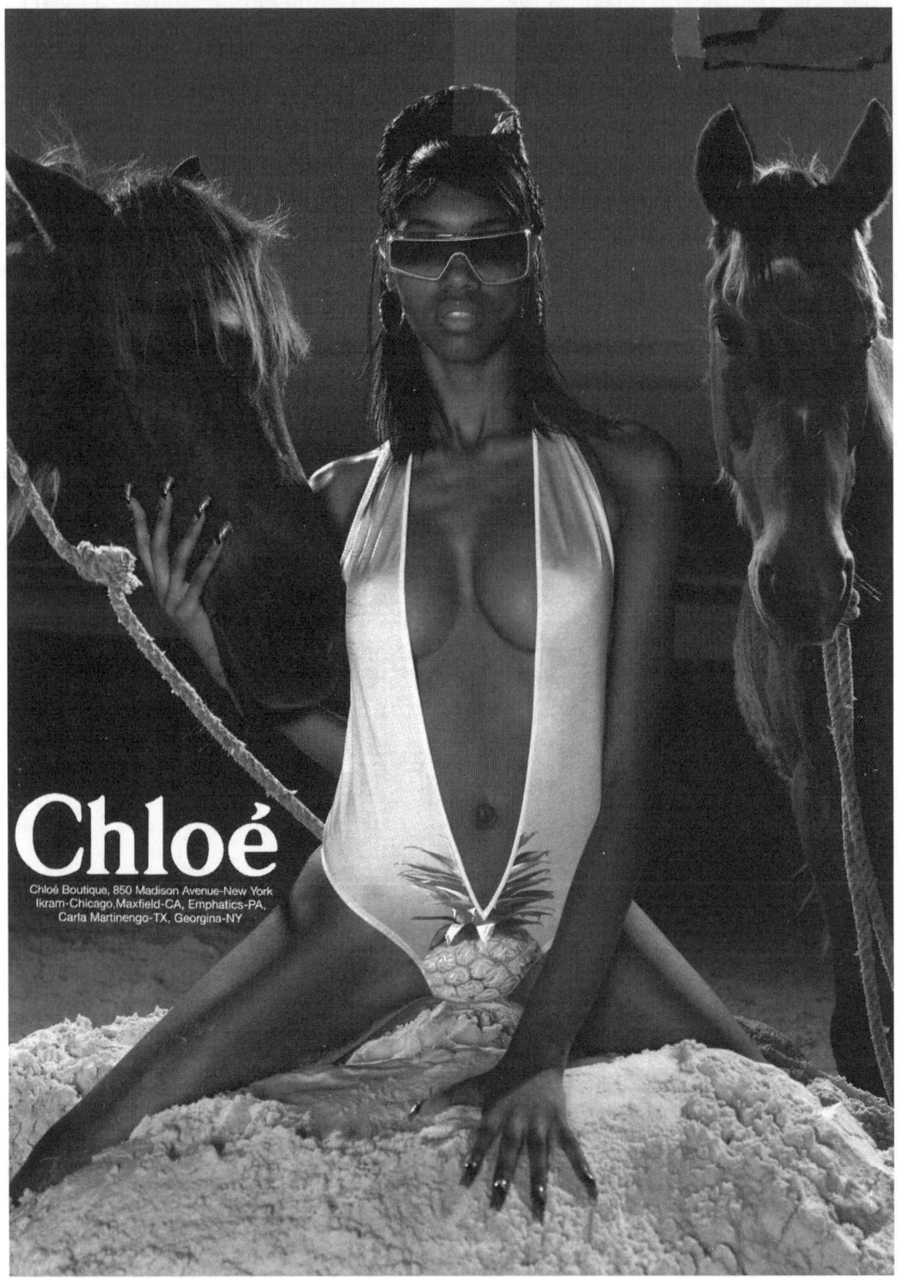

Figure 9.1: Chloé advertisement.

Source: Courtesy of photographer Donald Schneider.

and advertising imagery and more so by the *absence* of women of color from the ads. While an analysis of race is beyond the scope of this chapter, it is well worth identifying. Hierarchy and supremacy are clearly marks of pornography, and this ideology is reinforced through commercial messages as well. bell hooks (2000) points out a new racist regime lives in the in-between and absences in culture

> Ethnicity becomes spice, seasoning that can liven up the dull dish that is mainstream white culture. Cultural taboos around sexuality and desire are transgressed and made explicit as the media bombards folks with a message of difference no longer based on the white supremacist notion that 'blondes have more fun.' (hooks, 2000, p. 21)

Another advertisement needs to be discussed. Among the dozens of advertisements in the magazines only two featured an African American woman. No other racial or ethnic groups were represented. There is literature that discusses the framing of black women's sexuality in pornography (and by extension and example into these advertisements) (Collins, 1995; Mayall & Russell, 1995).

An ad, part of series for Chloé, shows a black woman straddling a small pile of sand, wearing a one-piece swimsuit that is v-shaped and open down the middle with a pineapple image at the base of her pelvis (Figure 9.1). She is wearing sunglasses so we cannot see her eyes, she is looking directly at the viewer, her lips are parted, and her nails are long as talons. On each side of her is a horse. The color scheme is browns and golds.

Summary

Advertising isn't the only social, economic, and cultural force responsible for how women's bodies are viewed in American society. But, as Kilbourne (1998), points out, advertising images contribute to social problems "by creating a climate within which the marketing of women's bodies—the sexual sell and dismemberment, distorted body image ideals, and children as sex objects—is seen as acceptable." A real problem is the socialization of children into acceptance of the pornographic stereotype and the reinforcement of that throughout their lives. Several areas of concern became evident in this study: (1) portrayals of women as girls that thereby sexualize children, (2) the normalization of violence, (3) the undermining of positive images and artful representations, and (4) the wide availability of these images.

In the video, "Slim Hopes," advertising critic Jean Kilbourne points out how pre-pubescent and pubescent children are eroticized in advertising through mainstream techniques for display. The models stand pigeon-toed, wear urchin hairstyles, and are underdeveloped or androgynous in appearance. According to McDonald (2001, p. 122), "the widespread use of these techniques blurs distinction between art, fashion, advertising, and pornography."

The plethora of images of the erotic promise of teen girls pervades American culture or what's being called the "**pornographication of the American girl**" (Junod, 2001). This pornographication extends beyond what we see in advertising. For example, pornography film director Gregory Dark, who directed Britney Spears in her videos, says this "seems not so much anomalous as inevitable" in what's being called "the lure of jail bait" (Junod, 2001, p. 133). A *Rolling Stone* cover featured Christina Aguilera with shorts unzipped and her "athletic tongue licking her lascivious lips" (Junod, 2001, p. 133).

In addition, advertising imagery that dresses women like little girls offers up a virtual pedophiliac's wet dream. The young girl becomes available in fantasy but is safely so thought of because she is in fact a woman. However, such thinking facilitates not only the sexualization of girls but also supports the ideology of lower class status for women as children. Bruce Weber's controversial photographs for Calvin Klein, which commonly portray a "youthful eroticism" (Harrison, 1991, p. 276), are in this category.

Another concern is the recurring level of violence (graphic, promised, and implied) evident in the ads. In the advertising analyzed, as well as many others too numerous to include, violence emerged as a dominant theme. Violence is one element that can be used to distinguish between soft- and hard-core pornography. This begs the question of whether or not fashion advertising has moved toward not only a pornographic stereotype but also whether the imagery qualifies as quasi-hard core. When discussing social behavior in what she termed our "rape-prone society" sociologist Jane C. Hood (1989) remarked that, in order to be effective in preventing assaults on women, criminals are not the ones to be targeted but rather, "advertisements portraying women as sex objects," or indeed of attractive abuse. According to Hood (1989), it is becoming increasingly difficult to tell the difference between *Playboy*, *Vogue*, or the *Sports Illustrated Swim Suit Edition* based on what we see, and "this has to be more damaging to women than frank pornography, which you at least know is pornography" ("Pornography," 1989). In the ideal presented by advertising, "our face becomes a mask and our body becomes a thing and turning a human being into a thing is often the first step toward justifying violence" (Kilbourne, 2000, p. 56).

While Europeans in general, and the French in particular, are known to be more lenient when it comes to nudity in advertising, in August 2001 the French said, "Enough!" in response to the Opium ad discussed earlier (Landau, 2001). A government minister concluded that many current fashion advertisements degrade women and ordered them stopped. For example, recent campaigns for clothing, shoes, and luxury goods showed "images of chained bodies covered in dirt, represented in animal poses, bruised faces, allusions to rape or domestic violence, sometimes with humor, sometimes without" (Landau, 2001). It wasn't nudity that was objectionable, rather the degrading and violent images that accompanied the bodies.

The proliferation of the pornographic stereotype in advertising images in American society coupled with wide acceptance has undermined efforts to establish feminist representations of the female body and positive feminist representations of human sexuality.

The consumption of the advertising and the women in the ads is as bell hooks (2000) calls it, "eating the other"; the psychological, spiritual, and phenomenological commodification of Otherness has been so successful because it is offered as a new delight. "Within commodity culture, ethnicity becomes spice seasoning that can liven up the dull dish that is mainstream culture" (hooks, 1992, p. 21). As such, consuming women of color in ads is a form of terrorism, the ingestion of the Other into the status quo, in their (implied) proper place. "Difference, as in spicy exotic foods, but over consumption destroys the difference we crave" (Probyn, 2000, p. 84).

Advertising, pornography, and popular culture have also affected representation of the naked female body in art. Adherence to prescribed sex roles is a key component of maintaining social order. The female body has, curiously and perhaps ironically, served as the locus of oppression. Relegating women to the status of sex objects is one way of ensuring participation in the established system of oppression.

Finally, it is important to stress that these images are easily accessible to all ages. Not confined to behind-the-counter locations, magazines such as *W, Elle,* and *Vogue* are widely available. The highly charged sexualized images presented in fashion advertising have inched along to the point where what we now see in doctor's offices, libraries, and on our own coffee tables is in fact pornographic, and widely available to every age, including children. In addition, fashion is a powerful force in shaping popular culture and fine arts as well as a borrower from them.

Society in general and women in particular, pay a heavy toll as a result of the generally unquestioned nature of these advertisements. Not from the actual images, but from the implications of these reductive and objectifying portrayals of women. As Turner (1984, p. 1) points out, drawing upon Marx, "society could not exist without the constant and regular reproduction of our bodies, and without their allocation to social places."

Who are the beneficiaries of these portrayals? Advertising agencies, clothing manufacturers, and magazine publishers. A defender of this imagery, Pascale Weil, associate director at Publicis Consultants says, "you always take the risk of pleasing some and offending others." Advertisements "tell a story about the product or brand, and for this to work the story must be connected to that product or brand in some obvious way." Cyril Marin le Quellec, commercial director at independent Paris agency Les Ouvriers du Paradis, says, "to sell perfume you have to show skin—that is where you put on your perfume." Graphic portrayals of women in mainstream fashion advertising show no signs of changing, either. One reason, as Asa Berger (2000, p. 57) points out, is that it (advertising) "has the uncanny ability to resist being affected by critiques of it. Attacking advertising is like throwing thumbtacks in the path of a herd of stampeding elephants." Another reason is the persistence of the belief (much like the belief in subliminal advertising) that sex sells, despite what the research tells us (Alexander & Judd, 1978; LaTour & Pitts, 1990; Jones, Stanaland, & Gelb, 1998; Shields, 1997). In fact the "bottom line" might be moving even further. Consider the example of contributing to the bottom line in fashion advertising with the bottom. When "everything from Burberry to Westwood, shoes to T-shirts, is being hawked with an ample helping of ass" (Fox, 2001, p. 32), so-called "butt-cleavage" is now part of Hollywood's best-dressed list as well as the Versace campaign discussed earlier. As tops push the boundaries of what is acceptable advertising imagery, bottoms are now paving the way for a new kind of bodily presentation. The new "cheek chic" is hardly surprising: but bottom, with its tender skin and unthreatening symmetry is the least obscene of the body parts that decency usually demands be hidden away" (Fox, 2001, p. 32).

Asa Berger (2000, p. 67) confirms that the use of sexual imagery in advertising shows no signs of slowing, if for no other reason than sex has become the commodity used in competition between advertising agencies. The amount of pornographic imagery escalates into something he calls "sexual clutter" (p. 66), where sexuality becomes so pervasive that the only way to get noticed from that point on is to use inreasingly explicit imagery. The law of diminishing returns eventually comes in. Where one type of imagery used to get our attention now it no longer gets so much as a passing glance. The "**sign wars**" that agencies engage in eventually may neutralize what we see as one company tries to "out sex" the other one. Solomon (1990, p. 69) sees sexual coercion in advertising as "a sign of a desperate need to make certain that clients are getting their money's worth."

Yet, **Keith Reinhard** (2001), chairman and CEO of DDB Worldwide Communications Group, Inc., was so alarmed by what he saw as the "gratuitous sex and gross potty humor found in a lot of advertising today," that he wrote an article targeted to his industry peers imploring them to rethink their use of sex to sell. Reinhard (2001) points out that what goes into an ad is a matter of taste and judgment of perceived taste among the public, acknowledging what is in good taste is a matter of individual choice, and that "sales have nothing to do with taste or decency." Too often, says Reinhard, advertising creative people are sent the message that "the more rude and shocking you can be, the more successful you'll be in advertising." He thereby offers a series of questions advertisers can ask of a creative concept that might be questionable:

1. What is the real intent of the ad? Is the goal to shock? Win awards? Create controversy?
2. Is the content relevant? "Breasts are important if you're selling sports bras. They are not important to the sales of beer."
3. Where and when will the message appear?
4. How 'artfully' is the questionable material presented?
5. Would I be proud to have my name associated with this ad or campaign? Would my teen-aged daughter be proud of me for doing it? Would I be proud to tell her I did it?

My goal in this chapter has been to provide evidence for what I am calling the pornographic stereotype in modern, mainstream fashion advertising. By using coding and categories that describe what constitutes pornography (both soft and hard core) in visual imagery it becomes clear that what is being presented is pornographic. Since advertisements, by their very nature, are designed to incite desire (in its many forms) in order to draw attention to a brand, the use of sexual appeal is a natural link to deep-seated, fundamentally human urges. Nevertheless, as Asa Berger (2000, p. 67) warns us, "we must never underestimate the power of sexual images to affect us in mysterious and powerful ways. There is so much vicarious sex in our lives that the "real thing" may be losing its appeal for a goodly number of people. Whether these "urges" are the result of nature or nurture is beyond the scope of this study. However, it appears that fashion advertising draws upon both. The impact conflates fashion and photography and advertising and pornography into a unified whole that normalizes viewing of women as only sexual, girls as sexually stimulating and available, and violence as the next level of activity and excitement. As Kuhner (2000) points out, "the mainstreaming of pornography is another symptom of the deepening rot that afflicts our society."

The purveyors of porn today are not the bohemian, burnt-out radicals of the 1960s; rather, it is being peddled by the bastions of corporate capitalism. The times have changed. And what makes this mainstreaming so disturbing is its availability to all ages at the supermarket and to our children on our coffee tables. This exists in a society where the visual is now the privileged mode of discourse.

In what might be the most important sentence in his classic work *Gender Advertisements*, Goffman (1979, p. ix) points out something very real and important for us to take away:

> Although the pictures shown here cannot be taken as representative of gender behavior
> in real life…one can probably make a significant negative statement about them, namely,
> that as *pictures* they are not perceived as peculiar or unnatural.

Questions for Discussion

1. What stereotypes of women are present in popular media?
2. Is the availability to children of fashion advertisements featuring naked or semi-naked women in popular magazines a concern?
3. Is advertising for fashion and women's presentation markedly different from other forms of advertising that use women's bodies?
4. How could an advertisement be constructed to sell clothing that doesn't rely on sex or innuendo? Do you think it could be successful?
5. What is your opinion of Reinhard's questions for art directors and copywriters?

Key Words

Advertising	Bits and pieces
Caught unawares	Cheesecake photographs
Conventions of Pornographic Photography and Gendered Codes	Description
Feminine qualities	Feminist approach
Frames	Gender displays
Gendered Codes	Hard-core pornography
Hierarchy	Interpretation
Invitation	Justice Stewart Potter
Keith Reinhard	Objectification
Pornographic stereotype	Pornographication of the American girl
Pornography	Re-presentations
Scopophilia	Sex appeal
Sign wars	Soft-core porn
Submission	Visual truth
Voyeurism	

CHAPTER TEN

❀ Women, Lipstick, and Self-Presentation

What lips my lips have kissed, and where, and why,
I have forgotten, and what arms have lain
Under my head till morning; but the rain
Is full of ghosts tonight,

Edna St. Vincent Millay

Red lips are not so red
As the stained stones kissed by the English dead.

Wilfred Owen

For the lips of a loose woman drip honey, and her speech is smoother
than oil;

but in the end she is bitter as wormwood, sharp as a two-edged sword.

Proverbs 5:3.

Sugared Plum, Double Fudge, Vanilla Brownie, and *Raspberry Glace* sound like temptations from a dessert cart, but instead these luscious sounding treats are names of lipstick shades. Estée Lauder's advertisements for its Clinique brand, for example, invite women to taste "deliciously sheer" shades such as Rich Cherry, Black Honey, Cherry Cola, Red Licorice, or to use a soft matte Butterscotch, Double Truffle, Ginger Goodie, Pink Chocolate, or Iced Punch lipstick. Other advertisements invite the wearer to experience "seduction," be a "tramp," or "X-pose" herself. Many women say that they won't leave home without it, feel empowered by wearing it, and, if asked to give up all makeup except for one item, say that they would keep their lipstick (Spicer, 2002, p. 11). Viene (As cited in Ragas & Kozlowski, 1998, p. 9) wrote, "I never leave home without my Swiss Army knife and a tube of lipstick. As far as I'm concerned, they're the only two weapons a woman needs."

The American cultural imperative of beauty prompts many women to doubt their self-worth and keeps attainment of the beauty ideal just out of reach. Over the last few years, scholars have examined women's relationships with food in terms of eating disorders (Hargreaves & Tiggemann, 2003), distorted body image (Abramson & Valene, 1991; Botta, 1999; Cusumano & Thompson, 1997; Field et al., 1999; Harrison, 2000, 2001; Harrison & Cantor, 1997; Levine, Smolak, & Hayden, 1994; Stice et al., 1994), and the influence of advertising and mass media (Anderson et al., 2001; Borzekowski, Robinson, & Killen, 2000; Harrison, 2001; Levine & Smolak, 1996; Owen & Laurel-Seller, 2000). Few scholars, however, have examined color names (Kahn & Miller, 2005; Zakia, 2002), and none has done work specifically with lipsticks.

This chapter presents the findings of a content analysis of more than 1700 lipstick names from 52 different manufacturers. Goffman's (1959) concept of **presentation of self** and impression management as theory and Barthes' (1982) **semiotic model** as method helped me to address the following research questions: (1) Under what major categories are lipsticks named? (2) What purpose does naming lipsticks serve? (3) What are the implications of lipstick names for women and society? Understanding how meaning is constructed through lipstick naming, as an extension of branding, is an important step toward apprehending the role of cosmetics in conflating femininity, self-esteem, and body image with the goals of hegemony.

Lip Service

More than merely functional, women's colored lips have served as metaphors for their supposed predation on men (Davis, 1991; Morris, 2004), as visual enticement for invited or uninvited sexual relations (Morris, 2004; Peiss, 1990), as projectors of attitude (Pallingston, 1999; Richlin, 1995), and as portals for pleasure (Brownmiller, 1984; Ragas & Kozlowski, 1998). According to anthropologists, the ideal female face "reflects a woman at her most fertile" (Hayt, 2005, p. E3). Moreover, "the lips remind us of the labia, because they flush red and swell when aroused, which is the conscious or subconscious reason women have always made them look even redder with lipstick" (Ackerman, 1993, p. 114).

Wearing lipstick can be viewed as a sign of social class (Peiss, 1990), as a satisfier of one of the signs of femininity (Brownmiller, 1984; Wolf, 2002), and at one time, as a marker of (supposed) morality (Beausoleil, 1994; Peiss, 1998; Smith, 1990). Therefore, "in the very process of growing up, female, a woman learns how to police the boundaries of her own looking and being a woman" (Black, 2004, p. 181). When these factors are then transferred to an object, such as lipstick, they become highly symbolic.

Before the 1920s, "nice girls" did not wear lipstick but when "nice girls did," wearing lipstick moved from being an affectation of prostitutes to serving as one of the indicia of aristocratic, sophisticated women. Although not completely free of its previous associations, lipstick wearing became a reminder of femininity rather than the façade of a "loose" woman. In 1931, a study found that 85% of college women wore lipstick (Woodhead, 2004, p. 197). As it was $2 billion industry then, Washington decided to levy a tax on cosmetics as luxury goods. In 1936, Virginia Jenckes, Democratic Representative from Indiana (Figure 10.1) argued that women needed to organize and protest what she saw as an unfair levy on an essential item (womenincongress.gov). By World War II, however, production of many products was limited and even banned from the marketplace in order to conserve essential resources (Black, 2004; Peiss, 1998). The 1942 ban of cosmetics lasted only 4 months due to public outcry and societal recognition of the role cosmetics played as a morale booster for "securing women's commitment" to the war effort (Black, 2004, p. 34). The pitch to women from cosmetics companies was "that one of the reasons we're fighting the war is for women to be beautiful" (Peiss, 2002, p. 240). This was reflected in the ample lips and glamour of 1940s film stars such as Veronica Lake, Lana Turner, and Rita Hayworth, as well as pin-up "girls" such as Betty Grable. After World War II, when women were sent back to domestica, cosmetics advertising turned to escapism and fantasy. In the 1950s and 1960s, when Betty Friedan's readers asked, "is that all there is?" cosmetics manufacturers replied, "yes, but you can escape day-to-day doldrums if you buy/wear this." The use of women's sexuality to sell products became a marketing norm.

Advertising campaigns connected with social rituals, such as age-based decisions about when a girl could begin wearing makeup, appealed to girls' natural curiosity and propensity to experiment with hairstyles, clothing, and cosmetics. Wearing makeup was a social lubricant for girls' interactions with peers and for establishing friendships (Black, 2004; Peiss, 1990).

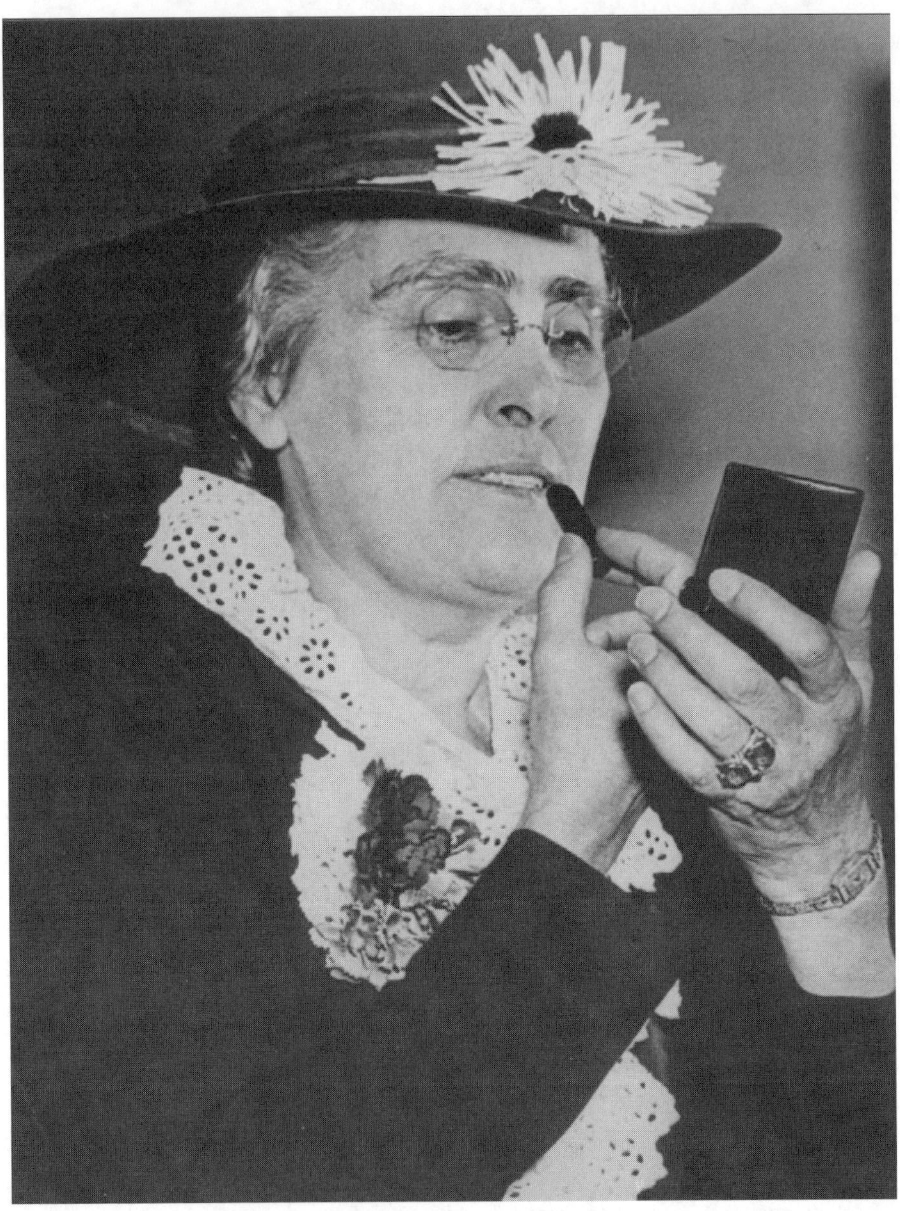

Figure 10.1: Virginia Jenckes (D-Indiana) applying lipstick, 1936.

Source: Used by permission, Collection of U.S. House of Representatives. *Women in Congress.*

Political critiques of cosmetics wearing and cosmetics companies gained momentum in the 1960s and 1970s (Brownmiller, 1984), and continue today. Under a system of advanced capitalism, cosmetics were viewed as tools designed to gain women's consent to their own (hegemonic) oppression. *Not* wearing makeup made a political statement and was viewed as a site of resistance. Social movements did not, however, deter the cosmetics business, which found a way to eroticize the "natural" look (which required makeup, of course). The always-opportunistic beauty advertising business appropriated "the 'liberated woman'" and thereby "the rejection of makeup among feminists was reinterpreted in the industry" (Black, 2004, p. 39). Scientifically (as opposed to beauty) based brands, for example, Clinique were introduced to take advantage of changes in attitudes, beliefs, and lifestyles. Thus, wearing lipstick continued to serve as a way of "calling attention to the most sexually charged part of the face," as a way of establishing identity, and as a way to signal availability (Ragas & Kozlowski, 1998, p. 49).

The "most sensual part of the [cosmetic] business," lipstick has proven to be one of the most economically reliable cosmetic categories and one of the few that benefits from hard times (Face lift, 2002, n.p.). Advertisers and consumers spend substantial amounts on lipstick, as 97% of women 18 to 24 years of age wear lip color (Platt, 2004). In 2005, American women spent more than $200 million on high-end lip-glosses and $279 million on prestige lipsticks (Singer, 2006). In 2004, more than $677 million was spent in mass-market sales of lipstick alone, and 2005 sales doubled 2004 levels (Hayt, 2005). Lipstick has the highest usage of all cosmetics—women bought an average of 8.5 tubes of lipstick in 2004 (Platt, 2004). It is the most shoplifted cosmetic (Ragas & Kozlowski, 1998); 98% of American women 18 to 34 years of age wear lipstick regularly, and the average woman will consume approximately 6 pounds of it in her lifetime (Ethridge, 2003). Lipstick sales have an inverse relationship with economic downturns and national calamity. During the Great Depression, for example, when food and other daily necessities were scarce, women still found money for the single cosmetic that would boost their morale (Ragas & Kozlowski, 1998). In fact, despite World War II, women were encouraged to use, and applauded for use of lipstick, as advertising reminded them of the importance of "keeping your femininity—even though you are doing a man's work" (Peiss, 1998, p. 240). Similarly, following the September 11, 2001, tragedy, fourth quarter sales of lipsticks increased more than 13% (van Dyk, 2001), and, despite the economic downturn, 2002 lipstick sales were up nearly 12% (Ethridge, 2003). A Dior dress might be out of reach, but a Dior lipstick might not be. According to Leonard Lauder, chair of Estèe Lauder, "when things get tough, women buy lipstick" (Lipsticks provide, 2001). Lauder supported this statement with what he called the "Leading Lipstick Indicator" (LLI). The LLI theory shows that, when consumers feel less than confident in the economy, they will turn to less expensive indulgences. For women, one indulgence consistently has been lipstick.

Whether it is a lipstick that promises to last all day or plump the lips, adorning lips with lipstick has played, and continues to play, an important role in many women's lives. The consistency of sales even during lean economic times suggests links among identity, appearance, cosmetics, and the fashion industry (Black, 2004). In the United States, since at least the 1920s, lipstick has been at the forefront of constantly shifting definitions and markers of ideal female beauty. The name of a color carries great weight in a woman's choice to buy (Kahn & Miller, 2005), and, by extension, the name affects not only whether a woman chooses a particular lipstick (Kahn & Miller, 2005) but also "how much she enjoys it" (Walker, 2005, p. 17). There are dozens of choices of brands, but "with a lot of makeup, there isn't really much to pay attention to besides color and texture, so a name that stands out means a product that stands out" (Begoun, as cited in Walker, 2005, p. 17).

Self-Declaration

A powerful component of participation in modern Western societies involves attention to the presentation of self. Goffman (1963) viewed the body as "integral to human *agency*"[italics original]. Three views comprise Goffman's (1963) declaration: (1) the body is a person's material property to be controlled and monitored, (2) meanings attributed to the body are determined by "shared vocabularies of body idiom" (Goffman, 1963, p. 35), such as "dress, bearing, movements and position, sound level, physical gestures such as waving or saluting, facial decorations, and broad emotional expressions" (p. 33), not under an individual's complete control, and (3) the body plays an important role in mediating reality in terms of self and social identity. This three-tiered approach suggests that the panoptic monitoring of physical appearance constructs the body as a malleable receptor and generator of individual and social meanings (Douglas, 1970; Foucault, 1979, 1980), as bearer of symbolic value (Bourdieu, 1984; Shilling, 1993), and as a symbolic material phenomenon (Shilling, 1993). Hence, bodies, and their constitutive parts, are carriers (sign-vehicles) and mechanisms through which social class, personality, and intent are conveyed. They work as "**predictive devices**" and are consistent with social norms regarding, for example, morality. It is the nature of the presentation of self to be promissory (Goffman, 1959). We want, for whatever reason, to be what others want us to be. Physical appearance can influence conduct toward us as an initial signal when complete information is otherwise unavailable to the surveyor.

An important cultural shift occurred in the United States at the beginning of the last century wherein the conceptualization of the female body moved from "laboring" to "desiring" (Turner, 1984, p. 3). In Western cultures, femininity is often regarded as "a 'natural' endowment of women," but it is also "a social construction motivated, in good measure, by power relations and financial gain" (Furman, 1997, p. 46). Through both symbolic and literal modeling of the accoutrements of femininity, women learn about new styles, codes of conduct, emotional responses, and social definitions of attractiveness, that is, how the self should be presented in everyday life. Appropriateness, "an all-encompassing concept which involves the negotiation of gender, class, ethnicity, and sexuality into identity" (Black, 2004, p. 181), is an aspect of this presentation of a self that is reified in mass media, particularly magazines, film, and now television. Bourdieu (2001) saw the appropriation of women's beauty akin to conformity, and, in this way, women are complicit in their oppression and the focus on physical appearance as a kind of "gentle violence" (Bourdieu, 2001, p. 11). The "aesthetic labor" of wearing cosmetics fulfills goals of the hegemonic process as it results in women taking the default position of an appearance-based self if, for no other reason, than that it is "appropriate," hence familiar and comfortable (Witz, Warhurst, & Nickson, 2003, p. 38).

The culture of beauty has never been only a regimen of self-appraisal and surveillance. Women have used makeup to declare themselves, "to announce their adult status, sexual allure, youthful spirit, political beliefs—and even to proclaim their right to self-definition" (Peiss, 2002, p. 269) to a point where cosmetics have become the "female equivalent of the power tie" (Ragas & Kozlowski, 1998, p. 75). As the physical self became routinely shaped, costumed, pierced, adorned, tattooed, exercised, and tanned, it became an increasingly important source, as well as a carrier, of information. The body, and thereby the lips, are, in a Bourdieuian perspective, the bearers of symbolic value, which are integrated into an analysis of the body as a material phenomenon (Shilling, 1993). Thus, the concept of "body" has lost its biological relevance, as it has become a highly malleable, socially constructed, product.

According to dominant ideological conventions and subsequent consumer response, happiness for women is equated with a thin, and above all a controlled, body that conforms to the rules and norms of the socially constructed view of femininity (Cusumano & Thompson, 1997; Harrison, 2001; Stice, Schupak-Neuberg, Shaw, & Stein, 1994; Williamson, 1978). To actualize the beauty imperative, women who seek validation, according to Western cultural expectations of physical appearance and affirmation of morality and status, must control their many appetites (Brumberg, 1998; Shilling, 1993; Wolf, 2002).

Making a Face

In *Decoding Advertisements,* Williamson (1978, p. 34) suggested that the "**fetishization of commodities**, and mystification of the meaning of products, can be decoded through the application of semiotics to reveal the disavowal of production/real human desires." Furthermore, it can be argued that commodity fetishism (and the production aspect of it) is decidedly gendered. Applying makeup (and other daily appearance practices) is part of the invisible, gender performative work that women do. By continually surveying themselves to be certain that they are projecting the image they desire, women engage in impression management and aspire to an ever-changing goal of realizing desired selves (Goffman, 1959). A woman who wears lipstick acts in such a way "intentionally or unintentionally to *express*" herself with the idea that "others will in turn be *impressed* in some way" by her [italics original] (Goffman, 1959, p. 2). Displays such as the made-up face communicate "acceptance and internalization of discursive practices" that are critical for women's success (Black, 2004, p. 114). They serve as visual reminders of **heteronormativity**. Such "embodied dispositions" reflect social position and "the habitus which underlies" it (Black, 2004, p. 114). This "to-be-looked-at-ness" (Mulvey, 2001, p. 397) aspect of impression management connects with women because "we live by inference" (Thomas, 1951, as cited in Goffman, 1959, p. 3). Making up literally constructs a mask, a persona, as a dramaturgical activity. According to **John Berger** (1977, p. 56), a woman

> … comes to consider the *surveyor* and the *surveyed* within her as the two constituent yet always distinct elements of her identity as a woman. She has to survey everything she is and everything she does because how she appears to others, and ultimately, how she appears to men, is of crucial importance for what is normally thought of as the success of her life.

Lipstick Signs

Barthes' (1982, p. 94) concept of myth as a system of communication and meaning suggests "every object in the world can pass from a closed, silent existence to an oral state, open to appropriation by society." This conceptualization of **semiology** "postulates a relation between two terms, a signifier and a signified," which produce the sign (Barthes, 1982, p. 97). In myth, the tripartite pattern of signifier, signified, and sign has a double function, it not only "makes us understand something…it imposes it on us" (Barthes, 1982, p. 102). Barthes used a rose as an example. Although red roses are used to signify passion, the flower itself (connotative level) is empty as a signifier; it has no meaning except that which a culture gives it. The resultant sign holds the meaning (denotative). In the case of lipstick, there is the oil wax base + coloring agents + trace amount of fragrance object (the signifier)—the raw material/physical object. By itself, before any socially constructed and agreed-upon characteristics are applied to the simple tube and contents, the object has no meaning. When meaning is applied, the result is the symbol/sign, such as lipstick. When red, for example, is the coloring agent, red + lipstick stand for (signify) specific emotions and actions, which then are "read" by the purchaser/user and by others within the context of a specific culture and set of beliefs. When mythical speech "points out and notifies" us of the sexual, moral, and class characteristics (signified) nature of the final object, the result is the sign—red lipstick (Barthes, 1982, p. 102).

Social class, morality, and sexuality are communicated internally and externally by brand but more specifically by color and name of the lipstick, which thereby emerges beyond a simple object. Essentially, form + meaning = concept. This is a crucial step in the process of building beliefs about an object; when it becomes normalized, the values seem natural or articulated (Hall, 1996). Lipstick as sign is an example both of "commodity fetishism…going beyond 'magic'" and the Marxian production process "because the goods being represented disavow not only production, but use value and also some levels of literal meaning" (Williams, 1980, as cited in Gamman & Makinen, 1994, p. 34). A fetish is also "a *fabrication*, an artifact, a labour of appearances and signs" [italics original] (Baudin, 1885, p. 5), and the "production of the image and the secondary production hidden in the process of its utilization" become one (de Certeau, 1984, p. xiii). Thereby, "lipstick manufacturers did not create an enhanced mouth, they created a pair of super labia" (Morris, 2004, p. 84), a doppelganger object of desire.

Through signifying practices, women make meaning from the cosmetics they choose; the lipstick-as-sign (and, by extension, the name of the color, tint, or shade) thereby becomes a commodity sign formed at the locus between a brand name and the object (lipstick). Fashion designer Diane von Fürstenberg (1998, as cited in Ragas & Kozlowski, 1998, p. 75) noted that "lipstick is to the face what punctuation is to a sentence and the act of applying [it] is steeped in sexual meaning." Then (Fürstenberg, 1988, as cited in Ragas & Kozlowski, 1998, p. 66) she added, "the name of a lipstick is like hope in a tube." It is at the juncture of the signifying practice and the commodity sign that we find a lipstick named *Drop Dead Red*.

Much of the information about lipstick reaches women through movies, store displays, peer groups, and advertising (primarily print, but increasingly via the

Internet). As a particularly powerful pedagogical force, advertising connects with women in different ways depending on self-perception and role-playing. It takes the "stuff of everyday life" and transforms it (Jhally, 1990, p. 31). Images of particular objects and materials from daily life are reconstituted in such a way that advertisers not only sell us consumer goods, but they also "sell us ourselves" in an environment "within which we and those goods are interchangeable" (Williamson, 1978, p. 13).

In modern societies, power flows not only from the top down in hierarchical form, but through the ephemera of everyday life (de Certeau, 1984; Turner, 1984). Lipsticks are no exception. In 1997, for example, the San Francisco Museum of Art show *Icons: Magnets of Meaning* contained 12 items of everyday life considered to be representative of American culture. Lipsticks were included because "they are icons. They work. Collectively we have been seduced by them, the need to have them" and because lipstick "allows us to make a face to meet the faces we meet, turning us into masks conforming to a mass image" (Betsky, 1997, p. 14). Through the socially constructed meaning of women's lips, "we find a new mode of investment which presents itself no longer in the form of control by repression but that of control by stimulation" (Foucault, 1980, p. 57).

A print advertisement has to make an immediate connection with the viewer, thereby employing signs and symbols that have been commonplace communicators in the society. Consumers often look to products for meanings needed to help construct, reconstruct, or sustain the image they have of themselves or would like to develop. Images and meanings are continuously drawn from the general culture and transferred back and forth between consumers and products. The associative process of **branding** used in advertising and marketing takes place when meaning is transferred to the object/sign. It is "the created image that has the hold on our most vibrant, immediate sense of what *is*, of what matters, of what we must pursue for ourselves" (Bordo, 1993, p. 103) and present to others. This transmutation works particularly well when joined with "emotional branding" (Gobé, 2001, p. xv) techniques (sounds, shapes, tastes, scents, and colors) (Klink, 2000) that often target women by engaging them "on the level of the senses and emotions" (Gobé, 2001, p. xv). Through embracing the sensual, advertisers have made lipstick "one of the sexiest products on Madison Avenue" (Ragas & Kozlowski, 1998, p. 49).

What's in a Name?

Names and everyday objects have power, as Michel de Certeau (1984) emphasized. Lipstick advertising, from the product itself to the naming of the color as part of branding, conveys information, triggers responses, activates thoughts, and evokes memories for the user of a product and those around her (Kahn & Miller, 2005). Lipstick names "draw upon the imagination first, then memory. They shock and fascinate us. They disturb us. Our lives are quiet. We like to be disturbed by delight" (Ackerman, 1993, p. 51). Department store brands, such as Estée Lauder, Clinique, Lancôme, Christian Dior, and Shiseido, convey an image of glamour and class communicated, in part, by what the brand name communicates about the wearer, where the products are available (higher end department stores), and what they cost ($12–$40 per tube). When makeup magnate Estèe Lauder named lipsticks, for example, she made "a color *do* something or put it in some location" with shades such as *Cinema Pink* and *Rosy Future* (Pallingston, 1999, p. 102). Revlon flirted early with some beautiful-but-dangerous names including *Fatal Apple, Paint the Town Pink*, and *Where's the Fire?* (Pallingston, 1999, p. 102). At M.A.C cosmetics (an Estèe Lauder company) makeup artists name the colors through a process of word association with characteristics such as *Envy, Integrity,* and *Virtue* (Pallingston, 1999, p. 102). Some "lipstick namers" look at a color and name it for the place, city, or country it evokes. The cosmetics company Lorac names some colors with locations and associations. *Malibu*, for example, is bright, clear, ands pink, whereas *New York* is dark, matte, and plum. Other companies draw upon particular films or past and present icons. Laura Mercier created the shade *M* for Madonna in her movie role as Evita Peron, and Della DePalma created a deep red reminiscent of the one worn by opera singer Maria Callas.

Lorac has created lipsticks named for particular celebrities such as *Winona* (Ryder), *Kim* (Basinger), and *Nicole* (Kidman), and then later made them available to the public (Pallingston, 1999). In the 1990s, companies such as Urban Decay and BeneFit parted ways with flowers, gems, seasons, and wines when they came out with anti-color colors such as *Ozone, Smog, Cement, Dirt*, and *But Officer.*[1] The resurgence of black lipstick in the early 1990s brought a touch of the theatrical and macabre with appellations such as *Damnation, Kiss of Death, Warlock, Sin,* and *Black Witch.* Fall 2005 brought, for example, matte stain colors such as *Cayenne, Candy, Cabernet*, and *Chili* (Singer, 2005).

Not only do colors and names of lipstick convey status, availability, and attitude, but also many of them refer to foods that are, by today's body ideal standards, off limits for most women. A *Triple Peach Pie, Double Chocolate Truffle*, or *Raspberry Soufflé* symbolically becomes forbidden fruit of contemporary femininity. These names "tend to stimulate the palate in addition to the eye or ear" through a phenomenon known as synesthesia (Zakia, 2002, p. 129), whereby a sensation, which would ordinarily occur in one sensory system occurs when another sensory system is stimulated.

Table 10.1: Lipstick Companies

Companies	Lipsticks	Companies	Lipsticks
Agnes B.	Lancôme	Cover Girl	Red Head's Fancy
Alexandra de Markoff	L'Oreal	Dior	Revlon
Almay	Laura Mercier	Elke Von Freudenberg	Rimmel
Annabelle Bloom	Lorac	English Ideas	RoC
Arden, Elizabeth	MProfessionals	Estée Lauder	Sans Spicos
Aveda	M.A.C.	Face Stockholm	Shiseido
Avon	Make-up Forever	Fetish	Shu Uemura
BeneFit	Manic Panic	Francois Nars	Smashbox
Black Radiance	Mawkins	Fudge	Stila
Bloom	Mary Kay	Garden Botanica	Sugar
Bobbi Brown	Mattese	Gayle Hayman	Sweet Georgia Brown
Body Shop	Maybelline	Givenchy	Tarte
Burt's Bees	Mavala	Guerlain	Three Custom Color Special
Calvin Klein	Max Factor	Hard Candy	Tommy Hilfiger
Chanel	Milani	Helena Rubenstein	Trucco
Charles of the Ritz	Molton Brown	Iman	Ultra Glaze
City Lights	Necessities	Isadora	Urban Decay
Clarins	Neutrogena	Jane	Ultima II
Clinique	Origins	Jordanna	Yves Rocher
Club Monaco	Poppy	Kanebo	Versace
Color Girl	Prescriptives	Kiehl	Wet 'n Wild
Color Strokes	Prestige	Kryolan	

The names of lipsticks and how they penetrate women's psyches as semiotic tools used in branding are the foci of the present study. As Gage (1999, p. 8) pointed out, "If color is to yield meaning, it must be named." Based on Goffman's (1959) concepts of presentation of self and impression management and Barthes' (1982) semiotic method for interpreting meaning, I studied the relationships among women, lipstick, food, and social expectations of femininity through an interpretive content analysis of the names of over 1,700 different shades and colors collected from the Web site lipstickpage.com. In a nonacademic analysis, Pallingston (1999) observed, "Lipsticks are most often named after foods, fantasy, places, flowers, times of the day, and various female archetypes" (p. 104). And, as displayed in advertisements, lipsticks are "purveyed more often as a food and drink ("Drenched with Moisture, try a lick of licorice!") than as agents of color" (Vlahos, 1979, p. 15). Those remarks stimulated the following research questions: (1) Under what major categories are lipsticks named? (2) What purpose does naming lipsticks serve? and (3) What are the implications for women and society? Or, to put it more simply, how do we get from a simple formula (oil wax base + coloring agents + trace amount of fragrance) presented in a 2-inch bullet-shaped tube, to something called *Double Truffle*?

The Lipsticks

The comprehensive Web site thelipstickpage.com has, "since 1995," been "entirely devoted to lipsticks" (http://www.thelipstickpage.com).[2] More than 1,700 colors sold by 44 manufacturers (see Table 10.1 for a complete list of companies) were listed at this site when I visited in 2004. These include both higher-end department store brands that cost about $15 to $40 per tube (e.g., Lancôme, Estèe Lauder, Chanel) and less expensive variety store brands that cost $2 to $6 per tube (e.g., Maybelline, Cover Girl, Wet 'n Wild). Quantitative content analysis and qualitative textual and content analyses were applied to thelipstickpage.com's named lipsticks (those with only numerical identification were removed from the sample). I thematically categorized the names (unit of analysis) given to the lipsticks and analyzed the meaning of the names according to Barthes' concept of signifiers and signified.

Categories

The coding categories I developed drew upon Pallingston's (1999, p. 104) presupposition that most lipsticks are named "after foods, fantasy, places, flowers, times of the day, and various female archetypes." These provided the first six categories for the research, and a preliminary examination of the data suggested eight additional classifications for a total of 14. These are defined as follows:

- *Color*: Straight-ahead color names.
- *Food:* Desserts, beverages (alcoholic and non-alcoholic), spices, and fruits.
- *Sex and Romance*: Words that refer to a woman's intentions, state of dress (or undress), or more romantic references.
- *Elements and Minerals*: Gems, minerals, and natural materials.
- *Emotions and Characteristics*: Emotions as well as personality and character traits.
- *Places*: Cities, countries, or locations, such as gardens.
- *People and Names*: Encompassed the archetype category but also went beyond this construct to include celebrity names, movie stars, characters, and other figures.
- *Flowers.* Flowers and flowering plants.
- *Objects*: Inanimate objects.
- *Darkside:* Names that evoked images of evil, darkness, witchcraft, and sorcery.
- *Arts and Media:* The names of artists, films, and related areas.
- *Times and Seasons*: Seasons and times of the day or year were included in this category as well as more holistic notions of time such as spring, May Day, and night.
- *Birds and Animals.* Living beings such as dove, fox, cat.
- *Other*: A variety of names did not fit under the other categories.

Findings

Table 10.2 shows that the top four categories of lipstick names were Food (24%), Color (20%), Sex and Romance (10%), and Elements and Minerals (9%). Names under the Food category included *Cherries Jubilee, Peach Melba, Apricot Fantasy, Grape Sorbet, Raisin Hell, Peach Mocha, Macaroon, Brown Sugar, Pumpkin, Toasted Almond, Rum, Sangria, Port, Brandy,* and *Double Matte Wine.* The color category was as simple as *Truly Red, Riot Red, Classic Coral, Pure Pink,* and *Rose.*

Sex and Romance was an interesting category. Names for these shades included *Buck Naked, See Through, Temptation, Sexy, Strip, Desire, Passion, Exhibitionist, Flesh, Primal, Vamp, Nymph, Coquette, Lust, Vixen, Tramp, Foreplay, Long Kiss,* and *Love Junky.* The fourth largest category, Elements and Minerals included *Sapphire Glitter, Platinum, Rocket Ruby, Garnet, 18K Gold,* and *Bronze Leaf.* Fantasy, broadly defined as "imagination unrestricted by reality" (Wordnet, 2005) could conceivably include every lipstick name, but in this case accounted for many

Table 10.2: Categories of Lipstick Names

Category	Number	Percent
Food	417	24
Color	345	20
Sex and romance	166	10
Elements and minerals	157	9
Emotions and characteristics	141	8
Other	138	8
People and names	85	5
Flowers	85	5
Places	54	4
Objects	49	3
Dark side	28	2
Arts and media	17	1
Birds and animals	17	1
Time and seasons	13	<1
Total	1,712	100

of the Sex and Romance colors. Lipsticks named for places accounted for 4% of the names (*Beach, Cafe, India, Alaska, Florida, Pasadena, Cuba, Long Island, Broadway*), and the "flowers" category contained 5% of the total (*Poppy, Rose, Geranium, Petunia, Spring Lilac*). The "times of day" category, which included seasons, accounted for less than 1% of names (*Autumn, Sunset Brown, Midnight,* and *Dusk*). Four lipsticks were named for "various female archetypes" (*Moon Goddess, Calliope, Venus,* and *Pale Venus*). The other ten categories accounted for 8% or less. Examples include categories such as Dark Side (*Black Witch, Fatal, Kiss of Death, Warlock, Blood Red, Asphyxia*), Birds/Animals (*Chinchilla, Pussy Cat*). Although the "Other" category accounts for 8% of the total, the names were ambiguous and adventitious enough that they could not be placed in the categories. Examples include *Big Bang, But Officer, SWF, Fluoride, Hypnotic, Epic, Road Stripe,* and *Graffiti*.

Summary

Women, cosmetics, and cultural definitions of femininity have an intimate shared history, one that includes coloring of lips and naming of lipsticks such as *Truly Toffee* and *Raisin Hell*. The research questions were (1) Under what major categories are lipsticks named? (2) What purpose does naming lipsticks serve? (3) What are the implications for women and society? The major name categories were Food, Color, Sex and Romance, and Elements and Minerals. These differ considerably from Pallingston's informal array ("foods, fantasy, places, flowers, times of the day, and various female archetypes"). This suggests that cosmetics companies and advertisers optimize women's emotional connections with food, particularly desserts and rich beverages, through lipstick in two ways: (1) by symbolically consuming the forbidden fruit and (2) by transforming oneself into the consumable. Pallingston (1999, p. 102) noted that, "In ancient cultures, the name of a thing was often one and the same with *being* that thing. Lipstick may be important in terms of becoming that thing—in either your mind or someone else's" [italics original]. **Bodily commodification** emerges from **brand commodification**, wherein lipstick-as-sign represents the "reduction of social meanings to exchangeable goods or services" (Holbrook, Block, & Fitzsimmons, 1998, p. 12), that is, lipstick substitutes for natural beauty as the basis for physical attractiveness. This **commodification** conjoins with consumption aimed at "appropriation of the body and transformation of…images into the commodified signs of self" (Langman, 1992, p. 61).

The fetishization of commodities (or commodity fetishism) of lipstick is thereby not only consumption of a lipstick as cosmetic, but also, through transference, consumption of the woman wearing it. Similarly, it functions as the symbolic consumption of the associated food, beverage, or characteristic. Williamson (1978, p. 70) described the commodified body phenomenon as an "**identikit**":

> In buying products with certain 'images,' we create ourselves…thus our lives become our own creations, through *buying* [italics original]; an indentikit of different images of ourselves, created by different products. We *become* [italics original] the artist who creates the face, the eyes, the lifestyle.

By using specific linguistic signs and symbols, lipstick names confer attitude, behavior, and/or access to a less fattening indulgence. Rather than directly applying her dessert to her hips (an old saying) a woman can instead "apply" the dessert to her lips. Goffman's (1959) concept of impression management and the presentation of self suggest that a woman applies color to her lips as a way of defining and presenting herself to the world and to herself. Several marketing strategies might attract a woman to a particular lipstick, such as brand name, the eye appeal of an in-store display, or a sense of what color looks best on her. However, when the decision to buy is made, the name of the color provides an avenue for making a statement and embodying an attitude, even if only the wearer knows the "truth" (Kahn & Miller, 2005).

What kind of picture do these lipsticks paint? Moreover, why are there more than 1,700 differently named lipsticks? What are the implications of this practice? Lipsticks matter, as they are one of the accoutrements of many women's everyday lives. Each year some shades and names are retired and others introduced. More important, however, is that the name given to a lipstick has hegemonic potential, the meaning and symbolic value of which were unpacked in the present study. The results of the present study are apposite to de Certeau's (1984) philosophy on the importance of the everyday because it is through the objects of everyday life that established views of gender and power are perpetuated and reinforced. Identification of the semiotic apparatus used to sell lipsticks demonstrates the conflation of the cultural imperative of appearing beautiful and desirable by wearing cosmetics as display:

> Because she is forced to concentrate on the minutiae of her bodily parts, a woman is never free of self-consciousness. She is never quite satisfied, and never secure, for desperate, unending absorption in the drive for a perfect appearance—call it feminine vanity—is the ultimate restriction on freedom of mind. (Brownmiller, 1984, p. 51)

Food, beverages, sex, and romance are essential components of human survival and desire. By applying *Truly Toffee* lipstick, a woman not only acts as subject but also as object, consumed and consumable. This culturally shaped means of communicating and embodying particular characteristics plays into the complicated conflation of appearance, identity, gender roles, beauty, and food. In this preliminary study I explored the naming of lipsticks and extended the analysis by inquiring into what purpose such naming serves in women's psychic space. As Davis (1991, p. 33) reminded us, "feminist theory on beauty needs to be grounded; that is, it must take the ambiguous, contradictory, everyday social practices of women as a starting point." Naming and branding of products is a meaningful part of advertiser-consumer connectedness. Women spend a great deal of money on lipsticks, as do the companies that develop and promote them. This research contributes to the limited literature on women and cosmetics in general, and lipstick in particular, both of which have significant economic, cultural, and sociological implications. The names of lipsticks serve as both visual and verbal reminders of what thin, attractive American women should not eat if they want to remain thin and attractive. Future researchers could examine branding, naming, and identity politics in relationship to advertisements for lipsticks and related products. The work of Bourdieu (1984) and others can inform a social-class-based analysis that could examine lipstick names by company and cost. In-depth personal interviews with women who do (and do not) wear makeup could yield important information. Shortcomings of the present study include the regular and unavoidable changes in lipstick names, inconsistent, in some cases, availability of certain shades due to seasonal campaigns, and availability of http://thelipstickpage.com. Although the site has been active since 1995, in the last few years it has changed in content and focus. For example, the site now features advertising for the lipsticks, which lessens its credibility as a research source. A potential shortcoming of the present study is that the coding categories are not mutually exclusive. However, given the nature of naming and the use of specific nouns and adjectives that refer to a quality or characteristic associated with a color or behavior, the findings are likely to be similar. Future research could examine naming according to, for example, high-end department store versus grocery, drugstore, and other retail level brands and could examine differences, if any, in names according to social class.

In many ways, women's lips and their coloring have served as tools of social control, a means of identifying the sinless from the sinful. Lipstick labels (names) as enticement and products that promise "the pleasures of fantasy and desire" are more than a system of commerce (Peiss, 1990, p. 6). They are more than the marketing and advertising behind them. When women "put on a face," or "put on war paint," they are not only acting in line with social prescriptions of feminine beauty but are also involved in a system of meaning that helps them to navigate the sea of changing conditions that are a part of postmodern social experience.

Questions for Discussion

1. Is it possible for a woman to wear makeup and be a feminist?
2. Are cosmetics targeted toward teen girls as well as grown women?
3. How do lipstick commercials advertise the product? Print advertisements?
4. Why do women wear lipstick?
5. What kind of information does lipstick wearing confer? Does the color matter?

Key Words

Bodily commodification	Brand commodification
Commodification	Fetishization of commodities
Heteronormativity	Identikit
John Berger	Michel de Certeau

Predictive device	Presentation of self
Semiology	Semiotic model

Endnotes

1. Apparently, this type of naming is nothing new. During the Renaissance, lip colors came in *Turkey, Horseflesh*, and *Beggar's Grey*. Mary Tudor wore *Old Medley,* and in England under the rule of King Edward VI, some colors were made official, such as *Merrey* (a mulberry) and his personal favorite *Raw Flesh* (Pallingston, 1999, pp. 109–110).

2. The Web site http://www.thelipstickpage.com changed in late 2004 to a forum. When I visited in early 2004 it was a comprehensive, non-commercial site. In 2006, it was re-launched with advertising.

Sun Also Rises: Stereotypes of the Asian American Woman on *Lost*

Asian women have been reduced to one-dimensional caricatures in Western representation…[which] obscures the social injustice of racial, class, and gender oppression.

Yen Le Espiritu

Jin: "Honey…I don't like being told what to do."
Sun: "Being told what to do was my life for four years…I didn't like it much either."
Jin: "Right. I don't suppose you did."

[When you watch TV] you want to think I could do that. I could be there. That could be me in five or six years. But you don't see anything of yourself.

Children Now.org

Sun-Hwa Paik is the beautiful dutiful daughter of a wealthy Korean industrialist. Although her family attempts match making, she meets and falls in love with the son of a poor fisherman, Jin Soo-Kwan. Despite social class differences, Jin gains Sun's father's permission for them to marry with the agreement that he will work for Mr. Paik. Mr. Paik asks Jin, "What would you do for my daughter?" "Even work for me?" Jin says he would and Mr. Paik wants to know why he should give his daughter to a man who sells his own dreams so easily. "She is my dream, sir," says Jin. They shake hands and Sun-Hwa Paik is passed to Jin Soo-Kwan. They marry, but do not live happily every after (Gates, 2005).

Jin's personality darkens the longer he works for Sun's father. One evening, Jin returns home and Sun insists on knowing what it is he does for her father. He tells Sun "his job was whatever Mr. Paik deemed it to be, for the sake of their marriage —leaving a stunned Sun outside, and leaving Jin to wash the blood off his hands" (lostpedia). Ready to leave her marriage, Sun plots an escape but has a change of heart at the airport when Jin shows the tender part of himself he has buried. She and Jin end up taking Oceanic Airlines' Sydney to Los Angeles flight 815. Nothing is the same after that. The plane crashes somewhere in the Pacific Ocean. Sun and Jin are among 46 survivors.

For fans of the hit network television series *Lost*, which ran from 2004–2010, Sun is one of several reoccurring characters (Figure 11.1). The complexity of *Lost*, its many characters, the use of flash forward, sideways, and backwards narrative techniques mean each individual has limited screen time. However, when he or she *is* the focus of an episode, the stories are deep and complex.

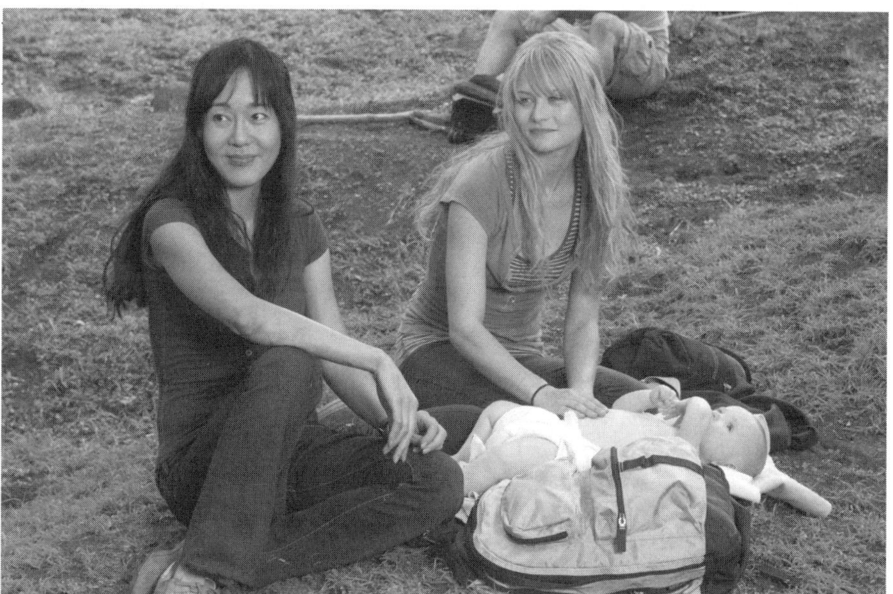

Figure 11.1: Sun (Yunjim Kim) and Claire (Emilie de Ravin) from ABC's *Lost*.

Source: photofestnyc.com

This is the case with Sun, one of the three Asian American actors on the show, a rarity on network or cable television.[1] Therefore, every moment viewers spend with her is precious and influential. Scholarly attention to issues of representation of race, ethnicity, and gender has not been at the forefront of academic interrogations of the show. In this chapter I suggest that while *Lost* liberates many of its characters from the confines of narrow, stereotypical portrayals, it nevertheless objectifies women in general, and race/ethnicity and womanhood in particular, into safe categories of expected gender and racial norms. In what follows I describe representations of Asian American women in media, with an emphasis on feminist **standpoint theory**. The representation of Sun (played by Yunjim Kim) on *Lost* serves as a case study for this analysis, a character who, "cries out for maturity and moral development" (Taliaferro & Kastrul, 2008, p. 79). I argue that she embodies the major stereotypes of Asian women (**Dragon Lady** and **China Doll**) as well as reinforces the Model Minority image. I draw on the first five seasons of *Lost* for illustrative quotes and examples of Sun's rotation between the two primary stereotypes of Asian women.

For purposes of this chapter, the following research questions are posited:

1. What is the history of the representation of Asian American women on television?
2. How is Sun, as the embodiment of Asian American womanhood, portrayed on *Lost*?

Getting Lost

Lost premiered in September 2004. Appealing to both men and women, more than 18 million viewers watched the first episode and, over its first seasons, the show averaged 15 million weekly viewers and top 20-prime time program status (Ahrens, 2006, D1). A critical success as well, during its first two seasons *Lost* received 19 Emmy nominations, including a best drama win in 2005. Lead actor Matthew Fox (Jack) said the show resonates because

> *Lost* is so much more about these characters being individually, personally, and spiritually lost than being lost on the island. It will test them as individuals. Maybe they will be finding themselves rather than being found. (as quoted in Adams, sec 13:4)

Lost is the story of survivors of an airplane crash, Oceanic Flight 815. For reasons no one can explain, the flight ends up 1,000 miles off course and then splits in two above a remote, off-the-map, South Pacific island. The show is the story of 46 survivors before, during, and after the crash as well as countless Others who came before them. Of the 14 premiere episode characters only four are women:

Shannon, the spoiled rich White girl; Claire, a lone, pregnant, White Australian woman; Kate, a White bank-robbing felon; and Sun, a quiet Korean wife.

The Sun character was not originally in the story, but when actor Yunjin Kim auditioned for the part of Kate, producer and writer J. J. Abrams liked her so much he wrote her into the story. There had been a discussion of a non-English speaking couple, but Kim's audition sealed it. Why a Korean couple? Perhaps because of increasing awareness of the spending power and likely attraction to the show for advertising among Asian Americans. Given the scarcity of representations of Asians and Asian Americans in media, each one merits particular attention and study. As Meyer and Stern (2007) point out, explanations for the paucity of research on Asians or Asian women has to do, in part, because portrayals such as model minority aren't necessarily viewed as problematic (at least on the surface). Furthermore, "it is problematic to speak of 'Asian' women as a monolithic or homogenous category" (Jiwani, 2005, p. 183). When she first read the script for the first episode of *Lost,* Kim expressed concern to the writer/producer J. J. Abrams, to whom she said, "Wait a minute, she's such a stereotypical character and that's not how it was described to me" (Surette, 2009, n.p.). Kim was promised that the character would develop during the course of the series. Therefore, "Sun's representation becomes important not only in terms of Asian visibility, but also as part of the ongoing political economy surrounding Asian American actors and roles in the television industry" (Meyer & Stern, 2007, p. 315). She is also said to have undergone the greatest character transformation on the show. Kim says of her role:

> She was a very mysterious, very veiled, subservient Korean wife, but you knew there was something more to her. And as the seasons went on, every time we'd flash back or flash forward to Sun and Jin's story, you got to find out more and more about her. It's been a thrilling ride for an actress to start with someone completely different and end up with where she is right now, I feel like they're two different characters. (Surette, 2009, n.p.)

The cast is multi-cultural—there are African American men and women, Latinas and Latinos, an Arab man, White men and women, as well as Sun and Jin. What is interesting about *Lost* is conflicts are rarely, if ever, about someone's race or ethnicity (Gaffney, 2008). Instead, Otherness is defined in some cases by longevity on the island or how much (or how little) is known about him or her. "*Lost* makes the notion of otherness explicit" (p. 140). There is a group referred to as "the Others" who occupied the island before the crash. What little is known about them is based primarily on conjecture, fear, and stories told by those who have encountered members of this group. Who exactly is an Other is slippery, which is consistent with constructions of Otherness, because, "for otherness to function…it must adapt to new moments. If static, it will lose its power" (p. 140).

As discussed in detail in earlier chapters, the construction of the Other happens through ideology. It is not a natural, normal, or eternal form of being; it just seems to be that way. Thus, ideology, as a system of beliefs, creates categories of people who are one of Us and are one of Them. All cultures do this, but the basis upon which these distinctions are made and the consequences of these markings vary considerably. On *Lost*, the many ways Otherness operates is demonstrated in "how it both creates fear and is created by fear, how it serves as a divide-and-conquer strategy, how it creates an "us versus them," and how those are associated with otherness are linked to savagery and to a lack of civilization" (Gaffney, 2008, p. 140).

Ideological Constructs of Asians

Ideological constructs of Otherness created in a hegemonic system use stereotypes as organizing tools. "Ideological state apparatuses" are social institutions such as church, religion, education, family and the mass media that disseminate and perpetuate particular versions of Asian-ness (Althusser, 1971). The stereotypes of Asian women as virgins or vamps and Asian men as effeminate or asexual are built from a past deeply immersed in issues of immigration and labor.

Between 1840 and 1930, more than one million men immigrated to the United States from Korea, Japan, China, the Philippines, and India to work. Viewed and treated as cheap laborers, U.S. immigration law regarded them as disposable, temporary, and exploitable workers. Chinese laborers were, for example, subject to violence as in the 1885 attack in Rock Springs, Wyoming in which 500 miners were attacked and 28 were massacred (Zinn, 2005, p. 266). Furthermore, laws forbid immigration of women out of fear they would stay (Espiritu, 2008). In 1882, Congress passed the **Chinese Exclusion Act** and, in 1924, prohibited all Asians from immigrating (Mansfield-Richardson, 2000).

Treatment and anti-Asian sentiment vacillated from group to group, depending on what was happening with U.S. relations, economic conditions, and war. For example, in February 1942, following the Japanese bombing of Pearl Harbor, "anti-Japanese hysteria spread in the government" (Zinn, 2005, p. 416). Franklin D. Roosevelt signed **Executive Order 9066** which gave the U.S. army the authority and power (without warrants, indictments, or hearings) to arrest every Japanese American living on the West Coast (110,000 people), remove them from their homes, and transport them to prison-like camps. Families were torn apart. Mothers and children were sometimes sent to one camp and fathers and older sons to another. Many of these individuals were long-time American residents and some were multi-generational citizens who were viewed as a threat simply by racial group association.

Out of the conditions of separation of families, either due to labor or perceived threat during wartime, constructions of race-based gender stereotypes arose. Men who worked on the railroads, in agriculture, and other occupations during the early days of immigration established "bachelor societies" (Sun, 2003, p. 657). As they were prohibited from bringing families to the United States or could not afford to live on their own, the men lived often in groups. As a result, they were seen as either asexual or a threat to White women. **Anti-miscegenation laws** (see Chapter 2) on the books in most states at the time prevented anyone from marrying across racial lines. Similar to the construction of Black men as predatory rape threats to White women, Chinese men were believed to possess an "undisciplined and dangerous libido" (Fung, 1996, p. 82). Prohibited from entering professions and high-paying occupations, many men took jobs doing so-called "women's work" as cooks, laundrymen, and domestic workers, further feminizing their image.

Emasculated images of Asian men were presented in mass media, particularly in films. Charlie Chan, a fat Chinese detective, was one extreme and the evil Dr. Fu Manchu, "a cruel, cunning, diabolical representation of the yellow peril" (Xing, 1998, p. 58) occupied the opposite position. These stereotypes were the only images most non-Asians saw of Asian men. The emasculated Asian American man is still present in advertising, television, and film today in characters such as the "nerdy Asian American adolescent math geniuses and brainy Asian American scientists who speak fortune-cookie English" (Cao & Novas, 1996, p. xvi) or camera-toting tourists. Even the martial arts experts sometimes played by Asians might be powerful and effective in their craft but aren't shown has having a romantic or loving side.

Asian American women were similarly typed as a result of historical conditions of immigration. When Asian men were prevented from bringing their families with them and women were kept from immigrating through legitimate channels, many sought sexual liaisons via prostitutes. Some Asian American women were already in residence in the United States, and others were brought under the auspices of finding work but were forced into prostitution. In 1870, estimates show 61% of the 3,536 Chinese women in California were prostitutes (Sun, 2003, p. 658). Even though the **Page Law** was passed in 1875 (preventing importation of prostitutes) Chinese women were nevertheless suspected of being sex workers and were subjected to harassment and violence (Espiritu, 2008).

U.S. military involvement in many Asian countries over the decades also reinforced the view of Asian women as prostitutes. Whether troops were located in the Philippines, Japan, Korea, Taiwan, or elsewhere, soldiers often engaged with women who were doing this work. This view of Asian men as inferior and asexual and Asian women as subservient or hypersexual served as confirmation of "White man's virility and superiority" (Espiritu, 2008, p. 13).

Foundations

Origins of the idea of Asian women as inferior can be traced to Edward Said's (1979) concept of Orientalism which means a prejudicial attitude of peoples in the West toward peoples of the East, informed by 18th and 19th century European imperialism and colonization.[2] According to Said, "the essence of Orientalism is the ineradicable distinction between Western superiority and Oriental inferiority" (p. 42). For most Westerners, particularly up until the last fifty or so years, the experience of peoples from the East or Asia has been second hand, via the media or other people's accounts. Therefore, the "pictures in their heads" often have/had little to do with reality (Lippmann, 1922/1961, p. 3).

In many early accounts, the West (America and Europe) was portrayed as developed, known, and superior whereas the East was "undeveloped, mysterious, and inferior" (Kim & Chung, 2005, p. 73). Orientalism, as a belief and practice, was used to justify colonization, domination, and oppression of people from Asian countries. As described in greater detail in Chapter 14, a variety of exclusionary laws and practices were applied to Asian immigrants depending on what was happening in America, that prevented them from immigrating, from studying for certain occupations, and from fully participating as U.S. citizens.

Prejudice (preconceived beliefs) was not only institutionalized through laws and legislation (discrimination), but also manifested in popular culture. In the early 20th century in America, common consumer items and memorabilia featured **Sinophobic** (fear of Chinese people and culture) caricatures. Stereotypical Chinese-couple salt and pepper shakers, for example, or porcelain China Doll figures exaggerated physical features and hyper-feminized both men and women (Kim & Chung, 2005). Such representations reinforced White Americans' feelings of superiority, strength, and sensibility. This "allowed them to lay both physical and sexual claim to the bodies of Orientals at home and abroad" (p. 74).

Asian women were especially constructed as inferior, as were women in general. White male heterosexual desire for Asian women was normalized in depictions in film in particular (Marchetti, 1993). Two primary constructions, that of a hyper-sexual and aggressive woman (**Dragon Lady**) and a submissive, child-like creature (**China Doll**), objectify women as the object of a male sexual gaze as well as a property (Gee, 1988; Lee, 1996; Marchetti, 1993).

Media portrayals reinforced these roles, particularly in film, but also in advertising, on television, and in popular culture. As discussed in earlier chapters, a stereotype is "a cognitive structure that contains the perceiver's knowledge, beliefs, and expectancies about some human group" (Hamilton & Trolier, 1986, p. 133). I add this also includes, at times, *lack* of expectations as well, particularly when it comes to gender stereotypes of women. A stereotype is part of "a schema for people we perceive as belonging to a social group" (Gorham, 2010, p. 17). Stereotypes function as scripts (schemata) through which we categorize in ways that give us fundamental characteristics of persons, places, or things in the world around us. Schemata are road maps, guides for objects (cars, couches), events (what we can expect or how we should behave at a wedding versus a funeral), and people. Thus, with limited amounts of invested mental effort, we can size up a situation or a person.

A feature associated with a schema is priming. A word or image or other feature can activate a schema. We come to expect these triggers and typically apply them to people or situations we're familiar with. If we consistently and persistently (as predicted by accumulation theory) are exposed to information that triggers associations we're likely to believe them to be "the truth." These **primed concepts** influence how we perceive and how we believe we should perceive information. Furthermore, we seek out information that is consistent with what we already believe. Schemata are organizational tools for our knowledge, beliefs, and attitudes as well as for expectations. Numerous studies of priming effects, such as use of particular words or images, reveal that stereotypes can be triggered even without our realizing it (Gorham, 2010). Thus, information we receive regularly in the media can influence what we think about others and ourselves. A stereotype, said, Walter Lippmann (1922/1961, p. 98) "precedes the use of reason," imposing "a certain character on the data of our senses before the data reach the intelligence." They shape our perceptions and are sometimes so strong that, even in the face of contrary evidence or experiences, remain because they become part of our beliefs. A study by Devine and Elliot (1995), for example, demonstrated that people select terms such as "lazy" or "poor" as traits of Blacks and, furthermore, that they tend to link them as being "natural tendencies." Thus, "an especially nasty characteristic of many stereotypes" is that they not only tell us what people of a particular group are like, they seem to explain *why* they are that way (Gorham, 2010, p. 19).

Feminist standpoint theory

If representations of minority men and women were wide and deep, a single narrow, hypersexualized, violent, or submissive portrayal wouldn't be particularly problematic. However, as is the case with race, gender, sexual, and other stereotypes, portrayals in media and popular culture tend to be polarized according to exaggerated characteristics. As a result, these one-dimensional figures stand in for the complexity and lack of uniformity that exists with real human beings. Who speaks for, stands in for, is given voice or face-time in media and popular culture is typically selected by those controlling media production. As Atkin (1992) notes

> social changes during the past twenty years thus may have contributed to changing media images of minorities. But true parity in representation will remain elusive so long as white cultural ideology— glorifying white norms, mores, and values—works to maintain a status quo for blacks [and other ethnic minority groups] as second-class citizens.

Ahlström (2005, p. 80) argues, "A great deal of knowledge and belief is produced in a social context." As described in the preceding section, stereotypes are cultural creations. Earlier chapters in this book explored representations of Arabs, Native Americans, African Americans, and women; television, film, advertising, and other forms of communication that have consistently and persistently corroborated in presenting limited and limiting views of members of these groups. "Stereotyped portrayals of African Americans and the unrealistic sanguine views of contemporary racial relations often presented in the mainstream media help perpetuate the racist myths held by ordinary White Americans" (Feagin, Vera, & Batur, 2001, p. 24). Thus the media play a key role in reinforcing limited and limiting images that influence behavior toward others and toward one's self. "The U.S. media are overwhelmingly White-oriented and White-controlled. White control of powerful institutions—from mass media to corporate workplaces to universities to police departments—signals White dominance to all members of the society" (p. 12).

Those who author television characters, for example, are usually members of dominant culture. **Feminist epistemology** argues that gender influences the way we understand and know the world. **Standpoint theory** predicts that subordinated groups such as women and people of color are subject to institutional and individualized forms of discrimination based on being members of these groups. Dominant social practices thus disadvantage particular groups by

> (1) excluding them from inquiry, (2) denying them epistemic authority, (3) denigrating their "feminine" cognitive styles and modes of knowledge, (4) producing theories of women that represent them as inferior, deviant, or significant only in the ways they serve male interests, (5) producing theories of social phenomena that render women's activities and interests, or gendered power relations, invisible, and (6) producing knowledge (science and technology) that is not useful for people in subordinate positions, or that reinforces gender and other social hierarchies. (*Stanford Encyclopedia of Philosophy,* 2009)

This theory also argues while the dominant group holds power in visible and invisible ways, particular forms of knowledge are situated among both the oppressed groups and the oppressor. The standpoint of the privileged group (dominant society) is one that sees lower status of other groups as normal, natural, and eternal; the disadvantaged group sees differences as socially contingent and changeable. This form of **critical theory** argues that more accurate representations are possible and necessary to change the status of marginalized groups. A standpoint is an accomplishment, not something that is automatically occupied by virtue of being a member of a group. Harding (1991, p. 127) notes

> women do not automatically occupy a feminist standpoint just by virtue of being women; a standpoint has to be achieved, and the way to achieve it is to raise one's consciousness through, among other things, a critical examination (which might very well be a self-examination) of the dominant institutional beliefs and practices that systematically disadvantage women and other traditionally marginalized groups.

Thus, Asian Americans are perpetually seen as "forever foreigners" by White majority culture (Aoki & Takeda, 2008, p. 143). Despite generations of participation in American culture and politics, Asian Americans are still regarded if not *from* another country as at least newly arrived. "You cannot look like an Asian and also look like an American," according to this view (p. 143). Many are asked, "Where are you from" based on physical appearance or "how did you learn to speak English so well," even though he or she is/was born in the United States. These are not questions asked of White Americans based on appearance alone.

Another generalized stereotype of Asian Americans is the model minority. This stereotype seems to have gained strength during the 1960s when stories were published in popular media such as the *New York Times Magazine* and *U.S. News & World Report* touting the work ethic of the high-achieving Asian American who "could overcome great obstacles" (such as discrimination, internment, bigotry, and other challenges) "and [still] succeed" (Aoki & Takeda, 2008, p. 145). Higher median income, high educational achievement, low rates of juvenile delinquency are all factors that bolster a "model" minority (and make members of other groups look lesser-than, for example, on SAT scores). This is a seemingly positive stereotype until one looks below the surface. As is the case with any stereotype, these are generalizations, which do not account for wide variation among Asian Americans as *individuals*. The idea of super success stories can disadvantage members of this group because of the perception that, for example, Asian American youth don't need grants for college or tutors. Conversely, Asian American students who aren't skilled in math (but might excel in art) often feel something is wrong. Thus, the stereotype is not only externalized but also internalized in ways that can contribute at least to feelings of uncertainty and can even be harmful or hurtful.

Representations of Asian American Women in Media

The 1990s were watershed years for Asian women in television. There was comedienne Margaret Cho on her short-lived situation comedy *All American Girl*, Ming-Na on the drama *ER*, and Lucy Liu in the comedy drama *Ally McBeal*.

Liu played Ling Woo an "articulate, high-powered, and acculturated" attorney, which ran counter to the many "off-the-boat refugee" images prevalent in news media of the time (Sun, 2003, p. 657). She gained visibility for Asian American women in her role. Liu went on to appear in the *Charlie's Angels* movies as well as in the Quentin Tarantino hit *Kill Bill II*. The Woo character broke the stereotypical China Doll role many Asian women occupied. However, she simultaneously reinforced the Dragon Lady. While all of the women on Ally McBeal were obsessed with sex, "Ling still stands out for her kinky sexual preferences and techniques" (p. 661).

After 2000, two programs offered Asian women roles with more depth; there was Keiko Agena on *Gilmore Girls* and Kristin Kreuk on *Smallville*. Arguably, the greatest character development took place on the sci-fi drama *Lost* (2004–2010) and the medical drama *Gray's Anatomy* (2005–present). Both of these programs have been huge hits for the networks, which discovered something: people of color tuned in, and White people didn't stop watching. In fact, ratings even went up on some of the shows. A collective, networking programming response of "Gee, maybe this whole diversity thing isn't such a bad idea, after all!" was felt for some time (Warn, 2007, n.p.).

Comedienne Margaret Cho's network television comedy show *All American Girl* lasted less than one season (1994). Between 1997 and 2002, other than a few news anchors and journalists, Lisa Ling on the daytime talk show *The View*, was the only Asian woman on prime-time television. Thus, there were no competing images to present a more balanced view of Asian women (Shimizu, 2007).

While today the number of Asian women on television is double what it was years ago, the number is still relatively small. When *Ally McBeal* ended in 2002, Liu moved to other programs such as ABC's *Cashmere Mafia* (January–February 2008). Lane Kim (Keiko Agena) appeared for seven seasons on *Gilmore Girls,* and Lindsay Price on *Lipstick Jungle* (2008–2009). The portrayal of Woo as "the over sexualized, evil seductress" reinforced the stereotype of Asian women because there were few to counteract it (p. 252). The short-lived crime drama *Women's Murder Club* (2007–2008) on ABC also featured an Asian woman in a lead role, as did *Vanished* (Ming-Na) (August–November 2008). Sandra Oh continues as Cristina Yang on *Grey's Anatomy's*, Michela Conlin is on *Bones*—doctors are, of course, model minority occupations. In its sixth and final season, *Lost*'s Yunjin Kim still appeared.

At the Web site TV.com, Sun is described as being of "two flavors": "as a sheltered wife of a dominating Asian man and a down-to-business, driven woman who will stop at nothing to achieve her goal" (Surette, 2010, n.p.). This description encompasses both of the major Asian American stereotypes as described in the next section.

Dragon Lady

"The wicked witch of the East, a reptilian dragon lady," is how *The New York Times* described Chinese Empress Tsu-his, who "ruled China from 1898 to 1908" (as quoted in Seagrave, 1992, p. 261). This image of the Asian (and by association Asian American) woman has been one of the most popular culture presentations over time. Consistent with the "forever foreigner" belief, a Dragon Lady can be either foreign or U.S. born.

The Dragon Lady ("prostitutes and devious madams") (Tajima, 1989, p. 309) is hypersexual, aggressive, opportunistic, and predatory. This **misogynistic** (anti-woman) stereotype is often presented as a gold-digger, going after (primarily) White men for their money and power. Strong, determined, out to get what she can in the world, the Dragon Lady is seductive but untrustworthy. It is "a stereotype of an East Asian female as mean, deceitful, domineering, or mysterious" (Herbst, 1997, p. 72).

One of the first portrayals of this stereotype in media was the first Chinese American movie star **Anna Mae Wong** in the 1924 blockbuster *Thief of Baghdad* (Walsh, 1924). Despite Wong's beauty and talent, she was usually cast in secondary roles, opposite White actresses such as Myrna Loy who appeared in yellow face (made to appear stereotypically Asian).

In modern times, Lucy Liu's Ling Woo character on *Ally McBeal* was pure Dragon Lady. As a Chinese-American Mandarin-speaking lawyer she harbored great sexual secrets and used her knowledge to tease and control men: "She is also the person who has a number of unknown sexual tricks (sexual finger sucking and the wax trick followed by the hair tickle) that she uses to keep her boyfriend interested without having to have intercourse with him because she does not like sweat" (p. 250). Woo is portrayed as "alien, evil, erotic, and hypersexualized" (p. 240).

The portrayal of Ling Woo attracted scholarly attention as "the embodiment of the Asian fantasy woman, the seductive temptress expert in eroticism who is knowledgeable in the art of sexual pleasure unknown to the Western world" (p. 72). Hamamoto (1994) describes Ling Woo as

> a neo-Orientalist masturbatory fantasy figure concocted by a white man whose job it is to satisfy the blocked needs of other white men who seek temporary escape from their banal and deadening lives by indulging themselves in a bit of visual cunnilingus while relaxing on the sofa. Ling sent a powerful message to white America that Asian American women are not to be trifled with. She runs circles around that tower of Jell-O who serves as her white boyfriend. She's competitive in a profession that thrives on verbal aggression and analytical skill. (p. 74)

China Doll/Geisha Girl

The second primary stereotype of Asian American women is the submissive, obedient, hard-working, childlike "Lotus Blossom Baby (e.g., China Doll, Geisha Girl) and the shy Polynesian beauty" (Tajima, 1989, p. 309). This type depends on the construction of White masculinity as a superior image to Asian male masculinity. She is "[d]emure, diminutive, and deferential" (Espiritu, 1997, p. 94). This stereotype has many of the characteristics of the model minority and has "spawned an entire marriage industry…the Filipino wife is particularly in vogue for American men who order Asian brides from picture catalogues" (Tajima, 1989, p. 309).

The movie *The World of Suzie Wong* (Quine, 1960) is an example of a single Asian woman embodying both stereotypes. On the one hand Suzie (played by Nancy Kwan), referred to as "the hooker with a heart of gold," displayed "shameless sexual desire.…Aggressive and manipulative traits…and [an] inability to resist White men" along with a diminutive figure, childlike behaviors, and naivety typical of the China Doll (Spade & Valentine, 2007, p. 261). The stereotype supports popular definitions of White masculinity and male dominance and reifies power.

Fiery Sun/ Submissive Sun

The second research question posited in this chapter: "How is Sun, as the embodiment of Asian womanhood, portrayed on *Lost?*" is explored in this section. In particular, how do racial and gender stereotypes of Asian womanhood emerge in relation to representations of Whiteness on the show?

Each episode of *Lost* presents viewers with different layers of a complex story of an island, different groups of people who have inhabited it, at different periods of time. Viewers of *Lost* learn about Sun's life prior to being a passenger on Flight 815 as they do all of the characters—by use of flashbacks, flash forwards, flash side-ways, and sidebars to the main story.

Season 1—Rising Sun

Early episodes of *Lost* present Sun as a little girl, a rich little girl, who is used to doing what she pleases, when she pleases, at least until she is caught. For example, when she accidentally breaks her father's glass ballerina she doesn't confess, rather accuses the maid and lets the maid be fired even though she could have prevented it by admitting she broke it, but she'd rather not confess the truth. This duplicity in Sun's nature appears repeatedly throughout the show's many seasons.

In the first five episodes of the series, Jin and Sun are established as "THAT Korean Couple, where he is controlling and nasty, and she is submissive and fearful, and no one can understand a word they say" (Stafford, 2006, p. 41). One of the first things Sun sets about doing when the survivors begin to accept that they may not be rescued is to create a garden. In several episodes Sun demonstrates knowledge of homeopathic herbs and traditional healing skills that are never explained. Whereas many of the passengers panic, dutiful Sun (and Jin) attend to practical matters. Sun has extensive knowledge of herbal medicine, is able to garden and produce vegetables under difficult circumstances, and is unafraid to get her hands dirty. She "gives Sawyer herbs to help his headaches, teaches Walt to brush his teeth with a plant, and is able to help Shannon's asthma attacks with eucalyptus she harvests" (Wood, 2007, p. 204). She creates healing remedies for Jin's hands and concocts a poison to sicken Jin so he won't go on a raft seeking help. She is a medicine woman, skilled in traditional ways in opposition to Jack's modern medical training. Sun's garden is also where she is most vulnerable. She is knocked out and kidnapped from there and it is where she finds out she is pregnant.

Jin and Sun's relationship "is a portrait of a whirlwind romance, a controlling father, and a difficult marriage" (Stafford, 2006, p. 41), but the greatest source of tension is Sun's father. Sun doesn't know exactly what Jin does for him, but "suspects it's dangerous, immoral, and illegal." And Jin won't tell her anything about it, which makes things worse between them. Prior to this episode, Sun is presented as submissive, with possible rebellious moments, but it becomes clear she is much deeper and more courageous and her father is the source of greatest tension.

But there is another side to Sun. Because of her ability to withhold information or release information on an as-needed basis, Jin believes Sun is submissive to his demands. Sun withholds from Jin that she is pregnant because of being told, while still in Korea, that she was unable to conceive. It is not until she learns he is the father that she reveals the news to him. Until it is absolutely necessary, Sun also keeps secret from Jin the fact that she speaks and understands English. In the episode "In Translation" (Gates, 2005) Jin and another survivor, Michael, are fighting and Sun yells, "Stop!" leading to Jin's humiliation and shock. When Jin finds out about her ability he is at first angry and rejects Sun for keeping this from him. Consider Sun in relationship to her husband, Jin. They "come from a culture that values highly certain kinds of honor and duty" (Wrisley, 2008, p. 51).

In these early episodes, Jin and Sun only speak Korean, which is subtitled in English for viewers. The couple keeps apart from the other survivors. The only other character who speaks to Sun is Michael, the sole African American on the show. This might be a nod to the historical tensions between Blacks and Koreans initiated in the 1980s in which a U.S. immigration influx brought many into historically Black neighborhoods, resulting in hostility between groups (Waldinger, 1999).

Michael assumes Sun speaks only Korean. A similar assumption is made in the Sydney airport by a couple sitting near Sun and Jin. The wife (Gina) observes Sun placing a napkin on Jin's lap:

GINA: If you ever catch me doing anything like that for you, shoot me.

JEFF: Don't knock it. Their divorce rate's 20 times lower than ours.

[Sun overhears them, then knocks a drink onto Jin. She tries to help and Jin asks where the bathroom is. Sun points, Jin exits).

GINA: My god, it's *Memoirs of a Geisha* come to life.

JEFF: Volume.

GINA: Relax, they don't speak English. (Bender, 2005)

Sun epitomizes qualities Collins (2000, p. 72) identifies as "the cult of true womanhood," comprised of four virtues: piety, purity, submissiveness, and domesticity. According to this view, these aspirational values were something women in the West were encouraged to work toward and women in the East are expected to attain. While a study of Western and Eastern values and femininity is beyond the scope of this chapter, it is important to note that so-called traditional versions of femininity and women's roles have undergone changes in Asian countries over the last several decades. "There is no single definition of femininity anymore," and Sun embodies several versions of this (Wood, 1994, p. 87). Given her upbringing, however, she is careful how and when she reveals them. The first time viewers meet her in the first episode when Jin demands, "You must not leave my sight! You must follow me wherever I go! Do you understand?" (Abrams, 2004). Sun nods obediently to Jin's instructions.

Characters of the shy, Lotus Blossom type are "utterly feminine, delicate and welcome respites from their often loud, independent American counterparts" (Tajima, 1989, p. 309). Sun is quiet, introspective in early episodes. However, she asserts herself when the need arises or in an emergency when she has no other choice.

Season 2—Mid-Day Sun

During the second season, Sun stands up to Jin. She tells him she doesn't like being told what to do and begins to take action. In the episode "Hunting Party," Sun tells Jin not to go with those looking for a missing Michael.

JIN: Honey...I don't like being told what to do.

SUN: Being told what to do was my life for four years...I didn't like it much either.

JIN: Right. I don't suppose you did. (Williams, 2006)

Once again she asserts herself, usually when her survival depends on it, but life on the island is getting more difficult, competitive, and uncertain.

Sun spends a lot of time in the garden during this season, creating food and cures for others. It becomes a precious and private place for her. Sun is attacked in her garden, and a worried Jin tears it apart when she returns to it, angry that she goes there to be by herself. He later tries to repair the tender place. Once he apologizes, Sun tells him she is pregnant (something the couple was told could not happen for them when in Korea). She swears she's never been with another man (she has). Jin is overjoyed with the news.

When Sun is assured by former Other Juliet (a pediatrician) that Jin is the father of her child, she becomes more assertive and aggressive, not only in her exchanges with Juliet but with everyone. She breaks up fights during Season 2 and demonstrates her skills as a sailor when she, Jin, and Sayid attempt a shore landing to rescue a member of the survivors abducted by the Others.

Season 3—Firey Sun

Sun demonstrates her self-protective skills when, aboard the sailboat, she shoots and kills one of the Others who boarded the ship. In the episode "The Glass Ballerina" (Edwards, 2006) Sayid, Jin, and Sun attempt to go ashore and infiltrate the camps of the Others who are holding Kate, Sawyer, and Jack prisoner. Sun begins standing up for herself and her ideas during Season 3. She tells Jin they should go in one direction, he disagrees and she argues with him. Later, she apologizes for disagreeing with him in front of Sayid, Jin says she shouldn't disagree with him at all. Jin also tells Sun he understands more English than she thinks he does. Rather than remaining threatened by a skill she possesses and he does not, Jin ends up respecting Sun and asks her teach him to speak English. In the same episode, aboard a sailboat, Sun shoots one of the Others who manages to board the ship. She does not hesitate to shoot and kill.

Later in the season ("Expose") Sun learns that it was not the Others who kidnapped her from her garden but fellow survivors Sawyer and Charlie (Williams, 2007). While Charlie and Sawyer are digging graves for a couple of diamond thieves who survived the crash, Charlie tells her it was Sawyer's idea to knock her unconscious and abduct her in order to scare other survivors. He tries to apologize, but she storms off, walks straight up to Sawyer, and slaps him. He asks if she will tell Jin what they did to her. She replies that if she did, they would have to dig another grave.

In the episode "D.O.C.," (Toye, 2007) Sun learns from Juliet that other women who became pregnant on the island (and their unborn babies) died. Juliet offers to help and escorts Sun to one of the Dharma Initiative Stations to do an ultrasound and determine the date of conception. They determine the baby was conceived off the island, that it is Jin's, and a happy Sun leaves. Juliet completes a tape recording for Ben about Sun and about other women in the group.

In a flashback, Sun is shown back in Korea, confronted by a woman who says she is Jin's mother. The woman blackmails Sun by threatening to reveal that she married a poor fisherman's son unless she is paid $100,000. Sun retrieves this money from her father, but in exchange, Jin will be made to do less-than-appropriate work. Jin discovers the money in Sun's purse; she lies and says it is for their honeymoon. She pays the woman and says if she ever says anything about Jin's paternity or their deal she will have her father kill her.

Sun also confronts Juliet about a tape recording made during Sun's pregnancy test. Juliet promises never to tell Jin about the paternity question.

Season 4—Eclipse

By the fourth season, Sun becomes even more assertive—she's admitted her affair, slapped Sawyer, and stood up to Jin's bossiness. She dreams of being pregnant, in pain, and fears losing the baby (Semel, 2008). When a group of outsiders lands on the island, headed by physicist Daniel Faraday, Sun walks up to him immediately, despite the apparent dangers of doing so. He asks if there is something he can help her with. She's reached the limits of her patience and silent expectations, is direct and no-nonsense:

> "I'm two months pregnant."
> "Oh you're—wow—uh, congratulations."
> Directly she asks, "So are you here to rescue us?"
> Faraday looks around and Sun says, "It's a simple question. Are you or are you not going to rescue us?"
> "Thing is, it's not really my call, Sun."
> "Then whose call is it?"

"Daniel doesn't answer.

Sun says, 'Thank you,' and walks away." (Semel, 2008)

Juliet tells Jin and Sun that other pregnant women have died on the island and they should get off it if they want their unborn child and Sun to survive. She decides that she and Jin should defect to a rival group led by John Locke. Sun is determined to find answers about women and pregnancy on the island and thus leaves the camp. Jin follows her and Juliet tries to stop them by telling Jin "Sun was with another man. She thought the baby was his." Jin is angry, storms off, but, reminded by another survivor of the value of marriage, he forgives Sun. He tells Juliet, "Where Sun go, I go," reflecting a newly born appreciation for her instincts. Finding no other way to keep Sun in the camp, Jin walks up to Juliet, slaps her face, and goes back to the camp. Later, Jin forgives Sun and says, "I'll do all it takes to protect you and the baby. I promise."

Season 5—Fire

As *Lost* progressed through five seasons, Sun also rose in prominence in the series. Kate, Jack, Hurley, Sun, Sayid, and Jin get to a tanker that is stalled in the ocean but is supposed to take them back to the United States. A room full of explosives is discovered on the ship and the group tries to escape aboard a helicopter. The chopper takes off just in time to avoid being part of the explosion, but Jin is left behind and presumed dead. Sun is distraught and secretly vows to kill Benjamin Linus (leader of the Others) to avenge Jin's death.

While not a full Dragon Lady (she doesn't overly use her sexuality), Sun is "cunning and manipulative" when she needs to be (Sun, 2003, p. 659). This trait, immortalized by Anna Mae Wong, means she "exudes exotic danger" (Chihara, 2000, p. 26). Her secretiveness and ability to slyly move about are useful when she wants to influence people to achieve her goals.

Inklings of her independence from both Jin and her father are evident when Sun stops obeying Jin's every command, demonstrating independence of thought (which she's had all along) in deeds. Her clothing changes from buttoned up and down cardigans and slacks in early episodes to a bikini by the end of the first episode (although Jin insists she become clothed). When Sun returns to the United States and then Korea, she is seen in body forming suits, sleeveless dresses, and very feminine modern clothing.

In season 5, the Oceanic Six (Kate, Jack, Sun, Sayid, Hurley, and baby Aaron) return to Los Angeles (Sun goes to Korea first where she has her baby) in order to try to rebuild their lives. Sun is determined to avenge Jin's death and leaves her daughter in Korea with her parents to confront and kill Benjamin Linus. Sun is shown in a hotel in Los Angeles receiving what appears to be a box of chocolates but instead of sweets, the box contains a gun.

During a confrontation with Benjamin Linus by most of the Ocean Six, Sun takes an aggressive step in seeking justice/vengeance. Standing at a marina, Jack, Ben, and others are arguing. The camera shows Sun in her car, considering getting out of it. She looks at a photograph of her baby, gets out of her car, walks straight up to Linus, and pulls out a gun. Linus, who is struggling to get everyone back to the island, convinces Sun that Jin is still alive by showing her his wedding band. He promises Sun if she returns with him to the island she and Jin will be reunited.

Summary

According to the 2000 census, Asian Americans comprise approximately 4% of the U.S. population. However, they are less than 1% of television characters and most of these are minor roles (Fung, 1996; Gerbner, 1998; Meyer & Stern, 2007). Furthermore, when Asian Americans are seen on television, they continue to be mostly portrayed in stereotypical roles, even if the stereotype has positive connotations such as the model minority. Representations of Asian American women on television have increased over the years, particularly on network television dramas (Meyer & Stern, 2007). However, relative to their proportion of the overall population, the roles are few and far between, and as of yet, none is a lead, but rather secondary or supporting characters.

As discussed in earlier chapters reasons why limited/limiting representations in media develop and persist can be found in historical circumstances within which racial, ethnic, sexual or other differences were established. That human beings create Us and Them is not news. However, the ubiquity of the mass media over the last 50 years distributes, reinforces, and reifies information about non-majority culture in ways never before possible. It is interesting that a television program in which one of the main story lines is an ongoing exploration of what Otherness and Others are should also contain a limiting number of racial minorities who are also limited in terms of character development. These roles not only establish the hierarchy on the fictional island but also reflect those in the world beyond that of *Lost*. Edward Said (1979, p. 42) said, "the essence of Orientalism is the ineradicable distinction between western superiority and Oriental inferiority." This is one of the primary functions of stereotypes, to reflect a society's social structure and signify its power relations (Hall, 1997). The research questions posited at the beginning of this chapter were as follows:

1. What is the history of the representation of Asian American women on television?

2. How is Sun, as the embodiment of Asian American womanhood, portrayed on *Lost*?

This chapter examined the historical underpinnings for the development of all Asian Americans in American culture with an emphasis on the primary stereotypes of Asian women: Dragon Lady and China Doll. On one level it can be argued that Sun breaks the stereotypical mold of Asian women on television, and yet, she goes back and forth between the two extremes. At times she is domestic (gardens, uses herbs) and submissive (lets her husband speak for her), and other times she is manipulative, calculating, and deliberate. She always has secrets.

Similar to the Self-sacrificing Senorita described in Chapter 7, Sun is often submissive to her husband and yet wields a kind of quiet but potentially deadly power. In many ways, Sun's way of being is juxtaposed with the other characters. Sun is the antithesis of Kate. Where Kate is reactive, outspoken, rebellious, a lawbreaker, unpredictable, sexual, and manipulative, Sun is steady, clear-minded, not impulsive, but measured. In an interview, actress Yunjim Kim said

> in the very beginning, we were sort of portrayed as a bad stereotype of an Asian couple—the subservient wife and domineering husband. But I kept on saying that you have to watch the characters because they will continue to grow, and you will see the reason why he is treating her that way and why she is reacting that way. In the beginning, I was really concerned that the whole Asian community would be turned off. (King, 2005, n.p.)

Sun would not have been on the fateful flight were it not for a change (or rather return) to a gentler temperament Jin shows at the airport, giving her a single flower as he had when they first courted. Sun had planned to escape both her father and Jin at the airport by creating a distraction. She had had an affair, paid off a blackmailer, and was familiar with a way of doing business that was much more subtle, but potentially more deadly, than Kate. Sun mourns for the Jin she married; however, she also evolves as the show reveals her earlier life and demands of life on the island and subsequent rescue and return. In the final season viewers could decide whether she was really a balance between Dragon Lady and China Doll or if this Sun set more deeply in the psyche of viewers.

Questions for Discussion

1. Are there stereotypes of women in other racial/ethnic groups that are comparable to the Dragon Lady? China Doll?
2. Does the model minority stereotype benefit Asian Americans? Or harm them?
3. What roles do Asian men occupy on network prime time television?

4. What groups of people are considered by census information to be Asian American?

5. Does Said's concept of Orientalism apply to groups other than Asians?

Key Words

Anti-miscegenation laws	China Doll
Chinese Exclusion Act of 1882	Critical theory
Dragon lady	Executive Order 9066
Feminist epistemology	Misogynistic
Page Law	Primed concepts
Sinophobic	Standpoint theory
Anna Mae Wong	

Endnotes

1. I use the terms Asian and Asian American in this chapter to refer both to individuals who are new to America and those who reside in the country as "Asian/American….It is "a choice between two terms, their simultaneous and equal status, and an element of indecidability, that is as it at once implies both exclusion and inclusion" (Palumbo-Liu, 1999, p. 1). Thus, Asian/Americans have historically and contemporarily remained "foreigners" within their own country.

2. The term "Oriental" has been misapplied to Asians as it actually means people from the Middle, rather than Far, East.

Coon Songs: The Black Male Stereotype in Popular American Sheet Music (1850–1920)

The Coon caricature…portrays black men as lazy, ignorant, and obsessively self-indulgent; these are also traits historically represented by the word nigger.

Pilgrim & Middleton

The events which transpired five thousand years ago; five years ago or five minutes ago, have determined what will happen five minutes from now; five years from now or five thousand years from now. All history is a current event.

John Henrik Clark

It seems as if the entire history of race relations could be told through the naming of black music.

Karen Sotiropoulos

We want to argue, with this work, that there is one old race battle that we're still fighting. That is the battle for blacks to be recognized as fully human.

Jennifer Eberhardt

On January 20, 2009, Barack Hussein Obama became the 44th president of the United States. A globally significant event—Obama was the first African American elected to this office—something only imagined a few years before. Many people were surprised that, even in 2008, the country would elect a Black man to office. Does Obama's presidency mean racism is a thing of the past in America? Unfortunately not. In fact, during a television interview with Steve Kroft (as cited in Steele, 2008, n.p.) on the CBS television program *60 Minutes*, first spouse Michelle Obama replied to Kroft's question about her husband's safety and race:

> KROFT: This is a tough question to ask, but a number of years ago, Colin Powell was thinking about running for president, and his wife, Alma, really did not want him to run.
>
> MICHELLE OBAMA: Mm-hmm.
>
> KROFT: She was worried about some crazy person with a gun.
>
> MICHELLE OBAMA: Mm-hmm.
>
> KROFT: Is that something that you think about?
>
> MICHELLE OBAMA: I don't lose sleep over it, because the realities are that, you know, as a black man, you know, Barack can get shot going to the gas station, you know. So, you know, you can't—you know, you can't make decisions based on fear and the possibility of what might happen. We just weren't raised that way.

Steve Kroft nodded in sad agreement.

On February 18, 2009, a *New York Post* editorial cartoon showed a chimp shot to death by police. The caption read: "They'll have to find someone else to write the next stimulus bill." The cartoon created both furor and dialogue about the nature of caricature, editorial cartooning, and race. *The Post* defended this representation by saying the chimp image was included because it referred to a story that same week about a primate in Connecticut that attacked its owner's friend and was subsequently killed by police. This reference was combined with the unpopularity among conservatives of Obama's proposed $787 billion economic stimulus bill. Nevertheless, critics contended that the horrors of slavery, racism, and racist representations are too recent and too tender to transcend what was, to some, a stab at ironic humor.

If all **caricatures,** defined as "grotesque or ludicrous representation of persons or things and "an exaggerated or debased likeness, imitation, or copy, naturally or unintentionally ludicrous" (*Oxford English Dictionary*), exaggerate features for comedic purposes, how is a representation of someone such as Barack Obama different from one of Hillary Clinton? When faced with complaints that his cartoons looked too "simian," *Post* editorial cartoonist Sean Selanos, responded in what, in its own way, is self-stereotyping: "Being the typical American editorial cartoonist—doughy, White, middle-aged—I'm more than willing to accept that I don't know what may or may not be offensive. But editorial cartoons are supposed to be offensive, and provocative. We're entering new waters here. What can you use or not use?" According to columnist Jesse Washington (2009, p. A1), "drawings of President Barack Obama…must contend with America's history of degrading racial imagery, from ape comparisons to enormous 'Sambo' lips."

In a rare public apology, the *News* owner media titan Rupert Murdoch said, "Over the past couple of days, I have spoken to a number of people and I now better understand the hurt this cartoon caused. It was not meant to be racist, but unfortunately, it was interpreted by many as such" (Pérez-Peña, 2009, n.p.). In this chapter I argue that the long history of racist stereotypes of African Americans as apelike and other derogatory representations cannot be erased by an election. While many politicians, including former President George W. Bush, have been shown as monkeys, when portraying an African American politician the allusion is not only mammalian. The trope of the trade for editorial cartoonists might be use of caricature and juxtaposition, but mixing elements with tropes of a powerful racial past can be explosive. Gottschalk and Greenberg (2008, p. 69) write,

> When a caricature of an individual becomes a symbol used by outsiders to depict a group, the image passes from caricature to stereotype. If an American political cartoon critiqued Henry Kissinger's political opinions while portraying him with exaggerated bushy hair, unusually large glasses, and a heavier than actual German accent, these would be understood as an acceptable caricature. However, should the cartoon depict him as Jew with the exaggerations common to anti-Semitic images, it would become an unacceptable stereotype. The same could be said about a caricature as an African American of Dr. Martin Luther King Jr.

Clearly, the symbiotic relationship between negative caricatures of Black people, apes, and the n-word still exists. Pilgrim and Middleton (2001, n.p.) write, "A racist society created nigger and continues to feed and sustain it; however, the word no longer needs racism, at least brutal and obvious forms, to exist. Nigger now has a life of its own." Despite efforts to re-appropriate the term by hip hop and rap artists, the word lives on in all its negativity.

A minority individual serving in the nation's most powerful position represents a seismic shift in voters' beliefs about who can and should lead and who should follow in American and global politics. But if Obama was the most qualified for the position, why was his election exceptional? Have there not been qualified minorities prior to 2008? If a common representation of a politician is a monkey, why was the *Post*'s cartoon unacceptable? Answering these questions is a goal of this chapter which examines the not-too distant past in terms of the representation of African Americans in American popular media in general, and in one historical cultural artifact in particular: the Coon stereotype on sheet music covers during the period 1850–1920, the period immediately preceding, including, and following the "**coon craze**" in theatre and music. Rather than an analysis of the lyrics, although the two are related, this case study focuses on the visual Coon stereotype, a representation related to the simian, arguing that this caricature is so deeply embedded in the American psyche that contemporary representations are unable to transcend its power.

In the findings of a six-study series discussed later in this chapter, the researchers argue "that examining the subtle persistence of specific historical representations...may not only enhance contemporary research on dehumanization, stereotyping, and implicit processes but also highlight common forms of discrimination that previously have gone unrecognized" (Goff, Eberhardt, Williams, & Jackson, 2008, p. 292). A visual semiotic analysis of 1305 pieces of sheet music from 1850–1920 retrieved from the Brown University Library and National Digital Library Project, Library of Congress reveals the historical underpinnings of this persistent, limiting, and narrow view of African American men before, during and after slavery.

The images discussed in this chapter are, in some cases, more than 100 years old. They are, however part of the foundation for the *idea* of Blacks as a sub-human type that formed the primary source of information for Whites about Blacks for decades. The quote by Pan-Africanist historian John Henrik Clark from the beginning of this chapter bears repeating here:

> The events which transpired five thousand years ago; five years ago or five minutes ago, have determined what will happen five minutes from now; five years from now or five thousand years from now. All history is a current event. (as cited in Bender, 2002, p. 161)

Thus, simply because time has passed does not mean cultural memory has been erased, particularly for those whose lives have been and remain forever impacted by the effects of limiting beliefs. Illustrative examples are used that demonstrate the centrality of racism to the commercial and editorial missions of music and theatre producers of the period 1850–1920.

The popularity of so-called "parlor music" at the time, along with that performed on the live stage allows us to take the temperature of the times in terms of White racial attitudes toward Blacks. According to a Web site about African American sheet music:

> Unlike many other sorts of published works, sheet music can be produced rapidly in response to an event or public interest, and thus is a source of relatively unmediated and unrevised perspectives on quickly changing events and public attitudes. Particularly

significant in this collection are the visual depictions of African Americans which provide much information about racial attitudes over the course of the nineteenth and early twentieth centuries.

The following sections present a discussion of research about race and a brief discussion of slavery and two important ways that oppression is enacted. This is followed by an exploration of representations of Black men in popular culture in general and the Coon stereotype in particular. The chapter concludes with an analysis of sheet music covers.

Racing Images

It is nighttime. A young White professional woman walks down the street. Her route is illuminated by a shimmering veil of streetlights. Walking toward her is a Black man, dressed in a track suit, hands in his pockets. At the same moment she sees him, he sees her. She holds her purse tighter. He removes his hands from his pockets. Her mind races with images of riots, news stories about crime, and dangers of the inner city. His mind swims with images of White women accusing Black men of attacking them, of police indiscriminately arresting them based on vague physical profiles and of lynchings. She tries to make eye contact; he lowers his gaze. They pass without incident. She is a woman alone at night and vulnerable. He is Black, male, and suspect. What does she know about Black men? Perhaps only what she has seen, heard, and read in the media. What experiences does he have with White women? He grew up told to stay away from them, that association meant trouble. In his grandparents' days, it could mean death by hanging or worse. This description of the thirty-second video *Passing*, encapsulates the narrative of Black/White; male/female; oppressor/oppressed relationships.

Narratives are the mental visual and verbal "tapes" that play in our heads. Some are written for and taught to us when we are children. Others are the result of first-hand personal experiences with people the same and different from ourselves. Together they form a **master narrative**, a scripting of human thought and behavior intended to guide "appropriate" interactions on the basis of sex, race, gender, ethnicity, or other distinctions. This **ideology** inevitably positions one person as right and good and the Other as wrong and bad. As described in Chapters 1 and 2, the threat of uncertainty is rarely based on actual experience but on what we are told and taught about others in mass media stories that form part of a shared cultural mythology, authored in ways to maintain order by maintaining distinctions. Unfortunately, once written, these narratives remain remarkably stable over time.

In a pioneering 1933 study of racial and ethnic stereotyping in the United States, 100 Princeton University undergraduates were asked about prevailing stereotypes of racial and ethnic groups (Katz & Braley, 1933). The researchers found that Blacks were consistently described as "lazy," "superstitious," and "happy-go-lucky," even if the participants had little to no contact with African Americans. In 1951, the study was repeated and the same attitudes and beliefs persisted. Due to the efforts of the **Civil Rights Movement** in the 1960s, Whites' attitudes about and toward Blacks improved, but a sizable number of Whites still held traditional, racist views of Blacks. A 1990 study by the National Opinion Research Center found that most of the White, Hispanic, and other non-Black respondents in the study demonstrated negative attitudes toward African Americans. For example, 78% said that Blacks were more likely than Whites to "prefer to live off welfare" and "less likely to prefer to be self-supporting" (diversityweb.org, n.d.). Furthermore, two thirds said Blacks were more likely to be lazy; more than half said Blacks were prone to violence; and more than half also said Blacks were less intelligent than Whites.

Martin Gilens, a Yale University political scientist, argued many White Americans believe that Blacks receive welfare benefits more often than Whites do and that "the centuries old stereotype of Blacks as lazy remains credible for a large number of White Americans" (1999, p. 3). He claimed that opposition to welfare programs results from misinformation and racism, with Whites assuming their tax money is being used to support lazy Blacks. Gilens (1999, p. 6) blames the media in part for "pictures of poor Blacks are abundant when poverty coverage is most negative, while pictures of non-blacks dominate the more sympathetic coverage."

Authors such as Omni and Winant (1994) refer to racism and constructions of race as "racial projects" (p. 60) that members of society learn, learn about, and are subjected to as part of the process of socialization. Thus, as discussed in Chapters 2 and 3, race and gender become commonsense ways of interpreting the world around us and imagining our place in it. The "vast web of racial projects" thus mediates between how an individual engages with and is engaged by the world. Whiteness, or the absence of racial Otherness, becomes the default category by which membership in other racial groups is measured. Furthermore, heterosexual Whiteness becomes the standard by which other groups and identities are determined. Whiteness thus becomes a "masculinist ideal," and Others are labeled either as feminine (non-threatening) or hyper masculine (threatening/animalistic). These racial and sexual tropes become fixed through the process of stereotyping.

While Black stereotypes might seem to be a historical artifact more comfortably relegated to a museum, they are still alive and well today when considering socially and culturally constructed definitions of Black masculinity. As Mercer (1994, p. 176) notes, drawing on the work of Homi Bhabha, "an important feature of colonial discourse is its dependence on the concept of 'fixity' in the ideological construction of otherness." Furthermore mass media stereotypes of Black men—as criminals, athletes, and entertainers—bear witness to the contemporary repetition of the colonial fantasy in the rigid and limited grid of representations through which Black male subjects become publicly visible. Ten stereotypes of Black sexuality continue to be reproduced (July, 1995). They are *idées fixes*, ideological fictions and psychic fixations, about the nature of Black sexuality and the 'otherness' it is constructed to embody.

1. Blacks are more sexual than other races.
2. Blacks are more promiscuous.
3. Black sex is pornographic.
4. Blacks are sexually adventurous.
5. Black women are hot, wild, and dangerous.
6. Black women "just gotta have it" [and can't get enough sex]
7. Black men can keep going, and going, and going.
8. Black men are more physically endowed than [men of] other races.
9. All Black men lust [for] White women.
10. All Black women desire White men.

Where did these beliefs originate? That is the subject of the next section.

Slavery and the ideology of oppression

For nearly 300 years, from 1607 until it was outlawed in 1865, slavery was institutionalized in America. While a complete telling of the history of slavery is beyond the scope of this chapter, two interrelated phenomena are keys to understanding the foundation upon which the symbolic representation of enslaved peoples rests. The first is based on the concept of the **colonizer** and **colonized** articulated by Memmi (1991), and addresses the co-colonizing influence of oppression. The second explores the articulation of symbolic oppression as expressed in the commercial products of colonialism.

The first phenomenon involves the experience of slavery. Enslavement of Africans by English colonists began in the United States in the early 1600s, ending with the passage of the Thirteenth Amendment to the United States Constitution (1865). For more than three centuries, one group of humans organized, enslaved as indentured servants, regarded as property, abused, humiliated, and murdered hundreds of other people who were brought against their will to the American colonies to work, primarily in the tobacco and cotton culture of the American South.

How many women, men, and children were enslaved? Between the 16th and 19th centuries, nearly 12 million individuals were taken from their homes in Africa and shipped to different parts of the world (Segal, 1995, p. 4). From the original population of approximately 645,000 people shipped to the United States, by the 1860 census, there were more than 4 million enslaved people. According to the 1860 U.S. census, in the 15 states in which slavery was legal, of the 12 million people living there, 4 million were slaves. While not all slaves were Black (some were Native American and a few were White), most were of African origin. Ironically, since these individuals were not regarded as human beings, rather as property, records were fairly well kept. An example is a January 20, 1840[1] bill of sale for payment of $500 for a Black man. The note reads:

> Rec'd of Judge S. Williams his notes for five hundred Dollars in full payment for a negro man named Ned which negro I warrant to be sound and well and I do bind myself by these presents to forever warrant and defend the right and Title of the said negro to the said Williams his heirs or assigns against the legal claims of all persons whatsoever. Witness my hand and seal this day and year above written.

Eliza Wallace [seal]

Africans were treated and traded like property, as livestock, and sold at auction in just the same manner as were cows and pigs. When the slave trade was closed in the mid-1800s, some slaveowners began treating them somewhat better if, for no other reason, the price for an individual became high. A slaveowner wrote:

> The time has been that the farmer could kill up and wear out one Negro to buy another; but it is not so now. Negroes are too high in proportion to the price of cotton and it behooves those who own them to make them last as long as possible. (as cited in Dusinberre, 1995, p. 206)

Slaves worked primarily with cotton and tobacco but also in many other industries as carpenters, mechanics, blacksmiths, ironworkers, lumberjacks, domestic workers, and in construction. Marlon Rigg's (1987) documentary *Ethnic Notions* describes how southern slaveholders often convinced themselves that, without their protection, Africans would perish, that the enslavement was a way, in fact, of helping them. Part of this delusional rationalization involved constructing slaves as forever childlike, which further fulfilled the idea of indebtedness, dependency, and voluntary compliance. John C. Calhoun went so far as to proffer "**Slavery as a positive good**." In an 1837 speech to the United States Senate he argued

> In every civilized society one portion of the community must live on the labor of another; learning, science, and the arts are built upon leisure; the African slave, kindly treated by his master and mistress and looked after in his old age, is better off than the free laborers

of Europe; and under the slave system conflicts between capital and labor are avoided. The advantages of slavery in this respect will become more and more manifest, if left undisturbed by interference from without, as the country advances in wealth and numbers.

At the same time slaveholders wove a narrative that supported their actions, slaves were forced to find ways to survive. Some chose adaptation (Mungazi, 1996; Memmi, 1991), which gives the colonizer (the slaveholder in this case) the sense that imposition of power and control has been a success. Furthermore, adaptation gives the colonizer "a false sense of security as he begins to base his actions on the illusion that the mind of the colonized has been controlled" thereafter not having to worry "about resistance or revolt" (Mungazi, 1996, p. 61). In the introduction to Albert Memmi's (1991) classic book *The Colonizer and the Colonized,* Jean-Paul Sartre (1957, p. xxvi) asks

> How can an elite of usurpers, aware of their mediocrity, establish their privileges? By one means only: debasing the colonized to exalt themselves, denying the title of humanity to the natives, and defining them as simply absences of qualities—animals, not humans. This does not prove hard to do for the system deprives them of everything.

Figure 12.1 is a photograph of separation of services by race. The "colored" drinking fountain demonstrates the segregation of the time.

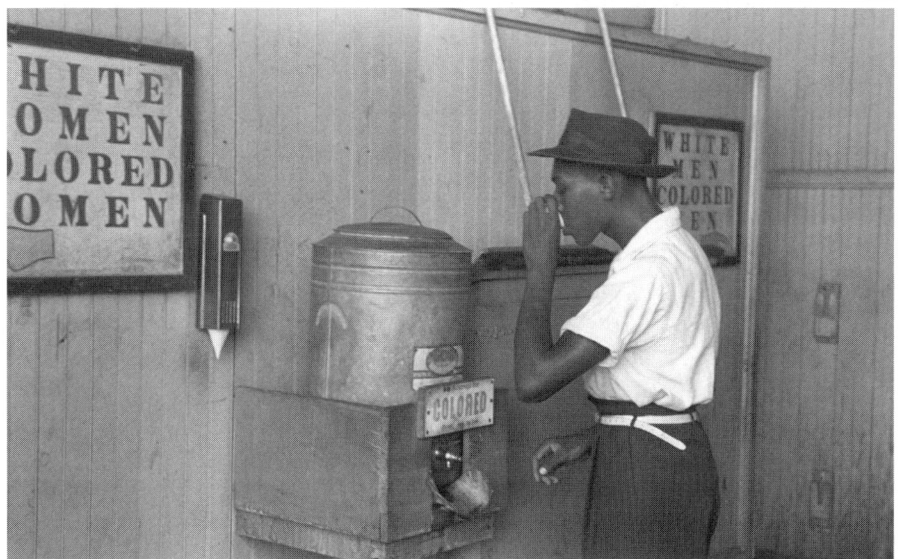

Figure 12.1: Man drinking at "Colored" water cooler in streetcar terminal, Oklahoma City, Oklahoma, July 1939.

Source: Russell Lee, photographer. Library of Congress.

The second avenue for enacting oppression is through widespread cultural reproduction of stereotype-enforcing and reinforcing imagery. Thus, items and artifacts of everyday life, such as posters, advertisements, memorabilia, and everyday speech reify limiting, one-dimensional constructions of Otherness. At the end of the 19th and turn of the 20th century, many Whites feared what the end of slavery would mean—the understandable anger of African Americans. In 1824, James M. Green described free Blacks as "a mass of ignorance, misery, and depravity," and "a dangerous foe." Furthermore, Green emphasized, even if free, Blacks could never be the equal to Whites, "with a few honorable exceptions, they degenerate in proportion as they are indulged," he said. In 1825, a New York pastor, William McMurray, stated that free African Americans were "low and immoral" and "doomed by the indelible mark which the hand of God has placed upon them, to be contemned and despised." Thus, African Americans were considered "evil" and it was thought that they "contaminated themselves…they extend their vices to all around them, to the slaves, and the Whites….A common evil confers a right to consider and apply a common remedy" (as cited in Bacon, 2007, p. 28).

These kinds of statements, sermons, and actions reinforced exclusionary practices that kept civil rights such as access to education and quality health care from African Americans for generations. As a result, laws were enacted in an effort to control the whereabouts of and access to resources by newly freed individuals. These became known as Jim Crow laws.

If anything, after overt racism became if not illegal, certainly considered immoral, stereotypes became more ingrained and present. As more African Americans entered parts of society they had been previously excluded from, what might not, what might not have been overtly practiced by Whites as discrimination settled deep inside as racist attitudes. The mass media were also developing at this time. Printing and mass distribution of daily newspapers, early forms of radio, magazines, and mass production of goods and services were accompanied by the development of symbolic representations of people of color, in particular, Blacks. According to Sartre (1957, p. xxvi), "colonialist practice has engraved the colonialist idea into things themselves; it is the movement of things that designates colonizer and colonized alike."

Once slaveholders could no longer legally oppress Blacks, some maintained the "slavery as a positive good" belief symbolically. Post-slavery, symbolic oppression spread like wildfire throughout American popular culture. Around 1830, what had been a survival route for Black artists (singing, dancing, and performing) was appropriated by White culture into the Black-face minstrel show. **Black face**, the application of Black theatrical make-up by Whites to imitate Blacks as a form of parody or caricature. The painful irony of this is reflected in this statement by

Frederick Douglass (October 27, 1848), who described White performers who did this as, "the filthy scum of White society, who have stolen from us a complexion denied to them by nature, in which to make money, and pander to the corrupt taste of their White fellow citizens" (as cited in Lott, 1993, p. 15).

The songs from these shows, as well as other pieces of music composed specifically for at-home performance, were written down, printed, distributed, and sold in the form of **sheet music**. The covers of this music visually depicted the central themes of the songs using caricature as the art form to convey meaning, illustrating Sartre's (1957, p. xxvi) statement of "colonialist practice [of engraving] the colonialist idea into things themselves."

Historical representation of black men in popular culture

The "earliest consistent pattern of American racist caricature" began around 1815 on broadsides (Lapsansky, as cited in Bacon, 2007, p. 28). Broadsides are wide sheets of paper that are folded, then mailed or delivered door to door or posted. An example of racist broadsides is a series produced by Edward Clay that mocked Black speech and physical appearance, including dress, implying that individuals who were achieving beyond working-class status were "stepping out of their place" in society. Court reporters also made fun of Blacks, and notoriously racist visual and verbal portrayals ran in the White press, "White newspaper coverage of African Americans in the 1820s often mocked them, placed excessive emphasis on criminal acts, or focused on reports of illicit activity" (Bacon, 2007, p. 30).

There are two primary stereotypes of Black men, as described in Chapter 4: the Sambo and the Coon. The Sambo was portrayed as childlike, asexual, docile, ineffectual, inarticulate, lazy, easily frightened, an individual incapable of taking care of himself—a stereotype that satisfied the common justification for slavery and segregation. The Coon stereotype developed out of slavery, when a master pushed the slave to do as much work as possible, and, naturally, the enslaved person resisted working and sought to avoid punishment (which could be brutal, even fatal) as much as possible. Who wouldn't give as little as possible of themselves under the conditions Blacks were made to endure? Resistance was demonstrated through attempts to run away and by being slow, not doing good work, and even ruining tools. Slaveowners pushed slaves to work from sun up to sun down, with little rest, little food, in deplorable conditions. This developed into a belief that slaves were genetically unable to produce quality work, to care about conditions, and were simply incapable of caring for themselves or others. Having the desire not to perform for one's captor did not mean slaves didn't work hard. They did, often driven to their deaths by overseers who whipped, tortured, punished, and exploited them. The Coon was sometimes presented as oversexed, with a powerful imposing physique, wily intelligence, and unbridled sense of courage. The root of today's Black criminal stereotype can be traced to the Coon.

In addition, "the Coon caricature, for example, portrays Black men as lazy, ignorant, and obsessively self-indulgent; these are also traits historically represented by the word nigger" (Pilgrim & Middleton, 2001, n.p.). Historian Donald Bogle (1973/1994, p. 8) describes the Coon, played theatrically by Stepin Fetchit as follows:

> Before its death, the coon developed into the most blatantly degrading of all black stereotypes. The pure coons emerged as no-account niggers, those unreliable, crazy, lazy, subhuman creatures good for nothing more than eating watermelons, stealing chickens, shooting crap, or butchering the English language.

Ethnophaulism is a term that describes a disparaging expression about a person or group. It is seen and heard in milder forms such as "you people" (Gundykunst, 2005, p. 330) as well as derogatory expressions such as "wetback," "kike," "jap," and "spic" which are the linguistic propellants of prejudice. The verbalization of racism in this form is **hate speech**. There are three forms of ethnophaulism: (1) disparaging nicknames (nigger, squaw, chink), (2) explicit group devaluations ("Jew down the price"), and (3) and ethnic names as disparagement "dago slop," "Irish confetti," and "Polish Tourister" (Ehrlich, 1973, p. 22). While all groups of people suffer disparaging stereotypes and names, "no American group has suffered as many racial epithets as have Blacks: coon, tom, savage, picanniny, mammy, buck, sambo, jigaboo, and buckwheat are typical" (Pilgrim & Middleton, 2001).

One of the most enduring ethnophaulisms is the word "nigger." Etymologically, the N-word can be traced to the Latin word *niger*, meaning Black. In English this word became *Negro*, which simply means Black in Spanish. Regardless of origins, and possible phonetic spelling of a White Southern mispronunciation of Negro, "by the early 1800s it was firmly established as a denigrative epithet. Almost two centuries later, it remains a chief symbol of White racism" (Pilgrim & Middleton, 2001). Many of these ethnophaulisms became so common as to be represented visually in the form of widely and popularly circulated caricatures. "Coon moneyboxes, not only encouraged saving, but also the belief that all Africans possessed gaping mouths, and wide rolling eyes" (Verney, 2003, p. 12).

Seemingly justified oppression supported the racial hierarchy that placed Whites at the top, and thus conferred power and resources along with a sense of this being the "natural" order of things. Anti-black images undergirded the system of oppression and were seen in everyday objects such as Mammy and Uncle Tom salt and pepper shakers, racists brand labels, and postcards that, "portrayed Blacks with bulging, darting eyes, fire-red and oversized lips, jet Black skin, and either naked or poorly clothed" (Pilgrim & Middleton, 2001, n. p.). White children were inoculated with this info early on. The N-word wasn't used in all of these but in some. For example:

> In 1874, the McLoughlin Brothers of New York manufactured a puzzle game called 'Chopped Up Niggers'. Beginning in 1878, the B. Leidersdory Company of Milwaukee, Wisconsin, produced Nigger Hair Smoking Tobacco—several decades later the name was changed to Bigger Hair Smoking Tobacco. In 1917, the American Tobacco Company had a Nigger Hair redemption promotion. Nigger Hair coupons were redeemable for cash, tobacco, S. & H. Green stamps, or presents. A 1916 magazine advertisement, copyrighted by Morris & Bendien, showed a black child drinking ink. The caption read, 'Nigger Milk.' (as cited in Ewen & Ewen, 2007, p. 342)

In the late 1800s, a form of highly popular music, performed by, often written by, and usually sung by Black musicians was heard throughout White society. The pejoratively named "coon song," featured "lyrics in 'Negro dialect,' caricaturing American life, set to the melodious strains of ragtime music" (p. 11). The first "coon songs," "All Coons Look Alike to Me" (Hogan, 1896), and "Mister Johnson, Turn Me Loose" (Harney, 1896) surpassed minstrelsy in their demeaning portrayals of African Americans. The lyrics "… presented Blacks as objects of ridicule, and depicted Black men in particular as being addicted to the vices of drunkenness, gambling, gluttony, and stealing" (Verney, 2003, p. 9). The year 1896 is considered by many to be the year the "coon craze" (Jasen & Tichenor, 1989, p. 12) took over, and the music remained popular through the first years of the 20th century and "achieved" the status of "national pastime" (Verney, 2003, p. 9).

The Coon Craze

Coon song

> A genre of comic song, popular from around 1880 to the end of World War I, with words in a dialect purporting to be typical of black American speech. (*New Grove Dictionary of American Music*)

Black actors and musicians participated in this form of oppression at great personal cost. Popular novels of the time used terms such as "darkies," "spades," "niggers," and "jigaboos" in this midst of "virulently racist storylines" (Verney, 2003, p. 9). Also called Negro music, slave songs, and sorrow songs, Coon songs drew on melodies sung by slaves and overheard by Whites that influenced both black and white music till today, including the blues, gospel music, spirituals, jazz, hip-hop and rap. Although composers such as Will Marion Cook sought to document the early music, what sold at the time was syncopated rhythms and racist imagery that characterize the "coon song" (Sotiropoulos, 2006, p. 81). White American mainstream culture was wild about ragtime music, was imitating Black speech and dance, and was enthralled with the **minstrel show**. The minstrel show contained comic acts, music, and a variety of forms of entertainment. This form of theatre brought what was socially off limits to "proper" Whites, city back streets, jazz joints, and, as jazz pianist Willie "the Lion" Smith pointed out, "the bad words and all the hell-raisin they heard about in the red-light district" (as cited in Levine, 1978, p. 178).[2] Thus, gender, class, and sexuality were brought to the table along with race and jazz. Ragtime and the minstrel show linked them all. The show also brought these interlocking aspects of difference together in places White folks permitted themselves to go—the live stage and clubs. After the Civil War ended, Blacks were permitted to perform but in a horrible self-satire, also in blackface. This paradox provided opportunities for some Black performers and musicians to earn a living at their art, yet, at the same time, the presentation reinforced stereotypes about Blacks generally and Black men in particular, making them the brunt of jokes. Singing and dancing in "coon style" and laughing and parodying "coon men" was sad, and the sadness came when the term entered the popular vernacular and men were called "coon" off stage. A January 2, 1909 editorial in the paper *Freeman* titled "Coon Songs Must Go," attested to this:

> What was meant for a jest is taken seriously. Before the show came the people were afraid to call a black man a 'coon.' Or they may have wanted to show him respect by calling him 'colored.' But now they think it's all right and he won't mind, because it's all in fun and it's all in the songs.….In this way 'coon' songs have done more to insult the Negro and cause his white brethren to have a bad opinion of good Negroes as well as bad Negroes, than anything that has ever happened." (as cited in Abbott & Seroff, 2007, p. 37).

In many ways the Coon of minstrel shows became a tragic comic figure. He was lazy, disinterested in working, slow in talking, mispronounced even the simplest of words, and was sometimes shown as a Dandy. While Mammy knew her place to be in the kitchen and/or caring for the White family and Sambo similarly selflessly served Whites, the Coon character did not know his place.

Thomas Dartmouth "Daddy" Rice was a White performer who is said to be the first to appear on stage as a Black man. One story of the origin of this character is that Rice saw an old, crippled Black man who walked with difficulty (other stories say it was a young boy) but who moved in a way that Rice saw as imitable. In 1828, he took on an exaggerated character called **Jim Crow**. This character became popular all over the world and became part of minstrel shows from coast to coast. White audiences appeared to enjoy a White man portraying an incompetent singing, dancing Black fool. After 1838 the expression Jim Crow entered the popular lexicon to describe segregationist laws, customs, and practices. Not as offensive as the word "nigger," but certainly as degrading, the term later became more descriptive of oppressive laws than of an offensive character. Rice and his imitators in minstrel shows influenced public opinion about African Americans and "helped to popularize the belief that Blacks were lazy, stupid, inherently less human, and unworthy of integration" (Pilgrim, 2000, n.p.). According to Pilgrim (2000, n.p.)

> The minstrel coon's goal was leisure, and his leisure was spent strutting, styling, fighting, avoiding real work, eating watermelons, and making a fool of himself. If he was married, his wife dominated him. If he was single, he sought to please the flesh without entanglements.

Black-face imitations, caricatures on products and in popular culture became widespread after the mid-late 1800s when slavery was formally eliminated but symbolically persisted. After 1877, after Reconstruction, through the 1960s, Jim Crow persisted as a pattern of oppression and prejudice throughout the United States. In more ways than one, it was Whites who benefited from the construction and perpetuation of the Coon stereotype no matter who played the role:

> The colored man writes the 'coon' song, the colored singer sings the 'coon' song, the colored race is compelled to stand for the belittling and ignominy of the 'coon' song, but the money from the 'coon' song flows with ceaseless activity into the white man's pockets. (From "Tom the Tattler," *Freeman*, August 24, 1901, as cited in Abbott & Seroff, 2007, p. 11)

From Live Stage to Home Parlor

While people enjoyed going to theatre and watching performances of Coon songs by Black and White artists, there was a growing culture of listening to music at home. Edison's phonograph was one source of entertainment but so was duplicating songs that audiences heard in the restaurants and clubs. **Parlor music** became a popular form of in-home entertainment in middle- and upper-class homes. Most typically played on the home piano and sung by amateur vocalists, these often sentimental, sometimes patriotic tunes, came in printed form. "Whether topical, political, or romantic, the illustrations [were] designed to entice potential buyers of sheet music" (Calderisi, 2005, p. 440). Demonstrable ability to sing and play instruments became a status symbol. Amongst the body of work performed at home was the Coon song, as popularity of parlor music ran parallel with the live stage versions. What the home musician played from was sheet music, which is still produced today. According to Cohen and Krushwitz (1990), sheet music has the following characteristics:

- Written for home use
- Usually performed and popularized in some form of secular stage entertainment and afterward performed or listened to in the home
- Composed and marketed with the goal of financial gain
- Designed to be performed and listened to by persons of limited musical training and ability
- Produced and disseminated in printed form, on an individual song-by-song basis (p. 345).

Popular sheet music offers two forms of representation: "the iconographic and pictorial representation" as seen in "cover art, and the lyrics reflecting current popular sentiments." The Coon caricature appeared on printed forms of the music that people could purchase in stores and perform in their own homes. Sometimes the cover images came from the song's title. "American racial prejudice has been reflected with particular virulence in the sheet music of the last half of the nineteenth century and early part of this century. Indeed, at the time, a category of music known as "coon songs" held Blacks up to caricature, ridicule, and insult in near-scatological terms" (Cohen & Krushwitz, p. 346).

Sheet music analysis

For this chapter, a visual semiotic analysis was conducted of 1305 pieces of sheet music retrieved from the Brown University Library and National Digital Library Project, Library of Congress. The period of the study, 1850–1920, covers the time immediately before, during, and after what has been called the "Coon Craze" for minstrel shows and popular music, both performed and printed. This collection

> includes many songs from the heyday of antebellum black face minstrelsy in the 1850s and from the abolitionist movement of the same period. Numerous titles are associated with the novel and the play *Uncle Tom's Cabin*. Civil War period music includes songs about African American soldiers and the plight of the newly emancipated slave. Post-Civil War music reflects the problems of Reconstruction and the beginnings of urbanization and the northern migration of African Americans. (Library of Congress African-American Sheet Music, 1850–1920 collection)

Of the 1305 pieces, more than 200 have the word "Coon" in the title and dozens more include the word "nigger." In many cases, the lyrics, which were not analyzed, use these terms as well. Several examples are described below that show the nature of the portrayals. Most of the music is printed using red, green, and brown which might be reflective of color printing technology of the time but does provide interesting visual contrasts between skin color, the coolness of green and its agrarian associations and the power of red as a hot, vital color.

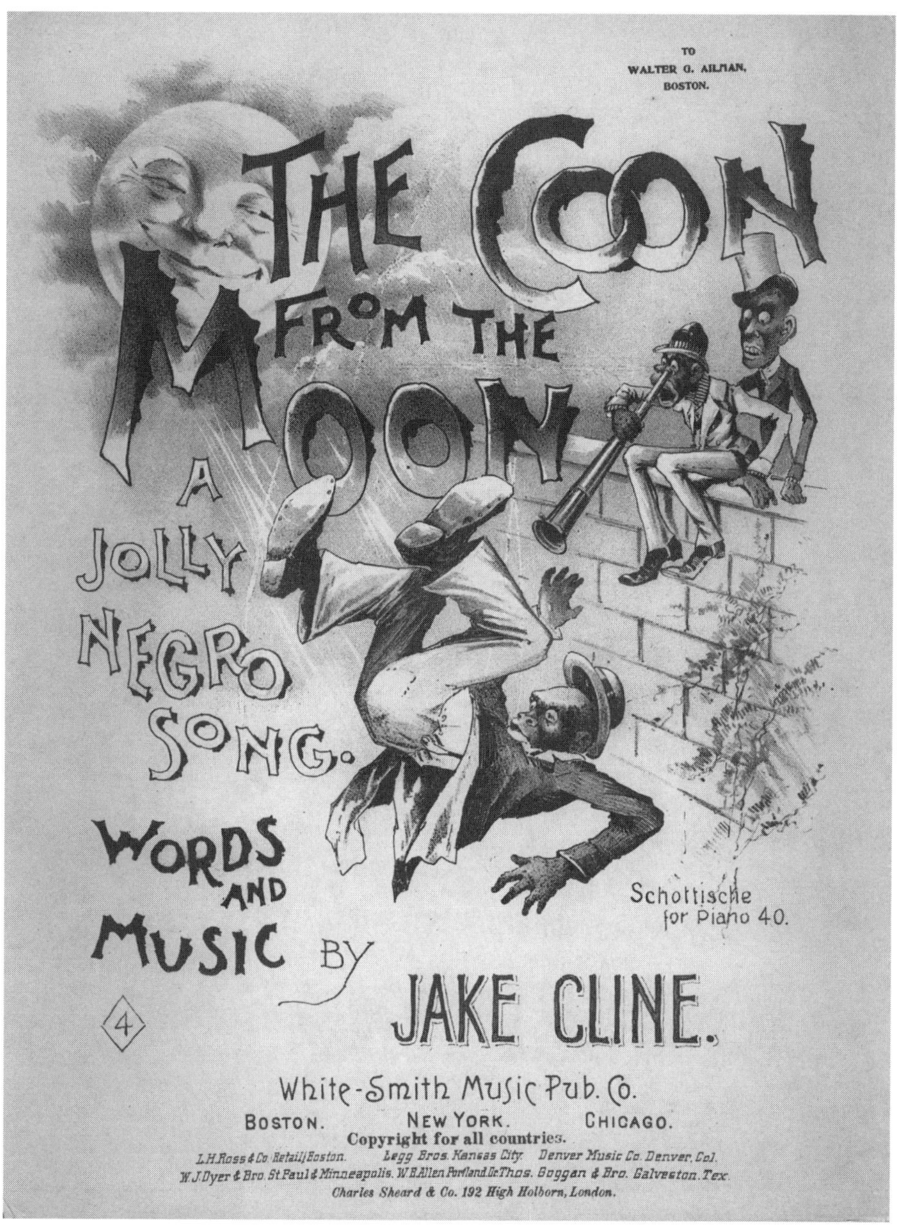

Figure 12.2: *The Coon from the Moon: A Jolly Negro Song.* Words and music by Jake Cline. Originally published Boston: White-Smith Music Pub. (1894).

Source: Reprinted with permission Sheet Music Collection, The John Hay Library, Brown University.

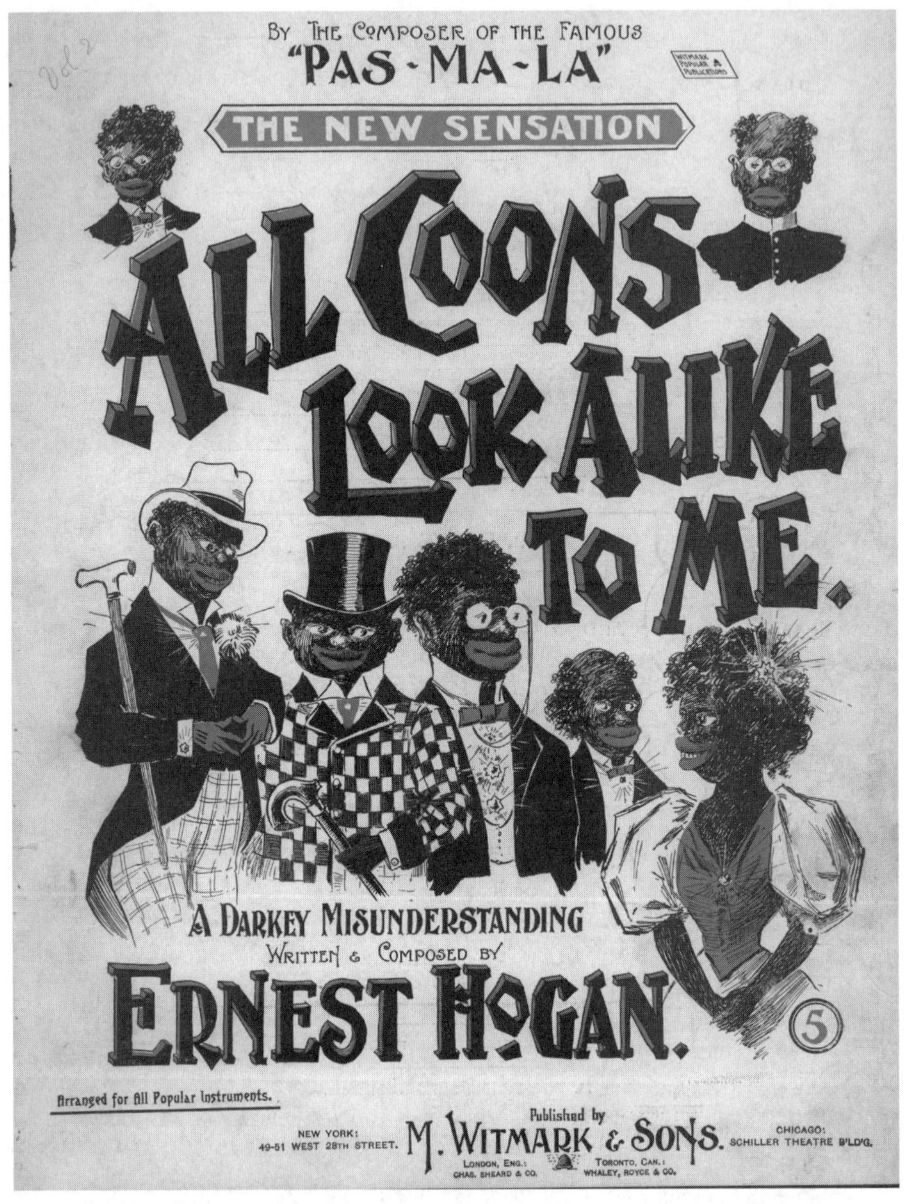

Figure 12.3: *All Coons Look Alike to Me: A Darkey Misunderstanding.* Words and music by Ernest Hogan. New York: M. Witmark & Sons, c1896.

Source: Reprinted with permission Sheet Music Collection, The John Hay Library, Brown University.

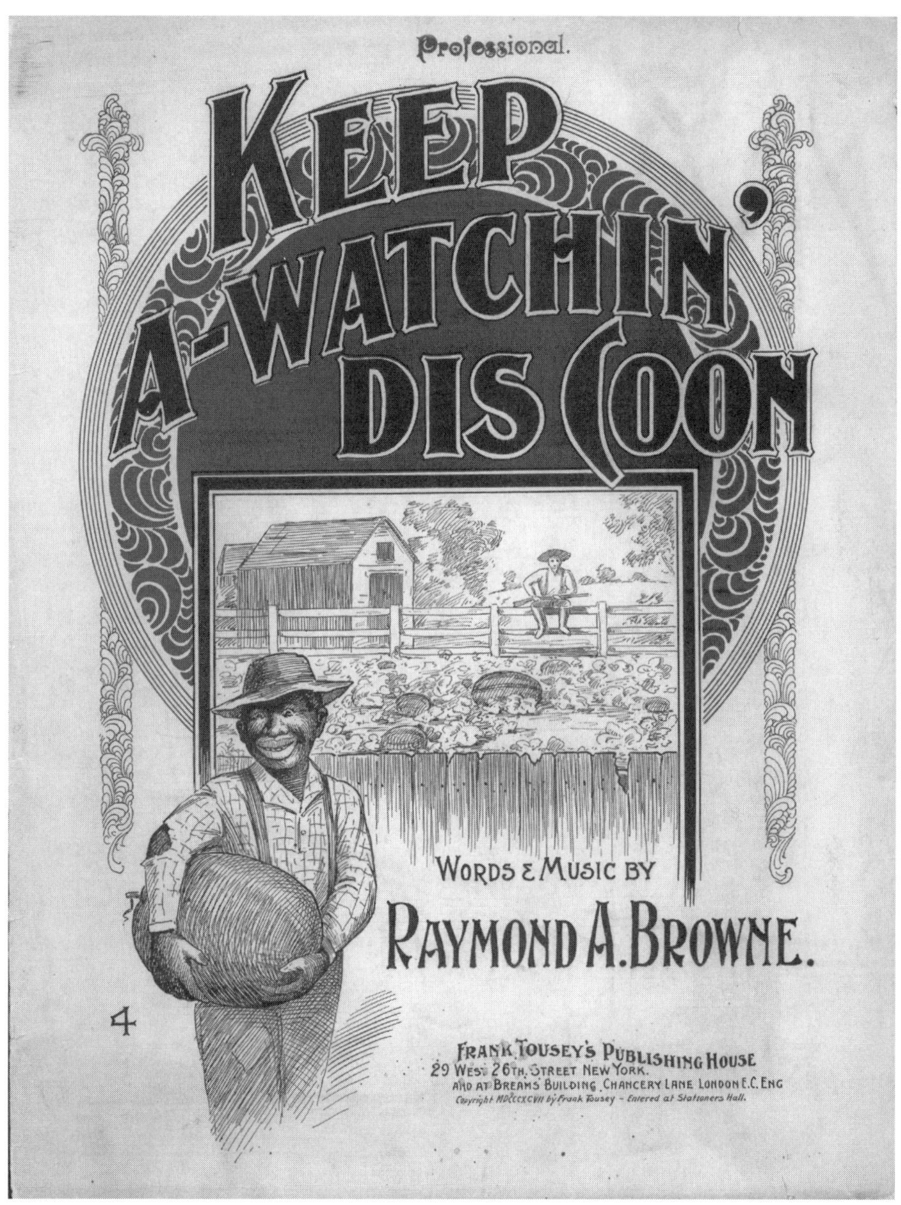

Figure 12.4: *Keep A-Watchin' Dis Coon.* Words and Music by Raymond A. Browne. New York: Frank Tousey's Publishing House, ©1897.

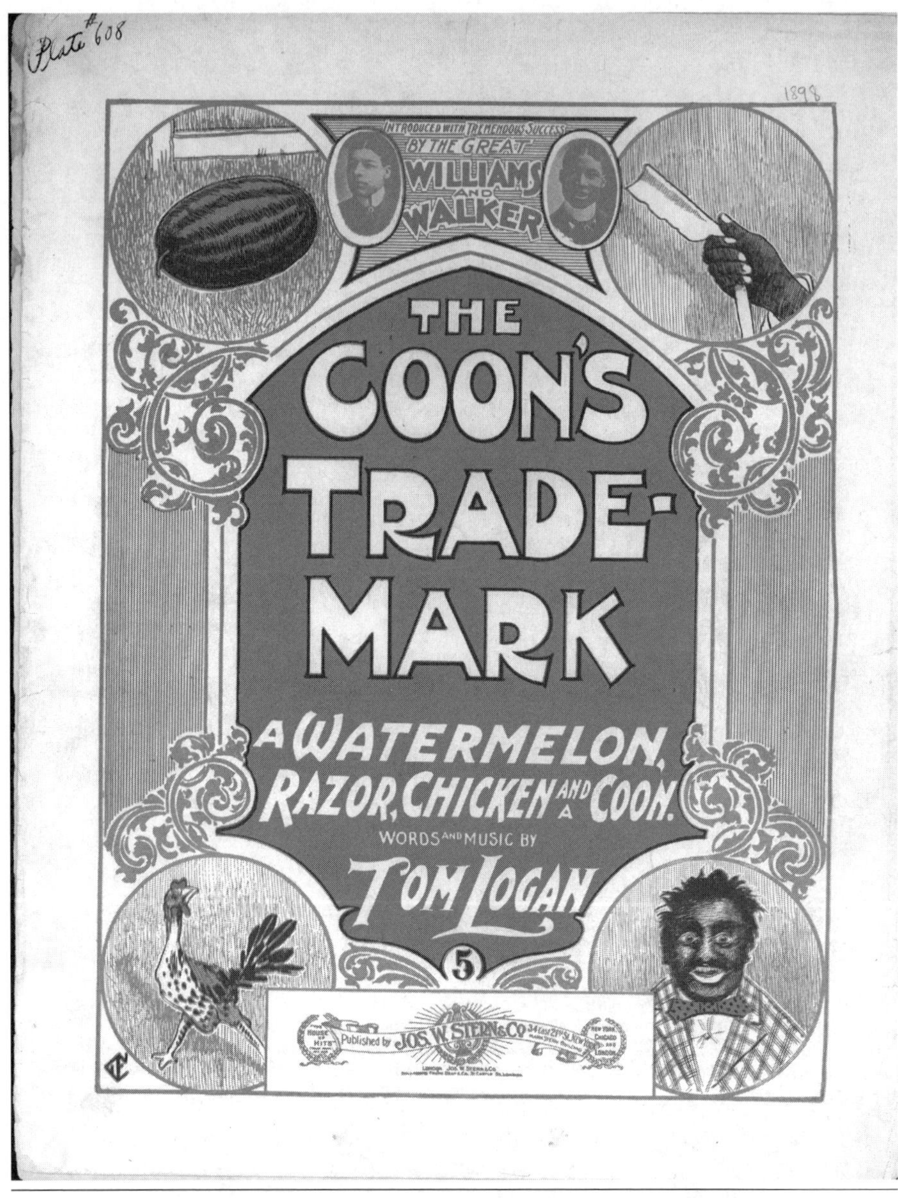

Figure 12.5: *The Coon's Trademark: A Watermelon, Razor, Chicken and a Coon.* Words and Music by Tom Logan. New York: Jos. W. Stern & Co., ©1898.

Source: Reprinted with permission Sheet Music Collection, The John Hay Library, Brown University.

The first example (Figure 12.2) is from a piece of sheet music from 1894 titled "The Coon from the Moon: A Jolly Negro Song." This early piece shows three happy Blacks being silly and content, playing childlike jokes on one another. The song's first line is "I'm a nigger, I'm a coon," and the second line of the chorus is, "There's that nigger, there's that coon" bringing together the image and the words as synonymous.

The second sheet music cover is from 1896 for "All Coons Look Alike to Me: A Darkey Misunderstanding" (Figure 12.3). On this cover, the song is described as a "new sensation" and features seven individuals, one of whom is a woman, with exaggerated facial features, comically put-together city clothing. This is one of the most (in)famous of the Coon songs. It demonstrates the insidiousness of the stereotype and illustrates Memmi's (1957/1991) concepts of oppressor and oppressed—the song's composer was African American.

"Keep A-watchin' Dis Coon," shows the agrarian Black who is shown on the farm, but raiding the watermelon patch. The implication is that he cannot be trusted not to steal (Figure 12.4).

Another cover image is another apparent "coon misunderstanding," for the song "You Ain't de Only Coon in Town" from 1897. The first line of the chorus is: "Oh, I don't know ma honey you ain't so good." A similar song, "My Watermelon-Boy" was published in 1899.

An 1898 piece of sheet music brings together themes of violence and thievery in the song "The Coon's Trademark: A Watermelon, Razor, Chicken and a Coon" by Tom Logan (Figure 12.5). The first line of the song is: "Now listen and a fact I'll show." The first line of the chorus is: "All coons need their razors." The song establishes these elements as a crucial part of the Black man and forever binds him to these stereotypical items. It is the malignant culmination of a number of trends that have been illustrated dating from the pre-minstrel period, yet its depiction of Black male violence it is quite different, and more ominous, than the exaggerated, blustering fights in the songs of the 1830s.

This illustration of the Black man is full of the stereotypical artifacts of the period: the bully's dandified dress, the chicken, and the omnipresent razor. A curious inclusion in some coon sheet music is the figure of the fleeing policeman. Facial features indicate that he is meant for a stereotyped Irishman—another ethnic group that did not escape caricaturing at the time. An 1885 song, "De Coon Dat Had De Razor," portrayed similar interactions.

Finally, one of the most frightening visual images of the covers is "Coon, Coon, Coon," touted as the "most successful song hit of 1901" (Figure 12.6).

With Edison's development of the phonograph in 1877, "coon songs" migrated to recorded cylinder versions and "were among the more popular early recordings"

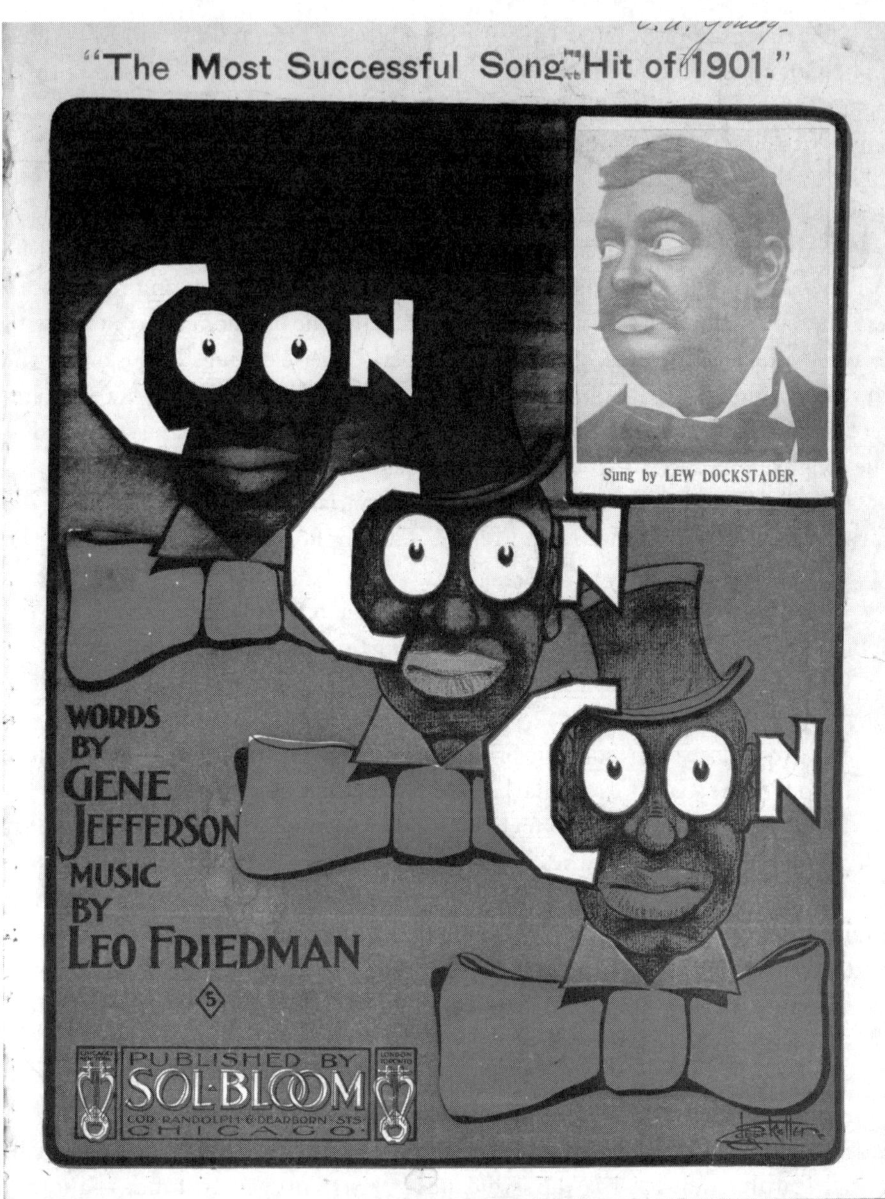

Figure 12.6: Coon, Coon, Coon. Words by Gene Jefferson and music by Leo Friedman. Chicago: Sol Bloom, c1900.

Source: Reprinted with permission Sheet Music Collection, The John Hay Library, Brown University.

(Verney, 2003, p. 10), sometimes performed by Blacks, such as Bert Williams, but usually by Whites imitating Blacks. The Coon character traveled to the silver screen between 1910–1911 in a series of short comedies with the Rastus figure. This character's "desire to avoid work and responsibility was exceeded only by his appetite for chicken and watermelon" (p. 10). At the same time, mass production and marketing increased and distribution grew. Store shelves were filled with packaged goods bearing labels filled with racially stereotypical imagery, such as those "reassuring" images from the Old South of mammy cooks (Aunt Jemima, Mrs. Butterworth), caretakers, butlers, chefs (Cream of Wheat), and servants. These were viewed at the time as more authentic and credible characters to emblazon product boxes and cans since "Blacks were seen as possessing a natural understanding of household work because of their slave heritage" (Verney, 2003, p. 11). The Coon stereotype was so pervasive that Utah, Oregon and Washington had a chain of restaurants called Coon Chicken Inn, each bearing the logo of "a grinning Black waiter" who appeared not only on the exterior of the establishments, but also on the menus, plates, napkins and other items.

In 1915, D. W. Griffith's racist film, *Birth of a Nation,* was one of the first forms of visual mass media to present what had been verbally (in writing and speech) constructed as the powerful, predatory, hypersexual Black man. The dark imposing Coon thereafter became a stock character.

Summary

"This was actually some of the most depressing work I have done," said researcher Jennifer Eberhardt about the findings of six studies at Stanford University and Pennsylvania State University in 2008 involving mostly White male undergraduates. "This shook me up. You have suspicions when you do the work—intuitions—you have a hunch. But it was hard to prepare for how strong [the black-ape association] was—how we were able to pick it up every time" ("Discrimination," 2008, n.p.). The article, "Not Yet Human: Implicit Knowledge, Historical Dehumanization and Contemporary Consequences," published in the *Journal of Personality and Social Psychology,* describes the findings of the six studies. In one, researchers flashed pictures of the faces of Blacks and Whites as is done in the Implicit Association Test.

The researchers found that "Black-ape linkages still influence people subconsciously and impact their judgment particularly in the case of African American suspects and defendants" ("Discrimination," 2008, n.p.). Among the college-age students, even those who claimed to have no knowledge of historical images that associate African Americans and apes, "were quicker to associate Blacks with apes than they were to associate Whites with apes," a finding that has significant implications for everyday interactions as well as criminal justice outcomes. "This Black-ape association alters visual perception and attention, and it increases endorsement of violence against Black suspects." The researchers concluded that, although explicit references to African Americans as apes have been removed from popular culture and media, covert, coded versions still exist in language and in shared cultural memory. "Perhaps subtle metaphors that go largely unnoticed in the media continue to have great effect—and even be linked to life-and-death decisions."

In the fifth study in this series, 115 White male undergraduate students were primed with words typically associated with apes (such as chimp, monkey, gorilla) and big cats (panther, tiger, lion). Big cats were used because of their association with violence and Africa. After viewing these, subjects watched a video similar to the *COPS* television show, depicting several police officers violently beating a man of undetermined race. A mugshot of either a white or a black man was shown at the beginning of the clip to indicate who was being beaten, with a description conveying that, although described by his family as "a loving husband and father," the suspect had a serious criminal record and may have been high on drugs at the time of his arrest.

After viewing the program, students were asked to rate how justified they felt the beating was. Those who thought the suspect was White were no more likely to condone the beating when they were primed with either big cat or ape. However, "those who thought the suspect was Black were more likely to believe the beating was justified if they had been primed with ape words than with big cat words. Taken together, this suggests that implicit knowledge of a Black-ape association led to marked differences in participants' judgments of Black criminal suspects" ("Discrimination," 2008, n. p.).

Does this affect how suspicious someone is depending on his or her race or whether or not he or she is likely to be a suspect of a crime and what treatment is justified? Yes, said the researchers who then studied news stories between 1979 and 1999 in the *Philadelphia Inquirer* and found that African Americans who had been convicted of capital crimes were four times more likely than Whites convicted of the same crimes to be described with "ape-relevant" language such as "barbaric," "savage," "brute," "beast," or "wild." Those who were most described in these terms were more likely to be executed for their crimes.

As recently as the 1990s, California state police euphemistically referred to cases involving young Black men as N.H.I.—No Humans Involved, according to a study (Wynter, 1994, p. 42). In another case, a police officer involved in the 1991 Rodney King beating had been in a discussion twenty minutes prior about a domestic dispute with a Black couple and referred to the situation as "something right out of (the movie) *Gorillas in the Mist*" (Cannon, 1999, p. 222).

Even in 2009, the effects of "dehumanization and animal imagery [that] have been used for centuries are still employed in order to justify violence against many oppressed groups. African Americans are still dehumanized; we're still associated with apes in this country. That association can lead people to endorse the beating of Black suspects by police officers, and I think it has lots of other consequences that we have yet to uncover" ("Discrimination," 2008, n.p.).

Research also suggests that who or what is considered racist and who suffers the effects of discrimination varies significantly by race. According to an ABC News/*Washington Post* poll released in January 2009, twice the number of Blacks than Whites felt that racism remains a significant problem in the United States, and twice the number of Whites than Blacks felt Blacks had achieved racial equity (Fletcher & Cohen, 2009, A06). In January 2008, a CNN poll reported that 72% of Whites feel Blacks overestimate felt-discrimination, and 82% of Blacks feel Whites underestimate the amount of discrimination against Blacks. Quite different visions. Whose is the "real" truth? Project Implicit, described in Chapter 2 is a Harvard University-based online test in which users can put their own biases to the test by categorizing White and Black people's faces with good and bad qualities or things.[3] According to a study produced by the project (Baron & Banaji, 2005), White children as young as six show an **implicit bias**, defined as "socio-cognitive attitudes towards other-race groups that are exempt from conscious awareness"

Table 12.1: Implicit Bias

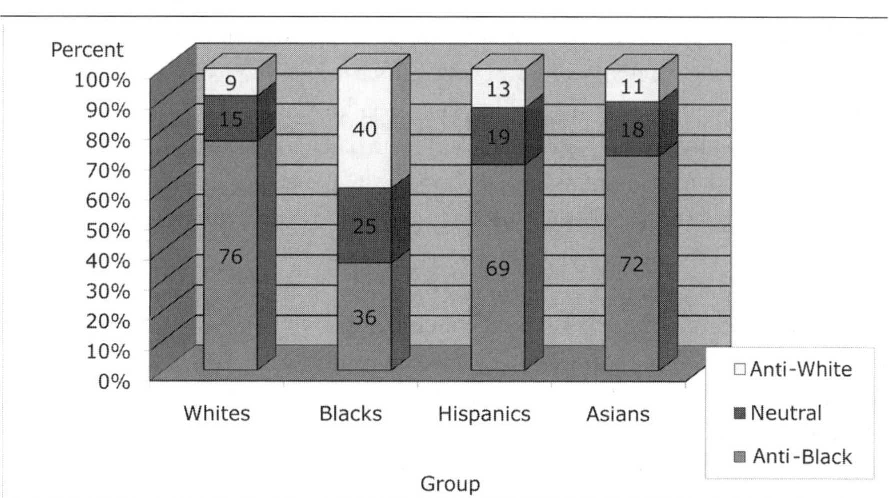

Source: Project Implicit (https://implicit.harvard.edu/implicit)

(Lebrecht, Pierce, Tarr, & Tanaka, 2009, n.p.), and in tests taken at the site between 2000 and 2006, 76% of Whites show anti-black racial biases, whereas Blacks showed some, but were more evenly split between anti-White and anti-Black. Table 12.1 reveals findings from the Project Implicit study indicating the percentage of people who more easily categorized White people's faces with positive things and Black people's with negative. The "neutral" category indicates people who were roughly equal in their categorizing. In a *New York Times* article Charles M. Blow (2009) analyzes the discrepancies in beliefs about and experiences of discrimination between Blacks and Whites:

> Racism exists along a spectrum. On one end is the mere existence of racial bias. Harvard's Project Implicit, an online laboratory, has demonstrated that most of us have this bias, whether we are conscious of it or not. Somewhere in the middle of the spectrum are the conscious expressions of that bias in the form of prejudices. On the other end, at the extreme, are deliberate acts of racial discrimination based on those prejudices. That's where the racists dwell. Think of it this way: You know that you could cheat on your taxes; acknowledging that you are tempted to do so reveals a frailty, but only the act of cheating is a crime.

As described in Chapter 2, our minds automatically categorize based on our actual experiences and the information we receive from other sources. Even if we think of ourselves as unbiased, the quick response time necessary in tests such as Project Implicit and others helps us tap into the deeply engraved social stereotypes all people hold. Our brains operate in a split second in what Malcolm Gladwell (2005, p. 32) calls "thin slicing," before we can consciously stop it. A study of White doctors found that many have an implicit anti-Black/pro-White bias and that Black doctors showed almost no bias (Sabin, Nosek, Greenwald, & Rivara, 2008); furthermore, studies show "U.S. Blacks are more likely than Whites to die from strokes, diabetes, cancer and heart attacks. Other studies have shown this disparity persists even when factors such as education level, incomes and insurance coverage are equal" ("Study Finds," 2008). Clearly our basic hardwiring combined with contemporary material deeply entrenched in the collective unconscious has not evolved to the point of stopping this reaction. These differences would explain in part why many people didn't understand the problem with the February 2009 editorial cartoon.

Some readers of this book can remember the time when Blacks were not permitted to ride at the front of busses, were prohibited from attending the same schools and colleges as White students, and were segregated into separate divisions of the armed forces. To other, younger readers, overt discrimination against African Americans might seem like a phenomenon of the distant past, one only referenced in history books and films. However, despite tremendous progress through the Civil Rights Movement of the 1960s and ongoing, constant activism and vigilance on the part of affirmative action proponents in the decades since, discrimination on the basis of difference is still very much a part of the American psyche and system.

Efforts on the part of the African American community have resulted in the removal of much racist memorabilia and representations from media, popular culture, and commercial interests, such as brand logos. However, "if you look at some political cartoons of Condoleezza Rice, Barack Obama and Colin Powell, you see that they are represented in ape-like caricature," noted Goff (Goff, Eberhardt, Williams, & Jackson, 2008). Because the depiction is not explicit it is not seen as offensive. "But not seeing Blacks as humans leads to implicit—or subconscious—bias, leading to support of stereotyping and other forms of discrimination again African Americans," he said. "Old-fashioned prejudice involves deliberate action and beliefs. By studying implicit knowledge and how it functions, we can study the mechanisms in hopes of remedying dehumanization's savage consequences" ("Discrimination," 2008, n.p.).

In February 2009, Attorney General Eric H. Holder, Jr. called America a "nation of cowards" because "average Americans, simply do not talk enough with each other about race" (Wall, 2009, n.p.). While the inevitable controversy ensued about what bravery and cowardice mean, it was an important statement and Holder had a point—that in order to make headway into changing the way people interact with one another, to experience each other first hand, not through representations, and thus to change institutionalized practices that discriminate, we need to have real time conversations. It is confusing and uncomfortable to talk about race. To admit holding prejudices and biases is embarrassing, to say the least. And yet, we all do. Why? There are two primary reasons (Blow, 2009). First, people are so concerned about appearing prejudiced that, according to a Tufts University and Harvard Business School study, many Whites, some as young as 10 years old, avoided talking about race even when the topic is appropriate. What is also interesting is that Blacks thought that Whites who avoided talking about race were more prejudiced than those who did. Second, to interrupt the process of automatic prejudice is "cognitively and emotionally" exhausting. People who try not to appear or be perceived as prejudiced get tired of doing so, so the amount of invested mental effort people are willing to exert is limited and limits simply talking about racial issues.

We do have a choice in how to respond to this signal of the 2009 caricature controversy. The hope, as was evidenced by young people's participation in the election of Obama, is a generational change in the way race is viewed and that race matters. Young people were essential in getting Obama elected and can play a pivotal role in not making the same representational mistakes in how the media portray a president. Conservative radio talk-show host Rush Limbaugh asked, "What are we supposed to talk about that would satisfy these people?" Many things. For example, playing devil's advocate, Denis Staunton (2009, p. 10) of the *Irish Times* responds:

> Are the black students supposed to sit with the white students and ask the white students what it's like being white? Are the white students supposed to say to black students, 'what is it like being black? Do you compare notes and figure out which you'd rather be? What is it we're supposed to talk about? Do the gay students talk to the straight students, find out what it's like to be gay, find out what it's like to be straight'? Such conversations might, as Holder suggests, be uncomfortable but if Americans want to finally overcome the divisions that have caused the country so much pain and created so much mutual suspicion, it doesn't sound like a bad place to start.

In a 2009 study of White/Black racial bias, researchers found that teaching White people how to distinguish Black people's faces, how to see Black people as individuals, decreased White people's discrimination (Lebrecht, Pierce, Tarr, & Tanaka, 2009). Not a radical exercise. How those who create visual representations navigate these waters remains to be seen. What matters is not forgetting the relatively recent past in which such images in popular forms such as sheet music informed and reinforced stereotypical views of African Americans.

Questions for Discussion

1. Are editorial cartoonists obligated to consider the historical, cultural, economic realities of those they portray?

2. "The problem is, cartoonists make their living by making fun of people—especially presidents—and exaggerating their features and foibles" (Washington, 2009, p. A1).

3. Can you identify any parallels with representations from the past and modern images of Black men in the media?

4. Are there any parallels in implicit bias with views of people of the opposite sex?

5. Can you think of any representations of African Americans that still exist today on consumer products?

Key Words

Black face	Caricature
Civil Rights Movement	Colonizer
Colonized	Coon Craze

Ethnophaulism	Hate speech
Ideology	Implicit bias
Jim Crow	Master narrative
Minstrel Show	Narrative
Parlor music	Sheet music
Slavery as a positive good	

Endnotes

1. January 20 was also the date for the inauguration of President Barack Obama into office as the nation's first African American president.

2. For a detailed history of musical theatre of this time period, see http://memory.loc.gov/ammem/collections/sheetmusic/brown/aasmsprs1.html for an extensive timeline.

3. You can try the Implicit Association test yourself at https://implicit.harvard.edu/implicit/demo/taketest.html

CHAPTER THIRTEEN

❈ Homosexuality and Horror: The Lesbian Vampire Film

In a hundred years of movies, homosexuality has only rarely been depicted on the screen. When it did appear, it was there as something to laugh at—or something to pity—or even something to fear. These were fleeting images, but they were unforgettable, and they left a lasting legacy. Hollywood, that great maker of myths, taught straight people what to think about gay people…and gay people what to think about themselves.

Russo, 1987

For without the exploitation of body-matter of women, what would become of the symbolic process that governs society?

Irigaray, 1985, p. 85

But first, on earth as Vampire sent,
Thy corse shall from its tomb be rent;
Then ghastly haunt thy native place,
And suck the blood of all thy race,
There from thy daughter, sister, wife,
At midnight drain the stream of life;
Yet loathe the banquet which perforce
Must feed thy livid living corse; …
Wet with thine own best blood shall drip,
Thy gnashing tooth and haggard lip.

Lord Byron, 1813

Imagine belonging to a group whose members are primarily presented in cinema as aliens, predators, monsters, and mutants. In representations ranging from supernatural to abnormal, film portrayals of gays and lesbians have historically relied upon coding characters in ways insider audiences will understand with hopes that the references will be missed by those opposed to this form of sexuality. As with other stereotypes, limiting and limited media representations of homosexual men and women tend to focus on a particular characteristic that gets taken out of context and magnified to present all members as if everyone were the same. Depictions of sexual preferences in media have evolved over the years as have representations of race and ethnicity. Homosexuality, according to Gartner (2001, p. 94) did not appear as a scientific term until 1869. Heterosexuality, much like Whiteness, was also constructed or "invented" as a normative concept and is hard to see as one among a variety of sexual preferences because it is the established norm of mainstream society and thereby, media representations. Naturalized by patriarchal ideology, being heterosexual in life and in art is taken to be the "normal" way. Until 1973, the American Psychological Association listed homosexuality as a mental disorder, thus **pathologizing** being gay and lesbian as an illness (Conger, 1975).

From the late 1960s to the early mid-1980s, gay and lesbian images on television, in film, and in magazines moved from nearly complete invisibility toward at least a contested presence. The Civil Rights Movement of the 1960s was not only about issues of equality and race but also gender, sexuality, and other characteristics by which people were discriminated against. Martin Luther King's famous march in Washington in 1963 and his 1965 participation with students in Selma, Alabama, were hugely significant events for human rights in general, and for African Americans in particular. For the gay and lesbian community, however, another event marked a key transition point. On June 9, 1969, New York City police raided a gay bar in Greenwich Village. Gays, lesbians, trans-gendered, and bisexual persons who were tired of being harassed and arrested stood up to this force. For three days riots erupted, after which the Gay Liberation Front was organized. Gayness started coming out of the closet and onto newspaper pages and television screens of the world.

While gay characters, when they appeared at all in media, remained in secondary roles and often died by the end of an episode, they were, however, increasingly visibile. Then, in 1981, the AIDS epidemic was recognized. Television news media were processing how to report the epidemic, how to intelligently discuss transmission and strategies to curtail its spread and not reinforce stereotypes. However, concern with advertising revenues outweighed public health concerns. When sympathetic portrayals of gay men suffering AIDS were seen, they were of afflicted White, middle to upper-class men, thus cloaking the real diversity and disparities in AIDS diagnosis and treatment. AIDS was presented as a gay problem, when in fact, as is the case with all disease, it knows no boundaries.

Movies have always provided an important voice for representations of gays and lesbians. This chapter examines a specific kind of film—the horror film, and more specifically—the **lesbian vampire film**. The goal is to understand how alternative sexualities are coded and performed within the conventions of film. The necessity of coding homosexual references is explained in a brief history of the **Hollywood Production Code System** of the 1930s–1960s. This self-regulatory system forced filmmakers to find creative ways of coding sexual, among other kinds of content, that was deemed inappropriate. This section is followed by a discussion of homosexuality in film, the horror film as a specific genre within which sexuality could be played with, and a description of three films in which female same-sex relationships are presented in the sub-genre of lesbian **vampire** films. In this chapter I raise the question of whether female vampires in general, and lesbian vampires in particular, are positive or negative representations of women, women's sexuality, and power in an "(in) famously tenacious trope" (Cairns, 2006, p. 37).

This chapter draws on psychoanalytic interpretation of homosexuality in film by exploring lesbian vampires through the lens of Creed's (1993) concept of the "monstrous-feminine" and Kristeva's (1982) "**abject**" in **horror**. While a seemingly obscure venue for referencing sexuality, "outside of male pornography, the lesbian vampire is the most persistent lesbian image in the history of cinema…the association of vampirism with lesbianism is far-reaching and long-lived" (Weiss, 1992, p. 84). The premise is that in horror films, lesbian vampires are used as metaphorical embodiments of that which is too unthinkable for mainstream society to consider under any other guise. This conflation of sexuality and appetite for sex and blood is ripe for analysis. While there are few representations of lesbians in media, "the combination of 'lesbian' and 'vampire' is a happy one since both figures are represented in popular culture as sexually aggressive women" (Creed, 2003, p. 59). If one takes the view that filmic monsters represent repressed content of the taboo, the desired, and the unspoken, as anthropologist Mary Douglas (1996) notes, "monsters…are unnatural relative to a culture's conceptual scheme of nature. They do not fit the scheme; they violate it." And yet, violating the scheme can be exciting, and that allure is often repressed. Whatling (1997, p. 93) said, "The heady combination of desire and repulsion, fascination and abjection, illustrates the double-bind between cultural oppression and sexual fantasy."

Censoring Sex and Sexuality

During the early 20th century, Hollywood was growing rapidly and so was the celebrity lifestyle that surrounded it. Ideas flowed into the United States from Europe about food, fashion, and lifestyles that were different than mainstream America's. Films of the era reflected new ways of thinking and America's evolving morals. Press coverage of wild Hollywood parties, films advertised with language alluding to sex, questionable language, and dangerous ideas, led to citizens organizing out of fear of the deleterious effects celluloid might be having on them and their children. (Figure 13.1)

Three scandals in Hollywood prompted industry self-regulation in anticipation of the federal government stepping in and formalizing a censorship process (Lewis, 2002). The first ignominy was the 1921 manslaughter trial of comedian Roscoe "Fatty" Arbuckle, who was charged with the death of an actress at a Hollywood party. The second controversy concerned the murder of director Desmond Taylor in 1922 and the discovery that he was bisexual. The third event

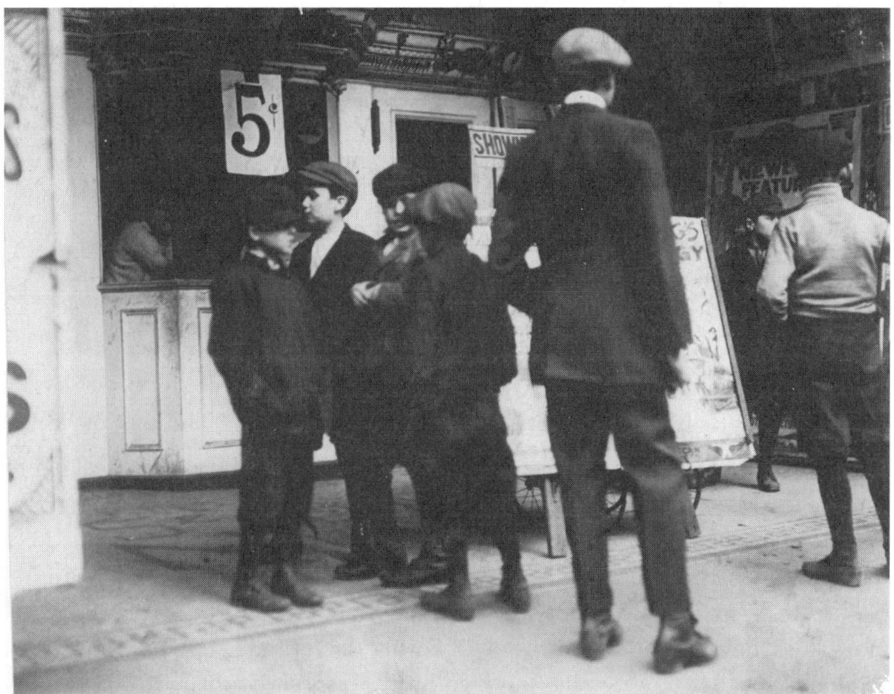

Figure 13.1: "Going to the Movies." (1912) 2:30 P.M. Jersey City, New Jersey.

Source: Louis Wickes Hine, Photographer, November 1912. *Library of Congress.*

was the 1923 drug-related death of actor Wallace Reid. In addition to sex scandals, other events and more drug-related Hollywood deaths, the public came to believe that Tinsel Town was Sin City and completely out of control. Public outrage over the "immorality" of Hollywood, subsequent leniency in films, and the rise of local and state censorship boards, resulted in the creation of the **Motion Picture Producers and Distributors Association** in 1922 (this group became the **Motion Picture Association of America** in 1945). A group of producers and filmmakers hired attorney and former U.S. Postmaster General Will H. Hays to head the association. From 1934 to the 1960s, films were rated by this agency to ensure their "suitability" (the MPAA film rating system still in use today is a descendent of this era). One of Hays' first acts was to ban Arbuckle from appearing in films and to institute a morality clause for anyone working in the movie industry. In 1927, he compiled a list of topics, subjects, and areas that filmmakers would be smart to avoid using. Initially, the movie studios and the association agreed to thirteen elements to be avoided in film that became known as the **Hays Formula**. These topics were those:

1. That dealt with sex in an improper manner
2. Were based on white slavery
3. That made vice attractive
4. That exhibited nakedness
5. With prolonged passionate love scenes
6. That were predominantly concerned with the underworld
7. That made gambling and drunkenness attractive
8. Which might instruct the weak in methods of committing crime
9. That ridiculed public officials
10. Which offended religious beliefs
11. That emphasized violence
12. That portrayed vulgar postures and gestures
13. That used salacious subtitles or advertising (Miller, 1994, pp. 37–38)

Members of the filmmaking group agreed to submit all materials related to films to the Hays committee for review. New titles could be required; scenes could be altered or cut. In the first year of the code's enforcement, 67 treatments were rejected, and, by the time this particular formula was changed in 1930, 125 stories, books, scripts and plays were kept from production. Not all studios played by the Hays rules, however, and many began ignoring the formula. As a result, in 1927, a "Don'ts and Be Carefuls" list was created of 36 specific subjects to be avoided (Landay, 2002, p. 96) (Figure 13.2).

The technology of sound in pictures that resulted in talking pictures ("talkies") first appeared in 1927 and produced a perceived need for additional regulatory

Resolved, that those things which are included in the following list shall not appear in pictures produced by the members of this Association, irrespective of the manner in which they are treated.

1. Pointed profanity—by either title or lip—this includes the words "God," "Lord," "Jesus" "Christ" (unless they be used reverently in connection with proper religious ceremonies), "hell," "damn," "Gawd," and every other profane and vulgar expression however it may be spelled
2. Any licentious or suggestive nudity—in fact or in silhouette; and any lecherous or licentious notice thereof by other characters in the picture
3. The illegal traffic in drugs
4. Any inference of sex perversion
5. White slavery
6. Miscegenation (sex relationship between the white and black races)
7. Sex hygiene and venereal diseases
8. Scenes of actual childbirth—in fact or in silhouette
9. Children's sex organs
10. Ridicule of the clergy
11. Willful offence to any nation, race or creed

And it be further resolved, That special care be exercised in the manner in which the following subjects are treated, to the end that vulgarity and suggestiveness may be eliminated and that good taste may be emphasized:

1. The use of the flag
2. International relations (avoiding picturing in an unfavorable light another country's religion, history, institutions, prominent people and citizenry)
3. Arson
4. The use of firearms
5. Theft, robbery, safe cracking, and dynamiting of trains, mines, buildings, etc. (having in mind the effect which a too-detailed description of these may have upon the moron)
6. Brutality and possible gruesomeness
7. Technique of committing murder by whatever method
8. Methods of smuggling
9. Third-degree methods
10. Actual hangings or electrocutions as legal punishment for crime
11. Sympathy for criminals
12. Attitude toward public characters and institutions
13. Sedition
14. Apparent cruelty to children and animals
15. Branding of people or animals
16. The sale of women, or of a woman selling her virtue
17. Rape or attempted rape
18. First-night scenes

Figure continued on next page

Figure continued from previous page

19. Man and woman in bed together
20. Deliberate seduction of girls
21. The institution of marriage
22. Surgical operations
23. The use of drugs
24. Titles or scenes having to do with law enforcement or law-enforcing officers
25. Excessive or lustful kissing, particularly when one character or the other is a "heavy."

Figure 13.2: "The Don'ts and Be Carefuls" Mast, 1982, pp. 213–214.

Published in October 1927 by the Motion Picture Producers and Distributors of America

enforcement. By the early 1930s Catholic theologian Father Daniel Lord was brought in to help write a morality code to be applied to language used in films. The Hays group asked audiences to sign a pledge to "remain away from all motion pictures except those which do not offend decency and Christian morality" (quoted in "Legion of Decency," 1934, n.p.). On March 31, 1930, the board of directors of the Motion Picture Producers and Distributors Association formally adopted what became known as the **Hays Code** and the Studio Relations Committee (SRC) was created in 1930 to enact it. In 1934, the guidelines became known as the Motion Picture Production Code in order to ban any questionable representations or words as well as "unacceptable ideas…most notable those that seriously questioned the status quo" (Miller, 1994, p. 9). What was deemed morally acceptable and unacceptable in films was spelled out. Three general areas were covered by the code, with specifics defined under each one:

1. No picture shall be produced that will lower the moral standards of those who see it. Hence the sympathy of the audience should never be thrown to the side of crime, wrongdoing, evil, or sin.
2. Correct standards of life, subject only to the requirements of drama and entertainment, shall be presented.
3. Law, natural or human, shall not be ridiculed, nor shall sympathy be created for its violation.

In 1934, the Production Code Administration developed its own **Seal of Approval**. Members of this group studied scripts, sent memos, and revised versions of the scripts indicating any character, scene, word, costume, or other aspect that was deemed anything other than a clearly heterosexual, monogamous relation. "Moral clauses" were written into actors' contracts. In some cases, studios forced actors to marry one another to keep up public appearances of heterosexuality. This code was not only about representations of gays in films, but about all sex and sexuality. Any kiss had to take place with closed mouth and last only a few seconds. If a couple kissed and they were in bed, one of the character's feet had to touch the floor. Sex was not erased from films at this time but instead was more often referred to or implied. Metaphors such as burning logs in a fire stood in for the passion of love. A scene quickly moved from a kiss to the two people smoking cigarettes. Audiences learned to make the associative leap from one scene to the next and fill in the blanks.

Scenes of homosexual desire were explicitly banned after 1934. According to Benshoff and Griffin (2004, p. 304), "queer moments" were written into films. "Connotative homosexuality," that is, representing homosexuality through cues and **codes** rather than denotative (explicit) references, was the direction of Hollywood for the next three decades. From the 1930s–1950s, public outrage ensued about immorality in Hollywood. Church and women's groups protested which resulted in more self-censorship and the creation in 1933 of the **Catholic Legion of Decency**, intended to identify and combat objectionable content in films. It was renamed the National Legion of Decency as a result of the 1952 case of ***Joseph Burstyn, Inc.* v. *Wilson*,** which involved banning Roberto Rossellini's film *The Miracle*, because it involved a religious man's inappropriate behavior with a young woman. The film was banned in New York, but Joseph Burstyn, a film distributor, took the case to the U.S. Supreme Court where the court ruled against religious censorship (Miller, 1994).

Neither the Hays Code nor the Catholic Legion had the power to enforce their rules, rather these were suggestions, albeit strong ones. Eventually, filmmakers found alternative ways to communicate their messages or chose to disregard the system entirely. In 1961, the code was amended to allow discussions of homosexuality, as long as it was conducted "with care, discretion, and restraint" (Russo, 1987, p. 48). The first film to explore this was *The Children's Hour* (1962) starring Shirley MacLaine, in which a girl's school teacher hangs herself once her sexuality is revealed. This ending points to significant treatment of homosexuality in film—pathologizing someone who is gay or lesbian. For example, characters might maintain effeminate traits, such as the killers in Hitchcock's *Rope* (1948) or Norman Bates in *Psycho* (1960), but they also crossed dressed and were killers. Beginning in the mid-1950s and continuing to the 1960s the dominant perception of homosexuality was no longer that it was criminal, but that it was a psychiatric disease. In this view, individuals could be pitied but never be cured. *Rebel Without a Cause* (1955) is often cited as one of the first films to depict a homosexual teenager, Plato (played by Sal Mineo). Originally the film contained more daring content, but once reviewed by the Production Code office, it was determined to have homosexual themes and was re-edited. Nevertheless, careful viewers can still read the innuendo and intent of the film.

Some scholars argue that trying to work around all the regulations complicated ways of coding sexuality (Noriega, 1990). Sometimes other issues were used as metaphorical stand-ins for homosexuality. For example, homosexuality was recast under the guises of the evils of gossip, alcoholism, or anti-Semitism. Thus, in the 1950s, a "conspiracy of silence" began in Hollywood.

These strategies point to an underlying storyline that has persistently followed gays and lesbians in film: if a character is or seems homosexual, he or she is dead by the end of the movie from murder, suicide, or disease. Often the villains, the predatory queer men and women, were eliminated because of their transgressions. Gay women were often coded in roles such as prison guards. Eleanor Parker, for example, played a naive inmate in *Caged* (1950) who was preyed upon by a sadistic female guard. In *The Haunting* (1963), actor Claire Bloom falls in love with another woman, a psychic (played by Julie Harris), when they visit a haunted mansion.

Homosexuality in media

As is true for all minorities, the absence of portrayals can have nearly as much negative emotional and social impact as stereotypical ones. To be eliminated from the cultural stage or assigned to marginalized roles is called **symbolic annihilation.** No one is physically harmed in this form of erasure, but certainly the exclusion is profound. Advertising dollars keep the media machine running, and many television programmers, film producers, and magazine editors are afraid of alienating audiences by featuring gays and lesbians in content (unless of course the medium is gay oriented). In 1990, for example, the very successful drama *Thirtysomething* lost over $1 million and half its advertising revenue for running an episode in which two men kiss in bed. The program *Roseanne* suffered similar consequences when it showed an on-screen lesbian kiss. When Ellen DeGeneres announced herself as a lesbian on her situation comedy *Ellen,* advertisers such as Wendy's, Chrysler, and others pulled their commercials. The program didn't last much longer, and thereafter the comedian was labeled as a *gay* actor, not simply an actor who also happens to be gay.

Increased recognition of the spending power of gays and lesbians has resulted in cable television's taking notice. In the last few years, programs such as *Queer Eye for the Straight Guy, the L Word*, and *Queer as Folk* (a BBC adaptation) ran on cable TV. *Will & Grace*, a popular network television program, featured an openly gay male character (who was straight in real life), but there was little discussion of gay relationships or romance in the show. The primary interaction is with the heterosexual female lead. Films follow this pattern with a straight woman/gay man friendship/relationship in movies such as *My Best Friend's Wedding* (1997), *The Next Best Thing* (2000), and *Object of My Affection* (1998). While these programs might be seen as a step in the right direction of including more gay and lesbian characters in entertainment media, the comedic sidekick status or marginalization of their sexuality in the role still privilege and prioritize heterosexuality and present homosexuality as an appropriate subject of ridicule, scorn, and the brunt of jokes.

Homosexuality in film

> Sissy characters in movies were always a joke. There's no sin like being a woman. When a man dresses as a woman, the audience laughs. When a woman dressed as a man, nobody laughed. They just thought she looked wonderful. Quentin Crisp (*The Celluloid Closet*, 1995)

Vito Russo's (1981) book *The Celluloid Closet* was made into a powerful documentary in 1995. Both the film and the book explore when, if, and how movies, particularly Hollywood films, portrayed lesbian, gay, and transgender characters. The film poignantly begins with the scene of two men dancing together in a Thomas Edison silent film *The Gay Brothers* (1895). The documentary demonstrates that, while themes of same sex relationships have been presented in films, homosexuality as lived experience was and remains to a considerable extent pathologized. Traditionally, Hollywood has served and appealed to mainstream views. The **Classic Hollywood formula** is one of the most typical presentations of relationships in films and is constructed around the dynamics of a female/male couple struggling to connect. Sometimes there is a lover's triangle, but what complicates things is not usually a character's sexual proclivity but issues around monogamy. Ordinarily the forbidden nature of encounters focuses on honesty and trust or the lack thereof. Thus, the heteronormative nature of Hollywood motion pictures presents this form of relationship as the only acceptable and/or normal one. Thus, heterosexuality enjoys privilege, as described in Chapter 2, as it is not unusual for heterosexual couples in film to kiss, to flirt, to make public their affections and desires. Gay-ness is presented as first and foremost sexual. Even when same sex relationships are presented in film, gay and/or lesbian characters, rarely, if ever, live happily every after. As such, this film formula works to ideologically shape and support the status quo.

An additional issue is how to represent homosexuality without relying on worn stereotypical notions of who a gay person is or what he or she looks like. Judith Butler (1999) argues that gender is a performative act, that identity and sexuality are constituted, particularly when they vary from the heterosexual norm. Masculinity and femininity are emphasized according to codes and conventions socially constructed that focus on hair, clothing, and appearance, to tell the audience who is a "real" woman and who is a "real" man. Thus "real" women are demure, quiet, very thin, and "real" men are assertive, strong, and vocal.

"Appropriate" sexual behavior in America has always been defined through the lens of religion. Monogamy is the Christian norm that holds to strict rules and codes about who can have sex with whom (i.e., one man/one woman), under what circumstances, and only for the purpose of procreation. Thus, a "proper" relationship, marriage, sexual encounter, and partner are all defined. While this arrangement is taught as the norm, this does not mean portrayals of this form of partnership go uncriticized. As discussed earlier, throughout the history of cinema, for example, codes and conventions have been applied to regulate sexuality onscreen and, at certain times, to eliminate homosexuality completely from the camera's lens.

Because filmmakers must get their films made if they want to tell their stories and they want them to be financially successful, they have largely shied away from presenting homosexual relationships. In particular, obvious and overt references to homosexuality in film have been rare, frequently criticized, banned, and if present at all, limited to a hug or kiss. As with other portrayals of individuals set apart from the mainstream, gay characters in films have been coded and stereotyped in particular ways.

During the early years of Hollywood filmmaking (1890s–1930s), gay characters were the objects of scorn, ridicule, and jokes. The **sissy/pansy** was the most popular character whose flamboyance and apparent asexuality presented him as non-threatening to heterosexual men's masculinity and to their claim on women. This effeminate character was often expressed in roles of hairdressers, costume designers, florists, and other stereotypical occupations and was quite visible in the 1920s and early 1930s on stage and screen. In the era widely known as **pre-code Hollywood**, one of the first portrayals of bisexual characters was in the 1914 film *A Florida Enchantment*. This early silent film more implied than showed the relationship between characters but was followed by the more explicit representation in *Exit Smiling* (1926), the first feature-film appearance of Franklin Pangborn, who appeared in covertly gay roles throughout the 1930s and 1940s (Fristoe, n.d.). Other actors include Tyrell Davis as a dance instructor in *Our Betters* (1933).

Scary sexuality

Genre theory is a method for analyzing films, along with semiotic and mythic analyses. This chapter invokes these perspectives but also draws on genre theory for its concerns with three primary elements: "audience, institution, and text" (Hockley, 2001, p. 179). These interconnected elements are jointly involved in how a film is received, decoded, coded, and analyzed by audiences. Regardless of genre "it is the combination of the familiar and the fresh, the universal and the unique, together with a finely tuned veil between them that generates strength in film" (Slater, 2005, p. 3). As is true of all myths, these stories are presented and represented under new guise and yet remain relevant due to the enduring power of myth.

As discussed in Chapter 1, the mass media draw upon ancient collective myths for contemporary story telling. Myths function "by demonstrating order," they tell cultural tales about life, death, birth, and other big topics in ways that make sense to us, and have made sense to us, since time immemorial (Ausband, 1983, p. 5). Myths function by giving us an "experience both of accord with the social order, and of harmony with the universe" (Campbell, 1975, p. 5).

A genre, identifiable in literature and film, tells "familiar stories with familiar characters in familiar situations" (Grant, 2007, p. 1). Genres have distinct conventions (and ways of addressing their audiences). Examples of film genres include romantic comedy, action/adventure, drama, horror, and pornography. Before there were western films, there were western novels. Conventions are "frequently used stylistic techniques or narrative devices typical of (but not necessarily unique to) particular genre traditions" (p. 10). Thus, particular ways of talking, the use of certain kinds of music, ways of dress, and camera angles all communicate the overall nature of the film to the audience. Conventions thus "function as an implied agreement between makers and consumers to accept certain artificialities" (p. 10). In film noir, it is often raining, dark; people speak in low tones, and in conventionalized ways that might seem out of place in other movies. The classic horror narrative is as follows:

> A monster is made or arrives in a village/town/city, wreaks havoc on its inhabitants, especially the heroine, and is destroyed by a bold and impressive hero, with the aid of an older man. The relationship between the monster and hero plays out a number of oppositions, such as inhuman versus human, uncivilized versus civilized, sexual versus asexual, and monstrous versus normal. (Berenstein, 1996, p. 2)

Horror films are exciting, they take us places in our bodies and imaginations we might not otherwise travel and yet do so, within the safe space of a movie house or our living rooms. A common element (convention) found in horror movies is a monster—some dark, threatening, unknown someone or something that keeps us perched on the edges of our seats, ever vigilant for the well-being of the movie's star and, in some ways, for ourselves. Horror connects us to parts of ourselves we would rather not acknowledge, such as feelings of powerlessness in an overwhelming and uncertain world, of alienation, of sexuality, of what is forbidden, and above all, our fear of death. The horror film is one of the most consistent, persistent, and resilient movie forms whose roots extend back to its origins in mythology and stories, both oral and written, particularly in literary genres (Crane, 1994; Ursini, 2000).

The horror genre is home to alternative ways of thinking and being. The veil between the world of the known and unknown, the trusted and feared, the acceptable and unacceptable is at its thinnest there. Horror films are both hiding places and public forums whose stories draw strength from the human fear of death, anxiety about the unknown present, the paradox of empathy, and identification with what Freud called the **uncanny**. There is something familiar yet frightening in what we fear, it both attracts and repels. Thus, within these films, we often find expressions of not only alternative ways of living (and dying) but also of ways of expressing sexuality, hetero, homo, bi, and trans. According to Voytilla (1999, p. 74)

> Effective horror preys on our most primitive fears: the unknown, powerlessness, alienation, dehumanization, mutilation, and death. The more universal the fear (dark basements, crowds, heights, bugs, chain saws), the stronger the audience's identification, and the more effective the horror.

The Monstrous-Feminine

> She caressed me with her hands, and lay down beside me on the bed, and drew me towards her, smiling; I felt immediately delightfully soothed, and fell asleep again. I was wakened by a sensation as if two needles ran into my breast very deep at the same moment, and I cried loudly. *Carmilla* (Le Fanu, 1872/1993, p. 246)

"Horror," says Ursini (2000, p. 5), "is based on recognizing in the unfamiliar something familiar, something attractive even as it is repulsive." It might be the Frankenstein monster's longing for friendship, a vampire's desire for erotic union, or a mummy's search for a lost love. Horror shows us that reality is a construction and suggests death might not be a permanent state. It invites the possibility of eternal life, which those we love might return to us, and the element of surprise in what seems like fantasy might in fact be real. Fear, a central affective goal of horror, is a deeply primal emotion used to motivate, it "explodes from inside our psyche when encountering a vision which touches our deepest emotions" (p. 5). This is the ground Kristeva (1982) called "the abject," the fertile fodder in which that which has been repressed, below the level of consciousness, dark, rich, and hidden, can be found. It is a familiar Other rooted in our minds, our psyches, "in our fears and obsessions" (Silver & Ursini, 2000, p. 4).

Some of what we fear, Freud said, are the residue and remnants of everyday experiences, some of which are deeply rooted in a shared psychic past that draws on terrors as old as our reptilian memory. Freud (1919/2003, pp. 240–241) noted, "everything which now strikes us as 'uncanny' fulfills the condition of touching those residues of animistic mental activity within us and bringing them to expression." We can tell this has happened when scenes in movies provoke "goose bumps" on our skin or the hair stands up on the back of our necks.

Women are represented as monsters in films in many ways. The female monster or "**the monstrous-feminine**" (Creed, 1993, p. 1) appears as witch (*Carrie*, 1976), as possessed (*The Exorcist*, 1973), as castrating mother (*Psycho*, 1960), as beautiful murderer (*Basic Instinct*, 1992; *Fatal Attraction*, 1987), as other-than-human animal (*Cat People*, 1942), as part-human part-monster (*Alien*, 1979), and as vampires (*The Hunger*, 1983). These stories build on ancient myths that paint a picture of a certain kind of woman as evil. The *Random House Dictionary* defines vampire as a woman who "unscrupulously exploits, ruins, or destroys the men she seduces," that is, the origin of the term "vamp." Joseph Campbell (1991, p. 55) elaborates:

> There is a motif occurring in certain primitive mythologies, as well as in modern surrealist painting, and neurotic dream, which is known to folklore as 'the toothed vagina'—the vagina that castrates. And a counterpart, the other way, is the so-called 'phallic-mother,' a motif perfectly illustrated in the long fingers and nose of the witch.

This terrifying portrayal of women as monsters, whose sexual organs contain teeth that can emasculate a man and are of temperaments that must be tamed, has haunted women for hundreds of years. Blamed for diseases, natural disasters, political unrest, male impotence, and the failure of crops, women have suffered and been murdered as witches, cast out and killed, unfairly blamed for problems that were the result of an entire society's doing. Creed (1993, p. 7) uses the term "monstrous-feminine" as the substitute for "female monster," to separate her from the usual male monster figure. While most monsters in film are male, coding women as monstrous, yet simultaneously as objects of desire, operates in ways that ease men's fears yet entertain them by using the bodies of women in sexual ways:

> In this respect, it could well be maintained that it is woman's sexuality, that which renders them desirable—but also threatening—to men, which constitutes the real problem that the horror cinema exists to explore, and which constitutes also and ultimately that which is really monstrous. (Neale, 1980, p. 61)

Many Western myths originate with Greek goddesses, who not only had their good, creative sides but also their bad, destructive natures as well. Unlike the one-dimensional, concretized meanings of stereotypes, these archetypes were multi-dimensional, complex beings who represented life and death, love and hate, good and evil.

Women's representations in media in general are stereotyped primarily in one of two ways: as virgin or vamp (Benedict, 1993). The horror film takes this framing a step further. The "'monstrous-feminine' emphasizes the importance of gender in the construction of her monstrosity" (Creed, 1993, p. 3). By the 1970s, sexuality and sadism were combined in a marked way—the lesbian vampire of the horror film. Horror's "key generic ingredients [are]: a limp and possibly tortured body; the promise of a scary performance; a monstrous figure; a resistant and frightened woman; and an eager male spectator" (Berenstein, 1996, p. 6). But this scenario is that of the typical horror film in which gender roles are assured. What if the monstrous figure is female who is advancing on an unwilling (or in some cases willing) female victim? There is a specialized **sub-genre** in film in which the monster is a woman—the lesbian vampire film.

It is the monstrous woman who has the power—the power to seduce, to kill, to maim—and ultimately is killed by the end of the movie. If we add the additional birdcage wire of homosexuality, the lesbian vampire is yet another step removed from being human and thus controllable.

The Abject

A study of lesbian vampires in film presents an intriguing opportunity to explore this coding. The horror film and the horrible female character is an opportunity to explore the simultaneous fascination and fear dynamic men have with female sexuality (Neale, 1980). Feminist theorist Julia Kristeva (1982) articulated this ambiguity as "abjection," as in that which does not "respect borders, positions, rules," which "disturbs identity, system, order" (p. 4). Abjection separates out and excludes someone from society who, by whatever criteria, is positioned as Other to the dominant order. It includes religious abominations such as "sexual immorality and perversion; corporeal alteration, decay and death; human sacrifice; murder; the corpse; bodily wastes; the feminine body and incest" (Creed, 1993, p. 9). All of these acts are typical conventions of the horror film genre, which is an illustration of abjection in at least three ways:

1. Through use of corpses, decay, and bodily fluids such as blood.
2. The idea of a "border" between what we know to be real and what we are uncertain of as real. Sometimes it is uncertainty of who is human (or not), who is dead (or not), who is normal (or not), who can be trusted (or not).

3. A dominant maternal figure, who either through her rejection or feeding of a character, or the violation of taboos such as incest and other sexual prohibitions, misperforms her role as an acceptable woman (Kristeva, 1982).

Taking a bite out of film

Sometimes after an hour of apathy, my strange and beautiful companion would take my hand and hold it with a fond pressure, renewed again and again; blushing softly, gazing in my face with languid and burning eyes, and breathing so fast that her dress rose and fell with the tumultuous respiration. It was like the ardor of a lover; it embarrassed me; it was hateful and yet overpowering; and with gloating eyes she drew me to her, and her hot lips traveled along my cheek in kisses; and she would whisper, almost in sobs, 'You are mine, you shall be mine, and you and I are one for ever'. (Le Fanu, *Carmilla,* 1872/1964)

The first cinematic portrayal of a lesbian was the representation of female-identified desire in the 1929 G. W. Pabst film *Die Büchse der Pandora* (*Pandora's Box*) (Berenstein, 1999, p. 303). The relationship, which is entirely implied, is between a countess and the woman she loves. In most cases the implication or enactment of lesbian love is punished in film. In films as early as Jacques Deval's *The Girls' Club* (1936) to the *The Children's Hour* (1962), *Basic Instinct* (1983), and others, the woman who feels or expresses love for another woman typically commits suicide, is banished to a mental hospital, or dies. In *The Children's Hour* (1962) (based on a 1934 Lillian Hellman play), Shirley MacLaine's character realizes she feels more than friendship for Audrey Hepburn's character. Exposed, the MacLaine character kills herself.

Sexual ambiguity is another theme amplified in many film genres. For example, Marlene Dietrich (*Morocco*, 1930) and Greta Garbo (*Queen Christina*, 1933) played with their appeal to both men and to women. Dressing in drag, teasing male and female characters, these classic beauties kissed, touched, and taunted audiences.

The allusion to sexual interaction or at least attraction is also evident in the 1940 Alfred Hitchcock classic *Rebecca*, in which the caretaker character is seen caressing the previous Mrs. de Winter's undergarments. Implication and implicitness might have had more to do with the Hollywood Production Code described earlier, which was well in place by the time of this film's creation. Throughout the 1950s–1970s, films such as *Touch of Evil* (1958) and *The Haunting* (1963) toyed with audience understandings of the relationships between characters and the power of the glance and the touch to communicate. This dance is still evident in films such as *The Color Purple* (1985) and *Fried Green Tomatoes* (1991). These films require "reading against the grain of mainstream images of lesbians" (Berenstein, 1999, p. 305).

The horror story *The Vampyre* (1819) and the stories by Edgar Allan Poe (*Tell Tale Heart, Pit and the Pendulum*), Mary Shelley (*Frankenstein*), Robert Louis Stevenson (*The Strange Case of Dr. Jekyll and Mr. Hyde*), and Matthew Lewis (*The Monk)* speak across generations, culture, and time, reappearing in new forms every day. The vampire story, the most famous of which is Bram Stoker's novel *Dracula*, is built largely from folktales and legends. Many people believe the first reference to vampires came from Bram Stoker's book. While a very important piece of literature in this regard, it was not the source of the first stories of encounters with and between female vampires. According to Silver and Ursini (1997), lesbian vampire films draw primarily on one of two sources: (1) Sheridan Le Fanu's novella *Carmilla* (1872/1964), the story of a countess who survived centuries by feeding on young women, and (2) the historical figure Countess Elizabeth Bathory, a 16th century Hungarian woman who was accused of killing more than 600 virgins and bathing in their blood, which she thought would maintain her youth and beauty.

Lesbian vampires first appeared in 19th century English romantic literature. The 1817 poem "**Christabel**" by Samuel Taylor Coleridge, relies on vampire allusion. The main character Christabel encounters another woman (Geraldine) late at night, under the full moon, in a forest. She invites Geraldine to stay at her home. In typical vampire fashion, Geraldine cannot cross the threshold into the family's castle unless invited in by Christabel. She does so, taking Geraldine into her bedroom. Once there, Geraldine undresses Christabel and herself. She reveals her body to Christabel who cannot help but kiss her breast. Uncertain whether she dreamed the encounter or not, the next morning Christabel is ashamed of her feelings but is weak. Geraldine grows stronger. In the end, Christabel is abandoned.

The first vampires were based on darker sides of goddesses, particularly aspects of life, death, blood, decay, and dangerous sexuality (Keesey, 2006). According to Pam Keesey in *Daughters of Darkness* (2006), the female vampire figure was based on the Judeo-Christian view of women as the embodiment of evil. Adam's first wife, Lilith, and his second wife Eve are both thought to be the downfall of men and represent challenges to and destruction of patriarchal society. Each defied authority, rebelled, and was punished by pain and blood. Both male and female vampires are afflicted with unquenchable appetites for sex and blood. Straight or gay, the female is seductive, sexual, and irresistible to both men and women—"the female vampire is she who steps outside the realm of acceptable 'feminine' behavior" (Keesey, 2006, p. 8).

It was during the 1970s wave of vampire films that the female figure came to prominence. Possibly a backlash to the hard-earned and newly won rights and freedoms following the sexual revolution and women's civil rights movements of the 1960s, films in general began to more openly explore themes of violence, sex, and death. Many vampire films of the 1970s combined the female vampire with a ravenous sexual appetite (including *Shadow of the Werewolf* and *Sex and the Vampire*). In these movies, women are presented as powerful predators, who feast on virginal victims, particularly if they are lesbians, thus are the monstrous-feminine. When a woman is cast as a vampire in these films, she is almost always at least bisexual and frequently a lesbian.

In the following section, three films are described that serve as benchmarks for studying female same-sex relationships when coded as vampires during and after Production Code Hollywood: *Dracula's Daughter* (1936), *The Vampire Lovers* (1970), and *The Hunger* (1983).

Dracula's Daughter (1936)

To say that the horror genre presents sexuality as heterosexual, bisexual, or homosexual is to only read the films denotatively. Connotatively they are more complex, "for the genre is not only home to representations of that depict the breakdown of heterosexuality; it also portrays a wide spectrum of sexualities in the process" (Berenstein, 1996, p. 24). Dracula, and the many male vampires, appear to be men who seduce women but also feed on other beings and can, at will, shape shift into wolves or bats. The vampire appears to be human, but not fully so; appears to be alive but is not fully that either. The level of eroticism varies by film. The predatory nature of vampires conveys a different kind of meaning to the seductions and attacks. A film that illustrates the slippery nature of sexuality and preference is the Hollywood Production Code era film *Dracula's Daughter* (1936).

In this film, Countess Marya Zaleska (Gloria Holden) is desperate for a cure for her malady—she drinks blood and kills virgin girls. She appeals to a psychiatrist for help. In thinly veiled allusions, the Countess describes her desires, her efforts to overcome them but is unsuccessful in conquering her urges. While instructed to exert better self-control and face the evil within her, Zaleska attacks a young woman whom she has lured to her art studio (Figure 13.3). At one level, the film could be described as a complex presentation of the **transference** phenomenon in therapy, where unrequited love of her psychiatrist drives her to seek out alternate relationships. On another, it presents same-sex desire as an incurable mental disorder that is inevitably doomed.

A film reviewer described Zaleska as follows:

> She is not a nice person; she goes around at night giving the eye to sweet young girls through her hypnotic power aided by the magic of a jeweled ring. After she taps their jugular veins for a couple of quarts she calls it a night and goes back to her studio.

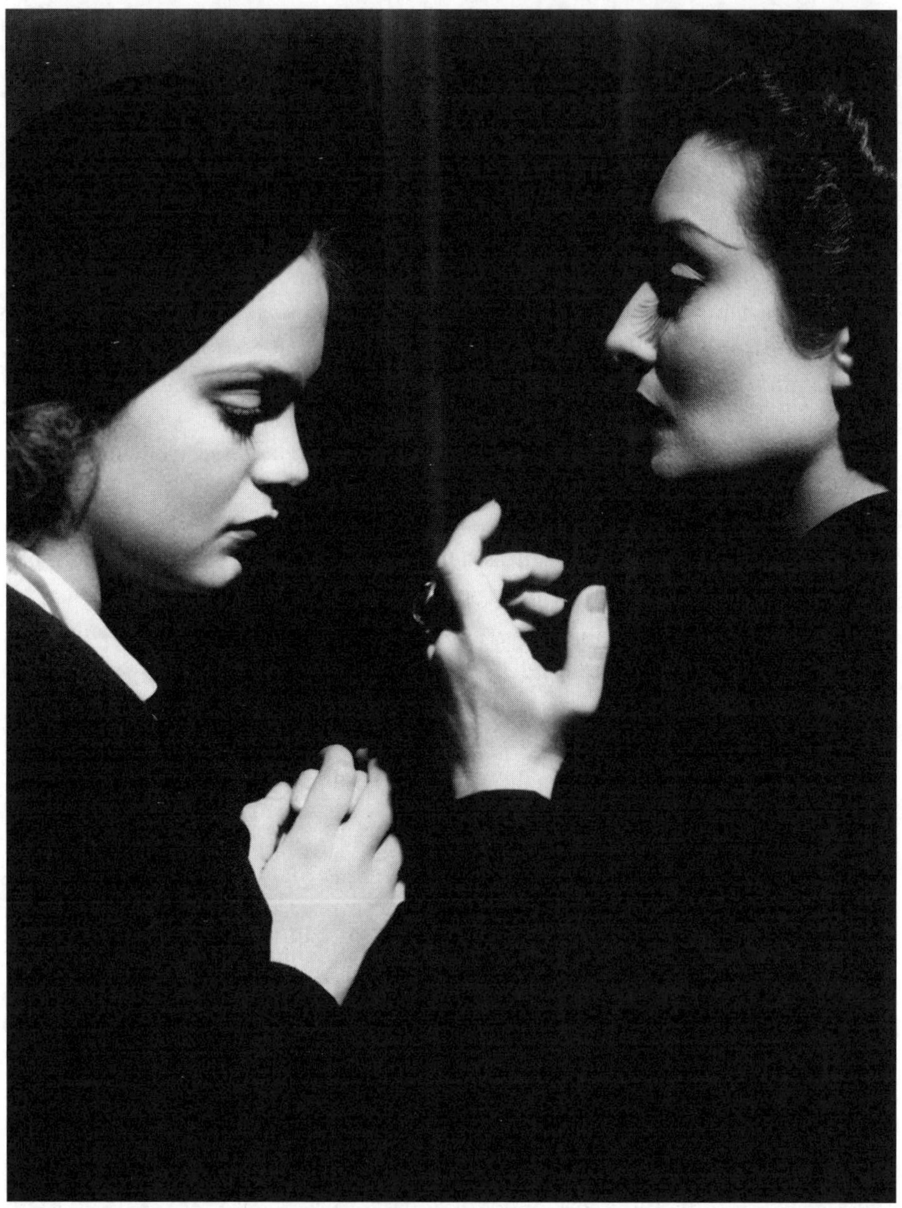

Figure 13.3: Screenshot from *Dracula's Daughter* (1936): Countess Zaleska puts an innocent girl under her spell. Directed by Lambert Hillyer. Shown from left: Nan Grey (as Lili) and Gloria Holden (as Countess Marya Zaleska, a.k.a. Dracula's Daughter).

Source: photofestnyc.com

Zaleska is a monstrous female who preys upon other women. Coding the Zaleska character as straight or gay, human or inhuman is limiting, because the horror genre works on definitions of sexuality by embellishing "them with perversions that defy and exceed traditional categories of human desire" (Bernstein, 1996, p. 27).

The Vampire Lovers (1970)

The Vampire Lovers stars Ingrid Pitt as Mircalla, the daughter of the countess in Le Fanu's (1872/1964) novel (Figure 13.4). In the story, Mircalla manages to elude a famous vampire killer. She seduces young women but eventually is hunted down and killed. Whereas she is a sensual, erotic, female vampire, the men in the movie are cold and puritanical. The film plays with contrasts of female versus male sexuality, portraying the former as passionate and expressive and the latter as sterile and repressed. Creed (1993, p. 61) argues that Mircalla fulfills the monstrous-feminine model because she threatens, "to undermine the formal and highly symbolic relations of men and women essential to the continuation of patriarchal society."

The female lesbian vampire not only seduces her victims, but unlike the male vampire/Dracula figure, more often than not transforms them into vampires as well, thus "she…threatens to seduce the daughters of patriarchy away from their proper gender roles" (p. 61). As does Countess Zaleska, this female vampire also fulfills Kristeva's (1982) concept of the abject—she disturbs the sexual and gender order, has an appetite for bodily fluids, does not adhere to laws of day or night worlds, nor does she follow dictates of sexual conduct. Like the male vampire, Mircalla also crosses the boundaries between animal and human (transforming into a wolf and a bat) and between living and dead. She is both and neither at the same time. She completes the **vagina dentata** by growing fangs with which she attacks, penetrates, and withdraws in order to feed on the blood of her victims. Unlike the 1936 film, we see the gore, penetration, and extraction. And blood is a key symbolic fluid in the construction of the female and lesbian vampire—it is shed, taken, consumed, and smeared. Kristeva (1982, p. 96) adds

> Blood, indicating the impure, takes on the 'animal' seme of the previous opposition and inherits the propensity for murder of which man must cleanse himself. But blood, as a vital element, also refers to women, fertility, and the assurance of fecundation. It thus becomes a fascinating semantic crossroads, the propitious place for abjection, where *death* and *femininity*, *murder* and *procreation*, *cessation of life*, and *vitality* all come together.

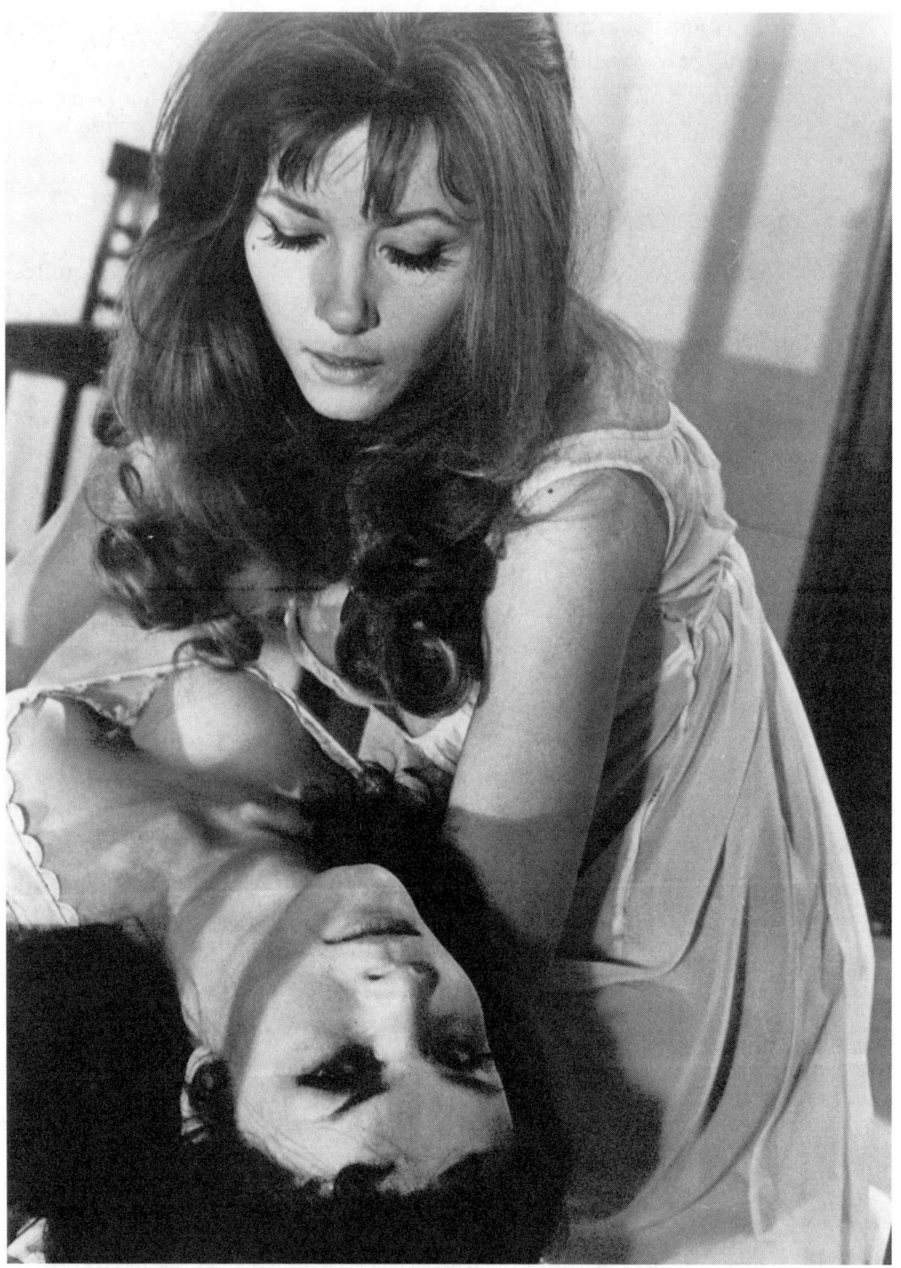

Figure 13.4: Screenshot from *The Vampire Lovers* (1970). Directed by Roy Ward Baker [shown Ingrid Pitt (left) and Kate O'Mara (right)].

Source: photofestnyc.com

The Hunger (1983)

By the 1980s, America's cultural emphasis was on individual pleasure; this was the era of the "Me-Generation." This attitude is reflected in the 1983 film *The Hunger*, which fulfills Kristeva's (1982) third quality of the abject because the lead figure is a beautiful, powerful vampire, played by Catherine Deneuve (Figure 13.5). Both foundational stories, the one of Carmilla and the legend of Countess Bathory, are articulated in this movie. French film star Deneuve plays Miriam Blaylock, a seductive, powerful woman who seeks her immortality through blood and has been staying young and beautiful for more than 2,000 years. Blaylock seduces both men and women with equal vigor. Her partner of two centuries, John (played by David Bowie), is equally elegant and similarly seductive.

The duo collects victims from nightclubs, luring them back to their chic apartment. These two do not have the traditional fangs but rather use a small instrument worn around their necks like a precious jewel, to cut their victims' throats. John was transformed into a vampire by Miriam and relies upon her to maintain his youth. One day he realizes that immortality may not be his as promised. Susan Sarandon plays Sarah, who is brought in to the relationship in order to replace John as Miriam's next lover.

Jealousy and competition ensue, and Miriam does not survive to see another millennium. What is notable in the film is that there is none of the usual moral sense of wrongness. The fear produced is more of aging than of becoming a vampire. The homoeroticism of the film was used to generate controversy and audiences. Roger Ebert (1983) panned its perhaps over-the-top emphasis on fashion and form, but noted that

> This movie has so much would-be elegance and visual class that it never quite happens as a dramatic event. There's so much crosscutting, so many memories, so many apparent flashbacks, that the real drama is lost—the drama of a living human being seduced into vampirism.

Just as *The Vampire Lovers* (1970) marks a radical change in the depiction of lesbian vampires onscreen to more overt than Code-era *Dracula's Daughter*, so too does *The Hunger* (1983). Fangs are absent, the word vampire is never used, and many of the typical vampire-genre conventions are absent—garlic, capes, and bats. Beautiful things, lovely music, and the finer aspects of life surround the almost-sympathetic Miriam and John, who live in an exquisite apartment. The vampire stereotype-breaking was brought further forward in *Interview with the Vampire* where the ideas of garlic, crosses, castles, and lack of reflections in mirrors were tossed to the dustbin of history and lore. In *The Hunger*, Miriam embodies the abject—she is a mother to John, denies him his needs, feeds on and is fed by Sarah. As John grows old she refuses to kill him, saying there is no death for him, but

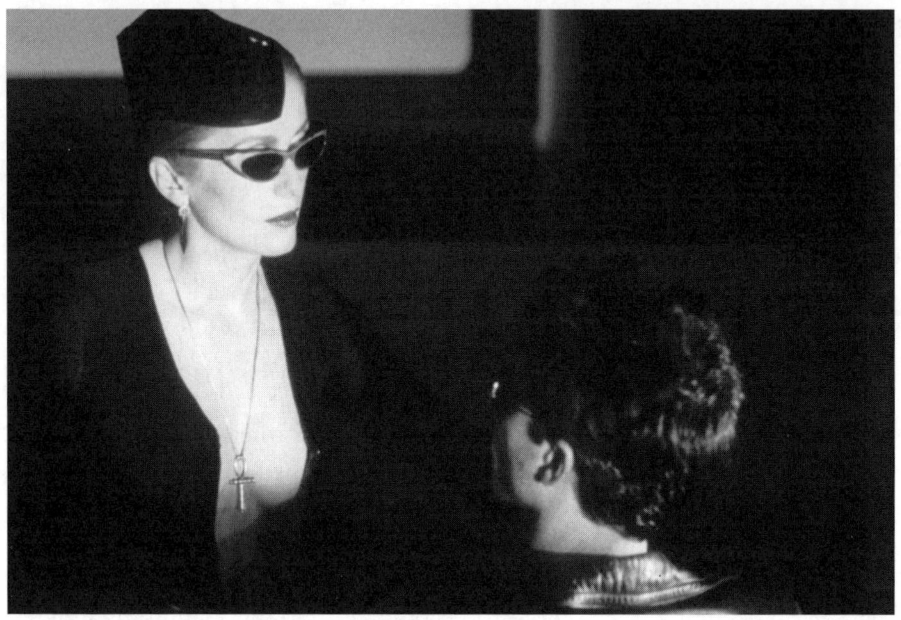

Figure13.5: Screenshot from *The Hunger* (1983). Directed by Tony Scott. Shown Catherine Deneuve (left) and David Bowie (right).

Source: photofestnyc.com

places him in a casket, as she has other lovers. Taboo violation is evident in bodily fluids (blood as food), the female body as sexual, a collapse of boundaries between who is deemed an appropriate sexual and life partner, and the clear pleasure Miriam takes, akin to oral sex, by sucking a victim's blood. "Orality, death, incest," three major categories of taboo are violated in *The Hunger* (Creed, 1993, p. 71). Add the element of *lesbianism* to the mix and the abjection is complete. Horror is instructive not only "in terms of what should and should not be done by adolescents, it is illustrative of what cannot be stopped among adults, such as homosexuality and the failure to conform to conventional gender roles" (Berenstein, 1996, p. 18). Thus, for mainstream acceptance, the vampires must be destroyed in the end.

Summary

That the lesbian vampire movie has developed into a sub-genre of the gay vampire film says something interesting about portrayals of same sex relationships and film. While movies such as *Interview with the Vampire* brought mass attention to the homoerotic qualities of vampire-ness, the appeal of women having sex (or something) with one another has fared better and longer. The sado-erotic quality of a woman feeding on and with other women transcends same-sex appeal but capitalizes on the appeal of pornography, "since the lesbian vampire genre can allow nudity, blood, and sexual titillation in a 'safe' fantasy structure" (Zimmerman, 2004, p. 73). Films such as *Dracula's Daughter* (1936), *The Vampire Lovers* (1970), and *The Hunger* (1983) all built on the *Carmilla* story structure in this way. Yet, many of the stereotypes of lesbians remain intact, furthered in the horror genre. The message remains clear: "lesbianism is sterile and morbid; lesbians are rich decadent women who seduce the young and powerless" (p. 74).

While women in the 1970s benefited from the activism that preceded this time and asked for more representation in the workplace and on the screen, some critics suggest that the lesbian vampire was used as vehicle to express "a fundamental male fear that woman-bonding will exclude men and threaten male supremacy" (Zimmerman, 1981). Therefore, lesbianism would necessarily be constructed as monstrous, as vampiric. The role of the lesbian vampire "is to contain attraction between women within the same boundaries of sexual violence" as rape of a woman by a man in order "to force it into a particular model of sexuality" (p. 75). Thus, the lesbian vampire "rapes" her victim by violating her innocence and draining her of her life force, that is, her femininity. The majority of lesbians in film in general are White. Many are also interested in men and as such

> the lesbian vampires of the cinema are not solely female identified, nor do they always pursue their victims in explicitly sexual ways. What renders them lesbian is their preference for females and their association with enduring stereotypes: They are usually aggressive, nonreproductive, sexually and socially aberrant, and conventionally masculine in behavior. (Berenstein, 1999, p. 303)

A more positive view is that the lesbian vampire genre offers a glimpse of female power and pleasure. Hanson (1999, p. 184) suggests:

> As I look at lesbian vampire films, I am no longer struck by their misogyny, but quite the opposite. They do not always follow the predictable track-and-kill traditions of the vampire genre, and lesbian desire often functions as a destabilizing and derailing force in the paranoid narrative that seeks to demonize and contain it. Some of the more complicated examples of the genre present a number of entertaining and intriguing possibilities for lesbian and feminist fantasy.

Clearly the sub-genre blurs the lines between expected roles of male and female, masculine and feminine. This raises provocative questions about the assumptions inherent in gender:

> As the primary site of erotic experience in *Dracula*, the mouth equivocates, giving the lie to the easy separation of the masculine and the feminine...are we male or are we

> female? Do we have penetrations or orifices? And if both, what does that mean? (Craft, 1997, pp. 445–446)

Fear of the emasculating power of women, the assumption that a woman, given enough freedom, would do this, is evident in the coding of the lesbian vampire. Kristeva's (1982) complex argument about the psychoanalytic function of the horrible and Creed's (1993) "monstrous-feminine" suggest that the aberrant is central to understanding the function of horror found in visual expression of shared fears and desires such as the lesbian vampire film.

While the horror film permits, and even encourages, gender-bending, transgression of expected sex and gender roles, it can operate as "a site of ideological contradiction and negotiation" (Berenstein, 1996, p. 10). But to rely on that oversimplifies the socio-political circumstances real men and women live in every day. "Horror is committed to the maintenance of the status quo, in terms not only of gender roles but also of social structures, institutions, and belief systems in general" (p. 10). It is a useful and sometimes satisfying site of transgression and convention but nevertheless is the product of media business whose primary intention is to fill seats and rent DVDs.

Although this chapter discusses only three films from three eras, it is an important part of genre theory to acknowledge that no single film should be considered alone, but rather one should keep in mind that films are created during specific sets of historical circumstances. In the horror film "gender is less a wall than a permeable membrane" (Clover, 1992, p. 46). The slippery nature of sex and gender roles in the horror film is one of the characteristics of the **genre** as is a **doubling** of female monsters as both woman and fiend that is facilitated by what the viewer brings to the filmic moment:

> There is a sense in which the woman's look at the monster is more than simply a punishment for looking, or a narcissist fascination with the distortion of her own image in the mirror that patriarchy holds up to her; it is also a recognition of their similar status as potent threats to a vulnerable male power. (Williams, 1984, p. 90)

A goal of this chapter, and this book, is to suggest that identities are not only imposed from without but also constructed from within. Intersecting with race, gender, and class, sexualities are similarly regarded as "multiple, unstable, and fluid social constructions" (Yep, Lovaas, & Elia, 2003, p. 4). The representation of lesbian sexuality in the horror film, therefore, contributes to the aim of Queer Theory, which is

> not to abandon identity as a category of knowledge and politics but to render it permanently open and contestable as to its meaning and political role. . . . [D]ecisions about identity categories become pragmatic, related to concerns of situational advantage, political gain, and conceptual utility. The gain, say Queer theorists, of figuring identity as permanently open as to its meaning and political use is that it encourages the public

surfacing of differences or a culture where multiple voices and interests are heard. (Seidman, 1996, p. 12)

Thus the mass media in general, and this genre and sub-genre of film in particular, present a version of sexuality that can be read by audiences in at least two ways: as resistance and liberation or as oppression and colonization. This by no means suggests that the ideal way to represent homosexuality or bisexuality or, for that matter, heterosexuality, is through the use of monsters. I do suggest that it is possible to look to media to destabilize categories of identity and use them to build a stronger sense of self. Gloria Anzaldúa (2002, p. 541) speaks to this time as one of opportunity:

We stand at a major threshold in the extension of consciousness, caught in the remolinos (vortices) of systemic change across all fields of knowledge. The binaries of colored/ white, female/male, [heterosexual/homo-sexual], mind/body are collapsing. Living in nepantla, the overlapping space between different perceptions and belief systems, you are aware of the changeability of racial, gender, sexual, and other categories rendering the conventional labelings obsolete. Though these markings are out worn and inaccurate, those in power continue using them to single out and negate those who are "different" because of color, language, notions of reality, or other diversity. You know that the new paradigm must come from outside as well as within the system.

Questions for Discussion

1. Do you think the Hollywood Production Code was a good idea? Would it be useful today?
2. Can you think of other ways of coding information in films, other than sexual preference?
3. Is the representation of same-sex female sexual attraction in vampire films positive or negative?
4. Why do you believe it has been so difficult getting programs featuring gay and lesbian characters on broadcast television?
5. Why are bisexuals so rarely seen on television?

Key Words

Abject	Catholic Legion of Decency
"Christabel"	Classic Hollywood Formula
Doubling	Genre
Genre Theory	Hays Code
Hays Formula	Hollywood Production Code

 Television News Coverage of "Day without an Immigrant"

No one is illegal.

Elie Wiesel

"Keep ancient lands, your storied pomp!" cries she
With silent lips. "Give me your tired, your poor,
Your huddled masses yearning to breathe free,
The wretched refuse of your teeming shore.
Send these, the homeless, tempest-tost to me,
I lift my lamp beside the golden door!"

Emma Lazarus

A screaming baby girl has been forcibly weaned from breast milk
and taken, dehydrated, to an emergency room, so that the nation's
borders will be secure.

New York Times (March 17, 2007)

On January 28, 1948, the U.S. Immigration and Naturalization Service (INS) arranged for 28 Mexican nationals to be returned to Mexico. These individuals had either overstayed their work permits or had entered the United States illegally.

Airline Transport Carriers, a California-based airline service, contracted for a wide variety of services, one of which was to return "**deportees**" (illegal migrant workers).[1] The pilot, Francis C. Atkinson of Long Beach, California was an experienced flyer; his wife was the flight attendant, but for some reason, the crew flew the wrong plane that morning. They were to take an airplane certified for 32 people but instead, took one designed only to carry 26, one that was overdue for a safety inspection. Due to a defective fuel pump, something that would have been caught during inspection, the plane crashed, killing all aboard. Witnesses saw at least nine people leap to their death. Afterward, only about half of the passengers were identifiable and were buried in a mass grave.[2] A radio announcer reporting the incident said, "It's not such a tragedy since they were just deportees" (Cohen, 2003, p. 2).

Most newspaper accounts of the crash contained only crewmember names and referred to the Mexicans collectively as "deportees" (*New York Times*, 1948). When singer, songwriter, and activist **Woody Guthrie** heard of the omission of the names, he wrote a poem. Later, music teacher Martin Hoffman scored the music. It has been recorded and performed by many artists since. Guthrie noticed in news accounts what went unsaid as much as what was. This example illustrates the importance of language in constructing how an issue or people is/are told and remembered. Framing, which is discussed in detail later in this chapter, is a way of selecting and telling a story in such a way that it presents a particular point of view to readers, viewers, or listeners. Frames "organize experience" (Goffman, 1997, p. 147). In terms of understanding mass media,

> … framing is a powerful concept for explicating the activities of journalists and news organizations. It also provides leverage for understanding the behaviors of public relations specialists, 'spin doctors,' and other elites and professionals whose job it is to produce congenial concepts, beliefs, and opinions among the broader public. (Nelson, Clawson & Oxley, 1997, p. 577)

Since the time when White, mostly male, explorers arrived on the shores of North America (more than 500 years ago), "Us," has been seen through the lens of Whites, and the "Them" was and is everyone else, including at times, White women. A great deal of social science research is founded on the premise that all the constructions of racism, sexism, ageism, and able-ism are about power—who has it, who wants it, and who wants to keep it. Ultimately, these propagandist strategies employ powerful metaphors and build on fear. But what is behind the sense of power? In this chapter I argue that *fear* is the motivator, fear that can escalate to the point of mass hysteria. Examples include Nazi Germany's attempts to exterminate Jews, European Americans' efforts to eliminate indigenous people, "**ethnic cleansing**" in the former Yugoslavia, murders of Tutsis and Hutus in

Rwanda, and the horrors of Darfur. These are, unfortunately, only a few examples of the extent to which human projection onto other human beings can go. The following sections include a brief journey through U.S. **immigration** history, followed by the specific case of Latina/o immigration in California, culminating in a discussion of news media coverage of May 1, 2006, the Day without an Immigrant.

In this chapter I propose a **Fear Theory of Stereotyping** that says group belonging, Us-ness, includes uniform attitudes, beliefs, and behaviors that make a clear distinction between an "Us" and a "Them." People thereby perceive themselves as belonging to and possessing the same qualities and characteristics of other members of the group and those who do not as being "Other." Thus, as described in earlier chapters, women, men, and children who, for whatever reason, are defined as "different" from the proscribed norm, are marked as part of a false dualism that similarly constructs Us as good and Them as evil. The mass media play an important role in the cultivation, perpetuation, and amplification of fears and perceptions of scarcity.

What is the U.S. track record when it comes to immigration? Who has traditionally immigrated? How were they treated? That is the subject of the next section that takes a summary look at U.S. immigration by examining six specific periods identifiable by the patterns in countries of origins, motivations, and lived experiences of immigration.

U.S. Immigration History

1790–1820

Between 1790 and 1820 many people sought home ground in America because, according to Thomas Paine it was "the **asylum** for the persecuted lovers of civil and religious liberty from every part of Europe" (as quoted in Foner, 2005, p. 77). Most immigrants at this time came from Europe. The first U.S. census (in 1790) tallied 3.9 million people. Of these, English people accounted for the largest immigrant group, along with 20% from Africa (85,000), followed by Scottish-Irish (50,000), French (40,000), German (25,000), and Irish (25,000). Native Americans were not counted and the Africans were, of course, slaves. At the time, immigration rules and authority was with the states. In 1790, Congress established the **Naturalization Act** that stipulated, "…Any alien, being a free white person, may be admitted to become a citizen of the United States…." In 1808, Congress banned slavery and claimed the authority to establish rules about naturalization.

During the early 1800s, the influx of immigrants slowed, although there was a surge of French refugees from Haiti. The War of 1812 also slowed immigration. However, in 1814, immigration swiftly resumed. Major port cities such as New York became hubs for thousands of British, Irish, and Western Europeans coming to the United States. Conditions were often terrible on board the trans-Atlantic ships. In 1819, Congress passed the **Steerage Act** requiring ship captains to maintain passenger records (manifests) and create more humane conditions for immigrants.

1820–1880

During America's Industrial Revolution, citizens moved westward. Immigrants continued to arrive along the Eastern seaboard but also increasingly along the west coast as well, many coming from Asia drawn to the excitement and opportunities for jobs associated with the California Gold Rush. Irish immigrants came in great numbers not only hoping for an opportunity to become successful but also fleeing devastating famine and extermination efforts in their homeland. This tragedy, which left more than 1.5 million dead from famine in Ireland, resulted in nearly 3 million coming to America. In addition, nearly 3 million people came from Germany, 2 million from Great Britain, and 1 million from the Austro-Hungarian Empire. By 1860, more than 4 million Africans had been shipped to the United States as slaves (see Chapter 12 for more information on this topic).

When times turned economically tough in America, it was the immigrant who paid the price for his or her "Otherness." Viewed in good times as needed workers, in hard times immigrants were commonly viewed as usurpers of jobs from "real" Americans, many were cast out, attacked, and even killed. Life in the United States was experienced quite differently than imagined. Sadly, this phenomenon hasn't changed very much.

Traveling to America from Europe improved dramatically in the late 1800s. Steam power made the arduous trip shorter. Immigrants began coming from a wider variety of countries: from Italy (4.6 million), the Russian Empire (3.3 million), as well as from the Middle East and Africa. It was increasingly common during this era for entire families to immigrate, rather than one person, usually a man, leading the way as in prior decades. Some, who had arrived earlier, had by now earned enough money to bring their families over.

1880–1930

For those who were able to find their way into the country, ethnic communities sprang up in cities such as New York and Boston, where an immigrant could find community amongst those who spoke his or her language and could help him or her find work. Between 1880 and 1930, more than 27 million people immigrated to the United States, and about 20 million of them came through **Ellis Island,** the place most associated with U.S. immigration.

In 1890, journalist Jacob A. Riis' book *How the Other Half Lives: Studies Among the Tenements of New York,* was published by Charles Scribner's Sons.[3] A pioneering work of photojournalism, it became part of the **muckraking** literature of the day. Muckraking is defined in this case in a positive sense as a form of investigative journalism, although it did have its sensationalistic appeal. In Riis' case, as "a reporter-reformer who liked to tell stories," his work exposed the horrors of the squalor in New York City's slums to middle- and upper-class people (Miraldi, 1990, p. 9). It was not uncommon then, nor unfortunately is it today, for those in the more economically able social classes to be unaware of the conditions of those less materially fortunate than themselves. Riis, a Danish immigrant, was unemployed until he established himself as a police reporter and photographer and wrote about the conditions of documented and undocumented immigrant life in images and in words. Riis collected statistics and sketched and eventually took pictures. Figure 14.1, "Bandit's Roost," is one of Riis' (1888) photographs.

The book contains 15 half-tone images and more than 40 drawings based on the photographs. Flash photography was available and Riis was able to capture aspects of tenement life normally kept in the dark. The book also revealed the conditions of sweatshop laborers, including children. Riis' publication reached the wealthy in a medium they were comfortable with (a book). This was information about the poor many of them preferred not to see or hear. While the book tends toward the stereotypical, it appears Riis was well intended and his message was heard—that immigrant people, given the same opportunities for education, housing, and health care, could join, be on par intellectually with the upper other half. But that the upper "other half" had to *see,* through photographs and descriptions of the extreme poverty and suffering, before they would be moved to care.

> There came a time when the discomfort and crowding below were so great, and the consequent upheavals so violent, that it was no longer an easy thing to do, and then the upper half fell to inquiring what was the matter. Information on the subject has been accumulating rapidly since, and the whole world has had its hands full answering for its old ignorance. (J. Riis, 1890)

During the years 1880–1930 the immigrant experience changed considerably, particularly for Asians. For example, in 1882, Congress passed the Chinese Exclusion Act, which severely limited immigration. This Act made it very difficult, if not impossible, for earlier immigrants to bring their wives and families over. Across the American West, "thousands of Chinese people were violently herded

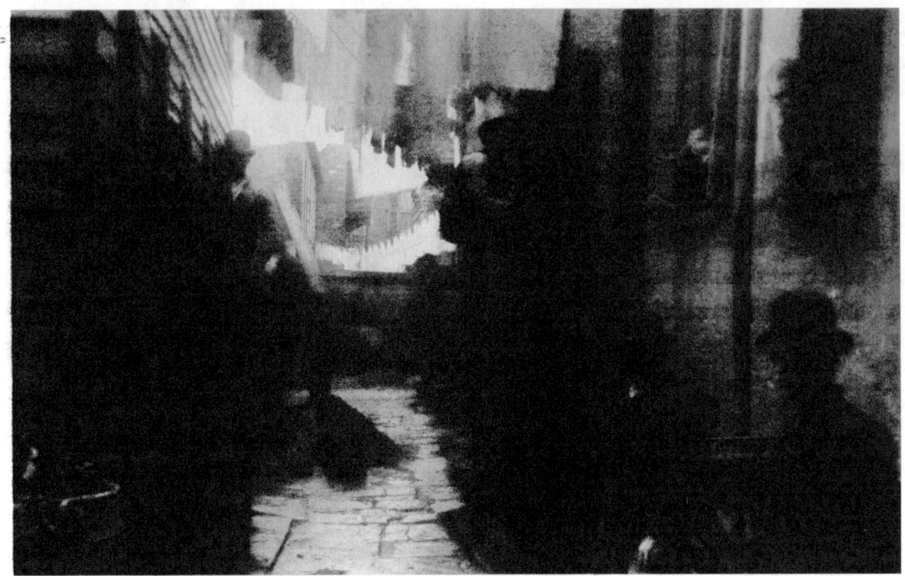

Figure 14.1: "Bandit's Roost" by Jacob A. Riis (1888).

Source: Photo courtesy of The Museum of Modern Art/Licensed by SCALA / Art Resource, New York.

onto railroad cars, steamers, or logging rafts, marched out of town or killed" along the Pacific coast and in the Rocky Mountains (Pfaelzer, 2007, p. xxv). The **Geary Act** of 1892 required Chinese immigrants to carry identification cards in order to prove they were in the United States legally, otherwise they faced deportation. This act prompted fear of the "Yellow Peril," fueled by the House Committee on Immigration and Naturalization who reported that, after 1892,

> There will be no law to prevent the Chinese hordes from invading our country in numbers so vast as soon to outnumber the present population of our flourishing states on the Pacific slope…to make this country their temporary home, where in a few years they can accumulate enough to live the balance of their days in China in comparative ease. (As quoted in Pfaelzer, 2007, p. 294)

A *Los Angeles Times* article of the day added

> If we can keep out the Chinese, there is no reason why we cannot exclude the lower classes of Poles, Hungarians, Italians and some other European nations, which people possess most of the vices of the Chinese and few of their good qualities, besides having a leaning towards bloodshed and anarchy which is peculiarly their own. (p. 294)

The Geary Act was also called the **"Dog Tag Law,"** a Chinese vice consul of the time commented:

> If you have a dog, a black and tan, a Llewellyn setter, a pointer, you buy a license tag for
> it and fasten it to the dog's collar, and the number in the dog's tag is its immunity from
> arrest by the poundman. Under the Geary bill the laboring Chinese carry their number
> in their pocket and any man who so desires may stop them and demand to see their
> 'tag'…. We ask that our Government protect its children. (as quoted in Pfaelzer, 2007,
> p. 294)

The Chinese response was a remarkable example of collective action. More than 7,000 lawsuits were filed over the 10 years following the Exclusion Act, and many were successful, resulting in what was "perhaps the largest organized act of civil disobedience in the United States" (Pfaelzer, 2007, p. 289). In *Driven Out: The Forgotten War against Chinese Americans,* Pfaelzer (2007, p. 246) documents these lawsuits, saying "The Chinese brought these suits as part of a strategy for coercing a nation to obey its own laws. Despite the violence and the limits on access to the courts, they acted as if legal judgments could be impartial." Pfaelzer argues the treatment of the Chinese in America under the Exclusion Act, once explored, constituted a form of ethnic cleansing, defined as "expulsion of an 'undesirable' population from a given territory due to religious or ethnic discrimination, political, strategic or ideological considerations, or a combination of these" (Bell-Fialkoff, 1993, n.p.) similar to other times in the United States and elsewhere.

With the advent of World War I (1914–1918), however, attitudes toward particular immigrants from specific European countries changed. Suspicion, **ethnocentrism** (a tendency to evaluate people from other cultures as less worthy than one's own), **xenophobia** (fear or hatred of strangers and/or foreigners) all reared their ugly heads. In the 1920s, for example, several laws limited the flow of immigrants, despite the life and death circumstances that brought people to America's shores. Thousands fled massacres in Europe, such as Eastern Europeans, Russians, and Armenians.

In the 1920s, the flood of immigrants was slowed by quotas, which

> … favored Anglo-Saxons, kept out black and yellow people, limited severely the coming
> of Latins, Slavs, Jews. No African country could send more than 100 people; 100 was
> the limit for China, for Bulgaria, for Palestine; 34, 007 could come from England or
> Northern Ireland, but only 3,845 from Italy; 51, 277 from Germany, but only 124 from
> Lithuania; 28,567 from the Irish Free State, but only 2,248 from Russia. (Zinn, 2003,
> p. 382)

While it was the Roaring Twenties, a time full of fanciful clothing and attitudes, the fun and shenanigans were amongst only a select few. For many people, it was a time filled with fear. For example, in 1924, the **Ku Klux Klan** grew in popularity, with more than 4.5 million members. Unemployment was relatively low in the early to mid-1920s, there were jobs to be had and yet the class system was becoming firmly established. The bulk of workers were in hourly jobs, factory work, and sometimes in poor conditions. There were bitter labor struggles at the time among coal miners and textile workers. While Riis' vision of improved living conditions for immigrants in New York City prompted some changes, in 1928 New York City Mayor LaGuardia toured the poor sections of the city and said, "I confess, I was not prepared for what I actually saw. It seemed almost incredible that such conditions of poverty could really exist" (as quoted in Zinn, 2003, p. 385). Things went from bad to worse for many people. In 1929, due to stock market speculation, a generally unsound economy, and extreme inequities in income distribution (the richest 5% of the population held nearly one-third of the nation's personal income), the economy tanked. Bad news for everyone, particularly for ethnic and racially identified laborers in what is known as the **Great Depression.**

1930–1950

By the time of the Great Depression (1929–1939), jobs were scarce for everyone. Some immigrants returned to their homelands. Others were forced to. By the late 1930s a new group of immigrants began arriving, also fleeing persecution in Europe. Many of the people fleeing Nazi persecution were turned away due to the restrictive immigration polices that remained in place, carried over from the 1920s.

When America entered World War II, immigration hopefuls from Italy and Germany were detained. Japanese, including resident and American born, were shipped to detainment camps. It was not until 1988 that the U.S. government would officially apologize for this heinous act. After WWII, President Harry Truman declared in a State of the Union Address in 1947, "I urge the Congress to turn its attention to this world problem in an effort to find ways whereby we can fulfill our responsibilities to these thousands of homeless and suffering refugees of all faiths." Thus, in 1948 Congress passed the **Displaced Persons Act**, which opened up the nation to thousands of refugees.

From the 1940s through the 1950s, the number of foreign-born residents declined from 12% to 7% of the total U.S. population (U.S. Census, 1999). There were some exceptions. For example, failed revolutions in Europe resulted in more than 38,000 Hungarians seeking solace in the United States as the first among many Cold War refugees. The 1945 **War Brides Act** allowed foreign-born wives of U.S. citizens to immigrate and was extended, in 1946, to include fiancées. In 1948, the Displaced Persons Act allowed individuals forced to leave their home countries during World War II to immigrate to the United States; 200,000 Europeans, among whom were 17,000 orphans, were the first to arrive. This act was extended and another 200,000 people arrived in 1950.

1950–2001

With the beginning of the Korean War in 1950, immigration was prohibited to anyone who was or was thought to be Communist. The 1952 **McCarran-Walter Immigration Act** returned the nation to a quota system for a period, limiting the number of immigrants to approximately 155,000. In 1953, the **Refugee Act** opened immigration to include non-Europeans. The year 1954 saw the offensively titled **Operation Wetback** enacted that forced thousands of undocumented individuals to return to Mexico. Prior to that, between 1944 and 1954, more than 1 million people had crossed the Rio Grande into the United States.

By 1965, during the civil rights movement, there was again a call for immigration reform and the quota system was dismantled. The immigration law was eased in 1965 and 2004, and nearly 900,000 individuals emigrated from Korea. President Lyndon Johnson signed the **Hart-Celler Act** into law, which replaced the quota system (which had favored Western Europeans) with one that offered an immigration opportunity to people around the world. In 1965, under the **Nationality and Immigration Act Amendments**, Asian immigration quadrupled, particularly among refugees from Southeast Asia. Cuban refugees were also seeking a way out of political turmoil. Policies that privileged professionals, such as lawyers, doctors, nurses and high tech experts, drew immigrants from all over the world. These skilled workers, many of whom were women, were often the beginning of a chain that would eventually bring entire families to the United States. During this time, nearly 4.3 million individuals came from Mexico, another 1.4 million from the Philippines, nearly 1 million each from Korea, the Dominican Republic, and India. From Vietnam came 700,000 individuals, 720,000 from Cuba and 650,000 from Canada.

Throughout the 1970s–1990s, there was increased emphasis on crime (Zinn, 2003). In nearly every city the contrast between the haves and have-nots was increasingly visible. No longer did a college education guarantee employment. Over this period of time, "never before was there such a general withdrawal of confidence from so many elements of the political and economic system" (Zinn, 2003, p. 640). America had come out of a war that lacked patriotic fervor and unity. Unlike earlier times, people were not joining together in the struggles. But the rise of giant corporations and dissociation of people from the means and ways of production were leading to general cultural malaise that would serve to divide, not unify; generate suspicion, not trust.

Although restrictions on immigration eased through the 1960s, economic fears in the 1990s saw renewed tightening. Corporations were downsizing or moving operations to other countries, and jobs in America were lost, many to Mexico, where it was/is cheaper to produce products. Immigrants crossing into the United

States were increasingly blamed for taking jobs and benefits from U.S. citizens. Under President Clinton, legislation was passed that removed welfare benefits from legal and illegal immigrants such as food stamps and payments to the elderly. Deportation happened regularly, to many who sought asylum such as Guatemalans and El Salvadorians who had escaped death squads. Because the United States gave aid to those nations, these people were denied status as "political" refugees. In 1996, both Congress and President Clinton moved to pass an "Anti-Terrorism and Effective Death Penalty Act" that would allow the deportation of any immigrant convicted of a crime, no matter how serious (or not) or how long ago it had happened. Clearly, the Statue of Liberty's statement of welcome to the "tired… huddled masses yearning to breathe free" did not apply to everyone.

2001 and after

There is no doubt that the immigration experience has and continues to have a profound effect on the political, economic, cultural, and psychological landscape of many countries, the United States and Europe included. More recent immigration to the United States has generated a variety of tensions about ethnic and cultural identity of resident immigrant groups and the newly arrived. In 2000, New York City was home to nearly 3 million foreign-born residents, the most in its history ("Population," 2009). Some keep their dollars and experiences here and others send some back home to help relatives and friends. Due to global technologies, many of the new immigrants can keep in touch with family and friends by cell phone, by videophone, and by the Internet. However, after September 11, 2001, the quality of life for people who adopted America as home and hoped to stay or even simply visit here, changed radically. The quote below, which is testimony of a Latino advocate in Birmingham, Alabama (Nguyen, 2007, n.p.) provides a snapshot of what life is like in the 21st century for many U.S. immigrants:

> There are local ordinances allowing databases on tenants, tracking how many people live in an apartment complex, their social security numbers, etc. At the same time, we've seen Alabama militia arrested because they were hoarding weapons and planning to attack Latinos. A radio host on 1070 AM was telling people in his shows before the May 1 vigils that what we can do to undocumented persons is to go and shoot all of them… In the city of Hoover, when they put people in jail they check their background, and they have the authority to do that. And the state patrol has been trained to enforce federal law. More and more people get arrested for something, a DUI, or running a red light, and when they are in jail they refer them to Immigration and Customs Enforcement.

Framing Immigration

The idea of immigrants, both legal and undocumented, taking something, anything, of what already established Americans deem as theirs, has contributed to a racist mindset that is consistent with how the media portray so-called aliens/outsiders. Once a person's status is determined to be an "illegal," an "alien," or otherwise undocumented, he or she becomes Other, thereby an object rather than subject of consideration—a **persona non grata**. As discussed in earlier chapters, disregard of Others by using minimizing discourse speaks to the power of humankind descriptors in establishing who is one of Us and who is one of Them. **Discourse**, as defined by Foucault (1969/1989, p. 12) is a "way of constituting a meaning." Combined with social practices, discourses "are more than ways of thinking and producing meaning. They constitute the 'nature' of the body, unconscious and conscious mind and emotional life of the subjects they seek to govern (as quoted in Weedon, 1987, p. 108). Furthermore, discourse is a hegemonic tool that enacts, sustains, and legitimates hierarchical social relations (Santa Ana, 2002). For example, exclusionary policies, laws, and other practices construct and contribute to the Us versus Them mentality.

As Chapters 1 through 4 describe, humans are territorial beings who erect borders, both psychological and physical, to maintain distinctions and reify differences. The fortified wall between Mexico and the United States is an example. Every year hundreds of men, women, and children die trying to cross this 2,000-mile line. Some perish from exposure to heat or dehydration. Others drown in the Rio Grande trying to make their way into the United States. Border control agents kill others, accidentally and intentionally. Since the mid-1990s, the number of deaths associated with this risky trek has more than doubled to 472 persons between 1995 and 2005. The majority of deaths are near Tucson, Arizona, one of the areas with the most crossings. Because of heavy patrolling of some areas of the border, many people seek out this remote passage. Warning signs posted near the California/Mexico border alert drivers of the possibility of people running across the highway. Signs are intended to warn people who are considering traveling across the desert of the risks of heat (115 degrees in the summer), snakes, and no drinkable water. The people are called by derogatory colloquial names such as wetbacks, illegals, and spics.

Crossing Guards

Latina/os are the largest minority group in the United States (15.5%), or about 47 million people (**Pew Hispanic Research Center**, 2007). About 25% of this group is composed of unauthorized immigrants, many of whom arrived as much as 30 years ago. Of unauthorized individuals living in the United States today, nearly half entered the country legally, through ports or across borders where they satisfied entry requirements. Many enter(ed) on visas that authorize(d) a specific time period of residence. Others came as visitors. The term "illegal alien" describes individuals who overstay their visas. Some entered the country by crossing remote border areas on foot, hiding in vehicles, and wading across rivers. Table 14.1 shows the many modes of entry into the United States.

While patterns of ancestry in the United States vary widely by country, nearly one third of all the country's immigrants reside in California.

The Rand Institute, a California-based think tank, conducted a three-year study of 30 years of immigration in California in terms of the interaction between immigration and other economic and demographic trends since the 1960s. The study, "New Immigrants, New Needs: The California Experience" (1997) "...profiles the changing character of recent immigrants and considers their contribution to the economy, their effects on other workers and the public sector, and their educational and economic success." Its findings can provide lessons for other states, the nation, and even other countries.

The study found some interesting things that impact not only the experience of new immigrants, but also how the increased numbers will potentially affect California's economy. For example, both legal and **illegal immigration** into California over the last 30 years has increased exponentially. During the 1970s, more than 1.8

Table 14.1: Modes of Entry for the Unauthorized Migrant Population (2005)

Entered legally with inspection	Non-immigrant visa overstayers	4 to 5.5. million
	Border crossing card violators	250,000 to 500,000
	Sub-total legal entries	4.5 to 6 million
Entered illegally without inspection	Evaded immigration inspectors and border patrol	6 to 7 million
	Estimated Total Unauthorized Population in 2006	11.5 to 12 million

Source: Pew Hispanic Center. Estimates based on the March 2005 Current Population Survey Department of Homeland Security reports.

million individuals entered the state, which, at that time, was a dramatic increase, more than during any preceding decade. However, in the 1980s and 1990s that figure doubled, even with California's economic difficulties. The result is that immigrants constitute more than a quarter of California's residents and workers, which has been a benefit for some of the state's employers. Place of origin of immigrants to California has changed over the years. About half come from Central America and Mexico, and a third from Asia (see Table 14.2).

Many are refugees from persecution and war in their native countries. Some don't arrive with the language or education skills needed to thrive, are younger than immigrants in the past, and often have several children with them. Treatment and work conditions of these young people are of great concern. This influx has contributed disproportionately to California's employment growth. The economic disaster that began in the early 2000s has had a significant impact on immigrant and working class people.

Table 14.2: The Origins of California's Immigrants (the Invisible Workforce)

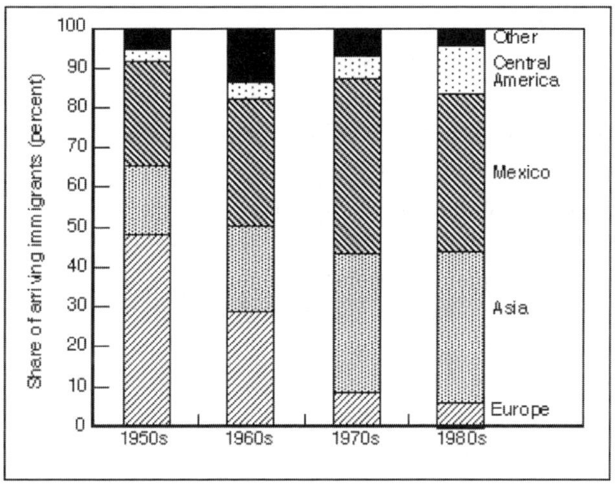

Source: Rand Institute on Education & Training

Undocumented, Unauthorized, and Essential

The country lacks resources to deport the estimated 12 million undocumented immigrants who are here—and their loss would decimate the economy. (*Boston Globe*, March 9, 2007)

There are approximately 7 million unauthorized workers in the United States today, nearly 3 million of whom arrived between 2000 and 2005. This group makes up nearly 5% of America's labor force and works in specific sectors of the job market: construction and services such as janitors, dental assistants, and restaurant personnel. The largest employer is the construction industry, which employs approximately 500,000 unauthorized migrants[4] who arrived between 2000 and 2005 for an overall total of more than 1 million workers. Other individuals who arrived during this same period constitute workers in the hospitality industry, building maintenance, landscaping, manufacturing, retail, and agriculture industries. Desperate for jobs to earn money to send to family members, many individuals work for extremely low wages, becoming part of an **"invisible" workforce**.

According to the Pew Hispanic Center, average weekly earnings for unauthorized men who arrived between 2000 and 2005 was $280 (it was about $100 more per week for those who arrived before 2000). Legal immigrants earn more—legal permanent residents (green card) earned approximately $700 per week. Immigrants are paid less than domestic workers, at all skill and ability levels, even though they are equally productive. Thus, the cost of labor is held low. Many undocumented workers feel vulnerable. In some cases they are the sole support of family and friends back home. If found to be in the United States illegally, they would be deported and the entire family would suffer. Many endure at the least difficult if not deplorable working conditions and treatment in order to stay, undetected, in the United States. It is at immigration law issues, says Cohen (2003, p. 8), "where racism meets sexism and homophobia, where patriotism meets patriarchy, all combining into a virulent nationalism in defense of the white...nuclear family."

Many individuals who legally immigrate to the United States take jobs far below their skill levels. These lower-level jobs carry with them lower wages, and thus immigrant skills are often undervalued (Chiswick, 1978). According to the New Immigrant Pilot Survey (Akresh, 2008, p. 435), 50% of legal immigrants "experience occupational downgrading." Furthermore, as noted in a *Washington Post* article:

> Throughout the Washington area these days, the person behind the wheel of any taxi cab or the counter of any hamburger stand may well be a foreigner who once did something much more elevated for a living: A Pakistani engineer, a Bolivian high school teacher, a Filipino accountant or, perhaps, a Vietnamese army officer (Constable, 1997, B03).

The immigration experience involves more than economics, however. Significant life changes such as relocation can have a significant impact on health and psychological well-being. Challenges of language skills, cultural differences, and treatment by a host culture upon arrival are all sources of stress, even under the best of circumstances. In some cases, a resident immigrant community is already in place when the newcomer arrives, which can ease the transition. In the

American Northwest and in Alaska, for example, other family members, particularly those who long ago set up communities such as Mexicans, Russians, and Chinese, have preceded recent immigrants. Several factors influence the kind of experience immigration will be for an individual and his or her family members (Bleakley & Chin, 2004; Chiswick, Lee, & Miller, 2003; Cobb-Clark & Kossoudji, 2000; Jasso & Rosenzweig, 1990). These include:

- Background and reasons for emigrating
- Immigrant or refugee status
- Adjustment issues
- Family and cultural supports
- Cultural differences
- Language issues
- Economic status
- Marketability of skills in U.S. economy
- Acceptance by U.S. mainstream society

The Patriot Act (Executive Order 13224), proposed by Congress and signed into law by President George W. Bush less than two months after the September 11, 2001 disaster, has had significant impact on individual civil rights. The law intended to lock down assets of so-called foreign nationals who "commit or pose a significant risk of committing acts of terrorism" ("U.S. Report," 2001) and or other entities who provide "support, services, or assistance to, or otherwise associate with, terrorists and terrorist organizations, their subsidiaries, front organizations, agents and associates." But the implications of this act go beyond issues of national security and significantly impact civil and immigrant rights when these individuals are seen as threats to national security. Over time, the media and internal government investigative bodies uncovered the harsh conditions suspected terrorists and innocent immigrants were subjected to who were arrested, detained and summarily denied rights to legal representation. For example, a 2003 report issued by internal investigators of the U.S. Justice Department substantiated charges against a federal prison doctor who told an inmate during a physical examination, "if I were in charge, I would execute every one of you" because of "the crimes you all did" (Shenon, 2003, n.p.).

The report also said, in the six-month period that ended on June 15, 2003, the inspector general's office had received 34 complaints of civil rights and civil liberties violations by department employees that it considered credible, including accusations that Muslim and Arab immigrants in federal detention centers had been beaten (Shenon, 2003, n.p.). Other examples include dehumanizing photographs taken by military officers of sex violence and other humiliations of prisoners at Abu Ghraib prison, mistreatment of prisoners (in some cases resulting in suicides) at Guantanamo Bay, Cuba are a few examples of uncovered U.S. government actions summarily denied but later found to be true, inciting investigations of "intelligence gathering" techniques (i.e., torture) of suspected conspirators.

Furthermore, a report issued in January 2007, the first full investigation of immigrants under domestic detention, focused on "detention standards for health care, environmental health and safety, conditions of confinement and reports of abuse" (Henry, 2007, n.p.). The report included findings such as rapes, denial of due process, beatings, and torture.

> At the Passaic County Jail (New York), detainees complained of horrible conditions, as well as physical and verbal abuse by guards. Incidents of the use of jail dogs on detainees were exposed by a National Public Radio report.
>
> A former detainee said Tuesday that lack of a proper grievance system had made getting responses to complaints difficult. "There was no system to complain," said Peter Ali, 39, a Guyanese who now lives in Queens, N.Y. "There's no system in the jail, my lawyers had to do it for me, file complaints from the outside. You have no idea of the torture in that place. One day they'd take the food, they take sheets and blankets away when it was cold, but if we complained, nobody listened to us."

A 2007 national telephone survey of Latinos by the Pew Hispanic Research Center revealed that all Latinos are feeling the impact of increased efforts by the U.S. government to step up enforcement of immigration measures. According to the study, approximately 50% worry about deportation (whether they are citizens or not) for friends, family, and themselves. Life is more difficult now, says another group, and, because of lack of immigration reform, many feel an overall negative impact on their lives such as increased difficulty finding housing, jobs, using government services, or traveling. As with any group of people, there are a variety of opinions about immigration including enforcement measures, treatment by authorities, access to services, and quality of life issues.

In December 2005, the U.S. House of Representatives passed an enforcement bill that, in the spring, went to the U.S. Senate. The bill, the Border Protection, Antiterrorism and Illegal Immigration Control Act of 2005, did not pass in the Senate. It was also known as the **Sensenbrenner Bill** named after its House of Representatives sponsor, Wisconsin Republican Jim Sensenbrenner. The bill identified areas of border protection, prosecution, limitations to citizenship opportunities for immigrants, and contained provisions too numerous to list here. As with discussion around the Comprehensive Immigration Reform Act of 2007, such bills would authorize the U.S. government to tighten border policies and increase enforcement by officers, require a new class of visa, affect temporary guest workers, and create a new division to explore the status of immigrants.

The U.S. Senate divided unauthorized individuals into two groups: long-term illegal immigrants (in the country five or more years and eligible for some form of legalization), and short-term illegal immigrants who would be forced to leave but could then apply for temporary work permits. While public opinion remained relatively consistent about immigration, immigrants, and policies over this period, one group stood out as finding immigration a major problem and a growing concern—Republicans. This was a finding of a major spring 2006 survey along with an almost even divide among Americans about whether immigration is or is not positive for the country; some feel the levels are about right, others feel too many people are immigrating. A majority of Americans believe that illegal immigrants take jobs that citizens do not want (Pew Hispanic Center). A May 2006 Zogby Interactive poll found that American voters were nearly as concerned about immigration (32%) as they were about terrorism and the Iraq war (37%). This fear was sharply divided along partisan lines. More than half of the Republicans surveyed said their biggest concern was immigration while 10% of Democrats felt this way (they were more concerned about the war, prescription drugs, and healthcare) (UPI, 2006, n.p.).

Framing can be used for an issue or an individual word, the goal being to define or redefine it in order to accomplish the goals of the organization. An example is the expression "Global Warming" versus "Climate Change" or "Illegal Alien" versus "Undocumented Worker." Frames carry and contain ideologies, both positive and negative, their energies fueled by how normal and natural, hence unremarkable, the words seem. They allow "individuals to locate, perceive, identify, and label" activities taking place in their worlds (Goffman, 1997, p. 21). As Schütz noted (as quoted in Goffman, 1997, p. 151).

> We speak of provinces of meaning and not of sub universes because it is the meaning of our experience and not the ontological structure of the objects which constitutes reality….For we will find that the world of everyday life, the common-sense world, has a paramount position among the various provinces of reality, since only within it does communication with our fellow-men become possible.

Social change movements often use framing to achieve a particular understanding of a concept, ideal, or "province of meaning." Achievement of the group's goal takes place through **frame alignment**, of which there are four types: **frame bridging**, **frame amplification**, **frame extension**, and **frame transformation** (Snow & Benford, 1988, 198), described briefly below:

1. Frame bridging is the "linkage of two or more ideologically congruent but structurally unconnected frames regarding a particular issue or problem" (Snow, Rochford, Worden, & Benford, 1986, p. 467). It brings together people and/or groups that might have similar points of view on an issue but who might not have a way of connecting or "bridging the sometimes different

> views and concerns among numerous heterogeneous groups" (Snow, 2004, p. 390).

2. Frame amplification is "the clarification and invigoration of an interpretive frame that bears on a particular issue, problem, or set of events" (Snow et al., 1986, p. 469). This step involves energizing beliefs, values, and ideals around a topic.

3. Frame extensions acknowledge that articulation and amplification occur within a given social context and that there are benefits to reaching outside the boundaries of a specific frame to include views beyond their borders.

4. Frame transformation is an adjustment when the current frame "may not resonate with, and on occasion may even appear antithetical to, conventional lifestyles or rituals and extant interpretive frames" (Snow et al., 1986, p. 473).

Thus, as interpretive schemata, frames construct "the world outside" through the use of signs, symbols, and spectacle in news media and entertainment. Several scholars have examined how frames function in focusing news media's, and thereby the public's, attention on specific issues (Gans, 1979/2005; Gitlin, 1980; Tuchman, 1978). **"Master frames"** are thus malleable constructions that can be adjusted depending on need and context (Snow & Benford, 1988, p 198). The mass media distribute messages and by framing them, through headlines, story choices, and selection of particular images, they influence the way we think about a person, place, or thing. Typically people, places, and things are characterized in ways that are consistent with dominant values and beliefs. "The media's selection of data makes a significant contribution to the outcome of each person's thinking… [T]he media do not control what people prefer, they influence public opinion by providing much of the information people think about and by shaping how they think about it" (Entman, 1989, p. 361). Thus, by studying media texts, we can learn about how meaning is constructed. Often what the media fail to do is contextualize events, people, or activities. Due to deadline pressures, rather than providing in-depth information that could give viewers a way of thinking about something, not in isolation, but part of an ongoing dialogue, news media typically present sound bites and visual snippets instead. Jesus Martin-Barberó (1993, p. 52) argued, "The alarmist rhetoric of the mass media imperialist colonization of popular culture fails to explain the everyday heterogeneous actions of the people on the ground." As a result, when an event happens such as the deportee tragedy, many viewers lack understanding of the significance of the erasure of individual workers from the story.

Framing the Day

On May 1, 2006, thousands of immigrants (legal and otherwise) took to America's streets as a sign of solidarity. On this "Day without an Immigrant" (El Gran Paro Estados Unidos), which coincided with International Worker's Day, students and laborers took the time away from their studies and jobs. The genesis of this demonstration of unity came, according to the *New York Times* (2006, n.p.)

> ...from an idea hatched by a small band of grass-roots advocates in Los Angeles, inspired by the farm worker movement of the 1960s led by Cesar Chavez and Bert Corona. Through the Internet and mass media catering to immigrants, they developed and tapped a network of union organizers, immigrant rights groups and others to spread the word and plan events tied to the boycott, timed to coincide with International Workers' Day.

In major cities, including Los Angeles, Chicago, New York, Denver, Atlanta, Las Vegas, Philadelphia, and Washington, D.C., organized events brought as many as 1 million people to the streets both as participants and as allies in order to bring attention to pending immigration bills, the need for solidarity, and to emphasize the sheer number of people who participate in America's invisible workforce. Several marchers carried both the American and the Mexican flag, which served to ignite the anger of some viewers who saw this as failure to adapt to American ways. Television news media focused primarily on the experiences of Mexican and Latin American workers, positioning the demonstrators as a potentially hysteric mass of humanity on the brink of eruption.

Many of the people hailed from Mexico, but marchers came from other countries as well. Why, based on news coverage in cities all over the nation, was the face of immigration brown? One reason is Latinas/os are the fastest growing minority group in the United States.[5] By 2050, census projections estimate the Hispanic population will reach 105 million, a quarter of the total population of the United States, rising from only 10 million Latinas/os in the 1980s. The number reached 23 million by 1990. In 2006, this diverse group of people had approximately $700 billion in disposable income, and that figure is expected to reach $1 trillion in the next few decades.

The mass media commonly employ metaphors to make connections between non-literal denotations in order to suggest a similarity, thereby providing the lingua franca for reinforcement of these beliefs. Used as symbolic equivalents, metaphors used in Anglo news stories frame immigrant peoples in ways that support dominant culture's view of them as "Other." Discourse used to characterize immigration creates and supports hierarchal social structure through this cognitive processing. Thus metaphors, as instruments of social control, are politically useful as ways of constructing, over time, common ground for the collective unconscious as a way of identifying who is "Other" to the majority with power. The metaphors used to frame the "Day without an Immigrant" were probably not consciously selected by reporters, for example, but are strategically propounded by political speakers.

Propaganda, as described in Chapter 6, is a useful tool for constructing the Other. By presenting a one-sided point of view that presents all members of a group as the same and dangerous, propaganda supports dominant ideology that benefits from categorization of people into clearly identifiable groups. Most human beings would find it impossible to intentionally cause serious harm to another human being. However, by using psychological techniques of propaganda, the "Other" is dehumanized (made non-human), and then becomes an object or a thing that stands in the way of or is likely to affect the dominant group's ability to hold on to and retain power and resources. Others are "constructed by those who do the Othering, by those who reflect upon that Othering, and by the Others' own representations of themselves" (Wilkinson & Kitzinger, 1996, p. 15). In a market-driven capitalist economy such as the United States, when the bottom line is the arbiter of value and worth, real or imagined scarcity is at the core of the construction of the generalized "Other," someone who is not one of "Us," someone who possesses the characteristics the Us-group doesn't like about itself. This articulation of the collective unconscious supports prejudice, oppression, exclusion, and sometimes the use of violence against the constructed Other. Simone de Beauvoir (1949/2010, p. 6) noted

> no group ever sets itself up as the One without at once setting up the Other over against itself. [To t]he native of a country all who inhabit other countries are 'foreigners' Jews are 'different' for the anti-Semite, Negroes are 'inferior' for American racists, aborigines are 'natives' for colonists, proletarians are the 'lower class' for the privileged.

Words Matter

As part of the natural human way of creating systems and categories, people get sorted and placed into categories as well with particular (usually negatively evaluated) characteristics. This process of connecting characteristics with all members of a particular group serves as the basis of hierarchical ordering as well as criteria for inclusion and exclusion. Racist discourse, constructed from metaphor sustains hierarchical patterns of power and institutionalized sources of oppression. If, as Foucault argued, the root power of metaphor is sustained discourse, the consistent, persistent, and corroborated construction of the Other is realized in ways that rarely question these assumptions. If we don't apply a critical lens to the images we see, sounds we hear, and words we read, the people and the constructions can become invisible. Sometimes this means reading between the lines, hearing and seeing what isn't as well as what is said, as when President George W. Bush spoke to the issue of national language:

> I think the national anthem ought to be sung in English, and I think people who want to be a citizen of this country ought to learn English and they ought to learn to sing the national anthem in English. (George W. Bush, April 28, 2006)

In 2002, Santa Ana studied metaphors used to describe California's 1994 Proposition 187 campaign (restriction of public services for undocumented immigrants), Proposition 209 (affirmative action's death), and 227 (bilingual education's death). His analysis of the *Los Angeles Times'* and other newspapers' coverage of these issues illuminated an alarming trend: metaphorical language reinforced stereotypes of Latino immigration. In *Brown Tide Rising*, Santa Ana (2002) asserts,

> the major metaphors characterizing immigration and immigrant in contemporary public discourse were, respectively, DANGEROUS WATERS and ANIMALS. The former metaphor invoked the enduring NATION AS HOUSE…Other secondary metaphors that also were seen with some frequency included the IMMIGRANT AS SOLDIER (attacking the HOUSE), AS WEED, and AS DISEASE metaphors, and, more to the point, often helped along the propositions' passage.

Fairclough (1989, p. 108) identified four kinds of products of discourse that become naturalized:

1. Definitions of words (for Latinos, race, language, citizen)
2. Based on Goffman's dramaturgical metaphor, stage directions of social interaction.
3. Who has access to the stage, its boundaries?
4. What is the social actor's identity?

Using Santa Ana's analysis as a model, and Fairclough's forms of discourse, all-day coverage of five news-oriented television networks: ABC, CBS, NBC, CNN, and FOX was examined. Print media heralded the day as follows: *USA Today* marked May 1 as "On Immigration's Front Lines" and the *New York Times* announced, "With Calls for Boycott by Immigrants, Employers Gird for Unknown." *Time* magazine emphasized the secrecy (not invisibility) of workers. The cover story was titled, "Inside America's Secret Workforce." This was followed by the next issue, featuring a Statue of Liberty with her hand held up as if to keep someone or something away, "Who gets to be an American: Inside the immigration debate that is dividing the nation." Emphasizing the conflation between labor's show of solidarity for the work they perform, terrorism, and border law disputes, *Newsweek* labeled the day as an "Immigration Dragnet," "Border War," and "Immigration Divide."

The ubiquitous Sunday newspaper insert, *Parade,* offered their empathy with immigration: the May 1, 2006 edition featured blond-haired Misha Barton, star of *The OC,* about the trials and tribulations of being an immigrant from England.

Television broadcasts, however, claimed the day in their own way, naming their day-long coverage in ways much as they do wars. ABC announcers used expressions such as "Pride and division," "Protests polarize," "Immigration clashes," and described the crowds as "suddenly swollen and screaming." Visuals on all of the networks emphasized the size of crowds, how crowded the events were, tensions within and without the event, and ultimately as a sea of Hispanic humanity pouring into America's streets. All networks locked on images shot from above.

CBS's coverage from Los Angeles emphasized the growing size of crowds throughout the day, along with the following commentary from LAPD Commander Louis Gray, Jr., the "incident commander": "I've been on the force 38 years and I've never seen a rally this big."

Fox News also emphasized Los Angeles' crowds, titling the event "The Cost of Freedom." The dialogue said:

> From a bluff at MacArthur Park, not far from downtown Los Angeles, the stream of people can seem like a marching line of ants dressed in white and carrying mostly the red, white, and blue…thus far they have successfully shut down the famous Wilshire Blvd. in preparation for the march to La Brea.

Although terrorists and terrorism had nothing to do with the event, newscasters nevertheless used it as an opportunity to bring up the issue. In one case the announcer said, "Senators up for re-election this year are being forced by the debate [border] to juggle the demand from voters for tighter borders to keep out terrorists."

CNN, who titled the event "Immigration Nation," then "Out of the Shadows," followed by "Border Disorder—Crossing the Line," emphasized, "They are coming." "Millions of people will take to America's streets in possibly unprecedented numbers." On Anderson Cooper's *360 Degrees,* he said, "hundreds of thousands demand immigration reform; Kids skipped school. Men and women walked off their jobs. Others didn't bother going to work. Businesses shut down for lack of patrons or employees. Throngs of immigrants and advocates took to the streets of many U.S. cities on Monday to protest proposed immigration laws, and the sites represented a veritable where's where of American metropolises."

The ancient Roman philosopher and political theorist Cicero said metaphor occurs "when a word applying to one thing is transferred to another, because the similarity seems to justify the transference" (as cited in Purcell, 1996, p. 150). Contemporary linguist George Lakoff's work demonstrates how discourse and metaphor work as hegemonic instruments but is also a "crucial measure of the way that public discourse articulates and reproduces societal dominance and relations." For example, when Santa Ana (2002, p. 20) described a news story about the number of immigrants receiving benefits, the metaphorical description read: "it's like overloading the lifeboats of a sinking ship." As discussed in Chapter 2, a metaphor is a "conceptual mapping from a semantic source domain to a different semantic target domain" (Santa Ana, 2002, p. 26). The source domain is what we can easily think about, such as love. Target domains are most often conceptual—hidden from our senses or even unknown. We borrow these to "get a handle on"—our "heads around"—complicated concepts. For example, we describe being in love as madness, as hell, as heaven, and other terms that don't literally happen, we don't actually go crazy when we're in love, but it seems like it sometimes. People understand the link. Lakoff and Johnson's (1980) conceptual mapping helps explain the retrieval system people use that constitute conceptual elements used to make sense of the social and spiritual worlds, via commonly used and understood metaphors.

Public discourse about outsider Others is frequently framed by metaphors. The effect of some forms of framing is to dehumanize human beings in the public eye by referring to them in nonhuman ways, as something rather than as someone. Visual and verbal metaphors in media that refer to immigrants as an invasion, as dangerous moving waters, armed invasion, dangerous diseases, animals, insects, and weeds, seem unremarkable because doing so is so familiar to most of us. Toine van Teeffelen (1994) speaks to this power:

> In its metaphoric meaning racism compares and contrasts the domains of the self and the other…when applied skillfully, metaphors can have a strong impact due to their 'literary' quality and visual concreteness (p. 384). This rhetorical thrust allows them to emphasize particular elements and linkages and simultaneously to de-emphasize others. Since they organize the understanding of cause and effect, symptom and essence, and especially praise and blame, metaphors can be employed to service political aims or interests. When thus used as ideological devices, they privilege, and when turning into common sense, naturalize particular accounts of reality (p. 385).

The New Immigrant Experience

The Joseph Rowntree Foundation (Robinson & Reeve, 2006) issued a report addressing what is known about new immigrant settlement experiences in the United Kingdom, much of which is transferable to the U.S. experience. The report brought to light important issues that today's immigrants face in terms of housing and the importance of establishing an established community. For example, even for those who are legal immigrants, the quality of housing, often inner city, in which new immigrants reside is often poor, and, as a result individuals feel excluded, besides the health and safety realities of these areas. Thus, "the challenges raised by living in such locations can be compounded by the problems that some new immigrants encounter accessing the care, support, and assistance they require."

Despite this, it is important to note, according to the report, the reservoir of strength and vitality that the neighborhoods can provide when established populations are in place. "These neighborhoods are often home to other immigrant households and established minority ethnic populations and can be rich in various resources vital to helping new immigrants meet the challenge of satisfying their material needs, coping with hostility and discrimination." Also, "New immigrants settling in neighborhoods with a more limited history of minority ethnic settlement appear more prone to harassment, abuse and violence." There are also significant adjustment issues within cultures: these include **culture shock**, being bombarded with an overwhelming number of experiences resulting in, at the least, extreme homesickness, fear of not having enough to eat or drink, fear of being cheated, and fear of being arrested and deported. Thus, these communities are essential in helping new immigrants make their way into a new country and life by providing support, services, and social cohesion needed to maintain a strong neighborhood and sense of belonging. An important consideration is media portrayals of new immigrants. The report states, "local reporting can in some instances compound national media stereotypes, thereby fuelling animosity and hostility within receiving populations and creating tensions between population groups" (Robinson & Reeve, 2006, n.p.).

Summary

The United States is reputed to be a country to which individuals and groups seeking asylum from persecution and war can come. The idea of asylum is old and carries with it values considered basic principles of international law, identified by the United Nations **"Universal Declaration of Human Rights"** adopted in 1948. It contains 30 articles that speak to rights, respect, and responsibility for treatment of human beings by other human beings, beginning with Article 1 that states:

> All human beings are born free and equal in dignity and rights. They are endowed with reason and conscience and should act towards one another in a spirit of brotherhood.

And Article 2 begins:

> Everyone is entitled to all the rights and freedoms set forth in this Declaration, without distinction of any kind, such as race, colour, sex, language, religion, political or other opinion, national or social origin, property, birth or other status.

However, particularly since September 11, 2001, politics and practice do not always match. U.S. policy on refugees states that a person will not be accepted into the country for a refugee program if he or she has a relative living in another country unless that country has denied admission. In 1996, for example, approximately 92,000 Cuban/Haitian individuals (called entrants because they had been processed out of their home country) came to the United States (United Nations High Commissioner of Refugees (UNHCR).

As described earlier in this chapter, visual and verbal discourse analysis, as method, is a useful tool for identifying coded terms and phrases that signify that something else going on during an exchange. **Discourse analysis** of "talk and texts" also includes a discussion of the consequences of particular word choices (McKinlay & Potter, 1987, p. 443). Thus, "discourse embodies unreflected and naturalized ideological assumptions" (Santa Ana, 2002, p. 17), which is "the articulated social order to which people are normally oblivious" (p. 18). It is what is taken to be common sense, natural. The hegemonic view of liberation was supported, as it had been in Santa Ana's (2002) study; it is evident in the visual and verbal narratives on "The Day without an Immigrant." Although a small number of examples are mentioned in the analysis, it is important to remember that these stills and moving images appeared on the nation's television screens for the entire day. The "sea" of humanity shown pouring into the streets, around corners, with shirts and banners emblazoned with empowering terms filled the airways with hope and pride.

In the midst of national discussions about the future of thousands of individuals already contributing to the nation's economy, perhaps as productive non-citizens, it was a show of strength and a demonstration of enthusiasm for this place that purports to welcome those who wish to come.

In an effort to counteract stereotypes of immigrants after September 11, a national coalition created a Web site and series of short films to correct misunderstandings of who America's immigrants are. The mission of "I am a Proud American" reads

> We are Americans, working hard to positively contribute to our families and communities across the nation. We are democrats, republicans, and independents. We are lawyers, factory workers, union stewards, doctors, military members. Many of us serve the public on a daily basis in our workplace. We have dark skin, light skin, blond hair, green eyes, black hair, blue eyes. We are your neighbor, your co-worker, your complete stranger, and perhaps even a close or distant member of your family. We are you.

In a commercial from the campaign, which was launched after 9/11, a Hispanic man is shown mowing the lawn of a giant house in an apparently affluent neighborhood. A woman pulls up in a BMW and asks him how much he charges to landscape the yard. His reply: "Why would I charge to landscape my own yard?" An on-screen message appears: "I am an American." (Fox News, 2006).

These messages are important efforts to counteract misinformation about the role of immigrants in American culture. It is easy to forget that for many of us, our own origins can be traced to Ellis Island and other ports of entry. The Fear Theory of Stereotyping described at the beginning of this chapter predicts that when people face challenges (economic, social, political, psychological) that seem insurmountable and naturally become frightened, a normal response is to blame someone else. A typical target, throughout human history, is anyone who can be constructed as Other. If there are barriers to communication such as language, cultural customs, or other identifiable ways of being that can be used to mark someone as an outsider, we surely will. In Riis' (1890, p. 1) book he pointed out that

> long ago it was said that "one half of the world does not know how the other half lives." That was true then. It did not know because it did not care. The half that was on top cared little for the struggles, and less for the fate of those who were underneath, so long as it was able to hold them there and keep its own seat.

Knowing this, can we not move now to ending this cycle of fear and blame?

Questions for Discussion

1. Did any members of your family immigrate from Europe, Asia, Africa or elsewhere?
2. What is your opinion about the numbers of immigrants that should be allowed to enter the United States?
3. What is the greatest concern about immigration today?
4. How do entertainment media present immigrants?
5. Were/are slaves considered immigrants?

Key Words

Asylum	Culture shock
Deportees	Discourse
Discourse analysis	Displaced Persons Act
Dog Tag Law	Ellis Island
Ethnic cleansing	Ethnocentrism
Fear Theory of Stereotyping	Frame alignment
Frame amplification	Frame bridging

Frame extensions	Frame transformation
Geary Act of 1892	Great Depression
Hart-Celler Act	Illegal immigration
Immigration	Invisible workforce
Ku Klux Klan	Master frames
McCarran-Walter Immigration Act	Muckraking
Nationality and Immigration Act Amendments	Naturalization Act
Operation Wetback	Persona non grata
Pew Hispanic Research Center	Refugee Act
Sensenbrenner Bill	Steerage Act
Universal Declaration of Human Rights	War Brides Act
Woody Guthrie	Xenophobia

Endnotes

1. This term identifies those who lack the required paperwork or have overstayed his or her visa.

2. Out of respect for the individuals who died, names are listed here. First, those who were identifiable: Ramon Perez, Jesus Santos, Ramon Portello, James A. Guardaho, Guadalupe Ramirez, Julio Barron, Jose Macias, Martin Navarro, Apolonio Placentia, Santiago Elisandro, Salvadore Sandoval and Manuel Calderon. Unidentifiable: Francisco Duran, Rosalio Estrado, Bernabe Garcia, Severo Lara, Elias Macias, Tomas Marquez, Louis Medina, Manuel Merino, Luis Mirando, Ygnacio Navarro, Roman Ochoa, Alberto Raygoza, Guadalupe Rodriquez, Maria Rodriguez, and Juan Ruiz.

3. The entire text of the book is available online at http://www.authentichistory.com/postcivilwar/riis/contents.html

4. The term "unauthorized migrant" comes from the Pew Hispanic Center's terminology, which includes "some persons who have temporary permission to reside in the U.S. or whose immigration status is unresolved." Labor Force Status Fact Sheet. April 13, 2006.

5. The terms Hispanic, Latina/o, Mexican American and other designations are used because individual preferences vary. Chicana/o is typically reserved as a political activism term.

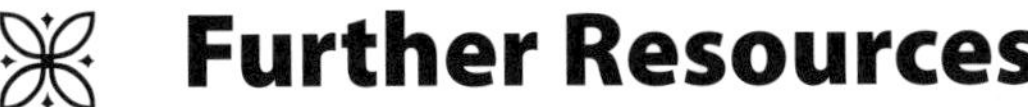# **Further Resources**

African American/Black

Internet

Africa and Slavery—African History: http://www- sul.stanford.edu/depts/ssrg/africa/history/ hislavery.html

African American Celebrities: http://www.africanamericans.com/BlackCelebsetal.htm

African American Filmmakers, African American Films:http://www.lib.berkeley.edu/MRC/ africanambib2.html

African American Holocaust: http://www.maafa.org/index.html

African American Media: http://www.unc.edu/~haman/media.htm

African American Mosaic: The African-American Mosaic: http://www.loc.gov/exhibits/african/ intro.html

African Americans in Motion Pictures, The Past and the Present: http://www.liu.edu/cwis/cwp/ library/african/movies.htm

African Americans in the Movies: http://www.lib.berkeley.edu/MRC/AfricanAmBib.html

African American Studies Research Guide: http://www.library.yale.edu/rsc/af-–am/

American Pictures: http://www.american-–pictures.com/english/index.html

Black Collegian: http://www.black-–collegian.com/

Black Enterprise: http://www.blackenterprise.com/

Black Entertainment Television: bet.com

Black Film Center Archive: http://www.indiana.edu/~bfca/websites.html

Black News.com: http://www.blacknews.com/

Black Press USA.com: http://www.blackpressusa.com/

Blaxploitation Film: http://www.blaxploitation.com/

Bunche Center for African American Studies at UCLA: http://www.bunche.ucla.edu/newsite/ index.html

Center for Media and the Black Experience: www.webcom.com/nattyreb/hype

Entman and Rojecki Index of Race and Media: http://www.press.uchicago.edu/Misc/Chicago/210758.html

Essence magazine: http://www.essence.com/

The Face of Slavery: http://www.photographymuseum.com/faceof.html

Gender, Race, and Ethnicity in Media: African Americans: http://www.uiowa.edu/~commstud/resources/GenderMedia/african.html

History of Jim Crow: http://www.jimcrowhistory.org/

Images of African Americans from the 19th Century: http://digital.nypl.org/schomburg/images_aa19/main.html

International Women of Color: www.IWMF.org

Jim Crow Museum of Racist Memorabilia. Ferris State University: http://www.ferris.edu/news/jimcrow/menu.htm

Movies, Race and Ethnicity: African Americans: http://www.lib.berkeley.edu/MRC/imagesafam.html

National Association of Black Journalists: http://nabj.org/

National Association of Black Owned Broadcasters: http://www.nabob.org/

National Black Media Coalition: www.bin.com/assocorg/nbmc/nbmc.htm

National Newspaper Publishers Association: http://www.nnpa.org/news/default.asp

Oprah Winfrey: http://www.oprah.com/index

Quarterly Black Review: http://www.qbr.com/

Slavery Fact Sheet. Digital History: http://www.digitalhistory.uh.edu/historyonline/slav_fact.cfm

Slavery and the Making of America. PBS: http://www.pbs.org/wnet/slavery/

Southern Freedom Movement: http://www.crmvet.org/crmlinks.htm

Stereotypes of African Americans (essays and images): http://www.authentichistory.com/diversity/african/

Tavis Smiley: http://www.pbs.org/kcet/tavissmiley/

Tony Brown: http://www.tonybrown.com/

U.S. African American History: http://vlib.iue.it/history/USA/african-american.html

U.S. Census: http://www.census.gov/population/www/socdemo/race/black.html

Vibe: http://www.vibe.com

Visualizing Otherness. The Center for Holocaust and Gender Studies. Racist and Discriminatory Views of Afro-Americans in Popular Culture: http://chgs.umn.edu/histories/otherness/otherness3-1.html

Young African Americans Against Media Stereotypes: http://www.yaaams.org/

Readings

Abernathy-Lear, G. (1994). African Americans' criticisms concerning African American representations on daytime serials. *Journalism Quarterly.*

Bobo, J. (1995). *Black women as cultural readers*. New York: Columbia University Press.

Campbell, C. P. (1995). *Race, myth and the news*. Thousand Oaks, CA: Sage.

Chideya, F. (1995). *Don't believe the hype: Fighting cultural misinformation about African-Americans*. New York: Plume.

Coleman, R. M. (Ed.). (2002). *Say it loud! African American audiences, media, and identity*. New York: Routledge.

Corea, A. (1995). Racism and the American way of media. In J. Downing, John, A. Mohammadi, & A. Sreberny-Mohammadi (Eds.), *Questioning the media: A critical introduction*. Thousand Oaks, CA: Sage.

Cosby, C. O. (1994). *Television's imageable influences: The self-perceptions of young African Americans*. Lanham, MD: University Press of America.

Dates, J. L., & Barlow, W. (Eds.). (1993). *Split image: African Americans in the mass media*. Washington, D.C.: Howard University Press.

Dennis, E. E., & Pease, E. (Eds.). (1997). *The media in black and white*. Piscataway, NJ: Transaction.

Dormon, J. M. (1988). Shaping the popular image of post–Reconstruction American Blacks: The 'Coon Song' phenomenon of the Gilded Age. *American Quarterly, 40*, 450–471.

Downing, J. (2000). 'The Cosby Show' and American racial discourse. In T. Van Dijk, Entman, R., & Rojecki, A. (Eds.), *The black image in the white mind: Media and race in America*. Chicago: University of Chicago Press.

Entman, R. (1990). Modern racism and the images of blacks in local television news. *Critical Studies in Mass Communication, 7*(4), 332–345.

Essed, P. (1991). *Understanding everyday racism: An interdisciplinary theory*. Thousand Oaks, CA: Sage.

Gray, H. (1995). *Watching race: Television and the struggle for 'Blackness.'* Minneapolis, MN: University of Minnesota Press.

hooks, b. (1992). *Black looks: Race and representation*. Boston: South End.

hooks, b. (1995). *Killing rage: Ending racism*. New York: Henry Holt.

Jhally, S. & Lewis, J. (1992). *Enlightened racism: The Cosby Show, audiences, and the myth of the American Dream*. Boulder, CO: Westview.

MacDonald, J. F. (1992). *Blacks and White TV: Afro Americans in television since 1948* (2nd ed.). Chicago: Nelson-Hall.

Smitherman-Donaldson, G. (Ed.). (1988). *Discourse and discrimination*. Detroit, MI: Wayne State University Press.

West, C. (1993). *Race matters*. Boston. Beacon.

Films

(Film titles preceded by an asterisk indicate documentaries made primarily for educational, rather than entertainment, purposes.)

Ali. (2001). (2001). Dir. Michael Mann.

Amazing Grace. (1974). Dir. Stan Lathan.

Amazing Grace. (2006). Dir. Michael Apted.

*American Gangster. (*2007). Dir. Ridley Scott.

Amistad. (1998). Dir. Steven Spielberg.

Amos 'n' Andy Show (Radio & Television). (1928–1953)

Amos and Andy: Anatomy of a Controversy. (1983). Dir. Stanley Sheff.

Band of Angels. (1957). Dir. Raoul Walsh.

Barriers. (1998). Dir. Alan Baxter.

Bataan. (1943). Dir. Tay Garnett.

bell hooks.(1997). *Cultural criticism & transformation.* Dir. Sut Jhally.

Beloved. (1998). Dir. Jonathan Demme.

Beverly Hills Cop. (1984). Dir. Martin Brest.

Big Momma's House. (2000). Dir. Raja Gosnell.

Bingo Long Traveling All-Stars & Motor Kings. (1976). Dir. John Badham.

Bird. (1988). Dir. Clint Eastwood.

Birth of a Nation. (1915). Dir. D. W. Griffith.

Black & White. (1991). Dir. Boris Frumin.

Black Legion. (1936). Dir. Archie L. Mayo.

Black like Me. (1964). Dir. Carl Lerner.

Booty Call. (1997). Dir. Jeff Pollack.

Borderline. (1930). Dir. Kenneth MacPherson.

Bring It On. (2000). Dir. Peyton Reed.

Brother from Another Planet. (1987). Dir. John Sayles.

Brother to Brother. (2004). Dir. Rodney Evans.

Bulworth. (1998). Dir. Warren Beatty.

Cabin in the Sky. (1943). Dir. Vincente Minnelli.

Car Wash. (1976). Dir. Michael Schultz.

Carmen Jones. (1954). Dir. Otto Preminger.

Catfish in Black Bean Sauce. (2000). Dir. Chi Muoi Lo.

Check and Double Check. (1930). Dir. Melville W. Brown.

Clara's Heart. (1988). Dir. Robert Mulligan.

Classified X. (1997). Dir. Melvin van Peebles.

Claudine. (1985). Dir. John Berry.

Collateral. (2004). Dir. Michael Mann.

Color Purple. (1985). Dir. Steve Spielberg.

Coming to America. (1988). Dir. John Landis.

The Cotton Club. (1984). Dir. Francis Ford Coppola.

Crash. (2004). Dir. Paul Haggis.

Crown Heights. (2004). (TV). Dir. Jeremy Kagan.

Defiant Ones. (1958). Dir. Stanley Kramer.

Dirty Dozen. (1967). Dir. Robert Aldrich.

Dreamgirls. (2006). Dir. Bill Condon.

Dreamworlds3. (2007). Media Education Foundation.

Driving Miss Daisy. (1989). Dir. Bruce Beresford.

Tha Eastsidaz. (2000). Dir. Michael Martin.

Edward Said: On Orientalism (1998). Dir. Sut Jhally.

Emperor Jones. (1933). Dir. Dudley Murphy.

Far from Heaven. (2002). Dir. Todd Haynes.

Fear of a Black Hat. (1992). Dir. Rusty Cundieff.

Fireman of the Follies-Bergere. (1928). Dir. Eric le Guen.

For Love of Ivy. (1968). Dir. Daniel Mann.

Framing an Execution: The Media & Mumia. (2001). Dir. Sut Jhally.

Freedom Song. (2000). Dir. Phil Alden Robinson.

Freedom Writers. (2007). Dir. Richard LaGravenese.

The French Way. (1940). Dir. Jacques d Baroncelli.

Game over: Gender, Race, and Violence in Video Games. (2001). Dir. Nina Hunteman.

Ghosts of Mississippi. (1996). Dir. Rob Reiner.

Glory. (1989). Dir. Edward Zwick.

Gone with the Wind. (1939). Dir. Victor Fleming.

Great White Hope. (1970). Dir. Martin Ritt.

Green Pastures. (1936). Dir. Marc Connelly & William Keighley.

Guess Who? (2005). Dir. Kevin Rodney Sullivan.

Guess Who's Coming for Dinner? (1967). Dir. Stanley Kramer.

Hallelujah. (1929). Dir. King Vidor.

Hip-hop: Beyond Beats and Rhymes. (2006). Dir. Byron Hurt.

Home of the Brave. (1949). Dir. Mark Robson.

The Hurricane. (1999). Dir. Norman Jewison.

Hustle & Flow. (2005). Dir. Craig Brewer.

I Am a Man: Black Masculinity in America. (1998). Dir. Byron Hurt.

I Spy. (1965–1968). (TV).

Imitation of Life. (1934). Dir. John M. Stahl.

Imitation of Life. (1959). Dir. Douglas Sirk.

In the Heat of the Night. (1967). Dir. Norman Jewison.

Intruder in the Dust. (1949). Dir. Clarence Brown.

Jerico. (1937). Dir. Thornton Freeland.

Just Another Girl on the I.R.T. (1992). Dir. Leslie Harris.

Kansas City. (1995). Dir. Robert Altman.

Lady Sings the Blues. (1972). Dir. Sidney J. Furie.

Lilies of the Field. (1963). Dir. Ralph Nelson.

The Little Colonel. (1935). Dir. David Butler.

Littlest Rebel. (1937). Dir. David Butler.

Livin' Large. (1991). Dir. Michael Schultz.

The Long Walk Home. (1991). Dir. Richard Pearce.

Lost Boundaries. (1949). Dir. Alfred L. Werker.

Love Jones. (1997). Dir. Theodore Witcher.

Manderlay. (2005). Dir. Lars von Trier.

Mandingo. (1975). Dir. Richard Fleischer.

Member of the Wedding. (1953). Dir. Fred Zinnemann.

Mississippi Burning. (1988). Dir. Alan Parker.

Mississippi Masala. (1991). Dir. Mira Nair.

Monster's Ball. (2001). Dir. Marc Forster.

Murder on the Bayou: A Gathering of Old Men. (1987). Dir. Volker Schlondorff.

Native Son. (1951). Dir. Pierre Chenal.

Negro Soldier. (1943). U.S. War Department.

New Orleans. (1947). Dir. Arthur Lubin.

No Way Out. (1950). Dir. Joseph L. Mankiewicz.

Nothing but a Man. (1964). Dir. Michael Roemer.

Odds Against Tomorrow. (1959). Dir. Robert Wise.

A Patch of Blue. (1965). Dir. Guy Green.

The Pawnbroker. (1965). Dir. Sidney Lumet.

Pursuit of Happyness. (2006). Dir. Gabriele Muccino.

Pinky. (1949). Dir. Elia Kazan.

Precious. (2009). Dir. Lee Daniels.

Pressure Point. (1962). Dir. Hubert Cornfield.

Purlie Victorious. (1963). Dir. Nicholas Webster.

Putney Swope. (1969). Dir. Robert Downey.

Ragtime. (1981). Dir. Milos Forman.

Raisin in the Sun. (1961). Dir. Daniel Petrie.

Redemption. (2003). Dir. Vondie Curtis Hall.

Rush Hour. (1998). Dir. Brett Ratner.

St. Louis Blues. (1929). Dir. Dudley Murphy.

Sanders of the River. (1935). Dir. Alexander Korda.

Secrets & Lies. (1996). Dir. Mike Leigh.

Separate but Equal. (1991). Dir. George Stevens, Jr.

Sergeant Rutledge. (1960). Dir. John Ford.

Shadows. (1959). Dir. John Cassavetes.

She' Done Him Wrong. (1933). Dir. Lowell Sherman.

Show Boat. (1936). Dir. James Whale.

Show Boat. (1951). Dir. George Sidney.

Six Degrees of Separation. (1993). Dir. Fred Schepisi.

Soldier's Story. (1984). Dir. Norman Jewison.

Something New. (2006). Dir. Sanaa Hamri.

Song of the South. (1946). Walt Disney Animation.

Sounder. (1972). Dir. Martin Ritt.

South Central. (1992). Dir. Steve Anderson.

Storm Warning. (1950). Dir. Stuart Heisler.

Stormy Weather. (1943). Dir. Andrew L. Stone.

Stuart Hall: Race, the Floating Signifier. (1996). Dir. Sut Jhally.

Stuart Hall: Representation and the Media. (1997). Dir. Sut Jhally.

They Call Me Mr. Tibbs. (1970). Dir. Gordon Douglas.

This Rebel Breed. (1960). Dir. Richard L. Bare.

A Time to Kill. (1996). Dir. Joel Schumacher.

To Kill a Mockingbird. (1962). Dir. Robert Mulligan.

To Sir, with Love. (1966). Dir. James Clavell.

Tougher than Leather. (1988). Dir. Rick Rubin.

Trading Places. (1983). Dir. John Landis.

Uncle Tom's Cabin. (1903). (1914). Silent. Dir. Edwin S. Porter.

Walking Tall. (1973). Dir. Phil Karlson.

What Happened in the Tunnel. (1903). Dir. Edwin S. Porter.

Wild Style. (1982). Dir. Charlie Ahearn.

Women of Brewster Place. (1988). Dir. Donna Deitch.

The Young One. (1960). Dir. Luis Bunuel.

Zebrahead. (1992). Dir. Anthony Drazan.

Blackface in films

Babes in Arms. (1939). Dir. Busby Berkeley.

Babes on Broadway. (1941). Dir. Busby Berkeley.

Bamboozled. (2000). Dir. Spike Lee.

Birth of a Nation. (1915). Dir. D. W. Griffith.

Blonde Venus. (1932). Dir. Josef von Sternberg.

Check and Double Check. (1930). Dir. Melville W. Brown.

Classified X. (1997). Dir. Melvin Van Peebles.

Color Adjustment. (1992). Dir. Marlon Riggs.

Ethnic Notions. (1987). Dir. Marlon Riggs.

Holiday Inn. (1944). Dir. Mark Sandrich.

Hollywood Shuffle. (1987). Dir. Robert Townsend.

The Jazz Singer. (1927). Dir. Alan Crosland.

Littlest Rebel. (1937). Dir. David Butler.

Neighbors. (1920). Dir. Buster Keaton and Eddie Cline.

Othello. (various versions).

Show Boat. (1936). Dir. James Whale.

Southern Fried Rabbit. (1943). (Animation).Dir. Friz Freleng.

Uncle Tom's Cabin. (1903). Dir. Edwin S. Porter.

Uncle Tom's Cabin. (1927). Dir. Harry A. Pollard.

Whoopee! (1930). Dir. Thornton Freeland.

Ziegfeld Follies. (1946). Dir. Vincente Minnelli.

Arab American

Internet

Arab American demographics: http://www.aaiusa.org/arab-americans/22/demographics

American-Arab Anti-Discrimination Committee: http://www.adc.org/

Arab American Institute. http://www.aaiusa.org/

Arab American Market: http://www.allied-media.com/Arab-American/Arab_Organizations.htm

Arab American National Museum: http://www.arabamericanmuseum.org/

Wingfield, M., & Karaman, B. (1995). Arab stereotypes and American educators. Retrieved from http://www.adc.org/index.php?id=283

Readings

(2006). *Arab media in the information age.* Emirates Center for Strategic Studies and Research.

Ahmed, Akbar S. (2002). Hello, Hollywood: your images affect Muslims everywhere. (The West and Islam). *New Perspectives Quarterly, 12,* 73–75.

Akram, S. M. (2002). The aftermath of September 11, 2001: The targeting of Arabs and Muslims in America. *Arab Studies Quarterly, 61*(58).

Alter, Jonathon. (1995, May 1). Jumping to conclusions, *Newsweek, 125,* 55.

Bazzi, Mohammad. (1995, August). The Arab menace. *The Progressive, 59,* 40.

Curtiss, R. H., & Hanley, D. C. (2001). Dr. Jack Shaheen discusses *Reel bad Arabs: How Hollywood vilifies a people.* In R. H. Curtiss & D. C. Hanley (Interview), *Washington Report on Middle East Affairs, 20*(5), 103.

Dobkin, B. A. (1992). Paper tigers and video postcards: The rhetorical dimensions of narrative form in ABC news coverage of terrorism. *Western Journal of Communications, 56,* 143–160.

Edwards, B. T. (2001). Yankee pashas and buried women: Containing abundance in 1950s Hollywood orientalism. *Film & History, 31*(2), 13–24.

Ezroura, M. (2005). The images of 'Other' in American cinema: The meaning of poking fun at Others in *Ishtar. Indian Journal of American Studies, 25*(2), 55–62.

Georgakas, D. (Ed.). (1995). The Arab image in American film and television. *Cineaste, 17*(1), 1–24.

Ghareeb, E. (1983) *Split vision: The portrayal of Arabs in the American media.* Washington, D.C. American-Arab Affairs Council.

Goodstein, L. (1998, November 1). Hollywood now plays cowboys and Arabs; with Arab-Americans cast mostly as Muslim extremists, anti-defamation groups are beginning to speak out. *The New York Times,* Sect. 2, col 1.

Hammond, A. (2007). *Popular culture in the Arab world.* Cairo: American University in Cairo Press.

Karim, K. (2000). *Islamic peril: Media and global violence.* Toronto: Black Rose.

Khatib, L. (2006). *Filming the modern Middle East: Politics in the cinemas of Hollywood and the Arab world.* London: I. B. Tauris.

Kressel, N.J. (1987) Biased judgments of mass media: A case study of the Arab-Israeli dispute. *Political Psychology, 8,* 211–224.

Landau, J. M., (1958). *Studies in the Arab theatre and cinema.* Pittsburgh, PA: University of Pennsylvania Press.

Leipoid, L. E. (1973). *Folk tales of Arabia.* Minneapolis, MN: T. S. Danson.

Loshitzky, Y. (2000). Orientalist representations: Palestinians and Arabs in some postcolonial film and literature. In E. Hallam & B. V. Street (Eds.), *Cultural encounters: Representing 'otherness'* (pp. 51–71). New York: Routledge.

Majaj, L. S. (2003). Reel bad Arabs. *Cineaste, 28* (4), 38–39.

Malkmus, L., & Armes, R. (1991). *Arab and African film making.* London: Zed.

Mandel, D. (2001). Muslims on the silver screen. *Middle East Quarterly, 8*(2), 19–31.

Martin, L. J. (1985). The media's role in international terrorism. *Terrorism: An International Journal, 8,* 127–143.

Masri, R, & Abunimah, A. (2001). The media's deadly spin on Iraq. In *Iraq Under Siege.* Boston: South End.

Michalek, L. (1989). The Arab in American cinema: A century of Otherness. *Cineaste, 17*(1), 3–9.

Morris International, (1980). *The Arab image in Western mass media.* London: The 1979 International Press Seminar.

Nacos, B. L., & Torres-Reyna, O. (2003). Framing Muslim-Americans before and after 9/11. In P. Norris, K. Montague, & M. R. Just (Eds.), *Framing terrorism* (pp. 133–158). New York: Routledge.

Paulson, A. (2003, April 10). Rise in hate crimes worries Arab-Americans. *Christian Science Monitor.* Retrieved from http://www.csmonitor.com/2003/0410/p01s03-ussc.html

Said, E. (1981). *Covering Islam: How the media and the experts determine how we see the rest of the world.* New York: Pantheon.

Sakr, N. (2007). *Arab media and political renewal: Community, legitimacy, and public life.* London: I. B. Tauris.

Sakr, N. (2007). *Arab television today.* London: I. B. Tauris.

Semmerling, T. J. (2006). *'Evil' Arabs in American popular film: Orientalist fear.* Austin, TX: University of Texas Press.

Shafik, V. (1999). *Arab cinema: History and cultural identity.* Cairo: American University in Cairo Press.

Shafik, V. (2007). *Popular Egyptian cinema: Gender, class, and nation.* Cairo: American University in Cairo Press.

Shaheen, J. (1987). The Hollywood Arab (1984–1986). *Journal of Popular Film and Television, 14*(4), 148–157.

Shaheen, J. (2008). *Guilty: Hollywood's verdict on Arabs after 9/11.* Fowlerville, MI: Olive Branch.

Shaheen, J. G. (1984). *The TV Arab.* Bowling Green, OH: Bowling Green State University Popular Press.

Shaheen, J. G. (2001). *Reel bad Arabs: How Hollywood vilifies a people.* New York: Olive Branch.

Shipler, D. K. (1986). *Arab and Jew: Wounded spirits in a promised land.* New York: Penguin.

Wall, J. M. (1997, October 15). Stereotypes in and out. *The Christian Century, 114*(28), 899.

Films

Ali Zaoua. (2000). Dir. Nabil Ayouch.

Arab Americans. (Multicultural Peoples of North America). (1993). Part of a 15-part series. Schlessinger Video Productions..

Arab Diaries. (2000, 2001, 2002). Five-part series: Birth, Youth, Love & Marriage, Work & Money, and Home, or Maids in my Family. Dirs. Suheir Farraj, Abbas Hashim, Abeer Esber, Mai Masri, James Longley. Mohamed Bakri, and Tony Stark.*The Arab World.* (1991). Series. Dir. Bill Moyers*The Battle of Algiers (La bataille d'Alger).* (1965). Dir. Gillo Pontecorvo.

The Battle for Islam. (2006). Dir. Ziauddin Sardar.

Beyond borders: Arab feminists talk about their lives—east and west. (2000). Dir. Jennifer Kawaja

*Beyond the Veil. (1998). *The Born-Again Muslims; The Holy Warriors; The New Cold War?*

*Bush's War. (2008). Prod. Michael Kirk. *PBS Frontline.*

Camera Afrique; Camera Arabe. (1983). (1987). Dir. Ferid Boughedir.

Control Room. (2004). Dir. Jehane Noujaim.

Coverup: Behind the Iran Contra Affair. (1998). Dir. Barbara Trent.

Death in Gaza. (2006). Dir. James Miller.

Death of a Princess. (2005). Dir. Antony Thomas.

Edward Said: On orientalism. (1998). Dir. Sut Jhally.

Edward Said, The Last Interview (2004).Dir. Mike Dibb.

Edward Said: The myth of the clash of civilizations. (1998). Dir. Sut Jhally.

Exiles: Edward Said. (1988). Dir. Christopher Sykes.

Fahrenheit 9/11. (2004). Dir. Michael Moore.

Ghosts of Abu Ghraib. (2007). Dir. Rory Kennedy.

Gunner Palace. (2004). Dir. Michael Tucker and Petra Epperlein.

Hajj: Drinking from the Stream. (1992). Dir. Claire Dannenbaum.

Has America Failed in Iraq? War, Torture, and Accountability. (2004). UC Berkeley Graduate
    School of Journalism

Iraq for Sale: The War Profiteers. (2006). Dir. Robert Greenwald.

The Islamic Mind with Seyyed Hossein Nasr (World of Ideas with Bill Moyers). (1990). Dir. Bill Moyers.

The Media and Democracy in the Arab World. (2000). Al Jezeera.

Muslim Women Talk Sex. (2006). Dir. Sophie Jeanneau.

Myth of the "Clash of Civilizations." (1998). Dir. Edward Said.

No End in Sight. (2007). Dir. Charles Ferguson.

Not in My Name. (2002). Prod. Igal Hecht.

Out of Place: Memories of Edward Said. (2006). Dir. Makoto Satô.

Peace, propaganda, and the promised land: U.S. media and the Isralei-Palestinian conflict. (2003).
    Media Education Foundation.

Perfumed Garden, The. (2000). Dir. Jag Mundhra.

Persepolis. (2007). Dir. Vincent Paronnaud and Marjane Satrapi.

Power of Nightmares: The Rise of the Politics of Fear, The. (2006). Dir. Adam Curtis.

Pupil of Her Hand, In the Palm of Her Eye, The. (1994). Dir. Claire Dannenbaum.

Reel Bad Arabs: How Hollywood Vilifies a People. (2006). Media Education Foundation.

Road to 9/11, The. (2005). Dir. Sabin Streeter.

Return to Kandahar. (2003). Dir. Mohsen Makhmalbaf.

Return to Kirkuk: A Year in the Fire. (2007). Dir. Karzan Sherabayani.

Selves and Others: A portrait of Edward Said. (2003). Dir. Emmanuel Hammon.

Towelhead. (2007). Dir. Alan Ball.

Uncovered: The Whole Truth About the Iraq War. (2003). Dir. Robert Greenwald.

Where in the World Is Osama Bin Laden? (2008). Dir. Morgan Spurlock.

Asian/Americans

Internet

Asian American Children and the Media: http://sitemaker.umich.edu/psy457_tizzle/asian_american_children

Asian American Film: http://www.asianamericanfilm.com/

Asian American Journalists Association: http://www.aaja.org/

Asian American Males in Mass Media: http://sitemaker.umich.edu/psy457_tizzle/asian_american_men

Asian American Policy Review: http://www.hks.harvard.edu/aapr/

Asian American Women in Mass Media:http://sitemaker.umich.edu/psy457_tizzle/asian_american_women

Asian American Studies Association (UCLA): http://www.aasc.ucla.edu/default.asp

Asian Pacific Islander Caucus: http://www.ou.edu/education/edahdtan/apincore/

Children of the Camps: http://www.pbs.org/childofcamp/index.html

Japanese American History Archives: http://www.amacord.com/fillmore/museum/jt/jaha/jaha.html

Model Minority: http://www.modelminority.com/

Model Minority Stereotype: http://sitemaker.umich.edu/psy457_tizzle/the_model_minority

National Asian American Telecommunication Association: http://www.museum.tv/archives/etv/N/htmlN/nationalasia/nationalasia.htm

Readings

Anwar, F. (1994, February). Bhaji on the beach. *Sight and Sound, 4*(2), 47–49.

Bhatia, N. (1998). Women, homelands, and the Indian diaspora. *Centennial Review, 42*(3), 511–526.

Bai, Y. (2008). Remarkable: The image of Chinese Americans in current film and television. *Chinese Studies in History, 41*(3), 67–75.

Bhavnani, K.-K. (2000). Organic hybridity or commodification of hybridity? Comments on *Mississippi Masala. Meridians: Feminism, Race, Transnationalism, 1*(1), 187–203.

Book, E. W. (1992). The East is hot: U.S. audiences line up for films with a Chinese flavour. *Far Eastern Economic Review, 156*(51), 34–36.

Budd, D. H. (2002). *Culture meets culture in the movies: An analysis East, West, North, and South, with filmographies.* Jefferson, NC: McFarland.

Chan, A. B. (2001). 'Yellowface': The racial branding of the Chinese in American theatre and media. *Asian Profile, 29*(2), 159–177.

Chan, J. (2001). *Chinese American masculinities: From Fu Manchu to Bruce Lee.* New York: Routledge.

Chua, L. Y. (1999). The cinematic representation of Asian homosexuality in *The Wedding Banquet. Journal of Homosexuality, 36*(3/4), 99.

Chung, H. S. (2006). *Hollywood Asian: Philip Ahn and the politics of cross-ethnic performance.* Philadelphia: Temple University Press.

Ciecko, A. (1999). Representing the spaces of diaspora in contemporary British films by women directors. *Cinema Journal, 38*(3), 67–90.

Deng, P. (2002). *Identities in motion: Asian American film and video.* Durham, NC: Duke University Press.

Desai, J. (2004). *Beyond Bollywood: The cultural politics of South Asian diasporic film.* New York: Routledge.

Feng, P. (1995). In search of Asian American cinema. (Race in contemporary American cinema, part 3). *Cineaste, 21*(1/2), 32–36.

Ghymn, E. (2000). Asians in film and other media. In E. M. Ghymn (Ed.), *Asia American studies: Identity, images, issues past and present* (pp. 135–150). New York: Peter Lang.

Gopinath, G. (1997). Nostalgia, desire, diaspora: South Asian sexualities in motion. *Positions: East Asia Cultures Critique, 5*(2), 467–489.

Haddad, J. (2001). The laundry man's got a knife! China and Chinese America in early United States cinema. *Chinese America: History and Perspectives, 2001*, 31–46.

Hagedorn, J. (1994, January-February). Asian women in film: No joy, no luck. *Ms., 4*(4), 74–79.

Hamamoto, D. Y. (1994). *Monitored peril: Asian Americans and the politics of TV representation.* Minneapolis, MN: University of Minnesota Press.

Heine, S. (1997). Sayonara can mean 'hello': Ambiguity and the Orientalist butterfly syndrome in postwar American films. *Post Script: Essays in Film and the Humanities, 16*(3), 17–35.

Hoppenstand, G. (1992). Yellow devil doctors and opium dens: The yellow peril stereotype in mass media entertainment. In J. Nachbar & K. Lause (Eds.), *Popular culture: An introductory text* (pp. 277–291). Bowling Green, OH: Bowling Green State University Popular Press.

Hornaday, A. (1994). Feminism meets the diaspora—*Bhaji on the Beach* directed by Gurinder Chadha and starring Kim Vithana, Sarita Khajuria, Shaheen Khan, and Lalita Ahmed. *Migration World Magazine, 22*(5), 45.

Hsing, C. (1998). *Asian America through the lens: History, representations, and identity.* Walnut Creek, CA: AltaMira.

Huey-Long Song, J., & Dombrink, J. (1996). Good guys and bad guys: Media, Asians, and the framing of a criminal event. *Amerasia Journal, 22*(3), 25–46.

Jiwani, Y. (2005).The Eurasian female hero(Ine): Sydney Fox as relic hunter. *Journal of Popular Film and Television, 32*(4), 182–191.

Kang, L. H.-Y. (1993). Desiring of Asian female bodies: Interracial romance and cinematic subjection. *Visual Anthropology Review, 9*(1), 5–21.

Koppedrayer, K. (2005). Hindu diasporic consciousness: Srinivas Krishna's Masala. *Psychology and Developing Societies, 17*(2), 99–120.

Lee, J. F. J. (2000). *Asian American actors: Oral histories from stage, screen, and television.* Jefferson, NC: McFarland.

Lee, R. G. (1999). *Orientals: Asian Americans in popular culture.* Philadelphia: Temple University Press.

Marchetti, G. (1993). *Romance and the "yellow peril": Race, sex, and discursive strategies in Hollywood fiction.* Berkeley, CA: University of California Press.

Marchetti, G. (2004). From Fu Manchu to M. Butterfly and Irma Vep: Cinematic incarnations of Chinese villainy. In M. Pomerance (Ed.), *Bad: Infamy, darkness, evil, and slime on screen.* Albany, New York: SUNY Press.

Maslin, J., & Singh, J. K. (2003). Globalization, transnationalism, and identity politics in South Asian women's texts. *Michigan Academician, 35*(2), 171–188.

Mehta, B. (1996). Emigrants twice displaced: Race, color, and identity in Mira Nair's *Mississippi Masala.* In D. Bahri & M. Vasudeva (Eds.), *Between the lines: South Asians and post-coloniality* (pp. 185–203). Philadelphia: Temple University Press.

Minh-Ha T. P. (2005). The Asian invasion (of multiculturalism) in Hollywood. *Journal of Popular Film and Television,* Fall, *32*(3), 121–132.

Moon, K. R. (2005). *Yellowface: Creating the Chinese in American popular music and performance, 1850s–1920s.* New Brunswick, NJ: Rutgers University Press.

Most, A. (2000). You've got to be carefully taught: The politics of race in Rodgers and Hammerstein's *South Pacific. Theatre Journal, 52*(3), 307–338.

Punathambekar, A. (2005). Bollywood in the Indian-American diaspora: Mediating a transitive logic of cultural citizenship. *International Journal of Cultural Studies, 8*(2), 151–173.

Robinson, K. (1996). Of mail-order brides and 'boys' own tales: Representations of Asian-Australian marriages. *Feminist Review, 52,* 53–68.

Russell, C. (2005). New women of the silent screen: China, Japan, Hollywood. [Introduction to special issue]. *Camera Obscura, 60*(4), 1–13.

Rzepka, C. J. (2007). Race, region, rule: Genre and the case of Charlie Chan. *PMLA: Publications of the Modern Language Association of America, 122*(5), 1463–1481.

Sawhney, C. R. (2001). 'Another kind of British': An exploration of British Asian films. *Cineaste, 26*(4), 58–61.

Shah, H. (2003). Asian culture and Asian American identities in the television and film industries of the United States. *Simile, 3*(3), 1–10.

Shim, D. (1998). From yellow peril through model minority to renewed yellow peril. (Asians in popular media)(constructing (mis)representations). *Journal of Communication Inquiry, 22*(4), 385–410.

Singh, J. K. (2003). Representing the poetics of resistance in transnational South Asian women's fiction and film. *South Asian Review, 24*(1), 202–219.

Wong, L. (1991, May). Remodeling Asian Media. *Afterimage, 18,* 14–15.

Yue, A. (2000). Asian-Australian cinema, Asian-Australian modernity. *Journal of Australian Studies, 24*(65), 189–199.

Films

[Cho, Margaret] I'm the One That I Want (2000). Dir. Lionel Coleman.

Agent Yellow. (2006). Dir. Christine Choy.

All Orientals Look the Same. (1986). Dir. Valerie Soe.

Ameriasians. (1998). Dir. Erik Gandini.

Anatomy of a Springroll. (1992). Dir. Paul Kwan & Arnold Iger.

Ancestors in the Americas: Chinese in the Frontier West, an American Story. (1998). Dir. Loni Ding.

Ancestors in the Americas: Coolies, Sailors, Settlers. (1996). Dir. Loni Ding.

Bend It like Beckham. (2002). Dir. Gurinder Chadha.

Betrayal, The. (2008). Dir. Ellen Kuras & Thavisouk Phrasavath

Better Luck Tomorrow. (2002). Dir. Justin Lin.

Bhaji on the Beach. (1993). Dir. Gurinder Chadha.

Black Hair and Black-eyed. (1994). Dir. Julie Whang.

Bollywood Bound: Finding Fame and Identity in India's Filmmaking Capital. (2002). Dir. Nisha Pahuja

Broken Blossoms or The Yellow Man and the Girl. (1919). Dir. D. W. Griffith.

California Roll. (2005). Dir. Stanley Lim.

Chan Is Missing. (1982). Dir. Wayne Wang.

Changing Face: Cosmetic Surgery of the Asian Eyelid. (1995). Dir. Clarence Ting, Tami Wong, Suzanne Shimoyama.

The Cheat. (1931). Dir. George Abbott.

Children of the Camps. (1999). Dir. Satsuki Ina.

The Color of Fear. (1994). Prod. Lee Mun Wah.

Come See Paradise. (1990). Dir. Alan Parker.

Dim Sum. (2002). Dir. Jane Wong.

Double Happiness. (1994). Dir. Mina Shum.

Eat a Bowl of Tea. (1989). Dir. Wayne Wang.

From Opium to Crysanthemums: Lao Tong and the Hmong People. (2000). Dir. PeÅ Holmquist.

I Got This Way from Eating Rice. (1995). Dir. Nguyen Tan Hoan.

Great Wall, A. (1986). Dir. Peter Wang.

I'll Love You When You're More Like Me: Selected Videos (1996–2000). Dir. Nguyen Tan Hoan.

Joy Luck Club. (1993). Dir. Wayne Wang.

Lost in Paradise: Native Hawaiians. (1993).

Masala. (1991). Dir. Srinivas Krishna.

Meeting at Tule Lake. (1994). Dir. Scott T. Tsuchitani

Mississippi Masala. (1991). Dir. Mira Nair.

My America, or, Honk If You Love Buddha. (2007). Dir. Regina Park.

My Beautiful Laundrette. (1985). Dir. Stephen Frears.

No Hop Sing, No Bruce Lee: What Do You Do When None of Your Heroes Look Like You? (1998). Dir. Janice Tanaka.

Picture Bride. (1994). Dir. Kayo Hatta.

Punjabi Cab. (2004). Dir. Liam Dalzell.

Rabbit in the Moon. (1999). Dir. Emiko Omori.

Rain of Ruin: The Bombing of Nagasaki. (1995). Dir. Stephen Segaller.

Roots in the Sand. (1998). Dir. Jayasri Majumdar Hart.

Sammy and Rosie Get Laid. (1987). Dir. Stephen Frears.

**Say I Do: Unveiling the Stories of Mail-order Brides.* (2002). Dir. Arlene Ami.

Sayonara. (1957). Dir. Joshua Logan.

Separate Lives, Broken Dreams: The Saga of Chinese Immigration. (1994). Dir. Jennie F. Lew.

Sex, Love, & Kung Fu. (2001). Dir. Kip Fulbeck.

Shepherd's Pie & Sushi. (1996). Dir. Mieko Ouchi.

The Slanted Screen. (2006). Dir. Jeff Adachi.

Slaying the Dragon. (1988). Dir. Deborah Gee.

South Pacific. (1958). Dir. Joshua Logan.

**Stories My Country Told Me: with Maxine Hong Kingston.* (1996). Films for the Humanities..

Wedding Banquet. (1993). Dir. Ang Lee.

Western Eyes. (2000). Dir. Ann Shinn.

What's Wrong with Frank Chin? (2005). Dir. Curtis Choy.

When East Meets East. (1997). Dir. Kalli Paakspuu.

**Where Strangers Become Neighbours: The Story of the Collingwood Neighborhood House and the Integration of Immigrants in Vancouver.* (2007). Dir. Giovanni Attili and Leonie Sandercock .

Who Is Albert Woo? (2003). Dir. Hunt Hoe.

Year of the Dragon. (1975). Dir. Portman Paget.

Year of the Dragon. (1985). Dir. Michael Cimino.

You? (1998). Dir. Janice Tanaka.

Hispanic/Latino/a

Internet

Association of Hispanic Advertising Agencies: http://www.ahaa.org/

Gender, Race and Ethnicity in Media-Latin Americans in Media:http://www.uiowa.edu/~commstud/resources/GenderMedia/latin.html

Hispanic Online: http://www.hispaniconline.com/

Hispanic Enterprise Magazine: http://hol.hispaniconline.com/HE/2007_10/Index.html

Hispanic Magazine: http://hol.hispaniconline.com/HispanicMag/2007_11/index.html

Latinitas magazine: http://www.latinitasmagazine.org/

Latinos and Media Project: http://www.latinosandmedia.org/

National Association of Hispanic Journalists: http://www.nahj.org/home/home.shtml

National Association of Latino Independent Producers: http://www.nalip.org/

National Council of La Raza: http://www.nclr.org/

National Hispanic Media Coalition: http://www.nhmc.org/

U.S. Census Bureau: "Facts on the Hispanic or Latino Population": http://www.census.gov/pubinfo/www/NEWhispML1.html

Readings

Alarcón, N., Castillo, A., & Moraga, C. (Eds.). (1993). *The sexuality of Latinas*. Berkeley, CA: Third Woman.

Anzaldúa, G. (1987). *Borderlands/La frontera: The new mestiza*. San Francisco: Aunt Lute.

Benavides, R. (Ed.). (1993). *Antología de cuentistas chicanas: Estados Unidos, de los '60 a los '90*. Chile: Editorial Cuarto Propio, 1993.

Blea, I. (1990). *La Chicana and the intervention of race, class, and gender*. New York: Praeger.

Castillo, A. (1994). *Far from God*. New York: Plume/Penguin.

Castillo-Speed, L. *Chicana studies index: Twenty years of gender research, 1971–1991*. Berkeley, CA: Chicano Studies Library.

Castillo-Speed, L. (Ed.). (1995). *Latina: Women's voices from the borderlands*. New York: Touchstone.

Cisneros, S. (1994). *My wicked, wicked ways*. New York: Knopf.

Córdova, T. (Ed.). (1990). *Chicana voices: Intersections of class, race and gender*. Albuquerque, NM: University of New Mexico Press.

Espinosa, M. (1995). *Dark plums*. Houston, TX: Arte Público.

García, C. (1992). *Dreaming in Cuban*. New York: Knopf.

Gómez, A. (Ed.). (1983). *Cuentos: Stories by Latinas*. New York: Kitchen Table Press.

Hernandez, G. (1991). *Chicano satire: A study of literary culture*. Austin, TX: University of Texas Press.

Horno-Delgado, A. (1989). *Breaking boundaries: Latina writings and critical readings*. Amherst, MA: University of Massachusetts.

Howe, F. (Ed.), (1992). *Tradition and the talents of women*. Champaign, IL: University of Illinois Press.

Jussawalla, F., & Way, R. W. (Eds.). (1992). *Interviews with writers of the post-colonial world*. Jackson, MS: University Press of Mississippi.

Markert, J. (2007). The George Lopez Show: The same old Hispano? *Bilingual Review, 28*(2), 148–165.

Martínez-Conde, J. (1992). *Literatura y sociedad en el mundo chicano*. Madrid: Ediciones De La Torre.

Mendoza, F. D. (1994). *Marina de la Cruz: Radiografía de una emigrante*. Santo Domingo, Dominican Republic: Editora Taller.

Mohr, E. (1982). *The Nuyorican experience: Literature of the Puerto Rican minority*. Westport, CT: Greenwood.

Moraga, C., & Anzaldúa, G. (Eds.), (1983). *This bridge called my back: Writings by radical women of color*. New York: Kitchen Table.

Ortiz, C. J. (1989). *The line of the sun*. Athens, GA: The University of Georgia Press.

Ortiz. C. J. (1995). *Latin deli: Telling the lives of barrio women*. New York: W.W. Norton.

Ponce, M. H. (1993). *Hoyt Street: Memories of a Chicana childhood*. New York: Anchor Books.

Rebolledo, T. D. (Ed.). (1994). *Hispanas in New Mexico, their images and their lives.* Albuquerque, NM: El Norte.

Robinson, C. (1992). *No short journeys: The interplay of cultures in the history and literature of the borderlands.* Tucson, AZ: The University of Arizona Press.

Saldívar, R. (1990). *Chicano narrative: A dialectics of difference.* Madison, WI: University of Wisconsin Press.

Sanchez, M. (1985). *Contemporary Chicana poetry: A critical approach to an emerging literature.* Berkeley, CA: University of California.

Santiago, E. (1993). *When I Was Puerto Rican.* Reading, MA: Addison-Weley.

Solá, M. (1990). *Aquí cuentan las mujeres.* Río Piedras. P.R. Ediciones Huracán.

Soto, G. (Ed.). (1993). *Pieces of the heart: New Chicano fiction.* San Francisco: Chronicle.

Sutton, C. (1987). *Caribbean life in New York City: Sociocultural dimensions.* New York: Center for Migration Studies.

Vigil, E. (1982). *Thirty an' seen a lot.* Houston, TX: Arte Público.

Viramontes, H. M. (1995). *Under the feet of Jesus.* New York: Dutton.

Films

A Day without a Mexican. (2004). Dir. Sergio Arau.

A Walk in the Clouds. (1995). Dir. Alfonso Arau.

Against all Odds. (Contra todo). (2006). Dir. Michel Franco, Karim Raoul, Dora Pena, & Yuri Makino.

Alambrista! (The Illegal). (1977). Dir. Robert M. Young.

All About My Mother (1999). Dir. Pedro Almodovar.

America 101. (2005). Dir. Mark A. Russell.

American Family. (TV Series). (2002). 20th Century Fox.

American Me. (1992). Dir. Edward James Olmos.

Amores Perros (2000). Dir. Alejandro Gonzalez.

And the Earth Did Not Swallow Him. (1994). Dir. Severo Perez.

Ballad of Gregorio Cortez. (1982). Dir. Robert M. Young.

The Border. (1979). Dir. Christopher Leitch.

The Border. (1982). Dir. Tony Richardson.

Border Incident. (1949). Dir. Anthony Mann.

Border Town. (2006). Dir. Gregory Nava.

Born in East L.A. (1987). Dir. Cheech Marin.

Bread and Roses. (2000). Dir. Ken Loach.

Break of Dawn. (1988). Dir. Isaac Artenstein.

Butterfly (La Lengua de las Mariposas). (2000). Dir. Jose Luis Cuerda.

Bronze Screen: 100 years of the Latino Image in American Cinema. (2002). Dirs. Nancy De Los Santos and Alberto Domínguez.

Captain from Castille. (1947). Dir. Henry King.

Chico and the Man. (TV Series). (1978). The Komack Company.

La Ciudad (The City). (1998). Dir. David Riker.

Colors. (1988). Dir. Dennis Hopper.

Crash (2004). Dir. Paul Haggis.

Crossover Dreams. (1985). Dir. Leon Ichaso.

Duel in the Sun. (1946). Dir. King Vidor.

El Mariachi. (1992). Dir. Robert Rodriquez.

El Matador. (2003). Dir. Joey Medina.

El Norte. (1983). Dir. Gregory Nava.

El Super. (1979). Dir. L. Ichaso & Orlando Jimenez-Leal.

English as a Second Language (2005). Dir. Youssef Delara.

Flying Down to Rio. (1933). Dir. Thornton Freeland.

Frida (Frida, naturaleza viva). (1984). Dir. Paul Leduc.

Frida. (2002). Dir. Julie Taymor.

Gay Desperado. (1936). Dir. Rouben Mamoulian.

Girlfight. (2000). Dir. Karyn Kusama.

Hangin' with the Homeboys. (1991). Dir. Joseph B. Vasquez.

Havoc. (2005). Dir. Barbara Kopple.

Heroes from another Country (Heroes de otra patria). (1998). Dir. Ivan Dariel Ortiz.

Hot tamales live. (2002). Prod. Kiki Melendez.

I Am Joaquin (Yo Soy Joaquin). (1969). Dir. Luis Valdez.

Juarez. (1939). Dir. William Dieterle.

La Bamba. (1986). Dir. Luis Valdez.

Like Water for Chocolate (1992). Dir. Alfonso Arau.

Lone Star. (1996). Dir. John Sayles.

Maid in Manhattan. (2002). Dir. Wayne Wang.

Manito. (2002). Dir. Eric Eason.

Mi Familia. *(My Family)*. (1995). Dir. Gregory Nava.

Mi Vida Loca. (1993). Dir. Allison Anders.

Milagro Beanfield War. (1988). Dir. Robert Redford.

Nueba Yol. (1995). Dir. Angel Muniz.

The Old Gringo. (1989). Dir. Luis Puenzo.

Once upon a Time in Mexico. (2003). Dir. Robert Rodriquez

The Party Line. (1996). Dir. Mario Barrera.

The Perez Family. (1995). Dir. Mira Nair.

Pretty Vacant. (1996). Dir. Jim Mendiola.

Quinceanera. (2006). Dir. Richard Glatzer & Wash Westmoreland.

Real Women Have Curves. (2002). Dir. Patricia Cardozo.

Ring, The. (1952). Dir. Kurt Neumann.

Road Dogz. (2001). Dir. Alfredo Ramos.

Rum and Coke. (2000). Dir. Maria Escobedo.

Saludos Amigos. (1942). Writers. Homer Brightman & Ralph Wright.

Salt of the Earth. (1954). Dir. Herbert J. Biberman.

Scarface. (1983). Dir. Brian DePalma.

Selena. (1991). Dir. Gregory Nava.

Short Eyes. (1987). Dir. Robert M. Young.

Smile Now, Cry Later. (2001). Dir. Jose Quiroz & Eduardo Quiroz.

Solas (Alone). (1999). Dir. Benito Zambrano.

Spanglish. (2004). Dir. James L. Brooks.

Stand and Deliver. (1987). Dir. Ramon Menendez.

Star Maps. (1997). Dir. Miguel Arteta.

Strangers in the City. (1962). Dir. Rick Carrier.

Talk to Her. (2002). Dir. Pedro Almodovar.

The Three Burials of Melquiades Estrada. (2005). Dir. Tommy Lee Jones.

This Rebel Breed. (1960). Dir. Richard L. Bare.

Three Caballeros. (1959). (Animation). Disney.

Touch of Evil. (1958). Dir. Orson Welles.

Traffic. (2000). Dir. Stephen Soderbergh.

Two Women on the Verge of a Nervous Breakdown. (1988). Dir. Pedro Almodovar.

Undefeated. (2003). Dir. John Leguziamo.

Viva Zapata! (1952). Dir. Elia Kazan.

A Walk in the Clouds. (1995). Dir. Alfonso Arau.

Walkout. (TV). (2006). Dir. Edward James Olmos.

Wassup Rockers. (2005). Dir. Larry Clark.

Week-end in Havana. (1941). Dir. Walter Lang.

West Side Story. (1961). Dir. Jerome Robbins and Robert Wise.

Zoot Suit. (1981). Dir. Luis Valdez.

Gay, Lesbian, Bi-Sexual, Trans-Gender

Internet

The Advocate: http://www.advocate.com/

AfterEllen.com

American Gay & Lesbian Alliance Against Defamation (GLAAD). Glaad.com

Gay and Lesbian Online Media: http://www.gaywiredmedia.com/

Gay Media Database: http://www.gaydata.com/

Gender, Race and Ethnicity in Media: LesBiGay

http://www.uiowa.edu/~commstud/resources/GenderMedia/gaymedia.html

Queer Sighted: http://www.queersighted.com/

Raising Our Voices—Queer Asian Women's Response to Relationship Violence (Report) http://www.endabuse.org/programs/display.php3?DocID=208

Readings

(2008, September 07). The Hunger. *Moria: Science Fiction, Horror, and Fantasy Film Review.* Retrieved from http://www.moria.co.nz/index.php?option=com_content&task=view&id=1924Itemid=1

Alwood, E. (1996). *Straight news: Gays, lesbians and the news media.* New York: Columbia University Press.

Barale, M. A. (1997). When lambs and aliens meet: Girl-faggots and boy-dykes go to the movies. In D. Heller (Ed.), *Cross-purposes: Lesbians, feminists, and the limits of alliance* (pp: 95–106). Bloomington, IN: Indiana University Press.

Barnhurst, K. (2007). *Media Q: Media/queered: Visibility and its discontents.* New York: Peter Lang.

Barrios, R. (2003). *Screened out: Playing gay in Hollywood from Edison to Stonewall.* New York: Routledge.

Battles, K., & Hilton-Morrow, W. (2002). Gay characters in conventional spaces: Will and Grace and the situation comedy genre. *Critical Studies in Media Communication, 19*(1), 87–106.

Bay-Cheng, S. (2001). 'An illogical stab of doubt': Avant-garde drama, cinema, and queerness. *Studies in the Humanities, 28*(1/2), 82–93.

Beam, J. (1991). Making ourselves from scratch. In E. Hemphill (Ed.), *Brother to brother: New writing by Black gay men.* (pp. 261–262.) Boston: Alyson.

Becker, E. (1995). Lesbians and film. In C. K. Creekmur & A. Doty (Eds.), *Out in culture: Gay, lesbian, and queer essays on popular culture* (pp. 25–43). Durham, NC: Duke University Press.

Becker, R. (2006). *Gay TV and straight America.* Piscataway, NJ: Rutgers University Press.

Becker, E., Michelle C., Lesage, J., & Rich, R. B. (1985). Lesbians and film. In P. Steven (Ed.), *Jump cut: Hollywood, politics, and counter cinema.* New York: Praeger.

Behar, R. (1995). Queer times in Cuba. *Bridges to Cuba/Puentes a Cuba* (pp. 394–415). Ann Arbor, MI: University of Michigan Press.

Bell-Metereau, R. L. (1993). *Hollywood androgyny* (2nd ed.). New York: Columbia University Press.

Benshoff, H. M. (1997). *Monsters in the closet: Homosexuality and the horror film.* New York: St. Martin's.

Benshoff, H. M. (2006). *Queer images: A history of gay and lesbian film in America.* Lanham, MD: Rowman & Littlefield.

Benshoff, H. M., & Griffin, S. (2004). *America on film: Representing race, class, gender, and sexuality at the movies.* Malden, MA: Blackwell.

Berenstein, R. J. (1996). *Attack of the leading ladies: Gender, sexuality, and spectatorship in classic horror cinema.* New York: Columbia University Press.

Berenstein, R. J. (1999). Film, mainstream. In B. Zimmerman & G. E. Haggerty (Eds.), *The encyclopedia of lesbian and gay histories and cultures* (pp. 303–305). Oxford, UK: Taylor & Francis.

Berry, C. (2001). Asian values, family values: Film, video, and lesbian and gay identities. *Journal of Homosexuality, 40*(3/4), 211–231.

Bould, M. (2002). Not in Kansas any more: Some notes on camp and queer SF movies. *Foundation: The International Review of Science Fiction, 31*(86), 40–50.

Bourne, S. (1996). *Brief encounters: Lesbians and gays in British cinema, 1930–1971.* London: New York: Cassell.

Braun, E. (2007). *Frightening the horses: Gay icons of the cinema.* London: Reynolds & Hearn.

Bronski, M. (1998). *The pleasure principle: Sex, backlash and the struggle for gay freedom.* New York: St. Martin's.

Bronski, M. (Ed.). (1996). *Taking liberties: Gay men's essays on politics, culture, and sex* (pp. 369–386). New York: Masquerade.

Brook, V. (2006). Puce modern moment: Camp, postmodernism, and the films of Kenneth Anger. *Journal of Film and Video, 58*(4), 3–15.

Bryant, M. (1997). Auden and the homoerotics of the 1930s documentary. *Mosaic: A Journal for the Interdisciplinary Study of Literature 30*(2), 69–92.

Bryant, W. M. (1997). *Bisexual characters in film: from Anais to Zee.* New York: Harrington Park.

Burns, R. (1995). Dracula's daughter: Cinema, hypnosis, and the erotics of lesbianism. In K. Jay (Ed.). *Lesbian erotics.* New York: New York University Press.

Burston, P. (1995). *What are you looking at?: Queer sex, style, and cinema.* New York: Cassell.

Burston, P. (Ed.). (1995). *Queer romance: Lesbians, gay men and popular culture.* London: Routledge.

Burt, R. (1997). The love that dare not speak Shakespeare's name: New Shakesqueer cinema. In L. E. Boose & R. Burt (Eds.), *Shakespeare, the movie: Popularizing the plays on film, TV, and video* (pp. 240–268). New York: Routledge.

Butler, J. (1999). Gender is burning: Questions of appropriation and subversion. In S. Thornham (Ed.), *Feminist film theory: A reader* (pp. 336–349). New York: New York University Press.

Cagle, C. (1997). Imaging the queer south: Southern lesbian and gay documentary. In C. Holmlund & C. Fuchs (Eds.), *Between the sheets, in the streets: Queer, lesbian, gay documentary* (pp. 30–45). Minneapolis: University of Minnesota Press.

Cairns, L. (2006). *Sapphism on screen.* Edinburgh, UK: Edinburgh University Press.

Case, S.-E. (1989). Toward a butch-femme aesthetic. In L. Hart (Ed.), *Making a spectacle: Feminist essays on contemporary women's theatre* (pp. 282–299). Ann Arbor, MI: University of Michigan Press.

Castenada, L., & Campbell, S. B. (2005). *News and sexuality.* Thousand Oaks, CA: SAge.

Castiglia, C. (1990). Rebel without a closet. In: J. A. Boone & M. Cadden (Eds.), *Engendering men: The question of male feminist criticism* (pp. 207–221). New York: Routledge.

Castiglia, C. (2000). Sex panics, sex publics, sex memories. *Boundary 2: An International Journal of Literature and Culture, 27*(2), 149–75.

Cestarao, G. P. (2004). *Queer Italia: Same-sex desire in Italian literature and film.* New York: Palgrave Macmillan.

Champagne, J. (1994–1995). Psychoanalysis and cinema studies: A 'queer' perspective. *Post Script: Essays in Film and the Humanities, 14*(1–2), 33–44.

Champagne, J. (1997). Dancing Queen? Feminist and gay male spectatorship in three recent films from Australia. *Film Criticism, 21*(3), 66–89.

Champagne, J. (1997). 'Stop reading films!' Film studies, close analysis, and gay pornography. *Cinema Journal, 36*(4), 76–97.

Chu, W. R. (1997). Some ethnic gays are coming home: Or, the trouble with interraciality. *Textual Practice, 11*(2), 219–35.

Ciasullo, A. M. (2001). Making her (in)visible: Cultural representations of lesbianism and the lesbian body in the 1990s. *Feminist Studies, 27*(3), 577–610.

Clarkson, J. (2005). Contesting masculinity's makeover: *Queer Eye,* consumer masculinity, and 'straight-acting' gays. *The Journal of Communication Inquiry, 29*(3), 235–255.

Claussen, D. S. (2002). *Sex, religion, media.* Lanham, MD: Rowman & Littlefield.

Clover, C. (1992). *Men, women, and chainsaws: Gender in the modern horror film.* Princeton, NJ: Princeton University Press.

Clum, J. M. (2002). *'He's all man': Learning masculinity, gayness, and love from American movies.* New York: Palgrave.

Coffman, C. E. (2006). *Insane passions: Lesbianism and psychosis in literature and film.* Middletown, CT: Wesleyan University Press.

Cohan, S. (2005). *Incongruous entertainment: Camp, cultural value, and the MGM musical.* Durham, NC: Duke University Press.

Corber, R. J. (1993). *In the name of national security: Hitchcock, homophobia, and the political construction of gender in postwar America.* Durham, NC: Duke University Press.

Corber, R. J. (1997). *Homosexuality in cold war America: Resistance and the crisis of masculinity.* Durham, NC: Duke University Press.

Cover, R. (2000). First contact: Queer theory, sexual identity, and 'mainstream' film. *International Journal of Sexuality & Gender Studies, 5*(1), 71–89.

Crane, J. L. (1994). *Terror and everyday life: Singular moments in the history of the horror film.* Thousand Oaks, CA: Sage.

Creed, B. (2000). The naked crunch: Cronenberg's homoerotic bodies. In M. Grant (Ed.), *The modern fantastic: The films of David Cronenberg* (pp. 84–101). Westport, CT: Praeger.

Creed, B. (2003). *The monstrous-feminine: Film, feminism, psychoanalysis.* New York: Routledge.

Creekmur, C., & Doty, A. (1985). *Out in culture: Gay, lesbian, and queer essays on popular culture.* Durham, NC: Duke University Press.

Daniel, L., & Jackson, C. (Eds.). (2003*). The bent lens: A world guide to gay & lesbian film*. Boston: Alyson.

Davies, J., & Smith, C. R. (1997). *Gender, ethnicity and sexuality in contemporary American film*. Edinburgh, UK: Keele University Press.

De Lauretis, T. (1994). *The practice of love: Lesbian sexuality and perverse desire*. Bloomington, IN: Indiana University Press.

Derry, C. (1996). Gay lives through gay eyes. *Harvard Gay & Lesbian Review, 3*(2), 20–23.

Dhaenens, F. (2008). Slashing the fiction of queer theory: Slash fiction, queer reading, and transgressing the boundaries of screen studies, representations, and audiences. *The Journal of Communication Inquiry, 32*(4), 335–347.

Dittmar, L. (1997). Of hags and crones: Reclaiming lesbian desire for the trouble zone of aging. In C. Holmlund & C. Fuchs (Eds.), *Between the sheets, in the streets: Queer, lesbian, gay documentary* (pp. 71–90). Minneapolis, MN: University of Minnesota Press.

Dixon, W. W. (2003). *Straight: Constructions of heterosexuality in the cinema*. Albany, NY: SUNY Press.

D'Lugo, M. (1996). From exile to ethnicity: Nestor Almendros and Orlando Jimemez-Leal's *Improper Conduct*. In C. A. Noriega & A. M. Lopez (Eds.), *The ethnic eye: Latino media arts* (pp. 171–182). Minneapolis, MN: University of Minnesota Press.

Doty, A. (1993). *Making things perfectly queer: Interpreting mass culture*. Minneapolis, MN: University of Minnesota Press.

Doty, A. (2000). *Flaming classics: Queering the film canon*. New York: Routledge.

Douglas, M. (1996). *Purity and danger: An analysis of concepts of pollution and taboo*. New York: Praeger.

Dudrah, R. K. (2006). *Bollywood: Sociology goes to the movies*. Thousand Oaks, CA: Sage.

Dyer, D. (1991). Believing in fairies: Author and the homosexual. In D. Fuss (Ed.), *Inside/out: Lesbian theories, gay theories* (pp. 185–201). New York: Routledge.

Dyer, R. (1977). *Notes on stereotyping. Gays and film*. New York: Zoetrope.

Dyer, R. (1990). *Now you see it: Studies on lesbian and gay film*. New York: Routledge.

Dyer, R. (1994). Idol thoughts: Orgasm and self-reflexivity in gay pornography. *Critical Quarterly, 36*(1), 49–63.

Dyer, R. (2002). *The culture of queers*. London; New York: Routledge.

Dyer, R. (Ed.). (1977). *Gays and film*. New York: Zoetrope.

Ebert, R. (1983, May 03). The Hunger. *Chicago Sun-Times*. Retrieved March 06, 2009, from http://rogerebert.suntimes.com/apps/pbcs.dll/article?AID=/19830503/REVIEWS/305030301/1023

Eberwein, R. (1995). Disease, masculinity, and sexuality in recent films. *Journal of Popular Film and Television, 22*(4), 154–61.

Ehrenstein, D. (1998). *Open secret: Gay Hollywood, 1928–1998*. New York: William Morrow.

Erni, J. N. (2003). Run queer Asia run. *Journal of Homosexuality, 45*(2/4), 381–384.

Fejes, F., & Petrich, K. (1993). Invisibility, homophobia and heterosexism: Lesbians, gays and the media. *Critical Studies in Mass Communication, 10*(4): 396–422.

Foster, D. W. (1997). *Sexual textualities: Essays on queer/ing Latin American writing.* Austin, TX: University of Texas Press.

Foster, D. W. (2003). *Queer issues in contemporary Latin American cinema.* Austin, TX: University of Texas Press.

Friedman, J. C. (2007). *Rainbow Jews: Jewish and gay identity in the performing arts.* Lanham, MD: Lexington.

Freud, S. (1919). *The uncanny.* J. Strachey (Trans.). London: Penguin.

Fung, R. (1993). Shortcomings: Questions about pornography as pedagogy. In M. Gever, P. Parmar, & J. Greyson (Eds.), *Queer looks: Perspectives on lesbian and gay film and video* (pp. 355–367). New York: Routledge.

Gallagher, M. (2004). Queer eye for the heterosexual couple. *Feminist Media Studies, 4*(2), 222–226.

Gamson, J. (1996). The organizational shaping of collective identity: The case of lesbian and gay film festivals in New York. *Sociological Forum, 11*(2): 231–261.

Garber, M. (1995). *Vice versa: Bisexuality and the eroticism of everyday life.* New York: Simon & Schuster.

Geller, T. L. (2004). Queering Hollywood's tough chick: The subversions of sex, race, and nation in *The Long Kiss Goodnight* and *The Matrix. Frontiers: A Journal of Women Studies, 25*(3), 8–34.

Ginsberg, T. (1990). Nazis and drifters: Radical (sexual) knowledge in two Italian neorealist films. *Journal of the History of Sexuality, 1*(2), 25–50.

Gregg, R. (2003). Gay culture, studio publicity and the management of star discourse: The homosexualization of William Haines in pre-code Hollywood. *Quarterly Review of Film and Video, 20*(2), 81–97.

Griffin, S. (2000). *Tinker Belles and evil queens: The Walt Disney Company from the inside out.* New York: New York University Press.

Griffiths, R. (Ed.). (2006). *British queer cinema.* New York: Routledge.

Gross, L. (1996). Don't ask, don't tell: Lesbians and gays in the media. In P. M. Lester (Ed.), *Images that injure: Pictorial stereotypes in the media* (pp. 149–160). Westport, CT: Praeger.

Gross, L. (1996, April–May). Lesbians and gays and the broadcast media. *SIECUS Report, 24*(4), 10.

Gross, L., & Woods, J. D. (Eds.). (1999). *The Columbia reader on lesbians and gay men in media, society, and politics.* New York: Columbia University Press.

Gross, R. (1997). Hollywood as inspiration for the stage: The gay playwrights' perspective. In K. King (Ed.), *Hollywood on stage: Playwrights evaluate the culture industry* (pp. 212–215). New York: Garland.

Grossman, A. (2000). Homosexual men (and lesbian men) in a heterosexual genre: Three gangster films from Hong Kong. (Critical Essay). *Journal of Homosexuality, 237.*

Grossman, A. (2000). *Queer Asian cinema: Shadows in the shade.* New York: Harrington Park.

Grossman, A. (2000). The rise of homosexuality and the dawn of communism in Hong Kong film: 1993–1998. *Journal of Homosexuality, 149.*

Gunn, D. W. (2005). *The gay male sleuth in print and film: A history and annotated bibliography.* Lanham, MD: Scarecrow.

Gutierrez-Albilla, J. D. (2008). *Queering Buñuel: Sexual dissidence and psychoanalysis in his Mexican and Spanish cinema.* New York: Tauris Academic Studies.

Hadleigh, B. (1993). *The lavender screen: The gay and lesbian films: Their stars, makers, characters, and critics.* Secaucus, NJ: Carol.

Halberstam, J. (1998). *Female masculinity.* Durham, NC: Duke University Press.

Halberstam, J. (2005). *In a queer time and place: Transgender bodies, subcultural lives.* New York: New York University Press.

Hammer, B. (2001). Lesbian images in the classic film era: Beth Mauldin talks with a lesbian film documentarian. (Interview). *The Gay & Lesbian Review Worldwide, 8*(6), 29–31.

Hankin, K. (2002). *The girls in the back room: Looking at the lesbian bar.* Minneapolis, MN: University of Minnesota Press.

Harper, P. B. (1994). The subversive edge—*Paris Is Burning,* social critique, and the limits of subjective agency. *Diacritics—A Review of Contemporary Criticism, 24*(2/3), 90–103.

Harris, D. (1997). *The rise and fall of gay culture.* New York: Hyperion.

Hart, K. P. R. (1999). Gay male spectatorship and the films of Montgomery Clift. *Popular Culture Review, 10*(1), 69–82.

Hart, L. (1994). *Fatal women: Lesbian sexuality and the mark of aggression.* Princeton, NJ: Princeton University Press.

Hays, M. (2007). *The view from here: Conversations with gay and lesbian filmmakers.* Vancouver: Arsenal Pulp.

Helms, U. (2000). Obscenity and homosexual depiction in Japan. *Journal of Homosexuality, 39*(3/4), 127–47.

Hernandez, S. F., & Perriam, C. (2000). Beyond Almodovar: Homosexuality in Spanish cinema of the 1990s. In D. Alderson & L. Anderson (Eds.), *Territories of desire in queer culture: Refiguring contemporary boundaries* (pp. 96–111). Manchester, UK: Manchester University Press.

Holleran, A. (2001). Brief history of a media taboo. (Critical Essay). *Gay & Lesbian Review, 8*(2), 12.

Hollinger K. (1998). Theorizing mainstream female spectatorship: The case of the popular lesbian film. *Cinema Journal, 37*(2), 3–17.

Holmlund, C. (1991). When is a lesbian not a lesbian? The lesbian continuum and the mainstream femme film. *Camera Obscura, 25/26,* 145–178.

Holmlund, C. (1994). Cruisin' for a bruisin': Hollywood's deadly (lesbian) dolls. *Cinema Journal, 34*(1), 31–51.

Holmlund, C., & Fuchs, C. (Eds.). (1997). *Between the sheets, in the streets: Queer, lesbian, and gay documentary.* Minneapolis, MN: University of Minnesota Press.

Hood, R. L. (1995). The wildness of AIDS: Sexual identity and cultural politics in the new queer cinema. *Revista/Review Interamericana, 25*(1/4), 72–80.

Hoogland, R. C. (1997). *Lesbian configurations.* New York: Columbia University Press.

Howes, K. (1993). *Broadcasting it: An encyclopaedia of homosexuality in film, radio and TV in the UK, 1923–1993.* London; New York: Cassell.

Ince, K. (2002). Queering the family? Fantasy and the performance of sexuality and gay relations in French cinema, 1995–2000. *Studies in French Cinema, 2*(2), 90–98.

Irigaray, L. (1985). *This sex which is not one.* In C. Porter (Trans.). New York: Cornell University Press.

Jenkins, T. (2005). 'Potential lesbians at two o'clock': The heterosexualization of lesbianism in the recent teen film. *Journal of Popular Culture, 38*(3), 491–504.

Jones, D. (2002) *Horror: A thematic history in fiction and film.* London: Arnold.

Kabir, S. (1998). *Daughters of desire: Lesbian representations in film.* Washington, D.C.: Cassell.

Kavka, M. (2004). The queering of reality TV. *Feminist Media Studies, 4*(2), 203–231.

Keller, J. R. (1997). Masculinity and marginality in *Rob Roy* and *Braveheart. Journal of Popular Film and Television, 24*(4), 146–152.

Keller, J. R. (2002). *Queer (un)friendly film and television.* Jefferson, NC: McFarland.

Kristeva, J. (1982). *Powers of horror: An essay on abjection.* In L. S. Roudiez (Trans.). New York: Columbia University Press.

Kuzniar, A. A. (2000). *The queer German cinema.* Stanford, CA: Stanford University Press.

La Bruce, B. (1995). Pee Wee Herman: The homosexual subtext. In C. K. Creekmur & A. Doty (Eds.), *Out in culture: Gay, lesbian, and queer essays on popular culture* (pp. 382–88). Durham, NC: Duke University Press.

Lang, R. (2002). *Masculine interests: Homoerotics in Hollywood films.* New York: Columbia University Press.

Latham, R. (1998). Phallic mothers and monster queers. *Science Fiction Studies, 25*(1), 87–101.

Leff, L. J. (1999). 'Come on home with me': 42nd Street and the gay male world 1930s. *Cinema Journal, 39*(1), 3–22.

Leff, L. J. (2008). Becoming Clifton Webb: A queer star in mid-century Hollywood. *Cinema Journal, 47*(3), 3–29.

Lewis, T. (2007). 'He needs to face his fears with these five queers!': *Queer Eye for the Straight Guy,* makeover TV, and the lifestyle expert. *Television & New Media, 8,* 285–311.

Lim, S. H. (2006). *Celluloid comrades: Representations of male homosexuality in contemporary Chinese cinemas.* Honolulu: University of Hawai'i Press.

Lovaas, K., & Jenkins, M. M., (2007). *Sexualities & communication in everyday life: A reader.* Thousand Oaks, CA: Sage.

Love, H. K. (2004). Spectacular failure: The figure of the lesbian in *Mulholland Drive. New Literary History: A Journal of Theory and Interpretation, 35*(1), 117–32.

Lugowski, D. M. (1999). Queering the (new) deal: Lesbian and gay representation and the Depression-era cultural politics of Hollywood's production code. *Cinema Journal, 38*(2), 3–35.

Mayne, J. (2000). *Framed: Lesbians, feminists, and media culture.* Minneapolis, MN: University of Minnesota Press.

Meyer, M. D. E., & Kelley, J. M. (2004). Queering the Eye? The Politics of gay white men and gender (in) visibility. *Feminist Media Studies, 4*(2), 214–17.

Miller, T. (2005). A metrosexual eye on queer guy. *GLQ: A Journal of Lesbian and Gay Studies, 11*(1), 112–117.

Moon, M. (1998). *A small boy and others: Imitation and initiation in American culture from Henry James to Andy Warhol.* Durham, NC: Duke University Press.

Morris, B. J. (2000). *Girl reel: A lesbian remembers growing up at the movies.* Minneapolis, MN: Coffee House.

Murphy, T. F. (2000). *Reader's guide to lesbian and gay studies.* Oxford: Taylor & Francis.

Murray, T. (1993). *Like film: Ideological fantasy on screen, camera, and canvas.* New York: Routledge.

Oishi, E. (2003). Bad Asians, the sequel: Continuing trends in queer API film and video. *Millennium Film Journal, 41,* 33–41.

Patton, C. (1990). *Inventing AIDS.* New York: Routledge.

Pearson, K., & Reich, N. M. (2004). Queer eye fairy tale: Changing the world one manicure at a time. *Feminist Media Studies, 4*(2), 229–231.

Peele, T. (2001). *Fight Club's* queer representations. *JAC: A Journal of Composition Theory, 21*(4), 862–869.

Pendleton, D. (2001). Out of the ghetto: Queerness, homosexual desire and the time-image. *Strategies: A Journal of Theory, Culture, and Politics, 14*(1), 47–62.

Phillips, G. D. (1997). Blanche's phantom husband: Homosexuality on stage and screen. *Louisiana Literature: A Review of Literature and Humanities, 14*(2), 36–47.

Phillips, W. H. (2004). *Film.* New York: Macmillan.

Press, C., & Keesey, P. (2006). *Daughters of darkness: Lesbian vampire tales.* Berkeley, CA: Cleis.

Price, T. (1992). *Hitchcock and homosexuality: His 50-year obsession with Jack the Ripper and the superbitch prostitute: A psychoanalytic view.* Metuchen, NJ: Scarecrow.

Ringer, R. J. (1994). *Queer words, queer images: Communication and the construction of homosexuality.* New York: New York University Press.

Russo, V. (1987). *The celluloid closet* (2nd ed.). New York: Harper & Row.

Stacey, J., & Street, S. (2007). *Queer screen: A Screen reader.* New York: Routledge.

Stoker, B. (1997). *Dracula.* In N. Auerbach & D. J. Skal (Eds.). Norton Critical Edition. New York: W. W. Norton.

Streitmatter, R. (1995). *Unspeakable: The rise of the gay and lesbian press in America.* Boston: Faber & Faber.

Tudor, A. (1989). *Monsters and mad scientists: A cultural history of the horror movie.* Oxford: Basil Blackwell.

Ursini, J. (2000). Introduction. In A. Silver & J. Ursini (Eds.), *Horror film reader.* New York: Limelight.

Wardlow, D. L. (1996). *Gays, lesbians, and consumer behavior: Theory, practice, and research issues.* New York: Haworth.

Weiss, A. (1992). *Vampires and violets: Lesbians in the cinema.* London: Jonathan Cape.

Whatling, C. (1997). *Screen dreams: Fantasizing lesbians in film.* Manchester, UK: Manchester University Press.

Williams, L. (1984). When the woman looks. In M. A. Doane, P. Mellencamp, & L. Williams (Eds.), *Re-visions: Essays in feminist film criticism* (pp. 83–99). Frederick, MD: AFI Monograph Series, University Publications of America.

Zimmerman, B. (2004). *Daughters of darkness: The lesbian vampire on film.* In B. K. Grant & C. Sharrett (Eds.), *Planks of reason* (pp. 72–81). San Francisco, CA: Scarecrow.

Films

The Adventures of Priscilla, Queen of the Desert. (1994). Dir. Stephan Elliott.

Aimeé & Jaquar. (1999). Dir. Max Färberböck.

Beautiful Thing. (1996). Dir. Hettie Macdonald.

Before Night Falls. (2000). Dir. Julian Schnabel.

Billy's Hollywood Screen Kiss. (1998). Dir. Tommy O'Haver.

Birdcage, The. (1996). Dir. Mike Nichols.

Bound. (1996). Dirs. Andy Wachowski and Lana Wachowski.

Boys in the Band, The. (1970). Dir. William Friedkin.

Boys Don't Cry. (1999). Dir. Kimberly Peirce.

Boys on the Side. (1995). Dir. Herbert Ross.

Brokeback Mountain. (2005). Dir. Ang Lee.

Broken Hearts Club. (2000). Dir. Greg Berlanti.

Celluloid Closet. (1996). Dirs. Jeffrey Friedman & Rob Epstein.

Come Undone. (2000). Dir. Sébastien Lifshitz.

Cruising. (1980). Dir. William Friedkin.

Crying Game, The. (1992). Dir. Neil Jordan.

Desert Hearts. (1985). Dir. Donna Deitch.

Further off the Straight and Narrow: New Gay Visibility on Television, 1998–2006. (1997). Dir. Katherine Sender.

Go Fish. (1994). Dir. Rose Troche.

Gods and Monsters. (1998). Dir. James Whale.

Hedwig and the Angry Inch. (2001). Dir. John Cameron Mitchell.

If These Walls Could Talk. (1996). Dirs. Cher and Nancy Savoca.

If These Walls Could Talk 2. (2000). Dirs. Jane Anderson and Martha Coolidge.

The Incredibly True Adventure of Two Girls in Love. (1995). Dir. Maria Maggenti.

It Takes a Team! Making Sports Safe for Lesbian and Gay Athletes. (2004). Prod. It Takes a Team.

I've heard the mermaids singing. (1987). Dir. Patricia Rozema.

Kissing Jessica Stein. (2001). Dir. Charles Herman-Wurmfeld..

La Cage aux Folles. (1978). Dir. Edouard Molinaro.

L.I.E. (2001). Dir. Michael Cuesta.

Longtime Companion. (1990). Dir. Norman René.

Ma Vie en Rose. (1997). Dir. Alain Berliner.

Maurice. (1987). Dir. James Ivory.

Milk. (2008). Dir. Gus Van Sant.

Mulholland Drive. (2001). Dir. David Lynch.

My Beautiful Laundrette. (1985). Dir. Stephen Frears.

Mysterious Skin. (2004). Dir. Gregg Araki.

Off the Straight and Narrow: Lesbians, Gays, Bisexuals, and Television 1968–1998. (1998). Dir. Katherine Sender.

Opposite of Sex, The. (1998). Dir. Don Roos.

Paragraph 175. (2000). Dirs. Rob Epstein and Jeffrey Friedman.

Paris Is Burning! (1990). Dir. Jennie Livingston.

Parting Glances. (1986). Dir. Bill Sherwood.

Philadelphia. (1993). Dir. Jonathan Demme.

Queer as Folk. (TV). Showtime.

Rocky Horror Picture Show, The. (1975). Dir. Jim Sharman.

Silkwood. (1983). Dir. Mike Nichols.

Speak up! Improving the Lives GLBT Youth. United States. (2001). Prod. Sut Jhally.

The Talented Mr. Ripley. (1999). Dir. Anthony Minghella.

Times of Harvey Milk, The. (1984). Dir. Rob Epstein.

Tongues Untied. (1990). Dir. Marlon Riggs.

Torch Song Trilogy. (1988). Dir. Paul Bogart.

Transamerica. (2005). Dir. Duncan Tucker.

Trick. (1999). Dir. Jim Fall.

Walk on Water. (2004). Dir. Eytan Fox.

Wedding Banquet, The. (1993). Dir. Ang Lee.

Native Americans/American Indians

Internet

American Indian and Alaska Native (AIAN) Data and Links: http://factfinder.census.gov/home/aian/index.html

Cherokee Phoenix: (http://anpa.ualr.edu/indexes/cherokee_phoenix_index/cherokee_phoenix.htm)

Circle of Stories (http://www.pbs.org/circleofstories/)

Disney's 'Politically Correct' Pocahontas. http://library.berkeley.edu/MRC/Pocahontas.html

Gender, Race and Ethnicity in Media: Indigenous Peoples in the Mediahttp://www.uiowa.edu/~commstud/resources/GenderMedia/native.html

Indian Country Today. http://www.indiancountry.com/

Movies and Native Americans. http://www.americanwest.com/pages/namovies.htm http://library.berkeley.edu/MRC/imagesnatives.html

Native Americans in the Movies: A Bibliography of Materials in the UC Berkeley Library http://
www.lib.berkeley.edu/MRC/IndigenousBib.html

Native America sites and American Indian Library Association: (http://www.nativeculturelinks.
com/indians.html)

Native American Journalists Association (http://www.naja.com/)

Native Media: Film and video organizations, journals, newspapers, radio, and television: http://
www.nativeculturelinks.com/media.html

Native Networks: http://www.nativenetworks.si.edu/nn.htm

Pictures of Our Nobler Selves, by Mark Trahant available as PDF at http://www.freedomforum.
org/templates/document.asp?documentID=14530

RezNet (http://www.reznetnews.org/) News and Views by Native American Students

Readings

Adams, H. (2004). Quoted in M. Yellow Bird (2004). Cowboys and Indians: Toys of genocide,
icons of American colonialism. *Wicazo Sa Review 19*(2), 33–48.

Barthes, R. (1972). *Mythologies.* New York: Noonday.

Berkhofer, R., Jr. (1979). *The White man's Indian: Images of the American Indian from Columbus to
the present.* New York: Vintage.

Biber, B. (1984). *Early education and psychological development.* New Haven, CT: Yale University Press.

Coombes, R. J. (1998). *The cultural life of intellectual properties: Authorship, appropriation, and the
law.* Durham, NC: Duke University Press.

Cortese, A. J. (1999). *Provocateur: Images of women and minorities in advertising.* Lanham, MD:
Rowman & Littlefield.

Darian-Smith, K. (2002). Material culture and the 'signs' of captive white women. In B. Creed & J.
Hoorn (Eds.), *Body trade: Captivity, cannibalism, and colonialism in the Pacific* (pp. 180–194).
London: Routledge.

Dávila, A. M. (2001). *Latinos Inc. The Marketing and Making of a People.* Berkeley, CA: University
of California Press.

Dotz, W., & Morton, J. (1996). *What a character! 20th century American advertising icons.* San
Francisco: Chronicle.

Doxater, M. G. (2004). Indigenous knowledge in the Decolonial Era. *American Indian Quarterly,
28*(3/4), 618–633.

Dubinsky, K. (1999). *The second greatest disappointment: Honeymooning and tourism at Niagara
Falls.* New Brunswick, NJ: Rutgers University Press.

Green, M. K. (1993). Images of American Indians in advertising: Some moral issues. *Journal of
Business Ethics, 12,* 323–330.

Hill, R. (1992, May). The non-vanishing American Indian: Are the modern images any closer to
the truth? *Quill,* pp. 35–37.

King, C. R. (1998). Spectacles, sports, and stereotypes: Dis/playing Chief Illiniwek. *Colonial discourse, collective memories, and the exhibition of Native American cultures and histories in the contemporary United States* (pp. 41–58). New York: Garland.

King, C. R. (2001). Uneasy Indians: Creating and contesting Native American mascots at Marquette University. In C. R. King & C. F. Springwood (Eds.), *Team spirits: Essays on the history and significance of Native American mascots* (pp. 281–303). Lincoln, NE: University of Nebraska Press.

Larson, C. (1937). Patent-medicine advertising and the Early American press. *Journalism Quarterly, 14*(4), 337–339.

Mansvelt, J. (2005). *Geographies of consumption*. Newbury Park, CA: Sage.

McClintock, A. (1995). *Imperial leather: Race, gender, and sexuality in the colonial contest*. New York: Routledge.

Merskin, D. (1998). Sending up signals: A survey of American Indian media use and representation in the mass media. *The Howard Journal of Communication, 9*, 337–345.

Merskin, D. (2001). Winnebagos, Cherokees, Apaches, and Dakotas: The persistence of stereotyping of American Indians in American advertising brands. *The Howard Journal of Communication, 12*, 159–169.

Mihesuah, D. A. (1996). *American Indians: Stereotypes and realities*. Atlanta, GA: Clarity.

Morgan, H. (1986). *Symbols of America*. New York: Penguin.

Roediger, D. R. (2002). *Colored White: Transcending the racial past*. Berkeley, CA: University of California Press.

Rosaldo, R. (1989). Imperialist nostalgia. *Representations, 26*, 107–122.

Strickland, R. (1997, January 13). Coyote goes Hollywood. *Native Peoples*. Retrieved from http://www.nativepeoples.com/article/articles/174/1/COYOTE-GOES-HOLLYWOOD

van Dijk, T. A. (1996). *Discourse, Racism, and Ideology*. La Laguna, Mexico: RCEI Ediciones.

Films

Black Robe. (1991). Dir. Bruce Beresford.

Business of Fancy Dancing. (2002). Dir. Sherman Alexie.

Dance Me Outside. (1995). Dir. Bruce McDonald.

Incident at Oglala: The Leonard Peltier Story. (1992). Dir. Michael Apted.

Lakota Women: Siege at Wounded Knee. (1994). Dir. Frank Pierson.

Northern Exposure. (TV). Columbia Broadcasting Company.

Pow Wow Highway. (1989). Dir. Jonathan Wacks.

Images of Indians (1980): Five part program, 30 minutes each:

> *The Great Movie Massacre* (part 1)
>
> *How Hollywood Wins the West* (part 2)
>
> *Warpaint and Wigs* (part 3)
>
> *Heathen Injuns and the Hollywood Gospel* (part 4)
>
> *The Movie Reel Indians* (part 5)

Native films made by and starring Native actors

Black Elk Speaks

Buffalo, Blood, Salmon, and Roots (1976). Dir. George Burdeau's

Business of Fancy Dancing. (2002). Dir. Sherman Alexie.

Charley Squash Goes to Town. (1969). Dir. Duke Redbird.

Do Indians Shave? (1974). Dir. Chris Spotted Elk

George Horse Capture's *I'd Rather Be Powwowing.* (1981*).* Dir. Victor Masayesva, Jr.

The Great Spirit in the Hole. (1983). Dir. Chris Spotted Eagle.

Harold of Orange. (1984). Dir. Richard Weise.

Hopi Ritual Clowns. (1988), Dir. Victor Masayesva, Jr.

Hopiit '81. (1982). Dir. Victor Masayesva, Jr.

House Made of Dawn. (1972). Dir. Richardson Morse.

Images of Indians. (1980). (see above).

Itam Hakim, Hopiit. (1985). Dir. Victor Masayesva, Jr.

Navajo Talking Picture. (1986). Dir. Irene Bowman.

Ramona (1928) and *The Trail of the Shadow* (1917). Dir. Edwin Carewe.

Return of the Country. (1982). Dir. Bob Hicks.

Smoke Signals. (1998). Dir. Chris Eyre.

Yacqui Girl. (1911). Dir. James Young Deer.

Whites

Internet

Whiteness studies: http://www.uwm.edu/~gjay/Whiteness/index.html

Readings

Alberti, J. (1995, December). The Nigger Huck: Race, identity, and the teaching of *Huckleberry Finn. College English, 58*(8), 919–937.

Allen, T. (1994). *The invention of the white race.* New York: Verso.

Appiah, A., & Gutmann, A. (1998). *Color consciousness: The political morality of race.* Princeton, NJ: Princeton University Press.

Bay, M. (2000). *The white image in the black mind: African-American ideas about white people, 1830–1925.* New York: Oxford University Press.

Berger, M. (1999). *White lies: Race and the myths of whiteness.* New York: Farrar, Straus & Giroux.

Bernardi, D. L. (1996). *The birth of whiteness: Race and the emergence of U.S. cinema.* New Brunswick, NJ: Rutgers University Press.

Bonnett, A. (1999). *White identities: Historical and international perspectives.* New York: Longman.

Brodkin, K. (1998). *How Jews became white folks and what that says about race in America.* New Brunswick, NJ: Rutgers University Press.

Broeck, S. (1999). *White amnesia—black memory? American women's writing and history.* New York: Peter Lang.

Brown, H., Gilkes, M., & Kaloski-Naylor, A. (Eds.). (1999). *White? women: Critical perspectives on race and gender.* York, UK: Raw Nerve.

Caughie, P. (1999). *Passing and pedagogy: The dynamics of responsibility.* Chicago: University of Chicago Press.

Chideya, F. (2000). *The color of our future: Race for the 21st century.* New York: Harper Perennial.

Cuomo, C. J., & Hall, K. (Eds.). (1999). *Whiteness: Feminist philosophical reflections.* Lanham, MD: Rowman & Littlefield.

Curry, R. R. (2000). *White women writing white: H.D., Elizabeth Bishop, Sylvia Plath, and whiteness.* New York: Praeger.

Daniels, J. (1997). *White lies: Race, class, gender, and sexuality in white supremacist discourse.* New York: Routledge.

Davis, J. *The white image in the black mind: A study of African American literature.* New York: Routledge.

Delgado, R., & Stefancic, J. (Eds.).. (1997). *Critical white studies: Looking behind the mirror.* Philadelphia: Temple University Press.

Deloria, V. (1997). *Red earth, white lies: Native Americans and the myth of scientific fact.* Golden, CO: Fulcrum.

Dyer, R. (1997, June 27). Seeing the White. *Times Higher Education Supplement, 1286.*

Dyer, R. (Ed.). (2002). *The matter of images: Essays on representations.* New York: Routledge.

Evans, N. M. (2000). *Writing jazz: Race, nationalism, and modern culture in the 1920s.* New York: Routledge.

Fanon, F. (1994). *Black skin, white masks.* New York: Grove.

Ferber, A. L. (1999). *White man falling: Race, gender, and white supremacy.* Lanham, MD: Rowman & Littlefield.

Fishkin, S. F. (1995). Interrogating 'whiteness,' complicating 'blackness': Remapping American culture. *American Quarterly, 47,* 428–466.

Frankenberg, R. (1993). *White women/race matters: The social construction of whiteness.* Minneapolis, MN: University of Minnesota Press.

Gilroy, P. (2002). *Against race: Imagining political culture beyond the color line.* Cambridge, MA: Harvard University Press.

Giroux, H. (1997). Rewriting the discourse of racial identity: Towards a pedagogy and politics of whiteness. *Harvard Educational Review, 67*(2), 285–320.

Gubar, S. (2000). *Race changes: White skin, black face in American culture.* New York: Oxford University Press.

Hale, G. E. (1999). *Making whiteness: The culture of segregation in the South, 1890–1940.* New York: Vintage.

Hall, K. (1996). Beauty and the beast of whiteness: Teaching race and gender. *Shakespeare Quarterly,* *47*(4), 461–476.

Haney-Lopez, I. (2006). *White by law: The legal construction of race.* New York: NYU Press.

Hartigan, J. (1997). Establishing the fact of whiteness. *American Anthropologist. 99*(3), 495–506.

Hill, M. (Ed.). (1997). *Whiteness: A critical reader.* New York: NYU Press.

Hill, M. (2004). *After whiteness: Unmaking an American majority.* New York: NYU Press.

hooks, b. (1999). *Black looks: Race and representation.* Boston: South End Press.

Howard, G. R., & Nieto, S. (2006). *We can't teach what we don't know: White teachers, multiracial schools.* New York: Teachers College Press

Hughes, L. (1990). *The ways of white folks.* New York: Vintage.

Ignatiev, N. (1994, Nov/Dec). Interview. Treason to whiteness is loyalty to humanity. *Utne Reader, 66,* 82–87.

Ignatiev, N. (2008). *How the Irish became white.* New York: Routledge.

Jacobson, M. F. (1999). *Whiteness of a different color: European immigrants and the alchemy of race.* Cambridge, MA: Harvard University Press.

Jensen, R. (2005). *The heart of whiteness: Confronting race, racism, and white privilege.* San Francisco: City Lights.

Jurca, C. (2001). *White diaspora: The suburb and the twentieth-century American novel.* Princeton, NJ: Princeton University Press.

Keating, A. L. (1995, December). Interrogating 'whiteness,' (de)constructing 'race.' *College English, 57*(8), 901–918.

Kincheloe, J. L. (1999). The struggle to define and reinvent whiteness: A pedagogical analysis. *College Literature, 26*(3), 162–195.

Kincheloe, J., Steinberg, S. R., Rodriguez, N. M., & Chennault, R. E. (Eds.). (2000). *White reign: Deploying whiteness in America.* New York: Palgrave Macmillan.

Kivel, P. (2002). *Uprooting racism: How white people can work for racial justice.* New York: New Society.

Kolchin, P. (2002). Whiteness studies: The new history of race in America. *Journal of American History 89,* pp. 154–73.

Lamont, M. (1999). *The cultural territories of race: Black and white boundaries.* New York: Russell Sage Foundation.

Lazarre, J. Manrique, J. (1996). *Beyond the whiteness of whiteness: Memoir of a white mother of black sons.* Durham, NC and London, UK: Duke University Press.

Lipsitz, G. (1995, September). The possessive investment in whiteness. *American Quarterly, 47*(3), 369–386.

Lipsitz, G. (2006). *The possessive investment in whiteness: How white people profit from identity politics.* Philadelphia: Temple University Press.

Lott, E. (1995). *Love and theft: Blackface minstrelsy and the American working class.* New York: Oxford University Press.

Martin, J. (1996). Exploring whiteness: A study of self-label for white Americans. *Communication Quarterly, 44*(2), 125–145.

Mazie, M. (1993). To deconstruct race, deconstruct whiteness. *American Quarterly, 45*(2), 281–295.

McCarthy, C., Crichlow, W., Dimitriadis, G., & Dolby, N. (Eds.). (2005). *Race, identity, and representation in education* (2nd ed.). New York: Routledge.

McIntosh, P. (1990). White privilege: Unpacking the invisible knapsack. *Independent School, 49*(2), 31–36.

McIntyre, A. (1997). *Making meaning of whiteness: Exploring racial identity with white teachers.* Albany, New York: SUNY Press.

McKee, P. (1999). *Producing American races: Henry James, William Faulkner, Toni Morrison.* Durham, NC: Duke University Press.

McKinney, K. D. (2005). *Being white: Stories of race and racism.* New York: Routledge.

McKoy, S. S. (2003, September 22). When whites riot: Writing race and violence in American and South African culture. *Labour/Le Travail. Canadian Committee on Labour History, 55,* 331–332.

Morrison, T. (1993). *Playing in the dark: Whiteness and the literary imagination.* New York: Vintage.

Nakayama, T., & Krizek, R. (1995). Whiteness: A strategic rhetoric. *Quarterly Journal of Speech, 81,* 291–309.

O'Donnell, J., & Clark, C. (Eds.). (1999). *Becoming and unbecoming white: Owning and disowning a racial identity.* New York: Praeger.

Omi, M., & Winant, H. (1994). *Racial formation in the United States from the 1960s to the 1980s.* New York: Routledge.

Pfeil, F. (1997). *White guys: Studies in postmodern domination and difference.* New York: Verso.

Rasmussen, B. B., Nexica, I. J., Klinenberg, E., & Wray, M. (Eds.). (2001). *The making and unmaking of whiteness.* Raleigh, NC: Duke University Press.

Rich, A. (1995). Notes toward a politics of location. In A. Rich (Ed.), *Blood, bread, and poetry.* New York: W. W. Norton.

Rodriguez, N. M., &. Villaverde, L. E. (Eds.). (2000). *Dismantling white privilege: Pedagogy, politics, and whiteness.* New York: Peter Lang.

Roediger, D. (1994). *Towards the abolition of whiteness: Essays on race, politics, and working class history.* New York: Verso.

Roediger, D. (Ed.). (1999). *Black on white: Black writers on what it means to be white.* New York: Schocken.

Roediger, D. (2002). *Colored white: Transcending the racial past.* Berkeley, CA: University of California Press.

Roediger, D. (2007). *The wages of whiteness: Race and the making of the American working class.* New York: Verso

Rogin, M. P. (1998). *Black face, white noise: Jewish immigrants in the melting pot.* Berkeley, CA: University of California Press.

Sartwell, C. (1998). *Act like you know: African-American autobiography and white identity.* Chicago: University of Chicago Press.

Saxton, A. (2003). *The rise and fall of the white republic: Class politics and mass culture in nineteenth-century America.* New York: Verso.

Seshadri-Crooks, K. (2000). *Desiring whiteness: A Lacanian analysis of race.* New York: Routledge.

Sollors, W. (Ed.). (2000). *Interracialism: Black-white intermarriage in American history, literature, and law.* New York: Oxford University Press.

Stokes, M. (2001). *The color of sex: Whiteness, heterosexuality, and the fictions of white supremacy.* Durham, NC: Duke University Press.

Talbot, M. (1997, November 30). Getting credit for being white. *New York Times Magazine,* 147.

Traber, D. S. (2007). *Whiteness, otherness, and the individualism paradox from Huck to punk.* New York: Palgrave Macmillan.

Ware, V. (1992). *Beyond the pale: White women, racism, and history.* New York: Verso.

Ware, V., & Back, L. (2001). *Out of whiteness: Color, politics, and culture.* Chicago: University of Chicago Press.

Wiegman, R. (1999). Whiteness studies and the paradox of particularity. *Boundary 2, 26*(3), 115–150.

Williams, L. (2002). *Playing the race card: Melodramas of black and white from Uncle Tom to O. J. Simpson.* Cambridge, MA: Princeton University Press.

Winant, H. (1997, September/October). Behind blue eyes: Whiteness and contemporary U.S. racial politics. *New Left Review, 225,* 73–89.

Wise, T. (2007). *White like me: Reflections on race from a privileged son.* New York: Soft Skull.

Wong, L. M., Fine, M., Powell, L. C., & Weis, L. (Eds.). (1996). *Off white: Readings on race, power, and society.* New York: Routledge.

Wray, M., & Nevitz, A. (Eds.). (1996). *White trash: Race and class in America.* New York: Routledge.

Films

Blue-Eyed. (1996). Dir. Bertram Verhaag.

Color of Fear, The. (1995). Dir. Lee Mun Wah.

Dreamworlds3. (2007). Media Education Foundation.

Ethnic Notions. (1986). Dir. Marlon Riggs.

Family Name. (1998). Dir. Macky Alston.

Imitation of Life. (1932, 1934). Dir. John M. Stahl.

Jefferson's Blood. (2000). Prod. Thomas Lennon.

Pinky. (1949). Dir. Elia Kazan

Tim Wise on White Privilege: Racism, White Denial and the Costs of Inequality. (2008). Prod. Sut Jhally.

Other Topics

Myth and Media

Communication Studies Resources. University of Iowa: http://www.uiowa.edu/~commstud/resources

Cultural Studies Central: http://www.culturalstudies.net

Cultural Studies and Critical Theory: http://eserver.org/theory

Joseph Campbell Foundation: http://www.jcf.org

Journals and Cultural Studies Resources: http://www.maryflanagan.com/courses/journals.htm

Jung Page: http://www.cgjungpage.org

Mythic Resources: http://www.folkstory.com/resources.html

Myths, Dreams, and Symbols: Carl Jung: http://www.mythsdreamssymbols.com/carljung.html

Popcultures.com: http://www.popcultures.com

Religion, myth, and movies resources: http://www.lib.berkeley.edu/MRC/religionbib.html

Professional Organizations

American-Arab Anti-Discrimination Committee: www.adc.org

Asian American Journalist Association: www.aaja.org

Association of Hispanic Advertising Agencies: http://www.ahaa.org/

California Chicano News Media Association: http://www.ccnma.org/

Fairness and Accuracy in Reporting: www.fair.org/racism-desk

Hispanic Marketing & Communication Association: http://www.hmca.org/index.htm

The Maynard Institute for Journalism Education: www.maynardije.org

Race and Media: raceandmedia.com News Watch: newswatch.sfsu.edu

National Association of Black Journalists: www.nabj.org

National Association of Hispanic Journalists: www.nahj.org

National Council of La Raza: http://www.nclr.org/

Native American Journalist Association: www.naja.com

National Association of Latino Independent Producers: http://www.nalip.org/

National Latino Communications Center: http://clnet.ucla.edu/community/nlcc/

National Lesbian and Gay Journalists Association: http://www.nlgja.org/

Teaching about Difference and Diversity

Association of Women in Psychology: http://www.awpsych.org/

Ben Harper "Oppression"—see and hear on youtube: http://www.youtube.com/watch?v=C7-PEGo8o4

Boyhood studies: http://www.boyhoodstudies.com/

Cohen, J. (1999, October 1). Racism and mainstream media. Retrieved from http://www.fair.org/index.php?page=2527

Colorlines: colorlines.com

Diversity Web: http://www.diversityweb.org/

Facing History and Ourselves: http://www.facinghistory.org/campus/reslib.nsf

Feminist Law Professors: Sexism and the Media: Retrieved from http://feministlawprofs.law.sc.edu/?cat=21

Gender Public Advocacy Coalition: http://www.gpac.org/

Global War against Media Sexism: Retrieved from http://www.medialit.org/reading_room/article450.html

International Guide to Literature on Masculinity: http://www.mensstudies.info/RMBP.html

Media Portrayals of Men & Masculinity: http://www.media-awareness.ca/english/issues/stereotyping/men_and_masculinity/index.cfm

Men & Gender Issues: http://www.xyonline.net/

The Men's Bibliography: http://mensbiblio.xyonline.net/

National Center for Transgender Equality: http://www.nctequality.org/

National Coalition on Racism and National Sports: http://www.aimovement.org/ncrsm/

National Organization for women: http://now.org/

New America Media: Expanding the news lens through ethnic media: http://news.newamerica-media.org/news/

Post September 11 resources: www.griid.org/terrorism.shtml

The Psychology of Prejudice:http://www.understandingprejudice.org/apa/english/page11.htm

Race, racism, and the law: http://academic.udayton.edu/race/

Race—The Power of an Illusion: http://www.pbs.org/race/000_General/000_00-Home.htm

Racism and Psychology: http://www.apa.org/pi/oema/racism/homepage.html

Racism in Europe, Australia, Africa, Immigration, Globalization: http://www.globalissues.org/HumanRights/Racism.asp

Racism in the Media: http://www.media-awareness.ca/english/resources/articles/diversity/racism_media.cfm

Racism Watch/Znet: www.zmag.org/racewatch/racewatch.htm

Social Identity Theory: http://www.tcw.utwente.nl/theorieenoverzicht/Theory%20clusters/Interpersonal%20Communication%20and%20Relations/Social_Identity_Theory.doc/

Topics in Feminism: http://plato.stanford.edu/entries/feminism-topics/

Transgender Law Center: http://www.transgenderlawcenter.org/

Understanding Stereotypes: http://school.discoveryeducation.com/lessonplans/programs/stereotypes/

Universal Declaration of Human Rights: http://www.un.org/Overview/rights.html

Social Class

Internet

Applied Research Center: http://www.arc.org/

Center for Third World Organizing: http://www.ctwo.org/

Center for Women Policy Studies: www.centerwomenpolicy.org

Class Action: Building Bridges Across Class Divides: http://www.classism.org/

Class Matters: http://www.classmatters.org/

Feminist theory Website: http://www.cddc.vt.edu/feminism/

Gretchen Wilson. Official Web site: http://www.gretchenwilson.com/

Institute on Race and Poverty: http://www.irpumn.org/

People like us. Public Television: http://www.pbs.org/peoplelikeus/

Pew Research Center Social and Demographic Trends. Report: Inside the Middle Class: http://pewsocialtrends.org/pubs/706/middle-class-poll

Poverty Race Research Action Council: http://www.prrac.org/

Racial Wealth Divide: http://www.faireconomy.org/issues/racial_wealth_divide

Southern Poverty Law Center: splcenter.org

Women of Country: http://www.womenofcountry.com/

Readings

Adams, R., Brewer, R., Leondar-Wright, B., Lui, M., & Robles, B. (2006). *The color of wealth: How government actions widen the racial wealth divide.* New York: The New Press.

Aldrich, N. W., Jr. (1988). *Old money: The mythology of America's upper class.* New York: Alfred A. Knopf.

Alters, D. (2003). We hardly watch that rude, crude show: Class and taste in '*The Simpsons*.' In C. Stabile & M. Harrison (Eds.), *Prime time animation: Television animation and American culture.* New York: Routledge.

Amott, T., & Matthaei, J. (1991). *Race gender and work: A multicultural economic history of the women in the United States.* Boston: South End.

Andersen, M. L., & Taylor, H. F. (2005). *Sociology: Understanding a diverse society* (4th ed.). Belmont, CA: Wadsworth.

Anderson, C. (1994). *Black labor White wealth: The search for power and economic justice.* Edgewood, MD: Duncan & Duncan.

Anthias, F., & Yuval-Davis, N. (in association with Harriet Cain). (1993). *Racialized boundaries: Race, nation, gender, colour and class and the anti-racist struggle.* New York: Routledge.

Bell, D. (1992). *Faces at the bottom of the well: The permanence of racism.* New York: Harper Collins.

Benedict, H. (1992). *Virgin or vamp: How the press covers sex crimes.* New York: Oxford.

Berk, L. (1977). The great middle American dream machine. *Journal of Communication, 27*(3), 27–31.

Brooks, D. (2001). *Bobos in paradise: The new upper class and how they got there.* New York: Touchstone.

Brunsdon, C., D'Acci, J., & Spigel, L. (Ed.). (1997). *Feminist television criticism: A reader.* New York: Oxford.

Buis, K. (2007, June). Mrs. Trollope's America. *Vanity Fair.* Retrieved from http://www.vanityfair.com/magazine/2007/06/essay_winner200706

Butsch, R. (1995). Ralph, Fred, Archie and Homer: Why television keeps recreating the white male working-class buffoon. In G. Dines & J. M. Humez (Eds.), *Gender, race and class in media: A text-reader.* Thousand Oaks, CA: Sage.

Butsch, R. (2000). *The making of American audiences.* Cambridge: Cambridge University Press.

Carnoy, M. (1994). *Faded dreams: The politics and economics of race in America.* New York: Cambridge University Press.

Carter, C., Branston, G., & Allan, S. (Ed.). (1998). *News, gender and power.* New York: Routledge.

Chafel, J. A. (1995). Children's conceptions of poverty. *Advances in Early Education Day Care, 7,* 27–57.

Chafel, J. A. (1997). Societal images of poverty: Child and adult beliefs. *Youth & Society, 28*(4), 432–463.

Cole, H. (1999). *How to be: Contemporary etiquette for African Americans.* New York: Simon & Schuster.

Coleman, J. (1965). *Adolescents and the schools.* New York: Basic.

Collins, P. H. (1990). *Black feminist thought: Knowledge, consciousness, and the politics of empowerment.* London: Harper Collins.

Conley, D. (1999). *Being Black, living in the red: Race, wealth and social policy.* Los Angeles: University of California Press.

Croizet, J.-C., & Claire, T. (1998). Extending the concept of stereotype threat to social class: The intellectual underperformance of students from low socioeconomic backgrounds. *Personality & Social Psychology Bulletin, 24*(6), 588–594.

Crouch, S. (2008, December 19). The hip-hop inauguration. *The Daily Beast.* Retrieved from http://www.thedailybeast.com/blogs-and-stories/2008-12-19/the-hip-hop-inauguration/2/

Davis, A. (1990). *Women, culture, politics.* New York: Vintage.

De Santis, S. (1999). *Life on the line: One woman's tale of work, sweat, and survival.* New York: Doubleday.

Deloria, V., & Lytle, C. M., (1984). *The nations within: Past and future of American sovereignty.* Austin, TX: University of Texas Press.

DeMott, B. (1992). *The imperial middle: Why Americans can't think straight about class.* New Haven, CT: Yale.

DeMott, B. (1996). *Created equal: Reading and writing about class in America.* New York: Harper Collins.

Diamond, I., & Quimby, L. (Eds.). (1988). *Feminism and Foucault: Reflections on Resistance.* Boston: Northeastern University Press.

Domhoff, G. W. (2002). *Who rules America? Power and politics.* New York: McGraw-Hill.

Ehrenreich, B. (2001). *Nickel and dimed: On (not) getting by in America.* New York: Metropolitan.

Ellison, C. W. (1995). *Country music culture: From hard times to heaven.* Jackson, MS: University of Mississippi Press.

Espiritu, Y. L. (1997). *Asian American women and men.* Thousand Oaks, CA: Sage.

Feagin, J. R. (2001). *Racist America: Roots, current realities, & future reparations.* New York: Routledge.

Feagin, J. R., Vera, H., & Batur, P. (1995). *White racism: The basics.* New York: Routledge.

Frank, R. (1998). *Luxury fever: Why money fails to satisfy in an era of excess.* New York: Free Press.

Franklin, R. S. (1991). *Shadows of race and class.* Minneapolis, MN: University of Minnesota Press.

Fussell, P. (1992). *Class: A guide through the American status system.* New York: Touchstone.

Gilbert, C., & Quinn, E. (2000). *Homecoming: The story of African-American farmers.* Boston: Beacon.

Glenn, E. N. (2002). *Unequal freedom: How race and gender shaped American citizenship and labor.* Cambridge, MA: Harvard University Press.

Goad, J. (1999). *The redneck manifesto, America's scapegoats: How we got that way and why we're not going to take it anymore.* New York: Simon & Schuster.

Goldfield, M. (1997). *The color of politics: Race and the mainspring of American politics.* New York: New Press.

Gonzalez, J. (2000). *Harvest of empire: A history of Latinos in America.* New York: Viking.

Gose, E. (1997). *Color-blind (seeing beyond race in a race-obsessed world).* New York: Harper Collins.

Graham, L. O. (2000). *Our kind of people: Inside America's Black upper class.* New York: Harper Perennial

Greenwood, J. T. (2001). *Bittersweet legacy: The Black and White "better classes" in Charlotte, 1850–1910.* Durham, NC: University of North Carolina Press.

Hartman, C. (Ed.). (1997). *Double exposure: Poverty and race in America.* Armonk, New York: M.E. Sharpe.

Holtzman, L. (2000). *Media messages.* New York: M.E. Sharpe.

hooks, b. (1981). *Ain't I a woman? Black women and feminism.* Boston: South End.

hooks, b. (2000). *Where we stand: Class matters.* New York: Routledge.

James, J. & Farmer, R. (Eds.). (1993). *Spirit, space and survival: African American women in (white) academe.* New York: Routledge.

Jennings, J. (Ed.). (1994). *Blacks, Latinos, and Asians in urban America: Status and prospects for politics and activism.* New York: Praeger.

Kennedy, L. (2005, May). Commentary: Music, social justice, and market manipulations. An interview with Professor Tricia Rose. *Fish Rap.* Retrieved from http://www.triciarose.com/commentary_fishrap.shtml

Kitch, S. L. (1994). Straight but not narrow: A gynetic approach to the teaching of lesbian literature. In L. Garber (Ed.), *Tilting the tower: Lesbians/teaching/queer subjects* (pp. 83–95). New York: Routledge.

Kotlowitz, A. (1992). *There are no children here: The story of two boys growing up in the other America.* New York: Anchor.

Kozol, J. (1992). *Savage inequalities: Children in America's schools.* New York: Harper Perennial.

Lakoff, G. (2002). *Moral politics: How liberals and conservatives think.* Chicago: University of Chicago Press.

Lamont, M. (19982). *Money, morals, & manners: The culture of the French and the American upper-middle class.* Chicago: University of Chicago Press.

Leahy, R. L. (1983). Development of the conception of economic inequality: Explanations, justifications, and concepts of social mobility and change. *Developmental Psychology, 19*(1), 111–125.

Levine, L. W. (1990). *Highbrow lowbrow: The emergence of cultural hierarchy in America.* Cambridge, MA: Harvard University Press.

Lipsitz, G. (1998). *The possessive investment in Whiteness: How White people profit from identity politics.* Philadelphia: Temple University Press.

Lott, B. (2002). Cognitive and behavioral distancing from the poor. *American Psychologist, 57*(2), 100–110.

Lydon, C. (2008, December). Race and class: Hip-hop. Open Source with Christopher Lydon [Radio program]. Retrieved from http://www.radioopensource.org/race-and-class-hip-hop/

Lynes, R. (1954). *The tastemakers.* New York: Grosset & Dunlap.

Marable, M. (2000). *How capitalism underdeveloped Black America.* 2nd Ed. Cambridge, MA: South End.

Martinez, E. (1998). *De colores means all of us?: Latina views for a multi-colored century.* Cambridge, MA: South End.

Menchaca, M. (2002). *Recovering history, constructing race: The Indian, Black, and White roots of Mexican Americans.* Austin, TX: University of Texas Press.

Meyers, M. (1997). *News coverage of violence against women.* Thousand Oaks, CA: Sage.

Morritt, H. (1997). *Women and computer based technologies: A feminist perspective.* New York: University Press of America.

Moss, K. (2003). *The color of class: Poor whites and the paradox of privilege.* Pittsburgh: University of Pennsylvania Press.

Oliver, M. L. & Shapiro, T. M. (1995). *Black wealth/White wealth: A new perspective on racial inequality.* New York: Routledge.

Otis, G. L. (1999). *Our kind of people: Inside America's black upper class.* New York: Harper Collins.

Parenti, M. (1993). *Land of idols: Political mythology in America.* New York: St. Martin's Press.

Parker, G. M. (1997). *Trespassing: My sojourn in the halls of privilege.* Boston: Houghton Mifflin.

Queenan, J. (1998). *Red Lobster, White Trash, and the Blue Lagoon: Joe Queenan's America.* New York: Hyperion.

Robinson, R. (2000). *The debt: What America owes Blacks.* New York: Dutton.

Rodriguez, R. (1983). *Hunger of memory: The education of Richard Rodriguez.* New York: Bantam.

Roediger, D. (1991). *The wages of Whiteness: Race and the making of the American working class.* London: Verso.

Roediger, D. (1994). *Toward the abolition of Whiteness.* London: Verso.

Rose, M. (1989). *Lives on the boundary.* New York: Macmillan.

Ross, S. J. (1998). *Working-class Hollywood: Silent film and the shaping of class in America.* Princeton, N.J.: Princeton University Press.

Rymer, R. (2000). *American Beach: How progress robbed a black town (and nation) of history, wealth, and power.* New York: Harper Perennial.

Sayles, G. P. (1992). *How to marry the rich.* Berkeley, CA: Berkley.

Sayles, G. P. (1999). *How to meet the rich.* Berkeley, CA: Berkley.

Sennett, R., & Cobb, J. (1972). *The hidden injuries of class.* New York: Vintage.

Shapiro, T. (2004). *The hidden cost of being African American: How wealth perpetuates inequality.* New York: Oxford University Press.

Takaki, R. (1993). *A different mirror: A history of multicultural America.* Boston, MA: Little Brown.

Terkel, S. (1997). *Working: People talk about what they do all day and how they feel about what they do.* New York: New Press.

Thompson, B. (2001). *A promise and a way of life: White anti-racist activism.* Minneapolis, MN: University of Minnesota.

Veblen, T. (1994). *The theory of the leisure class.* New York: Penguin.

Ware, V. (1994). *Beyond the Pale: White women, racism and history.* London: Verso.

Weiss, M. J. (1994). *Latitudes & attitudes: An atlas of American tastes, trends, politics, and passions.* New York: Little Brown.

Wilson, W. J. (1999). *The bridge over the racial divide: Rising inequality and coalition politics.* Berkeley, CA: University of California Press.

Woods, T. A., Costes-Kurtz, B., & Rowley, S. J. (2005). The development of stereotypes about the rich and poor: Age, race, and family income differences in beliefs. *Journal of Youth and Adolescence, 34*(5), 437–445.

Wray, M., & Newitz, A. (Eds.). (1997). *White trash: Race and class in America.* New York: Routledge.

Zweig, M. (2000). *The working class majority: America's best kept secret.* Ithaca, NY: Cornell University Press.

Films

1900. (1976). Dir. Bernardo Bertolucci.

A Civil Action. (1998). Dir. Steven Zaillian.

A Raisin in the Sun. (1989). Dir. Bill Duke.

A Woman Called Moses. (1978). Dir. Paul Wendkos.

Adventures of Robin Hood, The. (1938). Dirs. Michael Curtiz and William Keighley.

Amistad. (1997). Dir. Steven Spielberg.

Antitrust. (2000). Dir. Peter Howitt.

At Play in the Fields of the Lord. (1991). Dir. Hector Babenco.

Ballad of Gregorio Cortez. (1983). Dir. Robert M. Young.

Barbarians at the Gate. (1993). Dir. Glenn Jordan.

Bastard Out of Carolina. (1997). Dir. Anjelica Huston.

Battle of Algiers. (1966). Dir. Gillo Pontecorvo.

Beloved. (1998). Dir. Jonathan Demme.

Blue Collar. (1978). Dir. Paul Schrader.

Bob Roberts. (1992). Dir. Tim Robbins.

Bopha! (1993). Dir. Morgan Freeman. .

Born in Flames. (1983). Dir. Lizzie Borden.

Born on the Fourth of July. (1989). Dir. Oliver Stone.

Bowling for Columbine. (2002). Dir. Michael Moore.

Braveheart. (1995). Dir. Mel Gibson.

Bread and Chocolate. (1974). Dir. Franco Brusati.

Breaker Morant. (1980).Dir. Bruce Beresford.

Breaking Away. (1979). Dir. Peter Yates.

Broadcast News. (1987). Dir. James L. Brooks.

Bulworth. (1998). Dir. Warren Beatty.

Cabaret. (1972). Dir. Bob Fosse.

Cabeza de Vaca. (1990). Dir. Nicolas Echevarria.

Cadillac Man. (1990). Dir. Roger Donaldson. (Car sales).

Casa de los Babys. (2003). Dir. John Sayles.

Casualties of War. (1989). Dir. Brian de Palma.

Chicken Run. (2000). Dirs. Peter Lord and Nick Park.

Chinatown. (1974). Dir. Roman Polanski.

Citizen Ruth. (1996). Dir. Alexander Payne.

Coal Miner's Daughter. (1980). Dir. Michael Apted. (coal mining, singer).

*Cocktail. (*1988). Dir. Robert Donaldson. (Bartender).

Convoy. (1978). Dir. Sam Peckinpah (Truckers).

Corn Is Green, The. (1945). Dr.: Irving Rapport. (Coal miners).

Country Boys. (2006). Dir. David Sutherland.

Cradle Will Rock. (1999). Dir. Tim Robbins. (Nanny).

Crooklyn. (1994). Dir. Spike Lee. (Musician and teacher).

Deadly Business. (1986). Dir. John Korty.

**Deadly Deception: General Electric, Nuclear Weapons, and Our Environment.* (1991). Dir. Debra Chasnoff.

Death of a Salesman. (1951). Dir. Laslo Benedek; (1985). Dir. Volker Schlondorff.

Dodes 'ka-den. (1970). Dir. Akira Kurosawa.

Driving Miss Daisy. (1989). Dir. Bruce Beresford.

El Norte. (1983). Dir. Gregory Nava.

Erin Brockovitch. (2000). Dir. Steven Soderbergh.

Follow Me Home. (1997). Dir. Peter Bratt.

Frankie and Johnny. (1991). Dir. Gary Marshall. (Cook and waitress).

Freedom Song. (2000). Dir. Phil Alden Robinson.

Full Monty, The. (1997). Dir. Peter Cattaneo. (Unemployed steel workers).

Gandhi. (1982). Dir. Richard Attenborough.

Glengarry Glen Ross. (1992). Dir. James Foley. (Real estate sales).

Gosford Park. (2001). Dir. Richard Altman.

Grapes of Wrath. (1940). Dir. John Ford.

Gung Ho. (1986). Dir.: Ron Howard. (Autoworkers).

Harlan County, U.S.A. (1976). Dir. Barbara Kopple.

Heat and Dust. (1983). Dir. James Ivory.

Hoop Dreams. (1994). Dir. Steve James.

Incident at Oglala: The Leonard Peltier Story. (1992). Dir. Michael Apted.

Jack and the Beanstalk: The Real Story. (2001). Dir. Brian Henson.

JFK. (1991). Dir. Oliver Stone.

Julia. (1977). Dir. Fred Zinnemann.

La Misma Luna/Under the Same Moon. (2008). Dir. Patricia Riggen.

Lagaan: Once upon a Time in India. (2001). Dir. Ashutosh Gowariker.

Lakota Woman: Siege at Wounded Knee. (1994). Dir. Frank Pierson.

Les Miserables. (1935). Dir. Richard Boleslawski.

Les Miserables. (1978). Dir. Glenn Jordan.

Les Miserables. (1995). Dir. Claude Lelouch.

Life or Debt. (2002). Dir. Stephanie Black.

Lone Star. (1995). Dir. John Sayles.

Los Olvidados/ The Young and the Damned (1950). Dir. Luis Bunuel.

Lumumba. (2001). Dir. Raoul Peck.

Malcolm X. (1992). Dir. Spike Lee.

Marie. (1985). Dir. Roger Donaldson.

Matewan. (1987). Dir. John Sayles.

Milagro Beanfield War. (1988). Dir. Robert Redford.

Missing. (1982). Dir. Costa-Gavras.

Modern Times. (1936). Dir. Charlie Chaplin.

Mr. Holland's Opus. (1995). Dir. Stephen Herek. (Teacher).

Mystic Pizza. (1988). Dir. Donald Petrie. (Waitresses).

Newsies. (1992). Dir. Kenny Ortega.

Nine to Five. (1980). Dir. Colin Higgins.

Norma Rae. (1979). Dir. Martin Ritt.

Northern Lights. (1979). Dirs. John Hanson, Rob Nilsson, and Jim Hanson.

Organizer, The. (1964). Dir. Mario Monicelli.

Panther. (1995). Dir. Mario Van Peebles.

Philadelphia. (1993). Dir. Jonathan Demme.

Quiet American. (2003). Dir. Phillip Noyce.

Rabbit Proof Fence. (2002). Dir. Phillip Noyce.

Reds. (1981). Dir. Warren Beatty.

Roger and Me. (1989). Dir. Michael Moore.

Romero. (1989). Dir. John Duigan.

Roots. (1977). Dirs. Marvin J. Chomsky and John Erman.

Rosewood. (1997). Dir. John Singleton.

Salaam Bombay! (1988). Dir. Mira Nair.

Sally Hemings: An American Scandal. (2000). Dir. Charles Haid.

Salt of the Earth. (1954). Dir. Herbert J. Biberman.

Salvador. (1986). Dir. Oliver Stone.

Sankofa. (1993). Dir. Haile Gerima.

School Ties. (1992). Dir. Robert Mandel.

Separate but Equal. (1991.) Dir. George Stevens, Jr.

Silkwood. (1983). Dir. Mike Nichols.

Sounder. (1972). Dir. Martin Ritt.

Spartacus. (1960). Dir. Stanley Kubrick. *Spartacus.* (1960).

Spitfire Grill. (1996). Dir. Lee David Zlotoff. (Diner cook).

State of Siege. (1973). Dir. Costa-Gavras.

Stonewall. (1995). Dir. Nigel Finch.

Strike. (1924). Dir. Sergei Eisenstein.

Swing Shift. (1984). Dir. Jonathan Demme. (Aircraft workers).

Take This Job and Shove It. (1981). Dir. Gus Trikonis. (Brewery worker).

Taxi Driver. (1976). Dir.: Martin Scorsese (taxi driver, waitress, prostitute).

Adventures of Robin Hood, The. (1938). Dirs. Michael Curtiz and William Keighley.

The Bee Movie. (2007). Dirs. Steve Hickner and Simon J. Smith. Animated film. Useful for
Marxist analyses.

The Bicycle Thief. (1949). Dir. Vittorio De Sica. (working class Italian).

**The Big One.* (1998). Dir. Michael Moore.

The Burning Season. (1994). Dir. John Frankenheimer.

The China Syndrome. (1979). Dir. James Bridges.

The Insider. (1999). Dir. Michael Mann.

The Killing Floor. (1985). Dir. Bill Duke.

The Long Walk Home. (1989). Dir. Richard Pearce.

The Nasty Girl. (1990). Dir. Michael Verhoeven.

Organizer, The. (1964). Dir. Mario Monicelli.

The Revolution Will Not Be Televised. (2003). Dirs. Kim Bartley and Donnacha O'Briain.

The Ruling Class. (1972). Dir. Peter Medak.

The Triangle Factory Fire Scandal. (1979). Dir. Mel Stuart.

The Ugly American. (1963). Dir. George Englund.

The War at Home. (1996). Dir. Emilio Estevez.

This Boy's Life. (1993). Dir. Michael Caton-Jones.

Thousand Pieces of Gold. (1991). Dir. Nancy Kelly.

Three Kings. (1999). Dir. David O. Russell.

Tin Men. (1987). Dir. Barry Levinson. (Aluminum siding sales).

Titanic. (1997). Dir. James Cameron.

Traffic. (2000). Dir. Steven Soderbergh.

Ulee's Gold. (1997). Dir. Vincent Nune. (Bee keeping).

Viva Zapata! (1952). Biography of Mexican revolutionary Emiliano Zapata.

Wag the Dog. (1997). Dir. Barry Levinson. *Wag the Dog.* (1997).

Wall Street. (1987). Dir. Oliver Stone. (Stock trading).

When the Levees Broke. (2006): Dir. Spike Lee. Documentary on New Orleans and Hurricane Katrina.

Working Girls. (1986). Dir. Lizzie Borden. (Prostitution).

Working Girl. (1988). Dir. Mike Nichols. (Secretary, White-collar office).

Z. (1969). Dir. Costa-Gavras.

Zoot Suit. (1981). Dir. Luis Valdez.

Immigration

Internet

American Friends Service Committee http://www.afsc.org/immigrants-rights/

Family Violence Prevention Fund: Immigrant & Refugee Women's Rights Project. http://www.endabuse.org/programs/immigrant/

Human Trafficking: A Hidden Shame http://www.endabuse.org/programs/display.php3?DocID=359

Immigration Solidarity Network http://www.immigrantsolidarity.org

Immigration Statistics by State http://www.gcir.org/about_immigration/usmap.htm

National Immigration Law Center http://www.nilc.org/

National Organizations for Immigrant Rights

Public Eye Immigrants' Rights Activist Kit http://www.publiceye.org/ark/immigrants/im_main.html

Readings

Anzaldúa, G. (1987). *Borderlands/La frontera: The new mestiza.* San Francisco: Aunt Lute

Bender, S. W. (2003). *Greasers and gringos: Latinos, law, and the American imagination.* New York: NYU Press.

Cambridge, V. C. (2005). *Immigration diversity and broadcasting in the U.S., 1990–2001.* Athens, OH: Ohio University Press.

Chavez, L. R. (2001). *Covering immigration: Popular images and the politics of the nation.* Berkeley, CA: University of California Press.

Craig, A. L. (1981). *Mexican immigration: Changing terms of the debate in the United States.* San Diego: University of California.

Ono, K.A., & Sloop, J. M. (2002). *Shifting borders: Rhetoric, Immigration, and California's Proposition 187.* Philadelphia: Temple University Press.

Santa, Ana, O. (2002). *Brown tide rising: Metaphors of Latinos in contemporary public discourse.* Austin, TX: University of Texas Press.

Simon. R. J., & Alexander, S. H. (1993). *The ambivalent welcome: Print media, public opinion and immigration.* New York: Praeger.

Skeldon, R. (1994). *Reluctant exiles? Migration from Hong Kong and the new overseas Chinese.* Armonk NY: M.E. Sharpe.

Soderlund, M. (2007). The role of news media in shaping and transforming the public perception of Mexican immigration and the laws involved. *Law and Psychology Review*, 31, 167–178.

Soruco, G. R. (1996). *Cubans and the mass media in South Florida.* Gainesville, FL: University Press of Florida.

Films

32nd Street (2007). Dir. Michael Kang; written by Michael Kang & Edmund Lee.

A Day Without a Mexican (2004). ("Mockumentary"). Dir. Sergio Arau.

A Slim Peace (2007). Dir. Yael Luttwak .

ABCD (2001). Dir. Krutin Patel.

America, America (1963). Dir. Elia Kazan.

An American Tale (1986). (Animation). Dir. Don Bluth.

Avalon (1990). Dir. Barry Levinson.

Bend It Like Beckham (2002). Dir. Gurinder Chadha.

**Beyond Belief* (2007). Dir. Beth Murphy.

Born in East L.A. (1987). Dir. Cheech Marin.

Bread and Roses (2000). Dir. Ken Loach.

Bride and Prejudice (2004) (Bollywood version).

Catfish in Black Bean Sauce (1999). Dir. Chi Moui Lo.

Combination Platter (1993). Dir. Tony Chen.

Coming to America (1988). Dir. John Landis.

Crossing Arizona (2005). (Documentary). Dir. Joseph Mathew.

**De Nadie* (2005). Dir. Tin Dirdamal.

Dim Sum: A Little Bit of Heart (1985). Dir. Wayne Wang.

Dirty Pretty Things (2003). Dir. Steven Knight.

Do££ar Dream$ (2000). Dir. Sekhar Kammula.

East Is East (1999). Dir. Damien O'Donnell.

Eat a Bowl of Tea (1989). Dir. Wayne Wong.

El Norte (1983). Dir. Gregory Nava.

Eve and the Fire Horse (2005). Dir. Julia Kwan.

Everything Is Illuminated (2005). Dir. Liev Schreiber.

Far and Away (1992). Dir. Ron Howard.

Flavors (2003). Dir. Raj Nidimoru & Krishna DK.

Forging a Nation (2007). Dir. David Blaustein.

French Kiss (1995). Dir. Lawrence Kasden.

Game 6 (2005). Dir. Michael Hoffman.

Gangs of New York (2002). Dir. Martin Scorsese.

The Gatekeeper (2004). Dir. John Carlos Frey.

God Grew Tired of Us (2006). Dir. Christopher Quinn.

The Godfather, Part I, II, III (1974) Dir. Francis Ford Coppola.

**Golden Venture* (2006). Dir. Peter Cohn.

Green Card (1990). Dir. Peter Weir.

Green Card Fever (2003). Dir. Bala Rajasekharuni.

The Guru (2002). Dir. Daisy von Scherler Mayer.

Heaven and Earth (1993). Dir. Oliver Stone.

House of Sand and Fog (2003). Dir. Vadim Perelman.

Household Saints (1993). Dir. Nancy Savoca.

Hyderabad Blues (1998). Dir. Nagesh Kukunoor.

I Remember Mama (1948). Dir. George Stevens.

The Immigrant (1917). Dir. Charlie Chaplin.

The Immigrant Garden (2001). Dir. C. Tad Devlin.

In America (2003). Dir. Jim Sheridan.

In Between Days (2006). Dir. So Yong Kim.

The Journey (1997). Dir. Harish Saluja.

The Joy Luck Club (1993). Dir. Wayne Wang.

The Keeper: The Legend of Omar Khayyam (2005). Dir. Kayvan Mashayekh.

The Kite Runner (2007). Dir. Marc Forster.

La Ciudad (The City) (1999). (Documentary). Dir. David Riker.

La Tragedia de Macario (2005). Dir. Pablo Véliz.

Lana's Rain (2003. Dir. Michael Ojeda.

Living on Tokyo Time (1987). Dir. Steven Okazaki.

Lone Star (1996). Dir. John Sayles.

**Lost Boys of Sudan* (2003).

The Mambo Kings (1992). Dir. Arne Glimcher.

Maria Full of Grace (Maria Ilena eres de Gracia) (2004). Dir. Joshua Marston.

Masala (1993). Dir. Srinivas Krishna.

Mississippi Masala (1992). Dir. Mira Nair .

Monsoon Wedding (2000). Dir. Mira Nair.

Moscow on the Hudson (1984). Dir. Paul Mazursky.

Music in My Heart (1940). Joseph Santley.

My Big Fat Greek Wedding (2002). Dir. Joel Zwick.

My Family (1995). Dir. Gregory Nava.

My Girl Tisa (1948). Dir. Elliott Nugent.

The Namesake (2006). Dir. Mira Nair.

Never Forever (2007). Dir. Gina Kim.

Night of Henna (2005). Dir. Hassin Zee.

Nybyggarna (The New Land) (1972). Dir. Jan Troell.

The Paper Wedding (1990). Dir. Michel Brault.

The Party (1968). Dir. Blake Edwards.

The Perez Family (1995) Dir. Mira Nair.

Pedro Nuestro (2007). Dir. Christopher Zalla.

Pieces of April (2003). Dir. Peter Hedges.

Popi (1969). Dir. Arthur Hiller.

Quinceañera (2005). Dir. Wash Westmoreland & Richard Glatzer.

Real Women Have Curves (2002). Dir. Patricia Cardoso.

Romántico (2005). Dir. Mark Becker.

Saving Face (2004). Dir. Alice Wu.

**Sentenced Home* (2007). Dir. Nicole Newnham.

Sophie's Choice (1982). Dir. Alan J. Pakula.

Spanglish (2004). Dir. James L. Brooks.

**Spellbound* (2002). Dir. Jeffrey Blitz.

Stand and Deliver (1988). Dir. Ramon Menendez.

Stranger Than Paradise (1984). Dir. Jim Jarmusch.

Sueño (2005). Dir. Renee Chabria.

Sweet Land (2006). Dir. Ali Salim.

The Terminal (2004). Dir. Steven Spielberg.

The Three Burials of Melquiades Estrada (2005). Dir. Tommy Lee Jones.

The Wedding Banquet (1993). Dir. Ang Lee.

Tortilla Soup (2000). Dir. Maria Ripoll.

Under the Same Moon (La misma luna). (2007). Dir. Patricia Riggen.

Utvandrarna (The Emigrants) (1971). Dir. Jan Troell.

West Side Story (1961). Dir. Robert Wise & Jerome Robbins.

Women and Appearance

Black Narcissus. (1946). Dirs. Michael Powell & Emeric Pressburger.

Breakfast Club. (1985). Dir. John Hughes.

Breakfast at Tiffany's. (1961). Dir. Blake Edwards.

Bride of Frankenstein. (1935). Dir. James Whale.

Butterfield 8. (1960). Dir. Daniel Mann.

Dangerous Liaisons. (1988). Dir. Stephen Frears.

Dishonored. (1931). Dir. Josef von Sternberg.

How to Marry a Millionare. (1953). Dir. Jean Negulesco.

The Ice Storm. (1997). Dir. Ang Lee.

La Cage aux Folles. (1978). Edouard Molinaro.

La Femme Nikita. (1990). Dir. Luc Besson.

Lifeboat. (1944). Dir. Alfred Hitchcock.

Lipstick. (1976). Dir. Lamont Johnson.

Postman Always Rings Twice. (1946). Dir. Tay Garnett.

Rocky Horror Picture Show. (1975). Dir. Jim Sharman.

Some like It hot. (1959). Dir. Billy Wilder.

The Three Faces of Eve. (1957). Dir. Nunnally Johnson.

Tootsie. (1982). Dir. Sydney Pollack.

Internet

About-Face.org. http://www.about-face.org/

Commercial closet. www.commercialcloset.org

Feminism Online. http://home.wanadoo.nl/~vidabo/FeminismOn-Line.html

Feminista. www.feminista.com/issues/

Genderads.com http://www.genderads.com/

What is sexism in advertising? http://web.cortland.edu/russellk/courses/prjdis/html/usmsxobj.htm

Women's bodies in sports ads. http://www.lclark.edu/~soan370/

Readings

Andersen, A. E. & DiDomenico, L. (1992). Diet vs. shape content of popular male and female magazines: A dose-response relationship to the incidence of eating disorders? *International Journal of Eating Disorders, 11*(3).

Austin, E. W., Roberts, D. F., & Nass, C. I. (1990). Influences of family communication on children's television-interpretation processes. *Communication Research, 17*(4), 545–564.

Baker, D, Sivyer, R., & Towell, T. (1998). Body image dissatisfaction and eating attitudes in visually impaired women. *International Journal of Eating Disorders, 24* (3), 319–322.

Becker, A. E., & Hamburg, P. (1996). Culture, the media, and eating disorders. *Harvard Review of Psychiatry, 4.*

Browne Graves, S. (1993). Television, the portrayal of African Americans, and the development of children's attitudes. In G. L. Berry & J. Keiko Asamen. (Eds.), *Children & television: Images in a changing sociocultural world* (p.p. 179–190). Newbury Park, CA Sage.

Comstock, G. & Strasburger, V. (1990). Deceptive appearances: Television violence and aggressive behavior. *Journal of Adolescent Health Care, 11,* 31–44.

Crouch, A., & Degelman, D. Influence of female body images in printed advertising on self-ratings of physical attractiveness by adolescent girls. *Perceptual & Motor Skills, 87* (2), 585–586.

Cusumano, D. & Thompson, J. K. (1997). Body image and body shape ideals in magazines: Exposure, awareness, and internalization. *Sex Roles, 37*(9/10).

Dietz, Tracy L. (1998). An examination of violence and gender role portrayals in video games: Implications for gender socialization and aggressive behavior. *Sex Roles, 38*(5/6), 425–442.

Dines, G., Jensen, R. & Russo, A. (Eds.) (1998). *Pornography: The production and consumption of inequality.* New York: Routledge.

Durkin, K. & Nugent, B. (1998). Kindergarten children's gender-role expectations for television actors. *Sex Roles, 38*(5/6), 387–402.

Gerbner, G., Gross, L., Morgan, M., & Signorielli, N. (1994). Growing up with television: The cultivation perspective. In J. Bryant & D. Zillmann (Eds.), *Media effects: Advances in theory and research* (p. 17–41). Hillsdale, NJ: Lawrence Erlbaum.

Gilbert, K. (1998). The body, young children and popular culture (pp. 55–71). In N. Yelland (Ed.), *Gender in early childhood.* New York: Routledge.

Grogan, S., Williams, Z., & Conner, M. (1996). The effects of viewing same-gender photographic models on body-esteem. *Psychology of Women Quarterly, 20* (4).

Guillen, E. O., & Barr, S. I. (1994). Nutrition, dieting, and fitness messages in a magazine for adolescent women, 1970–1990. *Journal of Adolescent Health, 15* (6), 464–472.

Harrison, K. (1997). Does interpersonal attraction to thin media personalities promote eating disorders? *Journal of Broadcasting & Electronic Media, 41.*

Harrison, K. & Cantor, J. (1997). The relationship between media consumption and eating disorders. *Journal of Communication,* 47 (1).

Hartung, L. (1997). Disordered eating patterns in relation to gender in the college environment. *Journal of the Am Diet Assoc, 97*(9), A-60.

Heilman, E. (1998). The struggle for self: Power and identity in adolescent girls. *Youth & Society, 30* (2), 182–208.

Heinberg, L. J., & Thompson, J. K. (1995). Body image and televises images of thinness and attractiveness: A controlled laboratory study. *Journal of Social and Clinical Psychology, 14*(4), 325–338.

Henderson-King, E., & Henderson-King, D. (1997). Media effects on women's body esteem: Social and individual difference factors. *Journal of Applied Social Psychology, 27* (5), 1407–1416.

Irving, L. M. (1990). Mirror images: Effects of the standard of beauty on the self- and body-esteem of women exhibiting various levels of bulimic symptoms. *Journal of Social and Clinical Psychology, 9* (2), 230–242.

Kalodner, C. R. (1997). Media influences on male and female non-eating disordered college students: A significant issue. *Eating Disorders: The Journal of Treatment and Prevention, 5* (1), 47–57.

Kilbourne, J. (1994). Still killing us softly: Advertising and the obsession with thinness. In P. Fallon, M.A. Katzman, & S. C. Wooley (Eds.) *Feminist Perspectives on Eating Disorders* (pp. 395–418). New York: The Guilford Press.

Levine, M. P., & Smolak, L. (1997). Media as a context for the development of disordered eating. In L. Smolak, M. P. Levine, & R. Striegel-Moore (Eds.), *Developmental psychopathology of eating disorders* (pp. 235–257). Mahwah, New Jersey: Lawrence Erlbaum.

Lucas, A. R., Beard, C. M., O Fallon, W. M., & Kurland, L. T. (1991). 50-year trends in the incidence of anorexia nervosa in Rochester, Minn.: A population-based study. *American Journal of Psychiatry, 148* (7), 917–922.

Millum, T. (1975). *Images of women: Advertising in women's magazines.* London: Chatto & Windus Ltd.

Murray, S. H., Touyz, S. W., & Beumont, Peter, J. V. (1996). Awareness and perceived influence of body ideals in the media: A comparison of eating disordered patients and the general community. *Eating Disorders: The Journal of Treatment and Prevention, 4* (1), 33–46.

Myers, P. N., Biocca, F. A. (1992). The elastic body image: The effect of television advertising and programming on body image distortions in young women. *Journal of Communication, 42*(3), 108–133.

Nemeroff, C. J., Stein, R. I., Diehl, N. S., & Smilack, K.M. (1994). From the Cleavers to the Clintons: Role choices and body orientation as reflected in magazine article content. *International Journal of Eating Disorders, 16* (2).

Ogden, J. & Elder, C. (1998). The role of family status and ethnic group on body image and eating behavior. *International Journal of Eating Disorders, 23* (3), 309–315.

Ogden, J., & Mundray, K. (1996). The effect of the media on body satisfaction: The role of gender and size. *European Eating Disorders Review, 4* (3), 171–182.

Peirce, K. (1990). A feminist perspective on the socialization of teenage girls through *Seventeen* magazine. *Sex Roles, 23* (9/10), 491–500.

Posavac, H. D., Posavac, S. S., & Posavac, E. J. (1998). Exposure to media images of female attractiveness and concern with body weight among young women. *Sex Roles, 38* (3/4), 187–201.

Rabak-Wagener, J, Eickhoff-Shemek, J., & Kelly-Vance, L. (1998).The effect of media analysis on attitudes and behaviors regarding body image among college students. *Journal of American College Health, 47* (1), 29–35.

Remafedi, G. (1990). Study group report on the impact of television portrayals of gender roles on youth. *Journal of Adolescent Health Care, 11,* 59–61.

Roberts, D. F. (1993).Adolescents and the mass media: From *Leave it to Beaver* to *Beverly Hills 90210. Teachers College Record, 94* (3), 629–644.

Schlenker, J., Caron, S.L., & Halteman, W.A. (1998). A feminist analysis of *Seventeen* magazine: Content analysis from 1945 to 1995. *Sex roles, 38*, 135–149.

Schupak-Neuberg, E., Shaw, H. E., & Stein, R. L. (1994). Relation of media exposure to eating disorder symptomatology: An examination of mediating mechanisms. *Journal of Abnormal Psychology, 103* (4).

Signorielli, N. (1989). Television and conceptions about sex roles: Maintaining conventionality and the status quo. *Sex Roles, 21*(5–6), 341–360.

Signorielli, N. (1990). Children, television, and gender roles: Messages and impact. Conference: Teens and television. *Journal of Adolescent Health Care, 11*(1), 50–58.

Signorielli, N. (1993). Television, the portrayal of women, and children's attitudes. In G. L. Berry Q & J. Keiko Asamen (Eds.), *Children & television: Images in a changing sociocultural world* (pp. 229–242). Newbury Park, CA: Sage.

Signorielli, N., McLeod, D., & Healy, E. (1994). Gender stereotypes in MTV commercials: The beat goes on. *Journal of Broadcasting & Electronic Media, 38*(1), 91–101.

Silverstein, B., Perdue, L., Peterson, B., & Kelly, E. (1986). The role of the mass media in promoting a thin standard of bodily attractiveness for women. *Sex Roles, 14* (9/10), 519–532.

Stice, E., & Shaw, H. E. (1994). Adverse effects of the media portrayed thin-ideal on women and linkages to bulimic symptomatology. *Journal of Social and Clinical Psychology, 13* (3), 288–308.

Tiggeman, M., & Pickering, A. S. (1996). Role of television in adolescent women's body dissatisfaction and drive for thinness. *International Journal of Eating Disorders, 20* (2), 199–203.

Turner, S. L. et al. (1997). The influence of fashion magazines on the body image satisfaction of college women: An exploratory analysis. *Adolescence, 32* (127), 603–614.

Waller, G. et al. (1994). Beauty is in the eye of the beholder: Media influences on the psychopathology of eating problems. *Appetite, 23*(3), 287.

Waller, G., & Hamilton, K., & Shaw, J. (1992). Media influences on body size estimation in eating disordered and comparison subjects. *British Review of Bulimia and Anorexia Nervosa, 6* (2), 81–87.

Williamson, J. (1985). *Consuming passions: The dynamics of popular culture.* New York: Marion Boyars.

Films

Killing Us Softly: Advertising's Image of Women. Dir. Sut Jhally.

Killing Us Softly III: Advertising's Image of Women. (2000). Dir. Sut Jhally.

Killing Us Softly IV: Advertising's Image of Women. (2010). Dir. Sut Jhally.

*Prêt-ê-Porter (*Ready to Wear*).* (1994). Dir. Robert Altman.

Slim Hopes. (1995). Dir. Sut Jhally.

Still Killing Us Softly: Advertising's Image of Women. Dir. Sut Jhally.

✤ Chapter References

Preface

Fiebig von-Hase, R., & Lehmkuhl, U. (1997). *Enemy images in American history.* New York: Berghahn.

Goffman, E. (1979). *Gender advertisements.* New York: Harper Collins.

Hogan, L. (2001). *The woman who watches over the world: A native memoir.* New York: W. W. Norton.

King, M. L., Jr. (1963). *I have a dream. Speech given on the steps of the Lincoln Memorial.* Retrieved from http://www.americanrhetoric.com/speeches/mlkihaveadream.htm

Lippmann, W. (1922). The world outside and the pictures in our heads. *Public Opinion.* New York: Harcourt Brace.

Lyotard, J.-F. (1984). *The postmodern condition: A report on knowledge.* In G. Bennington & B. Massumi (Trans.). Minneapolis, MN: University of Minnesota Press.

Nin, A. (1971). *The diary of Anaïs Nin.* G. Stuhlmann (Ed.). New York: Harvest.

Rumi, J. al-Din (1993). Elephant in the dark. In A. J. Arberry (Trans). *Tales from the Masnavi.* New York: Routledge.

Sigmund Freud and C.G. Jung. W. McGuire (Ed.). Princeton, NJ: Princeton University Press.

Chapter One: Introduction

Alfino, M., Caputo, J. S., & Wynyard, R. (1998). *McDonaldization revisited: Critical essays on consumer culture.* Santa Barbara, CA: Greenwood.

Allison, A. (1991). Japanese mothers and obentos: The lunch box as ideological state apparatus. *Anthropological Quarterly, 64*(4), 195–208.

Althusser, L. (1971). Ideology and ideological state apparatuses. *Notes toward an investigation in Lenin and philosophy and other essays.* New York: Monthly Review.

Althusser, L. (2001). Ideology and ideological state apparatuses. In V. B. Leitch et al. (Eds.), *The Norton anthology of theory and criticism* (pp. 1483–1509). New York: Norton.

Barthes, R. (1972). *Mythologies.* New York: Hill and Wang.

Barthes, R. (1973). *Mythologies.* New York: Hill & Wang.

Barthes, R. (1977). *Image, music, text.* Glasgow: Fontana/Collins.

Baudrillard, J. (1981) *For a critique of the political economy of the sign.* C. Levin (Trans.). St. Louis, MO: Telos.

Bennett, L. W. (1980). Myth, ritual and political control. *Journal of Communication, 30,* 166–179.

Berger, A. A. (2003). *Media and society: A critical perspective.* Lanham, MD: Rowman & Littlefield.

Berger, A. A. (2004). *Ads, fads, and consumer culture.* Lanham, MD: Rowman & Littlefield.

Berger, A. A. (2005). *Media analysis techniques.* Newbury Park, CA: Sage.

Berger, J. (1977). *Ways of seeing.* New York: Penguin.

Bird, E., & Dardenne, R. (1988). Myth, chronicle, and story. In J. Carey (Ed.), *Media, myth, and narratives* (pp. 67–85). London: Sage.

Bohnke, M. (2001). Myth and law in the films of John Ford. *Journal of Law and Society, 28*(1), 47–63.

Campbell, C. P. (1995). *Race, myth, and the news.* Thousand Oaks, CA: Sage.

Campbell, J. (1959). *Masks of gods: Primitive mythology.* New York: Penguin.

Campbell, J. (1988). *The power of myth.* New York: Anchor.

Chandler, D. (2007). *Semiotics: The basics.* New York: Routledge.

Coman, M. (2005). News stories and myth—the impossible reunion? In M. Coman & E. W. Rothenbuhler (Eds.), *Media anthropology* (pp. 111–120). Thousand Oaks: Sage.

Coman, M., & Rothenbuhler, E. W. (2005). The promise. In M. Coman & E. W. Rothenbuhler (Eds.), *Media anthropology* (pp. 1–12). Thousand Oaks, CA: Sage.

Cook, A. L. (2007). *Performing myth: Narrative-based communities in a globalizing matrix.* Dallas: University of Texas.

Denton, Kirk A. (1987). Model drama as myth: A semiotic analysis of "Taking Tiger Mountain by Strategy." In C. Tung & C. Mackerras (Eds.), *Drama in the People's Republic of China* (pp. 119–136). Albany, NY: State University of New York Press.

Doty, W. (2000). *Mythography: The study of myths and rituals.* 2nd ed. Tuscaloosa: University of Alabama Press.

Ebert, J. D. (2005). *Celluloid heroes & mechanical dragons—Film as the mythology of electronic society.* Christchurch, New Zealand: Cybereditions Corporation.

Eco, U. (1976). *A theory of semiotics.* Bloomington, IN: Indiana University Press.

Eliade, M. (1962/1988). *Myth and reality.* Long Grove, IL: Waveland.

Eliade, M. (1963). *Myth and reality.* New York: Harper and Row.

Eliade, M. (1967). *Myths, dreams, and mysteries.* New York: Harper Collins.

Erikson, E. (1950). *Childhood and society.* New York: W. W. Norton.

Flood, C. G. (1996). *Political myth: A theoretical introduction.* New York: Garland.

Freud, S. & Jung, C. G. (1974). *The Freud-Jung letters: the correspondence between Sigmund Freud and C.G. Jung.* W. McGuire (Ed.). Princeton, NJ: Princeton University Press.

Gaffney, K. (2008). "The Others are coming": ideology and otherness in *Lost*. In S. M. Kaye (Ed.), Lost *and philosophy: The island has its reasons* (pp. 136–146). Malden, MA: Blackwell.

Galician, M-L. (2004). Sex, love, and romance in the mass media. Mahwah, NJ: Lawrence Erlbaum.

Graham, K., & Dean, T. (1982). Myth and the structure of news. *Journal of Commuunication, 32*, 144–158.

Hall, S. (1986). On postmodernism and articulation: An interview with Stuart Hall. In L. Grossberg (Ed.), *Journal of Communication Inquiry, 10* (2), 45–60.

Harris, R. J. (2004). *A cognitive psychology of mass communication.* Mahwah, NJ: Lawrence Erlbaum.

Hillman, J. (1975). *Loose ends: Primary papers in archetypal psychology.* New Orleans, LA: Spring.

Hillman, J. (1985). *Speech given at National Arts Club.* Retrieved from http://www.esalen.org/air/essays/joseph_campbell.htm

Huitt, W. (1998, April). Measurement, evaluation, and research: Ways of knowing. *Educational Psychology Interactive.* Valdosta, GA: Valdosta State University

Huitt, W., Hummel, J., & Kaeck, D. (2001, May). *Measurement, evaluation, and research.* Retrieved from http://chiron.valdosta.edu/whuitt/col/intro/sciknow.html

Jameson, F. (1972). *The prison-house of language.* Princeton, NJ: Princeton University Press.

Jhally, S. (1997). *Advertising and the end of the world.* VHS. Media Education Foundation.

Jung, C. (1976). *The portable Jung.* In J. Campbell (Ed.), trans. R. F. C. Hull, New York: Penguin.

Jung, C. G. (1936/1976). *The archetypes and the collective unconscious.* G. Adler & R. F. C. Hull (trans.). *Collected Works, 9, pars. 87-110.* Princeton, NJ: Princeton University Press.

Kellner, D. (2005). Cultural studies, multiculturalism, and media culture. In G. Dines & J. Humez (Eds.), *Gender, race, and class in media: A text-reader* (pp. 9–20). London: Sage.

Kerlinger, F. (1973). *Foundations of behavioral research.* New York: Holt, Reinhart & Winston.

Knight, G. (1982). Myth and the structure of news. *Journal of Communication, 32*(2), 144–161.

Kuberski, P. (2008). Odyssey: Myth, technology, gnosis. *Arizona Quarterly: A Journal of American Literature, Culture, and Theory, 64*(3), 51–73.

Kuhn, T. (1962). *The structure of scientific revolutions.* Chicago: The University of Chicago Press.

Lasierra, M. (2008). Cronenberg: A modern Canadian myth. In W. R. Keller & G. Walz Marburg (Eds.), *Screening Canadians: Cross-Cultural perspectives on Canadian film* (pp. 135–159). Marburg: Universitatsbibliotheck.

Lewis, J. (2002). *Cultural studies—The basics.* London: Sage.

Liebes, T., & Blondheim, M.(2005). Myths to the rescue: How live televisions intervenes in history. In M. Coman & E. W. Rothenbuhler (Eds.), *Media anthropology* (pp. 188–198). Thousand Oaks, CA: Sage.

Lippmann, W. (1922). *Public opinion.* New York: Harcourt Brace.

Lule, J. (2005). News as myth: Daily news and eternal stories. In M. Coman & E. W. Rothenbuhler (Eds.), *Media anthropology* (pp. 101–110). Thousand Oaks, CA: Sage.

Malinowski, B. (1962). *Sex, culture, and myth.* New York: Harcourt Brace.

Mansfield, N. (2000). *Subjectivity: Theories of the self from Freud to Haraway*. New York: NYU Press.

Marvin, C., & Ingle, D. W. (1999). *Blood sacrifice and the nation: Totem rituals and the American flag*. New York: Cambridge University Press.

McElroy, S. C. (2004). *All my relations: Living with animals as teachers and healers*. Novato, CA: New World Library.

McRobbie, A. (1991). *Feminism and youth culture*. New York: Routledge.

Mansfield, N. (2000). *Subjectivity: Theories of the self from Freud to Haraway*. New York: NYU Press.

Miller, D. (1995). Comparativism in a world of difference: The legacy of Joseph Campbell to the postmodern history of religions. In S. Scholl (Ed.), *Common era: Best new writings on religion* (pp. 168–177). Ashland, OR: White Cloud.

Moore, T. (2003). Songs of unforgetting. *Parabola: The search for meaning*, pp. 6–9.

Peirce, C. S. (1931–1958). *The collected papers of Charles Sanders Peirce*. A. Burks (Ed.), Cambridge MA: Harvard University Press.

Piaget, J. (1969). *La psychologie de l'enfant*. New York: Basic Books.

Pines, M. (1982, October 13). How they know what you really mean. *San Francisco Chronicle*.

Radway, J. (1984). *Reading the romance: Women, patriarchy, and popular literature*. Chapel Hill, NC: University of North Carolina Press.

Rosteck, T., & Frentz, T. S. (2007). Myth and multiple readings in environmental rhetoric: The case of an inconvenient truth. *Quarterly Journal of Speech, 95*(1), 1–19.

Rothenbuhler, E. W. (2005). Ground zero, the firemen, and the symbolic touch on 9-11 and after. In M. Coman & E. W. Rothenbuhler (Eds.), *Media anthropology* (pp. 176–187). Thousand Oaks, CA: Sage.

Saussure, Ferdinand de (1916/1983): *Course in general linguistics*. In R. Harris (Trans). London: Duckworth.

Schorer, M. (1946). *William Blake: The poetics of vision*. New York: H. Holt and Company.

Schorer, M. (1960). The necessity of myth and mythmaking. In H.A. Murray (ed.), *Myth and Mythmaking* (pp. 354–358). New York: Macmillan.

Skinner, B. F. (1953). *Science and human behavior*. New York: Macmillan.

Stevens, A. (1994). *Jung: A very short introduction*. New York: Oxford University Press.

Thompson, J. (1995). *The media and modernity*. Cambridge, MA: Polity.

Thwaites, T., Davis, L. & Mules, W. (2002). *Introducing cultural and media studies: A semiotic approach*. New York: Palgrave Macmillan.

Tollefson, T. E. (1998). Cinemyths: Contemporary films as gender myth. In M. L. Kittelson (Ed.), *The soul of popular culture: Looking at contemporary heroes, myths, and monsters* (pp. 106–110). Chicago: Open Court.

Trbic, B. (2007). This is not a pipe: An introduction to representation. *Screen Education, 47*, 86-90.

Trimbur, J. (1993). Articulation theory and the problem of determination: A reading of lives on the boundary. *JAC, 13*(1). Retrieved from http://jac.gsu.edu/jac/13.1/Articles/3.htm

Voytilla, S. (1999). *Myth and the movies*. Studio City, CA: Michael Wiese Productions.

Walter, R. (n.d.). In the air. *Esalen Institute.* Retrieved, from http://www.esalen.org/air/essays/joseph_campbell.htm

Zehnder, S. M. & Calvert, S. L. (2004). Between the hero and the shadow: Developmental differences in adolescents' perceptions and understanding of mythic themes in film. *Journal of Communication Inquiry 28*(2), 122–137.

Chapter Two: Constructing Categories of Difference

(1999, January 20). In a surprising act of redemption, Denny's becomes a leader in diversity. *Washington Informer.* Retrieved September 26, 2010, from http://www.highbeam.com/doc/1P1-22430276.html

Blum, D. (2002). Heart to heart: Sex differences in emotion. In G. Colombo (Ed.), *Mind readings.* Boston: Bedford St. Martins.

Brown, A. (2010, March 8). Two AIG subsidiaries agree to settle discrimination case. *Law is cool.* Retrieved from http://lawiscool.com/2010/03/08/2524/

Campbell, J. (1988). Campbell and the power of myth with Bill Moyers. B.S. Flowers (Ed.). New York: Doubleday.

"Case profile: Coca-Cola lawsuit." Retrieved from http://www.business-humanrights.org/Categories/Lawlawsuits/Lawsuitsregulatoryaction/Lawsuits Selectedcases/Coca-ColalawsuitreracialdiscriminationinUSA

"Category," 1. *The Oxford English Dictionary.* (2nd ed.). 1989. OED Online. Oxford University Press. Retrieved February 26, 2009, from http://0-dictionary.oed.com.janus.uoregon.edu/cgi/entry/50034564?single=1&query_type=word&queryword=category&first=1&max_to_show=10

CIA World Factbook. (2008). Retrieved from https://www.cia.gov/library/publications/the-world-factbook/index.html

Deslatte, M. (2009, November 3). Louisiana interracial marriage-refusing judge Keith Bardwell quits. *Huffington Post.* Retrieved from http://www.huffingtonpost.com/2009/11/03/louisiana-interracial-mar_n_344392.html

"Difference," 1a. *The Oxford English Dictionary.* (2nd ed.). 1989. OED Online. Oxford University Press. Retrieved from http://0-dictionary.oed.com.janus.uoregon.edu/cgi/entry/50063748?query_type=word&queryword=difference&first=1&max_to_show=10&sort_type=alpha&result_place=1&search_id=uefq-BnNKK6-7279&hilite=50063748

Dozier, R. W. (2003). *Why we hate: Understanding, curbing, and eliminating hate in ourselves and our world.* New York: McGraw-Hill.

Farley, R., & Haaga, J. (2005). *The American people: Census 2000.* New York: Russell Sage Foundation.

Foreman, J. (2002, August 13). Women and stress. Retrieved August 05, 2010, from http://www.myhealthsense.com/F20020813_womenStress.html

Gaffney, K. (2008). "The others are coming": Ideology and otherness in *Lost.* In S. M. Kaye (Ed.), *Lost and philosophy* (pp. 136-147). Malden, MA: Blackwell.

Gladwell, M. (2005). *Blink: The power of thinking without thinking.* New York: Little Brown.

Hansen, C. H., & Hansen, R. D. (1988). Priming stereotypic appraisal of social interactions: How rock music videos can change what's seen when boy meets girl. *Sex Roles, 19,* 287–316.

Hart, A. J., Whalen, P. J., Shin, L. M., McInerney, S. C., Fischer, H. & Rauch, S. L. (2000). Differential response in the human amygdala to racial outgroup vs ingroup face stimuli. *NeuroReport, 2*(11), 2351–2355.

Hastorf, A. H., & Cantril, H. (1954). They saw a game. *Journal of Abnormal and Social Psychology, 49,* 129–134.

Jost, J., & Kay, A. C. (2003). Complementary justice: Effects of 'poor but happy' and 'poor but honest' stereotype exemplars on system justification and implicit activation of the justice motive. *GSB Research Paper, 1753.*

Jost, J. T., & Banaji, M. R. (1994). The role of stereotyping in system-justification and the production of false consciousness. *British Journal of Social Psychology, 33,* 1–27.

Kirsanow, P. (2006, April 12). 2,000 flavors and counting: The more race categories you add, the more pointless they are. *National Review Online.* Retrieved from http://www.nationalreview.com/comment/kirsanow200604120718.asp

Lakoff, G. (1987). *Women, fire, and dangerous things.* Chicago: University of Chicago Press.

Lakoff, G., & Johnson, M. (1999). *Philosophy in the flesh.* New York: Basic.

Lewis, T., Amini, F., & Lannon, R. (2000). *A general theory of love.* New York: Random House.

McFetridge, G. (1999). *Spiritual emergency and the triune brain.* Retrieved from http://www.peakstates.com/spiritual_emergency.html

Monahan, J. L., Brown Givens, S. M., & Shtrulis, I. (2003, May) *Priming and stereotyping: How mediated images affect perceptions in interpersonal contexts.* Paper presented at the annual meeting of the International Communication Association, San Diego, CA. Retrieved from http://www.allacademic.com/meta/p111711_index.html

Morrison, T. (1992). *Playing in the dark: Whiteness in the literary imagination.* Cambridge, MA: Vintage.

Moyer, K. E. (1976). *The psychobiology of aggression.* New York: Harper and Row.

O'Sullivan, K., & Wilson, W. J. (1988). Race and ethnicity. In N. J. Smelser (Ed.), *Handbook of Sociology* (pp. 223–242). Newbury Park, CA: Sage.

Rome, D. (2004). *Black demons: The media's depiction of the African American male criminal stereotype.* Westport, CT: Praeger.

Rubin, R. T., Reinisch, R. T., & Haskett, R. F. (1981). Postnatal gonadal steroid effects on human behavior. *Science, 211,* 1318–1324.

Samsup, J. (2003). The portrayal of public relations in the news media. *Mass Communication and Society, 6*(4), 397–411.

Siegel, J. S., Swanson, D., & Shyrock, H. S. (2004). *The methods and materials of demography.* Bingley, UK: Emerald Group.

Steele, C. (2006). Stereotype threat and African-American student achievement.In S. Szelenyi & D. B. Grusky (Eds.), *Inequality reader* (pp. 252–257). Boulder, CO: Westview.

Weis, L. (1995). Identity formation and the process of "othering": Unraveling sexual threads. *Educational Foundations, 9*(1), 17–33.

Whitesell, P. (2002, November 5). Speech given at the Michigan State Police Training Academy. Police Ethics and Self-Discipline. In *TUEBOR*. Publication of the Michigan State Police Training Division, *9*(2), Spring 2003, p. 1.

Wilber, K. (2000). *A brief history of everything*. Boston: Shambhala.

Yamato, G. (1995). *New voices from Aunt Lute*. Minneapolis: Aunt Lute.

Yamato, G. (1990). Something about the subject makes it hard to name. In In G. Anzaldúa (Ed.), *Making face, making soul: Creative and critical perspectives by women of color* (pp. 20-24). San Francisco, CA: Aunt Lute Books.

Chapter Three: Minorities, Meaning, and Media

(2003). Race—The power of an illusion. Produced by California Newsreel. Retrieved from http://www.pbs.org/race/000_General/000_00-Home.htm

(2004, July 28). Mass media and the African American criminal male stereotype. Indiana University News Release. Retrieved from http://newsinfo.iu.edu/news/page/print/1580.html

Agnew, V. (Ed.). (2005). *Diaspora, memory, and identity: A search for home*. Toronto: University of Toronto Press.

Allport, G. (1954). *The nature of prejudice*. Garden City, New York: Doubleday.

Alvarado, M., Gutch, R., & Wollen, T. (1987): *Learning the media*. London: Macmillan.

Basson, L. L. (2005). Fit for annexation but unfit to vote? Debating Hawaiian suffrage qualifications at the turn of the twentieth century. *Social Science History, 29*(4), 575–598.

Bates, B. R., & Garner, T. (2001). Can you dig it? Audiences, archetypes, and John Shaft. *Howard Journal of Communications, 12*(3), 137–157.

Bentham, J. (1785/1995). Panopticon. In M. Bozovic (Ed.), *The Panopticon Writings*. London: Verso.

Buriel, R. (1987). Ethnic labeling and identity among Mexican Americans. In J. Phinney & M. Rotheram (Eds.), *Children's ethnic socialization: Pluralism and development* (pp. 134–152). Newbury Park, CA: Sage.

Butler, J. (1990). *Gender trouble: Feminism and the subversion of identity*. New York: Routledge.

Clifford, J. (1994). Diasporas. *Cultural Anthropology, 9*(3), 302–338.

Cohen, R. (1997). *Global diaspora: An introduction*. London: University College London Press.

Comas-Diaz, L., & Green, B. (1994). Women of color with professional status. In L. Comas-Diaz & B. Greene (Eds.), *Women of color: Integrating ethnic and gender identities in psychotherapy* (pp. 347–388). New York: Guilford Press.

Courtney, W. H. (2000). Constructions of masculinity and their influence on men's well-being. *Social Science and Medicine, 50*, 1385–1401.

Douglas, M. (2002). *Purity and danger: An analysis of concept of pollution and taboo*. New York: Routledge.

Du Bois, W. E. B. (1989). *The souls of black folk*. New York: Penguin (Original work published 1903).

Fanon, F. (1952). *Black skin, White masks.* New York: Grove.

Fanon, F. (1965). *A dying colonialism.* New York: Grove.

Foucault, M. (1973). *The birth of the clinic.* New York: Pantheon.

Foucault, M. (1977). *Discipline and punish.* New York: Pantheon.

Foucault, M. (1980). *Power/knowledge: Selected interviews and other writings, 1972–1977.* New York: Pantheon.

Frable, D. E. S. (1997). Gender, racial, ethnic, sexual, and class identities. *Annual Review Psychology, 48,* 139–162.

Frye, M. (1983). Oppression. *The politics of reality: Essays in feminist theory* (pp. 1–16). Trumansburg, New York: The Crossing Press.

Gandy, O. H.,.Jr. (1998). *Communication and race: A structural perspective.* London: Arnold.

Gilroy, P. (1995). *The black Atlantic: Modernity and double consciousness.* Boston: Harvard University Press.

Goffman, E. (1968). *Aslyums.* New York: Penguin.

Hacker, A. (2003). *Two nations: Black and white, separate, hostile, unequal.* New York: Simon & Schuster.

Hall, S. (1997). *Representation: Cultural representation and signifying practices.* Thousand Oaks, CA: Sage.

Harker, R., Mahar, C., & Wilkes, C. (1990). *An introduction to the work of Pierre Bourdieu: The practice of theory.* New York: St. Martin's.

Harris, T., & Holdt, J. (1997). *Insights about oppression.* Retrieved from http://www.american-pictures.com/english/racism/oppression.htm

Hogg, M. A., & Abrams, D. (1990). *Social identification: A social psychology of intergroup relations and group processes.* London: Routledge.

Howarth, C. (2006). Race as stigma: Positioning the stigmatized as agents, not objects. *Journal of Community & Applied Social Psychology, 16*(6), 442–451.

Hua, A. (2005). Diaspora and cultural memory. In V. Agnew (Ed.), *Diaspora, memory, and identity: A search for home* (pp. 191–208). Toronto: University of Toronto Press.

Jay, G. (2007). *Whiteness studies.* Retrieved from http://www.uwm.edu/~gjay/Whiteness/index.html

Johnson, A. G. (2001). *Privilege, power and difference.* Mountain View, CA: Mayfield.

Johnston, R. J. (2000). *The Dictionary of Human Geography* (4th ed.). Malden, MA: Wiley-Blackwell.

Jones, A. (2002). *The feminist and visual culture reader.* New York: Routledge.

Jones, S. (n.d.). *The right hand of privilege.* Retrieved from http://www.multiculturaladvantage.com/recruit/diversity/white-men-diversity/Right-Hand-of-Privilege.asp

Jordan, C., & Weedon, G. J. (1994). *Cultural politics.* Malden, MA: Blackwell.

Judd, B., & Copley, S. (1971). *Meanings of history: Readings from American Heritage.* New York: American Heritage Publishing.

Jung, C. G. (1960). *The collected works.* In R. F. C. Hull (Trans.), *The structure and dynamics of the Psyche* (Vol. 8). Routledge: London.

Kinzer, S. (2006). *Overthrow: America's century of regime change from Hawaii to Iraq.* Honolulu, HI: University of Hawaii Press.

Leung, R. (2005). Torture, Cover-up at Gitmo? *60 Minutes.* CBS News. Retrieved from http://www.cbsnews.com/stories/2005/04/28/60minutes/main691602.shtml

Lippmann, W. (1922). *Public opinion.* New York: Harcourt Brace.

McIntosh, P. (1989, July/August). White privilege: Unpacking the invisible knapsack. *Peace and Freedom* (n.p.).

Leyens, J. P., Yzerbyt, V., & Schadron, G. (1994). *Stereotypes and social cognition.* New York: Sage.

Lorenz, H. S., & Watkins, M. (2000). Depth psychology and colonialism: Individuation, seeing through, and liberation. Paper presented at The International Symposium of Archetypal Psychology, Santa Barbara, CA.

Merton, R. J. (1976). Discrimination and the American Creed. In R. Merton (Ed.), *Sociological ambivalence and other essays.* New York: Free Press.

Merton, R. K. (1948). The self-fulfilling prophecy. *Antioch Review, 8,* 193–210.

Merton, R. K. (1949). Discrimination and the American Creed. In Robert McIver (Ed.), *Discrimination and the national welfare.* New York: Institute for Religious and Social Studies and Harper and Row.

Mill, J. S. (1864). *Dissertations and discussions: Political, philosophical, and historical* (Vol. 2). Boston: William V. Spencer.

Myrdal, G. (1977). *Social psychology: Theory and application of symbolic interactionism.* New York: McGraw-Hill.

Peters, J. D. (1999). *Speaking into the air.* Chicago: University of Chicago Press.

Peters, W. (dir.). (1985). *A class divided.* [Motion Picture]. United States. *Frontline.* Public Broadcasting Company.

Phinney, J. S. (1996). What do we mean? *American Psychologist, 51,* 918–927.

Reyhner, J. (2006). *American Indian/Alaska Native education: An overview.* Retrieved from http://jan.ucc.nau.edu/~jar/AIE/Ind_Ed.html

Schermerhorn, R. A. (1970). *Comparative ethnic relations: A framework for theory and research.* New York: Random House.

Shohat, E., & Stam, R. (1994). *Unthinking Eurocentrism: Multiculturalism and the media.* London: Routledge.

Smith, J. (1612/1910). A map of Virginia with a description of the country, the commodities, people, government and religion. In E. Arber (Ed.), *Travels and works of Captain John Smith.* Edinburgh: John Grant.

Stibbe, A. (2004). Health and the social construction of masculinity in *Men's Health* magazine. *Men and Masculinities, 7*(1), 31–51.

Stremlau, R. (2005). "To domesticate and civilize wild Indians": Allotment and the campaign to reform Indian families, 1875–1887. *Journal of Family History, 30*(3), 265–286.

Swartz, D. (1998). *Culture and power: The sociology of Pierre Bourdieu.* Chicago: University of Chicago Press.

Tajfel, H. (1981). *Human groups and social categories.* Cambridge: Cambridge University Press.

Taylor, C. R., & Stern, B. B. (1997). Asian Americans: Television advertising the 'model minority' stereotype. *Journal of Advertising, 26*(2), 47–61.

Turner, P. A. (1992). *Enlightened racism: The Cosby Show, audiences, and the myth of the American Dream*. Boulder: Westview.

Valdivia, A. (1999). La vida es loca Latina/o. *Critical Studies in Mass Communication, 16*(4), 482–485.

von Franz, M. L. (1995). *Projection and re-collection in Jungian psychology: Reflections of the soul*. Peru, IL: Open Court.

Williams, W. E. (2006, September 21). How do you define prejudice? *Portland Examiner*. Retrieved from http://www.examiner.com/a-300809-Walter_E__Williams__How_do_you_define_prejudice_.html

Yamato, G. (1998). *Something about the subject makes it hard to name*. Belmont, CA: Wadsworth.

Yellow Bird, M. (2004). Cowboys and Indians: Toys of genocide, icons of colonialism. *Wicazo Sa Review, 19*(2), 33–48.

Yetman, N. (2007). Diversity in the United States. In Healey, J. F. & O'Brien, E. (Eds.), *Race, ethnicity, and gender: Selected readings* (pp. 9–22). London: Pine Forge.

Zinn, H. (2005). *A people's history of the United States: 1492 to the present*. New York: Harper Perennial.

Chapter Four: Articulations of Difference

Adams, H. (2004). Quoted in M. Yellow Bird (2004). Cowboys and Indians: Toys of genocide, icons of American colonialism. *Wicazo Sa Review, 19*(2), 33–48.

Alvarado, M., Gutch, R., & Wollen, T. (1987). *Learning the media*. London: Macmillan.

Basson, L. L. (2005). Fit for annexation but unfit to vote? Debating Hawaiian suffrage qualifications at the turn of the twentieth century. *Social Science History, 29*(4), 575–598.

Bates, B. R., & Garner, T. (2001). Can you dig it? Audiences, archetypes, and John Shaft. *Howard Journal of Communications, 12*(3), 137–157.

Belenky, M. F., Bond, L. A., & Weinstock, J. S. (1991). *A tradition that has no name*. New York: Basic.

Bell-Jordan, K. E. (2008). Black.White and a Survivor of the *Real World*: Constructions of race on reality TV. *Critical Studies in Media Communication, 25*(4), 353–372.

Bobo, J. (1995). *Black women as cultural readers*. New York: Columbia University Press.

Brooks, D. (2001). *Bobos in paradise: The new upper class and how they got there*. New York: Touchstone.

Bullock, H. E. (1995). Class acts: Middle-class responses to the poor. In B. Lott & D. Maluso (Eds.), *The social psychology of interpersonal discrimination* (pp. 118–159). New York: Guilford.

Butler, J. (1999). *Gender trouble*. New York: Routledge.

Calloway, N. O., & Harris, O. N. (1977). *Biological and medical aspects of race*. Fairburn, GA: Diversified Industries.

Chandler, D. (n.d.). *Visual semiotics*. Retrieved from http://www.aber.ac.uk/media/Modules/MC30820/represent.html

Christensen, C. P. (1989). Cross-cultural awareness development: A conceptual model. *Counselor Education and Supervision, 28*, 270–287.

Coleman, L., & Rainwater, L. (1978). *Social standing in America.* London: Routledge and Kegan Paul.

Cookson, P. W., Jr., & Persell, C. H. (1985). *Preparing for power.* New York: Basic.

Coombes, R. J. (1998). *The cultural life of intellectual properties: Authorship, appropriation, and the law.* Durham, NC: Duke University Press.

Craig, S. (Ed.). (1992). *Men, masculinity, and the media.* London: Sage.

Dávila, A. M. (2001). *Latinos Inc. The marketing and making of a people.* Berkeley, CA: University of California Press.

de Beauvoir, S. (1949/1989). *The second sex.* New York: Vintage.

du Gay, P., Evans, J., & Redman, P. (Eds.), (2000). *Identity: A reader.* London: Sage.

Dyer, R. (1997). *White.* New York: Routledge.

Edwards, A. (1993). From Aunt Jemima to Anita Hill: Media's split image of Black women. *Media Studies Journal, 7,* 215–222.

Fiske, J. (1986). Television: Polysemy and popularity. *Critical Studies in Mass Communication, 3*(4), 391–408.

Fleming, V. (Director). (1939). *Gone with the Wind.* [Motion Picture]. USA: MGM.

Frow, J. (1995). *Cultural studies and cultural values.* Oxford, UK: Clarendon.

Frye, M. (1983). Oppression. *The politics of reality: Essays in feminist theory* (pp. 1–16). Trumansburg, New York: Crossing.

Fuller, L. (2001). Are we seeing things? The Pinesol lady and the ghost of Aunt Jemima. *Journal of Black Studies, 32*(1), 120–131.

Goings, K. W. (1994). *Mammy and Uncle Mose: Black collectibles and American stereotyping.* Bloomington, IN: Indiana University Press.

Goodchilds, J. (Ed.). (1991). *Psychological perspectives on human diversity in America.* Washington, DC: American Psychological Association.

Hacker, A. (2003). *Two nations: Black and white, separate, hostile, unequal.* New York: Simon & Schuster.

Hall, S. (1997). *Representation: Cultural representation and signifying practices.* Thousand Oaks, CA: Sage.

Hannaford, I. (1996). *Race.* Berkeley, CA: University of California Press.

Harker, R., Mahar, C., & Wilkes, C. (1990). *An introduction to the work of Pierre Bourdieu: The practice of theory.* New York: St. Martin's.

Hess, B. B., Markson, E. W., & Stein, P. J. (1995). *Sociology.* New York: Allyn & Bacon.

Hirschfeld, M. (1938). *Racism.* London: Gollancz.

Jhally, S., & Lewis, J. (1992). *Enlightened racism: The Cosby Show, audiences, and the myth of the American dream.* Boulder, CO: Westview.

Kates, S. M., & Shaw-Garlock, G. (1999). The ever-entangling web: A study of ideologies and discourses in advertising to women. *Journal of Advertising, 28*(2), 33–49.

Langston, D. (1992). Tired of playing monopoly? In M. L. Anderson & P. H. Collins (Eds.), *Race, class, and gender: An anthology* (pp. 110–120). Belmont, CA: Wadsworth.

Lee, J. (2003). Menarche and the (hetero)sexualization of the female body. In R. Weitz (Ed.), *The politics of women's bodies: Sexuality, appearance, and behavior* (pp. 82–99). New York: Oxford University Press.

Leonard, D. (2005, January 26). *Cashing in on the Other: Race, commodity, and surveillance of contemporary athletes.* Retrieved from http://www.popmatters.com/sports/features/050126-nikecommercials.shtml

Lippmann, W. (1922). *Public opinion.* New York: Harcourt Brace.

Manring, M. M. (1998). *Slave in a box: The strange career of Aunt Jemima.* Charlottesville: University Press of Virginia.

Martinez, L. (2007, September 10). *Latinos hot and bothered about the wrong image.* Retrieved from adage.com/bigtent

McIntosh, P. (1989, July/August). White privilege: Unpacking the invisible knapsack. *Peace and Freedom* (n.p.)

Nieman, Y. F. (2001). Stereotypes about Chicanas and Chicanos. *The Counseling Psychologist, 29*(1), 55–90.

North, S., Snyder, I., & Bulfin, S. (2008). *Being digital in school, home and community: Final report.* Melbourne: Monash University.

Offer, D., Schonert-Reichl, K. A., & Boxer, A. M. (1996). Normal adolescent development: Empirical research findings. In M. Lewis (Ed.), *Child and adolescent psychiatry: A comprehensive textbook* (2nd ed.). Baltimore, MD: Williams & Wilkins.

Phinney, J. S. (1996). What do we mean? *American Psychologist, 51,* 918–927.

Ramírez Berg, C. (1990). Stereotyping in films in general and of the Hispanic in particular. *Howard Journal of Communication, 2*(3), 286–300.

Roediger, D. R. (2002). *Colored White: Transcending the racial past.* Berkeley, CA: University of California Press.

Said, E. (1978). *Orientalism.* New York: Vintage.

Shreve, A. (2001). *Dateline Los Alamos.* Bioscience Division Special Issue. U.S. Department of Energy, Los Alamos National Laboratory. University of California.

Stern, B. (1999). Masculinism(s) and the male image: What does it mean to be a man? In R. Reichert & J. Lambiase (Eds.), *Sex in advertising: Perspectives on the erotic appeal* (pp. 215–228). Mahwah: Lawrence Erlbaum.

Strasburg, J. (2002, April 19). Abercrombie recalls T-shirts many found offensive. SF Gate. *San Francisco Chronicle.* Retrieved from http://www.sfgate.com/cgi-bin/article.cgi?file=/c/a/2002/04/19/MN102999.DTL

Swartz, D. (1998). *Culture and power: The sociology of Pierre Bourdieu.* Chicago: University of Chicago Press.

Taijfel, H., & Turner, J. C. (1986). The social identity theory of inter group behavior. In S. Worchel & L. W. Austin (Eds.), *Psychology of inter group relations.* Chicago: Nelson-Hall.

Turner, J. C., Oakes, P. J., Haslam, S. A., & McGarty, C. M. (1994). Self and collective: Cognition and social context. *Personality and Social Psychology Bulletin, 20*, 454–463.

Valdivia, A. (1999). La vida es loca Latina/o. *Critical Studies in Mass Communication 16*(4), 482–485.

Veblen, T. (1912/1994). *The theory of the leisure class.* New York: Penguin.

von Sternberg, J. (Director). (1932). *Shanghai Express* [Motion Picture]. USA: Paramount.

Waters, M., & Eschbah, K. (1995). Immigration and ethnic and racial inequality in the United States. *Annual Review of Sociology, 21*, 419–446.

Westerman, M. (1989, March). Death of the Frito bandito: Marketing to ethnic groups. *American Demographics, 11*, 28–32.

Williamson, J. (1978). *Decoding advertisements: Ideology and meaning in advertising.* New York: Marion Boyars.

Introduction to Section II

Du Bois, W. E. B. (1903). *The souls of Black folk.* Chicago: A. C. McClurg.

Guerrero, E. (2003). Foreword: Reversing the Lens. In J. Xing, & L. R. Hirabayashi (Eds.), *Reversing the lens: Ethnicity, race, gender, and sexuality through film* (pp. ix–xii). Boulder, CO: University Press of Colorado.

Chapter Five: Country Music and "Redneck Woman"

(2006, June 15). The rich, the poor, and the growing gap between them. *The Economist.* Retrieved September 27, 2010, from economist.com

(2007, April 14). Blue-collar downsizing. *Billboard*, 21.

n.a. (2006, June 15). Inequality in America. *The Economist.* Retrieved from http://www.economist.com/world/displaystory.cfm?story_id=7055911

Abbey, E. (1979). In defense of the redneck. In *Abbey's Road: Take the other.* New York: E. P. Dutton.

Aldrich, N. W., Jr. (1988). *Old money: The mythology of America's upper class.* New York: Alfred A. Knopf.

Alters, D. (2003). We hardly watch that rude, crude show: Class and taste in 'The Simpsons.' In C. Stabile & M. Harrison (Eds.), *Prime time animation: Television animation and American culture.* New York: Routledge.

Andersen, M. L., & Taylor, H. F. (2005). *Sociology: Understanding a diverse society.* 4th ed. Florence, KY: Thompson Wadsworth.

Andsager, J. L., & Roe, K. (1999). Country music video in country's year of the woman. *Journal of Communication, 49*(1), 69–82.

Aufderheid, P. (1986). Music videos: The look of the sound. *Journal of Communication, 36*(1), 57–78.

Ayers, W. (2009, February 10). In Radical cheer. *New York Times.* Retrieved August 3, 2010, from http://www.nytimes.com/2009/02/15/magazine/15wwln_Q4-t.html

Bakhtin, M. (1981). *The dialogic imagination: Four essays,* ed. M. Holquist (Ed.), C. Emerson & M. Holquist (Trans.). Austin: University of Texas Press.

Barthes, R. (1988). Textual analysis: Poe's 'Valdemar.' In D. Lodge (Ed.), *Modern criticism and theory* (pp. 172–195). London: Longman.

Barthes, R. (1994). *The semiotic challenge.* Berkeley: University California Press.

Berube, A. (1997). Sunset Trailer Park. In A. Newitz & M. Wray (Eds.), *White trash: Race and class in America* (pp. 15–40). New York: Routledge.

Blumberg, P. (1980). *Inequality in an age of decline.* New York: Oxford.

Bourdieu, P. (1993). *The field of cultural production.* New York: Columbia University Press.

Bourdieu, P. (1998). On male domination. *Le Monde Diplomatique.* Retrieved from http://monde-diplo.com/1998/10/10bourdieu

Boynton, R. S. (1995, November 6). The professor of connection: A profile of Stanley Crouch. *The New Yorker.* Retrieved August 05, 2010, from http://www.robertboynton.com/articleDisplay.php?article_id=30

Brooks, D. (2001). *Bobos in paradise: The new upper class and how they got there.* Clearwater, FL: Touchstone.

Bufwack, M. A., & Oermann, R. K. (2003). *Finding her voice: The saga of women in country music.* New York: Crow.

Buis, K. (2007, June). Mrs. Trollope's America. *Vanity Fair.* Retrieved from http://www.vanityfair.com/magazine/2007/06/essay_winner200706

Butsch, R. (1992). Class and gender in four decades of television situation comedies. *Critical Studies in Mass Communication, 9,* 387–399.

Butsch, R. (n.d.). Social class and television. *The Museum of Broadcast Communications.* Retrieved from http://www.museum.tv/archives/etv/S/htmlS/socialclass/socialclass.htm

Butsch, R. (1995). Ralph, Fred, Archie and Homer: Why television keeps recreating the White male working-class buffoon. In G. Dines & J. M. Humez (Eds.), *Gender, race and class in media: A text-reader.* Thousand Oaks, CA: Sage.

Butsch, R. (2000). *The making of American audiences.* Cambridge, MA: Cambridge University Press.

Butsch, R., & Glennon, L. (1983). Social class frequency trends in domestic situation comedy, 1946–1978. *Journal of Broadcasting, 27,* 77–81.

Chafel, J. A. (1997). Societal images of poverty: Child and adult beliefs. *Youth & Society, 28*(4), 432–463.

Chandler, C. R., & Chalfant, P. (1985). The sexual double-standard in country music song lyrics. *Free Inquiry in Creative Sociology, 13,* 1428–1433.

Clarke, B. (2003, March 12). The Dixie Chicks. *Guardian.* Retrieved from http://arts.guardian.co.uk/reviews/story/0,,912236,00.html

Cockburn, A., & St. Clair, J. (2007, November 16). The vices of Hillary Clinton. *Counterpunch.* Retrieved from http://counterpunch.org/cockburn11162007.html

CMA Marketing (1998). *Country Music Association.* Retrieved from http://www.countrymusic.org/marketing/hotfacts.html

CMAWorld.com. (2007, January 5). *Country music remains steady in 2006.* Retrievedfrom http://www.countrymusic.org/news_publications/pr_common/press_detail.asp?re=595&year=2007

Cole, H. (1999). *How to be: Contemporary etiquette for African Americans.* New York: Simon & Schuster.

Coleman, J. (1965). *Adolescents and the schools.* New York: Basic Books.

Collins, P.H. (1990). *Black feminist thought: Knowledge, consciousness, and the politics of empowerment.* New York: Routledge.

Cose, E. (1997). *Color-blind: Seeing beyond race in a race-obsessed world.* New York: Harper Collins.

Croizet, J.-C., & Claire, T. (1998). Extending the concept of stereotype threat to social class: The intellectual underperformance of students from low socioeconomic backgrounds. *Personality & Social Psychology Bulletin, 24*(6), 588–594.

DeMott, B. (1990). *The imperial middle: Why Americans can't think straight about class.* New York: William Morrow.

DeMott, B. (1992). *Created equal: Reading and writing about class in America.* New York: Harper & Row.

De Santis, S. (1999). *Life on the line: One woman's tale of work, sweat, and survival.* New York: Doubleday.

Diamond, I., & Quimby, L. (Eds.), (1988). *Feminism and Foucault: Reflections on resistance.* Boston: Northeastern University Press.

Domhoff, G. W. (2002). *Who rules America? Power and politics.* New York: McGraw-Hill.

du Gay, P., Evans, J., & Redman, P. (Eds.). (2004). *Identity: A reader.* London: Sage.

Eyerman, R., & Jamison. A. (1998). *Music and social movements: Mobilizing traditions in the twentieth century.* Cambridge: Cambridge University Press.

Fox, A. A. (2004). *Real country: Music and language in working-class culture.* Durham, NC: Duke University Press.

Frank, R. (1998). *Luxury fever: Why money fails to satisfy in an era of excess.* New York: Free Press.

Freeman, L. (1992). Social mobility in television comedies. *Critical Studies in Mass Communication, 9*(4), 400–406.

Fussell, P. (1992). *Class: A guide through the American status system.* New York: Touchstone.

Glennon, L., & Butsch, R. (1982). The family as portrayed on television, 1946–1978. In D. Pearl (Ed.), *Television and behavior: Technical reviews, 2.* Washington, D.C.: U.S. Dept. of Health and Human Services.

Goad, J. (1998). *The redneck manifesto: How hillbillies, hicks, and white trash became America's scapegoats.* New York: Simon & Schuster.

Goldberg, D. T. (1993). *Racist culture: Philosophy and the politics of meaning.* Cambridge, MA: Blackwell.

Goodwin, A. (1992). *Dancing in the distraction factory: Music television and popular culture.* Minneapolis: University of Minnesota Press.

"Harper Valley P.T.A." (1968). Tom T. Hall. (Writer). [Song]. US: Unichappell Music.

Herzig, J. (2003, October). Shania the crusader. *Glamour, 249.*

Hochschild, J. (1995). *Facing up to the American dream.* Princeton, NJ: Princeton University Press.

Holtzman, L. (2000). *Media messages.* New York: M.E. Sharpe.

hooks, b. (2000). *Where we stand: Class matters.* New York: Routledge.

Jabour, A. (2003). Negotiating boundaries of southern womanhood: Dealing with the powers that be. *Alabama Review.* Retrieved from http://findarticles.com/p/articles/mi_qa3880/is_200301/ai_n9207278

Jhally, S. (Writer/Director). (1991). *Dreamworlds: Desire, Sex, and Power in Music Video* [Motion picture]. United States: Media Education Foundation.

Jhally, S. (Writer/Director). (1995). *Dreamworlds II: Desire, Sex, and Power in Music Video* [Motion picture]. United States: Media Education Foundation.

Jhally, S. (Writer/Director). (2007). *Dreamworlds III: Desire, Sex, and Power in Music Video* [Motion picture]. United States: Media Education Foundation.

Johnson, S. L. (1888). *Wit and wisdom of Samuel Johnson.* New York: Clarendon.

Jones, S. (2002). *Pop music and the press.* Philadelphia: Temple University Press.

Jordan, A. (1992). Social class, temporal orientation, and mass media use within the family system. *Critical Studies in Mass Communication, 9*(4), 374–386.

Joyce, J. (1922/2002). *Ulysses.* New York: Dover.

Keel, B. (2004). Between Riot GRRRl and quiet girl: The new women's movement in country music. In C. M. Mccusker & D. Pecknold (Eds.), *A boy named Sue: Gender and country music* (pp. 155–177). Jackson, MI: University of Mississippi Press.

Kennedy, L. (2005). Music, social justice and market manipulations: An interview with Professor Tricia Rose. *Fish Rap.* Retrieved August 5, 2010, from http://www.triciarose.com/commentary_fishrap.shtml

Kitch, S. L. (1994). Straight but not narrow: A gynetic approach to the teaching of lesbian literature. In L. Garber (Ed.) *Tilting the tower: Lesbians/teaching/queer subjects* (pp. 83–95). New York: Routledge.

Kotlowitz, A. (1992). *There are no children here: The story of two boys growing up in the other America.* New York: Anchor.

Kozol, J. (1992). *Savage inequalities: Children in America's schools.* New York: Harper.

Lakoff, G. (2002). Moral politics: How liberals and conservatives think. Chicago: University of Chicago Press.

Lamont, M. (1992). *Money, morals, & manners: The culture of the French and the American upper-middle class.* Chicago: The University of Chicago Press.

Leahy, R. L. (1983). Development of the conception of economic inequality: Explanations, justifications, and concepts of social mobility and change. *Developmental Psychology, 19*(1), 111-125.

Leo's Lyrics Database. (n.d.). *Redneck Woman.* Retrieved from http://www.pcelebs.com/php/getimg.php?ti=gretchen

Levine, L. W. (1990). *Highbrow lowbrow: The emergence of cultural hierarchy in America.* Cambridge, MA: Harvard University Press.

Lipsitz, G. (1986). The meaning of memory. *Cultural Anthropology, 1*(4), 355-387.

Lott, B. & Saxon, S. (2002). The influence of ethnicity, social class, and context on judgments about U.S. women. *The Journal of Social Psychology 142/4*, 481–499.

Lydon, C. (2008, December). Race and class: Hip-hop. Open Source with Christopher Lydon [Radio program]. Retrieved February 22, 2009, from http://www.radioopensource.org/race-and-class-hip-hop/

Lynes, R. (1954). *The tastemakers.* New York: Grosset & Dunlap.

Malone, B. C. (2002). *Don't get above your raisin': Country music and the Southern working class.* Chicago: University of Illinois.

McLaurin, M. (n.d.). *Class consciousness in country music.* Retrieved from http://www.mtsu.edu/~baustin/class.htm

Moss, K. (2003). *The color of class: Poor whites and the paradox of privilege.* Philadelphia: University of Pennsylvania Press.

Mumbi Moody, N. (2007). Gretchen Wilson shows vulnerable side. *USA Today.* Retrieved from http://www.usatoday.com/life/music/2007-05-16-796705887_x.htm

O'Dell, D. (2000). Book review. *Journal of Southern History, 66*(1), 107–110.

Otis, G. L. (1999). *Our kind of people: Inside America's black upper class.* New York: Harper Collins.

Parenti, M. (1997). *Land of idols: Political mythology in America.* New York: St Martin's.

Peterson, R. A. (1997). *Creating country music: Fabricating authenticity.* Chicago: University of Chicago Press.

Queenan, J. (1998). *Red lobster, white trash, and the blue lagoon: Joe Queenan's America.* New York: Hyperion.

Rodriguez, R. (1983). *Hunger of memory: The education of Richard Rodriguez.* New York: Bantam.

Rose, S. (2005). 5 myths about the poor middle class. *The Washington Post.* Retrieved August 8, 2010, from http://www.washingtonpost.com/wp-dyn/content/article/2007/12/21/AR2007122101556.html

Rymer, R. (2000). *American beach: How progress robbed a black town (and nation) of history, wealth, and power.* New York: Harper.

Sayles, G. P. (1992). *How to marry the rich.* New York: Berkley.

Seiter, E., Borchers, H., Kreutzner, G. ,& Warth, E.-M. (Eds.). (1989). Don't treat us like we're so stupid and naive: Toward an ethnography of soap opera viewers. In *Remote control: Television audiences and cultural power.* London: Routledge.

Sennett, R., & Cobb, J. (1972). *The hidden injuries of class.* New York: Vintage.

Sherrill, J.S., DiPiero, B., & Robbins, D. (1989). There's too much month at the end of the money. [Song]. United States. Little Big Town Music.

Sklar, R. (1980). *Prime time America: Life on and behind the television screen.* New York: Oxford.

Stack, S., & Gundlach, J. (1992). The effect of country music on suicide. *Social Forces, 71*(1), 211–218.

Steeves, H. L., & Smith, M. C. (1987). Class and gender on prime time television entertainment. *Journal of Communication Inquiry, 11*(1), 43–63.

Swedberg, R. (1998). *Max Weber and the idea of economic sociology.* Princeton, NJ: Princeton University Press.

Taylor, E. (1989). *Prime time families*. Berkeley, CA: University of California Press.

Terkel, S. (1967/1997). *Division Street: America*. New York: Pantheon.

Terkel, S., & Kotlowitz, A. (1997). *Working: People talk about what they do all day and how they feel about what they do*. New York: New Press.

Thomas, S., & Callahan, B. (1982). Allocating happiness: TV families and social class. *Journal of Communication, 33*, 184–190.

Thompson, E. P. (1963). *The making of the English working class*. New York: Vintage.

Van Sickel, R. W. (2005). A world without citizenship: On (the absence of) politics and ideology in country music lyrics, 1960–2000. *Popular Music and Society, 28*(3), 313–331.

"Too much month at the end of the money." (2003). (Writers). Bob DiPiero, Dennis Robbins, & John Sherrill. [Song]. United States.

Veblen, T. (1912/1994). *The theory of the leisure class*. New York: Penguin.

Webb, J. H. (2004). *Born fighting: How the Scots-Irish shaped America*. New York: Broadway.

Weiss, M. J. (1994). *Latitudes & attitudes: An atlas of American tastes, trends, politics, and passions*. New York: Little, Brown and Company.

Weston, R. D. (1993). The redneck hero in the postmodern world. *South Carolina Review, 25*(2), 195–196.

Wilson, C. R., & Ferris, W. F. (1989). (Eds.), *Encyclopedia of southern culture*. Chapel Hill, NC: University of North Carolina Press.

Wilson, G. (2004). Redneck woman. *Lyrics*. Retrieved from http://www.stormfront.org/archive/t-132736Redneck_Woman.html

Wilson, G. (2006). *Redneck woman: Stories from my life*. New York: Grand Central.

Wolff, K. (2000). *Country music: The rough guide*. London: Penguin.

Woods, T. A., Kurtz-Costes, B., & Rowley, S. J. (2005). The development of stereotypes about the rich and poor: Age, race, and family income differences in beliefs. *Journal of Youth and Adolescence, 34*(5), 437–445.

Woolf, V. (1998). Three guineas. In *A Room of One's Own*. Oxford: Oxford World Classics.

Wray, M. (2006). *Not quite white: White trash and the boundaries of whiteness*. Durham, NC: Duke University Press.

Wray, M., & Newitz, A. L. (Eds.). (1997). *White trash: Race and class in America*. New York: Routledge.

Zweig, M. (2000). *The working class majority: America's best kept secret*. Ithaca, NY: Cornell University Press.

Chapter Six: The Construction of Arabs as Enemies

100 questions and answers about Arab Americans—A Journalist's Guide (2001). *Detroit Free Press*. Retrieved from http://www.adc.org

Balmer, R. (2003, March 27). Bush and God. *The Nation*, 7–8.

Carver, T. (2003, April 06). Bush puts God on his side. *BBC News*. Retrieved from http://www.news.bbc.co.uk

Chandler, D. (2002). *Semiotics: The basics*. London: Routledge.

El-Farra, N. (1996). Arabs and the media. *Journal of Media Psychology, 1*(2), 1–7.

Feehan, J. (2003, April 25). Patriot Act erodes freedom, activists say. *The Eugene Register-Guard*, C1.

Feldstein, F. P., & Acosta-Alzuru, C. (2003). Argentinean Jews as scapegoat: A textual analysis of the bombing of AMIA. *Journal of Communication Inquiry, 27*, 152–170.

Fiebig-von Hase, R. (1997). Introduction. In R. Fiebig-von Hase & U. Lehmkuhl (Eds.), *Enemy images in American history* (pp. 1–42). Providence, RI: Berghahn.

Fineman, R. (2003, March 10). Bush and God [Electronic version]. *Newsweek*, 22.

Fish, S. (2001, October 15). Condemnation without absolutes [Electronic version]. *The New York Times*, p. A19.

Gandy, O. H., Jr. (1998). *Communication and race: A structural perspective*. London: Arnold.

Gavrilos, D. (2002). Arab Americans in a nation's imagined community: How news constructed Arab American reactions to the Gulf War. *Journal of Communication Inquiry, 26*, 426–445.

Ghareeb, E. (Ed.). (1983). *Split vision: The portrayal of Arabs in the American media*. Washington, D.C: American-Arab Affairs Council.

Gill, A. M., & Whedbee, K. (1997). Rhetoric. In T. van Dijk (Ed.), *Discourse as structure and process* (pp. 157–184). London: Sage.

Green, M. (1993). Images of American Indians in advertising: Some moral issues. *Journal of Business Ethics, 12*, 323–330.

Guerrero, E. (1993). *Framing Blackness: The African American image in film*. Philadelphia: Temple University Press.

Hall, S. (1975). Introduction. In A. C. H. Smith (Ed.), *Paper voices: The popular press and social change, 1935–1965* (pp. 11–24). London: Chatto & Windus.

Hall, S. (1997). The spectacle of the "other." In S. Hall (Ed.), *Representation: Cultural representations and signifying practices* (pp. 223–279). London: Sage.

Hall, S. (2002). Quoted in D. Gavrilos, Arab Americans in a nation's imagined community: How news constructed Arab American reactions to the Gulf War. *Journal of Communication Inquiry, 26*, 426–445.

Hamada, B. I. (2001). The Arab image in the minds of western image-makers. *The Journal of International Communication, 7*(1), 7–35.

Hathout, M. (1999, March 29). Group looks to bridge gap. In. C. Jones (Ed.), *View*. Retrieved from http://www.viewnews.com.

Hopcke, R. H. (1989). *A guided tour of the collected works of C. G. Jung*. Boston: Shambhala.

Hyde, M., & McGuinness, M. (1994). *Introducing Jung*. New York: Totem.

Jackson, N. B. (1996). Arab Americans: Middle East conflicts hit home. In P. M. Lester (Ed.), *Images that injure: Pictorial stereotypes in the media* (pp. 63–66). Westport, CT: Praeger.

Kakutani, M. (2001, October 9). The Age of Irony isn't over after all. *The New York Times*, E1.

Kates, S. M., & Shaw-Garlock, G. (1999). The ever-entangling web: A study of ideologies and discourses in advertising to women. *Journal of Advertising, 28*(2), 33–49.

Keen, S. (1986). *Faces of the enemy: Reflections of the hostile imagination*. San Francisco: Harper & Row.

Kibbey, A. (2003). Editorial: Gender and the American ideology of war. *Genders Online Journal, 37*. Retrieved from http://www.genders.org

Lasswell, H. D. (1934/1995). Propaganda. In R. Jackall (Ed.), *Propaganda* (pp. 13–25). New York: New York University Press.

Lind, R.A., & Danowski, J. A. (1998). The representation of Arabs in U.S. electronic media. In Y. R. Kamalipour & T. Carilli (Eds.), *Cultural diversity and the U.S. media* (pp. 156–167). New York: NYU Press.

Lippmann, W. (1922). *Public opinion*. New York: Harcourt Brace.

Lyman, R. (2001, October 3). Bad guys for bad times: Hollywood struggles to create villains for a new climate [Electronic version]. *The New York Times*, E1.

Martin, L J. (1985). The media's role in international terrorism. *Terrorism: An International Journal, 8*, 127–143.

Max, D. T. (2001, October 28). The speech [Electronic version]. *The New York Times*, 32.

May, S., & Modood, T. (2001). Editorial. *Ethnicities, 1(3)*, 291–294.

McNamara, M., & George, L. (2001, September 19). After the attack: When evil itself becomes the primary foe. *Los Angeles Times*, A3.

Merskin, D. (2001). Winnebagos, Cherokees, Apaches, and Dakotas: The persistence of stereotyping of American Indians in American advertising brands. *The Howard Journal of Communication, 12*, 159–169.

Nacos, B. L., & Torres-Reyna, O. (2003). Framing Muslim-Americans before and after 9-11. P. Norris, M. Kern & M. R. Just (Eds.), *Framing terrorism: The news media, the government, and the public* (pp. 133–158). New York: Routledge.

Pagels, E. (1996). *The origin of Satan*. New York: Vintage.

Pilon, R. (2001, December 10). *Right, center, & left support free & open debate in wartime: Dissent does not give aid, comfort to enemy*. Remarks delivered at the National Press Club meeting, Washington, D.C., by the vice president for legal affairs and director, Center for Constitutional Studies, Cato Institute, Washington, D.C.

Said, E. S. (1997). *Covering Islam: How the media and the experts determine how we see the rest of the world*. New York: Vintage.

Shaheen, J. G. (1981). Images of Saudis and Palestinians: A review of major documentaries. In W. C. Adams (Ed.), *Television coverage of the Middle East*. Norwood, NJ: Ablex Publishing.

Shaheen, J. G. (1984). *The TV Arab*. Madison, WI: University of Wisconsin Press.

Shaheen, J. G. (1988). Perspectives on the television Arab. In L. Gross, J. Katz, & J. Ruby (Eds.), *Image ethics: The moral rights of subjects in photographs, film, and television* (pp. 203–219). New York: Oxford.

Shaheen, J. G. (1990, August 19). Our cultural demon—The "ugly Arab": Ignorance, economics create an unshakeable stereotype. *Des Moines Register*, A7.

Shaheen, J. G. (1995). TV Arabs. In P. Rothenberg (Ed.), *Race, class, and gender in the United States* (pp. 197–199). New York: St. Martin's.

Shaheen, J. G. (1998). We've seen this plot too many times. *The Washington Post*, C3.

Shaheen, J. G. (2001). *Reel bad Arabs: How Hollywood vilifies a people*. Northampton, MA: Olive Branch.

Spillmann, K. R., & Spillmann, K. (1997). Some sociobiological and psychological aspects of "Images of the enemy." In R. Fiebig-von Hase & U. Lehmkuhl (Eds.), *Enemy images in American history* (pp. 43–64). Providence, RI: Berghahn.

Spyrou, S. (2002). Images of the "other": 'The Turk' in Greek Cypriot children's imaginations. *Race, Ethnicity, & Education, 5*, 255–272.

Suleiman, M. W. (1988). The *Arabs in the mind of America*. Brattleboro, VT: Amana.

Suleiman, M. W. (1999). Islam, Muslims, and Arabs in America: The other of the other of the other. *Journal of Muslim Minority Affairs, 19*, 33–48.

Suspect sues for false arrest. (1995, November 10). *Eugene Register-Guard*, A3.

Takaki, R. T. (1993). A *different mirror: A history of multicultural America*. Boston: Little Brown.

Terry, J. J. (1985). *Mistaken identity: Arab stereotypes in popular writing*. Washington, D.C.: American-Arab Affairs Council.

Valbrun, M. (2003, April 15). More Muslims claim they suffer job bias. *The Wall Street Journal*, B1.

White House history: A non-partisan evaluation of the past. (2004). Retrieved from http://whitehouse.org/history

Worth, R. F. (2002, February 24). A nation defines itself by its evil enemies. *The New York Times*, sec. 4, 1.

Zinn, H. (1995). *A people's history of the United States 1492–present*. New York: Harper Perennial.

Chapter Seven: Perpetuation of the Hot Latina Stereotype in *Desperate Housewives*

(2007). An ugly turn. Blog post. Retrieved September 20, 2010, from http://centerofgravitas.blogspot.com/2007_01_01_archive.html

Aparicio, F. R., & Chávez-Silverman, S. (1997). *Tropicalizations: Transcultural representations of Latinidad*. Hanover, NH: University Press of New England.

Arredondo, P. (1991). Counseling Latinas. In C. C. Lee & B. L. Richardson (Eds.), *Multicultural issues in counseling: New approaches to diversity* (pp. 143–156). Alexandria, VA: American Association for Counseling and Development.

Arthur, K. (2006, March 28). *Housewives* carries ABC. *New York Times*, E5.

Askmen.com. (2005). *Eva Longoria* (online). Retrieved from http://www.askmen.com/women/actress_250/277_eva_longoria.html

Beltrán, M. C. (2002). The Hollywood Latina body as site of social struggle: Media constructions of stardom and Jennifer Lopez's 'Crossover butt.' *Quarterly Review of Film and Video, 19*, 71–86.

Bender, S. W. (2003). *Greasers and gringos: Latinos, law, and the American imagination*. New York: New York University Press.

Black, C. (Writer), & Grossman, D. (Director). 2004. Everyday a little death [Television series episode]. In M. Cherry (Executive producer), *Desperate Housewives*. American Broadcasting Company.

Cherry, M. (Writer), & McDougall, C. (Director). (2004). Pilot [Television series episode]. In M. Cherry (Executive producer), *Desperate Housewives*. American Broadcasting Company.

Cherry, M. (Writer), & Shaw, L. (Director). (2004). Ah, but underneath [Television series episode]. In M. Cherry (Executive producer), *Desperate Housewives*. American Broadcasting Company.

Cherry, M., Spezialy, T. (Writers), & Melman, J. (Director). (2004). Who's that woman? [Television series episode]. In M. Cherry (Executive producer), *Desperate Housewives*. American Broadcasting Company.

Cofer, J. O. (2005). The myth of the Latin woman: I just met a girl named Maria. In R. Riske-Rusciano & V. Cyrus (Eds.), *Experiencing race, class, and gender in the United States* (4th ed.). Boston, MA: McGraw-Hill.

Cortés, C. E. (1997). Chicanas in Film: History of an Image. In C. E. Rodriguez (Ed.), *Latin looks: Images of Latinas and Latinos in the U.S. media* (pp. 121–141). Boulder, CO: Westview.

Cunningham, A. (Writer). (2004). Come in, Stranger [Television series episode]. M. Cherry (Executive producer), *Desperate Housewives*. American Broadcasting Company.

Dávila, A. (2001). *Latinos Inc. The marketing and making of a people.* Berkeley, CA: University of California Press.

DeFleur, M. L., & Dennis, E. E. (1998.) *Understanding Mass Communication* (6th ed.). Boston, MA: Houghton Mifflin.

Del Castillo, A. R. (1998). Mexican gender ideology. In R. Delgado & J. Stefancic (Eds.), *The Latino/a condition: A critical reader* (pp. 499–500). New York: New York University Press.

Etten, K. (Writer), & Sanford, A. (Director). 2004. Your Fault [Television series episode]. In M. Cherry (Executive Producer), *Desperate Housewives*. American Broadcasting Company.

Fashionspot.com. (2005). Eva Longoria signs with L'Oréal (online). Retrieved from, http://www.thefashionspot.com/forums/archive/index.php/t-24613.html

Femalefirst.com. (2005). Desperate Housewives Eva Longoria face of L'Oréal. Retrieved from http://www.femalefirst.co.uk/fashion/5582004.htm

Fernandez, M. L. (2004, September 5). Desperation row [Electronic version]. *L.A. Times.* Retrieved from http://www.geocities.com/Hollywood/4616/lat0905b.html

FHM.com. (2004). Eva Longoria [Electronic version]. Retrieved from http://www.fhmus.com/girls/covergirls/290/

Foster, L. (2005, April 13). Former Gucci team links with Lauder. *Financial Times*, p. 30.

Gerbner, G., Gross, L., Morgan, M., & Signorielli, N. (1994). Growing up with television: The cultivation perspective. In J. Bryant & D. Zillmann (Eds.), *Media effects: Advances in theory and research* (pp. 43–67). Hillsdale, NJ: Lawrence Erlbaum.

Gil, R. M. (1996). Hispanic women and mental health [Electronic version]. In J. A. Sechzer, S. M. Pfafflin, F. L. Denmark, A. Griffin, & S. J. Blumenthal (Eds.), *Women and mental health* (pp. 147–159). *Annals of the New York Academy of Sciences 789.*

Goffman, E. (1956). *The presentation of self in everyday life.* New York: Doubleday.

Guzmán, I. M., & Valdivia, A. N. (2004). Brain, brow, and booty: Latina iconicity in U.S. popular culture. *The Communication Review, 7*, 205–221.

Hall, S. (1996). On postmodernism and articulation: An interview with Stuart Hall. In D. Morley & K. H. Chen (Eds.), *Stuart Hall: Critical Dialogues in Cultural Studies* (pp. 131–150). New York: Routledge.

Harris, M. (2005, April 18). Celebrities have no shame when shilling. *Ottawa Citizen*, D. 3.

Hedeggard, E. (2005, December 15). Eva Longoria: A year of 'sex' for the *Desperate Housewives* star [Electronic version]. *Rolling Stone*. Retrieved from http://www.rollingstone.com/poylon goria/?rnd=1126115925047&has-player=true

Hernandez, B. (2001, September 10). *Bel Hernandez discusses Latino stereotypes.* Retrieved August 08, 2010,from http://www.cnnstudentnews.cnn.com/2001/fyi/lesson.plans/09/10/bel.her-nandez/index.html

Hughes, S. (2004, 1 August). *Tough road to college for Latinas.* Retrieved August 08, 2010, from http://www.cbsnews.com/stories/2004/07/30/sunday/main633154.shtml

Hyde, J. S. (2005). Gender roles and ethnicity. In R. Riske-Rusciano & V. Cyrus (Eds.), *experienceing race, class, and gender in the United States,* 4th ed. (pp. 74–78). Boston, MA: McGraw-Hill.

Keck, W. (2005, April 13). Housewives look forward to long, hot summer. *USA Today.* Retrieved from http://www.usatoday.com/life/people/2005-04-13-housewives-instyle_x.htm

Keller, G. D. (1994). *Hispanics and United States film: An overview and handbook.* Tempe, AZ: Bilingual Review/Press.

King, L. M. (1974). Puertorriquenas in the United States: The impact of double discrimination. *Civil Rights Digest, 6*(2), 20–28.

Kraidy, M., & Goeddertz, T. (2003). Transnational advertising and international relations: U.S. press discourses on the Benetton 'We on Death Row' campaign. *Media, Culture, & Society, 25,* 147–165.

Lester, E. (1994). The 'I' of the storm: A textual analysis of U.S. reporting on democratic Kampuchea. *Journal of Communication Inquiry, 18,* 5–27.

López, A. M. (1991). Are all Latinas from Manhattan? Hollywood, ethnography, and cultural colonialism. In L. D. Friedman (Ed.), *Unspeakable images: Ethnicity and the American cinema* (pp. 404–424). Urbana, IL: University of Illinois Press.

L'Oreal (2005). Eva Longoria. Retrieved from lorealusa.com

Lott, B. & Saxon, S. (2002). The influence of ethnicity, social class, and context on judgments about U.S. women. *The Journal of Social Psychology, 142*/4, 481–499.

Lule, J. (1993). Murder and myth: *New York Times* coverage of the TWA 847 hijacking victim. *Journalism Quarterly, 70*(1), 26–39.

Lule, J. (1995). The rape of Mike Tyson: Race, the press, and symbolic types. *Critical Studies in Mass Communication, 12,* 176–196.

Markert, J. (2007). The *George Lopez Show*: Same old Hispano? *Bilingual Review, 28*(2), 148–165.

Mastro, D. E., & Behm-Morawitz, E. (2005). Latino representations on prime time television. *Journalism and Mass Communication Quarterly, 82*(1), 110–127.

Maximonline. (2003). *Girls of Maxim.* Retrieved from http://www.maximonline.com/girls_of_maxim/html/girl_1021.html

McKee, A. (2003). *Textual analysis: A beginner's guide.* Newbury Park, CA: Sage.

Mulvey, L. (2001). Visual pleasure and narrative cinema. In *Media and cultural studies: Key works* (pp. 393–404). Malden, MA: Blackwell.

Murphy, K. (Writer), & Shaw, L. (Director). (2004). Children will listen [Television series episode]. In M. Cherry (Executive producer), *Desperate Housewives.* American Broadcasting Company.

Noriega, C. (1992). *Chicanos and film: Representation and resistance.* Minneapolis, MN: University of Minnesota Press.

Oboler, S. (1998). Hispanics? That's what they call us. In Delgado & J. Stefancic (Eds.), *The Latino/a condition: A critical reader* (pp. 3–5). New York: New York University Press.

O'Neil, B. (2005). Carmen Miranda: The high price of face and bananas. In V. L. Ruiz & V. S. Korrol (Eds.), *Latina Legacies: Identity, biography, and community* (193-208). Oxford: Oxford University Press.

oyemag.com. (2005). Eva fever. *Open Your Eyes.* Retrieved from http://www.oyemag.com/eva.html

Papps, N. (2005, April 10). The Latina temptress. *The Sunday Telegraph*, p. 21.

Ramierez-Berg, C. (1990). *Latino images in film: Stereotypes, subversion, resistance.* Austin, TX: University of Texas Press.

Rios-Bustamante, A. (1992). Latino participation in the Hollywood film Industry, 1911–1945. In C. Noriega (Ed.), *Chicanos and film: Representation and resistance* (pp. 18–28). Minneapolis: University of Minnesota Press.

Rodriquez-Erastrada, A. I. (1992). Dolores Del Rio and Lupe Vélez: Images on and off screen: 1925-1944. In C. Noriega (Ed.), *Chicanos and film: Representation and resistance* (pp. 475–492). Minneapolis, MN: University of Minnesota Press.

Román, E. (2000). Who exactly is living *La Vida Loca*? The legal and political consequences of Latino-Latina ethnic and racial stereotypes in film and other media. *Journal of Gender, Race, and Justice, 4,* 37–65.

Torontofashion.com. (2004). *Ten new faces of fall.* Retrieved from http://toronto.fashion-monitor.com/news.php/news/2005041001eva_longoria

Valdivia, A. N. (1998). Stereotype or transgression? Rosie Perez in Hollywood film. *Sociological Quarterly, 39*(3), 393-395.

Valdivia, A. N. (2000). *A Latina in the land of Hollywood and other essays in media culture.* Tucson, AZ: The University of Arizona Press.

Wittstock, M. (2005). Mothers of suburbia [Electronic Version]. *Observer/Guardian.* Retrieved from http://observer.guardian.co

Chapter Eight: Commodified Racism and Brand Images of Native Americans

Adams, H. (2004). Quoted in M. Yellow Bird (2004). Cowboys and Indians: Toys of genocide, icons of American colonialism. *Wicazo Sa Review, 19*(2), 33–48.

Barthes, R. (1972). *Mythologies.* New York: Noonday.

Berkhofer, R. (Jr.). (1979). *The White man's Indian: Images of the American Indian from Columbus to the present.* New York: Vintage.

Biber, B. (1984). *Early education and psychological development.* New Haven, CT: Yale University Press.

Blalock, C. (1992). Crazy Horse controversy riles Congress: Controversies over Crazy Horse Malt Liquor and Black Death Vodka. *Beverage Industry, 83*(9), 173.

Burnham, P. (1992, May 27). Indians can't shake label as guides to good buys. *The Washington Times,* E1.

Calvert Research recommends dropping Liz Claiborne and Tootsie Roll from index. *Social Issues Reporter.* (October 2002). Retrieved from Lexis/Nexis database.

Coombe, R. J. (1998). *The cultural life of intellectual properties: Authorship, appropriation, and the law.* Durham, NC: Duke University Press.

Cortese, A. J. (1999). *Provocateur: Images of women and minorities in advertising.* New York: Rowman & Littlefield.

Crazy Horse. (2003). *Case Western Reserve University.* Retrieved fromhome.case.edu/~ijd3/authorship/crazyhorse.html

Darian-Smith, K. (2002). Material culture and the 'signs' of captive white women. In B. Creed & J. Hoorn (Eds.), *Body trade: Captivity, cannibalism, and colonialism in the Pacific* (pp. 180–194). London: Routledge.

Dávila, A. M. (2001). *Latinos Inc. The Marketing and Making of a People.* Berkeley, CA: University of California Press.

DeFleur, M. L., & Dennis, E. E. (1998). *Understanding mass communication.* Boston: Houghton Mifflin.

Domash, M. (2004). Selling civilization: Toward a cultural analysis of America's economic empire in the late nineteenth and early twentieth centuries. *Institute of British Geographers, 29,* 453–467.

Dotz, W., & Morton, J. (1996). *What a character! 20th century American advertising icons.* San Francisco: Chronicle.

Doxater, M. G. (2004). Indigenous knowledge in the Decolonial Era. *American Indian Quarterly, 28* (3/4), 618–633.

Dubinsky, K. (1999). *The second greatest disappointment: Honeymooning and tourism at Niagara Falls.* New Brunswick, NJ: Rutgers University Press.

Ellwood, I. (2002). *The essential brand book: Over 100 techniques to increase brand value.* London: Kogan Page.

Eyre, C. (2002, April 20). Eyre, Alexie premiers fill silver screen at Taos film festival. *Indian Country Today.* Retrieved from http://www.indiancountrytoday.com/content.cfm?id=1019314433

Foucault, M. (1977). *Discipline and punish: The birth of the prison.* In A. Sheridan (Trans.). New York: Random House.

Goings, K. W. (1994). *Mammy and Uncle Mose: Black collectibles and American stereotyping.* Bloomington, IN: Indiana University Press.

Green, M. K. (1993). Images of American Indians in advertising: Some moral issues. *Journal of Business Ethics, 12,* 323–330.

Hall, S. (1997). *Representation: Cultural representations and signifying practices*. London: Sage.

Hill, R. (1992, May). The non-vanishing American Indian: Are the modern images any closer to the truth?" *Quill*, 32–37.

Kates, S. M., & Shaw-Garlock, G. (1999). The ever-entangling Web: A study of ideologies and discourses in advertising to women. *Journal of Advertising, 28*(2), 33–49.

King, C. R. (1998). Spectacles, sports, and stereotypes: Dis/playing Chief Illiniwek. *Colonial discourse, collective memories, and the exhibition of Native American cultures and histories in the contemporary United States* (pp. 41–58). New York: Garland.

King, C. R. (2001). Uneasy Indians: Creating and contesting Native American mascots at Marquette University. In C. R. King & C. F. Springwood (Eds.), *Team spirits: Essays on the history and significance of Native American mascots* (pp. 281–303). Lincoln, NE: University of Nebraska Press.

Lacan, J. (1977). *Ecrits: A selection*. New York: W.W. Norton.

Land O'Lakes. (2000). Retrieved from http:www.landolakes.com

Larson, C. (1937). Patent-medicine advertising and the Early American press. *Journalism Quarterly, 14*(4), 337–339.

Leonard, D. (2005, January 26). *Cashing in on the other: Race, commodity, and surveillance of contemporary athletes*. Retrieved from http://www.popmatters.com/sports/features/050126-nikecommercials.shtml

Lippmann, W. (1922/1961). *Public opinion*. New York: Macmillan.

Manring, M. M. (1998). *Slave in a box: The strange career of Aunt Jemima*. Charlottesville, VA: University Press of Virginia.

Mansvelt, J. (2005). *Geographies of consumption*. Newbury Park, CA: Sage.

Mastro, D. E., & Behm-Morawitz, E. (2005). Latino representations on primetime television. *Journalism and Mass Communication Quarterly, 82*(1), 110–127.

McClintock, A. (1995). *Imperial leather: Race, gender, and sexuality in the colonial contest*. New York: Routledge.

McCracken, G. (1993). The value of the brand: An anthropological perspective. In D. Aaker & A. L. Biel (Eds.), *Brand equity in advertising: Advertising's role in building strong brands* (pp. 125–142). Mahwah, NJ: Lawrence Erlbaum.

Merskin, D. (1998). Sending up signals: A survey of American Indian media use and representation in the mass media. *The Howard Journal of Communication, 9*, 337–345.

Merskin, D. (2001). Winnebagos, Cherokees, Apaches, and Dakotas: The persistence of stereotyping of American Indians in American advertising brands. *The Howard Journal of Communication, 12*, 159–169.

Metz, S. & Thee, M. (1994). Brewers intoxicated with racist imagery. *Business and Society Review, 89*, 50–51.

Michigan Sugar Company. Retrieved from http://www.members.aol.com=asga=mon.htm

Mihesuah, D. A. (1996). *American Indians: Stereotypes and realities*. Atlanta, GA: Clarity.

Morgan, H. (1986). *Symbols of America*. New York: Penguin.

Oboler, S. (1998). 'Hispanics? That's what rhey call us.' In R. Delgado & J. Stefancic (Eds.), *The Latino/a condition: A critical reader* (pp. 3–5). New York: New York University Press.

Pyrillis, R. (2004, April 24). Sorry for not being a stereotype. *Chicago Sun-Times.* Retrieved from http://www.bluecorncomics.com/stharm.htm

Ramíerez-Berg, C. (1990). *Latino images in film: Stereotypes, subversion, resistance.* Austin, TX: University of Texas Press.

Rave, J. (2003, March 04). *Crazy Horse used to sell boobs and beer.* Retrieved from http://indianz. com/News/show.asp?ID=2003/03/04/rave

Roediger, D. R. (2002). *Colored White: Transcending the racial past.* Berkeley, CA: University of California Press.

Rosaldo, R. (1989). Imperialist nostalgia. *Representations, 26,* 107–122.

Said, E. (1978). *Orientalism.* New York: Vintage.

Schmitt, B., & Simonson, A. (1997). *Marketing aesthetics: The strategic management of brands, identity, and image.* New York: The Free Press.

Shamdasani, S. (2003). *Jung and the making of modern psychology: The dream of a science.* New York: Cambridge University Press.

Sioux Honey Association. (2000). Retrieved from http://www.suebeehoney.com

Smith, S. D. (2002, April). The ticker. *Money, 31*(4), 27.

Specktor, M. (1995, January 6). Crazy Horse exploited to peddle liquor. *National Catholic Reporter 31*(10), 3.

Staurowsky, E. J. (1998). The Cleveland Indians' use of the Louis Francis Sock Alexis story. *Sociology of Sport Journal, 15,* 299–316.

Strickland, R. (1997, January 13). Coyote goes Hollywood. *Native Peoples.* Retrieved from http:// www.nativepeoples.com/article/articles/174/1/COYOTE-GOES-HOLLYWOOD

van Dijk, T. A. (1996). *Discourse, racism, and ideology.* La Laguna, Mexico: RCEI Ediciones.

Walker, C. (2004, October 14). Crazy Horse descendants ask Paris strip club to stop using name. *The Associated Press State & Local Wire.* Retrieved from Lexis/Nexis database.

Westerman, M. (1989, March). Death of the Frito Bandito: Marketing to ethnic groups. *American Demographics, 11,* 28–32.

Williamson, J. (1978). *Decoding advertisements: Ideology and meaning in advertising.* New York: Marion Boyars.

Yellow Bird, M. (2004). Cowboys and Indians: Toys of genocide, icons of American colonialism. *Wicazo Sa Review 19*(2), 33–48.

Chapter Nine: The Pornographic Gaze in Mainstream American Magazine Fashion Advertising

(1989). Pornography of the mainstream. *Women Artists News, 14*), 23–33.

(1990). *Webster's New World Dictionary.* New York: Warner.

(17 July 2001). French women unhappy with sexist advertising. *Taipei Times*, http://www.taipae-itimes.com.

Alexander, M. W., & Judd, B., Jr. (1978). Do nudes in ads enhance brand recall? *Journal of Advertising Research, 18*(1), 47–50.

Alleti, V. (1999, May 11). Fashion photography takes over. *Village Voice*, 63.

Atwood, M. (1991). *The female body: Figures, styles, and speculations* In L. Goldstein (Ed) (p. 1), Ann Arbor, MI: University of Michigan Press.

Balsamo, A. (1995). *Technologies of the gendered body: Reading cyborg women.* Durham, NC: Duke University Press.

Barthes, R. (1983). *The Fashion System.* M. Ward & R. Howard. (Trans.). In C. Scott (Ed.), *The spoken image: Photography & language.* London: Reaktion.

Berger, A. A. (2000). *Ads, fads, and consumer culture: Advertising's impact on American character and society.* Lanham, MD: Rowman & Littlefield.

Berger, J. (1972). *Ways of Seeing.* London: British Broadcasting Corporation.

Bernbach, B. (2001). Taste in advertising. In K. Reinhard (Ed.), *Agency*, 31–32.

Bordo, S. (1993). *Unbearable weight: Feminism, western culture, and the body.* Berkeley: University of California Press.

Borgerson, J. L., & Schroeder, J. E. (2005). Identity in marketing communications: An ethics of visual representation. In A. J. Kimmel (Ed.), *Marketing communication: New approaches, technologies, and styles.* New York: Oxford.

Browne, A. (2001, July). Flesh for fantasy. *Jalouse*, 162–169.

Budgeon, S. (1994). Fashion magazine advertising: Constructing femininity in the 'postfeminist' era. In L. Manca & A. Manca (Eds.), *Gender & utopia in advertising: A critical reader* (pp. 55–70). Syracuse, New York: Syracuse University Press.

Burgin, V. (Ed.). (1982). *Thinking photography.* Atlantic Highlands, NJ: Humanities Press International.

Caputi, J. (2002). The pornography of everyday life. In G. Dines & J. Humez (Eds.), *Gender, race, and class in media* (pp. 434–450). Thousand Oaks, CA: Sage

Collins, P.H. (1995). Pornography and black women's bodies. In G. Dines & J.M. Humez (Eds.), *Gender, race, and class in media* (pp. 279–286). Thousand Oaks, CA: Sage.

Cortese, A. J. (1999). *Provocateur: Images of women and minorities in advertising.* Lanham, MD: Rowman & Littlefield.

Crary, J. (1990). *Techniques of the observer: On vision and modernity in the nineteenth century.* London: MIT Press.

da Silva, Martins, M.C. (1995). *Humor & eroticism in advertising.* San Diego, CA: San Diego State University Press.

Dines, G., & Jensen, R. (1998). The content of mass-marketed pornography. In G. Dines, R. Jensen, & A. Russo (Ed.), *Pornography: The production and consumption of inequality* (pp. 65–100). New York: Routledge.

Dines, G., Jensen, R., & Russo, A. (Eds.). (1998). *Pornography: The production and consumption of inequality.* New York: Routledge.

Dworkin, A. (1988). *Letters from the war zone.* New York: Dutton.

Dworkin, A. (2000). Against the male flood: Censorship, pornography, and equality. In D. Cornell (Ed.), *Readings in feminism and pornography* (pp. 19–44). Oxford, UK: Oxford University Press.

Falk, P. (1997). The Benetton-Toscani effect: Testing the limits of conventional advertising. In M. Nava, A. Blake, I. MacRury, & B. Richards (Eds.), *Buy this book: Studies in advertising and consumption* (pp. 64–83). New York: Routledge.

Foucault, M. (1980). Body/Power. In C. Gordon (Trans.). In C. Gordon, L. Marshall, J. Mepham, & K. Soper (Eds.), *Power/knowledge: Selected interviews and other writings 1972–1977* (pp. 55–62). New York: Pantheon.

Fox, E. (2001, July). Butt, seriously. *Jalouse*, 32.

"Gender," n. 3.b. *The Oxford English Dictionary.* (2nd ed.). 1989. OED Online. Oxford University Press. Retrieved from http://0-dictionary.oed.com.janus.uoregon.edu/cgi/entry/50093521?query_type=word&queryword=gender&first=1&max_to_show=10&sort_type=alpha&result_place=1&search_id=Jore-WhfblI-9424&hilite=50093521

Goffman, E. (1979). *Gender advertisements.* New York: Harper Collins.

Goldman, Robert (1992). *Reading ads socially.* New York: Routledge.

Hall, S. (1977). Culture, media, and the 'ideological effect.' In J. Curran, M. Gurevitch, & J. Woollacott (Eds.), *Mass communication and society* (pp. 315–348). London: Sage.

Harrison, M. (1991). *Appearances: Fashion photography since 1945.* London: Jonathan Cape.

Hood, J. C. (1989, May 16). Why our society is rape-prone. *New York Times,*

hooks, b. (1992). *Black looks: Race and representation.* Boston: South End Press.

Ingrassia, M. (2000, September 21). Risqué business. Magazine fashion ads push lewdness to the edge. *New York Daily News*, 64.

International Perfume Museum http://www.museesdegrasse.com/MIP/html_ang/histo_jXX.htm

Jhally, S. (1990). *The Codes of advertising: Fetishism and the political economy of meaning in the consumer society.* New York: Routledge.

Jhally, S. (1995). Image-based culture: Advertising and popular culture. In G. Dines & J. Humez (Eds.), *Gender, race, and class in media* (pp. 77–87). Thousand Oaks, CA: Sage.

Jones, M. Y., Stanaland, A. J. S., & Gelb, B. D. (1998). Beefcake and cheesecake: Insights for advertisers. *Journal of Advertising,* 27(2), 33–51.

Junod, T. (February 2001). Devil Greg dark. *Esquire,* 130–135.

Kilbourne, J. (1998). Beauty and the beast of advertising. *Media & Values* (Winter).

Kilbourne, J. (2000/2001). Hooked. In C. Simon. *Ms.* (December/January), 55–59.

Köhler, M. (1995). *The body exposed: Views of the body.* Switzerland: Edition Stemmle.

Kramer, H. (1975, December 28). The dubious art of fashion photography. *New York Times,* 28.

Kuhn, A. (1985). *The Power of the image: Essays on representation and sexuality.* London: Routledge.

Kuhn, A. (1995). Lawless seeing. In G. Dines & J. M. Humez (Eds.), *Gender, race, and class in media* (pp. 271–278). Thousand Oaks, CA: Sage.

Kuhner, J. T. (2000, July 25). Going soft on porn: Pornography enters American mainstream with AT&T's purchase of HOT network. *The Gazette* (Montreal), B3.

La Tour, M. S., & Pitts, R. E. (1990). Female nudity, arousal, and ad response: An experimental investigation. *Journal of Advertising, 19*(4), 51–62.

Landau, S. (2001, August 25). Porno-chic raises eyebrows. *New Straits Times.*

Leader, D., & Groves, J. (2000). *Introducing Lacan.* St. Leonards, NSW: Allen & Unwin.

Leibowitz, A., & Sontag, S. (1999). *Women.* New York: Random House.

Mayall, A., & Russell, D. E. H. (1995). Racism in pornography. In G. Dines & J. M. Humez (Eds.), *Gender, race, and class in media* (pp. 287–297). Thousand Oaks, CA: Sage.

McDonald, H. (2001). *Erotic ambiguities: The female nude in art.* London: Routledge.

McElroy, W. (1995). *A woman's right to pornography.* New York: St. Martin's.

McKinnon, C. A. (1991). *Toward a feminist theory of the state.* Cambridge, MA: Harvard University Press.

Newton, J. (2001). *The burden of visual truth: The role of photojournalism in mediating reality.* Thousand Oaks, CA: Sage.

O'Guinn, T. C., Allen, C. T., & Semenik, R. J. (2000). *Advertising.* (2nd ed.). Cincinnati, OH: South-Western College Publishing.

"Pornography," n.1. *The Oxford English Dictionary.* (2nd ed.). 1989. OED Online. Oxford University Press. Retrieved from http://0-dictionary.oed.com.janus.uoregon.edu/cgi/entry/50184353?single=1&query_type=word&queryword=pornography&first=1&max_to_show=10

Power, T. (2001). *Postmodernity and the body in fashion photography.* Retrieved from http://losthighway.dcu.ie/solas/des/bodyweb/tracy.html

Probyn, E. (2000). *Carnal appetites: Foodsexidentities.* New York: Routledge.

Pultz, J. (1995). *The body and the lens: The role of photojournalism in mediating reality.* Thousand Oaks, CA: Sage.

Reinhard, K. (2001). The taste debate. *Agency,* 31–32.

Ritchin, F. (1991). Unwrapped reality. *Aperture* (Winter), 120–121.

Saco, D. (1992). Masculinity as signs. In S. Craig (Ed.), *Men, masculinity, and the media* (pp. 23–29). Thousand Oaks, CA: Sage.

Sahlins, M. (1976). *Culture and practical reason.* Chicago: University of Chicago Press.

Schiarato, T., & Yell, S. (2000). *Communication and culture: An introduction.* Thousand Oaks, CA: Sage.

Schroeder, J. E., & Borgerson, J. L. (1998). Marketing images of gender: A visual analysis. *Consumption, market and culture, 2*(2), 161–201.

"Sex," n.1. *The Oxford English Dictionary.* (2nd ed.). 1989. OED Online. Oxford University Press. Retrieved from http://0-dictionary.oed.com.janus.uoregon.edu/cgi/entry/50221203?query_type=word&queryword=sex&first=1&max_to_show=10&sort_type=alpha&result_place=2&search_id=JOre-taNmRF-9216&hilite=50221203

Shields, V. R. (1997). Selling the sex that sells: Mapping the evolution of gender advertising research across the decades (pp. 71–109). *Communication Yearbook,* 20.

Solomon, J. (1990). *The signs of our times: The secret meanings of everyday life.* New York: Harper & Row.

Squires, C., Yamashio, J. P., Stirratt, B., & Wolin, J. A. (2000). *Peek: Photographs from the Kinsey Institute.* New York: Arena.

Steele, V. (1991). Erotic allure. *Aperture,* 81–96.

Stokstad, M. (1995). *Art history.* New York: H.N. Abrams.

Stratton, J. (1996). *The desirable body: Cultural fetishism and the erotics of consumption.* Chicago: University of Illinois Press.

Tickner, L. (1989). The body politic: Female sexuality and women artists since 1970. In R. Betterton (ed.), *Looking on: Images of femininity in the visual arts and media* (pp. 235–253). London: Pandora.

Turner, B. (1984). *The body and society: Exploration in social theory.* Oxford: Basil Blackwell.

Wilkes, A. (1991). The idealizing vision: The art of fashion photography. *Aperture* (Winter).

Williamson, J. (1978). *Decoding advertisements: ideology and meaning in advertising.* New York: Marion Boyars.

Yell, S. (2000). *Communication and culture: An introduction.* London: Sage.

Chapter Ten: What's in a Name: Women, Lipstick, and Self-presentation

Abramson, E., & Valene, P. (1991). Media use, dietary restraint, bulimia, and attitudes toward obesity: A preliminary study. *British Review of Bulimia and Anorexia Nervosa, 5,* 73–76.

Ackerman, D. (1993). *A natural history of the senses.* New York: Vintage.

Anderson, D. R., Huston, A. C., Schmitt, K. L., Linebarger, D. L., & Wright, J. C. (2001). Early childhood television viewing and adolescent behaviour: The recontact study. *Monographs of the Society for Research in Child Development, 66,* 1–146.

Barthes, R. (1982). Myth today. In S. Sontag (Ed.), *A Barthes reader* (pp. 93–139). New York: Hill and Wang.

Baudin, P. (1885). *Fetichism and fetich worshippers.* New York: Benziger.

Beausoleil, N. (1994). Make-up in everyday life: An inquiry into the practices of urban American women of diverse backgrounds. In N. Sault (Ed.), *Many mirrors: Body image and social relations* (pp. 33–57). New Brunswick, NJ: Rutgers University Press.

Berger, J. (1977). *Ways of seeing.* London: British Broadcasting/Penguin.

Betsky, A. (Ed.). (1997). *Icons: Magnets of meaning.* San Francisco: Chronicle.

Black, P. (2004). *The beauty industry.* London: Routledge.

Bordo, S. (1993). Hunger as ideology. In J. B. Schor & D. B. Holt (Eds.), *The consumer society reader* (pp. 99–114). New York: New Press.

Borzekowski, D. L. G., Robinson, T. N., & Killen, J. D. (2000). Does the camera add 10 pounds? Media use, perceived importance of appearance, and weight concerns among teenage girls. *Journal of Adolescent Health, 26,* 36–41.

Botta, R. A. (1999). Television images and adolescent girls' body image disturbance. *Journal of Communication, 49,* 22–41.

Bourdieu, P. (1984). *Distinction: A social critique of the judgment of taste.* London: Routledge.

Bourdieu, P. (2001). *Masculine domination.* In R. Nice (Trans.). Stanford, CA: Stanford University Press.

Brownmiller, S. (1984). *Femininity.* New York: Fawcett Columbine.

Brumberg, J. J. (1998). *The body project: An intimate history of American girls.* New York: Vintage.

Cusumano, D. L., & Thompson, J. K. (1997). Body image and body shape ideals in magazines: Exposure, awareness, and internalization. *Sex Roles, 37,* 701–719.

Davis, K. (1991). Re-making the she-devil: A critical look at feminist approaches to beauty. *Hypatia, 6*(2), 21–43.

de Certeau, M. (1984). *The practice of everyday life.* Berkeley, CA: University of California.

Douglas, M. (1970). *Natural symbols: Explorations in cosmology.* London: Cresset.

Ethridge, M. (2003, January 13). Madshopper column. *Akron Beacon Journal.* Retrieved from Lexis/Nexis.

Face lift. (2002, April 15). *Advertising Age.* Retrieved from Lexis/Nexis.

Field, A. E., Cheung, L., Wolf, A. M., Herzog, D. B., Gortmaker, S. L., & Colditz, G. A. (1999). Exposure to mass media and weight concerns among girls. *Pediatrics, 103,* 214–220.

Foucault, M. (1979). *Discipline and punish: The birth of the prison.* New York: Penguin.

Foucault, M. (1980). *Power/knowledge: Selected interviews and other writings, 1972–1977.* New York: Pantheon.

Furman, F. K. (1997). *Facing the mirror: Older women and beauty shop culture.* New York: Routledge.

Gage, J. (1999). *Color and meaning: Art, science, and symbolism.* Berkeley, CA: University of California.

Gamman, L., & Makinen, M. (1994). *Female fetishism.* New York: New York University Press.

Gobé, M. (2001). *Emotional branding: The new paradigms for connecting brands to people.* New York: Alworth.

Goffman, E. (1959). *The presentation of self in everyday life.* New York: Anchor.

Goffman, E. (1963). *Behavior in public places: Notes on the social organization of gatherings.* New York: Free Press.

Hall, S. (1996). On postmodernism and articulation: An interview with Stuart Hall. In D. Morley & K. H. Chen (Eds.), *Stuart Hall: Critical dialogues in cultural studies* (pp. 131–150). New York: Routledge.

Hargreaves, D., & Tiggemann, M. (2003). The effect of "thin ideal" television commercials on body dissatisfaction and schema activation during early adolescence. *Journal of Youth and Adolescence, 32*(5), 367–373.

Harrison, K. (2000). Television viewing, fat stereotyping, body shape standards, and eating disorder symptomatology in grade school children. *Communication Research, 27,* 617–640.

Harrison, K. (2001). Ourselves, our bodies: Thin-ideal media, self-discrepancies, and eating disorder symptomatology in adolescents. *Journal of Social and Clinical Psychology, 20,* 289–323.

Harrison, K., & Cantor, J. (1997). The relationship between media consumption and eating disorders. *Journal of Communication, 47,* 40–67.

Hayt, E. (2005, August 4). Kiss my puffy lips. *New York Times,* p. E3.

Holbrook, M. B., Block, L. G., & Fitzsimmons, G. J. (1998). Personal appearance and consumption in popular culture: A framework for descriptive and prescriptive analysis. *Consumption, Markets, and Culture, 2,* 1–55.

Jhally, S. (1990). *The codes of advertising: Fetishism and the political economy of meaning in the consumer society.* New York: Routledge.

Kahn, B., & Miller, E. G. (2005). Shades of meaning: The effect of color and flavor names on communication. *Journal of Consumer Research, 32,* 86–92.

Klink, R. R. (2000, February). Creating brand names with meaning: The use of sound symbolism. *Marketing Letters,* 5–20.

Langman, L. (1992). Neon cages: Shopping for subjectivity. In R. Shields (Ed.), *Lifestyle shopping: The subject of consumption* (pp. 40–82). London: Routledge.

Levine, M. P., & Smolak, L. (1996). Media as a context for the development of disordered eating. In L. Smolak, M. P. Levine, & R. Streigel-Moore (Eds.), *The developmental psychopathology of eating disorders* (pp. 235–257). Mahwah, NJ: Lawrence Erlbaum.

Levine, M. P., Smolak, L., & Hayden, H. (1994). The relation of sociocultural factors of eating attitudes and behaviors among middle school girls. *Journal of Early Adolescence, 14,* 471–490.

Lipsticks provide a bright spot in a dull economy. (2001, November 28). (Corporate press release). Estèe Lauder Companies, New York.

Morris, D. (2004). *The naked woman: A study of the female body.* New York: St. Martin's.

Mulvey, L. (2001). Visual pleasure and narrative cinema. In M. G. Durham & D. M. Kellner (Eds.), *Media and cultural studies: Keyworks* (pp. 393–404). Malden, MA: Blackwell.

Owen, P. R., & Laurel-Seller, E. (2000). Weight and shape ideals: Thin is dangerously in. *Journal of Applied Social Psychology, 30,* 979–990.

Pallingston, J. (1999). *Lipstick.* New York: St. Martin's.

Peiss, K. (1990). Making faces: The cosmetics industry and the cultural construction of gender, 1890–1930. *Genders, 7,* 143–169.

Peiss, K. (1998). *Hope in a jar.* New York: Holt.

Peiss, K. (2002). Miss America [Television series episode]. In M. Ferrari (Writer) & L. Ades (Director), *American Experience.* Retrieved from http://www.pbs.org/wgbh/amex/missamerica/filmmore/index.html

Platt, M. (2004, December). Lip wardrobes. *In Style,* 459.

Ragas, M. C., & Kozlowski, K. (1998). *Read my lips: A cultural history of lipstick.* San Francisco: Chronicle.

Richlin, A. (1995). *Pornography and representation in Greece and Rome.* New York: Oxford.

Shilling, C. (1993). *The body and social theory.* London: Sage.

Singer, N. (2005, August 25). Season of the painted lady. *New York Times*, E3.

Smith, D. E. (1990). *Texts, facts, and femininity: Exploring the relations of ruling*. London: Routledge.

Spicer, E. (2002, December 31). *Lipstick can be applied as war paint or a prelude to New Year's allure. Canada.com.* Retrieved from http://www.canada.com

Stice, E., Schupak-Neuberg, E., Shaw, H. E., & Stein, R. I. (1994). Relation of media exposure to eating disorder symptomatology: An examination of mediating mechanisms. *Journal of Abnormal Psychology, 103*, 836–840.

thelipstickpage.com, retrieved February 2004.

Turner, B. (1984). *The body and society: Exploration in social theory*. Oxford: Blackwell.

van Dyk, D. (2001, December 10). The recession is here. Sales are up. *Time* (n.p.) Retrieved from Lexis/Nexis.

Vlahos, O. (1979). *Body the ultimate symbol*. New York: Lippincott.

von Furstenberg, D. (1998). Cited in M. C. Ragas & K. Kozlowski. *Read my lips: A cultural history of lipstick*. San Francisco: Chronicle Books.

Walker, R. (2005, July 31). Color coding. *New York Times Magazine*, 17.

Williams, R. (1980). As cited in L. Gamman & M. Makinen (1994). *Female fetishism: A new look*. London: Lawrence and Wishart.

Williamson, J. (1978). *Decoding advertisements: Ideology and meaning in advertising*. London: Marion Boyars.

Witz, A., Warhurst, C., & Nickson, D. (2003). The labour of aesthetics and the aesthetics of organization. *Organization, 10*, 33–54.

Wolf, N. (2002). *The beauty myth*. New York: HarperPerennial.

Woodhead, L. (2004). *War paint: Madame Helena Rubinstein and Miss Elizabeth Arden, their lives, their times, their rivalry*. New York: Wiley.

Wordnet. (2005). Retrieved from http://dictionary.reference.com

Zakia, R. D. (2002). *Perception and imaging* (2nd ed.). Boston: Focal.

Chapter Eleven: Sun Also Rises: Stereotypes of the Asian/American Woman on *Lost*

Abrams, J. J. (Executive Producer). 2004. Pilot. In *Lost* [Television series episode]. In *Lost*. New York: ABC.

Adams, T. (2004, September 19). If we're not being rescued, let's all start new lives. *The New York Times,* 13/4.

Ahlström, K. (2005). Incorporating feminist standpoint theory. *Sats—Nordic Journal of Philosophy, 6*(2), 79–92.

Ahrens, F. (2006, May 13). With *Lost* experience, ABC moves beyond the island. *The Washington Post*, D1.

Althusser, L. (1971). Ideology and ideological state apparatuses. In B. Brewster (Trans.), *Lenin and philosophy and other essays* (pp. 121–176). New York: Monthly Review Press.

Aoki, A. L., & Takeda, O. (2008). *Asian American politics.* Cambridge, UK: Polity.

Atkin, D. (1992). An analysis of television series with minority lead characters. *Critical Studies in Mass Communication, 9*(4), 337–349.

Bender, J. (Director). (2005). Exodus [Television series episode]. In *Lost.* New York: ABC.

Cao, L., & Novas, H. (1996). *Everything you never knew about Asian American history.* New York: Plume.

Chihara, M. (2000, February 25). Casting a cold eye on the rise of Asian starlets. *The Boston Phoenix*, 26.

Children Now. (2001). *Fall colors 2000–2001: Prime time diversity report.* Oakland, CA.

Collins, P. H. (2000). *Black feminist thought.* New York: Routledge.

Devine, P. G., & Elliot, A. J. (1995). Are racial stereotypes really fading? The Princeton trilogy revisited. *Personality and Social Psychology Bulletin, 21*(11), 1139–1150.

Edwards, P. (2006). The glass ballerina [Television series episode]. In *Lost.* New York: ABC.

Espiritu, Y. L. (1997). *Asian American women and men: Labor, laws, and love.* Thousand Oaks, CA: Sage.

Espiritu, Y. L. (2008). *Asian American women and men: Labor, laws, and love.* Lanham, MD: Rowman & Littlefield.

Feagin, J. R., Vera, H., & Batur, P. (2001). *White racism: The basics.* (2nd ed.). New York: Routledge.

Fung, R. (1996). Looking for my penis: The eroticized Asian in gay video porn. In R. Leong (Ed.), *Asian American sexualities: Dimensions of the gay and lesbian experience.* New York: Routledge.

Gaffney, K. (2008). 'The Others are coming': Ideology and Otherness in *Lost.* In S. M. Kaye (Ed.), Lost *and philosophy: The island has its reasons* (pp. 136–147). Malden, MA: Blackwell.

Gates, T. (Director). (2005). In translation [Television series episode]. In *Lost.* New York: ABC.

Gee, D. (Director). (1988). *Slaying the dragon* [Film]. San Francisco: Cross Current Media and National Asian American Telecommunication Association.

Gerbner, G. (1998). *Casting and fate in '98. Fairness and diversity in television: An update and trends since the 1993 SG report* (A Cultural Indicators Project report to the Screen Actors Guild). Philadelphia: Temple University Press.

Gorham, B. (2010). The social psychology of stereotypes: Implications for media audiences. In R. A. Lind (Ed.), *Race/Gender/Media: Considering diversity across audiences, content, and producers* (pp. 16–24). 2nd ed. Boston: Allyn & Bacon.

Hall, S. (1997). *Representation: Cultural representations and signifying practices.* London: Sage.

Hamamoto, D. Y. (1994). *Monitored peril: Asian Americans and the politics of TV representation.* Minneapolis, MN: University of Minnesota Press.

Hamilton, D. L., & Trolier, T. K. (1986). Stereotypes and stereotyping: An overview of the cognitive approach. In S. L. Gaertner & J. F. Dovidio (Eds.), *Prejudice, discrimination, and racism* (pp. 127–157). New York: Academic.

Harding, S. (1991). *Whose science? Whose knowledge? Thinking from women's lives.* Ithaca, New York: Cornell University Press.

Herbst, P. (1997). *The color of words: An encyclopedic dictionary of ethnic bias in the United States.* Yarmouth, ME: Intercultural Press.

Jiwani, Y. (2005). The Eurasian female hero[ine]: Sydney Fox as *Relic Hunter. Journal of Popular Film & Television, 32*, 182–191.

Kim, M., & Chung, A. Y. (2005). Consuming Orientalism: Images of Asian/American women in multicultural advertising. *Qualitative Sociology, 28*(1), 67–91.

King, S. (2005, May 11). 'Lost' actress is no timid Asian woman, after all. *Honolulu Advertiser.* Retrieved from http://the.honoluluadvertiser.com/article/2005/May/11/il/il03a.html

Lee, J. Y. (1996). Why Suzie Wong is not a lesbian: Asian and Asian American bisexual women and femme/butch gender identities. In B. Beemyn & M. Eliason (Eds.), *Queer studies: An anthology.* New York: NYU Press.

Lippmann, W. (1922/1961). *Public opinion.* New York: Macmillan.

Mansfield-Richardson, V. D. (2000). *Asian-Americans and the mass media: A content analysis of twenty United States newspapers and a survey of Asian-American journalists.* New York: Garland.

Marchetti, G. (1993). *Romance and the 'yellow peril': Race, sex, and discursive strategies in Hollywood fiction.* Berkeley, CA: University of California Press.

Meyer, M. D. E., & Stern, D. M. (2007). The modern (?) Korean woman in prime time: Analyzing the representation of Sun on the television series *Lost. Women's Studies, 36*, 313–331.

Palumbo-Liu, D. (1999). *Asian/American: Historical crossings of a racial frontier.* Stanford, CA: Stanford University Press.

Patton, T. O. (2001). Ally McBeal and her homies: The reification of white stereotypes of the other. *Journal of Black Studies, 322*(2), 229–260.

Quine, R. (Director). (1960). *The world of Suzie Wong* [Motion picture]. United States: Paramount.

Said, E. W. (1979). *Orientalism.* New York: Vintage.

Said, E. (1993). *Culture and imperialism.* New York: Alfred A. Knopf.

Seagrave, S. (1992). *Dragon lady: The last empress of China.* New York: Alfred A. Knopf.

Semel, S. (2008). Ji Yeon. D.O.C. [Television series episode]. In *Lost.* New York: ABC.

Shimizu, C. P. (2007). *The hypersexuality of race: Performing Asian/American women on screen and scene.* Durham, NC: Duke University Press.

Spade, J. Z., & Valentine, C. G. (2007). *The kaleidoscope of gender: Prisms, patterns, and possibilities.* Thousand Oaks, CA: Pine Forge Press.

Stafford, N. (2006). *Finding* Lost: *The unofficial guide.* Toronto: ECW Press.

Stanford Encyclopedia of Philosophy. (2009). Feminist social epistemology. Retrieved, from http://plato.stanford.edu/entries/feminist-social-epistemology

Sun, C. F. (2003). Ling Woo in historical context: The new face of Asian American stereotypes on television. In G. Dines & J. M. Humez (Eds.), *Gender, race, and class in media* (pp. 656–664). (2nd ed.). Thousand Oaks, CA: Sage.

Surette, T. (2009, February 09). *Lost*'s Yunjin Kim: 'Expect a different Sun in Season 6.' *TV.com*. Retrieved from http://www.tv.com/losts-yunjin-kim-expect-a-different-sun-in-season-6/story/21304.html#

Tajima, R. E. (1989). Lotus blossoms don't bleed: Images of Asian women. In Asian Women United of California (Ed.), *Making waves: An anthology of writings by and about Asian American women* (pp. 308–317). Boston: Beacon.

Taliaferro, C., & Kastrul, D. (2008). What would you do? Altered states in *Lost*. In S. M. Kaye (Ed.), Lost *and philosophy: The island has its reasons* (pp. 77–88). Malden, MA: Blackwell.

Toye, F. E. O. (Director). (2007). D.O.C. [Television series episode]. In *Lost*. New York: ABC.

Waldinger, R. (1999). When the melting pot boils over: The Irish, Jews, blacks, and Koreans of New York. In C. A. Gallagher (Ed.), *Rethinking the color line: Readings in race and ethnicity* (pp. 287–298). Mountain View, CA: Mayfield.

Walsh, R. (Director). (1924). *The thief of Bagdad* [Motion picture]. United States: United Artists.

Warn, S. (2007, May 15). Network TV featuring more leading Asian American women, sky doesn't fall. *AfterEllen.com*. Retrieved from http://www.afterellen.com/blog/sarahwarn/network-tv-featuring-more-leading-asian-american-women-next-season

Williams, S. (Director). (2006). The hunting party [Television series episode]. In *Lost*. New York: ABC.

Williams, S. (Director). (2007). Expose [Television series episode]. In *Lost*. New York: ABC.

Wood, J. (2007). *Living* Lost *and why we're all stuck on the island*. New Orleans, LA: Garrett County.

Wood, J. T. (1994). *Gendered lives: Communication, gender, and culture*. Belmont, CA: Wadsworth.

Wrisley, G. (2008). The island of ethical subjectivism: Not the paradise of *Lost*. In S. M. Kaye (Ed.), Lost *and philosophy: The island has its reasons* (pp. 49–59). Malden, MA: Blackwell.

Xing, J. (1998). *Asian America through the lens: History, representations, and identities*. Walnut Creek, CA: AltaMira.

Zinn, H. (2005). *A people's history of the United States: 1492–present*. New York: HarperPerennial.

Chapter Twelve: Coon Songs: The Black Male Stereotype in Popular American Sheet Music (1850–1920)

(2008, February 07). Discrimination against blacks linked to dehumanization, study finds. *Physorg.com*. Retrieved from http://www.physorg.com/news121622948.html

(2008, October 29). Study finds physicians have subconscious bias for whites. Retrieved from http://www.redorbit.com/news/health/1594779/study_finds_physicians_have_subconscious_bias_for_whites/index.html

(2009, February 21). 'A nation of cowards.' The Attorney General's speech on race. *The Washington Post*. (Editorial). A12.

Abbott, L., & Seroff, D. (2007). *Ragged but right: Black traveling shows, 'coon songs,' and the dark pathway to blues and jazz.* Jackson, MI: University Press of Mississippi.

"All coons look alike to me." (1896). E. Hogan (Writer). [Sheet music]. London: M. Witmark & Sons.

American Memory Project. The Library of Congress. *African American Sheet Music, 1850–1920.* Retrieved from http://memory.loc.gov/ammem/collections/sheetmusic/brown/

Bacon, J. (2007). *Freedom's journal.* Lanham, MD: Lexington.

Baron, A. S., & Banaji, M. R. (2005). The development of implicit attitudes: Evidence of race evaluations from ages 6 and 10 and adulthood. *Psychological Science, 17*(1), 53–58.

Bean, A., Hatch, J. V., & McNamara, B. (Eds.). (1996). *Inside the minstrel mask: Readings in nineteenth-century blackface minstrelsy.* Middletown, CT: Wesleyan University Press.

Bender, S. (2002). *Greasers and gringos: Latinos, law, and the American imagination.* New York: NYU Press.

Blow, C. M. (2009, February 21). A nation of cowards? *New York Times.* Retrieved from http://www.nytimes.com/2009/02/21/opinion/21blow.html?_r=1&scp=1&sq=A%20nation%20of%20cowards&st=cse

Bogle, D. (1973/1994). *Toms, coons, mulattoes, mammies, & bucks: An interpretive history of Blacks in American films.* New York: Continuum.

African- American Sheet Music 1850–1920. Retrieved from Brown University Library and National Digital Library Project, Library of Congress. http://memory.loc.gov/ammem/collections/sheetmusic/brown/

Calderisi, R. (2005). *The trouble with Africa: Why foreign aid isn't working.* Pretoria, South Africa: Pretoria University Law Press.

Cannon, L. (1999). *Official negligence: How Rodney King and the riots changed Los Angeles and the LAPD.* Boulder, CO: Westview.

"Caricature, n.1" *The Oxford English Dictionary.* (2nd ed.) 1989. OED Online. Oxford University Press. Retrieved from http://0-dictionary.oed.com.janus.uoregon.edu/cgi/entry/5003351

Clarke, J. H. (2002). As cited in T. Bender. *Rethinking American history in a global age.* Berkeley, CA: University of California Press.

Cohen, E. S., & Krushwitz, A. L. (1990). Old age in America represented in nineteenth and twentieth century popular sheet music. *Gerontologist, 30*(3), 345–354.

Cort, C., Blair, J. & Friday, I. (Dirs.). (1993). *Passing.* [Documentary]. Berkely, CA: University of California Extension Center for Media and Independent Learning

Denton, K. A. (1987). Model drama as myth: A semiotic analysis of Taking Tiger Mountain by Strategy. In C. Tung & C. Mackerras (Eds.), *Drama in the People's Republic of China* (pp. 119–136). Albany, New York: SUNY Press.

Dusinberre, W. (1995). *Them dark days: Slavery in the American rice swamps.* New York: Oxford University Press.

Ehrlich, H. (1973). *The social psychology of prejudice.* New York: Wiley.

Ewen, E., & Ewen, S. (2007). *Typecasting: On the arts and sciences of human equality.* New York: Seven Stories.

Fletcher, M. A., & Cohen, J. (2009, January 19). Far fewer consider racism big problem. *The Washington Post*, A06. Retrieved from http://www.washingtonpost.com/wp-dyn/content/article/2009/01/18/AR2009011802538.html

Gilbert, G. M. (1951). Stereotyping persistence and change among college students. *Journal of Abnormal and Social Psychology, 46*, 245–254.

Gilens, M. (1999). *Why Americans hate welfare: Race, media, and the politics of antipoverty policy.* Chicago: University of Chicago Press.

Gladwell, M. (2005). *Blink: The power of thinking without thinking.* New York: Little Brown.

Goff, P. A., Eberhardt, J. A., Williams, M. J., & Jackson, M. C. (2008). Not yet human: Implicit knowledge, historical dehumanization, and contemporary consequences. *Journal of Personality and Social Psychology, 94*(2), 292–306.

Gottschalk, P., & Greenberg, G. (2008). *Islamophobia: Making Muslims the enemy.* London: Rowman & Littlefield.

Gundykunst, W. B. (2005). *Theorizing about intercultural communication.* Thousand Oaks, CA: Sage.

Harney, B. P. (1896). Mister Johnson, Turn Me Loose. *Sheet Music.* Retrieved from http://memory.loc.gov/diglib/ihas/loc.natlib.ihas.200035822/default.html

Hogan, E. (1896). All coons look alike to me. [Sheet music]. New York: M. Witmark & Sons.

How do Americans view one another? The persistence of racial/ethnic stereotypes. Retrieved from Diversityweb.org.

Jasen, D.A., & Tichenor, J. (1989). *Rags and ragtime: A musical history.* New York: Dover.

Jones, L. R. (1969). *Black magic poetry 1961–1967.* New York: Bobbs-Merrill.

July, W. H. (II). (1995, May). The ten biggest myths about black sexuality. *Upscale,* 44–47.

Katz, D., & Braley, K. (1933). Racial stereotypes of one hundred college students. *Journal of Abnormal and Social Psychology, 28*, 280–290.

Kennedy, R. (2002). *Nigger: The strange career of a troublesome word.* New York: Pantheon Books.

Leab, D. J. (1976). *From Sambo to Superspade: The Black experience in motion pictures.* Boston: Houghton Mifflin.

Lebrecht, S., Pierce, L. J., Tarr, M. J., & Tanaka, J. W. (2009). Perceptual other-race training reduces implicit racial bias. *Plos One.* Retrieved from http://www.plosone.org/article/info:doi%2F10.1371%2Fjournal.pone.0004215

Levine, L. L. (1978). *Black culture and black consciousness: Afro-American folk thought from slavery to freedom.* New York: Oxford.

Levy, L. S. (1976). *Picture the songs: Lithographs from the sheet music of nineteenth-century America.* Baltimore, MD: Johns Hopkins University Press.

Lott, E. (1993). *Love and theft: Blackface minstrelsy and the American working class.* New York: Oxford University Press.

McLaughlin, A. C. (1914). *Readings in the history of the American nation.* New York: D. Appleton.

Memmi, A. (1957/1991). *The colonizer and the colonized.* New York: Beacon.

Mercer, K. (1994). *Welcome to the jungle: New positions in Black cultural studies.* New York: Routledge.

Mungazi, D. A. (1996). *The mind of Black Africa.* Westport, CT: Greenwood.

Omni, M., & Winant, H. (1994). *Racial formation in the United States.* (2nd ed.). New York: Routledge.

Page, T. N. (1904). *The Negro: The southerner's problem.* New York: Charles Scribner's.

Palmore, E. (1962). Ethnophaulisms and Ethnocentrism. *American Journal of Sociology, 67,* 442–445.

Pérez-Peña, R. (2009, February 24). Murdoch apologizes in *Post* for cartoon of chimpanzee. *New York Times.* Retrieved from http://www.nytimes.com/2009/02/25/nyregion/25cartoon. html?_r=1&scp=2&sq=chimpanzee&st=cse

Pilgrim, D. (2000). Who was Jim Crow? Retrieved August 05, 2010, from http://www.ferris.edu/ jimcrow/who.htm

Pilgrim, D., & Middleton, P. (2001). *Nigger and caricatures.* Retrieved from http://www.ferris. edu/jimcrow/caricature/

Riggs, M. (Director). (1987). *Ethnic Notions* [Motion Picture]. United States.

Sabin, J. A., Nosek, B., Greenwald, A., & Rivara, F. (2008). Comparing physician implicit and explicit attitudes about race by gender, race, and ethnicity. Paper presented at the American Public Health Association annual meeting. San Diego, CA.

Sartre, J-P. (1957/1991). Introduction. *The Colonizer and the Colonized* (pp. xxi–xxix). New York: Beacon.

Segal, R. (1995). *The Black diaspora: Five centuries of the Black experience outside Africa.* New York: Farrar, Straus & Giroux.

Smith, S. (2005). *Household words: Bloomers, sucker, bombshell, scab, nigger, cyber.* Minneapolis: University of Minnesota Press.

Sotiropoulos, K. (2006). *Staging race: Black performers in turn of the century America.* Cambridge, MA: Harvard University Press.

Stamp, K. M. (1956). *The peculiar institution: Slavery in the ante-bellum South.* New York: Random House.

Staunton, D. (2009, February 21). Cartoonist's monkey business enrages African-Americans. *The Irish Times,* 10.

Steele, S. (2008). Shelby Steele on Michelle Obama's *60 Minutes* comments: She was "facilitating her race's manipulation of the American mainstream." *MediaMatters for America.* Retrieved from http://mediamatters.org/items/200801160005

Swan, R. J. (2003). *New Amsterdam gehenna: Segregated death in New York City, 1630–1801.* Brooklyn: Noir Verite.

Toll, R. C. (1974). *Blacking up: The minstrel show in nineteenth-century America.* Oxford University Press.

Turner, P. A. (1994). *Ceramic uncles & celluloid mammies: Black images and their influence on culture.* New York: Anchor.

Verney, K. (2003). *African Americans and U.S. popular culture.* New York: Routledge.

Wall, T. (2009, February 24). Americans are not cowards on race. Commentary. *CNN.* Retrieved from http://www.cnn.com/2009/POLITICS/02/24/wall.holder/

Washington, J. (2009, February 21). Drawing Obama tricky for cartoonists. *Eugene Register-Guard,* A1.

Worth, R. F. (1995). Nigger Heaven and the Harlem Renaissance. *African American Review, 29*(3), 461–473.

Wynter, S. (1994). No humans involved: An open letter to my colleagues. *Forum N.H.I.: Knowledge for the 21st Century, 1*(1), 42.

Chapter Thirteen: Homosexuality and Horror: The Lesbian Vampire Film

(1934, June 11). Legion of decency. *Time.* Retrieved from http://www.time.com/time/magazine/article/0,9171,762190-1,00.html

(2008, September 07). The Hunger. *Moria: Science Fiction, Horror, and Fantasy Film Review.* Retrieved from http://www.moria.co.nz/index.php?option=com_content&task=view&id=1 924Itemid=1

Anzaldúa, G. E. (2002). Now let us shift. In G. E.Anzaldúa and A. Keating (Eds.), *This bridge we call home: Radical visions for transformation* (pp. 540–578). New York: Routledge.

Ausband, S. (1983). *Myth and meaning, myth and order.* Macon, GA: Mercer University Press.

Benedict, H. (1993). *Virgin or vamp: How the press covers sex crimes.* New York: Oxford.

Benshoff, H. M., & Griffin, S. (2004). *America on film: Representing race, class, gender, and sexuality at the movies.* London: Blackwell.

Berenstein, R. J. (1996). *Attack of the leading ladies: Gender, sexuality, and spectatorship in classic horror cinema.* New York: Columbia University Press.

Berenstein, R. J. (1999). Film, mainstream. In B. Zimmerman & G. E. Haggerty (Eds.), *The encyclopedia of lesbian and gay histories and cultures* (pp. 303–305). London: Taylor & Francis.

Butler, J. (1999). *Gender trouble.* New York: Routledge.

Byron, G. G. (1813/2006). The Giaour. In *Fragment of a Turkish Tale.* ReadHowYouWant.com

Cairns, L. (2006). *Sapphism on screen.* Edinburgh, UK: Edinburgh University Press.

Campbell, J. (1991). *The masks of god: Creative mythology.* New York: Viking.

Clover, C. (1992). *Men, women, and chainsaws: Gender in the modern horror film.* Princeton, NJ: Princeton University Press.

Conger, J. (1975). Proceedings of the American Psychological Association for the year 1974: Minutes of the annual meeting of the Council of Representatives. *American Psychologist, 30,* 620-651.

Craft, C. (1997). *Another kind of love: Male homosexual desire in English discourse, 1850-1920.* Berkeley: University of California Press.

Crane, J. L. (1994). *Terror and everyday life: Singular moments in the history of the horror film.* Thousand Oaks, CA: Sage.

Creed, B. (1993). *The monstrous-feminine: Film, feminism, psychoanalysis.* New York: Routledge.

Douglas, M. (1996). *Purity and danger: An analysis of concepts of pollution and taboo.* New York: Praeger.

Ebert, R. (1983, May 03). The Hunger. *Chicago Sun-Times*. Retrieved October 20, 2010, from http://rogerebert.suntimes.com/apps/pbcs.dll/article?AID=/19830503/REVIEWS/305030301/1023

Freud, S. (1919/2003). *The uncanny*. In J. Strachey (Trans.). London: Penguin.

Fristoe, R. (n.d.). Screened Out. *Turner Classic Movies*. Retrieved fromhttp://www.tcm.com/thismonth/article/?cid=159623

Gartner, R. B. (2001). *Betrayed as boys: Psychodynamic treatment of sexually abused men*. New York: Guilford.

Grant, B. K. (2007). *Film genre*. London: Wallflower.

Hanson, E. (Ed.). (1999). *Out takes: Essays on queer theory and film*. Durham, NC: Duke University Press.

Hockley, L. (2001). Film noir: Archetypes or stereotypes? In C. Hauke & I. Alister (Eds.), *Jung & Film: Post-Jungian takes on the moving image* (pp. 177–193). Hove, East Sussex; New York: Brunner Routledge.

Irigaray, L. (1985). *This sex which is not one*. In C. Porter (Trans.). New York: Cornell University Press.

Jones, D. (2002) *Horror: A thematic history in fiction and film*. London: Arnold.

Keesey, P. (2006). *Daughters of darkness: Lesbian vampire tales*. Berkeley, CA: Cleis Press.

Kristeva, J. (1982). *Powers of horror: An essay on abjection..* In L. S. Roudiez (Trans.). New York: Columbia University Press.

Landay, L. (2002). The flapper film: Comedy, dance, and jazz age kinasthetics. In J. M. Bean & D. Negra (Eds.), *A feminist reader in early cinema* (pp. 221–250). Durham, NC: Duke University Press.

Le Fanu, J. S. (1872/1964). Carmilla. In *Best Ghost Stories*. New York: Dover.

———. (1993). *In a glass darkly*. R. Tracy (Ed.). London: Richard Bentley.

Lewis, J. (2002). *Hollywood v. hard core: How the struggle over censorship saved the modern film industry*. New York: NYU Press.

Mast, G. (Ed.). (1982). *The movies in our midst: Documents in the cultural history of film in America* (pp. 213–214). Chicago: University of Chicago Press.

McKee, R. (1997). *Story: Substance, structure, style, and the principles of screenwriting*. New York: Harper Collins.

Miller, F. (1994). *Censored Hollywood: Sex, sin, & violence on screen*. Nashville, TN: Turner.

Neale, S. (1980). *Genre*. London: British Film Institute.

Noriega, C. (1990). 'Something's missing here!' Homosexuality and and film reviews during the production code era, 1934–1962. *Cinema Journal, 30*, 20–41.

Phillips, W. H. (2004). *Film*. New York: Macmillan.

Press, C., & Keesey, P. (2006). *Daughters of darkness: Lesbian vampire tales*. San Francisco, CA: Cleis.

Russo, V. (1987). *The celluloid closet: Homosexuality and the movies*. New York: Harper & Row.

Seidman, S. (1996). Queer theory/sociology. Malden, MA: Wiley-Blackwell.

Silver, J., & Ursani, A. (1997). *The vampire film: From* Nosferatu *to* Interview with the Vampire. New York: Limelight.

Silver, A., & Ursini, J. (2000). *The horror film reader*. Milwaukee, WI: Hal Leonard.

Slater, G. (2005). Archetypal perspective and American film. *Spring, 73,* 1–19.

Stoker, B. (1997). *Dracula.* In N. Auerbach & D. J. Skal (Eds.). New York: W. W. Norton.

Tudor, A. (1989). *Monsters and mad scientists: A cultural history of the horror movie.* Oxford: Basil Blackwell.

Ursini, J. (2000). Introduction. In A. Silver & J. Ursini (Eds.), *Horror film reader.* New York: Limelight.

Voytilla, S. (1999). *Myth and the movies.* Studio City, CA: Michael Wiese Productions.

Weiss, A. (1992). *Vampires and violets: Lesbians in the cinema.* London: Jonathan Cape.

Whatling, C. (1997). *Screen dreams: Fantasizing lesbians in film.* Manchester, UK: Manchester University Press.

Williams, L. (1984). When the woman looks. In M. A. Doane, P. Mellencamp, & L. Williams (Eds.), *Re-visions: Essays in feminist film criticism* (pp. 83–99). Frederick, MD: AFI Monograph Series, University Publications of America.

Yep, G. A., Lovaas, K. E., & Elia, J. P. (2003). Introduction. Queering communication: Starting the conversation. *Journal of Homosexuality, 45*(2/3/4), 1–10.

Zimmerman, B. (1981, March). Daughters of darkness: Lesbian vampires. *Jump Cut, 24–25,* 23–24.

Zimmerman, B. (2004). Daughters of darkness: The lesbian vampire on film. In B. K. Grant & C. Sharrett (Eds.), *Planks of reason* (pp. 72–81). Lanham, MD: Scarecrow.

Chapter Fourteen: Television News Coverage of "Day without an Immigrant"

(1997). New immigrants, new needs: The California experience. *Rand Policy Institute Report.* Retrieved from http://www.rand.org/pubs/research_briefs/RB8015/index1.html

(2001, December 19). *U.S. report to the UN Counterterrorism Committee.* Retrieved from http://www.state.gov/p/io/rls/rpt/2001/6917.htm

(2007, March 15). Immigration misery. Editorial. *New York Times.* Retrieved from http://www.nytimes.com/2007/03/15/opinion/15thu1.html

(2007, March 17). Hypocrisy on immigration: A raid in New England reveals a broken system. Editorial. *Washington Post.* Retrieved from http://www.washingtonpost.com/wp-dyn/content/article/2007/03/16/AR2007031602119.html

(2007, December 19). 2007 National survey of Latinos: As illegal immigration issue heats up, Hispanics feel a chill. *Report by the Pew Hispanic Center.* Retrieved from http://pewhispanic.org/reports/report.php?ReportID=84

(2007, March 09). Needed: Immigration policy. Editorial. *Boston Globe.* Retrieved from http://www.boston.com/news/globe/editorial_opinion/editorials/articles/2007/03/09/needed_immigration_policy/

(2009). Population: The newest New Yorkers. *New York City Department of City Planning.* Retrieved from http://www.nyc.gov/html/dcp/html/census/nny_overview.shtml

Akresh, I.R. (2008). Occupational trajectories of legal U.S. immigrants: Down grading and recovery. *Population and Development Review, 34*(3), 435–456.

Archibold, R. A., (2006, May 02). Immigrants take to U.S. streets in show of strength. *New York Times* (n.p.). Retrieved from http://query.nytimes.com/gst/fullpage.html?res=9E01E6DD11 30F931A35756C0A9609C8B63&sec=&spon=&pagewanted=2

Bakhtin, M. (1973). *Marxism and the philosophy of language.* L. Matejka & I. R. Tutunik (Trans.). New York: Seminar.

Barthes, R. (1972). *Mythologies.* A. Lavers (Trans.). New York: Hill & Wang.

Bell-Fialkoff, A. (1993). A brief history of ethnic cleansing. *Foreign Affairs.* Retrieved from http:// www.foreignaffairs.com/articles/48961/andrew-bell-fialkoff/a-brief-history-of-ethnic-cleansing

Bleakley, H., & Chin, A. (2004). Language skills and earnings: Evidence from childhood immigrants. *The Review of Economics and Statistics, 86*(2), 481–496.

Bush, G. W. (2006, April 28). Album to showcase Spanish 'Star-spangled banner. *National Public Radio.* Retrieved from http://www.npr.org/templates/story/story.php?storyId=5369517

Chiswick, B. R. (1978). The effect of Americanization on the earnings of foreign-born men. *Journal of Political Economy, 86,* 897–922.

Chiswick, B. R., Lee, Y. L. L., & Miller, P. W. (2003). Schooling, literacy, numeracy, and labor market success. *Economic Record, 79*(245), 165–181.

Chu Miniter, P. (2007, November 11). A border agent (and immigrant) defies stereotypes. *USA Today.* Retrieved from http://www.usatoday.com/news/opinion/2007-05-07-oplede_n.htm

Cobb-Clark, D. A., & Kossoudji, (2000). IRCA's impact on the occupational concentration and mobility of newly-legalized Mexican men. *Journal of Population Economics, 13*(1), 81–98.

Cohen, S. (2003). *No one is illegal: Immigration control past and present.* Staffordshire, UK: Trentham.

Constable, P. (1997, June 29). Facing the harsh reality of the American Dream. *Washington Post*, B03.

de Beauvoir, S. (1949/2010). *The second sex.* C. Borde & S. M-C. (Trans). New York: Alfred A. Knopf.

de Saussure, F. (1966). *Course in general linguistics.* New York: McGraw-Hill.

Derrida, J. (1976). *Of grammatology.* G. C. Spivak (Trans). Baltimore, MD: Johns Hopkins University Press.

Douglass, F. (1950). The Constitution of the United States: Is it pro-slavery or anti-slavery?" In P. S. Foner (Ed.), *Life and writings of Frederick Douglass.* New York: International.

Entman, R. (1989). *Democracy without citizens: Media and the decay of American politics.* New York: Oxford University Press.

Fairclough, N. (1989). *Language and power.* London: Longman.

Foner, E. (2005). *Tom Paine and revolutionary America.* New York: Oxford University Press.

Foucault, M. (1969/1989). *L'archéologie du savoir* New York: Routledge.

Gans, H. (1979/2005). *Deciding what's news: A study of CBS evening news, NBC nightly news, Newsweek, and Time.* Evanston, IL: Northwestern University Press.

Gitlin, T. (1980). *The whole world is watching: Mass media in the making and unmaking of the New Left.* Berkeley, CA: University of California Press.

Goffman, E. (1997). *The Goffman Reader.* C. C. Lemert & A. Branaman. New York: Wiley.

Henry, S. (2007, January 17). *Herald News*. Facility lax in treatment of detainees, report finds. Retrieved from http://www.immigrantsolidarity.org/cgi-bin/datacgi/database.cgi?file=Issues &report=SingleArticle&ArticleID=069

I am an American. (n.d.) Retrieved from http://www.iamaproudamerican.com/index.cfm

Jasso, G., & Rosenzweig, M. R. (1990). The new chosen people: immigrants in the United States. Washington, DC: Russell Sage Foundation.

Lakoff, G., & Johnson, M. (1980). *Metaphors we live by.* Chicago: University of Chicago Press.

Martin-Barberó, J. (1993). *Communication, culture and hegemony: From the media to mediations.* Newbury Park, CA: Sage.

McHoul, A., & Grace, W. (1997). *A Foucault primer: Discourse, power and the subject.* New York: New York University Press.

McKinlay, A., & Potter, J. (1987). Model discourse: Interpretative repertoires in scientists' conference talk. *Social Studies of Science, 17*(3).

Miraldi, R. (1990). *Muckraking and objectivity: Journalism's colliding traditions.* Santa Barbara, CA: Greenwood.

Nelson, T. E., Clawson, R. A., & Oxley, Z. M. (1997). Media framing of a civil liberties conflict and its effect on tolerance. *American Political Science Review 91*, 567–583.

Nguyen, T. (2007). The war on immigrants. *RaceWire*. Retrieved from http://www.racewire.org/ archives/2007/11/the_war_on_immigrants.html

Payne, T. (1777/1995). *Collected writings.* (2nd ed.). E. Foner (Ed.). New York: Library of America.

Pfaelzer, J. (2008). *Driven out: The forgotten war against Chinese Americans.* New York: Random House.

Purcell, W. M. (1996). *Ars poetriae: Rhetorical and grammatical invention at the margin of literacy.* Columbia, SC: University of South Carolina Press.

Riis, J. (1890). *How the other half lives: Studies among the tenements of New York.* New York: Kessinger.

Robinson, D., & Reeve, K. (2006, February 15). Experiences of new immigration at the neighbourhood level. *Report. Joseph Rowntree Foundation.* Retrieved from http://www.jrf.org.uk/ publications/experiences-new-immigration-neighbourhood-level.

Santa Ana, O. (2002). *Brown tide rising: Metaphors of Latinos in contemporary American public.* Austin, TX: University of Texas Press.

Schutz, A., & Nathanson, M. (1962/1990). *Collected papers.* New York: Springer.

Shenon, P. (2003, July 21). Report on U.S. antiterrorism law alleges violations of civil rights. *New York Times* (n.p.). Retrieved from nytimes.com.

Snow, D. A. (2004). Framing processes, ideology, and discursive fields. In D. A. Snow, S. A. Soule, & H. Kriesi (Eds.). *The Blackwell companion to social movements* (pp. 380-412). New York: Wiley-Blackwell.

Snow, D. A., & Benford, R. D. (1988). Ideology, frame resonance, and participant mobilization. *International Social Movement Research*, 1, 197–219.

Snow, D. A., & Benford, R. D. (1992). Master frames and cycles of protest. In A. D. Morris & C. M. Mueller (Eds.), *Frontiers in social movement theory* (pp. 133–155). New Haven, CT: Yale University Press.

Snow, D. A., Rochford, E. B., Worden, S. K., & Benford, R. D. (1986). Frame alignment processes, micromobilization and movement participation. *American Sociological Review, 51*(4), 464–481.

Truman, H. S. (1947, January 06). *State of the Union.* Retrieved from http://www.let.rug.nl/usa/P/ht33/speeches/ht_1947.htm

Tuchman, G. (1978). *Making news.* New York: Free Press.

United States Census. (1999; 2000). http://www.census.gov

van Teeffelen, T. (1994). Racism and metaphor: The Palestinian-Israeli conflict in popular literature. *Discourse and Society, 5*(3), 381–405.

Vigdor, J. (2008, May 19). Needed: Immigration policy. *Boston Globe.* Retrieved from http://www.boston.com/bostonglobe/editorial_opinion/oped/articles/2008/05/19/choices_to_make_on_immigration_policy/

Weedon, C. (1987). *Feminist practice and poststructuralist theory.* New York: Basil Blackwell.

Wilkinson, S., & Kitzinger, C. (Eds.). (1996). *Representing the other: A feminism and psychology reader.* London: Sage.

Zinn, H. (2003). *A people's history of the United States.* New York: HarperCollins.

❋ **Index**

X

Y

Z